THE
GREAT
DEPRESSION

Also by Robert S. McElvaine

Down and Out in the Great Depression:
Letters from the "Forgotten Man"

THE GREAT DEPRESSION

America, 1929–1941

Robert S. McElvaine

BOOKS

Portions of "Pretty Boy Floyd" by Woody
Guthrie, Copyright © 1961 by Fall River
Music, Inc. All Rights Reserved. Used by permission.

Library of Congress Cataloging in Publication Data

McElvaine, Robert S., 1947–
  The Great Depression.

  Includes index.
  1. United States—History—1933–1945. 2. United
States—History—1919–1933. 3. United States—Social
conditions—1933–1945. 4. Depressions—United States—
1929. 5. United States—Economic conditions—1918–1945.
6. New Deal, 1933–1939. I. Title.
E806.M43 1983   973.91′6   82-40469
ISBN 0-8129-1061-3 (hardcover)
ISBN 0-8129-6343-1 (paperback)

Designed by Doris Borowsky

Manufactured in the United States of America

9 8 7 6 5 4 3 2 1

First Edition

FOR ANNE,
FOREVER

Acknowledgments

This book would not have been possible without the generous assistance over a period of years of numerous individuals and institutions. They cannot all be named here, but I want to express special thanks to some of them. The support of the National Endowment for the Humanities, in the form of a summer seminar in 1978, a summer stipend in 1979, and a year-long seminar in 1980–81, was essential to the completion of my research. A fellowship from the Eleanor Roosevelt Institute in 1975 allowed me to conduct much of the early research for the book. A Millsaps College Faculty Fellowship enabled me to devote the summer of 1982 to finishing the manuscript.

My exploration of the Great Depression began with my dissertation at the State University of New York at Binghamton. I owe a great debt to my advisers on that project, Charles Forcey, Richard Dalfiume, and Melvyn Dubofsky. My greatest intellectual obligation is to Professor Lawrence W. Levine of the University of California, Berkeley, in whose NEH summer seminar, "The 'Folk' in American History," my work was redirected toward the form in which it now appears. Larry Levine inspired me to become excited again about the topic; he is a model of scholarship and friendship.

Joan W. Scott of Brown University, who led a yearlong NEH seminar, "The 'New' Labor History," in which I participated, guided me in many ways to become a better historian. The criticism of other members of the seminars at both Berkeley and Brown was invaluable. James T. Patterson was also particularly helpful to me during my year at Brown. Discussions I had with E. P. Thompson, who was then a visiting professor at Brown, helped to shape in my mind the key concept of a popular view of economics based on morality. Professor Mark Estrin of Rhode Island College was of much assistance in expanding my understanding of the Depression-era cinema.

In addition to these scholars, the following people have read and criticized all or part of this book, although in some cases in rather different earlier drafts. I want to thank each of them, although I hasten to add that I did not always follow their suggestions and they should not be blamed for anything that remains in the book: Edward Akin of Mississippi College; David Bennetts of St. John's College; David Brody of the University of California, Davis; Jane Clary of Millsaps College; Len De Caux of Glendale, California; Otis Graham of the University of North Carolina, Chapel Hill; Naomi Lamoreaux of Brown University; Staughton Lynd of Youngstown, Ohio; Paul Murray of Siena College; Joyce Peterson of Florida International University; Phillip Scranton of Philadelphia College of Textiles and Science; Mary H. Stevenson of the University of Massachusetts, Boston; and James Weinstein of Chicago.

My colleagues in the Millsaps College history department—Ross Moore, Frank Laney, Charles Sallis, Ann Sumner Holmes, and Adrienne Phillips— have over the years been consistently helpful. I thank all of them.

I presented some of the ideas contained in this volume in papers given at annual meetings of the American Historical Association in 1972 at New Orleans and 1977 at Dallas, and in a paper I delivered at the 1980 meeting of the Organization of American Historians at San Francisco. I am grateful for the comments of other participants in those sessions, as I am to many of my students at Millsaps College over the past decade. My thinking on aspects of the Great Depression has been stimulated by student discussions in more ways than most of the students ever realized.

The unsung heroes of any book involving large amounts of research are the librarians and archivists who provide the essential assistance without which the project could not succeed. I owe my greatest debt in this regard to James F. Parks and his staff at the Millsaps-Wilson Library, including Lillian Cooley, Laurie Brown, and Floreada Harmon. William R. Emerson and the staff at the Franklin D. Roosevelt Library were always of great assistance on my many trips to Hyde Park. I also want to thank the staffs of the National Archives, the Library of Congress, the State University of New York at Binghamton Library, the Rockefeller Library at Brown University, the University of California at Berkeley Libraries, the New York Public Library, the New York State School of Industrial and Labor Relations Library, the Georgetown University Library, the Cornell University Library, the Jackson Public Library, the Georgia State University Library, the Atlanta Public Library, the Emory University Library, the County College of Morris Library, and the Louisiana State University Library.

During research trips and while writing the book I enjoyed the hospitality and conversation of many homes. I particularly want to thank Anna and John Lee and Carol and Charles Boyle of Fayetteville, Georgia; Joan and Charles Meehan of Landing, New Jersey; Rose and Robert Lee of Mahopac, New York; Kathy and Hugh Boyle of Rockville, Maryland; and Mary Ellen and Thomas Molokie of Readfield, Maine. They have all made the task of completing the book a far more pleasant one than it would have been without their company.

Typing of the manuscript was ably handled by Ann McCord, who also assisted me in many other tasks; Linda Cassedy; Pamela Sullivan; and Sara Hoagland.

Edward T. Chase has been everything an author could ask for in an editor, and his suggestions have improved the book in many ways. Jean Pohoryles and other staff members at Times Books also deserve special thanks.

My wife, Anne, has been the most important person throughout the long gestation period of the book. She helped in every way imaginable; the manuscript never would have been completed without her. Our children, Kerri, Lauren, and Allison, have been constant sources of inspiration and delight. My parents, Edward and Ruth McElvaine, helped and sustained me over the years of becoming a historian and writer. I only wish that my mother, who deeply loved history, had lived to see this book reach print.

Robert McElvaine
Clinton, Mississippi
August 1983

Contents

Foreword

A half century has now passed since Franklin D. Roosevelt launched his "New Deal." Yet the shadows of those times are very much with us today as our economy hovers on the edge of Depression conditions and conservatives attempt to reverse the policies set in motion by the New Deal. Most Americans in the 1980s are too young to remember the Great Depression. Perhaps this is why so many people were willing to follow Ronald Reagan down the path trod by Calvin Coolidge and Andrew Mellon prior to 1929. Be that as it may, no period in American history has more of importance to say to us today than does the Depression decade. Events in those years have determined the direction of our social and economic policies, our relationship to our government, and our political alignments ever since.

History has usually been viewed from the top, that is, through the eyes of elites, by examining the activities of governments and intellectuals. In recent years there has been a movement to write history "from the bottom up." Studies from this perspective have added greatly to our knowledge of the past. Few attempts, however, have been made to blend these two approaches. Both vantage points are needed to understand a given historical period. This is true of all eras, but it seems to me to be especially the case with the Great Depression, a time of enormous upheaval from below and dramatic innovation from above. This book combines social and political history so as to achieve a fuller comprehension of the biggest crisis Americans have faced in this century, the attempts to deal with that crisis, and the resulting alteration of the nation's attitudes and politics.

Political leaders can have important influences on the course of history, but they can succeed at leadership only if they move in the direction in which the people want to go. Franklin Roosevelt was one of those rare individuals who had a significant impact on history, but his leadership explains less about the changes the United States underwent in the 1930s than does a fundamental shift in the values of the American people.

Throughout our history there have been pendulum swings in public attitudes between self-centered individualism and concern with social problems. The values associated with acquisitive individualism have generally been popular among the more well-to-do, while the values associated with the idea that economics should be based on moral considerations have been more widespread among the working class. The American middle class has oscillated between these viewpoints, identifying its interests most commonly with those above them, whom they hoped to emulate. The Great Depression served to confirm the poor in their belief that moral considerations ought to have a role in economic practices. The Depression also led many in the middle class to identify their interests and values with those of the poor.

The impression that many people today have of the Depression is one of bleakness. This perception stems in part from the visual images that have survived from the decade: the stark, evocative black-and-white photographs taken for the Farm Security Administration (several of which are included in this volume) and the films of the thirties, almost all of which were also in black and white. One result of seeing the Depression through these media is to add to our impression of it as an era devoid of color. But that is only part of the picture. As Josephine Herbst has recalled, there was in the thirties "an almost universal liveliness that countervailed universal suffering."[1] Both the liveliness and the suffering are visible in the pages that follow.

This volume is aimed at a general audience as well as at professional historians. I have gone over ground that will be familiar to specialists. Without this, it would be hard to make a comprehensive statement understandable to the newcomer to the period. Along with the recapitulation of the known, the book contains much evidence from my own primary research, incorporates recent scholarship on the Depression by others, and offers a new interpretive framework. The focus is entirely upon the Depression and responses of the people—"ordinary" and "extraordinary"—to it. Foreign policy has been ignored except in those cases where it was directly related to the American Depression.

All sources of information are listed in the notes, but to avoid distraction in reading, these have been grouped in fairly large numbers, usually one for each section of a chapter.

THE
GREAT
DEPRESSION

1·Historical Currents and the Great Depression

One need not be a devotee of astrology or sunspot theories to recognize that certain rhythms seem to exist in our history. Many different types of business cycles have been traced over the years. During the nineteenth century, for example, major economic slumps occurred with disturbing regularity: 1819, 1837, 1857, 1873, 1893. Another economic collapse was beginning "on schedule" in 1914, when the outbreak of war in Europe revived the American economy.

3

Less universally accepted, but hard to deny when our history is viewed in its entirety, are periodic swings of mood, opinion, and values among the American people. An oscillation between the dominance of reform sentiment and standpattism has taken place throughout American history, with each wave of reform and each trough of reaction usually lasting between ten and twenty years. The opposing moods have been called by many names: Jeffersonian and Hamiltonian, democratic and aristocratic, liberal and conservative. The terms inevitably lead to confusion, because their meanings are so imprecise that the opposing names are sometimes used to describe the same policy. Jefferson's famous declaration in his first inaugural address, "We are all republicans—we are all federalists," hinted at the ambiguity. In a speech during his 1928 presidential campaign, Herbert Hoover restated the point: "We are a nation of progressives; we differ as to what is the road to progress." Precisely. But the differences over the meaning of progress and the best road to reach it are often great.

The fundamental difference was well stated by Jefferson. Some men, he declared, "fear the people, and wish to transfer all power to the higher classes of society." Others "consider the people as the safest depository of power in the last resort." Despite the frequent confusion over means, the goals of the former group are conveniently labeled conservative; those of the latter, who have been more concerned with the wrongs done to people than with the rights of property, are generally termed liberal. Given this admittedly loose distinction, American history in its broadest outline can be seen as consisting of periods of liberal reform punctuated by conservative breathing spaces. The peaks of reform were reached during the American Revolution, the ages of Jefferson and Jackson, the crusade against slavery, the Progressive era, the New Deal, and Lyndon Johnson's Great Society. The motive forces in the decline of reform eras seem to have been principally three: First, people eventually grow weary of social problems. They choose instead to withdraw into more personal interests. This sentiment was best summed up by the slogan Republicans used in the 1946 congressional campaign and several times since: "Had enough?" When a majority is sufficiently tired of the activism of such leaders as Jefferson, Lincoln, the Roosevelts, Wilson, Kennedy, or Johnson to answer "yes," a period of reaction sets in. Such notable ages in American history have been the Federalist era, the Era of Good Feelings, the 1840s and early 1850s, the Gilded Age, the 1920s, the 1950s, and the 1980s.

The second main factor in bringing a period of liberalism to a close is that the pace of change in our society outdistances a generation of reformers. Their ideas become dated. Much of their program has been put into effect, yet old problems remain and new ones arise. Some of those who seek change in their youth come to favor the status quo as they grow older.

A third reason for the decline of reform eras is that political leaders who start out committed to principles are likely, after time, to come to prefer, unlike Henry Clay, to be president (or congressman) to being right. Thus their zeal for the cause diminishes, and with it the reform era itself cools.

New reform eras arise for reasons similar to those that lead to the demise of their predecessors: a rejection of the dominant mood and a generational change. Just as people tire of calls for self-sacrifice, they eventually become upset with themselves after a period of hedonism and disregard for others. For some, at least, a time of reform offers an opportunity for personal redemption as well as for social change. If the public ultimately grows weary of activist leaders, it finally becomes bored or disgusted with the Adamses, Fillmores, Coolidges, Eisenhowers, and Reagans, too. Zealots of the right come to find office-holding as comfortable as do their liberal counterparts. And as a new generation arises the old battles are history and new configurations of problems bring forth new attempts at solutions.

The fact that at least some *new* solutions are sought in each wave of reform indicates that the often-used metaphor of a swinging pendulum is not quite suitable for describing changes in America's mood. No conservative era succeeds in wiping out all the gains of the preceding period of reform. The Republicans in the Eisenhower years were unable (and in many cases unwilling) to repeal the New Deal. The Reagan Republicans appeared for a time to be on the verge of dismantling the Great Society, if not the New Deal, but the public has proved unwilling to follow its reactionary leaders that far. Each liberal age is able to build upon some accomplishments of those that came before it. Some positions of the Reagan administration that are today considered extremely conservative would have been denounced as liberal in the 1920s.

The limits of the pulsations of national opinion here under discussion must be made clear. They do not, of course, involve everyone. Nearly 17 million Americans voted against Franklin Roosevelt in 1936; more than 27 million voted for Barry Goldwater in 1964. We are speaking of shifts between about 40 and 60 percent of the electorate, which seem to be the lower and upper limits of support for one viewpoint or the other. Nor are the shifts of mood usually as dramatic as we sometimes make them seem. The continued strength of some items on the progressive agenda during the 1920s, the "white backlash" of the 1960s, and the surprising popularity in opinion polls of many social programs in the 1980s are cases in point. It should also be plain that this is no simple argument about "history repeating itself." There has been a substantial variation in the length and intensity of periods of reform and reaction. All sorts of external factors ranging from economic conditions to wars to individual leadership can affect the timing and strength of reform waves. None of these qualifications, however, detracts from the usefulness of the concept of oscillations of public sentiment to an understanding of the American past. Those who remain skeptical of the idea may be persuaded by noting the startling accuracy of the following prediction Arthur Schlesinger, Sr., made in 1949: "We may expect the recession from liberalism which began in 1947 to last till 1962, with a possible margin of a year or two in one direction or the other. The next conservative epoch will then be due around 1978." And, it might now be added, liberalism can be expected to be in the ascendancy again in the 1990s, if not before.[1]

I have taken the time to go into this discussion of tides of public sentiment in some detail because the concept is vitally important to an understanding of Depression America. It is notable that the cycles of opinion appear to be unrelated to those of the economy. The two worst depressions in American history prior to the 1930s occurred in the long conservative period of the late nineteenth century. Populism was already strong when the Panic of 1893 hit, but it remained an overwhelmingly agrarian movement and did not become nationally dominant during the nineties. When reform did win majority support after the turn of the century, the United States was again enjoying prosperity. Prosperity gives middle-class reformers the security they feel is necessary to undertake change. The last great liberal uprising we have experienced, that of the 1960s, also took place in a period of great prosperity for middle-class Americans. Clearly hard times are not a prerequisite for reform. Indeed, only one of the major reform eras in American history occurred during a depression and, to state the same point differently, all of the major economic collapses save one happened during conservative eras. The one exception is the Great Depression of the 1930s, our worst depression, during which the New Deal, our most significant era of liberalism, took place. The so-far unique coincidence of the nation's economic and values cycles in the 1930s is a little-noted but critical fact about the history of Depression America.

Superimposed upon the economic and mood shifts are basic differences in class values. These are far from absolute, but as a rule of thumb, working-class people have been more likely to hold values centered on cooperation, sharing, equity, fairness, and justice than have their affluent countrymen. The latter have, throughout our history, been more likely to defend the marketplace as the sole determinant of the distribution of the economy's fruits. The poor—whether farmers or industrial workers—have generally been less willing worshipers at the shrine of Adam Smith. So long as the marketplace economy provided reasonable opportunities, they were likely to accept it. But during hard times or when maldistribution was especially evident, working-class people have tended to call for community or government action to supplement—or counteract—the marketplace. In short, they have believed that morality ought to have a role in the workings of the economy.

The basic reason for this difference is not hard to find. The self-interest of have-nots is better served by a more equitable distribution, whereas the self-interest of the wealthy is obviously better served by keeping things as they are. This in no sense makes the two positions ethically equivalent. The self-interest of the poor coincides with justice, that of the rich with injustice. The significance of this for the Great Depression is that it, like previous depressions, led the lower classes to demand government action to help them. Workers and farmers had made similar protests in the 1870s and 1890s. The key differences in the 1930s were that the country was "due" for a swing to more humanitarian values and that the depression was so much deeper, wider, and longer than previous slumps that a far larger segment of the middle class was directly affected and hence came to identify its interests with those of the poor. The combination of all these ingredients made the 1930s the time in which the values of compassion, sharing, and social justice became the most dominant that they have ever been in American history.

Each periodic depression that plagued the United States from the early nineteenth century through the 1930s was worse than the one before it. Many reasons for this could be cited, but one stands out as by far the most important. As the United States became less agrarian and more industrial, less rural and more urban, an ever-increasing percentage of its population became susceptible to the vagaries of the market economy. This is not to say that farmers were not victims of economic collapse—much of the history of the late nineteenth century and of the 1920s and 1930s makes plain that they were—but that people who *owned* farms and were not deeply in debt could at least feed their families during hard times. Stated simply, more and more people became *dependent* as the nation industrialized. Urban working-class people who rented their living quarters and whose income was derived entirely from wages found themselves in desperate straits when they lost their jobs and could find no other employment.

The Panic of 1893 was America's worst depression in the nineteenth century. Real income of Americans is estimated to have dropped some 18 percent between 1892 and 1894. That depression led to massive unemployment, which in turn fueled protest. Workers were angry and ready to undertake cooperative and, in some cases, radical action. These facts alarmed middle-class Americans, some of whom believed revolution might be imminent, particularly since the farm belts of the nation were seething with populism. Under the circumstances, middle America chose to cast its lot with business and dig in to defend economic orthodoxy. No quarrel on this would come from President Cleveland who, in vetoing the Texas Seed bill of 1887, which would have provided a scant $10,000 for relief of farmers hard-hit by drought, uttered the immortal words, "though the people support the Government the Government should not support the people." Cleveland, like most others in power in the 1890s, believed that depressions were natural events, part of the working of the business cycle, and therefore the government could do little about them. His formula for recovery (which was continued in all its essentials by his Republican successor, William McKinley) was to maintain sound money, preserve the sanctity of contracts, and cut federal spending. It has an uncannily familiar ring.

If the effects of the Panic of 1893 on the economy, workers, and business were dramatic, the depression's impact on American politics was equally spectacular. Although only one Democrat (Cleveland) had been elected president between 1860 and 1892, the Republicans had failed to establish themselves as a clear-cut majority party. Democrats won decisively in the House elections in 1890 and 1892, and Cleveland regained the White House in the latter year. This was the first time since Reconstruction that *either* party had held the White House and both houses of Congress simultaneously. But what seemed a happy occasion for the Democrats soon proved to be quite otherwise. It meant that their party was fully "in charge" when the panic struck. They were blamed, as the Republicans would be four decades later, for the economic collapse and had to pay the price at the polls. The elections of 1894 and 1896 saw what has been called "one of the greatest bloodless political realignments that this country has ever experienced." The shift of House seats from Democrats to Republicans in 1894 was the largest in modern history, exceeding even the transfer in the other direction in 1932. The political results of the Panic of 1893 clearly foreshadowed those of the Great Depression: the party in power was devastated and the opposition party became dominant for more than a generation. Woodrow Wilson's two victories under unusual circumstances notwithstanding, the Republicans remained the majority party from 1894 until a new economic collapse turned the tables on them in the early 1930s. For an earlier generation, Grover Cleveland and the Democrats represented what Herbert Hoover and the Republicans have stood for to so many Americans in the last half century. "I was a child of four during the Panic of '93," Walter Lippmann wrote two decades later, "and Cleveland has always been a sinister figure to me. His name was uttered with monstrous dread in the household . . . And to this day I find myself with a subtle prejudice against Democrats that goes deeper than what we call political conviction."[2]

Preindustrial America was, in historian Robert Wiebe's apt phrase, a nation of "island communities." What was dominant in the lives of people of all classes was the local community. Each community was to a large extent self-contained, its significant contacts with the rest of the nation infrequent. Given the large number of limited stages on which Americans performed, there was an abundance of leading roles. Each town had its local elite—its

merchants, bankers, clergymen, attorneys, physicians, editors, and so forth—
to whom the community looked for leadership. These elites, of course, enjoyed their status. But the existence of tight-knit communities with a shared
set of values was also beneficial to other groups. Several social and labor
historians have shown in recent years that nineteenth-century workers were
often able to use shared values to gain community support for strikes and fair
treatment.

The rapid industrialization of the United States during the late nineteenth
century upset this world. The development of national systems of transportation and communications, of highly concentrated industrial and financial
systems, and of mass circulation newspapers and magazines, along with the
explosion of urban populations, submerged the independence of the nation's
separate local communities. In the useful concept developed by nineteenth-
century German sociologist Ferdinand Tönnies, *Gemeinschaft*—the small,
personal community of the nineteenth century—was replaced by *Gesell-
schaft*, a large, anonymous society in which the importance of one's place and
achievements in the local context nearly dissolved.

The Progressive era in the broadest sense was an attempt to regain the old
values or construct new ones. Progressivism may have meant many different
things, but what tied it together was that all its manifestations were responses
to a common stimulus: the myriad effects of industrialization on traditional
American values. Because of the vast changes, even true conservatives found
it necessary to become reformers. The only way to preserve at least some of
the old world in the face of the upheaval being wrought by industrialization
was to try to make social changes that would compensate for some of the
economic changes. Paradoxically, by the beginning of the twentieth century,
it was necessary for a sincere conservative (that is, someone genuinely interested in preserving the old values, not simply an apologist for concentrated
wealth) to become a reformer, a "progressive." Such people saw "certain radical but strictly limited reforms as the only way to salvage the system."

For the middle-class reformer, alterations might be needed, but they could
not be undertaken safely during the economic crisis of the 1890s. By the turn
of the century, though, both prosperity and optimism had returned. The
United States had recovered from its worst depression to that time, had won a
"splendid little war," the Spanish-American War, that most believed was
fought for the highest, most unselfish objectives, and was emerging as a world
power. Under such conditions, it was possible for the "better sort" to attempt
to guide the discontent that had been so evident among farmers and workers
in the nineties into acceptable channels. Middle America could rediscover
poverty, as it seems to do once a generation. Thus, while progressivism had
important working-class, farmer, and corporate components, its dominant
form represented a "cautious uprising of the better classes." There can be little

doubt that most of these people sincerely wanted the "uplift" of the lower classes and a better, more honest, just, and moral society. They also wanted the beneficiaries to know to whom they should be thankful. Improvements were not to be won by the struggles of the lower classes, but to be bestowed as gifts from the moral, disinterested people above them. Much of what passed for progressivism was pushed by people who saw themselves as altruistic— they wanted to do good for others, not themselves. As Richard Hofstadter pointed out, populism had been a reform dictated by empty stomachs, while progressivism was a reform movement guided by the mind and heart.[3]

World War I not only brought the culmination of the Progressive era and intensified the reaction that followed, it also provided in several important ways the soil in which the seeds of the Great Depression and New Deal would germinate.

When the basically pacifist Woodrow Wilson finally took his country into the war in April 1917 he justified it, as he had to in order to convince himself and the American people, in the moralistic rhetoric of progressivism. "There is not a single selfish element, so far as I can see," Wilson said, "in the cause we are fighting for." Unlike other belligerents, Wilson insisted, the United States fought for altruistic purposes.

In addition to demonstrating to himself and a majority of his countrymen that it was "right" for the United States to enter the war, Wilson's use of the language of idealistic self-sacrifice as a rationale for participation had at least two other notable effects. It tied the war so tightly to progressive values that, if people became disillusioned with the war, they would also lose their faith in reform. Wilson's rhetoric also made the war seem an unprecedented example of national self-sacrifice and hence it served finally to release the combined guilt and moral energy that had been at the base of much of middle-class progressivism. Having at last paid their dues and made their sacrifices, Americans after the war could turn with somewhat clear consciences to personal concerns. The hedonistic, greedy, self-centered norms of the twenties, which played no small part in the coming of the Depression, were at least intensified by the wrapping of the war in the mantle of progressive moralism.

The war also created an international economic situation that helped bring on the Great Depression. Following Versailles there was an "unquenchable jingoism" throughout the industrial world. The reparations and war debts questions fueled dangerous international tension and weakened both the domestic economies of some European nations and the international economic structure. European countries became debtors to, rather than creditors of, the United States. Among other factors, this meant that these nations were no longer in a position to provide a good market for the surplus farm production of the United States.

The contraction of Europe's ability to buy American agricultural products aggravated another fundamental economic problem produced by the war. Wartime demand for food was great and the normal supply in Europe had been cut sharply. Both market forces and government policies led during the war to a vast increase in America's farm output. When wartime Food Administrator Herbert Hoover allowed the price of wheat to be set at $2.20 a bushel, farmers increased wheat acreage by nearly 40 percent and output by almost 50 percent. This in turn meant chronic "overproduction" in the 1920s, a massive agricultural depression during America's "prosperity decade," and a further dislocation in the world economic structure.

The First World War had other results with a direct bearing on the Great Depression. It represented what historian Henry May has called "the end of American innocence." The great optimism of the progressive years, as well as most of what was left of the old familiar values, was shattered by the war and the disillusionment of Versailles and the struggle over the League of Nations. Unmistakable clouds now hung over the previously sunny American horizon. "Those of you who did not live in that period before 1914, or are not old enough to remember it," clergyman John Haynes Holmes reminisced years later, "cannot imagine the security we enjoyed and the serenity we felt in that old world." Like most old worlds when they are gone, prewar America took on more of a glow than reality warranted, but the feeling of loss was a significant part of the mood of the twenties and the motive for the desire to return to "normalcy." The word itself, coined accidentally by Warren Harding during his 1920 campaign for the presidency, symbolized perfectly what the nation sought after the war: a return to a golden age that, like Harding's word, only resembled what had existed before.

To carry on the war effort, the United States government had embarked, for the first time, on serious social and economic planning. Indeed, it has been persuasively argued that the models for many programs and practices of the New Deal are to be found in wartime Washington rather than in the proposals of progressive reformers.

John Dewey, for one, took note in 1918 of "the social possibilities of war." The American economy was controlled in a completely unprecedented fashion during World War I. The War Industries Board, when placed under the leadership of Wall Street speculator Bernard Baruch early in 1918, held extensive powers over business during the war. The WIB tightly regulated and managed the economy, achieving remarkable results that many observers believed were proof of the efficacy of a planned economy.

Other precedents for New Deal actions are readily discernible in wartime practices. The National War Labor Board mediated labor conflicts. Workers were guaranteed the right to bargain collectively. Union membership increased by more than 40 percent between 1915 and the Armistice, and real earnings for laborers increased a modest 4 percent during the same period.

Major wars are sufficiently grave that orthodox thinkers are willing to suspend their dogma for the duration. Most American leaders who would not consider having an unbalanced budget in peacetime saw no alternative during the war. About half of the more than $32 billion cost of the war was met by borrowing. The rest was paid for through sharply increased taxes, including levies on corporate profits and a sharply graduated income tax (the latter made possible by the ratification of the Sixteenth Amendment in 1913). All of these wartime precedents were rummaged through for useful ideas when a different but equally momentous crisis had to be faced more than a decade later. [4]

The fanatical patriotism of World War I left a legacy that would play an important part in the decade ahead. The insistence on "100 percent Americanism" helped turn many people against anything with a hint of "internationalism" about it. This included Communists, Catholics, and Jews, all of whom became prime targets of the new Ku Klux Klan. The Klan of the 1920s represented a carry-over of the intolerance and reaction against progressivism, the war, and internationalism that had become so popular in 1919–20. It cannot be blamed for creating these feelings. Indeed it was, like so much else in the twenties, a business dictated by the marketplace. Its organizers were interested in nothing so much as making money through the sale of memberships. It was organized rather like a modern fast-food franchise, but in this case the product was not hamburgers but hatred. Accordingly, the Klan had to be willing to be intolerant of anyone the potential consumers did not like. Basically it was: "You don't like Group X? Well we don't either. Join us." This meant that while the KKK certainly exacerbated intergroup tensions in the twenties, it did not manufacture them. That a sizable part of the nation—principally in rural and small-town regions—continued for so long the passionate intolerance of the postwar period is closely related to another of the prominent realities of the twenties: the decline of rural America and its values.

The war itself was the last and greatest example of the progressive spirit of sacrifice. It was a mood that dissolved rapidly after the war. But the progressive-wartime state of mind carried through one last sacrifice before it expired: the Eighteenth Amendment. Although the fact would be forgotten quickly in the twenties, prohibition enjoyed solid majority support when the amendment sailed through state legislatures to ratification in January 1919. "Prohibition," *The New York Times* accurately observed, "seems to be the fashion, just as drinking once was." [5]

By definition, fashions change. Few have changed more rapidly than this one. The shift of opinion on drinking was one of the more dramatic examples of how, by the fall of 1920, much of America had tired of the whole idea of self-sacrifice. The temper of the twenties was to be vastly different from what had gone before.

Whenever the decade of the 1920s is mentioned, certain images come automatically to mind. Few periods are so clearly etched in the popular mind. It is difficult to think of the time as anything but the Roaring Twenties, the years of flappers, the Charleston, bathtub gin, petting parties, and the Stutz Bearcat. These were the days when America withdrew from the world and went into an orgy of self-indulgence. The decade has had more titles applied to it than any other similar time span in our history: the Jazz Age, the Prosperity Decade, the New Era, the Lost Generation, the Incredible Era, the Era of Excess, the Era of Wonderful Nonsense, the Dollar Decade, the Ballyhoo Years, and the Dry Decade.

Historians have been harsh in their views of the twenties. Typical are the comments of Henry Steele Commager and Richard B. Morris, editors of the generally authoritative New American Nation Series, in their introduction to the series' volume on the 1920s. "We think of the second and fourth decades of our century in positive terms, but of the third largely in negative," they rightly say. "The mark of failure is heavy on these years." "Not since the fateful decade of the 1850's," Commager and Morris devastatingly conclude, "had there been so egregious a failure of leadership in American politics." The reason for examining the decade, these noted historians suggest, is that "physicians study sickness rather than health."

The decade, though, was far more complex than the catchy names and flickering images suggest. It was a time of enormous contrasts. The staid, proper Puritan Calvin Coolidge was immensely popular in the age of the speakeasy and the rumble seat. It was a time of political conservatism and moral latitude, of great prosperity and grinding poverty.

The complexity has been more difficult to perceive with the twenties than with other periods because that decade's images are so sharp in the public mind. In view of what came after it, the Jazz Age took on the appearance of a carefree time. For some, this clouded hindsight with nostalgia; for others, it indicated a time in which the American people, and particularly their leaders, were treading water when they should have been swimming vigorously. Combining these images but emphasizing the latter, Malcolm Cowley remembered the twenties as "an easy, quick, adventurous age, good to be young in; and yet coming out of it one felt a sense of relief as on coming out of a room too full of talk and people into the sunlight of the winter streets."

For others who were young in the twenties, it has remained a golden age of freedom and opportunity, before the New Deal began to "ruin" the country. Most of us tend to have fond but distorted memories of the period of our youth. A generation now approaching middle age looks back on the 1950s as "Happy Days." Ronald Reagan was twelve years old when Calvin Coolidge succeeded to the presidency. Reagan's admiration for Coolidge remained undiminished nearly sixty years later when, in one of his first acts as president, Reagan ordered a portrait of Thomas Jefferson in the East Wing of the White House removed to make way for one of Coolidge. Four months after his own inauguration, President Reagan made it clear that Coolidge's were the presidential shoes he most hoped to fill. Reagan publicly praised his tight-lipped predecessor for cutting "taxes four times." During the Coolidge years, Reagan continued, "we had probably the greatest growth in prosperity that we've ever known."[6]

That President Reagan was overlooking what happened to "Coolidge Prosperity" less than eight months after Coolidge left office is plain. But the point here is that what Reagan—and, presumably, many if not most other Americans—remembers about the twenties is also misleading. The prosperity of the decade was real enough, yet it was anything but evenly spread.

With the timely passing of Warren Harding in 1923, Calvin Coolidge came to power, or more accurately, power came to Calvin Coolidge. He used little of it, though. Irving Stone put it well: Coolidge "aspired to be the least President the country had ever had; he attained his desire." As long as the nation prospered, few could argue with the Coolidge approach. Indeed, most people had no quarrel with it. "Coolidge's signal fault," biographer Donald McCoy has shrewdly observed, "was his pursuit of the policies approved by most Americans." There may be some questions about *why* Coolidge was so reassuring to the American public, but there is no doubt that he was.

The decline of Coolidge's reputation was a result of the Great Depression that followed his nearly six-year presidency. His refusal to worry about the problems of the future, along with his complete deference to business, was perceived by people with the benefit of hindsight as causes of the economic collapse. "If you see ten troubles coming down the road," Coolidge had said, "you can be sure that nine will run into the ditch before they reach you." This attitude epitomized the twenties; the consequences it helped to produce were grim. In his obituary for Coolidge, H. L. Mencken guessed that the former President "would have responded to bad times precisely as he responded to good ones—that is, by pulling down the blinds, stretching his legs upon his desk, and snoozing away the lazy afternoons." Mencken summed up the Coolidge years by saying: "There were no thrills while he reigned, but neither were there any headaches. He had no ideas, and he was not a nuisance." Although President Coolidge's policies were hardly *the* cause of the Depression, they made their contribution, and it would be difficult to disagree with Peter Levin's conclusion that "Coolidge, the success of his times, is a failure in history."[7]

In his veneration of businessmen, Calvin Coolidge was wholly representative of his times. Business leaders emerged from the war with greatly enhanced reputations. They had "lost some of the tarnish of the muckraking era" because of the excellent performance of American industry in war production. It was ironic, though, that the success of war production came under strict government control. That success was, nevertheless, used as an argument that the economy should be governed by the marketplace and the wisdom of independent businessmen.

The twenties cannot be comprehended without understanding that after two decades of reform sentiment, businessmen were once again in the saddle. But they were willing to be more flexible in the methods they used in dealing with workers, consumers, the general public, each other, and government. This attitude was reflected in a new vocabulary current among corporate leaders in the twenties. Such terms as "trusteeship," "service," "harmony," "social responsibility," "industrial statesman," "enlightened entrepreneur," and "industrial democracy" were heard frequently. "Welfare capitalism" was the order of the day.

One of the primary aims of welfare capitalism was to keep the workers happy. Contented workers were better workers and, if they saw the paternalism of the company as the source of their well-being, they could be kept subservient. The critical point about the welfare capitalism programs is that they were *given* by employers to "their" workers. Enlightened corporate leaders provided their employees with recreational facilities, athletic teams, company picnics, reading rooms, housing, insurance plans, opportunities to purchase company stock, and other fringe benefits. Since one of management's major problems was dealing with still unacculturated immigrants, many employers included "Americanization" programs (English and citizenship classes) among the benefits they offered employees.

The experiment in corporate welfare collapsed early in the Depression, but it served to confirm among workers the idea that economic relations ought to be based on justice. When the Depression made it clear that business was not so benevolent, workers would seek their justice elsewhere. In the meantime, though, welfare capitalism seemed to be making great strides. It made even as unlikely a convert as former muckraker and later Communist Lincoln Steffens. "Big business in America," Steffens wrote after the 1928 election, "is producing what the Socialists hold up as their goal: food, shelter, and clothing for all. You will see it during the Hoover administration."

Business was proclaiming a New Era of eternal prosperity and people were believing it. It was wonderful while it lasted, but he who prospers by claiming responsibility for good times is likely to be wiped out in hard times. Business was credited with everything good in the twenties; it was blamed for every-thing bad in the thirties. As deflated as the economy was in the Depression, it was not so deflated as the reputations of businessmen. They were, journalist Elmer Davis wrote in 1933, "about as thoroughly discredited as any set of false prophets in history, and most of them know it." Herbert Hoover may have said it best: "The only trouble with capitalism is capitalists. They're too damned greedy."[8]

From the end of the small depression of 1920–22 to the crash of October 1929, relatively few Americans would have dared to say such nasty things about capitalists. These, it seemed, were the biblical "seven years of great plenty." What soon came to be known as Coolidge Prosperity was the greatest economic boom the world had yet seen. It was a time in which, economics writer Stuart Chase noted, the businessman had replaced "the statesman, the priest, the philosopher, as the creator of standards of ethics and behavior." The businessman in the Coolidge years was "the final authority on the con-duct of American society," "the dictator of our destinies."

The priest was not merely replaced, the very Object of his worship was converted into a businessman. In the number-one best-seller of 1925 and 1926, *The Man Nobody Knows*, advertising executive Bruce Barton related how Jesus had "picked up twelve men from the bottom ranks of business and forged them into an organization that conquered the world." Christ was "the founder of modern business." "The parable of the Good Samaritan," Barton pointed out to his readers, "is the greatest advertisement of all time." The worship of business verged on the literal. "The man who builds a factory," President Coolidge intoned, presumably with his usual straight face, "builds a temple, the man who works there worships there." And on it went. Moses was said to have "appointed himself ad-writer for Deity."

It is not surprising that professional advertisers most often brought together business and religion. Those who wanted to market a product had, of course, to persuade consumers that it would do them some good. Advertisers planted and then harvested fears. Ads informed women that "health authorities . . . tell us that disease germs are everywhere." Fortunately, Lysol was available to protect the children. Another ad played upon the fear of mothers that they might not succeed. A "famous scientist" said: "Tell me what your children eat and I will show you the kind of men and women they will be!" Grape-Nuts were the solution. 'Twas admen that taught consumers' hearts to fear, and admen their fears relieved.

The growing power of advertising in the 1920s reflected more than the resurgence of business dominance. It was a sign of a fundamental change in the economy. The nation's industries had seemingly conquered the age-old problems of production. John Stuart Mill had expressed the nineteenth-century economic view when he said "if we can only produce enough, consumption will take care of itself." He was wrong. The key to the economy was now consumption. To stimulate sufficient consumption, advertising was essential. "We grew up founding our dreams on the infinite promises of American advertising," Zelda Fitzgerald later recalled. "I still believe that one can learn to play the piano by mail and that mud will give you a perfect complexion." Old habits of thrift and sacrifice, deeply ingrained in early stages of industrialism, now were to be altered, if not reversed, and advertisers would be the instructors in the new ways. All the virtues of the age of scarcity were now questioned. Even before the war some advanced thinkers were spelling out the new values that would win far more converts in the twenties. "The non-saver is now a higher type than the saver," economist Simon Patten wrote in 1907, "I tell my students to spend all they have and borrow more and spend that. It is foolish for persons to scrimp and save." Advertisers spread this new consumer ethic widely in the prosperity decade: Don't tighten our belts, loosen them—the more we spend the more prosperous we'll be. Many Americans brought up on the old virtues converted to consumerism in the twenties.

The relationship between expanding consumption and prosperity in the 1920s is clear. Productivity increased astronomically. Between 1920 and 1929 output per person-hour soared upward by 63 percent. If the economy was to stay afloat, someone had to buy these products. Many of them were new. Starting from a tiny base in 1922, sales of radios had increased by 1400 percent by 1929. There was a similar, if not quite so spectacular, explosion in sales of such household appliances as vacuum cleaners, electric irons, refrigerators, and washing machines. Such new industries helped greatly in producing the economic boom of the decade.

But no product was more representative of the mass consumption culture of the twenties than the automobile. Much of the twenties' prosperity was directly related to this industry. Between 1919 and 1929 the number of motorcars in the United States leaped from fewer than 7 million to more than 23 million. It was during the 1920s that the automobile became a "necessity" for Americans.[9]

The greatest seeming paradox of the 1920s centers on the attitudes of Americans toward "new" things. The decade's love of newness was hardly unique in United States history. We have always placed a premium on anything new. We were a new country in a new world, a new people, and we have seen such curiosities as a New Freedom, a New Nationalism, a New Deal, a New Frontier, a—or rather, many—New Souths, a New Left, a New Right, innumerable New Nixons, at least two New Federalisms, and even a New Conservatism. Manufacturers of well-established products feel constrained every few years to advertise them as "new, improved," or with "new ingredient X-17."

This persistent American affair with novelty reached special heights in the 1920s, the New Era. It was an age in which one fad displaced another with astonishing rapidity: mah-jongg, crossword puzzles, the teachings of Émile Coué, the wearing of open galoshes (which gave us the term "flappers" for those who wore them—a name that far outlasted the fad), marathon dancing, flagpole sitting. Each burned briefly, only to be replaced by another. A fad could move from "new" to passé in a matter of months. Being new was not enough; what was sought was the newest of the new.

Technologically also, the decade was a New Era. Henry Ford put it simply: "Machinery is the new Messiah." To prove his assertion, Ford perfected his assembly line to the point where, at the end of October 1925, a car came off the end of the line every 10 seconds, with a total of 9575 autos produced in a single day. By 1929 the ratio of cars to people in the United States was 1:5, and one-third of the nation's homes were equipped with radios. Inventions that had seemed impossible within the living memory of much of the population came quickly to be seen as necessities. Obviously, new was better than old.

Or was it so obvious? This same era of newness saw Warren Harding achieve the biggest landslide victory the nation had yet experienced by promising a return to normalcy. The Klan thrived by defending the old morality. And surely there was nothing "new" about Calvin Coolidge.

Some aspects of the New Era were not as pleasing as others. The new technology appeared to be beneficial, but many were not so sure about the new morality. Young and urban Americans seemed especially to be gripped by new ideas that were upsetting to their older and more rural fellow citizens. New gadgets might be one thing, but a New Woman was quite another. (What, after all, was wrong with the old one?)

Here again we are on ground that spreads throughout American history and is not peculiar to the 1920s. It is the clash between old and new values, between farm and city, between the garden and the machine. But this recurrent clash reached a particular crescendo in the 1920s. The revolutions in technology and morals came on top of the finding of the 1920 census that for the first time the nation's urban population exceeded the number of rural residents. Although the statistics are rather misleading, since the census classified as "urban" anyone living in a community of 2500 or more residents, the conclusion was in its own way as great a shock as had been the finding of the 1890 census that the frontier had closed. American values since before Jefferson had been rural values. What would happen now?

To many horrified Americans of traditional beliefs, the answer was all-too-apparent in the actions of the young people of the Jazz Age, especially the women. It was always expected that boys would be boys, and since they would be irresponsible, women had to assume, as *The Atlantic* stated in 1920, "the entire responsibility of the human race." But now young ladies—if that was the appropriate word—were beginning to smoke (some even in public), drink alcoholic beverages, wear rouge, lipstick, and daringly short skirts, bob their hair, ride in automobiles with men, use strong language, and engage—with men to whom they were not even engaged—in such unspeakable practices as kissing and . . . who could be sure what else? "Gazing at the young women of the period," historian Paula Fass has said, "the traditionalist saw the end of American civilization as he had known it." The president of the University of Florida verbalized the fears of many: "The low-cut gowns, the rolled hose and short skirts are born of the Devil and his angels, and are carrying the present and future generations to chaos and destruction."

Farmers and small-town residents, long accustomed to being hailed as the backbone of the nation, now found themselves ridiculed as hayseeds and hicks. An urban-industrial society that they neither liked nor understood was engulfing them. In the early twenties, farmers saw the last bulwarks of their values being attacked. Theirs was not the world of speakeasies, petting parties, rosary beads, or bagels. To rural Americans the city was the center of *sin*. It was associated with all evils: crime, prostitution, Catholics, Jews, immigrants, bootlegging, alcohol, Wall Street, and everything else that was wrong with

America. And, adding insult to injury, the cities were rapidly attracting the sons and daughters of the Middle Border, thus corrupting the last hope for the future.

Rural America seemed to be making its last stand in the twenties (actually its values would often be heard again). The struggle might be hopeless, but it must be carried on. It was a many-fronted war. The Ku Klux Klan and rural churches provided the foot soldiers. Such politicians as William Gibbs McAdoo and the aged William Jennings Bryan offered their skills as general officers. Battles took place on the fields of both sides, from New York City to Dayton, Tennessee.

The clearest sign that the old, rural values were on the defensive was that their champions began enacting laws to uphold the old ways. If the old morality worked properly, it would be self-enforcing; no laws would be needed. Turning to the law was an admission of defeat. A bill introduced in the Utah legislature in 1921 would fine and imprison persons (presumably females) who were caught in public wearing "skirts higher than three inches above the ankle." A proposed Ohio law would prohibit the sale of any "garment which unduly displays or accentuates the lines of the female figure." The *Ladies' Home Journal* called for the "legal prohibition" of jazz dancing. Numerous books and plays were banned in Boston—and elsewhere. And several states passed laws prohibiting the teaching of the theory of evolution.

To see the values conflict of the twenties merely as a struggle between groups, however, is to miss its most important aspect. The apparent paradox of a decade of loving everything "new" and Calvin Coolidge at the same time would be no paradox at all if we were dealing with distinct groups, one committed to the old and the other to the new. But in fact the tension between stability and change often took place within individuals. Here Henry Ford was the representative American of the 1920s. No one did more than he to destroy the old rural America, yet he continually tried to escape from the age he did so much to create. "It was," Ford affirmed in his autobiography, "an evil day when the village flour mill disappeared." He attempted to recreate the old world at his Greenfield Village, a replicated nineteenth-century farming community. There he employed a blacksmith, a cobbler, and a glassblower.

The irony goes even deeper. Henry Ford had gotten into tinkering with machines as a boy because he despised farm work. Here was the apotheosis of the American love-hate relationship with both farm and city. Ford did his best to try to reconcile the two, and to convince himself that his lifework had not really been destructive of the lifestyle he professed to favor. "You can't fix a dead horse with a monkey wrench," the nature-loving industrialist observed. "Unless we know more about machines and their use . . . ," he said, trying to persuade himself as much as others, "we cannot have time to enjoy the trees and the birds, the flowers and green fields." Ford went so far as to promote village industries at the same time he was building the enormous River Rouge plant. The ultimate symbol of his ambivalence, though, must have been the seventy-six-unit "bird hotel" he constructed at his estate. Each apartment was equipped with an electric heater and other mechanical devices.[10]

In times of rapid change—newfangled contraptions, new morality, new women—old values take on a *new* importance; they give people something to which they can cling. Thus Americans held fast to Calvin Coolidge, the security blanket of the 1920s.

If American farmers were roaring in the twenties, it was not in the same sense of the word that is usually connected with the decade. While other sectors of the economy recovered from the collapse of 1920–22, in agriculture that depression continued on until it blended into a new one at the end of the decade. Farm prices fell to a much greater extent than did the cost of industrial products. The relationship between the prices of farm and nonfarm commodities determines the welfare of farmers. In 1922 the farmer was at a 19 percent disadvantage compared to the price relationship that had prevailed in 1913. The gap narrowed only slightly over the rest of the decade. The nation's farm families, representing some 22 percent of the American people in 1920, received 15 percent of the national income in that year. Eight years later, farm families accounted for only 9 percent of national income. In 1929 annual per capita income of farm persons was $273; the average for all Americans was $750.

It seems significant that as the major economic group which shared least in the prosperity, farmers remained the most committed to "progressive" programs in the 1920s. The farm bloc pushed for government intervention, redistributive (in the direction of farmers, of course) taxation, and government waterpower projects.

Industrial workers found a bit more to roar about in the twenties than farmers did, but not much. For most working-class families in the decade, labor historian Irving Bernstein has said, "the appropriate metallic symbol may be nickel or copper or perhaps even tin, but certainly not gold." At first glance, workers seem to have shared in the decade's new material abundance. Many obtained cars, radios, and other trappings of at least modest prosperity. But despite surface appearances, the American economy of the 1920s was seriously out of balance, and workers as well as farmers bore the brunt of the cost of the maladjustments. In *Middletown*, their classic study of a "typical" middle American city (Muncie, Indiana), Robert and Helen Lynd found that work was very unsteady in "good times" as well as bad. In the prosperous year of 1923, more than one-quarter of a sample of Muncie workers had been laid off, 15 percent for more than one month. During the first three-quarters of 1924, when "times were bad," 62 percent of the same workers had been out of work, 43 percent for a month or more out of nine.

National unemployment figures cannot be stated accurately because government statistics were not collected on the subject. Estimates of nationwide unemployment at the height of Coolidge Prosperity vary from 5.2 percent to 13 percent. The class difference in views of the problem can be seen in Muncie. The wife of a prominent businessman stated the upper-class view: "I believe that anyone who really tries can get work of some kind." When jobs were scarce, though, Muncie workers became very fearful.

The conditions under which many Americans labored in the twenties are often obscured by the surface image of general prosperity. In 1929 the American wage earner had a longer workweek than did his counterpart in other industrialized nations. The American enjoyed almost no protection against the constant specter of unemployment. All the nations of Western Europe had gone further than the United States in acknowledging public responsibility in this area. By 1929 the United States stood with two underdeveloped countries, China and India, as the only major nations allowing women and children to work at night.

All of this said, however, it should not be concluded that prosperity had no effect on workers in the twenties. Despite the inequities, the material well-being of workers who had jobs was improving. "Ownership of a Model T," Irving Bernstein points out, "even if shared with the finance company, was more than entertaining: it inclined one to accept things as they were." Industrial workers were generally persuaded that they had never had it so good. "Falling prices and fuller employment," as E. P. Thompson has observed of a similarly prosperous period in England a century before, tend to "take the edge off" worker anger.

By 1923 unions had lost nearly 1.5 million members, a decline of almost 30 percent from the 1920 high. The loss of union membership during hard times was not unexpected. This was the usual pattern. What was unusual about the status of unionism in the twenties was that unions failed to regain members when prosperity returned. In the greatest period of prosperity the United

States had yet known, union membership stagnated and even declined a bit, hitting a low for the decade in 1929. It was the first period of prosperity in American history during which unions failed to increase their membership. There were several reasons for this reversal of form. Most important was that the prosperity was based principally upon increased productivity resulting from automated, assembly-line manufacturing. The number of person-hours worked *fell* by 7 percent between 1920 and 1929. This meant that despite the prosperity unemployment continued to be a problem. The persistent labor surplus made it difficult for workers to organize. The usual aspect of prosperity most helpful for unions—plentiful jobs—was absent during the twenties.[11]

If Calvin Coolidge himself made little use of his office, the same could not be said of his two leading Cabinet members, Herbert Hoover and Andrew Mellon. Hoover was, one contemporary quipped, "Secretary of Commerce and Undersecretary of all other departments." He provided much assistance for business. Hoover's role, though, seemed to be less important than that of Mellon, the Pittsburgh banker and industrial magnate who was secretary of the Treasury in the administrations of all three Republican presidents of the twenties. One of the richest men in America, Mellon strived unstintingly toward his major goal: the reduction of the tax "burden" on the rich. Until 1926 progressives in Congress were able to block Mellon's most generous proposals for his own class. Of Mellon's bill Senator George Norris said without much exaggeration, "Mr. Mellon himself gets a larger personal reduction than the aggregate of practically all the taxpayers in the state of Nebraska." Under Mellon's Revenue Act of 1926, a person with an annual income of $1 million had his taxes lowered from more than $600,000 to less than $200,000. Mellon's own income was considerably higher, and he benefited even more from his own program. Small taxpayers received minimal reductions. Nor did Mellon's munificence end there. He and the few people in his income bracket also enjoyed clandestine administrative refunds of taxes. Mellon was generous in granting tax credits, abatements, and refunds. Between 1921 and 1929 (when his activities were exposed by House Speaker John Nance Garner), $3.5 billion was granted to corporations and individuals friendly to the Republican party.

In the twenties, however, helping the rich was not a partisan issue. Pierre S. du Pont, president of E. I. du Pont de Nemours & Co., was—for understandable reasons—of the opinion that the rich should not bear the burden of taxation. Taxes, Du Pont reasoned, ought to be paid by the working class, not the "productive" class (which he defined as large employers). This view was shared by John J. Raskob, an executive of Du Pont, General Motors, and other corporations. In seeking a way to bring about their objective, these two eminent gentlemen, along with some wealthy associates, hit upon a brilliant scheme. They would seize control of the Democratic party and commit it to the repeal of prohibition. When this was achieved, they would place a tax on beer, the workingman's drink. Estimates indicated that such a levy could raise $1.3 billion. This would allow a further 50 percent cut in corporate and individual taxes. In short, Du Pont and friends would give workers beer, and with it they would also give them half the tax burden of the rich. It seemed to them to be a reasonable trade-off.

New York Governor Al Smith became the instrument of the Du Pont plan. When Smith won the 1928 Democratic presidential nomination, he named Raskob—who listed his occupation for Who's Who as "capitalist"—as chairman of the Democratic National Committee. Interestingly, Raskob had been up until that time a Republican. Despite Smith's loss to Hoover, Raskob owned the Democratic National Committee for the next four years. He and the Du Ponts still hoped to put their plan into effect in 1932.

Thus by the end of the twenties, Raskob seemed to be close to the mark when he said the only difference between the two parties was that the Democrats were wet and the Republicans were dry. He might have added that Republicans favored shifting taxes from the rich to the poor by means of a national sales tax (an idea that Mellon had been pushing since 1920), while the Democrats would try to achieve the same end by taxing beer. The conservative era had reached its zenith—or its nadir, depending upon one's point of view.[12]

2·Who Was Roaring in the Twenties?— Origins of the Great Depression

Far less has been written about the origins of the Depression than about its results. Some notion of the relative lack of attention to the Depression's causes can be seen in statements made by two of those scholars who have tackled the subject. "As a year," John Kenneth Galbraith wrote in the early fifties, "1929 has always been peculiarly the property of economists." Two decades later Peter Temin asserted that "economists have—with a few prominent exceptions—left the study of the

Depression to others." If the origins of the Depression are the special province of economists and they have left its study to others, it is apparent that the topic has not received its due.

Not that there is any dearth of explanations of the Depression's causes. The question of what brought on this worst economic catastrophe in our history is, naturally, one that cries for an answer. Being one whose economic philosophy leans toward emphasis on demand, I am pleased to point out that the strong demand for an explanation of the Depression's causes has called forth an abundant supply. There is, it should be clear, no contradiction between the existence of a bumper crop of theories and a relative paucity of careful study of the subject. "When people are least sure," as Galbraith has noted, "they are often most dogmatic." In a contemporary assessment, W. W. Kiplinger said: "The amazing lesson from this depression is that no one knows much about the real causes of ANYTHING."

More than a half century after the fact, there is no consensus on what caused the Great Depression. One of the principal reasons is that explanations of that increasingly ancient calamity are generally tied tightly to one's socioeconomic philosphy and, hence, to current political questions. Although there are many variations and nuances, "liberal" interpretations differ from "conservative" and "radical" explanations.

The debate over what produced the Great Depression is, however, not simply a convenient political weapon. It is far more serious. Our conclusions concerning the causes of the last depression greatly influence our attempts to prevent a new one and our economic policies intended to bring about sustained prosperity. The policies of the Reagan administration, for instance, are based at least in part on the "supply-side" view of the Depression's causes. In the liberal or Keynesian view, some of these same policies are precisely the ones that brought about the Depression.

Twice in recent years *The Wall Street Journal* has polled leading economists on the prospects of another Great Depression. The first such survey, conducted in connection with the fiftieth anniversary of the Panic of 1929, found a virtually unanimous opinion that nothing like a repeat of the Depression of the thirties was likely to happen "anytime soon." In the spring of 1982 that opinion held, but not nearly as firmly as it had less than three years earlier. Galbraith demonstrated the importance of interpretations of the causes of the Depression when he said: "Reagan is putting up a notable effort to have another Great Depression." Galbraith still doubted in early 1982 that the President would succeed in that effort. Still, it is clear that the growing fear of a new depression—some insisted the nation was already in one by the end of 1982—has made analysis of the origins of the last one a subject of intense interest.

Interpretations of the causes of the greatest economic collapse in the history of the industrial world divide into categories based on various criteria. One distinction is between those who seek to lay the blame on, or at least attach primary importance to, a single cause, and those who maintain that no one factor was responsible. A second split occurs between those who see the major problems originating within the United States and those who find the underlying causes abroad. A third basis for dividing interpretations of the Depression concerns fundamental economic philosophy. Those who now call themselves "supply-siders" see very different causes of the collapse from those we might broadly identify as "demand-siders." Perhaps a fourth division should be added—most observers believe that human errors of some sort caused the Depression and so it was avoidable. But some insist that it was inevitable, the result of the operation of inexorable business cycles. Although each of these divisions is important, they cut across each other. That is, someone who insists on a single primary cause might locate that cause at home or abroad, and might favor either a supply- or a demand-side explanation.

I offer a particular interpretation in the context of a narrative of the events leading up to the collapse. A few other theories demand comment because they are the most influential.

Among the simplest and, in some respects, most beguiling explanations of the Depression is the "law of compensation." In biblical terms, the seven fat years of "Coolidge Prosperity" had to be followed—and paid for—by seven lean years. (Unfortunately, the lean years turned out to be seven-cum-eleven.) Although this notion that bad times must alternate with good, or the related concept that the economy needs to "rest" periodically, has the attraction of obviating the need for any real explanation, it is easily enough disposed of. We have enjoyed much longer periods of relative prosperity since World War II, and the idea that the economy needed to rest is sheer nonsense. Unemployed workers were quickly more rested than they wanted to be, and most factories and machinery of the nation were in good condition, not in need of repair. A deeper explanation must be sought.

Milton Friedman and Anna Schwartz have provided one possibility. As part of their larger monetarist argument that prosperity is dependent upon the size of the money supply, they contend that the Great Depression was triggered by a "mild decline in the money stock from 1929 to 1930." The collapse, they say, broadened and deepened when "a wave of bank failures beginning in 1930" further contracted the money supply. The problem, they insist, was not that lack of confidence inhibited businessmen from borrowing, but that insufficient money was available. It was not that the horse would not drink, but that there were not enough watering holes to which he could be led. This monetarist explanation cannot be ignored. It can be refuted, though. Charles Kindleberger, in his overview of *The World in Depression*, rejected the unicausal monetarist interpretation. Peter Temin went further

and demonstrated that the facts plainly do not support the contention of a
shrinking money supply from 1929 to 1931. Interest rates declined and so did
prices, the latter more sharply than the reduction of the money supply, hence
the real money supply was actually growing slightly.

Herbert Hoover, who had some personal interest in the outcome of the
analysis, put forward the classic statement of the school that places responsibility in Europe. In his *Memoirs*, Hoover flatly stated that it "was not the fact"
that "the American stock-market slump pulled down the world." Instead,
Hoover found the original source of the Depression in World War I. The
Wall Street Crash, the former President admitted, had caused "a normal recession." But the "great center of the storm was Europe." Hoover specifically
pointed his finger at the European financial collapse of 1931 as the culprit that
turned the "recession" into the Great Depression. Although I do not agree
with this interpretation, it should not be dismissed out of hand. The Depression was, after all, a worldwide phenomenon. The causes Hoover cited may
have played a role, even if they also served the purpose of absolving him.

Others, such as economist Paul Samuelson, have found the origins of the
Depression in "a series of historical accidents." A species of this genus, sired
by Joseph Schumpeter, holds that the Great Depression was the consequence
of the unfortunate coincidence of several different types of economic cycles
reaching their low points simultaneously. These cycles include the fifty-year
"super" business wave detected in the 1920s by Russian economist Nikolai
Kondratiev, as well as a "normal" nine-year business cycle and a short-range
inventory cycle. All this may be statistically correct, but it is hardly satisfying
to the historical appetite. If there were "accidents" we need to explore them
carefully; if there is anything to the idea of economic cycles, we must nonetheless examine the particulars of what happened in 1929 and subsequent
years.

Undoubtedly the most prevalent view of the causes of the Depression has
been that which focuses upon a decline in spending—that is, in consumption, investment, or both. John Maynard Keynes gave this interpretation its
definitive expression. With various modifications it has been endorsed by Alvin Hansen, Thomas Wilson, J. K. Galbraith, and a host of others. With
further modifications, this interpretation forms the foundation for my analysis.

One thing most of the theories have in common is that they are based more
on impressionistic evidence than hard data. They assume their conclusions
and then explain the Depression on the basis of their assumptions. Only in
the last decade or so have attempts been made to approach the problem of the
Depression's origins through more scientific methods. Just as more careful
statistical analyses of the Depression have begun to emerge, however, there
has been a resurgence in the popularity of the original classical economic

view of the nature of the Depression. This is odd, since the latest versions of the old free-market viewpoint are strictly unscientific, seat-of-the-pants observations. Because of the influence this "supply-side" interpretation has had upon American economic policy in the 1980s, it deserves examination in some detail.[1]

American industrialization in the late nineteenth century was accomplished with little government planning. The rapid development of the United States was taken as the ultimate proof of the political economy of Adam Smith. Although much of what had been accomplished in the nation had been the result of cooperative efforts, by the 1920s reverence for the freely operating marketplace was high. America's plan for prosperity was planlessness—the Adam Smith notion that individual greed and striving led to collective harmony; the "invisible hand" guided all free-market activity.

Most Americans in positions of authority, whether in business or government, were devout believers in old-time economics when the Depression began. Their faith was so strong that it would not have been surprising to hear them joining in a hymn that went something like:

> *Give me that old-time economics,*
> *Give me that old-time economics,*
> *It was good enough for Bill McKinley,*
> *And that's good enough for me.*

Such men—few of them were of any other gender—literally took their economics as a matter of faith. They worshiped the marketplace as a god who moved in mysterious ways. He was a generally benevolent god, but he could also be a god of vengeance. Just as such "acts of God" as violent weather could not be controlled, neither could the economic storms that the marketplace sent our way. Only fools would try to bring the economy under human control and prevent such storms.

"So long as business activity goes on," Albert Wiggin, chairman of the Chase National Bank, told a Senate committee in 1931, "we are bound to have conditions of crisis once in so often." The committee chairman, Robert M. La Follette, Jr., then asked Wiggin if he thought "the capacity for human suffering is unlimited." "I think so," the banker replied. (It later came out, we might mention in passing, that during the fall of 1929, Wiggin used more than $6 million of Chase funds to finance an operation in which he sold short some 42,506 shares of stock in his own bank. In the process, while so many were being wiped out by the Crash, Wiggin netted the not inconsiderable profit of $4,008,538 from the decline in the value of Chase stock. The limits of his own capacity for suffering were not severely tested.)

Wiggin's view of the inevitable nature of depressions contrasted sharply with the glowing New Era forecasts of a few years before. Yet most "conservative" businessmen espoused such interpretations of the collapse. It was a period of chastisement. Americans had been extravagant in the twenties. "Now the piper would be paid his due." It might even be a blessing, a time of "beneficial readjustment." Andrew Mellon told Hoover that "a panic was not altogether a bad thing." "It will purge the rottenness out of the system," the Treasury secretary declared. "People will work harder, live a more moral life. Values will be adjusted, and enterprising people will pick up the wrecks from less competent people." Still, as Gilbert Seldes pointed out, "no one ever proposed to continue the depression in order to continue its benefits."

It is worth noting that most of those who were prepared to face the Depression with equanimity or saw it as a potentially healthy development were men of means. Wiggin and Mellon—like their counterparts in more recent times—were in a position to advocate liquidation, to suggest that it was time to bite the bullet. One assumes that they personally found more palatable fare. Those who, according to the conservative view, paid the price for the past extravagance were too often those who were entirely innocent of those excesses.

The initial reaction to the Depression among many was to "sit and wait with folded hands." "The great advantage of allowing nature to take her course," economics writer Stuart Chase noted in 1932, "is that it obviates thought." That may have been sufficient to recommend the course of inaction to comfortable folk, but as the Depression worsened, the do-nothing approach came to be totally discredited. Not only did the collapse expose men who worshiped the god of the marketplace to ridicule, but it also severely undermined classical economics. Since the discipline had not predicted the Crash, could not explain the Depression, and offered no way out other than waiting till it was over, most people began to look elsewhere for their economic theories. Eric Hobsbawm's characterization of the economic illiteracy of British leaders during the Depression, while perhaps a bit harsh, can be applied as well to their American counterparts: "Never did a ship founder with a captain and a crew more ignorant of the reasons for its misfortune or more impotent to do anything about it." The Depression's devastating impact on classical economics was so great that old-time economics remained in disfavor for most of the half century after 1929. There were always adherents of the old laissez-faire doctrine, and sometimes they even managed to make one of their sect a Republican presidential nominee. But until the 1970s there was something slightly disreputable, in an intellectual as well as a social context, about being an out-and-out laissez-faire advocate. If the adherents of this creed were ever to emerge from their catacombs and win more votes than Barry Goldwater did in 1964, they would have to find some way to explain the Depression on their own terms. The need was admitted by one of those who took up the quest. In attempting to write a book based on a revival of classical political economy, Jude Wanniski of *The Wall Street Journal* said, "it was necessary that I somehow demonstrate that the Crash of 1929 was consistent with classical theory."

When one sets out looking for evidence with which to support a preconceived theory, it is not surprising if he finds it. Nor is it particularly surprising that the evidence seems rather strained to the nonbeliever. What may be somewhat more astonishing, though, is the vehemence with which such a proselytizer is willing to push his scanty grounds for belief. One might assume that a writer in the 1970s who refers to Mussolini as "a conservative" has a gift for understatement. Such, alas, is not the case with Wanniski when it comes to advancing his unicausal explanation of the Depression or his faith in the Laffer Curve. More revealing of Wanniski's attitude might be his reference to children as "human capital."

To begin at the beginning, the reborn "supply-side" advocates of today are basing their beliefs on Say's Law. Jean Baptiste Say, an early nineteenth-century popularizer of classical economics, asserted that "a product created offers, from that instant, a market for other commodities to the full total of its value." More recently, supply-side guru George Gilder has had his children going around the house reciting: "Supply creates its own demand." On one level, these assertions are true enough. But in the way they are meant by modern "supply-siders" they amount to nonsense. If the assertion means that whenever something is produced that someone else is willing and able to buy, purchasing power equivalent to the price the second party will pay is created, of course this is true. Indeed, it is axiomatic. It could be restated: When something of value is created, value is created. To go beyond this, however, and suggest that "if we can only produce enough, consumption will take care of itself," is to go too far. It implies that no matter what we produce, in no matter what quantity, there will be a demand for it (at some price). This is absurd. The demand for many products is inelastic—and for some it does not exist. The answer supply-siders would give to this is that they are speaking of the economy as a whole and they mean that once something is produced the producer has gained the wherewithal to buy something else, so the whole economy ought to stay in balance. Unfortunately, this is not so either. The demand side, the question of distribution, cannot be ignored. This, in fact, was a large part of the problem in the late twenties. Too much of the value of what was being produced (and, hence, the effective demand) was going into too few pockets. This did not create a sufficient demand for the items the mass production economy was turning out.

To argue that supply creates its own demand is also to remove the role of advertising in creating demand. Advertising often creates its own demand, but supply does not. If we confine ourselves to demand in the economic sense—effective demand (desire backed by ability to buy)—it would be closer to the truth (although not entirely accurate) to say that demand creates its own supply.

But we get ahead of ourselves. The supply-side interpretation of the Depression must be addressed before we get into our own. Jude Wanniski and his supply-side coreligionists worship, like the rich men of the 1920s, at the altar of laissez faire. In his book *The Way the World Works*, Wanniski sees the free market as the ultimate in democracy. Through its workings, the "global electorate" exercises its franchise. The parliament of this global electorate, it appears, is the New York Stock Exchange, which doubles as its Kaaba. This may strike some as an unusual place to associate with democracy, but one must understand that votes are apportioned among the global electorate on a basis slightly different from the famous *Baker* v. *Carr* ruling. In the marketplace electorate, votes are distributed by the formula of one dollar, one vote, or perhaps, $100,000, one vote.

The stock market, Wanniski insists, is a "great, sensitive brain" governed by market forces in such a way that stocks can never be "overpriced" or "underpriced," but "at any moment, the market is fully priced." Such a view is not a scientific observation, but a statement of dogma. It sounds rather like Rousseau's mystical concept of the General Will: "The Sovereign, merely by virtue of what it is, is always what it should be."

Starting with revealed truth, Wanniski faced the task of finding a way to make the Depression conform. Since the market is supposed to work properly if left alone, the Crash meant, *ipso facto*, that there had been government interference. In Arthur Laffer's terminology, government interference takes a "wedge"—a slice of the pie of private transactions. Wanniski's job was to show that the Crash had been caused by the entrance of a wider "wedge" into the free economy. Wedges are usually taxes and regulations. Thanks to Andrew Mellon, Calvin Coolidge, and friends, these were not expanding in the late twenties. Hence the persistent problem for classical economists in explaining the Depression on their terms.

In 1977, Wanniski found the long-sought deus ex machina: the Hawley-Smoot tariff of June 1930. It had been there all along, of course, but was not on stage at the proper time. Practically everyone had agreed that the tariff increase was a terrible mistake and had made the worldwide Depression worse. It seemed impossible, though, to blame the crash of October 1929 on a law that was not enacted until eight months later. But Wanniski found a coincidence between some of the big drops in the stock market in 1929 and key Senate votes indicating that low tariff forces would be defeated.

One can readily imagine the thrill that Wanniski must have felt at finding the Grail. It is understandable that he allowed himself to be carried away with his enthusiasm. Yet on more sober examination his discovery, while interesting, seems less meaningful. If, as Wanniski insists, the market is "a great sensitive brain" that is guided by the perceptions—or "votes"—of masses of investors, it is hard to see how it could have responded so dramatically to information that went almost unnoticed at the time. As Wanniski himself says, "not a word appeared in the press making note of the remarkable coincidence" of a key tariff vote and the big drop of stock prices in the last hour of trading on October 23. He makes no mention of any words in the press about the similar remarkable coincidences of other days in the fall of 1929. To say that the market can react spectacularly to information the importance of which is not widely recognized is to deny Wanniski's own view of the market. In any event, many investors believed that higher tariffs would help rather than hurt business.

None of this is to say that the Hawley-Smoot tariff, to which we shall have occasion to return, was insignificant, or anything other than a disaster. But it cannot let classical economics off the hook. The tariff, it may be said categorically, was not the sole, or even the principal, cause of the Crash or the Great Depression. Wanniski must be given credit for the degree of his faith. His panacea of low taxes and low (or no) tariffs, he asserts, would have either prevented Mussolini and Hitler from coming to power or made them nice fellows as rulers. But for bad tax and tariff policies, Wanniski tells us, there would have been no Second World War. He even implies that Hitler became an expansionist only because he had a bad (high) tax policy. It would be nice if the world were so simple. [2]

Tariff policies were not at the root of the Great Depression, but international forces did play a role in causing the collapse. The trouble began with the World War and the drastic changes it made in the relative economic positions of the world's leading nations. Throughout the nineteenth century, Great Britain had been the world's dominant economic power. By the beginning of the present century, that position was being severely challenged by both the United States and Germany. The war temporarily eliminated Germany as a competitor, but it also weakened the British position and strengthened that of the Americans. Most significantly, the war converted the United States from a net debtor to a creditor nation. This change obligated the country to take more responsibility for the smooth operation of the international economy and to make adjustments in its other policies, including exports and tariffs.

As the leader of the world economy in the century prior to 1914, Great Britain had used its lending policies as a means of stabilizing the international situation. It had also clung to free trade for more than a half century. Doing so caused short-term disadvantages for some British manufacturers during economic slumps, but it helped prevent the sort of self-defeating tariff war that worsened the world depression in the early 1930s. In the 1920s the British were no longer able to act as the stabilizer of the world economy. That position should have gone to the United States, but American leaders did not want it, or rather, they wanted only part of it. Much of the historical debate over whether the United States was isolationist in the 1920s misses the point. The nation wanted all the advantages (and profits) of participation in world affairs, while minimizing the responsibilities that went with world leadership. American leaders sought to make their country an isolated participant in world affairs. They wanted to be in the world, but not of it. It did not work.

The World War also made for instability in the international economy because of the reparations and war debts problems. The Dawes Plan of 1924, the first of several international attempts to ease the reparations-debts problem, set in motion an arrangement whereby Americans lent money to Germany to pay reparations to France and others, who in turn made debt payments to the United States. Although American financiers had already made some large foreign loans before this, the Dawes loan started American foreign lending on a massive scale. Americans in the mid-twenties were new to the role of international financier and approached the market like "a sales department with a new article." The volume of American foreign lending soared to $900 million in 1924 and $1.25 billion in both 1927 and 1928. This large-scale lending accomplished several things: it provided an outlet for the excess incomes of wealthy Americans, it allowed reparations and war debts to be paid for a time, it offset tariff barriers, and it helped American producers secure overseas markets. This last function was similar to that of domestic credit; it helped an unbalanced economy avoid collapse for a few years, but ultimately made the Crash worse when it came.

American lending abroad slowed in 1928 and 1929, as the opportunities for money-making on Wall Street became more attractive than the interest rates of foreign loans. British lending in the 1800s had generally been countercyclical. When times were good, investment opportunities at home attracted British capital away from international loans, but during slumps the British expanded foreign lending. This policy had had an obvious stabilizing influence. American foreign lending in the twenties and early thirties, though, followed an opposite pattern: lending expanded during the early part of the boom and contracted drastically with the Depression.

By the late twenties, each country was seeking to advance its own interests, even if in the process it worsened the positions of others. In a delicate, interdependent world economy, these "beggar thy neighbor" tactics were suicidal. Nowhere should this have been more clear than in the United States. This country was trying nothing less in the 1920s than to be the world's banker, food producer, and manufacturer, but to buy as little as possible from the world in return. This attempt to eat the world and have it, too, was the epitome of a self-defeating policy. This is one of the two points on which the popular blaming of Herbert Hoover for the Depression has some validity. As secretary of Commerce, Hoover was a dynamo in promoting both foreign sales and foreign investment, yet he consistently favored high tariffs for the United States. Such attempts to assure a very "favorable" balance of trade cannot succeed for long. It is impossible, in fact, for a country to maintain a "favorable" balance of trade over a prolonged period. What all nations should strive for is a balance that is neither favorable nor unfavorable. If the United States would not buy from other countries, there was no way for others to buy from Americans, or to meet interest payments on American loans.

The weakness of the international economy and contradictory American foreign economic policy unquestionably contributed to the coming of the Great Depression. If the origins of the calamity are to be kept in perspective, though, it must be realized that while the world collapse was cutting $1.5 billion from American exports between 1929 and 1933, domestic contraction was slicing $12 billion from the American gross national product. Statistically, internal problems appear to have had an effect on the American Depression some eight times greater than did foreign ones. This is not to underestimate the significance of the nearly 10 percent of American GNP that went into exports in 1929. That $5 billion was of great importance, and the loss of a large portion of it undoubtedly affected domestic parts of the economy. But if we are to find the most telling causes of the Depression, we must look within the borders of the United States.[3]

In some respects, the agricultural problems of the 1920s were closely tied to the international difficulties just recounted. The fundamental problem facing the American farmer in the twenties was chronic overproduction of agricultural commodities around the world. ("Overproduction" in the economic sense, of course, does not necessarily mean that there was more food and fiber than the world's ill-fed and ill-clad multitudes could use. It refers only to more than there was a paying market for.) For some reason this excess agricultural supply did not create its own demand. This is especially extraordinary from the perspective of classical economics, because farm products were in as close to a genuine free market as existed. This was a big part of the farmers' problem. They still sold on a largely unregulated world market and had no control over the prices they received, but the companies from which they bought and the banks from which they borrowed were often in a position to dictate terms.

The more immediate cause of the farmers' troubles in the 1920s was World

War I. Here is Herbert Hoover's other small contribution to the origins of the Depression. During the war the American government, particularly in the person of Food Administrator Hoover, encouraged a vast increase in agricultural production. This was fine during the war, when European production was way down and demand was very high. But after the war the success of the wartime stimulation of increased production came back to haunt the nation's farmers. Added to this were increased mechanization and more specialization and intensive methods. Another little-noted but quite significant cause of overproduction of farm products in the twenties was the coming of the automobile and tractor on a large scale. Some 25 million acres previously used to grow feed for horses and mules was turned to other agricultural uses as the demand for beasts of burden declined. The result of all these factors was, as I noted earlier, that farmers struggled with a depression throughout the prosperity decade.

Although the farmer was declining in American society in the 1920s, his continuing importance to the economy must be recognized. In 1929 fully one-quarter of all employment in the United States was in farming. A solidly based prosperity could not leave out this segment of the population. If the whole economy was dependent upon agriculture, agriculture was particularly dependent upon the export market. More than one-quarter of American farm income in 1929 came from exports. The economy as a whole could be harmed by a sharp reduction in exports, but farming could be devastated by such an export drop. That is precisely what happened in 1929 and subsequent years.

The weak position of American farmers was exacerbated by their heavy burden of debt. The expansion of the war years had helped to double farm mortgages from $3.3 billion to $6.7 billion between 1910 and 1920. In the first five years of the twenties, another $2.7 billion was added to the total. When the debt burden is added to chronic overproduction and the perennial farmers' problems, such as uncertain weather, it is clear that the structural weaknesses in this quarter of the American economy were sufficiently grave as to pose a threat to the whole economy.

Until the middle of 1928 the abundance of credit, both at home for the farmers and abroad for those who bought their products, helped to keep the decidedly leaky craft that was American agriculture afloat. Beginning in 1928, though, the already overloaded ship had new weights dumped upon it. It began to sink. As American international lending declined, the ability of consuming countries to pay for imports of American foodstuffs dropped sharply. At the same time, the world market was becoming further glutted. The Soviet Union decided to begin large exports of wheat in 1928. The full impact of this decision on the world market was not felt until 1930, but it did not help the worldwide surplus.

Agriculture in the 1920s was more than a blemish on the face of Coolidge Prosperity; it was a vital segment of the economy that was falling further behind and increasingly unable to keep its consumption up to the level the rest of the economy required of it. Plainly this was not the trigger of the Depression, but it was an unsound feature of the fundamental business of the country.[4]

The structure of American business and industry itself—the crown jewel of Coolidge Prosperity—was another contributing factor in bringing on the collapse of that prosperity. The idealized American economy of small, freely competing units upon which much of the nation's economic thought and social philosophy was based was largely a thing of the past by the 1920s. In the preface to the classic study of corporate concentration in the twenties that he undertook with Gardiner C. Means, *The Modern Corporation and Private Property*, Adolf A. Berle put his finger on the crux of the phenomenon: "American industrial property, through the corporate device, was being thrown into a collective hopper wherein the individual owner was steadily being lost in the creation of a series of huge industrial oligarchies." By the end of the twenties, roughly two-thirds of the industrial wealth of the United States had passed "from individual ownership to ownership by the large, publicly financed corporations," Berle said. It was enough to make a red-blooded American uneasy, even in the midst of unprecedented prosperity.

In 1929, 200 corporations controlled nearly half of all American industry. The $81 billion in assets held by these corporations represented 49 percent of all corporate wealth in the nation and 22 percent of all national wealth. Moreover, the trend was rapidly in the direction of even more concentration. The estimates for three years earlier were that the same corporations held 45 percent of corporate and less than 20 percent of all national wealth. And by 1932, Berle calculated that 600 American corporations owned 65 percent of the nation's industry. The rest was "spread among millions of little family businesses." Some 2000 men, the active directors of the giant corporations, were in a position to dominate the life of the United States.

What the degree of concentration exposed by these figures meant, Berle and Means said, was that the political economy of Adam Smith, which had dominated American thinking for a century and a half, no longer applied. The competitive model drawn by Smith as the "great regulator of industry" was based upon the assumption of numerous small units whose prices were determined by market forces. This was not the case in the United States of the late 1920s, and so the market had lost its inherent tendency toward equilibrium.

The booming decade of the twenties saw a new headlong rush into corporate mergers. President Hoover's Committee on Social Trends reported that between 1919 and 1928 some 1200 mergers "involving the disappearance of over 6000 independent enterprises" had been registered.

Clearly a major cause of the unstable foundation beneath the prosperity decade was the dichotomy between the reality of massive concentration in American business and the classical economic model upon which policy was still being based. Coolidge and Mellon were playing by the rules of Adam Smith's pin factory at a time when Henry Ford's River Rouge plant was more indicative of the true nature of the economy. It would have been remarkable if disaster had not resulted from this discrepancy.[5]

One result of the use of eighteenth-century theories to deal with twentieth-century reality was a growing maldistribution of income in twenties America. No cause of the Great Depression was of larger importance.

According to the famous Brookings Institution study, *America's Capacity to Consume*, the top 0.1 percent of American families in 1929 had an aggregate income equal to that of the bottom 42 percent.* Stated in absolute numbers, approximately 24,000 families had a combined income as large as that shared by more than 11.5 million poor and lower-middle-class families. Fully 71 percent of all American families (a term that includes unattached individuals) in what was generally regarded as the most prosperous year the country and the world had ever known had incomes under $2500. At the other extreme, the 24,000 richest families enjoyed annual incomes in excess of $100,000 and 513 American families that year reported incomes above $1 million. Nor was the prosperity of the twenties narrowing the gap. On the contrary, the authors of the Brookings study concluded, it appeared that "income was being distributed with increasing inequality, particularly in the later years of the period." The income of those at the very top was increasing more rapidly than that of any other group. Late in the twenties, "a larger percentage of the total income was received by the portion of the population having very high incomes than had been the case a decade earlier." Between 1920 and 1929, per capita disposable income for all Americans rose by 9 percent, but the top 1 percent of income recipients enjoyed a whopping 75 *percent* increase in disposable income. The share of disposable income going to the top 1 percent jumped from 12 percent in 1920 to 19 percent in 1929. Here in stark statistics was one of the principal causes of the Great Depression.

Maldistribution of wealth in 1929 was even greater than that of income. Nearly 80 percent of the nation's families—some 21.5 million households—had no savings whatsoever. The 24,000 families at the top—0.1 percent—held 34 percent of all savings. The 2.3 percent of families with incomes of more than $10,000 controlled two-thirds of America's savings. Stock owner-

* A table comparing income distribution in 1929 with that in selected years since, down to 1981, appears in Chapter 15, page 331.

ship, as we shall see shortly, was even more concentrated. The top 0.5 percent of Americans in 1929 owned 32.4 percent of *all* the net wealth of individuals. This represented the highest concentration of wealth at any time in American history. The Depression and World War II cut into this concentration somewhat, and the amount held by the top 0.5 percent has hovered around 20 percent throughout the postwar years.

A large part of the reason for the growing gap between rich and poor was that productivity was increasing at a far faster rate than wages. In the decade ending in 1929 output per worker in manufacturing leaped upward by a remarkable 43 percent. In only six years between 1923 and 1929 manufacturing output per person-hour increased by almost 32 percent. During the same period, wages increased also, but only by 8 percent—a rate one-fourth as fast as the rise in productivity. With production costs falling rapidly, prices remaining nearly stable, and wages rising only slowly, the bulk of the benefits from increased productivity went into profits. In that same six-year period ending in 1929, corporate profits soared upward by 62 percent and dividends rose by 65 percent.

This, in cold figures, was the essence of the New Era. Prosperity was shared by fairly large segments—although certainly not all—of the populace, but in very unequal portions. The rich were getting richer at a much more rapid rate than the poor were becoming less poor. Government policies during the twenties were designed to achieve just this end. The unfavorable climate for labor unions made it more difficult for workers to obtain their share of the benefits of rising productivity. And Mellon's tax cuts for the wealthy helped to aggravate the gross disparity in income levels.

The maldistribution of income, although growing worse, was already marked in the mid-twenties, while prosperity reigned. Any interpretation of the origins of the Depression that places significant emphasis on maldistribution must account for the peaceful coexistence of prosperity with maldistribution in the years preceding the Crash. This is not as much of a problem as it may appear.

For the economy to remain on an even keel, it is of course necessary for total demand to equal total supply. Say's Law to the contrary notwithstanding, there was no automatic assurance that this would happen, especially in a mass production economy with a poor distribution of income. The balance could be achieved in a number of ways. The largest part of the demand side was made up of domestic consumption of nondurable and durable consumer goods. These categories range from food and clothing in the former to automobiles and houses in the latter. Almost all the income of more than three-fourths (the lower three-fourths, of course) of the American people went for these purposes. These people were doing their part to maintain prosperity.

They could do no more for the demand side of the balance unless they were paid more.

But what of the huge incomes of those at the top of the scale, most conspicuously the 24,000 families with annual incomes above $100,000? They bought consumer goods, too, and in far larger quantities than their less affluent neighbors. They could, however, be expected to eat only so much and buy only so many cars and houses. The income of the $100,000 per year man, we find by simple arithmetic, was 40 times greater than that of the above-average $2500 man. It was not reasonable to ask the former to eat 40 times as much or buy 40 Model A's (or 15 Cadillacs). The wealthy and nearly-so had to find other ways to use their money. Up to a point, this was beneficial. Saving and investment, as well as consumption, are necessary for the well-being of the economy. This, along with luxury spending, was the principal use to which excess profits were put in the twenties. Maverick economist William Trufant Foster may have gone too far when he said of the decade, "Far from having been profligate, the nation wasted its substance in riotous saving," but there was a serious point beneath the exaggeration. Investment remained at a high level throughout the years 1925–29, dipping below 15 percent of GNP only in 1928 (a threshold that investment did not break again until 1948). This high level of investment helped keep the economy in temporary balance during the boom years, but it was intensifying the long-term problem. That is, greater investment usually meant further increases in productivity. All other things being equal, this would be to the good. But when are all other things equal? Surely they were not in the twenties. Since the gains in productivity were not being fairly distributed, the heavy investment was making the problem of income distribution worse.

Other means existed for disposing of the supply for which there was insufficient domestic demand. Two of these came to be heavily relied upon in the twenties: exports and credit sales. We have already discussed the former. The purpose and effects of the latter were similar. The basic macroeconomic problem growing out of maldistribution was that those with the means to buy more of the products of mass production industry could satiate their needs and desires by spending only a small fraction of their incomes, while those whose needs and desires were not satisfied had no money. One obvious temporary solution was to let those who wanted goods to buy them without the money. Thus the installment plan arose for the first time on a massive scale. By the second half of the decade, it was possible to purchase cars, appliances, radios, furniture, and other expensive items on "easy monthly (or weekly) payments."

Convincing Americans to buy now and pay later required a reversal of many traditional American values. People brought up on the aphorisms of Poor Richard had to be weaned. Advertising was the medium through which this message was transmitted to American consumers. First, people had been convinced to consume rather than save. Now they must go further. The idea that a penny saved is a penny earned was passé. It was now to be: Spend the penny before you earn it. It was no longer necessary to save for a rainy day, since in the New Era of eternal prosperity the sun would always shine.

By the last years of the decade, three of every five cars and 80 percent of all radios sold were purchased with installment credit. Between 1925 and 1929 the amount of installment credit outstanding in the United States more than doubled, from $1.38 billion to $3 billion. In keeping with the live-for-today attitude of many Americans in the 1920s, as the President's Committee on Social Trends pointed out, time payment schemes allowed people "to tele-scope the future into the present." The device helped to put off the day of reckoning by unnaturally keeping up demand, but it made the collapse worse when it came. When the supply of consumers who could be persuaded to make time purchases and the credit of those customers were exhausted, the installment stopgap could no longer perform its service. What made matters worse, though, was the fact that all those carrying installment debt could no longer even use all of their regular wages or salaries for new buying; part of their current income was taken up paying off past purchases.

There were at least two other ways in which demand might have been brought into balance with supply. One possibility was for the government to buy the surplus through deficit spending. Suicide would have been a more welcome suggestion to most politicians, businessmen, and economists in the pre-Depression decade. The remaining solution was, if anything, more repul-sive to the powers-that-be than were peacetime deficits: higher taxes on the rich. Again it was William T. Foster who brazenly spoke the truth. In the interests of the rich (as well as of everyone else), he said, "we should take from them a sufficient amount of their surplus to enable consumers to consume and business to operate at a profit. This," Foster neatly added, "is not 'soaking the rich'; it is saving the rich." The rich, on the whole, chose to remain unregenerate.[6]

Under these circumstances, the New Era economy was peculiarly depen-dent on a continued high level of luxury spending and investment by those receiving a disproportionately large share of the national income. If some-thing caused a sudden loss of confidence by these affluent Americans, the whole economic structure might collapse, particularly if the decline in invest-ment and luxury spending coincided with a loss of foreign markets and a saturation of the credit-purchase market at home. Just such a confluence occurred in the fall of 1929.

American values, it should be plain by now, were undergoing important changes during the 1920s. Some were long-term and more or less permanent.

Others were part of recurring shifts in attitude. Among the latter, the most notable of the twenties was an unusually high degree of self-centeredness and emphasis on financial gain.

American society—or rather, a large portion of it—came in the twenties to be preoccupied with the single-minded pursuit of riches. A growing number of people accepted the proposition that "God intended the American middle class to be rich." (Had He not so intended, why had He made middle-class Americans with wallets and savings accounts?) The mood of the times was evident in the title of a 1929 article Democratic national chairman John J. Raskob wrote for the *Ladies' Home Journal*, "Everybody Ought to be Rich." The new convert to the Democracy had a plan whereby a company would be established to help the little fellow pool his meager resources with those of others like him, so they could enjoy the benefits of stock ownership and speculation. It was, doubtless, one of the more altruistic thoughts of the age. Cynics might point out that if more people could be gotten into the market, demand for stocks would keep rising and hence the boom and profits would be bigger and better for large speculators, of whose number Raskob was one. But who are we to question the motives of a man who would make everyone rich?

The values of the society were shown, albeit in a somewhat exaggerated form, in a 1929 *New York Times* ad offering the securities of the National Waterworks Corporation: "Picture this scene today, if by some cataclysm only one small well should remain for the great city of New York [how much could be charged for water?]—$1.00 a bucket, $100, $1,000, $1,000,000. The man who owned the well would own the wealth of the city." The thought of so many parched lips was surely enough to wet those of an investor.

As more and more Americans came to believe that "they were predestined . . . to become rich without work" and excess income accumulated in the accounts of many, the likelihood of the rise of large speculative bubbles increased. The medium of speculation was of little importance. As it happened, the first one to present itself in the mid-twenties was Florida real estate. Sunshine had already done wonders for southern California; the automobile and growing wealth put Florida within reach as a winter haven for the well-to-do of the Northeast. That much of the 1924–26 boom in Florida property was based on reality. The rest was largely fantasy, but a financial fantasy in which one could get rich quickly.

Some of the land sold in Florida at rapidly appreciating prices was genuinely attractive; much of it was not. But that was of no concern to most buyers once the bubble had begun to inflate. Roughly 90 percent of those who made purchases in the Florida land boom had no intention of ever occupying the property—or even of owning it for long. Its actual value (or the fact that it turned out to be in a swamp forty miles from the nearest beach) was immaterial. One bought the land not for its use value, but in the expectation that it could be sold shortly to someone else at a handsome profit. The new purchaser was not a fool, either. He bought for exactly the same reason. Anyone who stopped to consider the situation had to realize that this game had limits and the bubble was bound to burst. The trick was, though, to ride with the expansion as long as possible and get out before the collapse. Some did. But greed was what it was all about, and many investors were tempted into staying too long. Indeed, it could not have been otherwise, because as soon as any significant number decided the time had come to get out, it inevitably became that time.

It was grand while it lasted. In 1925 the *Miami Herald* carried more advertising than any paper anywhere in the history of the world ever had before. Soon it was over, though. In 1926 deflation of values set in, and it is extremely difficult for a speculative boom to start up again after it has begun to subside. Nature provided the mandatory exclamation point at the end of the Florida boom. Two vicious hurricanes ripped through the state in the summer of 1926 and destroyed any hope for a quick revival. For the remainder of the decade, while much of America boomed, Florida sat in the doldrums. Its land boom proved to be only the dress rehearsal for the decade's biggest speculative mania: the stock market. It was a tribute to the extent of confidence Americans had in their destiny to get rich that the popping of the Florida bubble was not sufficient to make people wary of another round of speculation.

Before we delve into the mysteries of the Great Bull Market, it must be made clear that while "speculation" and "boom" are often used in close proximity one to the other, there was nothing speculative about the economic boom of the Coolidge years. It was real. The boom was built on the foundation of new technology, especially upon the automobile. Numerous other industries surged forward in the twenties, holding on to the rear bumper of the automobile. Rubber, steel, oil, road construction, suburban housing, service stations, and many others were dependent upon automotive sales. When those sales tapered off, the boom slowed; when they dropped sharply, the boom turned bust. The automobile was so central to the economy, in fact, that most authorities identify Henry Ford's decision to shut down production for six months while he shifted from the Model T to the Model A as the chief cause of the recession of 1927. The genuine industrial boom helped to fuel optimism and the belief that anyone could get rich. As the Florida bubble deflated, excess profits were already moving on a large scale into the stock market.

It was not true, as was often heard in the late twenties, that "everyone's in the market." Roughly 4 million Americans owned stock in 1929, out of a population of approximately 120 million. Only 1.5 million of those stockholders had a sufficiently large interest to have an account with a broker. The bulk of the "stockholders" owned only a few shares. The distribution of dividends tells the story of concentration of stock ownership. Almost 74 percent of all 1929 dividends went to the fewer than 600,000 individual stockholders with taxable incomes in excess of $5000. Just under 25 percent went to the 24,000 taking in over $100,000 for the year, and nearly 6 percent of all dividends went to 513 individuals whose families reported an income of more than $1 million for the year.

The reasons for the great speculative boom of the late twenties have long been debated. One culprit often pointed to is the Federal Reserve Board's decision early in 1927 to lower the rediscount rate one-half point to 3.5 percent. The decision was based on the need to save international liquidity in the wake of Britain's overvaluation of the pound. Of course it also meant easier money at home. Surely this made stock speculation easier, but it did not cause it. The source of the Great Bull Market was the same as that of the Florida land boom that preceded it: the notion that it was easy to get rich quickly. Stocks, once bought principally on the basis of their earning power, came to be purchased only for resale after their price had risen. As with a swamp lot in Florida, the quality of a stock was largely immaterial, as long as prices continued to rise. That earnings were of little interest can be seen in the case of one of the "glamour" stocks of the age: Radio Corporation of America, which leaped from 85 to 420 during 1928, even though it had never paid a dividend. When the Fed reversed its easy-money policy in the spring of 1928, it had no effect on the market. By this time the lure of fantastic easy profits had become sufficiently bright that higher interest rates were no deterrent.

The Dow Jones industrial average rose from 191 early in 1928 to 381 in September 1929, a 100 percent increase in less than two years. By most standards, this represented more than reasonable returns, but it was no measure of the possibilities for gamblers during the period. The magic words of the fantasy land in lower Manhattan in those years were "margin" and "leverage." Buying stocks on margin was similar to buying an automobile on credit. The purchaser paid a part of the price—say 10 percent—and used the stock as collateral for a loan of the remainder. Just as installment credit stimulated industry, margin buying aroused the market. Such borrowing gave the customer leverage. An illustration will show how this worked. Suppose a buyer purchased on margin a share of the aforementioned RCA stock at the beginning of 1928, putting up $10 and borrowing the remaining $75 from his broker. At the end of the year he could have sold it for $420. The stock itself had appreciated by 394 percent, which wasn't bad; but Mr. X saw his $10 investment bring him $341.25 ($420 less $75 and 5 percent interest owed to the broker). His profit for the year was over 3400 percent!

It seemed too good to be true. It was. The miracle of leverage when prices were rising would operate in reverse if prices fell. The host of margin buyers could be wiped out quickly. What was more, the whole market in 1929 compounded the leverage idea as "investment trusts" proliferated and pyramids were erected from one end of Wall Street to the other. The investment trust existed for the sole purpose of owning stocks. It had no assets other than the securities of other companies. It, in turn, sold stock of its own. By the summer of 1929, such businesses were being piled one on top of another. More and more speculators saw them as centers of intelligence—or at least inside information—that could do a better job with a person's investments than he could do for himself. It seems that the investment trusts had become a kind of electoral college for Wanniski's "global electorate." The individual investor would buy—on margin—stock in Investment Trust A, which would buy—on margin—stock in Investment Trust B, which would buy—on margin—stock in "genuine" corporations. Here was "leverage" on a grand scale. The principal building material used on Wall Street in 1929 was credit. The economic equivalent of the 1926 Florida hurricanes could easily blow down such ill-built structures.

In the uncalm before the storm, Wall Street was attracting much of the available capital in the world. As the demand for call money (for brokers' loans to allow margin buying) rose, so did the interest rate. Eventually call money rates reached 10 and 12 percent, finally even touching 20 percent. Such returns on what seemed like utterly safe investments (the loans were secured by the stocks) were irresistible. The amount banks provided for brokers' loans actually declined in 1929, but that was more than made up for by the funds being made available by corporations. In particular, corporations with surplus capital (of which there was a great deal in the wake of the Mellon tax cuts and refunds) often found lending money on Wall Street a more attractive option than expanding their own production.

Foreign investors came to the same conclusion. Some observers charged that the New York Stock Exchange was sucking up all the money in the world. Of course funds used to purchase stocks did not vanish. For every buyer, a seller received money. This obvious fact did not mean, though, that Wall Street was not absorbing funds normally available for productive purposes. Most of the money used for speculation was held for that purpose on a continuing basis and was not offered for productive investment. Moreover, as the call money rate rose, credit for other purposes became very tight. Speculators might be willing to pay 12 percent interest, since they expected a far higher return; but companies considering expansion could not afford to borrow at such rates.

Brokers' loans—probably the best measure of the extent of speculation—sped upward from less than $5 billion in the middle of 1928 to nearly $6.5 billion at year's end. Six months later the total of outstanding brokers' loans was just over $7 billion. In the next three months—July through September

1929—they shot up by another $1.5 billion. Such massive speculation was obviously unhealthy. In his *Memoirs*, Herbert Hoover passed his judgment on speculators: "There are crimes far worse than murder for which men should be reviled and punished." But who would have done so in 1928 or 1929? It was not the speculators who were reviled in that fantastic time, but those who dared to criticize speculation. *The Wall Street Journal* reacted to one criticism in September 1929 by asking: "Why is it that any ignoramus can talk about Wall Street?"

Under the circumstances, government action to deflate the bubble was virtually impossible. Ending the boom would not only have been unpopular, it almost certainly would also have caused a bust. Bubbles are hard to deflate without popping them. If the choice is between a collapse now or later, politicians and regulators normally prefer to put off until tomorrow what they could do today. Thus in his last days as president, Calvin Coolidge issued a statement declaring that prosperity was "absolutely sound" and stocks were "cheap at current prices."

One observer pointed out that by the late twenties the broker's office had replaced the saloon; it had "the same swinging doors, the same half-darkened windows." The offices of one New York investment service even had a speakeasy-style peephole. It was a telling analogy. Stock speculation provided a legal spirit of intoxication in a time when intoxicating spirits were prohibited by the Eighteenth Amendment. By the fall of 1929, those who were guiding the market were driving under the influence. A terrible crash, to be followed by unpleasant sobering experiences and an awful hangover were the likely results.[7]

Contrary to popular impression, the Wall Street Crash of 1929 was not a single collapse of one or two days (Black Thursday and Black Tuesday, October 24 and 29, are usually identified), but a long, rolling downward slide that went on for weeks, from September 3 through November 13. There were brief upsurges after some of the worst days.

The speculative boom was, of course, dependent upon confidence. Confidence was a commodity, however, that was available in abundance in 1929. The bull market had suffered two sharp breaks, in December 1928 and March 1929, only to come back stronger than ever. Accordingly, it took a prolonged, devastating collapse to convince speculators that it was really over. Even after the collapse had started in the fall of 1929, the demand for confident statements kept bringing forth a plentiful supply. Noted economist Irving Fisher of Yale, for example, declared on October 15: "Stock prices have reached what looks like a permanently high plateau." As the decline degenerated into the Crash, a wide array of leaders repeated phrases containing the words "fundamentally sound."

Not everyone was so sure, though. Since taking office in March, President Hoover had tried on several occasions to warn against speculation. In April the President ordered his financial agent to sell some of Hoover's stocks, "as possible hard times coming." When the President issued his famous October 25 statement about "the fundamental business of the country" being "on a sound and prosperous basis," he reportedly declined a request from a group of bankers to say something specifically about the stock market.

The story of the Crash itself is summarized easily. The peak of the bull market was reached on September 3. Two days later there was a break. It was not too serious, and the general assumption was that it was just another "adjustment." Thereafter the market drifted generally downward, but unevenly. Optimism remained the official watchword, and speculators continued to flock into the market. Brokers' loans rose by more in September than ever before. Prices continued downward in early October. Then on Monday, October 21, the real rout began. Although far worse days were to come, the style of the next few weeks was set on this day. The volume was huge, causing the ticker to fall far behind. This added a terrible ingredient of uncertainty to the gathering panic. Knowing that prices were falling, but not knowing by how much, produced great fear and led many to sell quickly, before prices dipped further. Such sales, of course, added to the price declines.

Wednesday, October 23, although not as often noted as the 24th or the 29th, may have been the key day of the Crash. An hour before the closing bell, a slide began which saw the Dow Jones industrials lose 21 points in 60 minutes, wiping out all the fantastic advances of July and August. Greater losses and higher volumes would be registered on subsequent days, but October 23 was the trigger. After trading closed amid the hour-long scramble to sell, many investors concluded that this time the boom was really over. They would sell the next day, before it was too late. Once a sizable number of important investors decided the boom had ended, it had ended. It had all been built on expectations of rising prices. As soon as those expectations were reversed, the market had to fall. Adding to the deflationary pressures were a large number of margin calls, which forced many to sell who did not want to. (Since the stocks provided the security for the loans, when their value fell more money had to be put up to cover the loans.)

The voluntary and involuntary decisions to sell that evening took their toll when the market opened the following morning, October 24. If the image of a downward slide had been appropriate for earlier days, the metaphor for Black Thursday was that of the bottom falling out. A vast supply of shares for sale hit the market that morning, but they failed to create their own demand until prices had plummeted. Partial recovery was achieved in the afternoon when a group of leading bankers headed by Thomas W. Lamont of J. P. Morgan moved in to support prices. This calmed the situation and restored some confidence. In the afternoon most of the terrible losses were reversed. By the end of the day, *The New York Times* industrial average had climbed back to within 12 points of where it opened.

On Friday and Saturday prices stabilized. Then on Monday the 28th, everything fell apart. The Dow lost more than 38 points, nearly 13 percent of its value at the start of the day. The bankers' group threw in the towel that afternoon, admitting that it could not stem the collapse. The next day was the infamous Black Tuesday, October 29, 1929, usually cited as *the* day of the Crash. An unprecedented 16.4 million shares changed hands. At many points during the day, no buyers were available at any price. Even after a closing rally, the *Times* index was down another 45 points at the close.

The day after Black Tuesday saw a remarkable recovery in which two-thirds of Tuesday's losses were regained. But the Crash was far from over. After a short session on Thursday, the market closed for the rest of the week. When trading reopened on Monday, November 4, a startling new collapse set in. The *Times* industrials lost 22 points that day, 37 on Wednesday (the Exchange was closed on Tuesday for election day), and a total of 50 more points during the first three days of the following week. When the Crash bottomed out (for 1929—prices would go much lower in subsequent years of the Depression), the *Times* index had lost 228 points since the high point of September 3. Fifty percent of the value of stocks in the index had been lost in ten weeks. The New Era was over.

As J. K. Galbraith has pointed out, nothing was lost in the Crash "but money." Given the values of the day, though, many losers might have responded: "What else is there?" Americans soon found out what else there was. Industrial production fell by more than 9 percent from October to December 1929. American imports dropped by 20 percent from September to December. The Great Depression was under way.[8]

The unavoidable question must be asked again: Did the Crash cause the Depression? There are two correct answers. If it is meant as a "why" question, the answer is: "Of course not!" If it is a "how" or a "when" question, the response must be: "Yes, in part." "Whatever happens in a stock market," Milton Friedman has declared, "it cannot lead to a great depression unless it produces or is accompanied by a monetary collapse." Although I disagree with Friedman's exclusive emphasis upon monetary factors, his statement is a useful one. He is absolutely right in contending that a stock market collapse is unlikely to produce a large depression by itself. But the stock market, fantasy land though it had become in 1929, was not operating in a vacuum. Wall Street's connections with other parts of the economy meant that the Crash would do more than merely reflect the weaknesses in the economic structure. Among other things, the fragile economy was heavily dependent upon confidence and the spending and investment of the well-to-do. These were precisely the things that the Crash most effectively undercut.

The fact is that, despite all the statements about fundamental soundness, both the domestic and international economies were fundamentally unsound by the late 1920s. When someone becomes ill after "catching a chill," it is not the cold itself that causes the sickness. Rather the cold reduces the body's resistance to microorganisms already present in it, which then are able to cause the illness. Some such role is the proper one to assign to the Crash. The cold wind that swept through lower Manhattan in October and November 1929 lowered the economy's resistance to the point where already existing defects could multiply rapidly and bring down the whole organism. The Crash is important in explaining how and when the Depression happened.

As for the question of where the Depression began, it clearly started in the United States. The American collapse need not have set off a worldwide depression had the United States not been the leader of the world economy. But it was. This placed certain responsibilities on the United States—responsibilities that, in the main, the nation shunned. When the United States cut lending and erected higher tariff walls, the world economy faltered further. Doubtless the world situation—sparked by American actions—in turn made the Depression worse in this country. Cause and effect should not be reversed. Geographically, the origin and spread of the Depression went in just the opposite direction from that traced by Herbert Hoover.

By far the most important question about the origins of the Depression is why? Unicausal explanations simply cannot stand up. When an American today develops cancer, it is usually impossible to say precisely what caused it. Such environmental factors as diet, chemicals, radiation, and tobacco, to name a few, may be among the possible causes. The "typical" American's environment is filled with carcinogens. The same was true of the nation's economy in the 1920s. Yet it is often possible in studying the cancer patient's life to identify things that were more likely than others to have done the most damage. Exposure to some carcinogens is more apt to be sufficient cause of the disease than others. This seems to have been the case with the Great Depression as well.

The causes of the Great Depression were many, sufficiently so that they have required a long chapter to explore. In the end, though, the greatest weight must be assigned to the effects of an income distribution that was bad and getting worse. Michael Harrington has succinctly stated the problem: "The capitalist genius for production was on a collision course with the capitalist limits on consumption." A recent statistical analysis of the origins of the Depression has concluded that, although the data are not sufficient to answer many questions, they do point toward the belief that "the Depression was the result of a drop in autonomous expenditures, particularly consumption." The most persuasive reasons for that drop have to do with poor distribution of income. It seems more than coincidental that the shares of income going to the upper reaches of American society have been appreciably smaller in the years of postwar prosperity than they were in 1929. (See table, page 331.)

Maldistribution was only one among many roots of the Great Depression, but it was the taproot. It led to both underconsumption and oversaving, and it helped fuel stock speculation. Maldistribution was the most important factor in the greatest paradox of the Depression. As eloquently stated in a 1932 article in *Current History:*

> We still pray to be given each day our daily bread. Yet there is too much bread, too much wheat and corn, meat and oil and almost every other commodity required by man for his subsistence and material happiness. We are not able to purchase the abundance that modern methods of agriculture, mining and manufacture make available in such bountiful quantities. Why is mankind being asked to go hungry and cold and poverty stricken in the midst of plenty?

Here was the central question of the Depression.[9]

3· In the Right Place at the Wrong Time?— Herbert Hoover

The public memory of many of our presidents is clouded by myth, often to the point where it is very difficult to convince anyone that a given leader was different from his popular image. Some presidents—Washington, Lincoln, the Roosevelts, to name a few—are the subject of generally positive myths, others negative images. No past president, though, has suffered quite as much abuse as Herbert Hoover. He is used as an example of a poor leader, a weak president, an awful politician. Russell Baker's Aunt Pat informed her young nephew of some of the sins of President Hoover in 1932: "People were starving because of Herbert Hoover. My mother was out of work because of Herbert Hoover. Men were killing themselves because of Herbert Hoover, and their fatherless children were being packed away to orphanages . . . because of Herbert Hoover."

There has been a method to the mythology of Herbert Hoover. He has served Democrats for a half century in the same way the "Bloody Shirt" issue was used by Republicans in the decades following the Civil War. Blaming Hoover for the Great Depression, and implying (or actually saying) that he was a man who would provide relief for banks but not people, a president who would feed foreigners but would let his own people starve, were useful reminders that the Republican party was the party of little compassion, big business, and great depressions. (Some of the stereotypes, incidentally, may be more justified when applied to subsequent Republicans rather than to Hoover.) The ultimate use of the negative Hoover symbol may have been David Levine's cartoon on the cover of the *New York Review of Books* in June 1970. It showed a man removing a Nixon mask to reveal Hoover underneath.

References to the "Hoover Depression" just will not go away. In congressional hearings in the spring of 1982, South Carolina Senator Ernest Hollings read a statement by Treasury Secretary Donald Regan asserting that President Reagan's budget was "a blueprint for growth and prosperity." Hollings exclaimed: "That's Hoover talk, man!" As the economic collapse of the early 1980s worsened, more and more people were heard to mention the names "Reagan" and "Hoover" in the same breath. In September 1982, House Speaker Tip O'Neill called Reagan "Hoover with a smile." Such implications of similarity between the two men are unfair—to Hoover.

Nor are the bitter attacks on poor Hoover the sole property of Democrats and liberals. "Supply-side" economist Jude Wanniski charges: "Most one-term Presidents only have time for one truly disastrous decision but Herbert Hoover squeezed in two." (He refers to Hoover's signing of the Hawley-Smoot tariff and his tax increase of 1932.) Wanniski is not content with these charges. He goes on to imply that Hoover's tariff was responsible for bringing Hitler to power! Even *The Wall Street Journal* has lambasted Hoover in recent years. The temptation is strong to say that with such a host of enemies on opposing sides, Hoover must have been doing something right. This is not necessarily so, but the diversity of Hoover's critics ought at least to make us more curious about his philosophy and actions.

My purpose here is not to reverse the Hoover image but to examine Herbert Hoover so that his role in the Great Depression can become more comprehensible.

Until the publication of several highly competent works in the last decade or so, finding the "real" Herbert Hoover was no easy task. Hoover's own

Memoirs were done very carelessly and are chock-full of errors, beginning with an incorrect date for his own birth and carrying through, according to biographer David Burner, hundreds of other mistakes. Even with the recent scholarship, many facts about Herbert Hoover remain beyond our knowledge. He was a very private person, and less can be said about his inner life than we would like to know in order to paint an accurate portrait. Since the opening of the Hoover papers in the 1960s, however, it has become possible to offer a reassessment of Hoover and to do so with some confidence.[1]

Prior to 1929, Hoover was a symbol, as he has been since; but before the Crash he symbolized something vastly different from what he came to stand for later. Herbert Hoover was the foremost example of the idea of the New Era. Much of the public seemed to agree that he was the perfect man for the presidency: an expert, an engineer, a businessman, a "nonpolitician," a humanitarian. Optimism was the order of the day in the late twenties, and it was no coincidence that Hoover entitled the volume of his speeches from the 1928 campaign "The New Day." But, like Henry Ford, Hoover was not only a symbol of the new that people so loved in the twenties; he also seemed to embody the old ways. His image was a "highly successful blend of modern and traditional themes."

And image is the proper word. Hoover was the first important figure in American politics to use the techniques of modern public relations on a massive scale. His publicity agents were so successful in selling their product that Hoover was generally seen in the twenties as a "human symbol of efficiency," a super businessman who could solve any problems that might arise. "We were in a mood for magic," journalist Anne O'Hare McCormick recalled of Hoover's inauguration. "We had summoned a great engineer to solve our problems for us; now we sat back comfortably and confidently to watch the problems being solved."

The image-makers had worked wonders for Hoover. But in the process they "oversold" him and created a dangerous situation. Hoover recognized the problem just before he took office, when he told a newspaper editor that he feared "the exaggerated idea the people have conceived of me. They have a conviction that I am a sort of superman, that no problem is beyond my capacity." "If some unprecedented calamity should come upon the nation," the President-elect went on, ". . . I would be sacrificed to the unreasoning disappointment of a people who expected too much."

In the twenties, the public conception of Hoover rivaled that of Henry Ford as the perfect embodiment of the American Dream. Orphaned and very poor at the age of nine, Hoover was a self-made millionaire thirty years later. In the 1920s this dream seemed viable, but when the dream became a nightmare in the thirties, most people had no desire to be reminded of it. People in depressions are not likely to have kind views of self-made men. Ford and Hoover both learned this unpleasant lesson in the early thirties. [2]

The help of publicity agents notwithstanding, Herbert Hoover's career prior to reaching the nation's highest office was remarkable. In that background can be found the character traits that led Hoover to deal with the Depression in the way he did.

Born in 1874 into a hardworking Quaker family in West Branch, Iowa, Herbert Hoover's religious upbringing left a distinct imprint on him. The Friends were not opposed to worldly success, which they saw as the just reward for individual effort, but they held that one who was enriched by society owed a great obligation of service to his fellow citizens. The successful member of the Society of Friends has a trust to do good and to bring order to a part of the world. Quaker individualism was a long way from social Darwinism. Hoover expressed the belief well when he said that what was needed was "ordered liberty," not "individualism run riot."

Hoover's father died when Bert (as he was called by family and friends) was six, and his mother passed away less than four years later. Thereafter young Hoover was shuttled among the households of various relatives. At age eleven he joined relatives in Oregon. His life was beyond his control. As an adult Hoover constantly sought to impose order and stability on his surroundings, to gain personal control. The Friends among whom the future President grew up may have been friendly, but there was a definite lack of warmth around the boy. He was lonely and his boyhood was decidedly austere.

Young Hoover was poorly prepared for college, but the new Stanford University was in need of students and admitted him to its first class, despite a serious deficiency in English that would trouble him throughout his career. At Stanford, Hoover aligned himself with the poorer student faction—the "barbarians"—against the fraternity boys. In 1893, Bert Hoover ran for elective office for the first of only three times in his life. He won the race for Stanford student body treasurer, but did not offer himself to an electorate again until he sought the presidency of the United States thirty-five years later.

Hoover took his engineering degree from the new university when the nation was in the depths of the depression of the 1890s, and he found it necessary to accept a job as a laborer in a mine. Within a few months, though, he landed a position as an engineer with a British mining company operating in Australia. Over the next several years, Hoover worked in mining operations all over the globe, using his skills as an engineer to move into the business as a manager and promoter. It was not true, as his publicity agents later claimed, that he never knew failure in his mining and business ventures, but the degree of his accomplishment was great. It was revealing of Hoover that he never acknowledged the few failures interspersed in his overall success. At the age of twenty-nine, Hoover was a financier-promoter-geologist-engineer-metallurgist. He was internationally famous as "the Great Engineer." When the United States entered World War I, Hoover was worth $4 million. He held the opinion that if a man "has not made a million dollars by the time he is forty he is not worth much."

Having made his money, Hoover turned to his Quaker duty of service. In London when the war began, he was asked to assist Americans caught in Europe. He soon joined an effort to assist the people of Belgium, a neutral country overrun by German armies invading France. Hoover quickly "took charge" of the Commission for Relief in Belgium. Its achievement—and his—was phenomenal. The CRB fed more than 9 million people in Belgium and northern France over a period of nearly five years. The overhead costs were kept to an incredible one-half of 1 percent. And child mortality was actually lower in the area the CRB helped than it had ever been before. Here was efficiency! The experience confirmed Hoover's belief that voluntary action could meet any crisis. Ironically, though, 78 percent of the CRB's funds came from government help.

The subsequent service Hoover rendered as United States food administrator during the war and director general of the American Relief Administration after the Armistice only added to his renown. The former task involved a vast increase in American agricultural production and a huge effort to cut consumption. Hoover's agency conserved without resort to rationing, another example of the efficacy of voluntary action. And the postwar European relief effort saved upward of 100 million lives. Hoover had much of which he could be justly proud. After the Versailles conference, John Maynard Keynes singled out Herbert Hoover as "the only man who emerged from the ordeal of Paris with an enhanced reputation." "Never was a nobler work of disinterested goodwill carried through with more tenacity and sincerity and skill, and with less thanks either asked or given," Keynes declared. Hoover's agents could not have said it better, but it was essentially true. The tributes were effusive. The word "Hooverize," meaning to economize for a noble purpose, entered the language for a time. *Hooverstrassen* and other variants of streets named for him appeared in many European towns. Such uses of his name provide a graphic illustration of how different his reputation was in 1919 from what it became in 1933, when the most common derivative was "Hooverville."

To Americans as well as Europeans, Hoover was a hero, a "gruff humanitarian" who could accomplish miracles. "I think," Brand Whitlock, the progressive former mayor of Toledo, wrote of Hoover to Secretary of War Newton Baker in 1917, "he is precisely the man that the liberal movement in America, as you and I understand it, needs . . . his hardness is all on the surface." Other progressives agreed. "He is truly a wonder, and I wish we

could make him President," wrote Woodrow Wilson's assistant secretary of
the Navy in a 1920 letter. "There couldn't be a better one." It was an opinion
the writer, Franklin D. Roosevelt, would eventually alter, but not until after
Hoover was in the White House. In 1928, FDR still referred to Hoover as "an
old personal friend."

Hoover was the Great Progressive Hope for 1920. He appeared to be just the
ticket—a "hardheaded moralist," that wonderful paradox so loved by Americans, the "practical idealist." Although most of his relatives were Republicans, Hoover had never been actively involved in politics. Progressives in
both parties wanted to claim him. The Democrats, desperately in need of a
superman to replace Wilson and stem the Republican tide, might have nominated Hoover. But at the end of March of the election year he finally publicly
announced his Republican affiliation and his willingness, under certain conditions, to be drafted. *The New York Times* translated the meaning of Hoover's
statement: "In effect, Mr. Hoover tells the Republican party he would like to
belong to [it] if [it] will be the kind of a party to which he would like to belong.
And that, if he belongs to it, he would have no objection to leading it." The
Republican bosses were not interested.

When Warren Harding began to form his Cabinet, he said he wanted the
"best minds." The progressive Hoover was appointed to Commerce, balancing the arch-conservative Mellon (of whom Harding had never heard before
the appointment was suggested to him) at Treasury. Hoover's talents and
ideals had a new showcase, one in which it could be seen just what sort of
progressive he was.[3]

In his post at Commerce during the eight years of the Harding-Coolidge
administrations, Herbert Hoover demonstrated both his character and his beliefs in ways that clearly prefigured his tragic presidency. The department
itself moved from the shadows to the center stage of government activity.
Whether Mellon was, as his friends insisted, "the greatest Secretary of the
Treasury since Alexander Hamilton" (which, it may be helpful to point out,
they meant as a compliment) or only the greatest since Carter Glass (who had
held the post under Wilson), Hoover was the greatest secretary of commerce
in our history. "There is reason to doubt," TRB wrote in *The New Republic* in
1925, "whether in the whole history of the American government a Cabinet
officer has engaged in such wide diversity of activities or covered quite so
much ground."

Hoover had no use for the strict laissez-faire attitude of the nineteenth
century. As early as 1909 the future President declared, "The time when the
employer could ride roughshod over his labor is disappearing with the doctrine of 'laissez faire' on which it was founded. The sooner the fact is recognized, the better for the employer." He often said that the root problem in our

economic system was the unfair distribution of income between labor and capital. Nor did Herbert Hoover believe the government's role in the economy ought to be minimized. He emphatically did not think that the business cycle was "natural" and so could not be mitigated by government action. He proposed a dynamic program for dealing with the depression of 1920–22 and, thanks to Hoover, President Harding took more action at that time than had ever been tried by any previous president in the face of economic collapse. Government actions, such as public works spending, should provide a "balance wheel" for the economy, Hoover maintained. After his 1928 victory Hoover called for a "prosperity reserve fund" in which excess government income in times of prosperity would be held for use in providing jobs during hard times. This amounted to a small-scale countercyclical proposal, seven years before the publication of Keynes's *General Theory*.

Hoover's views on taxation were similarly far removed from the Coolidge-Mellon philosophy. He told Harding that income from the securities of the "well-to-do" ought to be taxed at a higher rate than "earned" income. "I would like to see," Hoover wrote in 1924, "a steeply graduated tax on legacies and gifts . . . for the deliberate purpose of disintegrating large fortunes." Hoover opposed taxes on necessities and believed that the lower and much of the middle class should be free of taxation. In direct contradiction to such people as Du Pont, Raskob, and Mellon (not to mention the present-day leaders of Hoover's party), he said the burden should be borne by the rich. It should be seen as their social duty.

Hoover was clearly not a strong champion of unrestricted capitalism. In his often-mentioned but seldom-read 1922 book, *American Individualism*, Hoover insisted that the key to the American system was equality of opportunity. He had no truck with the belief that people really were equal, an idea he wrote off as "the claptrap of the French Revolution." For Hoover's conception of the American system as just to be accurate, he had to argue that everyone in the "race" had an equal start and played by the same rules. Thanks to "free and universal education" and the government acting as "umpire of fairness," candidate Hoover contended in 1928, each "runner" had a fair chance. Those who won were those who deserved to win. Given Hoover's assumptions, this might seem to be a fair system. But it should be noticed that despite all the qualifications and regulations, Hoover had worked his way back into dangerous proximity of social Darwinism.[4]

If the rationale for Hoover's system approximated that of social Darwinism, however, his vision was well separated from dog-eat-dog, devil-take-the-hindmost individualism. Here was not "rugged individualism," but what Hoover saw as a uniquely American blend of opposites, a nation of "socially responsible individualists." "I believe we in America are developing a new economic thought, a new basis of community action . . . cooperation," Hoover wrote. He downplayed the differences among conservatism, liberalism, and progressivism. All aimed, or should aim, at his goal of equality of opportunity. One day he would find that opposites could not be united so easily.

The emphasis on the American system may seem strange from one who spent so much time abroad. As with Thomas Jefferson, however, extensive foreign travels served to confirm Hoover's belief in the superiority of American ways. One of the clearest effects of Hoover's contacts with foreign systems was his conviction that government intervention in the economy, although necessary, must be strictly limited. "I have witnessed not only at home but abroad," the Republican candidate said in 1928, "the many failures of government in business. I have seen its tyrannies, its injustices, its undermining of the very instincts which carry people forward to progress." Hoover wanted a moral economy, by which he meant an efficient one, a progressive economy in the sense of achieving the most progress. Too much reliance on the national government to solve problems, he fervently believed, would endanger progress and efficiency, and subvert liberty as well. By "liberty," though, he did not mean what the anti–New Deal "Liberty League" of the mid-thirties meant. "As to the Liberty of the Wall Street Model," he wrote in 1934, "I am not for it . . . they give no consideration to the fact that property or the power over property can be used to abuse Liberty. It can be used to dominate and limit the freedom of others."

What Herbert Hoover was grappling with was one of the fundamental problems of the United States in the twentieth century: how to apply our Jeffersonian heritage in a highly concentrated, urban industrial setting. Hoover spoke much in the language of Jefferson, Jackson, and Lincoln, but he understood that he lived in a different age. Individualism no longer meant "go it alone." His ideal remained people ruling themselves, through voluntary cooperation. It was—and is—an attractive concept. Hoover was naive, but that, in a way, is refreshing. He clung to the belief that people could be gotten voluntarily to cooperate, share, and help their neighbors, that coercion was unnecessary. It may be more of a commentary on our age than on Hoover that most of us today do not understand him.

But Herbert Hoover was not one to admit failure or that his ideals were unworkable. Throughout his career, as biographer Joan Hoff Wilson has noted, Hoover had a large "capacity for self-delusion where failure was involved." In his business career he had a tendency "of ignoring, dismissing, whitewashing, or even falsely claiming success for those inevitable financial failures common in any speculative profession." At least one of his mining ventures in Australia, for example, was a large failure. As he would not admit failure in business, neither would he in ideas. Herbert Hoover constructed his values into a closed system and would not let events or facts upset his ideal vision. His system—unlike the real world—was based on rationality, but he was irrational in his defense of it.

Here is one of the great Hoover ironies. Although he was the Great Engineer, the objective scientist who said all that was needed to make the government work was to collect the facts, he came finally to reject those facts that did not support his viewpoint. It is impossible to understand Herbert Hoover and his reaction to the Depression without seeing that he was that rarest of politicians, a man of principle. He was an idealist who firmly (and rightly) believed that means cannot be separated from ends. This was admirable up to a point. But his method proved disastrous during the Depression when crisis conditions demanded results without much concern about method.

The ends desired by Herbert Hoover were not so different from those sought by Franklin Roosevelt. All the public images to the contrary notwithstanding, Hoover was not opposed to helping Depression victims and did not favor letting the "unfit" fend for themselves. What Hoover sought was the sort of vast voluntary effort that he had witnessed during the war. He wanted people to rise to the challenge through charitable organizations. His pleas were answered. Private giving in the United States reached a record level in 1932. What Hoover desperately wanted to avoid was not assistance for the poor, but the demoralizing effects of a federal dole, which he believed would be "to lower wages toward the bare subsistence level and to endow the slackers." The President insisted, though, that his first priority was to prevent suffering. "I am willing to pledge myself," he declared in February 1931, "that if the time should ever come that the voluntary agencies of the country together with the local and state governments are unable to find resources with which to prevent hunger and suffering in my country, I will ask the aid of every resource of the Federal Government. . . ." But Hoover said he had "faith in the American people that such a day [would] never come." Exactly. Hoover by this time was operating on faith, not facts.

It was not that Hoover rejected all facts and always refused to take pragmatic action. He finally accepted the conclusion that voluntary action would not save the nation's banks, so he agreed to government intervention to help them. He continued, though, to reject federal relief for the unemployed. "In the one case," as historian Albert Romasco has pointed out, Hoover "faced the facts as he found them and acted; in the other, he persistently denied the facts and refused to act." The President was willing to handle the banking crisis pragmatically, but remained idealistic in dealing with unemployment. Hoover seemed to many Americans to be splitting ideological hairs while people starved.

In a similar vein, President Hoover endorsed a $45 million appropriation to feed the livestock of Arkansas farmers during the 1930 drought, but rejected a grant of $25 million for food for the farmers and their families. As in the case of unemployment relief, the President was worried about destroying people's self-reliance and "spiritual responses." Hogs and bankers, it seemed, were in one category, while farmers and the unemployed were in another. Hoover saw no danger of undermining the independence and self-respect of the former group, but was more solicitous of the latter's spiritual health.

It was not that there was anything inherently wrong with Hoover's ideals, but that he held to them so tenaciously, if sometimes inconsistently. In upholding his values no matter what and refusing to go along with the demands of the American people during the Depression, Herbert Hoover became, in biographer Joan Hoff Wilson's words, "the remembered reactionary and forgotten Progressive."[5]

The reasons for Hoover's politically suicidal adherence to his principles must be sought in his character and psychological makeup. Herbert Hoover's greatest virtue may have been his consistency; his worst defect was his rigidity. These are, of course, two terms for what is basically the same quality. If we choose to say that a person is tenacious, unshakable, or steadfast we are usually praising him; to call him stubborn, obstinate, or pigheaded is to condemn him. Other terms, such as inflexible, uncompromising, or adamant, might be used in either a positive or negative sense. Hoover was all of these things—or this one thing—but whether it is good or bad depends not only upon the adjective chosen but also upon the conditions under which one is unyielding.

Herbert Hoover became so unbending in his commitment to his beliefs that he was willing to contradict the obvious. Despite all the evidence of the gross inadequacy of local relief efforts, Hoover said in his December 1931 State of the Union address that "Our people are providing against distress from unemployment in true American fashion by magnificent response to public appeal and by action of the local governments." Richard Hofstadter explained Hoover's apparent mental process well: "Because, on his postulates, his program should have been successful, he went on talking as though it were, and the less his ideas worked, the more defiantly he advocated them."

Hoover's commitment to his ideas was so strong that when they had failed completely by mid-1932, he could offer only to try the same ideas over again. In the end, his rigidity was a matter of pride. In 1962, two years before his death, Hoover wrote to a friend: "The world has gone bye [sic] you and me. However it is some satisfaction that you and I have gone through the agonies of these years without 'deviations.'" Herbert Hoover "stayed the course."

Next to his refusal to "deviate," Hoover's most notable characteristic was his apparent scientific detachment. He seems to have been a man of little personal warmth. His great humanitarian efforts involved masses of people and were acts of administrative efficiency, not personal contact. He evidenced little emotion or empathy with individual sufferers. Much of his life before entering Harding's Cabinet had been spent roaming the globe, often entailing long absences from his family. While we still do not know very much about his private life, there are many indications that it was nearly as impersonal as his public appearance. In the New Era none of this was held against Hoover. His image as "efficiently cold-blooded" suited the public mood in the 1920s. During the Depression, though, compassion came to be more highly prized than detached efficiency.

In order to be efficient, it is usually thought necessary to be a hard worker. This Herbert Hoover was. The contrast with Coolidge is overwhelming. Hoover hated idleness, an attitude that helps to account both for his despising the "idle rich" and his fear of the "dole" creating an "idle poor." He would not be idle himself. Smashing his immediate predecessor's precedent of long vacations, Hoover panicked at the very idea and tried to avoid vacations entirely. If forced to take one, he would hurry from one sightseeing spot to the next at breakneck speed.

Herbert Hoover was that unusual—but far from unique—person who is both shy and possessed by a passion for publicity. He had, according to David Burner, "the need of an orphan to show the world he had made good." Hoover wanted credit for what was accomplished, but he also was, or wanted to be, humble, as befits a Quaker. A private person with a large ego runs certain risks. Bernard Baruch pointed out Hoover's problem, while overstating it. Hoover had, the financier asserted, "delusions of grandeur—he really believes all the wonderful things he has written about himself."

Any man who craves success and fears failure to more than the ordinary degree is likely to be hypersensitive to criticism, and Hoover was no exception. Coolidge's policy was "If you don't like it, don't read it." Hoover was incapable of assuming this attitude. One critic in 1931 said that the President was "thin-skinned and sensitive." The same could have been said of him before the Depression, when there was far less provocation from detractors. The political life may have held great attractions for such a man, but it was not the best life for him.[6]

"Politics," wrote William Allen White in a marvelous mixed metaphor, "is one of the minor branches of harlotry, and Hoover's frigid desire to live a virtuous life and not follow the Pauline maxim and be all things to all men, is one of the things that has reduced the oil in his machinery and shot a bearing." Certainly the general assessment is that Herbert Hoover was a poor politician. The weight of the evidence supports that view, but more than a few grams can also be counted on the other side of the scale.

Republican congressional leaders were generally hostile to Hoover. They questioned his "Republicanism"—the nonpartisan stance that pleased so many voters did not meet the approval of party leaders. Senate majority leader James E. Watson of Indiana was barely on speaking terms with the President.

"How can a man follow the President unless he has St. Vitus's dance?" Watson asked. Isolationists and "patriots" in Congress questioned the "Americanism" of the citizen-of-the-world in the White House. In a private 1931 letter, California's Hiram Johnson referred to Hoover as "the Englishman in the White House."

Congressional distaste for Hoover was generously reciprocated. He once called Congress "that beer garden up there on the hill," and cited one senator as "the only verified case of a negative IQ." After the Depression began, the President saw the proper role for Congress as that of spectator. There was, in his opinion, no need for legislation, so Congress was just an annoyance to a recovery plan that would be a cooperative effort of the White House and business leaders.

A poor relationship with Congress can often be overcome if a president has the public behind him. But here Hoover's political weaknesses manifested themselves. After all the wonderful publicity work of earlier years, Hoover as president was unable to present himself to advantage. He always insisted upon writing his own speeches. It was a serious mistake, as the activity consumed huge amounts of time and yielded generally poor results. Hoover's prose was, one historian has noted, always "suggestive of a light fog moving over a bleak landscape." Nor did the content of some of his statements help his standing with the public. Some of the things he said appeared callous, disingenuous, or just plain stupid. In March 1930 the President announced, without any statistics upon which to base the assertion, that the worst of the unemployment would be over within sixty days. He was trying to build confidence and may have believed it, so we will forgive that one. Less understandable was his declaration a few months later to a visiting group of public works advocates: "Gentlemen, you have come sixty days too late. The Depression is over." On another occasion Hoover told the press that things were not so bad: "The hoboes, for example, are better fed than they have ever been. One hobo in New York got ten meals in one day." At least the President was still wedded to statistical precision, even if his sources of information were slipping to the sort of anecdotes later so favored by Ronald Reagan. In writing his *Memoirs*, Hoover made the fascinating statement that during the early thirties "many persons left their jobs for the more profitable one of selling apples."[7]

Had Calvin Coolidge run and won in 1928, he would have been president for longer than anyone who had served before him. As the country neared the crest of the wave called Coolidge Prosperity, the incumbent President seemingly could have had reelection for the asking. He did not ask. On one of his long vacations, in the Black Hills of South Dakota, on August 2, 1927, Coolidge took the most surprising action of his presidency. He summoned reporters and as they filed by him he handed each one a small slip of paper reading:

"I do not choose to run for President in nineteen twenty-eight." Reporters asked for further comment, but Coolidge said "None" and proceeded to lunch.

The most intriguing reasons for Coolidge's decision to step down center on the possibility that he foresaw what was coming. First Lady Grace Coolidge put it most succinctly: "Poppa says there's a depression coming." By the accounts of both Mrs. Coolidge and Senator Watson, the President believed that times were changing and that he was better suited to the passing than the coming era. "I know how to save money," Mrs. Coolidge said her husband told a member of the Cabinet, ". . . Perhaps the time has come when we ought to spend money. I do not feel that I am qualified to do that." "From this time on," Coolidge told Watson, "there must be something constructive applied to the affairs of government, and it will not be sufficient to say, 'Let business take care of itself.'" Coolidge knew he was not the man to undertake such a constructive policy.

A simpler explanation for President Coolidge's decision is that, never energetic, he had grown increasingly tired. Being president had become more of a burden than the novelty it had once been. On the way back from issuing his statement, Coolidge told Republican Senator Arthur Capper of Kansas: "Ten years in Washington is longer than any other man has had it—too long!" This cautious Yankee was not one to wear out his welcome.

If the nation must do without Coolidge, what better choice could there be than Herbert Hoover? If "something constructive" must be done, Hoover was the man to do it. He won the Republican nomination handily.

The Democrats met in Houston and managed to bind over the wounds of four years earlier sufficiently to nominate Al Smith on the first ballot. It has often been said that Smith had no chance to win because he was a Catholic, an urbanite, and an opponent of prohibition. This is only partially correct. That Smith had no chance to win is true, but the principal reason had nothing to do with his religion, origins, or positions on issues. At the height of Republican prosperity, no Democrat, even a Methodist born in a log cabin in Indiana who was as dry as the Sahara and a member in good standing of the Klan, could have defeated Hoover. This is not to say that these issues may not have hurt Smith, or even that one of them might not have been sufficient in itself to cause his defeat. The point is simply that they were unnecessary to Hoover's victory; the prosperity issue—"A Chicken in Every Pot, Two Cars in Every Garage"—was decisive.

Something momentous was taking place in American political life in 1928. In much of the country Al Smith was ridiculed for his background working in the Fulton Fish Market, his poor education and grammar, his Lower East Side pronunciation. Cartoons portrayed him as an urban ruffian, a man who would disgrace the Office of President of the United States. This was a direct reversal of an earlier development in American politics in which the poorly educated, ungrammatical country roughneck—symbolized by Andrew Jackson—became the embodiment of American democracy. Then the urban enemy was pictured as cultured, educated, an undemocratic "professor," the role for which John Quincy Adams seemed well cast in 1828. A century later, though, the East and the city had taken on a very different character in the rhetoric of rural America. Perhaps more important, the "ploughman" of whom Jefferson had spoken so reverently and whom Jacksonians had elevated above the professor—the simple working man looked down upon by the elite—had moved to the city and exchanged his plow for an assembly-line wrench. The effects of this change were fully apparent for the first time in the Depression decade.

It was not plain that Smith was the more liberal and Hoover the more conservative candidate in 1928. Despite their vastly different backgrounds both men were "administrative progressives." It was no coincidence that both wound up bitter opponents of the New Deal. Smith and Raskob spared no effort in trying to "out-Coolidge" Hoover. Smith followed the advice of his predecessor as Democratic presidential nominee. "When will we get done with the fool idea that the way to make the party grow is to scare away everybody who has an extra dollar in his pocket?" John W. Davis asked in 1925. "God forbid that the Democratic party should become a mere gathering of the unsuccessful!" If God was not interested in forbidding it, Smith and Raskob were. Their attempt to repeal prohibition and shift the tax burden to the poor spent $7 million, compared to the $9 million Hoover effort. This was a spending ratio far better than the Democrats usually enjoy, but it did them little good at the polls.

For his part, Hoover ran a mildly progressive campaign. Despite the mildness of his progressivism, it was enough to upset many Wall Streeters. Hoover was known to favor a cooling of stock speculation. Although they would have preferred Coolidge—or Mellon—"the Interests" had to settle for Hoover, who spoke in favor of public power and labor unions and against strike-stopping injunctions. Franklin Roosevelt wrote letters to businessmen warning that Hoover had "shown in his own Department a most alarming desire to issue regulations and to tell businessmen generally how to conduct their affairs." Business interests, FDR assured his friends in that line, would be safer with Smith than with Hoover in the White House. It was all to no avail.

In September, Roger Babson warned that "if Smith should be elected with a Democratic Congress we are almost certain to have a resulting business depression in 1929." It was a warning similar to the one in the probably apocryphal story about the man who was warned in 1964 that if he voted for Barry Goldwater the United States would become deeply involved in Vietnam and the nation would be torn apart. A few years later the man ran into the person who had made the warning and said to him: "You were right. I voted for Goldwater and all those terrible things happened."

Hoover crushed Smith by more than 6 million popular votes and won the electoral college by a greater margin than Harding had eight years before. The outcome—if not its magnitude—was entirely predictable months before the ballots were cast. (It is tempting to speculate that some dry, anti-urban, anti-Catholic Democrats may have dropped their opposition to Smith on the grounds that anyone they nominated was going to lose, so he might as well be a Catholic, whose religion could be blamed for the defeat, making another Catholic nominee unlikely for years to come.) The 1928 Republican victory was so decisive that the party's domination seemed assured for another generation. The title of an article by the Democratic National Committee's former publicity director expressed the political wisdom of the day: "Will the Democrats follow the Whigs?" Like the similar inquiries about the Republicans after 1936, 1964, and 1974, this question was premature. In accepting his nomination, Hoover had declared: "We in America today are nearer to the final triumph over poverty than ever before in the history of any land. The poorhouse is vanishing from among us. . . . We shall soon with the help of God be in sight of the day when poverty will be banished from this nation." It was a statement that came back to haunt Hoover more than any other. The candidate had left himself few outs. It soon became apparent that God either was not a Republican or had decided that the Great Engineer needed no help. In any event, God offered to take none of the blame for the Depression. Herbert Hoover was left to answer alone when prosperity, rather than poverty, was banished from this nation.[8]

Herbert Hoover's presidency began with great expectations. This, of course, could be said of most, if not all, administrations. But hopes were especially high in 1929. For many, the greatest hope was the return of progressivism after eight years of conservative Republican rule. Among the new President's more interesting symbolic acts were the closing of the White House stables and the retirement of the presidential yacht. Before his first week in office ended, Hoover openly declared that "excessive fortunes are a menace to true liberty by the accumulation and inheritance of economic power."

Within a few months Hoover's plans were upset by the Crash. Previous presidents—with the partial exception of Harding (and that mostly at Hoover's urging)—had followed a simple policy in dealing with economic depressions: they waited. This was in keeping with the mystical approach to economics—the belief that the business cycle was "natural" and beyond the ability of men to influence. Adam Smith's invisible hand would automatically correct economic problems.

Sitting and waiting were alien to Herbert Hoover's temperament. His great confidence in humankind's abilities—and his own—led him to believe that action could mitigate the effects of an economic downturn. He moved swiftly and boldly to stem the decline. Hoover sought to create a business-labor-government partnership that would reverse the usual behavior of depression periods. Within a month of the October 1929 stock market crash, President Hoover began a series of conferences with leaders in all fields. He got employers to pledge not to cut wages. This, he hoped, would maintain purchasing power. If wages were to fall, it should happen only after prices had dropped. If workers were assured that their real wages would not decline, they might be persuaded to buy. The usual inclination in hard times is, of course, to cut back and save as much as possible. Hoover and the business group he organized, the National Business Survey Conference, urged Americans to reverse their frugal habits and spend the nation back to prosperity.

Along similar lines, the President sharply increased spending for public works. In 1931 public works expenditures reached the unheard-of sum of $700 million. In the past, such government spending had, like personal buying, been cut in depressions. Hoover's initial response amounted to joining with business and other leaders in what Walter Lippmann called "an open conspiracy not to deflate." The hope was that the Wall Street crash could be isolated and that everyone else could proceed as if it had not happened.

The essential ingredient needed for rapid recovery, President Hoover firmly believed, was confidence. What mattered was not reality, but the expectations of businessmen. The President wasted no time in launching his confidence offensive. "The fundamental business of the country, that is production and distribution of commodities," Hoover declared on the day after Black Thursday, October 24, 1929, when the bottom fell out of the stock market, "is on a sound and prosperous basis." Less than a month later the President assured the nation that "any lack of confidence in the economic future or the strength of business in the United States is foolish."

His understandable desire to engender confidence led Hoover down a disastrous path. He hoped that prediction of prosperity would be father to the fact. But his optimistic talk backfired when it quickly proved to be groundless. Hoover's statements then looked at best ridiculous, at worst heartless and fabricated. Soon the President and his cohorts were publicizing only those statistics that were reassuring. And when no numbers fitting that description were available, they began to imply that such favorable figures existed. Hoover's quest for confidence became desperate. In the fall of 1931 he took time off to go to Philadelphia for a World Series game. The only purpose of the trip was to try to convince people that normal times were returning.

The idea of bringing about recovery through building confidence was not a foolish one. Three underlying problems thwarted the plan: First, the collapse was far worse than almost anyone realized, and optimistic talk is a drug that either works in the initial dose or not at all. The Great Depression was too serious a disease to be cured instantly by an injection of confidence. The second reason for the failure of Hoover's prescription was that he was not the proper physician to administer it. The President talked optimism, but he looked and acted pessimistic. "He took an unnecessarily dark view of situations," Baruch contended. It was one of Hoover's most striking contrasts with Roosevelt, and a trait that was most inopportune during the Depression.

The third problem with the business-confidence approach was that it proved to be self-defeating. Hoover concluded that the most essential factor in restoring an optimistic business climate was balancing the budget. "The course of unbalanced budgets is the road of ruin," he declared. The President therefore devoted much of his energies in 1931 and 1932 to the goal of a balanced budget, which was hopeless under the circumstances. Yet, as Hoover himself had recognized in less frantic times, cutting spending and raising taxes diminished purchasing power and made the situation worse.

As Hoover's hopes collapsed with the economy, his rigidity grew more pronounced. He began to sound more like his reactionary adversaries than the generally progressive man he had always been. "We cannot legislate ourselves out of a world economic depression," the President told a press conference in May 1931, "we can and will work ourselves out." A month later Hoover told an Indianapolis audience that the notion that we could get out of the Depression by congressional action was similar to believing that we could "exorcise a Caribbean hurricane by statutory law." This was a far cry from the 1929 Hoover, who insisted that business cycles were *not* like the weather, and were susceptible to human remedies. A year later, the same President who earlier had so greatly increased public works expenditures was denouncing one of the relief bills before Congress as "an unexampled raid on the public treasury." "We cannot thus squander ourselves into prosperity," Hoover lectured. [9]

The Depression was bringing forth a "new Hoover," clearly an outgrowth from the same roots as the old one, but with different and less attractive foliage.

It should be apparent by now that although Herbert Hoover was taken as a symbol for the New Era, his views were at wide variance with those of the Coolidges, Mellons, and Raskobs. As the Commerce secretary during Coolidge Prosperity and the nominee of the Republican party in 1928, Hoover became associated with a constellation of beliefs to which he did not adhere— at least not fully. Progressive social worker Lillian Wald protested in 1928 that in the campaign Hoover was working with men he had previously said "made him vomit." There was no great affection between Coolidge and Hoover. "Mr. Coolidge was a real conservative," Hoover later remarked, "probably the equal of Benjamin Harrison. . . . He was a fundamentalist in religion, in the economic and social order, and in fishing." Hoover drew a line between himself and any man so conservative that he fished with worms. During the 1928 campaign, the two men appeared together and barely talked. (Donald McCoy explains the relationship between them in an interesting fashion: "If Coolidge disliked Herbert Hoover, it must be remembered that he disliked many men.") Hoover's view of Mellon was even less charitable. He believed—with ample evidence—that the Treasury secretary was a hopeless reactionary. The new President retained the old secretary of the Treasury only because of the trouble that would be raised in business circles if he let him go.

In the late thirties, Herbert Hoover pleaded that he not be made "a whipping boy for the 'New Era.'" "I was," he wrote to Mrs. Sinclair Lewis in 1937, "neither the inventor nor the promotor nor the supporter of the destructive currents of that period." Hoover insisted that he was merely the New Era's "'receiver' when it went into collapse." This seemingly self-serving statement was actually very close to the truth. As a progressive (of sorts) in 1928, Hoover was out of step with his times. The greatest of all the Hoover ironies is that he remained out of step by changing not with the times, but against them. Conservatism was popular when Hoover was elected and he was wrongly seen as a conservative. As the Depression caused that philosophy to lose its popularity, Hoover was unjustly blamed for being a conservative. Always overly sensitive to criticism, the President moved further to the right to defend a record that was not his, but Coolidge's and Mellon's. In defending that record, Hoover increasingly made it his own.

In a very complex way, several of Hoover's character traits came together to put him on a collision course with the American people. His own record of success ill equipped him for dealing with failure. Hence he naturally became more conservative as economic conditions worsened. His sensitivity to criticism enhanced his natural rigidity and caused him defensively to embrace positions he had not really held but was being blamed for. Hoover's need to be in control and to get credit led him to reject proposals from Congress and others. As the American people moved leftward, Hoover was in no position to place himself at the head of the parade. Accordingly, he marched in the opposite direction.

By the 1932 campaign, President Hoover had become an almost full-fledged conservative, or at least he sounded like one. His speeches were "a defense of a record, not a plan for reconstruction." The once great progressive was reduced by the later stages of the campaign to shivering and trembling with emotion while he delivered bitter, desperate speeches. Roosevelt's ideas, the President wildly charged, represented "the same philosophy of government which has poisoned all Europe . . . the fumes of the witch's cauldron which boiled in Russia." The Democrats, Hoover angrily asserted, had become "the party of the mob." "Thank God," he said, "we still have some officials in Washington that can hold out against a mob." [10]

Herbert Hoover's place in history, like that of most leaders, was determined more by external events than by his own character and actions. No president who suffered the misfortune of being in office when the Great Depression began would have been likely to be remembered favorably. Yet the damage such circumstances do to one's reputation need not be as bad as in Hoover's case. Grover Cleveland did almost nothing to counteract the Panic of 1893; Herbert Hoover took bold action in the face of the Panic of 1929. But Cleveland's reputation has generally fared better than Hoover's. A recent survey of scholars of the presidency rated Cleveland thirteenth and Hoover twenty-first among our presidents.

"When all is said and done," Hoover wrote in an autobiographical fragment during the First World War, "accomplishment is all that counts." Held up to his own yardstick, Hoover failed. But if the assessment is left at that, we miss his very large historical significance. Observers have long argued whether Hoover was the last of the old presidents or the first of the new. It is a fascinating question, but if one is to be fair and accurate it must finally be begged or straddled. He was both.

Hoover was, in truth, neither the last of the old nor the first of the new; he was a transitional figure between the two. He played a critical—though thankless—historical role in breaking with the past and giving moderate change a chance to succeed. He rejected the old economic fatalism, got the government involved (within his strict limits), and allowed a more-than-fair test of the idea that business could act cooperatively to bring about recovery. The failure of both the Coolidge planless economy and Hoover's voluntary cooperation opened the way for the New Deal's government-directed plans. Before people will accept what they see as extreme programs, moderate ones must be shown to be insufficient. This was one of Hoover's chief contributions. Thanks to his efforts, no one could justly complain (although of course many protested without good cause) that the government intervened without giving the private sector a chance to recover on its own. The New Deal owed its wide support in no small measure to the failures of Hoover's policies.

But Herbert Hoover's accomplishments went beyond this negative achievement. Many of the things that he tried proved to be forerunners of the New Deal. The Reconstruction Finance Corporation, of which Hoover made only limited use, became one of the more important agencies of the New Deal. He began—although with extreme reluctance—the move to public assistance. His 1930 call for a $25 million loan to the Department of Agriculture to provide seed and feed for struggling farmers was a precedent for government assistance. Despite his complaints about "raids on the federal treasury," Hoover finally signed a much watered-down version of the Wagner-Garner relief bill in July 1932. It was another precedent Hoover did not want to set, but he did.

In many other particulars, Hoover took hesitant steps in the directions in which New Dealers would leap in subsequent years. Decades later, New Deal architects Raymond Moley and Rexford Tugwell gave Hoover credit for inventing "most of the devices we used." Hoover himself explicitly approved in 1935 the concepts of deposit insurance (although only in emergencies) and the Securities Act. Moley said flatly a few months prior to his death that "Herbert Hoover originated the New Deal." In 1974, Tugwell said, "We didn't admit it at the time but practically the whole New Deal was extrapolated from programs that Hoover started." Thomas Dewey said to Hoover, long after the fact, "I have a suspicion that you would have signed practically all the legislation that FDR signed." The former President considered the statement for a minute and responded, "I think I would have." Such statements made with long hindsight exaggerate the distance Hoover traveled, but they serve as useful reminders that the differences between Hoover and Roosevelt were more over means than ends, more of style than substance. They demonstrate that the frequent politically motivated contrast between Hoover the hopelessly reactionary demon and Roosevelt the faultless progressive saint has little historical basis.

Hoover is often compared to other presidents, usually unfavorably. The most frequent presidential names that come up when similarities to Hoover are being discussed are the likes of McKinley, Coolidge, Nixon, and more recently, Reagan. This is as misleading as it is unjust. The twentieth-century President to whom Hoover bore the most resemblance is Jimmy Carter. Both Hoover and Carter were "nonpoliticians," or tried to give that impression. Each was skilled at using new techniques—Hoover's use of mass publicity, Carter's mastery of the reformed Democratic delegate-selection process—to rise from political obscurity to the presidency. They worked the respective systems and defeated the "politicians" of their day. Both were masters of detail, incredibly hard workers, and lovers of statistics. Each tried to do almost everything himself. Each successfully portrayed himself as an expert, an engineer, a technician who could make the government work smoothly. Efficiency was the strong suit of each. In both cases their nonpolitician status initially raised them in the public's esteem. (Carter's "I'm not a lawyer" line was always good for a hand—or at least appreciative smiles—in 1975 and 1976.) But this quality that was once viewed so positively turned with a vengeance against both presidents.

"He does not understand the game," one journalist wrote, "and seems totally unable to think his way through a situation in advance. Moreover, he is dreadfully handicapped by the personal hostility of most of his own party leaders." A comment on Jimmy Carter in 1979? No, one on Herbert Hoover in 1929. Neither Hoover nor Carter understood the need to "stroke" congressional leaders and both had dreadful relations with important senators in their own parties. Each man favored rational over political solutions and hence was able to solve little.

Both Hoover and Carter were highly intelligent men, but unable as president to be convincing to the public. Both were, as president, poor speakers. Each was a humanitarian and wanted to make the government more compassionate. Both qualify as that paradoxical American breed, the "conservative progressive." The presidencies of both were judged to be failures by voters, who sharply rebuked each man after a single term.

And yet, while such analogies can be helpful, they should not be pushed too far. Jimmy Carter's handicaps as a politician seem sufficiently large to have prevented him from being a successful president under almost any circumstances. The feeling persists, on the other hand, that Herbert Hoover might have succeeded under different conditions. Hoover was long judged to be a prophet after his time. More recently, scholars of both left and right have argued that he may have been a prophet ahead of his time. Perhaps he was both, or more simply a prophet at precisely the wrong time. To argue that some of his ideas—such as community-based cooperative efforts—might have relevance today is not to say that they could have worked during the Depression.

It has often been speculated that had Hoover won the presidency in 1920— which is not a particularly farfetched idea—he might have served two highly successful terms and retired as "one of the most admired chief executives in all American history." And Charles Evans Hughes contended in 1931 that had Coolidge "chosen to run" again, the people would have looked "upon Hoover as a potential deliverer from suffering" in 1932. Whether he could then have delivered the people from their suffering is a valid question, but it may well be that Herbert Hoover simply had the misfortune of being in the right place at the wrong time.[11]

4·Nature Takes Its Course: The First Years of the Depression

Although the term "depression" had been used to describe earlier economic slumps, it came to be particularly associated with the years following the collapse of 1929. Ironically, the person most responsible for this association was Herbert Hoover himself. The President consciously used the word as part of his psychological campaign to keep up confidence. He believed "depression" had a less ominous ring to it than the more common previously used words "panic" and "crisis." Such semantic games have been played by presidents and their aides ever since, often with more success than Hoover had with his choice of words.

After the Crash, President Hoover did more than issue optimistic statements; he also held optimistic conferences. The conferences were at least partially successful. The President asked business to maintain wage rates and keep up investment. He also called for lower taxes. This was a much better approach to a depression than any previous president had employed. "Keynes could not have done better," as one economic historian has said. For more than a year, many businesses kept their pledges not to cut wages. Upon emerging from one of Hoover's business conferences in November 1929, Henry Ford told reporters that he would do his part by *raising* daily wages to $7 and launching a $25 million expansion of his operations. A greater demonstration of confidence could not be asked for, but it did little good. While many corporations refrained from wage cuts, investing heavily in the future was a more optimistic step than most were willing to take. Gross investment in the United States fell by 35 percent from 1929 to 1930 and at the same rate from 1930 to 1931. In 1932 investment in the American economy almost ceased, dropping 88 percent from the greatly deflated 1931 level and totaling only $800 million (down from $16.2 billion in 1929).

Nor did wage maintenance produce the desired effect. One reason was that as demand fell corporate leaders saw no alternative but to cut production. Rather than slicing wages, they reduced payrolls. Wages remained stable for a time for those who had jobs, but that number was shrinking. Under these circumstances, aggregate purchasing power was falling even while that of many individual workers held steady (or, as prices began to fall, actually increased). But even those who kept their jobs reduced their buying out of fear that their turn to be laid off would come soon. As an economist said in 1931, "The employed have not dared spend what they have lest they be walking the streets next month." "The basis of this fear," he pointed out, was "the insecurity which characterizes the incomes of the great masses of the population." The contrast with the mass psychology of the twenties was striking. When the outlook had been sanguine, large numbers of Americans had been willing not only to spend most of their current incomes, but to commit future income through installment purchases. Once the Depression was under way, this psychology reversed itself completely.

Declining consumption and investment were the keys to the worsening depression. But Hoover was not wrong in placing a great emphasis upon confidence. Prosperity in the twenties had been built on faith in the future. It seemed logical that what the depressed economy needed was a "fix" of faith. Business leaders at Hoover's November 1929 conferences committed themselves to an optimistic view, but if one followed the sage advice John Mitchell gave forty years later and watched what they did rather than what they said, it soon became clear that the supply of optimism, unlike that of so many commodities, fell far short of the demand. Many businessmen actually expected the worst and prepared for it. Their preparations helped ensure that the worst would, in fact, happen. Business retrenchment was the order of the day in 1930 and 1931. Demand was down and inventories were unsold. The only sensible course for the individual company to follow was to cut production and prices. In the aggregate, though, the effect of many such separate actions was to deflate the economy further. When production was cut, more people lost their jobs. This reduced demand more, both directly and indirectly (by increasing insecurity). The futher drop in demand would lead to new slowdowns in production, more layoffs, and so on in an ever-deepening spiral.

The thinking of individual businessmen was well illustrated in testimony given by Daniel Willard, president of the Baltimore & Ohio Railroad, before a Senate subcommittee in 1931. "We have had to discontinue our purchases," Willard told the committee. Replacement of rails normally was at the rate of 60,000 to 80,000 tons a year. In 1931, he said, it would not be more than 15,000. "We are not painting any buildings. We are not doing a thing that we can help in order that we may preserve, as far as possible, our financial status." Who could blame companies for following such a policy? They had no real choice. The trouble, again, was that steps that were sensible—even necessary—for separate units in the economy weakened the economy as a whole. It was a classic example of the fallacy of composition: an action, like standing up at a football game, that can help an individual harms everyone if everyone does it. So it was with attempts by companies to secure their own financial positions during the Depression.

Despite the pledges made at the presidential conferences, investment dropped precipitously, and construction, which had been falling at an accelerating pace since its peak in 1925, sank by 26 percent in 1930, 29 percent in 1931, and 47 percent in 1932. In addition to the slashes in investment and construction, the drop in demand also led to a decline in prices. This was moderate at first, with the Consumer Price Index falling by 2.6 percent in 1930. The next year, though, saw an additional price decline of 9 percent. By the time the economy hit bottom in 1933, consumer prices had fallen 18 percent from their 1929 level. Maintaining wages in the face of falling prices was no easy task for the businessman. In May 1930, Henry Ford hinted that the united wage maintenance front had some cracks. "Issuing optimistic statements on the one hand and lowering wages on the other," the automaker warned, "is a sure way to prevent betterment." Despite the cracks, the no-wage-reduction plan remained widely in effect until the late summer of 1931. Then it, like the economy around it, collapsed. When U.S. Steel announced in September a 10 percent wage reduction, other companies hastily joined in breaking ranks. Ford himself, who had eagerly sought publicity when he

raised wages, very quietly cut his pay rates in October 1931. The wage maintenance plan, the *Commercial & Financial Chronicle* declared, had "proved a
flat failure."

That conclusion would be hard to dispute. The magnitude of the collapse
was unprecedented. There was a brief recovery of sorts in early 1930. On May
1, President Hoover said: "I am convinced we have passed the worst and with
continued effort we shall rapidly recover." That month marked instead the
end of the weak recovery. By the close of the year everything—except unemployment—was down sharply. Statistics tell only a small part of the story, but
they are startling. From the top of prosperity in 1929 to the bottom of depression in 1933, GNP dropped by a total of 29 percent, consumption expenditures by 18 percent, construction by 78 percent, and investment by an
incredible 98 percent. Unemployment rose from 3.2 to 24.9 percent. By almost any standard, the United States was in its worst crisis since the Civil
War.[1]

Although most of the blame for failing to reverse the collapse finally fell on
Herbert Hoover, it was in fact everyone's concern. The President did not, as
historian Albert Romasco reminds us, "struggle to overcome it in some sort of
splendid isolation." Congress, businessmen, the general public—and even
some economists—had ideas on how to deal with the Depression.

On Hoover's right flank were some businessmen and archconservatives
who favored the "proven" policy used by Grover Cleveland: sit it out; wait for
natural forces to bring about recovery. The classic statement of this approach
was Andrew Mellon's: "Liquidate labor, liquidate stocks, liquidate the farmers, liquidate real estate." The Treasury secretary based this formula on an
odd, mistaken memory of the Panic of 1873, which he told Hoover had ended
quickly "and in twelve months the whole system was again working at full
speed." Mellon was only eighteen at the time and may perhaps be forgiven
this gross historical error. It is less easy to absolve him for either his tax policies in the twenties or his attitude toward the Depression.

Quite willing to let the collapse take its "natural" course, Mellon had
somehow not foreseen this healthy cleansing of the economy. A year before
the Crash he had declared: "There is no cause for worry. The high tide of
prosperity will continue." Of course for Mellon himself the ebb in the tide
was slight. Born into a family of substantial means, Mellon had increased the
family fortune through banking, steel, aluminum, oil, real estate, and other
enterprises. He was one of the richest men in the world. Still, he believed that
greedy New York bankers were responsible for the Crash. His verdict: "They
deserved it." At least Mellon was as good as his word. He recommended that
manufacturers curtail output, and he did just that in his own plants. The
Treasury secretary was, as Galbraith has observed, "a passionate advocate of

inaction." This was not Herbert Hoover's style. Hoover was especially outraged when, in 1931, Mellon refused a presidential request, as part of Hoover's effort to get bankers to help each other voluntarily, to contribute a
million dollars to an emergency fund to save the Bank of Pittsburgh. If
Mellon would not volunteer, what chance did voluntarism have?

While Hoover did not agree with Mellon's deflationary inaction as an approach to the Depression, the Treasury secretary was far from alone in his old-
fashioned beliefs. The hand of the "liquidationists" was strengthened by the
extreme fear of inflation that survived the terrible German experience of 1923.
Even moderate programs that involved inflation seemed terrifying. A year
after the Crash, Senate Democratic leader Joseph T. Robinson of Arkansas
wrote to Bernard Baruch that the only solution was to "sit steady in the boat."
"I grow more and more impressed," Robinson told the Democratic financier,
"with the necessity of conservative action. . . ." Baruch, as might be expected,
was of the same mind: "No government agency . . . can cure this situation."
In 1930 and 1931 there was, in fact, something approaching consensus in
business and political circles to follow Mellon's prescription. Even the President accepted—at least in public—Mellon's contention that the first priority
in restoring business confidence must be balancing the budget.

"The fact that we have let nature take its course," declared the Stock Exchange's Richard Whitney, "may augur well for the ultimate prosperity of the
country." One business representative said in 1931 that since the Depression
was "a business ailment," "the remedy, if one is to be found, must be a
business remedy." This might strike some as a curious logic: "Physician, heal
thyself!" Yet it was a widespread attitude. At least equally common among the
well-to-do and their political representatives was the refusal to admit that a
serious problem existed. Such sentiments were to be expected from administration spokesmen, who had to be professional confidence builders, but they
were common enough even among lesser folk. A Maryland building contractor, for example, wrote to Hoover in 1931, "of this fact I am very positive, that
there is *not five percent* of the poverty, distress, and general unemployment
that many of your enemies would have us believe."

Others realized that there *was* a good deal of poverty and distress, but
thought it best if no one mentioned it. A Syracuse automobile dealer was one
of those who subscribed to the "out of sight, out of mind" formula. "I believe," he wrote to a government official in 1931, "that if you could see your
way clear to discontinue your publicity on unemployment and its kindred
evils, the return of prosperity would be less hampered." An apparently wealthy Minnesota man contended that talk of starvation could not "help but have
a depressing effect." And a New Jersey woman found the "UNEMPLOYED"
signs used by apple sellers unsightly and tending to retard progress. Some
seemed to think that recognizing the collapse's existence bordered on dis-

loyalty. "I'm sold on America. I won't talk depression," read buttons worn by Cincinnati residents.

Some—including on occasion Secretary Mellon—went beyond trying to ignore the Depression and attempted to make a case that it was actually beneficial. Erstwhile popular hero Henry Ford was one of the leading offenders in this regard. In the fall of 1930 he declared that it was "a good thing the recovery is prolonged. Otherwise people wouldn't profit by the illness." The Depression, Ford said shortly thereafter, was a "wholesome thing in general. If we could only realize it, these are the best times we ever had." These were opinions that seem to have come more easily to Ford than to the unemployed.

In comparison with the Mellonites—and with his presidential predecessors in hard times—Herbert Hoover was extraordinarily active. But, being a man of principle, he would go only so far. His basic concept was to utilize the government as a catalyst for voluntary cooperative action in the private sector. Organizations formed with Hoover's blessings—the Federal Farm Board (established before the Crash), the National Business Survey Conference, and the National Credit Corporation—attempted to make voluntarism work. In view of the enormity of the economic disaster, it should have been no great surprise that they failed. In attempting to stabilize prices through temporary purchases of surplus farm production, the farm board lost $345 million and wound up in 1931 with farmers angrier and farm prices lower than when it started. Optimism was the National Business Survey Conference's business, its *only* business. It was a product that simply could not be moved by 1931, and the organization was quickly dissolved. This test of voluntary business action was such a failure that Hoover, who had once been bullish on the organization, neglected even to mention it in his *Memoirs*.

Herbert Hoover was nothing if not persistent. The failure of voluntarism in agriculture and industry did not dissuade him from trying the idea with bankers. Created at the President's behest in October 1931, the National Credit Corporation amounted to a final test for voluntary cooperation. Within two months of its inception the NCC was an unmistakable flop. Hoover said years later that the bankers' association quickly "became ultraconservative, then fearful, and finally died. . . . Its members—and the business world—threw up their hands and asked for government action." For bankers, at least, such action would soon be forthcoming. In his recollection, the former President had hit upon an important point. Bankers, who were essential to a restoration of confidence, were fearful themselves. Like businesses, banks worked to improve their individual positions, but this weakened the economy as a whole. Banks seeking stronger, more liquid positions were loath to help weaker banks. As the latter failed, depositor confidence in the institutions in general declined, placing further pressures on all banks. They also reduced available credit. The latter fact, however, was of little immediate importance in the last two years of the Hoover administration. The nearly total lack of confidence meant that very few businesses wanted to borrow money, regardless of its availability. As Ogden Mills, Mellon's successor as Treasury secretary, said in 1932, there was "more to fear from frozen minds than frozen assets."

It was a singular misfortune that a president as committed to confidence as Hoover was so incapable of instilling it. Hoover did keep trying, though. Early in 1931 he said: "What this country needs is a good big laugh. There seems to be a condition of hysteria. If someone could get off a good joke every ten days, I think our troubles would be over." What humor there was, though, was likely neither to lift the spirits nor please the President. An example: "Business is improving," says the straight man. The comedian responds: "Is Hoover dead?"

In the fall of 1930, Hoover announced formation of the President's Emergency Committee for Employment (PECE), with Colonel Arthur Woods, an old right-thinking Hoover friend who had organized relief activities during the 1921 slump, as its chairman. As part of the confidence campaign, the committee was a marvelous example of positive thinking. Even the name was well chosen: "emergency" meant the crisis would not last long, and "employment" avoided emphasizing the negative "unemployment." The PECE was the President's committee—a classic Hoover organization. The purpose was "to soothe the nation, not to alarm it." The committee collected and passed along ideas and sketchy information, always accentuating the positive. No attempt was made to collect reliable statistics on such critical subjects as unemployment levels and local availability of relief funds. The PECE's information (like that of Ronald Reagan) was anecdotal rather than accurate. Thus Colonel Woods was able to declare: "The country as a whole has responded most heartily to the emergency. Evidence is pouring in that communities are organizing to meet their own problems." This statement was true enough, as far as it went. Many communities *were* organizing heartily. But the implication that this would be sufficient to meet the mushrooming needs was highly misleading.

The Emergency Committee lasted until August 1931, when it was transformed into the President's Organization for Unemployment Relief (POUR). Named as new chairman was Walter S. Gifford, president of AT&T. This amounted more to a facelift than to a change of policy or function. The intention remained to manipulate public psychology to bring about a return to optimism. While attempting to spread cheer, POUR did try to help local groups raise money to help the unemployed. The main thrust of POUR was advertising. Major periodicals contributed space and leading advertising agencies provided talent. The results can be judged from the following copy, which appeared beneath a picture of an unemployed worker in a POUR ad:

They tell me there's five or six million of us—out of jobs. I know that's not your fault, any more than it is mine. But that doesn't change the fact that some of us right now are in a pretty tough spot—with families to worry about—and a workless winter ahead.

Understand, we're not begging. We'd rather have a job than anything you can give us.

We're not scared, either. If you think the good old U.S.A. is in a bad way more than temporarily, just try to figure out some place you'd rather be. . . .

I'll see it through—if you will!

How much encouragement those among the jobless who were either insufficiently frugal to have kept up their magazine subscriptions or lucky enough to find a periodical in a trash can derived from such ads cannot be said with certainty. It does seem likely that the ads were helpful in collecting funds for local relief.

Chairman Gifford was called before a Senate subcommittee in January 1932. He provided assurances that local relief groups were prepared to meet the needs of the winter. Quotas for contributions, Gifford said, had "gone over the top." Gifford told the committee: "My sober and considered judgment is that at this stage . . . Federal aid would be a disservice to the unemployed." Gifford was uninterested in learning of actual needs, unemployment levels, and the like. He told the senators that he did not think "the data would be of any particular value." As the POUR director continued to paint his brightly hued landscape, Democratic Senator Edward P. Costigan of Colorado became exasperated. "You are always hopeful!" he exclaimed. "I find it pleasant, Senator, to be hopeful," Gifford responded. [2]

On the ground, where relief was desperately needed, it was both less pleasant and less hopeful than in the circles frequented by Gifford. The President and his committees continued to insist that state and local agencies had the situation in hand. These claims were based on reports from the governors. This source was less then reliable, as governors are not in the habit of admitting that their states are beyond their control. Those in positions to know conditions were less sanguine. At the time Gifford was giving his cheerful assessments, his claims—and Hoover's—were directly contradicted by the head of the Association of Community Chests and Councils. "I am stating that the funds we have are altogether inadequate to meet the situation," declared Arthur T. Burns, "and we are not yet aware that local public funds have been appropriated in any such amount as to meet the situation."

In point of fact, it was beyond the realm of possibility for states and localities to meet the enormous need for relief by the beginning of 1932. In most places funds were completely exhausted. People would not readily tolerate tax increases in the midst of a depression. Borrowing through bond issues was a possibility, but few buyers could be found for the bonds. And in many states constitutional restrictions that would take years to alter prohibited unbalanced budgets. In 1932 only eight states provided any form of unemployment compensation, and none of these even nearly approached adequacy.

The Hoover administration remained adamantly opposed to federal relief. Secretary of War Patrick J. Hurley spoke the typical language of the administration in June 1932, when he argued that "to give a gratuity to an individual, is divesting men and women of their spirit, their self-reliance. It is striking at the very foundation of the system on which this nation is builded." This may have been true, but it was clear that one could not subsist on spirit and self-reliance for long. The Hoover argument was dependent upon the invalid assumption that the degree of suffering was still manageable on an individual basis. Hurley demonstrated this connection when he went on to say: "I disagree with all who think that there is not still opportunity for the man with the nerve and the capacity and the desire."

Misconceptions in high places covered the gamut from the possibility of getting jobs, through the adequacy of local relief funds, to the degree of acute suffering among the unemployed. "Nobody is actually starving," Hoover always contended. As in most of his perceptions of Depression conditions, the President was mistaken. Relatively few people literally starved, but genuine hunger was widespread. One study of health in eight cities found that families with a fully employed member had 66 percent less illness than those of the unemployed. Desperate people took desperate steps to feed themselves. In rural areas hungry people sometimes turned to eating weeds. Less appetizing were the urban scenes of men digging through garbage cans and city dumps. A Chicago widow followed the practice of removing her glasses before using rotting meat; in this way she avoided seeing the maggots she was eating.

Many of the nation's more fortunate people were genuinely concerned about the plight of the unemployed. Generous contributions to local relief funds made this point clear. Some of the philanthropic impulses of the well-off were more ambiguous, though. Several proposals were made, for example, to feed the unemployed with leftovers from the tables of the affluent. In 1932 a midwestern newspaperman suggested that the needy be fed with "the side dishes of vegetables, half bowls of soup, half cups of coffee, portions of rolls . . . and all the rest that is left on plates by restaurant patrons." Some such suggestions were undoubtedly made tongue in cheek, but similar ideas were actually put into practice in some localities. Princeton University's eating clubs were among those generous enough to send their table scraps to the poor.

A growing discontent among the jobless (and those who feared they soon might be) was evident in many of their statements, including the letters they sent to Hoover and his committees. Of course working-class Americans were far from agreed on what the Depression's causes and solutions were. Opinions ranged from "All this country needs is assurance that the law of supply and demand can work," to finding the major cause of the collapse in "the placing of property rights above human rights." Some searched for culprits, human or supernatural. A nearly illiterate Illinois man who warned that "the Emty Stomack does not Recogniz no laws," * placed the blame on the devil. Many Americans who had come to believe that Herbert Hoover was Lucifer in disguise would have agreed. From the other side of the political fence, a New Haven Republican suggested that the Wall Street Crash and Depression had their "origin in the subtle schemes and manipulations of the interests and institutions represented by Alfred E. Smith and his friend Raskob."

The search for a Satan, in the form of elephant, donkey, or Wall Street octopus, was all too common in the early Depression years. A good many workers, though, came to believe that it was not individual demons but the whole hellish system that had caused their troubles. A Pennsylvanian wrote to Hoover in 1932 that it was the capitalists who were "responsible for this unemployed situation," and so they should be made to pay the cost of remedying it. A Denver man made the point that "purchasing power is not lost but redistributed and now rests in the hands of a few." He did not suggest altering that situation drastically, but others did demand legislation giving everyone his fair share. A poorly educated New Yorker said in late 1930, "I am neither an anarchist, socialist, or communist—but, by God, at times I feel as if I should affiliate myself with the radicals."[3]

The picture that many contemporaries have given us of the mood of the downtrodden in the Hoover years is one of defeat, resignation, and self-blame. Hitchhikers picked up by author Sherwood Anderson apologized for their condition. Marquis Childs wrote in January 1933: "What is surprising is the passive resignation with which the blow has been accepted; this awful pretense that seeks to conceal the mortal wound, to carry on as though it were still the best possible of all worlds." Childs saw something quite the opposite of class consciousness. "Sympathy," he said, "is all too often an ill concealed form of triumph, a kind of 'Thank God, someone is worse off than we are.'"

* Throughout the book, letters from "ordinary" people are reproduced exactly as they were written, without corrections in spelling or grammar.

The sad acquiescence of a farmer at the foreclosure of his estate was shown when he said only, "The Lord gave and the Lord has taken away." Louis Adamic, speaking of American workers, wrote in 1931: "I have a definite feeling that millions of them, now that they are unemployed, are licked." *The New Yorker* summed up the contemporary view in mid-1931: "People are in a sad, but not a rebellious mood."

To a large extent, all of this was true. The initial reactions to the Depression on the part of many of its victims were bewilderment, defeat, and self-blame. Glad to believe themselves responsible for whatever success they had enjoyed in the twenties, many "ordinary" people found themselves during the early Depression in a position similar to that of businessmen and Republicans. Having taken credit for the good, they had little choice but to accept responsibility for the bad. As they groped for some way to understand the calamity that had befallen them, however, some of the unemployed began to work toward values quite different from the egoism that had dominated the twenties.

Discontent remained amorphous in the Hoover years, but the potential for the development of a value system stressing morality, justice, equality, and compassion was beginning to appear. "Oh why is it," a December 1930 letter asked Colonel Woods, "that it is allways a bunch of overley rich, selfish dumb, ignorant money hogs that persist in being Senitors, legislatures, representatives Where would they and their possessions be if it were not for the Common Soldier, the common laborer that is compelled to work for a starvation wage." The writer went on to complain: "In the Public Schools our little children stand at salute and recite a 'rig ma role' in which is mentioned 'Justice to all' what a lie, what a naked lie."[4]

It is plain that in its first years the view of the Depression from below was rather different from the way it appeared in Washington or on Wall Street.

While slowly growing discontent in society's lower ranks was of obvious concern, Americans of the upper ranks had other troubles in 1930 and 1931. Many people believed that the Depression was somehow caused by European events. Cutting ourselves off from the contagion of the rest of the world seemed a possible way out. As it happened, it was instead a way to get in deeper.

A world economic conference in Geneva in 1927 had recognized the threat that tariffs posed to the functioning of the world economy. The conference reached agreement on a tariff truce. It was an idea somewhat like the nuclear freeze proposals of the early 1980s. The hope was that a truce would provide a climate in which meaningful tariff reductions could take place. Tariffs were, however, as American as apple pie, or at least as American as the Republican party. High import levies were, as Joseph Schumpeter put it, "the household remedy" of the Grand Old Party. Although Herbert Hoover did not march in lockstep with his party, he was "solid" on the tariff. The candidate pledged in 1928 that, as part of his program to help farmers, he would seek higher duties on agricultural commodities. True to his word, the new President called a special session of Congress, beginning in April 1929, for the purpose of "selective revision" of the tariff. But the hearings on the bill were not restricted to questions involving agricultural duties. Hoover and the congressional Republican leadership failed to keep control over the bill. The traditional backscratching process that had turned so many previous attempts at tariff reform into higher duties began to operate. In the view of one early student of the enactment of the new tariff, Hoover must bear a heavy share of the blame: "To manage pressure is to govern, to let pressures run wild is to abdicate."

Talk on the tariff for public consumption centered upon helping the American farmer and "equalizing" production costs at home and abroad. Both arguments amounted to nonsense. There should have been no doubt that farmers would lose more from increased costs of articles they bought than they would gain from price increases for their products, most of which faced little foreign competition in the domestic market. As one historian noted, "Far more farmers wore shoes than sold hides." An American Farm Bureau Federation study indicated that American farmers would gain $30 million from the increases in agricultural tariffs and lose $330 million. The "equalizing costs" concept was a wonderful political tool, but was impossible of realization. In any event, such arguments were a smokescreen. What the organized business interests sought, simply, was to exclude foreign competition so they could charge more for their products.

The special session dragged on, through the Crash, without settling the tariff question. Opposition by Democrats and insurgent Republicans blocked the increases sought by the special interests. Some Republicans even blamed the Crash on Democrats' opposition to high tariffs. When the regular session began a few weeks later, the high tariff forces pushed harder. The resulting Hawley-Smoot tariff, which Hoover signed into law in June 1930, was the highest in American history, with *ad valorem* rates jumping from an already high 33 percent to more than 40 percent.

Before its passage, economist (and later U.S. Senator from Illinois) Paul Douglas drafted a statement denouncing the bill and quickly obtained the signatures of more than one thousand economists representing 179 institutions of higher learning and all but two states. The statement pleaded for congressional rejection of the bill or, failing that, a presidential veto. The economists' arguments that the high tariff would "injure the vast majority of our citizens" and that "countries cannot permanently buy from us unless they are permitted to sell to us" were unassailable. It is understandable, of course, that many people might not take the views of a thousand economists too seriously in 1930, but on this point they were right, as events soon showed. Other nations rapidly retaliated and the world depression grew worse.

The Hawley-Smoot Act, conceived in 1929, was the last will and testament of the New Era's "every man for himself" ethic. It was motivated, as tariffs almost always are, by the greed of special interests. Fittingly, this relic of the prosperity decade left as a further legacy of the twenties a deepening of the Depression that other aspects of that era had already produced.

With the new tariff war, the focus of economic problems shifted to the international arena. Herbert Hoover contended for the rest of his life that the United States economy was recovering in the spring of 1931, when the collapse of the European banking system plunged this nation, along with the rest of the world, deeper into depression. In fact an *extremely* modest improvement was registered in the first months of 1931, but stock prices and other indicators hit new lows in April and continued with brief pauses to plunge until the bottom was hit in 1932 and early 1933.

The international crisis of 1931, like that of 1914, began in Austria. In May it was announced in Vienna that a major bank, the Kreditanstalt, had lost during the preceding year an amount equal to the total of its capital reserves. The bank remained open with assistance from the Rothschilds, the Austrian government, and the Austrian Nationalbank. The news, however, precipitated a banking crisis in Germany. The domestic political situation in Germany was tense, with great pressure on the government from both Nazis and Communists. Chancellor Heinrich Brüning argued that the nation was on the verge of bankruptcy and could not continue to make reparations payments. The idea was to get relief on reparations in order to defuse the Nazi attacks on the government. A financial crisis would help make Brüning's point. The act worked too well. A run on German banks led in mid-July to the failure of one of the nation's leading financial institutions and the temporary closing of all banks in the country.

One reason that all this was of more than academic interest in the United States was that a complete German collapse would have taken many American banks with it. Chase and the Guaranty Trust Company, for example, each had placed nearly half of their capital in German securities. This was, of course, foolish (it bears disturbing similarities to the massive lending by American banks to Third World countries in the late 1970s and early 1980s), but the Germans were offering especially high interest rates and there was a shortage of investment opportunities in the United States.

While the German banking crisis was unfolding, President Hoover issued a proposal for a one-year moratorium on all intergovernmental payments. The French, who had not been consulted before Hoover's announcement, were outraged, although they finally agreed to go along. The German government, however, felt itself obliged to make increasingly jingoistic statements in order to undercut the Nazi appeal. When Berlin began talking of military parity, it gave rise to fears in France and elsewhere that freeing the Germans of their reparations obligations would enable them to put the money saved into arms. The hoped-for consequences of the "breathing space" provided by the Hoover moratorium never materialized. By the second half of 1931, most of the world's leading countries were consumed by supernationalism.

The final blow of the international crisis of 1931 came in September when, after a prolonged run on the overvalued pound, the British abandoned the gold standard. This was followed immediately by heavy conversion of dollars into gold. The pressure certainly did not help the weak American economy, and the fall in prices, imports, and industrial production accelerated.[5]

Herbert Hoover's insistence that the Depression was ending early in 1931 and continued only because of the European financial crisis is unacceptable. There can be no question, though, that foreign problems added to the woes of the depressed United States.

Politics in a democracy ought to be a mirror of social and economic life. As values change, so should the political complexion of the nation. The appearance of this reflected image is not always immediate, however.

In 1930, American voters had their first significant opportunity to react to the altered conditions brought by the Depression. The results were not encouraging for President Hoover or his party. Republican House losses were their worst since 1922, when another economic slump had hurt the party in power. The Republicans did remain the majority party, winning 54.1 percent of the popular major party votes for House seats, compared with 57.4 percent two years before. But their margin of control in both houses was paper thin. In the Senate, the Republican majority dropped from 17 before the election to one after it. In the House, where Democrats picked up more than 50 seats in 1930, the Republican margin was so small that it had vanished after by-elections were held in the 13 months between the election and the convening of the Seventy-second Congress. Eleven of the 13 new senators elected in 1930 were Democrats, and progressives of both parties fared well.

When the Seventy-second Congress convened in December 1931, Hoover seriously considered allowing the Democrats to organize both houses so that they would have to share responsibility (and blame) for economic policies. This idea can be viewed as a bold stroke of genius or sign of lack of leadership. It might have helped the country to reduce partisanship in determining how to deal with the crisis. It might have helped Hoover politically in 1932 by allowing him to take a page from the as yet unwritten 1948 book of Harry Truman. Although it is highly unlikely that he could have pulled it off, Hoover might have been able to get off the defensive by attacking a Democratic Congress. However that might be, the idea was surely unrealistic. Neither party would go for it. Republican senators were not prepared to give up their committee chairmanships in order to help either the nation or Hoover's chances for reelection. And Democrats, sensing victory in 1932, had, as political scientist Arthur W. MacMahon pointed out at the time, "no wish to incur premature responsibility." It was a Republican depression, and Democrats wanted to keep it that way. It was the old idea of giving one's opponents enough rope to hang themselves.

Although there are indications that in private Hoover said he believed moderate deficits might be as necessary in depressions as in wars, he concluded that this position was politically untenable. The deficit for fiscal 1932 was the largest, as a percentage of federal expenditures, in peacetime American history. It approached 60 percent of spending, more by this measure than even the Reagan deficits of the early 1980s. As the Depression slashed normal revenues, the only way to balance the budget was to raise taxes. Both Mellon and his successor, Ogden Mills, were longtime advocates of a sales tax, the regressive nature of which held great appeal for the wealthy. The desperate need for new revenue if the budget was to be balanced appeared to give them their chance. The battle lines were drawn over the issues of taxation—and a national sales tax in particular—as the critical issue Congress would decide in preelection 1932.

At first it did not appear likely to be much of a battle. Democratic leaders deferred to Bernard Baruch, whose differences on the subject with Mellon, Mills, and Raskob were negligible. Democratic Speaker of the House John Nance Garner, publisher William Randolph Hearst, and Jouett Shouse, director of the Democratic National Committee, all endorsed the sales tax idea. Their argument was simply that it was essential to balance the budget and a sales tax was the only way to raise sufficient revenues. Democratic leaders were so anxious to place the tax burden upon those least able to pay that they allowed Mills to maneuver them into accepting responsibility for authorship of the idea.

Given the bipartisan support, some sort of sales tax seemed certain. But one quarter had not yet been heard from: the people. It was apparent to many Americans that the purpose of the sales tax was to "soak the poor." Some of its advocates made little attempt to hide this. The sales tax was "proper," said Hudson Motors' board chairman Roy Chapin, "since the lower income brackets pay nothing to the maintenance of the National Government." As it happened, though, the view of proper redistribution subscribed to by Chapin and so many business and political leaders was not shared by those upon whom the tax would fall. A large number of Americans perceived that "the interests" were trying to substitute the sales tax for income and corporate taxes. "It's a wonder," said Socialist leader Norman Thomas, "they don't put a tax on tickets to the breadline." (Forty years later, members of the Reagan administration suggested almost that: to tax unemployment benefits.)

An unprecedented volume of mail poured into congressional offices. Constituents denounced the sales tax in no uncertain terms and, making democracy work as it ought to, obliged their representatives to defeat the proposal. The events of March 18–24, 1932, in the House were truly remarkable. Prompted by the largely spontaneous outpouring of sentiment from their constituents, congressmen rebelled against their leaders. Amidst cheers, foot stomping, whistling, and wild applause, progressive Republicans united with Democrats in voting to increase income taxes, surtaxes, and estate taxes. Shouts of "soak the rich!" and "conscript wealth!" rose from the House floor. Complaining of "a runaway House," Democratic leader Henry Rainey declared with more than a little exaggeration: "We have made a longer step in the direction of communism than any country in the world ever made except Russia."

When the sales tax itself came before the House, opponents defeated it handily, 223–153. The battle showed that the people had moved far ahead of Congress in their quest for fairer economic arrangements. The tax bill had become a symbol, as one lobbyist put it, "of the struggle between those who have and have not." For once, the latter won.

But *what* did they win? The Revenue Act of 1932 has often been denounced as one of Hoover's greatest mistakes. Raising taxes in a depression has come to be unthinkable (although not "undoable," as Congress showed in 1982) in subsequent decades. Many economists have blamed the further worsening of the Depression in 1932–33 on the new higher taxes. Jude Wanniski goes so far as to attribute to them the bank panic of early 1933, which he says was caused by people withdrawing deposits to pay their 1932 taxes. Leaving such silly arguments aside, the effects of the tax increase must be assessed.

The 1932 tax bill enacted the largest peacetime percentage increase in taxes in American history. Thanks to the protests from the public, however, that burden did not fall directly upon the mass of consumers, although there were a substantial number of "manufacturers' excise taxes" on specific products, which amounted to hidden sales taxes. Corporate income taxes of 1.75 percent would not seem to have approached the point of diminishing returns on the Laffer Curve. And the raising of surtaxes to 55 percent on incomes in excess of $1 million would not appear likely to have been discouraging to very many people. Did an estate tax of 45 percent on legacies of more than $10 million put a serious brake on industriousness? Even after the Revenue Act of 1932, the vast majority of Americans paid no federal income taxes whatsoever. Only about 15 percent of all American families and unattached individuals experienced the tax bite. A family of four earning $20,000—a very sizable income in those days—paid taxes at an effective rate of only 8.1 percent.

The notion that the Revenue Act of 1932 was an economic disaster is highly questionable. Parts of it were certainly counterproductive, but most of its sections were reasonably well conceived. Later changes in 1935 and 1936 were not nearly as dramatic as the 1932 legislation, which, as one economist has said, "essentially set the tax structure for the entire period up to the Second World War." One thing can be said with assurance: any harmful effects of the final act were far less than would have been caused by a sales tax, which would have reduced consumption directly.

The great failing of Hoover's fiscal policies was in not spending enough, rather than taxing too much. Even on spending though, the criticism is often too harsh. Hoover's spending of $700 million on public works in 1931 was a large step toward subsequent New Deal levels. When it came to relief spending, however, Hoover remained adamant. If anything, he grew more hostile to the idea. The President came to believe a huge work relief program might be as demoralizing as a dole. His objections easily prevailed in January 1932.

The same alteration in public mood that was evident in the outcry over the sales tax soon made itself felt on the question of relief. The momentum for federal assistance for Depression victims became irresistible. After relief measures had passed both houses by comfortable margins, Senator Costigan rightly pointed out that "legislation which was taboo in January is sanctified in June." The President vetoed the bill and obtained a version more to his liking, which he signed into law late in July. The sustained veto could not hide the fact that Hoover had lost on the question of principle. In his veto message, the President declared: "Never before has so dangerous a suggestion been seriously made to our country."

The results of the sales tax and relief battles showed that by 1932 the shift away from the self-centered values of the twenties was well under way. "Leaders" were far behind the public mood and had to scramble to catch up with their "followers." The growing values of compassion, justice, and equality were an important backdrop to the election of 1932, as well as to the rest of the Depression decade.

Until the results of that election took effect, however, the Hoover administration remained in charge. That its values were out of step with the public mood was amply demonstrated in the handling of relief under the newly passed Emergency Relief and Construction Act. Hoover's people were placed in the awkward position of administering a program to which they were philosophically opposed. The result was that the very limited federal funds made available for relief and public works were granted in the most parsimonious manner. Before a state's governor could apply for a loan (for such they were, not grants), he had to sign an oath of poverty. Then federal officials nitpickingly went over the application to see what they could reject. In short, a destitute state was to go through the same sort of humiliating experience that greeted the individual who sought assistance.[6]

The oft-noted contrast between the Hoover administration's favorable attitude toward assistance for bankers and its reluctance to help the poor centers on the most important institution created in the Hoover presidency, the Reconstruction Finance Corporation.

When the National Credit Corporation fizzled in the fall of 1931, voluntarism had had its last chance. Bankers themselves were, as Hoover said, clamoring for government action. The result was the creation of the RFC, the boldest move Hoover made in the way of government intervention to combat the Depression. The model was the War Finance Corporation. In finally taking action based on the war analogy, Hoover was recognizing that the collapse was more severe than he had previously admitted. The war analogy was important, too, because it emphasized the temporary nature of the proposed agency.

While the RFC was unquestionably a new departure, it was also based firmly upon Hoover's earlier assumptions. Business confidence was still seen as the key to recovery. "After all," Ogden Mills asked at the Senate committee hearings on the RFC bill, "what is credit but confidence?" Moreover, the President still believed the essence of the crisis to be financial. And by emphasizing credit, Hoover was still working through the private sector. Noting these continuities, some observers go on to assert that Hoover had not changed his mind about government intervention at all. Elliot Rosen points out that while the President was pushing for the establishment of the RFC, he was simultaneously slashing the budget for public works: "RFC had really served as a camouflage for the achievement of federal fiscal retrenchment of a catastrophic nature."

This, in effect, is what *happened*; it goes too far, though, to contend that it was what Hoover *intended*. Believing confidence to be central to recovery and credit to confidence, the President was sincere in his advocacy of the RFC. His assumptions were wrong, but that does not mean that he was deceitful. The purpose of the RFC was to make government credit available to banks and other financial institutions. This, its backers hoped, would loosen credit throughout the economy and bring about recovery. Had the underlying assumptions been correct, it might have worked. The fundamental mistake was to think that the credit problem was one of supply. Given the paucity of purchasing power, businesses were not interested in obtaining loans. Expansion was the last thing on the minds of most businessmen in 1932. And bankers, fearful that their own positions were insufficiently liquid, were not anxious to make new commercial loans. In short, an enlarged supply of credit would not create its own demand. Hoover and the RFC were on the wrong side of the equation.

This is not to say that the RFC did no good in 1932. What it accomplished was to save the American banking system, albeit only temporarily. RFC loans held off the collapse of the banking system until the final weeks of Herbert Hoover's presidency, thereby providing Hoover's successor with both a crisis and an opportunity. (I shall come back to the banking crisis in more detail later, because it came to a head during the weeks just before Franklin Roosevelt took office.)

The controversy over banks versus people that plagued Hoover during 1932 reached its head in the summer and centered on the famous—or infamous—$90 million RFC loan to the Central Republic Bank of Chicago. Charles G. Dawes, president of the RFC and former Vice President of the United States, was a director of the bank. When the Central Republic appeared ready to go under in June 1932, Dawes resigned his RFC position and returned to Chicago to take over the affairs of his troubled bank. The only hope was massive assistance from the RFC. This was granted, not because of Dawes's relationship with the organization, but out of fear that the collapse of the Republic would take the rest of Chicago's banks—and quite possibly those of the whole nation—with it.

Although very likely justified from an economic standpoint, the Republic loan was a public relations disaster for Hoover. A few weeks before the loan was made, Chicago's mayor had brought a delegation to Washington seeking an RFC loan to the city so that teachers and municipal employees could be paid. The RFC had no statutory power to make loans to cities and refused the request. To the public, though, the appearance was clear: Hoover's RFC gave $90 million to a bank at the same time it denied a much smaller amount to the same city to pay its impoverished workers. Democratic campaign workers could not have invented a better piece of propaganda.[7]

That many people were prepared to believe the worst about the government and its agencies in 1932 was a reflection of how much the economy had deteriorated and the social fabric frayed by late in Hoover's term. Many observers were warning that the desperate conditions facing Americans might produce a revolution. Such predictions were more common among the potential victims than the putative revolutionaries. A few years later the "substantial businessfolk" of Muncie remembered they had feared in the winter of 1932–33 that their world was collapsing. "We all laugh about it now," one of them recalled in 1935, "but it was no joke then! At the time of the national bank crisis in 1933, when it seemed for a while that everything might collapse, many of us bought a great deal of canned food and stored it in our cellars, fearing a possible seige. One family I know bought enough for more than five years."

Wealthy businessmen were not alone in their forecasts of possible bloody upheaval. Prominent journalists and politicians agreed that revolution, rather than prosperity, might be right around the corner. William Allen White wrote in the fall of 1931 that effective relief would be "the only way to keep down the barricades in the streets this winter." Several normally conservative labor leaders joined in the predictions of revolution. American Federation of Labor President William Green warned in 1931: "When despite every effort to get employment, men and women find no opportunity to earn their living, desperation and blind revolt follow." Green saw evidence that such a situation was building at that time: "Throughout the width of our country these seeds of unrest are lying ready to be quickened by the radical propagandists or other irresponsible leadership." As his words reveal, the labor chief emphatically did not favor revolution. Rather, he was suggesting that if revolt was to be prevented, industry must change its ways and give workers a fair share of the profits.

By the spring of 1932, the AFL leadership had escalated its talk of approaching violence. Other leaders went further than Green. Speaking for the AFL, Federation Vice President Edward F. McGrady told a Senate subcommittee, "There will be a revolution in this country if nothing is done at once to create work for the unemployed or to meet their needs in some other way." If the administration refused, McGrady continued, "to allow Congress to provide food for these people until they do secure work, as far as I am personally concerned, I would do nothing to close the doors of revolt if it starts." Such strong language from the lips of so conservative a man as McGrady should have been enough to frighten those who had something to lose. If not, Green himself was back before a congressional committee, threatening a "universal strike" if Congress failed to remedy the situation. When Senator Hugo Black of Alabama asked, "That would be class war, practically?" Green replied, "It would be that . . . that is the only language that a lot of employers ever understand—the language of force." "If we do not get at the fundamentals in an orderly, constructive way," Green said in August 1932, "we shall be swept aside by a tide of revolt."

When Senator Tom Connally of Texas charged the War Department with concentrating troops near urban areas, the secretary of War "referred to Reds and possible Communists that might be abroad in the land." Some Americans were scared. Their worst fears never materialized, but the period was by no means entirely peaceful.

In the realm of discontent, the farmers had a long head start. The clouds of agrarian unrest had been gathering since 1920. Those clouds were mature enough to produce small but powerful storms of violence in the Hoover years. The rebellious farmers have, however, generally been pictured as conservatives defending private property rather than revolutionaries seeking fundamental change. Arthur Schlesinger, Jr., has said of the agrarian rebels, "Theirs, as they saw it, was the way not of revolution but of patriotism." But the evidence seems to point to a different conclusion. The leader of the National Farmers Union, John A. Simpson, said, "I feel the capitalistic system is doomed. It has as its foundation the principles of brutality, dishonesty, and avarice." Conservative Edward O'Neal of the American Farm Bureau Federation told Congress in the winter of 1932–33, "Unless something is done for the American farmer we will have revolution in the countryside in less than twelve months."

Perhaps the major difficulty concerning the farm unrest lies in Schlesinger's dichotomy between patriotism and revolution. It was a distinction that radical farmers did not make. As one elderly farmer participating in the Farm Holiday movement put it, "They say blockading the highway's illegal. I says, 'Seems to me there was a Tea-party in Boston that was illegal too. What about destroying property in Boston Harbor when our country was started?'" Talk of revolution, to these sons of the Middle Border, was the height of patriotism. Their nation had been born in revolution and some of its greatest heroes had glorified the right of revolution. "To the American," one journalist wrote in 1932, "revolution is a birthright, an inheritance that no power can take away, a privilege to be guarded most jealously. If he seldom exercises his privilege, he has not forgotten that the right and responsibility are his."

Rebellious incidents were by no means confined to agricultural areas. Organized looting of food became a nationwide phenomenon. In March 1930 over a thousand New Yorkers standing in a Salvation Army breadline suddenly charged two bakery trucks that were making a delivery at a nearby hotel. Bread and pastry were thrown into the street and the hungry men scrambled to get it. It was reported to be common practice for groups of thirty or forty jobless men to enter a store and demand food. "The chain stores as a matter of policy refrained from calling the police in order to keep the incidents out of the papers." In Detroit, people were often seen looting through broken store windows at night. In the drought-stricken areas of Arkansas in 1931, hungry residents used guns to force Red Cross officials (who seemed more worried about the possibility of non-needy impostors than feeding the desperate) to give out food. Hundreds of incidents like these could be recounted, but even that number would only scratch the surface of the rebellious mood many Americans had reached by 1932. It is almost certain that most of the small acts of lawlessness committed by bands of unemployed men were never recorded because in many areas newspapers would not print the stories. The editors, like the chain store managers, feared publicity might precipitate other such actions.

Two urban mass actions of 1932 were, however, far too large to go unnoticed. These were the March battle between workers and police at Dearborn, Michigan, and the summer encampment of World War I veterans in Washington.

On the frigid morning of March 7, 1932, some 3000 persons assembled in Detroit for a Communist-initiated march to the Ford River Rouge factory in Dearborn. Their purpose was to present a number of demands to the management of the Ford plant. Henry Ford had by this time fallen from his lofty perch of respect and was seen by many of the poor in the Detroit area (and throughout the nation) as a symbol of the old order's evils. The march proceeded uneventfully through Detroit, which was under the enlightened leadership of Mayor Frank Murphy. But when the Dearborn line was reached, a group of gendarmes from that Ford-controlled community ordered the demonstrators to turn back. After they refused the police shot tear gas at the crowd, which responded by hurling back stones and chunks of frozen dirt. The forces of law and order retreated to the factory, where firemen began dousing the crowd with freezing water from their hoses and the police resumed their tear gas barrage, this time mixing it with gunfire. One petitioner was killed at this point and the crowd removed to a nearby field. There the police opened fire again, killing three more demonstrators and seriously wounding fifty others.

This remarkable flash of class conflict ended five days later with a common funeral for the deceased protesters. Some 40,000 persons viewed the four bodies lying beneath a red banner presenting a picture of Lenin and the words "Ford Gave Bullets for Bread." The bodies were lowered into their graves as a band played the "Internationale."

The most significant aspect of the battle at River Rouge is that the actual fighting was initiated not by the workers but by those taking their orders from business leaders. As the editor of the Amalgamated Clothing Workers' *Advance* said, "The outrageous shooting at defenseless, peaceably marching unemployed workers in front of Henry Ford's Dearborn plants best shows that the masters won't wait till the slaves will take matters into their own hands."

The same point was made even more clearly several months later when the federal government used force to expel peaceable veterans of World War I from Washington. It all began in the spring of 1932, when a group of veterans in Portland, Oregon, began a march on Washington. Their purpose was to obtain the immediate payment of bonuses Congress had agreed to pay in 1945 to veterans of the European conflict. Many veterans insisted that immediate payment of the money would stimulate the economy and so help end the Depression. Styling themselves the Bonus Expeditionary Force (after the American Expeditionary Force, which had been their name in France in 1918), the group set out for Washington, riding freight cars and subsisting on handouts. By the time the Portland group arrived in the District of Columbia, many other veterans had taken up the idea and were en route to the capital. Eventually their number grew to more than 20,000. Under the pressure of these people who lobbied with their feet, the House passed a bill for immediate payment of the bonus. The Senate, however, defeated the measure. Some veterans gave up and went home, but others decided to stay in Washington. They built shacks on the Anacostia Flats and sent for their families. All continued in relative calm until Congress adjourned. On the final day of the session, the veterans massed at the Capitol, expecting to see Hoover, who had firmly refused to meet with any of them. But at the last moment the President decided not to make the traditional visit to the congressional adjournment ceremonies. Their quest for the moment fruitless, some veterans began to leave the city.

Others did not move quickly enough to suit some in positions of authority. At the end of July an incident in which a policeman started shooting at unarmed veterans, one of whom was killed, provided a pretext for action. General Douglas MacArthur, disobeying orders from Hoover, decided to drive the Bonus Army out of the District. The veterans were given one hour to remove themselves, then MacArthur's troops began throwing tear gas and prodding the slow moving with bayonets. A seven-year-old boy who tried to go back to his tent for his pet rabbit was stabbed in the leg by a soldier who shouted, "Get out of here, you little son of a bitch!" The pathetic "Army" was quickly driven out of Washington by MacArthur's brave legions. After his glorious victory in the Battle of Anacostia Flats, the general was beside himself with self-congratulation. MacArthur insisted that the "mob" was driven by "the essence of revolution." He asserted that it was "beyond the shadow of a doubt" that the Bonus Army had been about to seize control of the government. Actually the veterans had been prepared to seize nothing larger than MacArthur's imagination. The fears of those in power had again magnified the danger.

One of the final ironies of the Hoover administration was that the President was blamed for the brutal eviction of the Bonus Army. Hoover let MacArthur get away with insubordination—encouraging a habit that the general would continue to exercise—and publicly took responsibility for the action. This was part of a calculated campaign move to the right. By this time the President's knack for assessing situations wrongly was well developed. Moving to the right in 1932 put him on a collision course (or more accurately, a rapidly diverging course, since the public mood was already far to Hoover's left) with a majority of the people, who were definitely traveling in the opposite direction.

Revolution was not yet likely in 1932. But an unemployed store clerk who had written to the PECE to warn Hoover that he had better take action soon, "before we have to do something desperate," touched on a critical point. Talk was cheap, and few of those who spoke or wrote radical words were ready to man the barricades. It was not, after all, the protesters who initiated the violence at Dearborn and Washington. But the restless words did show that faith in the economic system was beginning to erode. [8]

The person elected president in 1932 would have what might well be the last chance to save the system through peaceful change. It was one of history's critical moments. The time has come for a detailed look at the man upon whom that burden—and opportunity—fell.

5·The Lord of the Manor: FDR

The man for whom a majority of the poor voted in 1932 was far from being one of them. Born into one of the few remaining pockets of landed aristocracy in post–Civil War America, that of the Hudson River country gentleman, Franklin Delano Roosevelt never wanted for anything that money could buy. This background is the single most important element in understanding Roosevelt's career, beliefs, ability to deal with the Depression, and extraordinary relationship with the people, especially the poor.

One of the main differences between the social development of the United States and that of such European nations as Great Britain and Germany was the lack of a powerful landed aristocracy in America. Before the Civil War, the southern planters represented something of an American aristocracy; but the war and Reconstruction destroyed their power. Thus America's rising capitalists in the late nineteenth century faced no effective counterforce such as that provided by the English Tories or the Prussian Junkers. The latter aristocratic groups checked the worst abuses of the British and German industrialists. They did this for two reasons: first, their sense of noblesse oblige led to a degree of paternalistic care for the poor; second, the aristocrats resented the rising power of the bourgeoisie and pushing social reform was a way to strike back at the new rich. Many social welfare laws that were enacted in America only in the 1930s had British and German counterparts dating from thirty to fifty years earlier.

Significantly, when American social legislation was finally put on the books, it was pushed through by a landed aristocrat. Although the United States lacked a powerful *class* of aristocrats, it did possess certain *individual* patricians of great influence. The Roosevelt family is, perhaps, the best example of this limited American aristocratic paternalism. Theodore Roosevelt was a leading figure in the new paternalistic, nationalistic liberalism of the Progressive era. His relative, Franklin, brought those ideas to fruition. The wealth of the Roosevelts has led to much confusion about their loyalties. Throughout his career FDR was critical of businessmen. "Business must get out of politics," he declared in 1911. He saw Wilson's 1916 victory as "the debacle of plutocracy." The twenties found him calling for keeping "the control of our government out of the hands of professional money-makers" and denouncing "the old money-controlled crowd." Neither such statements nor his far stronger denunciations of businessmen in 1936 indicated that Roosevelt was a traitor to his class. He never considered himself in the same group with the money-makers. His money was already made. "These millionaires," Roosevelt said in a 1939 letter, clearly indicating that despite his wealth, he did not associate himself with the group, "are a funny crowd. They are perfectly willing to go along with lip service to broad objectives, but when you ask them to help put them into effect by any form of practical means, they howl in opposition and decline to suggest any other course."

Throughout his political career, from his earliest days in the state senate, Franklin Roosevelt was an unrelenting conservationist. This was a revealing reflection of his patrician background. The lord of the manor has an obligation to maintain and preserve the land. As a country gentleman, FDR believed in conserving more than forests. He took a neofeudal, paternalistic view of "his" people. During the 1932 campaign he said privately that people who came to hear him speak had "the frightened look of children." His background enabled Roosevelt to see himself as a true friend of the forgotten man. But it was a particular type of friendship, one based not on equality but on noblesse oblige. It was a characteristic of FDR, as it has been of most twentieth-century liberals, to speak of "community" but to see control of the national community as resting with a strong president who embodies the desires and needs of the people. It is fitting that a system with such feudal overtones was perfected by the Squire of Hyde Park. British diplomat Nigel Law made a point critical to understanding FDR when he said that Roosevelt "was a perfect example of the English Country Gentleman."[1]

Franklin Roosevelt's background was different from that of almost all presidents—save his relative, Theodore—since John Quincy Adams. Our first six presidents were all aristocrats. Andrew Jackson changed that by emphasizing his "common man" origins. Thereafter, it helped to put a log cabin in one's past, even if none had actually been there. Henceforth, an elite heritage was taken as a severe political handicap. In this regard, Franklin Roosevelt's disability was large, but he had a way of turning handicaps to his advantage.

In his "centenary remembrance" of FDR, distant relative Joseph Alsop argues that the Roosevelts were not American aristocrats. They were "nice people," but were not at the "apex of the pyramid." Strictly speaking, this is true, at least in terms of wealth. Roosevelt's father, James, was "comfortable," but his attempts to attain really great wealth had been thwarted by the depressions of the 1870s and 1890s. (His experience with economic depression was somewhat different from that of his younger son.) James Roosevelt left an estate of $300,000. His wife, Sara Delano Roosevelt—one of eleven children—inherited approximately $1 million from her father. This may strike some readers as placing the Roosevelts among the "nice people," indeed, particularly when one remembers how much a million dollars was worth in the late nineteenth century. But this was a long way from the apex of the pyramid. By way of comparison, Cornelius Vanderbilt left an estate of between $70 million and $100 million. The difference is apparent in the contrast between the extravagant, gaudy display of the various Vanderbilt mansions—notably the one built for the Commodore's grandson, Frederick, just up the road from the Roosevelt estate in Hyde Park—and the "very nice" comfort of the lesser Roosevelt mansion.

In another sense, however, Alsop's contention that the Roosevelts were not aristocrats will not wash. The very contrast between the Roosevelts and Delanos on the one hand, and the Vanderbilts on the other, makes the point. The former were "old money"; the latter demonstrated in their ostentatious style the newness of their wealth. Aristocracy, after all, is not measured in terms of wealth alone. The ancestry of the Roosevelt and Delano families placed them, without question, at the top of the social order. Sara Delano

Roosevelt, a student in the genealogy of the two families, claimed relationship to numerous European aristocrats and at least a dozen *Mayflower* passengers. Among the more interesting ancestors she listed were William the Conqueror and Anne Hutchinson. Sara Roosevelt did not exaggerate when she remarked that her son had "had many advantages that other boys did not have."

That Franklin Roosevelt had this type of deep aristocratic heritage, rather than that of the self-made man or the nouveau riche, was of great importance. It provided him with a fundamental security and self-assurance. In addition, such people were customarily taught that their birthright carried with it the obligation of being good citizens. They had a duty of stewardship. Franklin Roosevelt's achievement was to expand the concept of stewardship and combine it with a heavy dose of democracy, thus uniting Jefferson and Jackson.

The man who would accomplish this remarkable political feat was the product of the second marriage of James Roosevelt, to Sara Delano. If not a June–December match, it was at least a July–October one. The future President's father was fifty-four, his mother twenty-eight, when FDR was born in 1882. The maternal influence on the boy was far the greater. As the only child of a mother from a large family, young FDR was the center of attention. His mother, who took a Victorian view of power relationships between the sexes, served father and son alike. What Franklin failed to obtain from his parents, he was able to get from adoring servants. The boy rarely got into trouble as he always wanted to please and seemed to know what was necessary to do so, no small advantage for a politician.

It was a terrible but necessary sacrifice for one in her social position when Sara Roosevelt sent her son at the age of fourteen to the nation's most exclusive boarding school, Groton. Endicott Peabody had established the school for the purpose of instilling in boys of society's upper ranks "manly Christian character." The emphasis was not especially upon scholarship, but upon morality and vigor. Groton's effect on Franklin Roosevelt in both regards was perceptible. Rector Peabody preached constantly upon the need for a man, especially one from the privileged class, to *serve*. This was very much in keeping with what young Roosevelt had been taught at home. The emphasis upon physical vigor also left its imprint on FDR. His build was too slight to excel at football, but he always tried with all his might to succeed on the playing field. The Groton ideal was implicit in a comment that Grotonian Averell Harriman made about Peabody: "You know he would be an awful bully if he weren't such a terrible Christian." What the Reverend Peabody wanted, it seemed, was for his boys to grow up to be like Theodore Roosevelt. That also became the passionate goal of Teddy's young kinsman. The ideal may have placed an excess of stress on the "manly" and "physical," and not quite enough on the moral, but this was only a part of Franklin Roosevelt's education.

As a lover of sailing and an accomplished yachtsman himself, Franklin longed to go to Annapolis, but his parents objected. In the spring of 1898, when Cousin Ted and the rest of the nation got caught up in the excitement of a splendid little war with Spain, Franklin plotted with two other Groton boys to sneak away to Boston and enlist in the Navy. A mild case of scarlet fever nipped this romantic notion in the bud.

Harvard and the law, not Annapolis and the sea, were "proper" goals for a young gentleman. Harvard was, of course, an intellectual center, but not for all of its undergraduates. The other world at Harvard was that of the social elite: prep school backgrounds, parties, football, other extracurricular activities, and the "Gentlemen's C." It was to the latter Harvard world that young FDR naturally gravitated. He and a friend took a comfortable suite of rooms at one of the private dormitories and Franklin added a piano, even though he had never mastered the art of playing one.

Academically, Harvard's influence on the future President does not appear to have been overwhelming. He worked hard, but only sparingly on his studies. He took few of the easy, so-called football courses. Although he enrolled in several semesters of history, his knowledge of the subject upon leaving Cambridge seems to have been quite limited. In 1904, Roosevelt wrote an essay on Alexander Hamilton that was nothing more than hero worship and was replete with errors. His economics courses, fortunately, left even less of a long-term imprint.

At Harvard, as at Groton, most of Roosevelt's considerable energies were expended in nonacademic endeavors. He played scrub football and captained a club crew. Seeking the "strenuous" life, FDR took time to join the Harvard Republican Club in 1900 in order to work in support of Cousin Ted's campaign to become Vice President. Although he had completed coursework for a degree in three years, Franklin returned to Cambridge for a fourth year in order to edit the *Crimson*. If his editorials are a gauge of his concern for the world's problems at the age of twenty, the needle was pointing near "empty." Editor Roosevelt directed most of his attention to the need for school spirit and a winning football team. If, at this age, winning was not to Franklin Roosevelt what it would later be to Vince Lombardi ("everything"), it was close to it. He did not, however, always win. Most significantly, Roosevelt failed to be selected for Harvard's most elite club, Porcellian. This may have been the result of association with his nephew, who was involved in many escapades and who had just created a scandal by contracting what FDR biographer Frank Freidel calls "an unfortunate marriage." Whatever the cause of Roosevelt's rejection by Porcellian, many observers have contended it was one of the best things that happened to him. It may not have made him "more democratic" at the time, but it did reduce the additional elitist influences that the club might have had upon him.

While at Harvard, Roosevelt was entirely caught up in its atmosphere, but this does not seem to have had any large positive influences on his later career. Although he surely did not learn much about pragmatism in the courses he took, FDR, like most college students, obtained much of his education outside the classroom. Pragmatism was "in the air" at Harvard at the turn of the century and the future President may well have caught a dose of it. Otherwise, his Harvard experience was more something from which he had to escape than what made him what he subsequently became.

From Harvard, Roosevelt went on (as had Theodore, who was now President) to Columbia Law School. Before the end of his first year there, he had married his distant cousin (and the President's niece), Eleanor. Franklin's legal education made scant impression on him. When he passed the New York Bar Examination during his third year, he did not bother to complete his studies or take his degree. For the next few years, FDR settled into the pastimes of fathering children and being a legal clerk in a Wall Street law firm that specialized in defending corporations against antitrust suits. He was drifting into a life like that his father (who died while Franklin was a freshman at Harvard) had enjoyed. It was not long, though, before FDR decided that the footsteps he preferred to follow were those not of his father, but of Eleanor's uncle.[2]

In 1907 a group of clerks in the law firm for which Franklin Roosevelt worked discussed their ambitions. Roosevelt, one of the others later remembered, listed the steps he planned to take to reach his goal. "They were: first, a seat in the State Assembly, then an appointment as Assistant Secretary of the Navy . . . , and finally the governorship of New York." The clerk recalled FDR saying, "Anyone who is Governor of New York has a good chance to be President with any luck."

It was a blueprint that had already been shown to be workable. These were the stopovers Theodore Roosevelt had made (along with a stint as a war hero and a final pause at the vice presidency) en route to the White House. Why could not another Roosevelt, of another party, tread the same path? At twenty-five, FDR was quite confident of his abilities, his luck, and perhaps his destiny. The next few years did nothing to undermine that confidence.

When a possibility arose in 1910 that he might become the Democratic nominee for the state assembly seat from Dutchess County, Roosevelt could not resist. His attractions for the normally losing upstate New York Democrats were his name and his money. FDR soon found himself the victim of a "bait and switch" tactic. The incumbent assemblyman decided to keep his seat and if Roosevelt wanted to run, it would have to be for the senate. This was a more prestigious position, but had two major drawbacks: Uncle Ted had started in the assembly, not the senate, and—far more serious—the larger senate district was heavily Republican. Franklin decided to give it a try, anyway.

Thanks to the growing progressive/Old Guard split in the Republican party (between followers of TR and of President Taft), FDR had a chance. Waging a strenuous—what else?—campaign on progressive themes and getting considerable mileage out of both his name and an attention-grabbing red Maxwell touring car, Roosevelt won by just over a thousand votes out of more than 30,000 cast. The long journey to duplicate TR's achievement had begun. And FDR had picked up from Dick Connell, the local Democratic candidate for Congress, the habit of beginning speeches with "My friends."

Franklin Roosevelt quickly made a name for himself. His surname was already well known, of course, but he now had to create an identity of his own, albeit one closely linked with that of his relative. The younger Roosevelt's progressivism was at this point amorphous. In most respects it was not noticeably different from the "clean government" crusades so frequently identified with men of Roosevelt's background. Despite his worship of Theodore Roosevelt, Franklin was still closer in philosophy to Grover Cleveland. No sooner had he arrived in Albany, though, than Roosevelt was making "good government" sound new and courageous.

Joining with several other "progressive" Democrats, Roosevelt headed a faction that declared war on Tammany Hall. Holding the balance of power in the state senate, Roosevelt's group tied up the legislature for weeks by refusing to support Boss Charles F. Murphy's candidate for United States senator. (This was prior to the ratification of the Seventeenth Amendment and New York did not yet directly elect its senators.) In the end, the insurgents blocked Murphy's original candidate, but had another Tammany choice shoved down their throats. Nevertheless, Franklin D. Roosevelt had gained much statewide and national publicity and was widely hailed as an up-and-coming progressive in the Democratic ranks.

The youthful state senator continued to take every opportunity to gain publicity as a rising progressive star. Unlike the Tammany organization, Roosevelt supported Woodrow Wilson for the presidential nomination in 1912. When Josephus Daniels, Wilson's choice to head the Navy Department, met FDR on the morning of the inauguration, he asked him how he would like to become assistant secretary of the Navy. "How would I like it?" Daniels remembered Roosevelt blurting, "I'd like it bully well. It would please me better than anything in the world . . . the assistant secretaryship is the one place, above all others, I would love to hold." The delight of the playwright—even one guilty of plagiarism—at seeing his script followed so neatly is understandable.

Sitting at TR's desk in the Navy Department, Franklin was in a position to influence patronage in New York and get his name before the public periodically. It was a pleasant job for one who loved ships. When he visited a Navy vessel, the assistant secretary commanded a seventeen-gun salute and an honor guard. FDR loved it. He loved even more getting a chance to pilot destroyers he visited. Before long, though, the career script called for a new political move. Had he been able to win an endorsement from Wilson, Roosevelt would have run for governor of New York in 1914. Failing that, FDR attempted to alter Act II, Scene I, and took a fling at the available U.S. Senate seat. It was a mistake. Without Tammany support, the young reform candidate could not win the Democratic nomination. Roosevelt was crushed, both in and outside New York City. Overall, he lost by a ratio of nearly 3 to 1.

Fighting in a war was part of TR's prescription for the strenuous life. It was also, if one was resourceful enough to become a hero, a great help in reaching the White House. TR had employed his escapades with his Rough Riders to help elect him governor within a few months of the war. His account of the war, one wag said, should be entitled, "Alone in Cuba," by Theodore Roosevelt. Three years later, he was President of the United States. Given these considerations, it was to be expected that Franklin Roosevelt would attempt to resign his post and enlist as soon as the United States entered the World War. Perhaps with visions of a San Juan Hill somewhere in the north of France, FDR did just that: *attempted* to enlist. Wilson would no more hear of this than he would allow TR to raise a "Roosevelt Division." Franklin's superiors convinced him that his services were more valuable in Washington.

His fences with Tammany reasonably well patched, Roosevelt could probably have had the 1918 gubernatorial nomination and won the election. He declined, and Al Smith became governor. There was not too much danger that Roosevelt would be labeled a slacker, but he still hated to see a war go by without some personal adventure. FDR finally persuaded Secretary Daniels to send him on a mission to Europe. It gave the aspiring politician a chance to "see war" and even come briefly under hostile fire. When he returned, FDR planned to insist upon a commission so he could get into uniform before the war ended. His knack for contracting diseases, which had dashed his plans for enlisting in the Spanish-American conflict, now gave him influenza. By the time he recovered, it was too late; the Armistice was only a few weeks away. Roosevelt's next brush with serious disease was not to turn out as happily.

As always, Franklin D. Roosevelt's eyes were searching for opportunities to advance his political career. The situation in 1920 seemed singularly inauspicious for a progressive Democrat. The tide of public opinion had crested and was running rapidly in a conservative direction. The next stop in the Roosevelt script was to become governor of New York. But Democrat Al Smith was the incumbent. Roosevelt could have had the nomination for United States senator almost for the asking, but he was not at all sure he wanted it. A few friends and an occasional newspaper story actually boosted the man with the magic name for the Democratic presidential nomination. This was remarkable for someone whose total experience with elective office consisted of two years in the state legislature, but the talk was hardly serious.

Deciding that the time was not good for a progressive politician, Roosevelt had two options: he could change with the times and try to ride the conservative wave, or he could stake out a position as a future leader of Democratic progressives and wait for the next change in public mood. Both calculation and inclination pointed FDR toward the latter course.

Early in 1920 one of Roosevelt's friends tried to push a Hoover-Roosevelt ticket. The proposed second name on the slate had no objections to the idea, and after Hoover announced his Republicanism the possibility of FDR as a vice presidential candidate lingered. That the ambitious Roosevelt was interested may seem surprising. The vice presidency was not only a seat of obscurity, it was also a road to political oblivion. Unless an act of God or an assassin intervened, no one was likely to hear of the vice president again. Other than those who were elevated by the death of a president, no vice president since Martin Van Buren, nearly a century before, had ever gone on to win a major party presidential nomination. What was more, it was almost certain that the Democratic nominee in 1920 was not ever going to become vice president. The ticket was highly likely to lose in November.

All of this was well known to Franklin Roosevelt. His willingness to accept the vice presidential spot was a bold stroke. He expected to lose, but to build up a national following in the process. He could then go back and become governor of New York a few years later and win a presidential nomination when it would be worth having. It was a strategy that had never been tried. The subsequent political records of *losing* vice presidential candidates were even worse than those of winners. Only twice in the republic's early years had men lost a bid for the vice presidency and then been placed in the top spot on a major ticket. Charles C. Pinckney had lost as the Federalist vice presidential candidate in 1800 and been chosen to head the campaign four years later. His running mate in 1804, Rufus King, lost the vice presidency that year and again in 1808, but won the worthless Federalist presidential nomination in 1816. It was not a record to inspire others to try this route to the White House.

But Franklin Roosevelt was not a man who doubted the chances for his own success. Just because no one had ever lost a vice presidential race and gone on to become president was no reason to think *he* could not be the first. (FDR, incidentally, remains the only person ever to accomplish this feat.) Roosevelt went to the 1920 party convention in San Francisco in a more optimistic frame of mind than many other Democrats.

Much as New York's Republican bosses had been glad to kick Theodore Roosevelt upstairs (or *downstairs*) to a vice presidential nomination in 1900 in order to get rid of him, Boss Murphy agreed to support FDR for the second position on the party's national ticket. The degree of Murphy's enthusiasm for the man who had caused him so much trouble in the past decade was apparent in his comment to Democratic presidential nominee James Cox's campaign manager: "I don't like Roosevelt . . . but . . . I would vote for the Devil himself if Cox wanted me to."

The 1920 campaign was for Roosevelt the national counterpart of the anti-Tammany fight in 1911: his name had helped put him where he was; now he had to build a reputation of his own to go with the name. Despite a few grievous mistakes, Roosevelt was a bright spot in the 1920 Democratic debacle. He seemed to be in a good position to make his gamble pay off by returning at the head of a future national ticket. [3]

Several circumstances combined to make Franklin Roosevelt the man who could win the allegiance of so many of the down-and-out during the Great Depression. His patrician background with its supreme security and sense of stewardship was one; the influence of Eleanor Roosevelt was another. A third that is always mentioned, but which has generally been downplayed in recent years, was his struggle with polio. In searching for the basis of Roosevelt's compassion and his rapport with the downtrodden, the importance of this dream-shattering disease deserves heavy emphasis.

The results of the 1920 election showed unmistakably the direction of the country. FDR did not follow entirely on that conservative route, but he was sufficiently adaptable that he took up a position with a Wall Street firm. The following summer at Campobello, the exhausted Roosevelt was stricken with infantile paralysis. Both the local doctor and a Philadelphia specialist found vacationing at Bar Harbor misdiagnosed his illness, the latter prescribing precisely the wrong treatment and sending a $600 bill for his trouble. (Doctors who vacation at Bar Harbor are rarely inexpensive.)

The pain was excruciating. At first, as was to be expected, Roosevelt was in "utter despair, feeling that God had abandoned him." Until this point in his life, he had always gotten almost anything he wanted, effortlessly. Now he would have none of his desires—or so it seemed to others. But an upbringing in which a child usually gets his way if he is persistent is not all to the bad. It provided Roosevelt with his extraordinary self-confidence, tenacity, and optimism. He soon concluded that he *could* still attain his goals, only no longer would it be effortless.

Those who saw Franklin Roosevelt, before and after, as a "Mama's boy" did not understand his nature at all. In fact, had he been that, he would simply have vanished from political life. After his crippling attack, his mother strove constantly and ruthlessly to make him a lifelong invalid. In one sense, it was her fondest dream. She could care for her son at Hyde Park as she had for her elderly husband. But Franklin would have none of it. Part of his aristocratic heritage entailed stoic acceptance of hardship, not complaining. FDR had previously had little opportunity to practice this virtue, but now he performed it superbly. With the support of Eleanor, he refused to admit defeat—or even the possibility of defeat.

Eleanor Roosevelt was not without a powerful ally in her struggle to keep her husband looking ahead. Louis McHenry Howe, a newspaperman who had joined Roosevelt's entourage in 1912 and decided immediately that FDR was destined to be president, would not give up on that destiny. Until his death in 1936, Howe was a central figure in Roosevelt's political efforts. During the 1932 campaign for the presidency, Roosevelt supporter Robert Jackson gave what may be the best capsule description of Howe, as he directed the campaign from his cramped office. Howe, Jackson said, was "an implausible little man . . . 5 feet 4 or 5 inches tall, his frail cadaverous frame is topped by a face that is stretched taut about the skull underneath." "His age," Jackson continued, "defies computation; he could be forty, or fifty, or sixty. His clothes are a sartorial ruin, disorderly and in need of cleaning. He appears constantly on the verge of physical collapse."

Louis Howe clearly saw Franklin D. Roosevelt as the vehicle for a political rise that someone of Howe's appearance and qualities could never hope to accomplish on his own. But his devotion to FDR was not mere calculation. Roosevelt was his idol. Jackson suggested that the worship may have been partly "the instinctive reverence of the physically inferior man for the Apollo." After August 1921, Howe's hero no longer fit the role of Apollo, but the devotion and obsession with reaching the White House remained; perhaps it even intensified.

Roosevelt's political career scarcely skipped a beat when he was stricken with polio. Howe controlled the flow of information to newsmen, indicating that Roosevelt would recover completely. A month after the initial attack of the disease, Roosevelt accepted a position on the executive committee of the New York Democratic party. The road back to political prominence would be long and extremely difficult, but Roosevelt was determined to make the journey, even if he could not do it by foot.

The importance of Roosevelt being struck by a serious disability can be overestimated, but that importance was very great. Few if any events *totally* change a person after he has reached adulthood. A basic set of characteristics is already well formed and subsequent developments react upon that base. Frances Perkins has been criticized for asserting that Roosevelt "underwent a spiritual transformation during the years of his illness." That term does imply too much. FDR's religious faith appears to have changed little. It was, Eleanor Roosevelt later said, "a very simple religion. He believed in God and his guidance. . . . He could pray for help and guidance and have faith in his own judgment as a result." That simple, undogmatic faith, Mrs. Roosevelt believed, helped account for her husband's confidence in himself. Always convinced of his own destiny, FDR decided soon after he was taken ill that he "must have been shattered and spared for a purpose beyond his knowledge." It was a short step to concluding that God's purpose was what his had always been: to make him President of the United States.

Roosevelt's illness did change him in important ways. Determined always to succeed in politics, FDR had nonetheless been something of a carefree playboy before his paralysis. He seems to have become inwardly more serious afterward. Most of all, Roosevelt's suffering helped to broaden his patrician sense of stewardship into a more genuine sense of compassion. "The man emerged," Frances Perkins wrote, "completely warmhearted, with humility of spirit, and with a deeper philosophy. Having been to the depths of trouble, he understood the problems of people in trouble."

This was absolutely critical to Roosevelt's later relationship with victims of the Great Depression. It worked both ways. He was able to understand suffering in a way a country gentleman would not have otherwise been likely to. And, to the deprived, the smiling "only thing we have to fear is fear itself" attitude Roosevelt took in the face of the Depression was acceptable and uplifting only because he had overcome a terrible affliction himself. Without this "blessing in disguise," Roosevelt's jauntiness in the thirties would likely have turned people against him as an overprivileged man who did not understand life's hardships. When asked years later if he ever worried, Roosevelt responded: "If you had spent two years in bed trying to wiggle your toe, after that anything would seem easy." It cannot be seriously doubted that Roosevelt's paralysis changed him in more than the obvious physical ways. It enabled him to present voters with a magnificent success story, one with which people in the Depression could identify far more readily than they could with tales of business success.[4]

For all the qualifications, it can still be said that had Franklin Roosevelt not contracted polio, it is highly unlikely that he ever would have become the "man for the times" during the Great Depression. The disease was not alone, however, in providing FDR with sufficient compassion to deal with the collapse. He owed much of his success to his wife.

Anna Eleanor Roosevelt was Franklin D. Roosevelt's fifth cousin, once removed. FDR's great-great-great-great grandfather, Nicholas Roosevelt (1658–1742), of the first generation of the family born in the New World, was also Eleanor's great-great-great-great-great grandfather. Eleanor was the first child of Theodore Roosevelt's younger brother, Elliott, and his wife, the former Anna Hall. Eleanor's arrival in the world was not an entirely welcome event, at least to her mother. Both parents had wanted a "precious boy" and the little girl was "a more wrinkled and less attractive baby than average." This was not pleasing to Anna Hall Roosevelt, herself a beautiful woman. Moreover, Mrs. Roosevelt had a very difficult pregnancy and almost died. Eleanor began life under a cloud of guilt. Her mother never became reconciled to the little girl's appearance and called her "Granny."

Given this rejection by her mother, it was natural that Eleanor developed a strong affection for her father, a man of great expectations and little will-power, who frequently suffered from bouts with excessive quantities of alcohol. Her father's health problems led to long periods in Europe, during some of which Eleanor was left at home. She felt abandoned and unloved. On her fourth birthday, Eleanor told her father that she "loved everybody and everybody loved her." The first half of this was often the case later in her life, but Eleanor Roosevelt's love for everybody was, she must have often felt, unrequited.

Her one love as a child, her father, was frequently exiled. When Eleanor was eight her mother died—an event that seemed most important to her as a chance to live again with her father. But Elliott Roosevelt died two years later, leaving Eleanor with a feeling of complete loneliness. She was placed with her grandmother, who treated her poorly and put her under the authority of a cruel governess. Even as a child, Eleanor felt sympathy for the poor and rejected (with whom she felt an obvious kinship).

Attendance at the progressive Allenswood School outside London helped Eleanor's compassion blossom. When she returned home, she remade the acquaintance of her distant cousin, Franklin, whom she had met and played with on various occasions during their childhoods. They fell in love and Franklin shocked his mother on Thanksgiving, 1903, by telling her that he planned to marry Eleanor. Marriage was not what Sara Roosevelt had in mind for her pride and joy, at least not for another decade or so. She did all she could to break up the couple, but failed. They were married on St. Patrick's Day, 1905, in New York. Eleanor's uncle, the President of the United States, gave away the bride and, according to some accounts, strove to *be* the bride, as was his wont on most occasions. Marriage to the President's niece gave FDR even greater social prestige than he already enjoyed and brought him closer to the family of his idol.

In the first eleven years of their marriage, Eleanor gave birth to six children, an occupation that left her little time for further intellectual and social development. Her mother-in-law continued to dominate the family. Sara was turning Eleanor into a conventional young society matron. The two women were, in fact, rivals for the affections of both Franklin and the children. In revealing fashion, Franklin always tried to ignore the conflict between his wife and his mother, acting as if all were well.

Besides her close relationship to TR, Eleanor soon proved in other ways to be an important political asset to her husband. Although still quite shy, her thoughtfulness and kindness made many friends for Franklin in both Albany and Washington during his early career. She was not nearly as physically unattractive as many people who knew her only from unflattering photographs in later years believed, and what she lacked in outward beauty was more than made up by her warmth and "inner radiance." Eleanor's eyes "caressed one with sympathy and studied one with intelligence."

Work during World War I led Eleanor Roosevelt to become more independent. It also saw her make a commitment to public service and helping others. The sleeping princess, as Archibald MacLeish put it years later, had been awakened. But it was not the World War experience alone that changed Eleanor Roosevelt into an independent woman dedicated to social service; there was at the same time a private war.

Eleanor apparently had long seen conjugal relations of a physical nature as a duty rather than a pleasure. Such was the expectation—although surely not always the reality—for women who were products of the Victorian Age. Mrs. Roosevelt fulfilled the expectation. Sex, Eleanor later told her daughter Anna, was an ordeal to be borne. She bore the ordeal often enough during the first eleven years of her marriage; but after giving birth to six children, she wanted no more. This was entirely understandable, particularly since her children all weighed more than ten pounds at birth, and one, Elliott, was almost twelve pounds. Having no knowledge of birth control, and too shy to ask anyone, Eleanor Roosevelt saw abstinence as the only way. After early 1916, Franklin and Eleanor never again lived together as husband and wife.

In his 1956 biography of Roosevelt, James MacGregor Burns said that "rumormongers" spread a story that Franklin "had fallen in love with another woman and that Eleanor had offered him his freedom." Rumormongers are not always wrong. In the period beginning in 1916, FDR became increasingly fond of his wife's social secretary, Lucy Mercer, with whom he eventually started an affair. Miss Mercer, although penniless, was descended from one of the "best" families. The Washington elite, Elliott Roosevelt has said, would have placed Miss Mercer a few rungs higher than the Roosevelts on the social ladder.

Some encouraged the affair—Theodore Roosevelt's daughter, Alice, for one. She invited the clandestine couple to dinner, later saying with the cruelty for which she was noted: "He deserved a good time. He was married to Eleanor." Anxious to cause as much trouble as possible, Alice attempted to tell Eleanor about the situation. Mrs. Roosevelt already had her suspicions; the proof came in September 1918, when Franklin returned from his trip to see the war. His flu had progressed into double pneumonia and Eleanor unpacked his luggage. There she found a package of love letters that Lucy Mercer had written to Franklin while he was away.

Eleanor promptly offered her husband a divorce, as the "rumormongers" said. FDR was of a mind to accept this proposition and launch a more permanent adventure with Lucy. Two considerations dissuaded him. His mother told him that if he followed that course, she would cut off his money. Equally compelling was the undeniable effect that being divorced for adultery would have on his political career. It would end it. (On this subject, at least, voters are more liberal in Ronald Reagan's day than they were in Roosevelt's.) So an understanding was reached. Franklin agreed never to see Lucy again and Eleanor stayed on as his public partner, but not his private wife. She kept her part of the bargain; he did not keep his. FDR and Lucy stayed in touch over the years. He secretly provided a limousine for her during his 1933 inauguration. With the help of many friends, including his daughter Anna, and Bernard Baruch, Franklin saw Lucy often during the last years of his life. She was present at his death. Eleanor knew nothing about this until after FDR died.

In some respects her husband's infidelity was the sort of life-altering event for Eleanor that being stricken with polio would be three years later for Franklin. Eleanor Roosevelt now moved toward complete independence. She realized henceforth that advancing her husband's career was a means to advancing her own. The more prominent he was, the more good she might hope to accomplish through humanitarian endeavors. In 1932 she frankly said in an interview, "I never wanted to be a President's wife, and I don't want to now." She was, nevertheless, the best "President's wife" this nation has ever had.

Their lack of "normal" marital life notwithstanding, Franklin and Eleanor were a winning team. Their strengths complemented each other. Her compassion was a match for his ambition, and over the years, particularly after their great crises, each of these qualities began to rub off on the other spouse. It is almost certain that Franklin Roosevelt would not have become president without Eleanor's help; it is absolutely certain that if he had, he would not have been the same beloved, benevolent father figure that he became during the Depression. For Eleanor Roosevelt was at least as widely perceived as her husband as a person who genuinely cared for the fate of others. The letters that Depression sufferers wrote to her were every bit as laudatory as those written to FDR. Being First Lady gave Eleanor Roosevelt a wider arena in which to distribute her love.

For that is what it came down to. From her tragic childhood onward, Eleanor Roosevelt's life was a search for love. In seeking to be loved by others, she was lavish in spreading her own love, both widely and deeply. She was not the sort of person who claims to love "everybody," but has real affection for nobody. On the contrary, her general compassion was reflected in intensely warm, personal friendships with many individuals. She was, Joseph Lash writes, "a woman of great vitality, whose affectionate nature overflowed and . . . constantly sought opportunities to dispense love upon those she cared about and those who needed her love."

In recent years, the suspicion has arisen that at least one of those who needed her love may have had an unseemly amount of it lavished upon her. Many of the letters that were exchanged between Mrs. Roosevelt and Lorena

Hickok, an Associated Press reporter who was assigned to cover her in 1932 and became a great friend, suggest a passionate, physical relationship. Hickok gave Eleanor a ring, which—in a fascinating act symbolic of her private independence under her public role as Franklin's wife—she wore during the 1933 inauguration ceremonies. It is interesting to compare this secret act by Eleanor with FDR's secret provision of a car for Lucy Mercer on the same day. "Oh! I want to put my arms around you," Eleanor wrote to Hickok a few days later. "I ache to hold you close. Your ring is a great comfort. I look at it and think, she does love me, or I wouldn't be wearing it!"

There can be little doubt that Lorena Hickok did love Eleanor Roosevelt and desired to make that love physical. Given all we know of her quest for love and her problems with her husband, it would not stretch credibility to believe that such a desire was reciprocated. Yet, despite such passionate letters as the one quoted above, there is strong reason to believe that the sort of love Mrs. Roosevelt sought was neither heterosexual nor homosexual, but asexual. She wrote letters similar to those she sent Hickok to many other friends of both genders. What matters for a historical understanding of one of the most important figures in the twentieth century is her need for love and her expression of it for the downtrodden of the nation and the world. Helping others made her feel needed. Beyond that, it is not necessary to go into her personal life in an attempt to find conclusive answers.[5]

During the 1920s, Franklin Roosevelt and Al Smith, former opponents who later became bitter enemies, had an interlude of close political cooperation. In 1922 Roosevelt helped Smith regain the governorship he had lost in the Harding landslide. Two years later, Roosevelt became the titular head of Smith's campaign to win the Democratic presidential nomination. Smith asked Roosevelt to make his nominating speech before the convention in Madison Square Garden, and Roosevelt responded to the challenge of his first major address since his illness with a superb effort in which he called Smith the "happy warrior of the political battlefield." The speech helped Smith, although not enough to win the nomination that year. It helped Roosevelt more, by showing that he could not be written off as a political force.

He was, though, a man who had never held elective office higher than a seat in the state legislature, had lost his last two elections, labeled himself a progressive in a period of strong conservatism, and was partially paralyzed. It is certainly remarkable that such a man could continue to be a power in politics. There was, of course, the magic surname, but that cannot explain much. Theodore Roosevelt, Jr., also had the name—and a much closer association with the man who gave it its attraction—but his political career never got past an unsuccessful New York gubernatorial nomination in 1924. Far more than his name, his unceasing effort kept Franklin Roosevelt a force in the Democratic party. The reverse side of the coin of political banishment for a party is opportunity for one whose name is already known and who is tenacious at political work. Richard Nixon did much the same thing in the 1960s. Roosevelt undertook many unglamorous political tasks in the twenties. He kept up a voluminous correspondence with Democratic leaders around the nation. And as Nixon did four decades later, Roosevelt staked out a position for himself moderately to the side of center toward which he believed his party would have to lean if it wanted to regain power. "Hamiltons we have today," Roosevelt wrote in 1925. "Is there a Jefferson on the horizon?" It was a role he was most willing to accept, should it be offered.

In 1926, FDR declined all requests that he run for the Senate. He did not need another defeat on his record, and he had just started at Warm Springs, Georgia, what he hoped would be a cure for his paralysis. Two years later, the political outlook was no better, but Roosevelt's career took its last, decisive turn toward the White House anyway. He again nominated Smith, giving a speech aimed at the radio audience rather than the crowd in the Houston arena. This was a significant development in itself, for Roosevelt was the first major politician to understand how the new medium was changing politics. He sensed that the rousing speech that worked well in a large hall was not right for entering people's living rooms. (This was a lesson that Edward Kennedy had not yet learned in 1980.)

After Smith's nomination, New York and national Democratic leaders mounted increasing pressure on Roosevelt to run for governor. He wanted no part of it, principally because he realized that the Republican tide was at its peak in 1928 and he thought he would lose. Even if he won, serving as governor of New York would propel him toward the presidential nomination in 1932. Anticipating a continuation of Republican prosperity, both Roosevelt and Howe feared that 1932 was too early to win the White House. Howe had from the start of his planning pegged 1936 as *the* year. But the party leaders and Smith himself, believing that Roosevelt's upstate strength was needed for the presidential candidate to carry New York in 1928, would not take "no" for an answer. Thus one of the greatest Roosevelt ironies: for all the planning that he and Howe had done for nearly two decades, the decision that put FDR into a position to win the presidential nomination at a time when that turned out to be tantamount to election was forced upon him against his will, and over the strenuous objections of Howe. ("If they are looking for a goat," Howe said, "why doesn't Wagner sacrifice himself?") Roosevelt's belief in his destiny must have seemed confirmed by this twist of fate in which he took a giant step toward the White House in spite of himself.

While Al Smith was losing his home state in the 1928 presidential election, Franklin Roosevelt was narrowly winning the race to succeed Smith in Albany. The campaign and Roosevelt's activities as governor dispelled fears (and carefully nurtured political propaganda) that he was physically incapable of carrying out the duties of an executive.

When the Depression began, Roosevelt's policies did not substantially differ from Hoover's. But the New York governor quickly developed a far more positive image. Roosevelt had done enough and the political tide had turned sufficiently against the Republicans that he won a smashing reelection victory in 1930, defeating his opponent by some 725,000 votes. "I do not see how Mr. Roosevelt can escape becoming the next presidential nominee of his party," said New York Democratic party chairman Jim Farley the day after FDR's 1930 victory, "even if no one should lift a finger to bring it about." Roosevelt no longer had any thought of trying to escape this fate, and many fingers were lifted over the next twenty months to bring it about. Increasingly, Governor Roosevelt took a more liberal position. "I believe the country is ready for a more progressive policy," Roosevelt wrote in 1931. During that year, while Hoover still clung to the hope that private philanthropy could meet relief needs, Roosevelt called for the creation of a Temporary Emergency Relief Administration. This organization was set up, with social worker Harry Hopkins as its executive director, but it provided little relief. In fact, Roosevelt's program for dealing with the Depression remained only slightly bolder than Hoover's. Roosevelt was the choice of progressives in 1932 largely because of the lack of alternatives. His liberalism was still timid, but in comparison with what others were doing, especially in Washington, it could be made to look daring. This he did rhetorically in the 1932 presidential campaign. It worked.[6]

As with most political figures, it is very difficult to find the real Roosevelt under his public mask, which almost always wore a smile. To most of those who knew him or met him, FDR's dominant characteristic was reducible to the word "charm." He was able to charm even those who opposed his policies or were not satisfied with the accomplishments of his programs. Millions of Americans credited Roosevelt for everything they liked, but blamed others for what upset them. This was especially noticeable among southerners, many of whom in the later thirties became uncomfortable with the New Deal but wanted to remain loyal to their party and President. "Now I understand how it was possible for my family to worship FDR despite all the things he had done during his administration that enraged them," southern journalist Florence King has written. ". . . It was very simple: Credit Franklin, better known as He, for all the things you like, and blame Eleanor, better known as She or 'that woman,' for all the things you don't like. This way, He was cleared, She was castigated, and We were happy."

Such reasoning was not confined to the South or to conservatives. Many working-class people who were discontented with the failure of the New Deal to go far enough wrote to complain . . . and at the same time to praise the President. "You send the stuff to Poor but we dont get It," protested a 1936 letter. The writer went on to say: "What wonderful man you have been I will always vote for you." After informing him that her family's children were suffering from undernourishment, a Californian told FDR in 1935: "You are the best president we ever had."

Whatever a Roosevelt supporter disliked was someone else's fault. For conservatives, the guilty party was likely to be Eleanor Roosevelt, Harry Hopkins, or Secretary of Agriculture Henry A. Wallace. For those on the left, blame was more frequently placed on relief administrators, Republicans, "Wall Street," "the Interests," or simply "them." In any case, the fault was not the President's. "I am sure the President," a Seattle man wrote, "if he only knew, would order that something be done, God bless him." Such letters became almost a litany:

> If only he knew about the starvation wages on WPA projects;
> If only he knew that people were not being paid when they were sick;
> If only he knew that food was being destroyed while people went
>   hungry;
> If only . . . If only He knew, then he would make everything right.

But he did not know. That was certain. Because if he did, he would do something, God bless him. Even people on the verge of starvation believed this. A mother of seven hungry children wrote to the President early in 1934: "You have tried every way to help the people." Another Californian complained of "slave wages," but wrote to FDR: "You are wonderful. But surely this treatment is unknown to you." A Chicago man was another of those who were sure the President could not "know whats going on around here." The treatment of relief clients, he said, was very unfair, but "we know that it is not your falt but is the foult of those who are working in the relief stations."[7]

Poor people were ready—even eager—to believe that local officials were destroying food and clothing to make the unemployed turn against FDR. "I'd give my heart to see the President," a destitute North Carolina woman told FERA investigator Martha Gellhorn in 1934. "I know he means to do everything he can for us; but they make it hard for him; they won't let him." Here the "they" who were at fault were left unenumerated.

This pervasive tendency to absolve Roosevelt and blame unnamed others for what one dislikes has still not died. Ronald Reagan, even while attempting to dismantle the New Deal, continued to speak of Roosevelt with obvious admiration. He told an interviewer on the occasion of the one hundredth anniversary of FDR's birth that "other people" caused the damage: "President

Roosevelt started administering medicine to a sick patient, but those people who then gathered around and became the structure of government had no intention of letting the patient get well and cutting him off the medicine." When he attacked the New Deal, Reagan carefully avoided mentioning Roosevelt by name.

President Reagan was well advised to refrain from direct assaults on the New Deal President. Franklin Roosevelt's popularity remains remarkable a half century after the beginning of his presidency. In January 1982 an NBC–Associated Press national survey found 63 percent of the American public still had a favorable opinion of FDR, compared to only 11 percent who had an unfavorable opinion—and this in the midst of the putative Reagan reaction.

The popularity of Franklin D. Roosevelt is unprecedented among twentieth-century American politicians. Four years after his death, more than 42 percent of a group of nearly one thousand Philadelphia residents named FDR as their first choice as the greatest person in history. Another 10.6 percent named him as their second choice. Finishing second in the survey was Abraham Lincoln, with only 8.5 percent of the first-place votes. George Washington was third with 5.1 percent. It is highly unlikely that a similar poll taken either during the thirties or today would obtain similar results. The findings are stunning all the same. The survey also showed that admiration for Roosevelt was highest among those whose economic class was listed as "lower," but that those listed as "middle" and "upper-middle" nominated him as a great man almost as frequently as did the lower-class people. Only among the "upper" economic group was there significantly less liking for the late President among Philadelphians in 1949.

Part of Roosevelt's popularity, doubtless, is attributable to the circumstances in which he held office. Few presidents whose administrations never faced a major crisis have been labeled "great" by many observers beyond their immediate families. Roosevelt experienced two of the nation's largest crises during his twelve-year reign: the Great Depression and World War II. Yet facing crisis does not guarantee popularity. Not even being in office when a crisis ends does that. Rutherford Hayes and William McKinley each had the good fortune to be in office when a depression begun under his predecessor came to an end. Although McKinley was certainly popular, his "greatness" was never rated on a level even remotely close to FDR's. (And this despite the fact that McKinley also had a "splendid little war" to advance his prestige.) Presiding over a war is no assurance of popularity, either, as the more recent experiences of Harry Truman and Lyndon Johnson attest. Richard Nixon spent much of his time in office trying to find—or create—major crises with which he could deal and so become a "great" president. The end of his presidency is a testament to the inadequacy of such an approach to popularity and greatness.

Hence we must search beyond the mere "good fortune" of facing a depression and a war in order to explain the extraordinary public affection for FDR. The answer seems to lie in the man's position and *Weltanschauung*. During hard times, people want a leader from a secure background. Roosevelt obviously met that requirement. But that is not enough. In the aforementioned 1949 study of Roosevelt's popularity in Philadelphia, Fillmore H. Sanford hypothesized that to underprivileged people "a tremendously powerful man who *still* is personally very human and who *still* champions the little man's cause is the truly admirable man." This, Sanford rightly concluded, was the way most of the forgotten Americans looked at FDR. "He was perceived," Sanford wrote, "as a warm, understanding man, a man with great power and status, a man with competence who was, withal, a champion of the little man."

No other American politician in this century has been able to play the part of the democratic patrician quite like FDR. The Kennedys, perhaps Robert more than his brothers, have come the closest; and Roosevelt's Republican kinsman did a good job in originating the role at the start of the century. But no one else has gotten quite the audience reaction or rave reviews that the Democratic Roosevelt received.

The combination of warmth and power allowed Franklin Roosevelt to remain popular with many working-class Americans almost without regard to his particular actions or policies. When Hoover said that all the country needed was a restoration of confidence, people jeered; when Roosevelt told them that they need fear nothing but "fear itself," people nodded their agreement and their spirits rose. "From his fresh mind and resolute utterance," *The New York Times* said editorially of Roosevelt after his inauguration, "the people accept, with great calm and fine spirit, what would have seriously upset them if it had been set forth by a dying Administration." Will Rogers captured the early attitude toward Roosevelt when he said: "The whole country is with him. Just so he does something. If he burned down the Capitol, we would cheer and say, 'Well, we at least got a fire started anyhow.'"[8]

To many working-class Americans, Franklin Roosevelt was the one great hope in the midst of despair. He could do no wrong. Martha Gellhorn's 1934 report from the Carolinas indicated the adoration of FDR in terms that would be difficult to improve upon:

> Every house I visited—mill worker or unemployed—had a picture of the President. These ranged from newspaper clippings (in destitute homes) to large coloured prints, framed in gilt cardboard. The portrait holds the place of honour over the mantel; I can only compare this to the Italian peasant's Madonna. And the feeling of

these people for the President is one of the most remarkable emotional phenomena I have ever met. He is at once God and their
intimate friend; he knows them all by name, knows their little town
and mill, their little lives and problems. And, though everything
fails, he is there, and will not let them down.

This admiration—love is not too strong a word—of poor Americans for
Franklin Roosevelt was something so powerful that in some cases it has survived for decades after his death. In 1981, *Southern Exposure* magazine published a recent photograph of a Kentucky coal mining family in their home.
On the wall above the family members is a wall hanging showing Jesus tending His flock. Above that hangs a picture of FDR.

The association of Roosevelt with Jesus or other religious figures was common among Depression victims. A Wisconsin woman who reported that a
three-year-old girl who was visiting her home had identified a picture of FDR
as "Saint Roosevelt" spoke for many when she wrote: "As long as Pres. Roosevelt will be our leader under Jesus Christ we feel no fear." Others referred to
the President as a new Moses. And for those who saw Roosevelt's place in the
Chain of Being as a bit lower than those of Christ and Moses, Abraham
Lincoln provided a convenient substitute. "My wife and I consider you to be
the most humane man to occupy the chair since Lincoln," an elderly Texan
wrote to FDR in 1935. An Arkansas Republican agreed: "Roosevelt has
proved himself to be one of the greatest humanitarians and the most Christian
of any President since Lincoln's time."

Even people who normally distrusted politicians had affection for FDR.
"Your husband is *great*," a Denver woman wrote to Mrs. Roosevelt in 1936.
"He seems lovable even tho' he is a 'politician.' I wish him all the success in
the world." Here was a critical point. Roosevelt was unquestionably a master
politician, but few viewed him that way. Rather, it was in his role as paternalistic guardian that he was most commonly seen. A textile worker spoke for
millions in 1934: "The president isn't going to forget us." Frequently letter
writers addressed the Roosevelts in their communications as father and
mother of the nation.

The personality, rhetoric, and actions of the Roosevelts all added to their
popularity among disinherited Americans. Ironically, however, conservative
businessmen and partisan Republicans may also have provided significant
assistance to FDR in winning worker support. People are often known by their
enemies. That the rich hated Roosevelt was all many poor citizens needed to
know to convince them that he was their friend. Opponents often made FDR
seem more radical than he was. Soon after Roosevelt's famous "Forgotten
Man" speech in 1932, his former ally, Al Smith, declared: "I will take off my
coat and vest and fight to the end any candidate who persists in any demagogic

appeal to the masses of the working people of this country to destroy themselves by setting class against class and rich against poor!" In a similar vein, the arch-conservative Liberty League probably added unwittingly to the President's popularity when it suggested early in 1936 that he sought "redistribution of income on a grand scale." The year before, Roosevelt aide Rexford Tugwell had asserted that a sweeping attack on the New Deal by the United States Chamber of Commerce was "perhaps one of the best things which has happened politically." He seems to have been right. An Indiana admirer wrote in a typical 1935 letter that she liked FDR because "his most bitter opponents are the (Rich) the Chambers of Commerce Principaly the manufacturers."[9]

It has often been said that Franklin Roosevelt was a pragmatist. In one of his more famous statements, he said at Oglethorpe University in May 1932: "The country needs and, unless I mistake its temper, the country demands bold, persistent experimentation. It is common sense to take a method and try it: If it fails, admit it frankly and try another. But above all, try something." But what he intended to try was *something*, not *anything*. In the proper sense of pragmatism, Roosevelt had a goal in mind. His experimentation was always aimed at particular, if often vague, ends.

John Dewey, one of the founders of pragmatism, insisted that Roosevelt's approach was not what he intended. "Experimental method is not just messing around nor doing a little of this and a little of that in the hope that things will improve," Dewey wrote in 1935. His criticism was generally well taken, but Roosevelt does seem to have had a more consistent end in view than Dewey or many Roosevelt critics gave him credit for. He was what might be called a "pragmatic humanist." His pragmatism was always rooted in compassion.

Like most political leaders, Roosevelt was no intellectual. Former Supreme Court Justice Oliver Wendell Holmes, in his ninety-third year, perceptively summarized FDR after talking with him in 1933. "A second-class intellect," the famous jurist stated, "but a first-class temperament!" That temperament, that personality, was able to lift the nation's spirits in the depths of the Depression. Perhaps more could have been accomplished by a first-class intellect, but under the circumstances a first-class temperament may have been more effective.

Several of the more noted intimations that Roosevelt was an intellectual lightweight went too far. Walter Lippmann said he considered Roosevelt "a kind of amiable boy scout." George Creel referred to him more accurately as "a gay, volatile Prince Charming." "His mind is quick and superficial," William Allen White wrote of Roosevelt in 1934. "Of this I am dead sure. He still smiles too easily for one who shakes his head so positively. I fear his smile is from the teeth out. . . . He is a fair-weather pilot. He cannot stand the storm." On this last point, White was obviously proven wrong. He was not far off, though, in seeing Roosevelt's mind as "quick and superficial." Roosevelt had always been able to read books at an incredible speed and easily retain the gist of their contents, but he was not given to deep reflection.

Franklin Roosevelt was a figure of great importance in the development of modern liberalism, but he was anything but a systematic thinker himself. Ironically, though Roosevelt was a longtime advocate of planning, he had no plan. He wanted simple answers, but he was quick to move from one expedient to another. On one occasion, for instance, President Roosevelt laughingly said: "I experimented with gold and that was a flop. Why shouldn't I experiment a little with silver?" But he never lost confidence. And that, perhaps, was the key to his popularity. FDR never expected anything that he did to go wrong. Although the only thing *he* had to fear may have been fear itself, his countrymen had far more tangible problems. Roosevelt was always reassuring, but he was not quite a Pollyanna. Like other liberals, he sought action. Roosevelt never denied problems, he simply asserted his capacity to solve them. People tended to believe him. One reason for this was his remarkable ability, first demonstrated at the 1928 convention, to utilize the radio. His personality and warmth came across the airwaves in extraordinary fashion. Even lifelong Republicans and veteran Roosevelt-haters have testified that while listening to his broadcasts they sometimes weakened to the point of almost believing him—a condition from which they usually recovered by the next morning when they read newspaper accounts of what he had said. The President was able to identify himself and his programs with the people, and to do so in a believable manner. "My friends," he would begin, and continue with such phrases as "you and I know . . ." When Roosevelt addressed "our problems" and illustrated them with touching stories, few Americans were able to resist his charms.[10]

What Franklin D. Roosevelt sought, he said in a 1932 speech, was "social justice through social action." It was an excellent statement of Roosevelt's political position *and* the dominant values of Depression America. The key to understanding FDR's political success is that his positions so often coincided with the values of a people struggling for economic—and in many cases, physical—survival. Roosevelt stated the relationship perfectly in his first inaugural address: "The people of the United States . . . have made me the present instrument of their wishes." This sounds like the sort of democratic hogwash that all politicians indulge in, and it probably was little more than that to Roosevelt when he said it. But it was an accurate forecast of the relationship between President and people during the next few years.

Why were Roosevelt and a majority of the American people on the same wavelength during the Great Depression? Did he sincerely want to help the nation, or was he oriented only toward self-advancement? These raise other questions that can no more be definitively answered about Roosevelt than they can in general. Doubtless Roosevelt, with his sense of stewardship, his democratic feelings, and his personal experience with suffering, really wanted to help the people; he also wanted to become president, be reelected, and go down in history as a great leader.

Whatever the particular mix of motivations, Roosevelt succeeded on all counts. The recent *Chicago Tribune* poll of presidential scholars impressionistically rated Roosevelt as the third best President of the United States. He came in second, behind Lincoln, on a composite of separate ratings for different qualities, and would have easily won the top overall ranking had it not been for his justifiably low score on "character/integrity." Roosevelt did receive the highest rating of all presidents for leadership.

Roosevelt had, we should hasten to add, numerous faults. John Gunther, in his largely hagiographic *Roosevelt in Retrospect*, offers a representative list: "dilatoriness, two-sidedness (some would say plain dishonesty), pettiness in some personal relationships, a cardinal lack of frankness . . . , inability to say No, love of improvisation, garrulousness, amateurism, and what has been called 'cheerful vindictiveness.'" Several of these flaws centered on one basic defect in Franklin Roosevelt, one unfortunately shared by most politicians. Lippmann had seen it at the beginning of 1932: "He is too eager to please." This led to FDR's "two-sidedness," his "cardinal lack of frankness," and his "inability to say No." Louisiana Senator Huey Long explained the problem during the period prior to Roosevelt's inauguration: "When I talk to him, he says, 'Fine! Fine! Fine!' Maybe he says 'Fine!' to everybody." FDR, Richard Hofstadter noted, "could say 'my old friend' in eleven languages."

That Roosevelt wanted to please everyone was a serious, if understandable, character flaw, and one that hurt him on many occasions. Perhaps more striking was his failure to recognize the problem. The most interesting revelations to come out of the tape recordings Roosevelt secretly made during the 1940 campaign demonstrate his remarkable ability at self-deception, at criticizing others for faults he himself exhibited to an even larger extent. "Of course, the trouble with Willkie, as you know, his whole campaign—the reason he's losing—," Roosevelt said in October 1940, "is that he will say anything to please the individual or the audience that he happens to talk to. It makes no difference what he's promised. J.P.M. [perhaps J. P. Morgan] . . . will come in and say, 'Now Mr. Willkie, please, will you, if elected, do thus and so?' 'Quite so!' Then somebody else comes in, and he says 'Of course I won't.'"

Along the same lines is the most damaging information to emerge from the tapes—Roosevelt's suggestion that his campaign workers "way, way down the line" spread rumors about Willkie's affair with a New York woman. The President further urged that word be spread that Willkie's wife had been paid to act during the campaign as if they were happily married. *"Now, now,"* FDR said, "Mrs. Willkie may not have been *hired*, but in effect she's been hired to return to Wendell and smile and make this campaign with him. Now whether there was a money price behind it, *I don't know*, but it's the same idea." [11]

At the very least, such a statement coming from the lips of a man who had had an affair beginning more than two decades earlier with a woman in whose arms he would die—and whose own spouse was a political partner, not a wife—was incredible hypocrisy. But these two 1940 statements together seem to indicate that Roosevelt actually failed to realize that he was guilty of the faults he pointed out in others.

It must be recognized not only that Roosevelt was far from perfect, but also that he did things in his personal and political life that were simply despicable. None of this, however, prevented him from being one of the few people who can truly be said to have personally changed the course of history. One need not be an advocate of the "great man" school of history (I emphatically am not) to argue that had Roosevelt not won the Democratic nomination in 1932, or had the unemployed bricklayer who attempted to assassinate him in February 1933 been a better marksman, the United States—and, presumably, the world—would be a different place today than it is. *How* it would be different cannot be said with any certainty, but Roosevelt personally had an important impact on the course of history during the ensuing years.

6·"And What Was Dead Was Hope": 1932 and the Interregnum

The probability of a Republican victory in 1932 was better than that of being dealt a royal straight flush in five-card-stud poker, but only marginally so. Most voters blamed either Herbert Hoover or big businessmen for the Depression. Both were inextricably bound up with the Grand Old Party; all three were sinking in a common embrace.

Association with financiers and industrialists was doubly damning for the Republican party. Not only were businessmen blamed for causing the Depression, their attitudes during the crisis showed them to be even more heartless and selfish than did the increasing revelations of their past shady dealings. While many poverty-stricken workers were contributing part of their meager wages to help the unemployed, the wealthy often refused to make any sacrifice. Henry Ford, erstwhile champion of high wages, insisted that businessmen had no responsibility for the jobless. Such prominent financiers as Albert Wiggin of the Chase National Bank and J. P. Morgan manipulated their incomes through such devices as the pretended sale of stock to their wives, so that they paid not a penny of tax in the early years of the Depression.

The Depression grew worse almost by the day in 1932. This was due, at least in part, to the draconian program of retrenchment that Hoover had instituted at the end of 1931, in his desperate attempt to restore confidence by balancing the budget. By May, Hoover's brief burst of optimism at the year's outset had expired. He was in the depths of despair, and privately predicted that a new collapse would occur within three weeks. A few weeks later, Charles G. Dawes resigned as head of the Reconstruction Finance Corporation and returned to Chicago to prepare not only for the likely failure of his bank, but for the possible crash of the whole system. Perhaps for the first time, the true dimensions of the Depression were dawning on administration leaders. Hoover's social and economic beliefs may have been the right ones, but their chance had passed. People were no longer willing to wait. The public did not understand the causes and solutions of unemployment, but people could judge policies by results. They had little tolerance for anyone who claimed current policies were working when, in fact, more jobs were being lost. One indication of how desperate the situation was came in June when Chicago Mayor Anton Cermak told a House committee that the federal government still had a choice: it could send relief, or it could send troops.

Under the circumstances, Herbert Hoover was an almost certain loser in 1932, but so was any other Republican. Some in the party hoped that Hoover would follow Coolidge's precedent and "choose not to run." This, one party official said, would make it possible to "look forward to the nomination of Coolidge or Dawes. . . . The effect would be electrical. There would be no stopping us." The man who expressed this view suffered from an overdose of wishful thinking. The idea that they could restore Coolidge Prosperity by bringing back Coolidge was a measure of how desperate the Republicans were in 1932. The people were in no mood to buy such nonsense that year. "We are in a new era to which I do not belong," Coolidge himself said a few months later, shortly before his death, "and it would not be possible for me to adjust myself to it." This may have been the most penetrating of all Coolidge's notable statements of wisdom.

The Republicans could not repudiate Hoover without appearing to accept blame for the Depression. Few of the party's delegates who gathered in Chicago in June were enthusiastic about Hoover; fewer still sincerely believed he had much chance of winning a second term. Nowhere in the city, it seemed, was a picture of Hoover displayed, not even in the convention hall. Slides of the President flashed on a screen during the demonstration following the placing of his name in nomination. Such quick flashes apparently were all the Republicans wanted as reminder of their candidate. Significantly, the Hoover demonstration ended with the playing of "California, Here I Come, Right Back Where I Started From." Few doubted that this was an appropriate, if embarrassing, choice. The most impressive, though rather questionable, endorsement was carried by one of those seconding Hoover's nomination. Brought "fresh" from the Lincoln Memorial was this message from the sixteenth President: "If you see him, speak to Hoover for me and say that this road is the one I traveled." It may have seemed to some of the cheerless delegates that the only enthusiasm for Hoover came from beyond the grave.[1]

Democrats had every reason to be optimistic. After more than a decade in the political wilderness, the party expected to win. Nevada Senator Key Pittman spoke for Democrats everywhere: "I am tired of being in the minority. I want to win." The likelihood of victory meant the struggle for the nomination would be even more fierce than was the party's custom. As far as most party regulars were concerned, though, the most important qualification for a candidate was that he be able to capitalize on the people's hatred for the incumbent without alienating many voters himself. In short, the party needed someone who looked like a president. The twin disabilities of death and Republicanism having made Warren Harding unavailable, Governor Franklin D. Roosevelt of New York was the front-runner.

Many were looking for a hero to save the nation. Teddy had been a hero; why not another Roosevelt? It might seem strange that people looking for a "man on horseback" turned to a man in a wheelchair. But the aura of the heroic seemed to many to surround this second Governor Roosevelt of New York.

Although FDR was the clear front-runner, that was no guarantee of victory. The party's requirement that its nominee win two-thirds of the convention votes, rather than a simple majority—a rule instituted a century earlier to allow southern Democrats to veto candidates unacceptable to them—meant that Roosevelt's nomination was far from a certainty. Such Republicans-in-Democratic-clothing as the party's millionaire national chairman, John J. Raskob, feared the New York governor. They generally grouped behind FDR's predecessor as governor, Alfred E. Smith. Since his 1928 loss to Hoover, Smith had been hobnobbing with the rich and in the process lost whatever progressive tendencies he had ever possessed. H. L. Mencken later wrote that Smith had "ceased to be the wonder and glory of the East Side and [become] simply a minor figure of Park Avenue." Progressive Republican Harold Ickes of Illinois said in the spring of 1932 that Smith had become "an enthusiastic little brother of the rich." On the other side of the Democratic party, some agrarian reformers from the South and West were skeptical of Roosevelt. They backed the candidacy of Speaker of the House John Nance Garner of Texas. Garner also attracted another type of Democrat. "Unconsciously, what they want," a political writer said early in 1932, "is a Democratic Coolidge, and they instinctively feel that Garner is their man. They are not wrong." By the summer, however, it was apparent that in their developing mood the voters wanted no Coolidge of any kind. Garner faded rapidly after assuming leadership of the drive to adopt a sales tax. He failed to win support because he hooked his wagon to a horse (or, rather, a Hearst) going in the wrong direction. Despite his "populist" reputation, Garner joined with the conservative forces of Bernard Baruch and William Randolph Hearst. Garner had little choice, since Roosevelt had already preempted much of the progressive support and the Texan needed Baruch's financial backing, but in the context of 1932 this move to the right was fatal to his chances for attracting popular approval.

Roosevelt's early advisers—Louis Howe, Jim Farley, and old Wilson confidant Colonel Edward House—carried him to the front of the pack, but they grew overly optimistic and almost lost the nomination. When it became clear to Roosevelt that this team was not making sufficient progress with delegates to assure winning the necessary two-thirds and that they were certainly not capable of developing solutions to the nation's economic problems, FDR sought to widen his staff. Governor Roosevelt's legal counsel, Samuel I. Rosenman, suggested in March that a group of academic advisers be formed. Although leery of such people, Roosevelt agreed and asked Raymond Moley of the Columbia Law School to assemble a group of professors. Thus was conceived the assemblage of academics that New York Times reporter James Kieran later dubbed the "Brains Trust." The group was to play a crucial role in Roosevelt's 1932 victories and in shaping the New Deal.

The key figure in the Brains Trust (the plural was used originally, although subsequently it came more often to be "Brain Trust") was Raymond Moley. Moley grew up in the populist-progressive tradition in small town Ohio. At the age of ten, he was already an avid follower of William Jennings Bryan, and considered himself an enemy of "the Interests" and "Wall Street." By the time he was sixteen, Moley owned an often-read copy of Henry George's Progress and Poverty. When he began his doctoral studies at Columbia in 1914, Moley came under the spell of historian Charles A. Beard, thus becoming even more solidly progressive than he had been before. For a time he flirted with socialism. After taking his degree in political science, Moley became an expert on criminal justice, eventually returning to Columbia. There he came to know Louis Howe and, through him, he met Roosevelt in 1928.

Moley's first important collaboration with Roosevelt was the "Forgotten Man" radio address early in April 1932. It set the tone for the campaign and the New Deal by reflecting the values that were emerging among the people as the Depression progressed. The speech created something of a sensation. It committed Roosevelt to a humane theme and program, including a much larger role for the federal government than it had ever before assumed in peacetime. The speech stressed the idea that the root cause of the Depression lay in the problems of farmers and the consequent lack of purchasing power in the rural–small-town half of the population. This placed Roosevelt clearly among those who saw lack of demand—underconsumption—as the key, and some form of redistribution of income as the solution. FDR attacked Hoover's recovery program as an elitist, trickle-down approach. What was needed instead, Roosevelt said, were "plans like those of 1917 [a reference to the American war economy, not the Russian Revolution] that build from the bottom up and not from the top down; that put their faith once more in the forgotten man at the bottom of the economic pyramid." "A real economic cure," Roosevelt declared, "must go to the killing of the bacteria in the system rather than to the treatment of external symptoms."

This struck some as radical talk. Senator Cordell Hull of Tennessee, a Roosevelt supporter, feared "another Bryan campaign of 1896." The most bitter attack came from Al Smith. "I protest," Smith declared, "against the endeavor to delude the poor people of this country to their ruin by trying to make them believe that they can get employment before the people who would ordinarily employ them are also again restored to conditions of normal prosperity." Smith was endorsing the trickle-down approach.

As the criticism from the right over the "Forgotten Man" speech rose, Howe, House, and other members of the inner circle told Roosevelt to back off, to take a conservative tack. Even progressive Senator Burton K. Wheeler of Montana recommended that Roosevelt clarify his position by saying that "in calling attention to the necessity of doing something for the foundation, he did not mean to criticize any proper efforts to repair the roof." Roosevelt rejected this advice and gave another stirring speech only five days after Smith's attack on him. In his Jefferson Day address at St. Paul, FDR called for "a real community of interest," "common participation . . . planned on the basis of a shared common life, the low as well as the high. In much of our present plans, there is too much disposition to mistake the part for the whole, the head for the body, the captain for the company, the general for the army," Roosevelt said. "I plead not for a class control, but for a true concert of interests."

Roosevelt's veteran advisers were looking backward; he and Moley were looking forward. FDR had an understanding, perhaps an instinctive one, that what would have been political suicide a few years before was just what many Americans wanted to hear in 1932. They had seen enough attempts at roof repair and were anxious for some foundation work. Roosevelt's "radical" speeches came in the month following the public outcry that had defeated the sales tax. Roosevelt and Moley must have understood that message from the public. Siding with the top of the pyramid was no longer the expedient thing to do. (This is not meant to imply that FDR's speeches were motivated mainly by expediency, but that he realized contentions that his position would be politically disastrous were mistaken.)

Roosevelt had based his promise of curing the nation's economic ailments on increasing the purchasing power of the farmer. The only trouble was that neither Roosevelt nor Moley could figure out how to do this. An economist with new ideas and some knowledge of agriculture was needed. Moley looked, naturally, to the Columbia faculty and found Rexford Guy Tugwell. Tugwell was the son of a modestly successful fruit grower and canner in up-state New York. He studied economics at the University of Pennsylvania, where he came under the influence of Scott Nearing and Simon N. Patten. He was especially impressed with the arguments of J. A. Hobson that under-consumption is a basic flaw of capitalism.

Always a maverick, Tugwell believed in experimentation and loved order and symmetry. As early as 1924, he was calling for a new experimental economics that rejected the divinity of Adam Smith. Tugwell was a firm believer in planning and government regulation of the marketplace to protect the consumer. He thought the planning done in the American economy during World War I was a step in the right direction. In 1927 he visited Russia and he later believed that he had seen the future there. Laissez faire, Tugwell believed, was nearing its end and social control was coming to the forefront. Eventually, he said, "business will logically be required to disappear. This is not an overstatement for the sake of emphasis; it is literally meant."

Rex Tugwell was the most radical of Roosevelt's academic advisers, but he was not at this point completely out of step with the others. Moley remembered that Tugwell's "original and speculative turn of mind made him an enormously exhilarating companion. Rex was like a cocktail, his conversation picked you up and made your brain race along." He may have also had this effect on Governor Roosevelt. Certainly he influenced the candidate, although not as much as Tugwell would have liked. The economist kept most of his more radical notions to himself when he was around Roosevelt, and was able to sell him on some less grandiose ideas.

The Tugwell influence was first apparent in FDR's speech at Georgia's Oglethorpe University in May. There Roosevelt spoke of the possibility of using "drastic means" to correct "the faults in our economic system." The candidate's famous "bold, persistent experimentation" statement was completely in line with Tugwell's thinking. Roosevelt aligned himself with the growing public hostility to bankers and greedy businessmen: "We cannot allow our economic life to be controlled by that small group of men whose chief outlook upon the social welfare is tinctured by the fact that they can make huge profits from the lending of money and the marketing of securities—an outlook which deserves the adjectives 'selfish' and 'opportunist.'" In the twenties many people had not considered those adjectives particularly damning. Roosevelt was wagering that they were taken as terms of opprobrium in 1932. They were. If we wanted our economic order to endure, Roosevelt told his audience, we must "bring about a wiser, more equitable distribution of the national income." The candidate had placed himself solidly in line with the set of values that Americans were embracing under the impact of the Depression. It is significant that this move to the left—for such it was— was made *after* Roosevelt had been crushed by Smith in the Massachusetts primary and was in need of reigniting his campaign.

The new emphasis of the Roosevelt campaign was crystallized in a long memorandum Moley wrote in May. In this document Moley called for a reorientation of the Democratic party toward humane, progressive policies and a lower- and middle-class base. Moley denounced the economic view that "sees to it that a favored few are helped and that some of their prosperity will leak through to labor, to the farmer, and to the small businessman." This, he said, was the reactionary view of the Republicans, but some Democrats (e.g., Al Smith) shared it. "There is," Moley continued, "no room in this country for two reactionary parties." What the people wanted, he asserted, was "not a choice between two names for the same reactionary doctrine. The alternative should be a party of liberal thought, of planned action, of enlightened international outlook, . . . of democratic principles."

Here was an outline of the principles of the New Deal (Moley used that term in the May memorandum, although without any emphasis), even to the point of suggesting the party realignment that Roosevelt attempted in 1938. Nothing Moley said was inconsistent with the general positions Roosevelt had taken for many years, but Moley organized and filled them out. They were in the background of the 1932 campaign and the early New Deal measures; they surged to the forefront in the Second New Deal of 1935 and Roosevelt's reelection campaign in 1936. By that time, though, Moley had taken a right turn and become distressed over Roosevelt's move in just the direction Moley himself had outlined in 1932.

By the time Moley wrote this memorandum, he had recruited the third and last member of the Brains Trust. Adolf A. Berle, Jr., was the son of a Congregationalist minister. The Social Gospel permeated the Berle household. Something of a prodigy, Berle took his B.A. at Harvard at age eighteen, his M.A. a year later, and a law degree at twenty-one. He had wanted to study history, but had heeded his father's unassailable argument that no one could expect to make a respectable living as a professional historian. Instead, young

Berle entered upon a law career, hoping to influence a change in the American economy that would put some of the teachings of the Social Gospel into practice.

Berle obtained a position at Columbia Law School in 1927 and received a grant that enabled him to hire an assistant, Gardiner C. Means, and study the influence of corporations on modern American life. When he joined Roosevelt's group of academic advisers, Berle became its most moderate member. With his Christian background, he believed that businessmen could be redeemed and made to act benevolently. Berle favored a federal incorporation act for the purpose of regulating corporations through a Federal Trade Commission with sharpened teeth.[2]

Feeling was running so high against the Republicans in 1932 that almost any Democrat could have won the presidential election. The only prominent Democrat capable of losing was Al Smith. His own backers recognized this, and Smith himself may have known it. Hoover was the perfect "issue." There was no point in raising the specter of Catholicism again and diverting attention from the Depression.

Yet diverting attention from the Depression was precisely what the people behind Smith had in mind. Raskob and his associates on the Democratic National Committee strove to ignore economic issues and concentrate on prohibition. The DNC was "trying to merge . . . with the Republican Party on everything except prohibition," Kentucky Democrat Alben Barkley charged. The zeal of this group for repeal was grounded in more than their taste for alcohol.

Whether or not Smith thought of himself as a serious contender, his key backers clearly never intended to nominate him in 1932. Their plan from the start was to use Smith as a major part of the "Stop Roosevelt" movement. They would deadlock the convention and bring forth Newton D. Baker, who had been Woodrow Wilson's secretary of War, as a "compromise." From the viewpoint of its authors, this was a neat script. The trouble was that Smith would not have enough votes by himself to deny the nomination to Roosevelt.

Politics, the cliché says, makes for strange bedfellows. This is especially so where attempts to prevent a nomination are concerned, since such efforts can provide the most disparate individuals with a common objective. In 1932 the "Stop Roosevelt" movement may not have brought anyone together in bed (although Smith indicated a willingness for such a liaison), but it made for a remarkable luncheon meeting. William Gibbs McAdoo, still hoping for the nomination that the Smith forces had denied him in 1924, had joined with Hearst behind the candidacy of John Nance Garner. It appears to have been McAdoo's goal to have a deadlocked convention make him the nominee. This coalition controlled the large California and Texas delegations and was critical for either stopping Roosevelt or putting him over the top. Bernard Baruch, who had no love for Roosevelt and less for his radical rhetoric, acted as matchmaker and invited Smith and McAdoo to a luncheon meeting in Baruch's suite at Chicago's Blackstone Hotel just before the convention. "Bernie, I don't like him," Smith is reported to have said of McAdoo to Baruch, "I don't trust him, but in this fight, I would sleep with a Chinaman to win and I'll come." Thus the desire to deny the nomination to Roosevelt brought together the bitter enemies of eight years before.

Such a shotgun marriage was by its nature unstable and subject to instant annulment prior to its consummation. Roosevelt was on the verge of losing the nomination. His only hope was to lure away one of the partners in the odd Smith-McAdoo alliance. A reconciliation with Smith was out of the question; it would have to be McAdoo and his allies, Hearst and Garner. Each of them had a reason finally, though reluctantly, to swing over to FDR. Baker was an open "internationalist," and anathema to Hearst. When the publisher realized that Baker's nomination would be the consequence of denying Roosevelt, Hearst became more favorable to FDR. Garner feared that a deadlocked convention would follow the 1924 pattern and destroy the party. McAdoo, though, remained the key. His basic reason for finally being willing to switch is evident in a simple statement in his autobiography published in the previous year: "I like movement and change." He wanted the nomination himself, but his first priority was to have a progressive nominee. Roosevelt fit that description; Baker did not.

The dynamics of a multiballot convention require that the front-runner gain strength on each ballot. This Roosevelt did on the second ballot, but he almost lost the nomination on the third ballot. That vote, held after an all-night session, saw the Mississippi delegation teeter on the brink of abandoning Roosevelt. The delegation, operating under the unit rule, was divided 10½ to 9½ for Roosevelt and had cast its 20 votes for him on the first two ballots. The Roosevelt leader in the state, Senator Pat Harrison, believing the convention adjourned, went to his hotel after the second ballot. As he got into bed, he turned on the radio and heard, "Mississippi passes." Harrison dressed quickly and raced the three miles back to the convention hall. In the meantime, Louisiana Senator Huey Long, who had earlier announced his support of Roosevelt by telling Senator Wheeler, "I don't like your sonofabitch, but I'll be for him," cajoled the Mississippi delegates and kept them from deserting. Roosevelt escaped the third ballot with a gain of five votes. Had Mississippi fallen, his cause probably would have been lost.

It was still far from won. Indeed, many people believed that Roosevelt's strength had peaked and Baker would be nominated. FDR himself telephoned Baker in the evening, prior to the fourth ballot, offering to help him. Soon thereafter, a tearful Jim Farley met with two of McAdoo's supporters and told them, "Boys, Roosevelt is lost unless California comes over on the next ballot." They replied that California would go for FDR, but not for a few more ballots. "Well, then," Farley said, "Newton D. Baker will be nominated. He is the interests' candidate, and you will be playing squarely into their hands if you wait. I tell you, unless California comes over on the fourth ballot, Roosevelt is lost and Baker will win!"

McAdoo was convinced. So was Garner. Despite the objections of many California and Texas delegates, the states would be swung to Roosevelt. It was none too soon. Just before the balloting began, Mississippi went over to the opposition. The anti-Roosevelt forces thought they had won. When California was called, though, McAdoo rose and said, "California came here to nominate a President." The meaning was clear. Roosevelt won, but Smith refused to release his delegates so that the nomination could be made unanimous. Garner was persuaded to take the vice presidency, an office the Texan later complained, according to published reports, was "not worth a pitcher of warm spit." (Garner is rumored to have actually used more colorful language.)

Franklin Roosevelt demonstrated his boldness by breaking with tradition and flying from Albany to the convention in Chicago to deliver his acceptance speech. It was a doubly symbolic act. It indicated the candidate's willingness to try new things; it also foreshadowed a campaign that would have more style than substance. In his speech Roosevelt told the delegates: "We will break foolish traditions and leave it to the Republican leadership, far more skilled in that art, to break promises."

Roosevelt's acceptance speech reflected Moley's influence. Several parts were taken almost directly from the adviser's May memorandum. Roosevelt spoke of the "Tory" idea that the rich should be helped in hopes that "some of their prosperity will leak through, sift through, to labor, to the farmer, to the small businessman." Again echoing Moley, Roosevelt said the people wanted a genuine choice. "Ours must be a party of liberal thought, of planned action, of enlightened international outlook, and of the greatest good to the greatest number of our citizens." Roosevelt also pledged himself "to a new deal for the American people." This phrase has generally been attributed to Samuel Rosenman, who is said to have inserted it in the speech draft the previous night, attaching no special significance to it. Historian Elliot Rosen, however, has made a convincing case that Raymond Moley was responsible for the "new deal" phrase, and that he intended it to be more than a rhetorical flourish. In a paragraph that was dropped at the last minute in order to use part of a draft by Howe, Moley proposed "a new deal" as "an emblem—a happy emblem of new purposes, renewed life, rededicated devotion . . . to the sorely tired people of this country." That the Roosevelt program came to be known as the New Deal was no journalistic accident.

All of this was in keeping with the shift to the left that had begun with the "Forgotten Man" speech. But other parts of the acceptance speech were slightly more conservative. The candidate promised help for "the top of the pyramid" as well as its base. The reason for this slight retreat is plain. Winning a general election is quite a different matter from winning a nomination. Splitting the party is often the mode of winning a nomination; uniting the party is necessary to win a general election. After the nomination is won, pontoon bridges must be rapidly constructed to replace the sturdier structures that the candidate found it necessary to burn in his campaign for the nomination. In the wake of his defeat in the Massachusetts primary, Roosevelt had been obliged to take the risk of alienating some within the party by moving to the left. Now a reconciliation with Raskob, Baruch, Smith et al., would be useful, so Roosevelt tried to be a bit more moderate. The campaign against Hoover, after all, was far more of a "sure thing" than had been that for the Democratic nomination. Fewer chances needed to be taken during the general election campaign.[3]

The middle of the road was shifting into the left lane with the worsening Depression. All of that area was occupied by Roosevelt. Hoover had available to him only the right shoulder. An unaccustomed spot for him, he tried to run his campaign there.

Hoover sincerely believed that the future of the nation depended on his reelection. This conviction, Secretary of State Stimson said, led to the President "losing his balance" in the summer and fall of 1932. It was small wonder that this happened. Many Republican candidates found it necessary or expedient to ignore Hoover—or worse. Some went so far as to allow backers to employ such slogans as the one used for South Dakota Republican Senator Peter Norbeck: "Elect Norbeck and Roosevelt." Just before the election, one telegram sent to Hoover carried the message: "Vote for Roosevelt and make it unanimous." By that time, observers reported that the President looked like a "walking corpse." His car had been the target of rotten eggs in Elko, Nevada. Huey Long added insult to such near injuries when he told a reporter that "the great trouble with the Democrats is that we have all the votes and no money." Long suggested that the Democrats could "sell President Hoover a million votes for half of what he is going to pay to try to get them. We can spare the votes and we could use the money."

The heavy toll taken on Hoover was reflected in his last speeches before the election. In Madison Square Garden on October 31, Hoover said the election was "a contest between two philosophies of government." His opponents, he charged, "are proposing changes and so-called new deals which would destroy the very foundations of the American system of life." The Democrats, Hoover said, wanted "to change our form of government and our social and our economic system." "We denounce any attempt to stir class feeling or class antagonisms in the United States," the President affirmed. Hoover even had the temerity near the end of his extremely long address to repeat his statement of four years earlier that we would "with the help of God, be in sight of the day when poverty will be banished from this Nation." God's help was Hoover's only hope for reelection.

With his opponent painting him as a radical, Franklin Roosevelt had little need to portray himself that way. There was, in fact, little call for him to say or do anything. Many party leaders urged Roosevelt to run a front porch campaign. "All you have got to do is to stay alive until election day," Garner told his running mate. He was probably right. But Roosevelts are not given to sitting out campaigns, whether the enemies be Spaniards, Democrats, Germans, or Republicans. So Franklin insisted on taking to the hustings, albeit somewhat less boisterously than had Cousin Ted.

Democratic conservatives still hoped to make prohibition the main issue of the campaign, thus taking the pressure off business and its responsibility for the Depression. Roosevelt came out against the noble experiment, but refused to allow the main spotlight to be shifted from Hoover and the Depression. Since his supporters had differing economic ideas, Roosevelt tried to steer a middle course that, while it would entirely satisfy no one, would alienate few and would commit him to nothing specific. Thus in Columbus, Ohio, the candidate seemed to attack Hoover for overregulation and call instead for more competition. At Topeka, Roosevelt gave an agriculture speech that included bits of all the various farm proposals. In the most notable speech of the campaign, given at San Francisco's Commonwealth Club, he reaffirmed his belief in a planned economy and called for a more equitable distribution of wealth. Not wishing to lose votes on either side of the tariff question, FDR took two proposed speeches on the subject, one protectionist, the other free trade, and astonished Raymond Moley by telling him to "weave the two together." Finally, in Pittsburgh, Roosevelt complained that the 50 percent increase in federal spending since 1927 was "the most reckless and extravagant past that I have been able to discover in the statistical record of any peacetime government anywhere, anytime." He called for reducing government expenditures by 25 percent and attacked Hoover for not balancing the budget and for trying "to center control of everything in Washington as rapidly as possible." The actions of presidents often bear scant resemblance to their campaign pledges, but the difference between the New Deal and this speech is a prime candidate—along with the chasm separating Ronald Reagan's 1980 promise to balance the budget by 1983 from his actual budget figures for the mid-eighties—for the largest such gap in American history. As his administration embarked on unprecedented deficit spending and centralization, Roosevelt and his advisers jokingly decided that the only way to get around the speech was to deny that he had ever been in Pittsburgh.

The Pittsburgh speech was an attempt to appease the Smith-Raskob faction. Roosevelt sought consensus during the campaign and got it. The conservative Democrats stuck with the party through the 1932 election, despite their fear that a Roosevelt victory would mean the end of an era: theirs. Keeping John Raskob in the same tent with Huey Long, and Al Smith under the same roof as William McAdoo, was quite a feat. It could not last forever.

The Roosevelt campaign in 1932 also had its more left-leaning statements. At Portland, Oregon, Roosevelt made what was probably his most radical-sounding statement of the campaign. Saying that he wanted "to protect the welfare of the people against selfish greed," he exclaimed: "If that be treason, my friends, then make the most of it!" These words of Patrick Henry had been suggested by Moley five months before. Roosevelt went on to defend his "radicalism" by reminding his auditors that their nation had been founded by revolutionaries: "My friends, my policy is as radical as American liberty."

Astute observers were upset by Roosevelt's vagueness. At the beginning of the election year Walter Lippmann, in one of his most famous columns, summed up the views many held of the New York governor. He was, Lippmann stated, "an amiable man with many philanthropic impulses, but he is not the dangerous enemy of anything." Rather than being a "crusader" or an "enemy of entrenched privilege," Lippmann wrote, Franklin Roosevelt was "a pleasant man who, without any important qualifications for the office, would very much like to be President."

But what did it matter? Hoover must be removed, so people had to vote for Roosevelt. There were other alternatives—Socialist Norman Thomas and Communist William Z. Foster, most notably—but Hoover and other conservatives helped Roosevelt overcome the danger of massive defection to the left. By lashing his opponent as one who would lead to drastic change, Hoover may have done more to win votes for Roosevelt than the Democrat did for himself. Drastic change was, after all, appealing to the masses of hungry, jobless people. Discontent was sufficient that upward of 5 percent of the electorate strongly considered voting for Thomas on the Socialist ticket, as the *Literary Digest* poll indicated. In the end, the Thomas vote was less than a million (2.2 percent) and Foster won just over one hundred thousand ballots. Thomas, at least, had a good deal more support, but many of his backers voted for FDR, fearing that in a two-party system Hoover might be reelected if they "threw their vote away" by marking the Socialist column. Roosevelt's landslide victory—the largest electoral margin since 1864—unquestionably was a mandate for a "new deal," though less a vote of confidence in Roosevelt himself. Most of all, the large Roosevelt vote was a repudiation of Hoover. Will Rogers pointed to this fact when he said most ordinary voters would like to be able to cast two ballots, one against Hoover and one against Roosevelt. No one really knew what to expect from the President-elect, but it seemed that any change had to be for the better.

The Democratic victory in 1932 was overwhelming. The shift from two years before was immense. Democrats gained 90 seats in the House and 13 in the Senate. Republicans won only 6 of 34 Senate races. All the Old Guard leaders and foremost defenders of big business who were up for reelection— James Watson, Reed Smoot, George Moses, Hiram Bingham—went down to defeat. The Democrats won their biggest advantage in the Senate since the Civil War. The turnaround in the House saw the Democrats go from 44.9 percent of the major party national votes in 1930 to 56.6 percent in 1932. The New Era was repudiated in no uncertain terms.

A fundamental change in American politics appeared to be under way. Henry Stimson said after the election that "the people of sobriety and intelligence and responsibility" had voted Republican, "yet we have the feeling that the immense undercurrent is against us." Stimson believed that "a very unworthy element of the nation [was] coming into control." From his viewpoint, this was just what was happening. "The mood of the country was such," wrote Commerce Secretary Roy Chapin, "that . . . perhaps we are lucky that we didn't get a Socialist or a Radical, instead of Roosevelt." The lower and middle classes to whom Moley and Roosevelt had said the Democrats must appeal had shifted their votes in decisive numbers.

Almost all of this political upheaval was anti-Hoover, although Roosevelt's lower-class–oriented rhetoric had some effect. Whether the Democratic gains in 1932 would be lasting or simply a one-time protest depended upon what Roosevelt and his congressional majorities did to deal with the Depression.[4]

While Americans waited from November 1932 to March 1933 to see what the Democrats would do, the economy continued to collapse. The interregnum between Hoover's defeat and Roosevelt's inauguration was the most critical such period since the lame duck months of James Buchanan, during which the nation awaited the start of Abraham Lincoln's presidency. As in 1860–61, events continued during the interregnum to worsen the situation facing the new President.

The winter of 1932–33 was the most desperate of the Depression. Hoover later insisted that recovery had begun in the summer and the new collapse was caused by uncertainty over Roosevelt. This was largely, although perhaps not entirely, nonsense. One-fourth of the nation's work force was unemployed. Funds available for relief were pitifully inadequate. Hoover still refused to agree to direct federal assistance, and Roosevelt had implied that Hoover was a spendthrift. It was not a time for much hope. By February, even those who had voted for Roosevelt were said to have little confidence that he would accomplish anything.

Conditions were particularly bad for farmers, who were now in the second decade of their depression. After the rest of the nation had joined their economic plight, farmers faced an even more difficult situation. By 1932 a bushel of wheat would fetch only 30 cents, down nearly 90 percent from the almost $3 it had brought twelve years earlier. And the farmer now had to deal not only with low prices for his products, but also with a general deflation, the late nineteenth-century nemesis of American agriculture. The combination meant that many farmers, crushed by long-term debt, were threatened by foreclosure.

Some met the danger with an old American expedient: direct action. Nooses were suggestively dangled over trees when judges attempted to hold foreclosure sales. In one such incident, an Iowa judge was momentarily hanged; but the farmers revived him and forced him to say: "O Lord, I pray thee, do justice to all men." Rather than depend upon the Lord to provide justice, other farmers took matters into their own hands. "Penny auctions" were one example of homegrown justice. Neighbors of a bankrupt farmer would prevent—by threat of force if necessary—realistic bids, buy back the farm for a nominal fee (often one dollar), and return it to the original owner. Such actions never became very common, but their repeated occurrence in the heart of the supposedly conservative Middle West gave rise to heightened fears of revolution. Many believed that Roosevelt would have the last opportunity to save capitalism and stave off revolution. Others—mainly in the business community—feared that Roosevelt's victory *was* the revolution.

Based on his campaign, however, no one could be sure what to expect from the President-elect. Accordingly, people of various viewpoints sought to commit him in advance to their own policies. Conservative Democrats again proposed a national sales tax designed to balance the budget at any cost—even that of further eroding purchasing power. Incredibly, the outrageous proposal won many supporters in the lame duck Congress. Roosevelt was unsure of his own policies, but he was sure he was against this regressive tax. The people's view on the subject had already been heard. The scheme was jettisoned once more.

Prior to the ratification of the Twentieth Amendment in 1933, a full session of each Congress was held after each election, with the old members still in office. These lame duck sessions never made any sense, as they allowed congressmen to continue making laws after they had been rejected by the voters. The last lame duck session, that of 1932–33, was the worst. Fully 30 percent of its members—144 representatives and 14 senators—either had been defeated or had not sought reelection. With the nation facing one of its worst crises, this was a wholly indefensible situation. Virtually nothing happened in the last session of the Seventy-second Congress, because both Hoover and Roosevelt preferred no legislation to any this rejected group would pass.

During the interregnum everyone, it seemed, was attempting to gain the President-elect's endorsement for schemes of the left or right. Perhaps the most persistent in trying to wed the incoming President to a particular set of policies was the man he had just defeated. Hoover's first such attempt came less than three weeks after the election. At this and subsequent meetings between the retiring and arriving chief executives, Hoover attempted to maneuver Roosevelt into endorsing the policies so recently repudiated by the electorate. It was politically impossible for Roosevelt to do this, so he contented himself with demonstrating his allegiance to the common man by puffing on cigarettes while Hoover smoked cigars.

By 1933, Hoover and the other guardians of the New Era were the subjects of ridicule and hatred. Calvin Coolidge's death at the beginning of January was followed by the spiritual demise of the men he had represented. Utility magnate Samuel Insull had fled to Europe in mid-1932, as his empire collapsed. In the ensuing months, evidence of his massive wrongdoing emerged, culminating in his early 1933 indictment for embezzlement. Insull could not understand his unpopularity. "What have I done," he asked, "that every banker and business magnate has not done in the course of business?" It was a pregnant question, but the offspring was not the one Insull had planned. A Senate investigation in January 1933 saw one banker after another parade before counsel Ferdinand Pecora. Most of them admitted to a long series of misdeeds. The prestige of bankers and big businessmen in general had already dropped at a rate similar to that of the stock market. Now that prestige, so great only a few years before, hit bottom.

The most startling of the early revelations of the Pecora committee surrounded Charles E. Mitchell, president of the National City Bank. He (like many other leading bankers, as it turned out) had done much speculation in the stock of his own bank. What was more, he did it with the bank's money. Faced with the prospect of a large tax liability in 1929, Mitchell sold stock in his own bank that he had used to secure a loan from J. P. Morgan. He "sold" the stock to his wife, for much less than he had paid for it, creating a huge paper loss and eliminating all of his tax obligation for the year. Mitchell was not a man without principles. Robbing his own bank was one thing, but he was not one to swindle his wife. He subsequently bought the stock back from her for the same price he had received, although the market value had by that time dropped tremendously. Before the Senate committee, Mitchell said: "I sold this stock, frankly, for tax purposes." He also told of the bank making available to its officers $2.4 million of the stockholders' money for interest-free loans with which to try to save their portfolios after the Crash. Mitchell was indicted, but later acquitted.

Mitchell's specific admissions may have created the biggest stir, but a larger picture of extreme greed among the nation's leading bankers emerged from the hearings: manipulated stock prices, trading in the stock of one's own bank, unsupportable holding companies, huge "loans" to bank officials, tax evasion, and so on. What remaining faith the public had in bankers expired.

So did many banks. The practices revealed by the Pecora investigation had spawned a banking system of startling weakness. Even in the prosperous twenties nearly 7000 banks had failed. Most of these, however, were small "country" banks and their failures were scarcely noticed in the prosperity decade. In 1930 the situation worsened. There were 1345 failures that year, including the large Bank of the United States in New York. Now it was every banker for himself. Strong banks tried to solidify their own positions (which, in a semantic paradox, they did by increasing their liquidity) rather than trying to save their weaker brothers. Most bankers were "unreconstructed individualists," believers in the mystical forces of the market. They would not lift a finger to help the banks that were going under because they viewed the latter as "bad" banks that deserved their fate.

This was all well and good, except that banking is built to an extraordinary extent upon confidence. Depositors were unable to distinguish the good bankers from the bad and came to distrust them all. More than 2000 banks failed in 1931. When Hoover's voluntary schemes to help the banks collapsed, government action came in the form of the RFC and the Glass-Steagall Act. Congress passed the latter measure in February 1932, while in a state of panic. Members of the Banking Committee told other House members that the nation's banking system was in such bad shape that the details could not be given to the full House—or the public.

These measures stabilized the system for a time, but Hoover made decreasing use of the RFC, and by the beginning of 1933 the American banking structure was tottering more ominously than ever. People fortunate enough to have savings at this point feared losing them in insolvent banks. Senator "Cotton Ed" Smith of South Carolina showed the state of his confidence by carrying all his remaining cash in a belt around his waist. After Henry Ford refused to take any action to save Michigan's banks, the state's governor declared a "bank holiday," a euphemism for closing all banks and preventing further withdrawals. Runs now spread rapidly from one bank to another, and state after state proclaimed bank holidays as panic gripped the nation anew.

President Hoover again insisted that Roosevelt endorse the Republican program and thus restore confidence. After narrowly escaping the February assassination attempt in Miami, however, the President-elect made it clear that he had no desire to kill himself politically. Moreover, Roosevelt probably believed that he was far more likely to restore confidence by taking fresh action when he assumed office than he would by endorsing anything the public associated with Hoover. The banking crisis continued to deepen and by March 4 the nation could only hope that the new President would be able to revive the nation's financial institutions as well as its spirits. [5]

7·"Action, and Action Now": The Hundred Days and Beyond

As he took office Franklin Roosevelt inspired a new, perhaps last, hope in the American people. The nation was paralyzed and so had been the President, but he had not given up. He had fought back to triumph over his illness; maybe he could lead America to do the same. Scant as this hope was, it was all the country had in March 1933.

Perhaps it would be enough, at least for a time. Arthur Krock reported in *The New York Times* the day before the inauguration that the mood in Washington was "distinctly hopeful." The capital —and the nation—anticipated the return of "leadership," for which Americans had "been clamoring for two years." Part of the reason for "the almost visible air of hope" on the eve of March 4 was the President-elect's "cheery demeanor." This represented a pleasant contrast to Hoover's increasingly sour public countenance. But far more than a smile was involved. Roosevelt had an opportunity greater than that greeting any new president in peacetime American history. The people were desperate for new leadership; they demanded change. Whatever Roosevelt wanted to do, as long as it was bold and seemed likely to ease the Depression and reduce inequality, would meet with the approval of most Americans. Washington "welcomes the 'new deal,' even though it is not sure what the new deal is going to be," Krock correctly reported. "It is ready to be enthusiastic over any display of leadership, any outline of a reconstruction program." The unusual, virtually unique, situation in which Roosevelt found himself was summed up perfectly by Krock when he wrote: "Not for years . . . has a new President been more likely to gain gratitude and praise beyond the merits of his accomplished program for the simple fact of being able to achieve any program at all."

The next day the nation's hopes seemed to be reflected in the capital's weather. The overcast skies of the preceding days remained, but the rains stopped and the forecast was for clearing the next day, symbolically showing what Americans unrealistically expected of their new leader. *The Times* pointed this out editorially on the morning of Roosevelt's inauguration: "He will be thought of as something of a miracle-worker."

The new President realized that the miracles could not be postponed. The day before he took office, the major states of New York and Illinois had joined most of the rest of the nation in declaring "bank holidays." Roosevelt skillfully used the banking crisis to aid his attempt to restore confidence in the American public. That goal was, of course, stated clearly in the most famous lines of his inaugural address: "So, first of all, let me assert my firm belief that the only thing we have to fear is fear itself—nameless, unreasoning, unjustified terror which paralyzes needed efforts to convert retreat into advance." Going on to assail the incompetence of bankers, the new President used his speech to demonstrate that he was on the side of "the people" and that he subscribed to the values of justice and compassion that were becoming dominant during the Depression. He condemned "unscrupulous money changers" who used "the lure of profit" to mislead people. They were "a generation of self-seekers." *
The implication was clear: whatever else it might be, the embryonic "new

---

* Edmund Wilson in his piercing memoir of the era, *The Shores of Light*, wrote of the Crash and the banks:

> To the writers and artists of my generation, who had grown up in the Big Business era and had always resented its barbarism, its crowding-out of everything they cared about, these years were not depressing but stimulating. One couldn't help being exhilarated at the sudden, unexpected collapse of that stupid gigantic fraud. It gave us a new sense of power to find ourselves still carrying on, while the bankers, for a change, were taking a beating.

deal" would emphasize cooperation rather than self-seeking. "The money changers have fled from their high seats in the temple of our civilization," Roosevelt declared. "We may now restore that temple to the ancient truths. The measure of the restoration lies in the extent to which we apply social values more noble than mere monetary profit."

Roosevelt's words were well attuned to the spirit of the time. His phrases echoed again and again the values and themes that Depression-era Americans were developing: "moral stimulation," "mad chase of evanescent profits," "minister to ourselves and to our fellow men," "honesty," "ethics," "unselfish performance," "evils of the old order." "If I read the temper of our people correctly," Roosevelt said, "we now realize as we have never realized before our interdependence on each other; that we cannot merely take but we must give as well." He *did* read the temper of the people correctly. It was a wonderful address, one that held the promise of a new and better direction for the United States.

But grand statements are usually far easier than grand accomplishments, and FDR rightly said: "This Nation asks for action, and action now." He quickly launched that action by calling Congress into an extraordinary session to begin only five days later (March 9) and by proclaiming a nationwide closing of banks. Out of the myriad of problems facing the country, events had chosen the first area with which Roosevelt had to deal. The way he handled the banking crisis was indicative of his basic approach to the economic catastrophe. Given the magnitude of the problem and his unprecedented support, Roosevelt could have done whatever he pleased with the unpopular "money changers" and their institutions. Had he wanted, as later critics so frequently charged, to lead the country toward socialism, he could have taken an important step by nationalizing the banking system. He did nothing of the sort. Instead, he submitted to Congress a distinctly unradical Emergency Banking bill drawn up largely by bankers and Hoover appointees in the Treasury Department. Both houses of Congress passed the bill without any study. When it was taken up—neither "debated" nor "considered" would be accurate words —in the House, a rolled-up newspaper had to be used to symbolize the proposed legislation until the still-wet copies of the bill arrived. Roosevelt signed the measure into law eight hours after its introduction in Congress. The act provided assistance to private bankers and gave them a government stamp of approval. "The President drove the money changers out of the Capitol on March 4th," a North Dakota congressman complained, "and they were all back on the 9th." Even this charge overstated Roosevelt's "war" on bankers. On the very morning of his inauguration he agreed to consult with leading "money changers" on how to solve the banking crisis.

To complete the process, Roosevelt took to the airwaves the following Sunday evening with the first of his "fireside chats." It was the most effective means of reaching the public yet devised. By early 1933 more than 16 million American familes (approximately 50 percent of the American population) owned radios. Radio networks reached into all significantly populated areas of the country. When the new President spoke people listened. An estimated 30 percent of the American radio audience heard the first fireside chat. "I want to talk for a few minutes with the people of the United States about banking," he began in his soothing, fatherly voice. The President went on to explain banking in terms that he and his listeners (and, as Will Rogers said, even bankers) could understand. He assured the people that those banks which reopened were sound. They believed him. When banks began to open the next morning deposits exceeded withdrawals. The stock market, when it reopened on the third day after the fireside chat, had its largest one-day increase in history. Prices went up by 15 percent. "Capitalism," Raymond Moley later declared, "was saved in eight days." The magic of Roosevelt's radio oratory had been amply demonstrated.

Roosevelt had refused to cooperate with Hoover to stem the banking collapse during the interregnum. If Roosevelt was to restore confidence after he took office, it was necessary to keep his distance from the rejected Hoover. A policy announced by the new President alone after March 4 was likely to be far more effective in restoring confidence than would the same policy proclaimed jointly with the old President before that date. Perhaps more significant were FDR's plans to institute a wide-ranging program of reforms. By allowing the banking crisis to worsen in the last weeks of Hoover's presidency, Roosevelt was creating a situation in which his program would be accepted with the least opposition. How conscious this motivation was cannot be said. The need to avoid tying himself to the sinking Hoover was, after all, in itself sufficient reason for Roosevelt's inaction prior to his inauguration. But that the Depression hitting bottom on the morning of March 4 made it easier for Roosevelt to win approval for his reforms is undeniable. "The very deterioration in the financial and economic position which has taken place in recent weeks," *The Wall Street Journal* declared on the morning of Roosevelt's inauguration, "has cleared some obstacles from his path. A common adversity has much subdued the recalcitrance of groups bent upon self-interest. All of the country over," this voice of interests not generally favorably disposed toward FDR went on, people "are now ready to make sacrifices to a common necessity and to accept realities as we would not have done three months ago."

The suggestion that Roosevelt may have at least semiconsciously allowed the banking crisis to deteriorate and consequent suffering to increase in order to win more approval for his reforms may sound like a damning accusation. It is, on the contrary, the best face that can be put on Roosevelt's refusal to work with Hoover on the crisis. FDR never believed that closing banks for a short period would cause serious suffering, anyway. And it would be easy to conclude that whatever problems were created by the banking crisis were a small price to pay for lasting reforms that would benefit far more people than were inconvenienced by the closed banks.

Whatever Roosevelt's reasons for waiting to act until he was in power, his banking bill was scarcely more daring than what Hoover wanted. "Our information from Washington is of terrific confusion," *Nation* editor Ernest Gruening wrote to Norman Thomas the day Congress passed the bill, "with the money changers whom Mr. Roosevelt drove out of the temples in his inaugural congregating in the White House and telling him what to do." Roosevelt was often almost populist in his penchant for condemning bankers, yet his views on banking were so conservative that he refused to support the most obvious method of restoring confidence: federal insurance of bank deposits. The Federal Deposit Insurance Corporation, a far more important reform than the Emergency Banking Act, was not to Roosevelt's liking. He unenthusiastically accepted it only at the end of the special session in June.

The conservative handling of the banking crisis was not only in keeping with Franklin Roosevelt's beliefs on the subject, it was also a way to reassure those on the new President's right, before he launched a program of reform without American precedent.[1]

The special session of Congress had been made necessary by the banking crisis, but Roosevelt's call for the session had included the subjects of economy and unemployment. This provided little hint of what was to come out of the ensuing hundred days, the most intense—although perhaps not the most significant (which in my view was the Second New Deal of 1935)—period of reform legislation in American history.

Franklin Roosevelt always liked to keep his opponents off balance by moving in one direction for a time before suddenly veering sharply the other way. He believed this was good politics. Thus the push for reform was preceded by a brief move toward the conservative side. Immediately after signing the banking act, the new President called for budget cuts aimed at saving $500 million. "For three long years," FDR told Congress, "the Federal Government has been on the road toward bankruptcy." Roosevelt sincerely believed that progressing toward a balanced budget was essential. Few dared to disagree with him. The memory of German inflation in 1923 was still vivid. Later wisdom would hold that attempting to cut spending was the reverse of what was needed to stimulate the economy, but the Economy bill passed over the protests of more than a third of the House membership. The Democratic caucus in the House refused to back the President on this conservative, counterproductive step, but Republicans combined with conservative Democrats pushed the bill through.

Little of substance was new in the first week of the New Deal. The most daring step FDR took was to call for and obtain legalization of 3.2 beer. Unkind critics later said this was symbolic of the entire New Deal approach: ease the pain, cloud the senses, but leave the basic problems untouched. Still, people were cheered. Rapid action helped calm discontent and reverse pessimism. Movement, at least in the short run, seemed more important than achievement—or even direction. The substance might not have been new, but the mood certainly was. At last things were happening. Roosevelt had lifted the nation's morale, Walter Lippmann wrote eleven days after the inauguration, to a level similar to that of the "second battle of the Marne in the summer of 1916."

In light both of what has been said here about the changing values of the American people and of the New Deal actions that subsequently won public approval, it may seem incongruous that a program so conservative that it would have pleased Calvin Coolidge or Ronald Reagan should have lifted the nation's spirits. Part of the explanation lies in Roosevelt's personality. People had confidence in him. Another portion of the answer is to be found in the very fact of action, which was bound to seem more likely to solve the Depression than the apparent inaction of the Hoover administration. Raymond Moley pointed to a third factor: "Hoover had always seemed to be an expensive President." The former chief executive was so despised that any seeming inversion of his practices was likely to be popular.

Yet none of this could last long. If President Roosevelt was to keep the faith of the American people, his actions would soon have to conform to their values. Most of all, his policies would have to show results in easing the Depression, or at least its effects. Toward that end Roosevelt quickly moved. Fortunately, his own inclinations toward planning and humanitarian reform coincided with the wishes of a growing number of Americans. The successful political leader is one who "leads" in the direction people are already going on their own.

So far the conservatives were doing most of the cheering. Roosevelt seemed almost to be Grover Cleveland reincarnated. In addition to aiding bankers, cutting budgets, and legalizing beer (which, it will be recalled, was the goal of the Raskob-Du Pont-Smith group that had so bitterly fought Roosevelt), the new President called for reorganization of the federal government to bring about greater efficiency, reduce waste, cut bureaucracy, and eliminate duplication. It must be this part of Roosevelt's program that Ronald Reagan recalls so fondly. Indeed FDR had fallen under the influence of a forerunner of David Stockman, a charming, fiscally conservative former congressman from Arizona, Lewis Douglas, who had become Roosevelt's budget director. Arthur Krock reported in *The Times* in May that Douglas was "the real head of the Roosevelt Cabinet." It seems significant, however, that the main target of Roosevelt's ax was the Commerce department with its services for business, while Reagan's aim has been principally at Health and Human Services, Energy, and Education.

Many of FDR's advisers, of course, were not as conservative as Lew Douglas. In choosing his Cabinet, Roosevelt had honored the usual considerations of geographical balance, but had avoided surrounding himself with potential political enemies or people with large reputations of their own. The President kept such men as Bernard Baruch, Newton Baker, and Al Smith out of the Cabinet. He considered all of them too conservative, but whether this was his primary reason for passing them over is uncertain. Each of them had been involved in the "Stop Roosevelt" effort and revenge may have been a more powerful motivation than genuine progressivism.

The people Roosevelt did put in his Cabinet were, with a few exceptions, hardworking progressives who would go along with the President's leadership. "Progressive," of course, could mean different things. Four of FDR's original Cabinet members were old Jeffersonian/Wilsonian progressives: Secretary of State Cordell Hull of Tennessee, Secretary of War George Dern of Utah, Attorney General Homer Cummings of Connecticut, and Commerce Secretary Daniel C. Roper of South Carolina. Although this group took three of what were usually considered the most important posts, it is significant that their names did not become as familiar to the public as did those of three more forward-looking liberals in lesser positions: Henry A. Wallace of Iowa at Agriculture and Harold Ickes of Illinois at Interior, both nominally Republicans, and Frances Perkins of New York at Labor, the first woman Cabinet member.

Another well-known progressive, Senator Thomas J. Walsh of Montana, had originally accepted the post of Attorney General. But the seventy-three-year-old Walsh, a widower, suddenly eloped to Havana. Whether because of the excitement of the honeymoon or for some other reason, he suffered a heart attack on the way back to Washington and died two days before Roosevelt took office. The new President replaced him with Cummings. After conservative Senator Carter Glass was eliminated from consideration at Treasury, Roosevelt turned to a flexible Republican, William Woodin. The choice for Postmaster General was never in doubt. That patronage-dispensing job went as a matter of course to the successful candidate's campaign manager, Jim Farley. Finally, in a nod toward Glass and the conservative Democrats, Senator Claude Swanson of Virginia was appointed Secretary of the Navy. (This opened the way for Glass's arch-conservative protégé, Harry F. Byrd, to be elected to the Senate.) The Navy Department being steeped in tradition, Roosevelt named yet another family member—Henry Latrobe Roosevelt—as assistant secretary.

Despite the important roles played by several Cabinet officers, it was not the department heads who gave the New Deal its special spirit. As Franklin

Roosevelt almost instantly turned the federal government into the center of activity in a depressed nation, thousands of ambitious and idealistic young men—and some women—flocked to Washington. It was that rarest of times when ambition and idealism could go hand in hand. These were the "New Dealers," the seemingly tireless young people of ideas who were bent upon changing the world and being part of the most dramatic transformation in their nation's history. In the 1920s an ambitious young man headed for Wall Street, "where the action was"; in the sixties, depending upon his orientation, he might go into the aerospace industry or social work; in the 1970s he was likely to enter petroleum geology. During the New Deal, though, he went into government. By the fall of 1933, colleges found that students were rejecting business training and asking for courses "which would point them toward the 'brain trust.'"

The excitement was contagious. "There is certainly a curiously exilerating [sic] feeling," wrote novelist Sherwood Anderson. Rex Tugwell called it a "renaissance spring," "a time of rebirth after a dark age." An "anything can be done" spirit—diametrically opposed to that of the later Hoover administration—took over. Many New Dealers wore their hair far longer than was the style, not through any desire to display nonconformity, but because they did not take the time to get haircuts; so much of more importance had to be done. Even festive occasions turned into serious discussions of social and economic problems and how best to solve them. "It's exciting and educational to be alive and asked out in Washington these days," one young man wrote several months after the start of the New Deal.

All of this represented a new development in American government. There had, of course, been intellectuals in the White House before. Franklin Roosevelt himself was far less of an intellectual than such predecessors as the Adamses, Jefferson, Theodore Roosevelt, and Wilson. But the concept that had begun to grow up during the Progressive era of a charismatic leader representing the desires of the people, setting a course of action, and surrounding himself with experts to carry out those actions was brought to fruition with the New Deal. Men with degrees from Columbia, Harvard, and Cornell, rather than from Tammany Hall or Hull House, were now to be in charge. Older leaders were not pleased with them. "They floated airily into offices, took desks, asked for papers and found no end of things to be busy about," complained old-timer George N. Peek, who headed the Agricultural Adjustment Administration. "I never found out why they came, what they did or why they left."

These eager young New Dealers were not, for the most part, those who drew up the Hundred Days legislation, but those who tried to implement it. The task of writing the new laws fell to Roosevelt's inner circle and, of course, congressional leaders. The former included Louis Howe and the Brains Trust of the campaign with several additions: Budget director Douglas; Secretaries Woodin and Wallace; Henry Morgenthau, Jr., who was governor of the Farm Credit Administration and later became Treasury secretary; Jesse Jones of the RFC and—from a distance—Professor Felix Frankfurter of the Harvard Law School. Although the stars of both soon faded, in the spring of 1933, Raymond Moley and Lewis Douglas were the President's most influential advisers.

As Roosevelt and his advisers pushed their ambitious reform program that spring, they had to consider the public mood and the attitude of Congress. Both had improved markedly since earlier in the year, but they were far from identical. Several historians have contended that Roosevelt had to operate in what Elliot Rosen calls a "conservative political climate." Roosevelt biographer Frank Freidel has said that FDR faced "a basically conservative electorate." This is simply wrong. Admittedly, the word "conservative" is amorphous, but the people as a whole were decidedly in the mood for change in 1933 and for several years thereafter. They may not have been precise about the direction they wanted that change to take, but it would be hard to make a case that it was not generally liberal.

Congress, with its southern committee chairmen, might more readily be labeled conservative. At heart, it undoubtedly was more conservative than the electorate in 1933. But it did not act that way. In some respects, as historian James Patterson has noted, the Seventy-third Congress "was considerably less orthodox than Roosevelt." There were many reasons for this. The two most obvious were the desperate situation of the nation's economy and Roosevelt's immense popularity. Slightly less apparent, but also important, was the large size of the freshman class in Congress. Most new members had been swept in by the reaction against Hoover, inaction, and conservatism. If they wanted to keep their seats, they were well advised to support dramatic steps to reverse the Depression. (In addition to the 1932 housecleaning, about a fourth of the members had first been elected in 1930. Thus more than half of the Seventy-third Congress had been elected in response to the Depression.) The new members also had many friends whom they needed to reward, if they were to build up political machines of their own. So did veteran Democrats, out of power for a dozen years. The voters wanted them to spend to provide jobs, and the New Deal programs created numerous new, non–Civil Service positions that could be dispensed to deserving Democrats. Conservatives in Congress may not have liked helping the poor, social programs, or deficits, but most of them had nothing against patronage.

This combination of factors, along with Roosevelt's political skills (for instance, his delay in making regular patronage appointments until after most of his legislative package had been approved), produced the most remarkable legislative accomplishment any American president has ever made in so brief a time. The House passed eleven key measures in the special session with a total of only forty hours of debate.[2]

The influence of Douglas combined with Roosevelt's own fiscal conservatism to shape a part of the early New Deal. But the President knew from the start that the applause of conservatives could not be his main objective. While they hailed his Old Deal, Roosevelt belatedly launched a new one. In keeping with his campaign contention that insufficient farm income was the root of the Depression, he turned to that problem. Quick action on agriculture was also necessary if a program was to be put into effect for 1933 crops. Spring had already arrived in the Deep South and was moving northward.

The agricultural crisis in early 1933 was almost as acute as that in banking. Farm income in 1932 was less than one-third of the already-depressed 1929 figure. The parity index showing the relative level of prices farmers received compared to prices for what they bought (1910–14 = 100) fell from a bad 89 in 1929 to a disastrous 55 in 1932. (It was even lower by the end of 1982.) "My candid opinion," Farmers' Union President John A. Simpson wrote to the President-elect in January 1933, "is that unless you call a special session of Congress . . . and start a revolution in government affairs there will be one started in the country. It is just a question of whether or not you get one started first."

Roosevelt's quick-but-conservative first actions bought him a little time in which to start that "revolution in government affairs," but only a little. During the campaign FDR had spoken carefully in order to keep the support of all major farm groups and of the advocates of the various schemes for solving the farm problem. This was good politics, but now Roosevelt had to choose. Or did he? Late in the campaign he had told a group of agricultural leaders that one of his first steps would be a move to raise farm prices. "I am going to call farmers' leaders together," one of them recalled the candidate saying, "lock them in a room, and tell them not to come out until they have agreed on a plan." This, in effect, is what he did in March.

Roosevelt required the leaders of all the major farm interest groups to accept the agricultural plan before it was brought to him. This meant that the President could take credit for success, but could shift the blame for failure to others. Such a plan might not make sense economically, but it was superb politics. Any farm bill, FDR told reporters, "is in the nature of an experiment. We all recognize that. My position toward farm legislation is that we ought to do something to increase the value of farm products and if the darn thing doesn't work, we can say so quite frankly, but at least try it." How much better, though, to have many approaches written into a bill that allowed the President and his agricultural advisers to choose which scheme might be best for given conditions in each crop at a particular time. This would further delay any choice among the various schemes.

Roosevelt had to make few compromises to get the agriculture bill he wanted. He satisfied conservatives by letting it be known beforehand that he would appoint George Peek, longtime champion of the McNary-Haugen dumping plan—the most favored farm panacea of the twenties—to head the farm program. This may have been politically wise in the short run, but it proved to be a terrible mistake. Peek was placed in charge of a program of which he basically disapproved.

As it emerged, the Agricultural Adjustment bill was an omnibus law that provided for bits and pieces of most of the various farm proposals then afloat. The basic concept, however, was clear: Farm prices would be raised by government-subsidized scarcity. The executive branch was permitted to choose the means it thought best to achieve this end. The principal method used was government-organized payments to farmers who agreed to take acreage out of production. The payments were to be funded by a tax on the processing of food products. The last point was perhaps the most controversial. It amounted to a regressive tax in a deflationary situation. "What will the great mass of consumers think of this form of sales tax, resting heavily on food?" *The New York Times* pointedly asked. But Roosevelt's popularity was so great that most people overlooked such problems.

It was not possible, though, to resist the demands of some groups. An Emergency Farm Mortgage Act was tied to the Agricultural Adjustment Act in order to provide relief for farmers in the form of mortgages at lower rates. Most important was the attempt by populist-descended politicians from the West and South to add inflation to the legislative package. It is often said that the advocates of inflation in the Senate forced Roosevelt to accept an amendment to the farm bill introduced by Senator Elmer Thomas of Oklahoma. This is inaccurate. The President wanted to have some means to bring about controlled inflation. He understood that it was necessary both to offset the deflationary effects of the Economy Act and the processing tax, and in order to increase farm income. Monetarism—a managed currency—was intended to be a part, but only a part, of the New Deal recovery program.

The need to move quickly to take the United States off the gold standard and begin a mild inflation was created by a new drain of American gold to foreign countries. While the United States remained on the gold standard with Great Britain off it, the dollar was considerably overvalued, particularly in relation to the pound. This put American products at a serious disadvantage in the world market. In addition, sentiment for inflation was growing rapidly in the Senate. Burton K. Wheeler of Montana pushed an amendment in mid-April that would have enacted the old Populist-Bryan demand of re-monetizing silver at a ratio of 16 to 1 to gold. Wheeler would probably have obtained a majority had it not been for Roosevelt's opposition.

What the President sought was the same sort of permissive legislation as the farm bill provided: a variety of means made available to him to raise prices, but none made mandatory. He also wanted it to appear that Congress was forcing him to accept inflation. Moley said in his diary that the administration wanted Wheeler's silver amendment to lose, but not by much. Roosevelt then agreed to a modified version of the Thomas Amendment (a version administration officials drafted), indicating that this was the only way to stop the Senate from passing mandatory legislation. This was at least misleading, but it served FDR's purposes well.

The so-called Thomas Amendment to the Agricultural Adjustment Act authorized the President, among other things, to remonetize silver, issue greenbacks, or lower the gold content of the dollar by up to 50 percent. Conservatives, whose overwrought fears of Roosevelt had been much calmed by the banking and economy measures, now fought off apoplexy. "We are on our way to Moscow," proclaimed one House member. Bernard Baruch saw it as "mob rule" perhaps "more drastic than the French Revolution." He complained that the only people whom inflation would help were "the unemployed, debtor classes—incompetent, unwise people." Budget Director Douglas went further. "Well, this is the end of Western civilization," he stated succinctly.

The defenders of Western civilization proved insufficiently numerous to stop the amendment. Roosevelt signed the Farm Relief Act, incorporating the Agricultural Adjustment Act (with the Thomas Amendment) and the Emergency Farm Mortgage Act, into law on May 12, 1933.

The delay in the enactment of the farm bill meant that the growing season was well under way before the Agricultural Adjustment Administration (AAA) could swing into action. The unpleasant task of ordering the destruction of crops fell to Secretary Wallace. He understood the need for eliminating "surplus" production in order to raise prices, but he never reconciled himself to it. Many other Americans never even understood the program's rationale. Particularly appalling to many was the slaughter of some 6 million piglets and 200,000 sows, and the plowing under of 10 million acres of cotton. What sense did it make to destroy food in a nation where millions were hungry and a world where hundreds of millions were starving? Very little perhaps, but no less than it did to have such poverty and want in the midst of abundance and unused capacity in the first place. The AAA concept of limiting production was no more incongruous than the economic system itself, which found no way to bring together idle workers and idle factories or hungry people and unsold crops.

The AAA proved to be less than an unqualified success. It remained voluntary. Farmers were induced, not coerced, to reduce acreage. In many cases large landowners took government payments for not planting their poorest land, but cultivated their better acres more intensively, producing as much or more on fewer acres. The idea of crop reduction was so powerful, though, that Nature itself soon provided assistance in reducing farm output. The AAA and the Dust Bowl combined to increase farm prices by 50 percent during Roosevelt's first term. Although raising prices had been the main objective, this limited success was hardly enough. Farm income did not again reach its poor 1929 level until the end of the Depression in 1941.

The drought may have helped raise farm prices, but that was small consolation to the roughly one million "Okies" who were driven off their land by the dry weather and farm mechanization. It was a process beyond understanding. When representatives of the landowners told tenants they must leave their farms, the latter often wanted to fight to defend their homes. But as John Steinbeck described it in *The Grapes of Wrath*, they could find no one to blame: "But where does it stop? Who can we shoot? I don't aim to starve to death before I kill the man that's starving me." But who was responsible? Steinbeck's character Muley Graves found the answer: "It ain't nobody. It's a company." So the Okies gathered their few possessions and headed for California. Most of them found the Golden State less hospitable than did another Depression-era migrant who prospered in Hollywood and was elected president forty-five years later.

Nearly as bad off as the Okies were those who remained behind in the South. Sharecroppers and tenant farmers in the region had long been the subjects of miserable exploitation. Fully one-fourth of the entire population of the South fell into these two categories. The AAA not only did little to help them, it actually worsened the plight of many. Under AAA rules, tenants and sharecroppers were supposed to get a fair share of the payments. These regulations were often ignored, and plantation owners evicted "their" tenants in order to collect AAA payments for taking the land out of production. The problems tenants had to face are evident in a letter one wrote in 1934: "I live on Brown place he Says I haft to move For he going to tear this Old house there no place I can find to move to . . . Shear crop for him he got half of Every thing he rais the paople that get orders Just haft to trade at Sertin Stores. . . ."

An attempt to improve the situation of tenants and sharecroppers was made in 1934 with the formation of the Southern Tenant Farmers' Union (STFU). This organization, largely confined to the Arkansas delta region, was backed by Norman Thomas and the Socialist party, but it was based entirely on local leadership. It sought, among other things, to force the AAA to obtain better treatment for nonlandowning farmers. An important group of AAA officials supported the sharecroppers and tenants, but these sympathetic bureaucrats were "purged" from the agency in 1935.

The AAA in its first years was a very modest success. Prices were raised, although certainly not enough. Roosevelt's hope that this could be the main route to recovery was never realized. Early in 1936 the Supreme Court in *United States* v. *Butler* declared the processing tax unconstitutional. A new drop in agricultural prices ensued and the administration was faced with the problem of finding other approaches to the perplexing farm problem.[3]

Easing the suffering of the at least 30 million Americans whose families were without regular incomes was, aside from the banking crisis, the most pressing need facing Franklin Roosevelt when he took office. The number of applicants for assistance had continued to grow, not only as a result of more layoffs, but also because both the personal resources and the pride of people long unemployed were reaching total exhaustion.

In 1932 private charity rose to its highest level in history and public spending for welfare was more than twice what it had been in the twenties. But these increases were not nearly enough to meet the unprecedented need. Almost all governmental expenditures were made at the local level, and in 1932 they equaled only $1.67 per resident nationwide. Federal relief was the only possible answer.

Prodded by Harry Hopkins, who was in charge of state relief efforts in New York, Roosevelt asked Congress late in March 1933 to create the position of Federal Relief Administrator. Senators Wagner, Costigan, and La Follette, who had been urging federal relief for years, submitted a bill to create a Federal Emergency Relief Administration (FERA), to make grants to the states. The initial appropriation for this purpose was $500 million. It should be noted that while this represented an important step beyond the Reconstruction Finance Corporation loans to the states, it was not a federalizing of relief. States would still administer the grants. Even so, conservatives roundly denounced the bill as "socialism." "God save the people of the United States," exclaimed a Maine representative. But in the view of most members of Congress the country had relied upon salvation from that source long enough; the bill passed quickly.

Harry Hopkins, then forty-two years old, Roosevelt's choice to run the FERA, remained the central figure in relief programs for the rest of the Depression, and during Roosevelt's second and third terms enjoyed power second only to that of the President himself. This man who came to be known as the "assistant president" was a person of remarkable contrasts. Reared in Iowa, Hopkins nevertheless had the appearance of the street-wise urban resident. His pale complexion did not seem to indicate one who had come from rural sunshine. After graduating from Grinnell College, Hopkins had taken a summer job at a New York settlement house. His experiences there launched him on a career in social work. But, like the New Deal itself, Hopkins was a do-gooder of a different sort. He was given to playing the ponies and was without formal religious affiliation. He may not have fit an earlier stereotype of a "moralist," that is, a "puritan," but he was driven by a genuine moral passion for helping others.

Hopkins had, Raymond Moley said, a "capacity for quick and, it should be added, expensive activity." This was apparent when he arrived in Washington. By the time he had been in his job for two hours, Hopkins had spent $5 million. When someone told him that a particular plan would "work out in the long run," Hopkins retorted: "People don't eat in the long run—they eat every day." As he saw it then and later, his job was to spend money quickly and disperse it among the neediest. This would "prime the pump" and start the economy working again. This approach was not universally favored by New Dealers. Interior Secretary Ickes had nothing against pump-priming, but he thought Hopkins favored "just turning on the fire-plug."

Ickes's beliefs were of much importance. While Hopkins's FERA made grants to the states for relief, Ickes was placed in charge of the Public Works Administration. This agency, created under Title II of the National Industrial Recovery Act, was given the task of expanding federally sponsored public works projects in order to provide employment and stimulate the economy. Originally intended, as its positioning in the recovery bill indicated, to go hand in hand with industrial planning, the PWA under Ickes quickly went its own way. In 1933 and 1934 the PWA, with its $3.3 billion appropriation, was a primary weapon against the Depression.

Harold Ickes had joined the Roosevelt Cabinet almost by chance. Although he actively sought the position, it had seemed very unlikely that Roosevelt would choose him. Nearly a generation older than Hopkins, Ickes was a veteran progressive who was picked to head the Interior Department when more prominent Republican progressives declined the job. It was a fortunate choice. A self-described curmudgeon, Ickes trusted no one and was very tight-fisted with the public's money. He saw the PWA as a means of bringing about recovery, but also as a way to provide valuable public projects for the American people. Unlike Hopkins, he would not spend for the sake of spending— or just for the sake of putting money in the pockets of the needy. This meant that much of the PWA appropriation went for materials, architects, engineers, and skilled workers. Private contractors often did the work. All this was to the long-term good. "We set for ourselves at the outset," Ickes said, "the perhaps unattainable ideal of administering the greatest fund for construction in the history of the world without scandal." For all practical purposes, the PWA attained that ideal. The agency registered an incredible record of efficient use of funds and left a great legacy of public structures, including the bridges on the hundred-mile causeway leading from the mainland to Key West, Florida; the Grand Coulee, Boulder, and Bonneville dams; the Triborough Bridge in New York City; and some 70 percent of all new educational buildings constructed in the United States between 1933 and 1939. It built municipal buildings, sewage systems, port facilities, and hospitals. Spending $1 billion, the PWA greatly improved the nation and helped many people get through hard times. In addition, the clear purpose of PWA projects and the careful expenditures kept the agency above much of the criticism leveled at other New Deal programs.

But the question remains of whether Ickes's efficiency was not counterproductive in the context of the employment crisis of the thirties. It is not pleasant to think of inefficiency as being positive and efficiency as negative, but this argument has been made with respect to the public works spending of the New Deal. It is not without merit, but it goes too far. An effective works program could conceivably accomplish both immediate economic and long-term construction purposes. This would have necessitated some spending on materials and planning, but would have concentrated the bulk of available funds in wages for the previously unemployed.

Most of the down-and-out were untouched by the PWA. Their main contact with federal efforts early in the New Deal was through direct relief. Scarcely anyone, including Roosevelt and Hopkins, liked the dole. Hopkins rightly held that direct relief took from people "their sense of independence and their sense of individual destiny." A group of relief clients in Michigan wrote to President Roosevelt in 1936, asking for work rather than a dole. "We are thankful for what we receive though." The last point was decisive in 1933. As much as most people might dislike direct relief, there was no immediate alternative if mass misery and even starvation were to be averted.

But Hopkins and the President, like the bulk of those on relief, preferred work relief to the dole. Giving a person something to do in exchange for his check "preserves a man's morale," Hopkins contended. "It saves his skill. It gives him a chance to do something socially useful." With such arguments, Hopkins convinced Roosevelt to launch a temporary work relief program in the winter of 1933–34. The idea was to tide the unemployed over the winter with small, quick projects until the PWA got into full gear.

The resulting Civil Works Administration was a phenomenal chapter in New Deal history. Within a month of its start, CWA had hired 2.6 million people, and at its peak in January 1934 it employed more than 4 million workers. Wages averaged over $15 a week—hardly sufficient, but 2.5 times the typical FERA payment. When the CWA began, Hopkins's field investigator Lorena Hickok found that it lifted people's spirits tremendously. "When I got that [CWA identification] card it was the biggest day in my whole life," a middle-aged former insurance man in Alabama told Hickok. "At last I could say, 'I've got a job.'"

But any program that spent so much so quickly on so many people in so many projects (about 400,000) was bound to involve waste. By February, many conservatives were denouncing the CWA for being rife with "petty graft" and "politics." Worse, in the view of some, it was said that many people on work relief projects were "beginning to regard CWA as their due—that the Government actually owes it to them. And they want more." Such reports alarmed the President. He feared that if the program continued it would "become a habit with the country." As spring arrived, Roosevelt ordered Hopkins to phase out the CWA rapidly. "Nobody is going to starve during the warm weather," Roosevelt declared with more confidence than comprehension.

The reaction from those who had been CWA workers was not so bland. In Minneapolis, riots broke out when CWA ceased operations. Less violent but equally distressed responses—strikes and demonstrations—occurred elsewhere. But the protests did no immediate good. It was back to FERA direct relief for the remainder of 1934.[4]

During the hectic first hundred days of his administration, Roosevelt's areas of concentration were generally dictated by necessity, not choice. There were, however, two areas that had long interested the President on which he moved quickly after his inauguration. These were conservation and public power development.

Like Cousin Ted, Franklin D. Roosevelt had a sincere interest in conservation. The patrician reformer came by his dedication to nature honestly. It was an area that one would expect to be of concern to a Hudson estate owner. At Hyde Park, FDR had overseen the planting of tens of thousands of trees. "The forests," Roosevelt declared in 1935, "are the 'lungs' of our land, purifying our air and giving fresh strength to our people." As governor of New York he had put up to 10,000 unemployed men to work on a reforestation program. As president, Roosevelt protected more national forestland than all his predecessors and greatly expanded the country's national parks, adding new ones from Shenandoah in Virginia to the Olympic National Park in Washington State.

No sooner had the banking crisis been weathered than Roosevelt moved to set up a national conservation program along the lines of his New York experiment. The result was the Civilian Conservation Corps, an agency that took young unmarried men from the relief rolls and put them to work in the woods. The idea seemed to Moley to be an attempt to find William James's "moral equivalent of war," but to the less philosophical Roosevelt it was simply part of his recurring dream of de-urbanizing America and returning to the old virtues. The President decided to act rapidly ("But look here! I think I'll go ahead with this—the way I did on beer") so that his favorite idea could slide through Congress while the honeymoon was still passionate.

Despite some criticism, especially from organized labor, of the $1 per day wage and of the question of military regimentation, the CCC bill sailed through Congress. Some disturbing undertones of militarism did exist in the CCC camps (particularly when the assistant secretary of war suggested that the

Army would gladly take over the CCC and make the boys "economic storm troops"), but in terms of "regimentation" the camps were probably little worse than the practice sessions of high school football teams. The accomplishments of the CCC were vast in protecting and restoring forests, beaches, rivers, and parks; providing flood control and disaster relief; and helping some 2.5 million young men survive the Depression with some degree of self-respect. The CCC, after some criticism at its inception, was the most widely praised of the New Deal programs. Roosevelt took justified personal pride in it.

Another of the new President's pet projects was public power, particularly the long-standing goal of federal operation of the Wilson Dam on the Tennessee River at Muscle Shoals, Alabama. Progressives, led by Senator George Norris of Nebraska, had tried since the end of World War I to achieve this goal, but had been thwarted by private power interests and Republican administrations. Roosevelt had committed himself to the idea, and after he won the election he astounded (and delighted) Senator Norris by proposing a program for the entire Tennessee Valley, a proposal that met Norris's fondest hopes but far exceeded what he had dared to think possible.

Roosevelt had long believed in planned land use. He saw the severely depressed, eroded, and nearly hopeless Tennessee basin as "an opportunity of setting an example of planning, planning not just for ourselves but planning for the generations to come, tying in industry and agriculture and forestry and flood prevention." This comprehensive development program fit perfectly into Roosevelt's utopian scheme for moving workers and work into the countryside. The result, the Tennessee Valley Authority, created in May 1933, was one of the great accomplishments of the New Deal.

The TVA produced power at its numerous hydroelectric facilities, but it did much more. The government-produced electricity made available a "yardstick" whereby private power rates could be judged. It also provided power for farms that had previously been without it and made possible the development of industry in the region. The dams were used in flood control, and comprehensive land-use programs were developed to reclaim the soil of the valley. Other programs provided for the education and "betterment" of the region's inhabitants. Remarkably, this was accomplished largely through "grass roots democracy," with many decisions being made by local residents.

TVA was a model of the best that could be accomplished under the planning philosophy espoused by many New Dealers. Its success, however, was largely due to its breaking away from the centralism favored by planners. Critics called the TVA "socialism," a term not likely to endear the program to the people of the valley. Yet the TVA was very popular in the areas it served. Roosevelt had foreseen why when Norris asked him how he would answer questions about the political philosophy behind the TVA. "I'll tell them it's neither fish nor fowl," FDR said, "but, whatever it is, it will taste awfully good to the people of the Tennessee Valley." It tasted so good, in fact, that private interests, particularly in the electric power field, lobbied successfully to prevent similar experiments elsewhere. (Roosevelt had spoken of such projects in "the watersheds of the Ohio, Missouri, and Arkansas Rivers and in the Columbia River in the Northwest.") The main reason the TVA was not replicated was not that it failed, but that it worked so well.[5]

Although the National Industrial Recovery Act came to be the centerpiece of the First New Deal legislation, and Franklin Roosevelt called it "the most important and far reaching legislation ever enacted by the American Congress," the President had not even planned to introduce an industrial recovery bill in the special session. He believed that reform of the relationship between business and government was desirable, but that it should not be rushed into and was not necessary to bring about general recovery. Still contending that agricultural income was the key to recovery, FDR thought the AAA, along with limited inflation and modest federal spending for relief and construction, would turn the economy around.

He was wrong. A month into the New Deal the economy began to slip again and it became clear that Congress would take action on recovery legislation even if the President did not submit a bill. Responding to what political journalist Ernest K. Lindley called "revolution boiling up from the bottom," the Senate passed a bill in early April introduced by Senator Hugo Black of Alabama. The Black bill, which had the support of the American Federation of Labor, would ban from interstate commerce any goods made by workers who labored more than a six-hour day or a five-day week. Sentiment was such that the thirty-hour bill appeared likely to be passed in the House as well. That would have put Roosevelt in an awkward position. He would not want to veto recovery legislation, particularly since it was backed by many Democrats. But Roosevelt did not like the bill because, unlike the measures the administration submitted, it was rigid. It did not simply grant powers to the President and leave their exercise to his discretion. And it said nothing about minimum wages, which seemed essential if the reduced hours were to increase purchasing power and stimulate recovery. Moley later recalled that Roosevelt believed, "what was needed was not to thin out the jobs then available, but a measure to create new employment and to stimulate industrial confidence."

In order to head off the Black legislation, the President gave the go-ahead for a recovery bill that would be acceptable to business, labor, and the administration. Moley asked General Hugh Johnson, a disciple of Bernard Baruch, former associate of George N. Peek, and a veteran of the War Industries Board, to draw up a draft. Another draft came from Senator Wagner and others. In typical fashion the President listened to the advocates of both sides and then told them to "shut themselves in a room, iron out their differences, and bring him a bill on which they could agree."

Conceived under circumstances in which its paternity could not be proved, the National Industrial Recovery Act (NIRA) was clearly of mixed parentage. Among the most important men involved in siring the bill, in addition to General Johnson and Senator Wagner, were Rexford Tugwell, Raymond Moley, Lewis Douglas, Undersecretary of Commerce John Dickinson, former New York Congressman Meyer Jacobstein, and labor attorney Donald Richberg. A group with such a mixture of beliefs inevitably produced an ambiguous, catchall piece of legislation. This was to be expected for other reasons as well.

The American people—and their President—were of two minds on the question of the proper basic organization of the economy. Newspaperwoman Dorothy Thompson, who was unfriendly toward the New Deal, summarized this problem well. "Two souls dwell within the bosom of the American people," she wrote in 1938. "The one loves the Abundant Life, as expressed in the cheap and plentiful products of large-scale mass production and distribution. . . . The other soul," Thompson rightly said, "yearns for former simplicities, for decentralization, for the interests of the 'little man,' revolts against high-pressure salesmanship, denounces 'monopoly' and 'economic empires,' and seeks means of breaking them up." These conflicting ideals represent what is perhaps the basic American paradox. Both are present not only in the society as a whole, but in most of the individuals who compose it. Americans love the benefits of bigness, but cherish the simpler, more personal economy of an earlier time. Our ideal is individualism, but we covet the efficiency and comfort provided by large organization. From time to time the conflict comes into the open, as it seemed to in the 1912 campaign between Woodrow Wilson's New Freedom, which emphasized a simple, competitive economy, and Theodore Roosevelt's New Nationalism, which advocated government-regulated bigness. More often, the two ideals coexist in a largely unrecognized and most uneasy alliance. The ideas of regulated concentration and a free competitive order may be logically inconsistent, but as historian Ellis Hawley has convincingly argued, "the two streams were so intermixed in the ideology of the average man that any administration, if it wished to retain political power, had to make concessions to both."

If there was one goal that Franklin Roosevelt's administration had, it was to remain in power. The recovery bill that came out of the "locked" room was, like most of the New Deal, based on politics, not economics. Politically, the bill had not only to satisfy both the impulse for regulation and that against monopoly, but also to win the support of those who would participate in the recovery plan. This included labor, but principally it meant businessmen. Like other Americans, most businessmen were somewhat ambivalent concerning questions of competition and regulation. They, too, paid lip service to the competitive economy, but many were convinced that its time had passed. During the Progressive era substantial numbers of forward-looking businessmen had come to realize that regulation might have a similar effect on them to that of briar patch on Br'er Rabbit. They began to see great possibilities in "business self-government." The key to the effects of regulation, after all, was in who did the regulating. More businessmen favored "self-government" after their experience with a regulated economy during the World War. The associational movement—the formation of cooperating organizations among corporations involved in the same industry—which was pushed by Herbert Hoover's Commerce Department in the twenties, represented a continuation of the idea of businesses regulating themselves. If Roosevelt's industrial recovery program could be seen as providing for this, it would enjoy substantial business support.

In the National Industrial Recovery Act, as in the AAA and the Thomas Amendment, Congress made few choices. Instead, it passed an "enabling" law, transferring great powers to the executive branch. The act created the National Recovery Administration (NRA), over which Roosevelt placed Hugh Johnson. The precise purpose of the organization remained in the eye of the beholder at the time of its creation in June 1933. It might seek genuine government planning in industry; it might try to restore and enforce competition, or it might allow business to set prices and divvy up markets without fear of prosecution under the Sherman Act. Any of these courses was possible; everything would depend upon how the NRA was administered. Laissez faire was over, and the state would play a far more prominent role, but what that part would be remained unclear.

As director, Hugh Johnson was in charge of casting. In keeping with Johnson's style, the opening scenes of the NRA resembled the choreography of Busby Berkeley. With Johnson one might have expected that the climax would have rivaled Cecil B. De Mille, but fortunately for the general, he was no longer with the project when the credits rolled.

The idea behind the NRA, quite simply, was to introduce rational planning into what had been a chaotic economic system. By providing balance to the economy, the NRA, it was hoped, would restore employment and prosperity. It amounted to an admission that the "unfettered marketplace" was no longer a viable means of governing the national economy. Under the NRA, each industry in the country would draw up a code of practices that would be acceptable. These would cover wages, working conditions, and as it turned out, prices and production. The promise of economic planning was sufficiently large that such left-liberal journals as The New Republic and The Nation warmly endorsed the NRA. The Nation went so far as to call it a promising step toward a "collectivized society." The NIRA had provided the new agency with licensing powers to coerce businesses into going along with the codes that were established. The basic idea was that envisioned by Theodore Roosevelt in 1912. In his second fireside chat, Franklin Roosevelt called the NRA "a partnership in planning" between business and government. The law gave business its demand for "constructive relief from the antitrust laws." (It is noteworthy that businesses always seem to be seeking "relief" from something. More recently, they have obtained "tax relief" and "regulatory relief." One may be forgiven for wondering how businessmen spell relief.) The NIRA also allowed "cooperative action among trade groups."

Most goals of the NRA were to be accomplished through the development of codes for each industry. Fearing constitutional problems and desiring business as well as public support, however, General Johnson made no attempt to use his authority to dictate codes to businessmen. Instead, he negotiated with them. The predictable result was that the largest companies in each industry drew up their own codes. In doing so, leaders of some 400 industries established provisions prohibiting sales "below cost." In practice, "cost" usually meant "reasonable price." Hence the agreements often amounted to government-sanctioned price fixing. Johnson himself pointed out how much better the NRA codes were for businesses than had been trade associations: "Now I am talking to a cluster of formerly emasculated trade associations about a law which proposes for the first time to give them potency."

In return for such a generous gift, businessmen were to allow labor-oriented reforms against which they had fought for decades. The minimum wages, maximum hours, improved working conditions, and elimination of child labor called for in NRA codes represented a definite advance for working Americans. (The blanket code that Johnson suggested for all industries until they worked out their specific codes called for a forty-hour maximum work-week and a 30 cents per hour minimum wage.) Companies often found ways to avoid collective bargaining, which was putatively provided for in section 7(a) of the Recovery Act. But even in this area the stage was set for subsequent, effective legislation in 1935. Therefore some of the long-term advantages of the NRA were substantial.

It did little, however, to bring about recovery. One of the great ironies of the New Deal is that its principal program for achieving economic recovery amounted to little more than a larger effort in what Hoover had been trying all along: pepping people up, restoring confidence. Johnson drew upon his experience with the War Industries Board and started a massive campaign to enlist Americans in a new campaign against a different sort of "Hun." He came up with the idea of having merchants and manufacturers who adhered to NRA standards display a symbol of their compliance, so that consumers would know with which businesses they should deal. The symbol Johnson hit upon was a blue eagle with the slogan "We Do Our Part." (Some industrialists were not anxious to display the bird. Henry Ford was reported to have said: "Hell, that Roosevelt buzzard! I wouldn't put it on the car.")

In the summer of 1933, Johnson treated the nation to a spectacle like nothing it had seen since the war—or at least since Charles Lindbergh's return from France. It was wartime patriotism all over again. The largest parade in the history of New York City saw 250,000 people march down Fifth Avenue for the Blue Eagle. Pledges like the war bond drives were called for and songs were composed:

Join the good old N.R.A., Boys, and we will end this awful strife.
Join it with the spirit that will give the Eagle life.
Join it, folks, then push and pull, many millions strong,
While we go marching to Prosperity.

How the Nation shouted when they heard the joyful news!
We're going back to work again, and that means bread and shoes.
Folks begin to smile again. They are happy and at ease,
While we go marching to Prosperity.

For a brief time in the summer of 1933 it was believable that the country *was* marching back to prosperity. During the months between Roosevelt's inauguration and the effective dates of the NRA codes in the fall, production and employment increased significantly. The index of factory production, which had hit a low of 56 in March, rose to 101 in July 1933. The gains were at least partially attributable to causes unrelated to the NRA: increased federal spending, Roosevelt's restoration of confidence, and perhaps, a "bottoming out" of the Depression. The promise of the NRA did have something to do with the boomlet of the summer of 1933, though. Unfortunately, in many ways that connection proved to be a negative development a few months later. Many manufacturers, believing that both prices and demand would rise with the NRA, sought to build up their inventories with goods produced by cheap labor before codes requiring higher wages went into effect. Many of those hired in the spring of 1933 were unemployed again by the fall.

The reverse side of high hopes is disillusionment. So it was when the Blue Eagle failed to soar to the expected altitude. Whatever economic gains might have resulted from increased wages were undercut by higher prices. Many believed the price increases that resulted from the suspension of competition actually outdistanced wage increases. Complaints of "NRA prices and Hoover wages" were common by early 1934. Huey Long and some labor leaders began saying the agency's initials stood for "National Run Around." William Randolph Hearst's version was "No Recovery Allowed."

Hopes that the NRA would prove to be labor's long-sought "Magna Carta" were also forlorn. Some labor leaders were able to make use of section 7(a) to rebuild unions decimated by twenties prosperity and thirties depression. John L. Lewis of the United Mine Workers launched a highly successful 1933 organizing campaign, basing his appeal on 7(a) and Roosevelt's popularity. "The President wants you to unionize," proclaimed organizers who remained cunningly vague as to whether the president referred to was FDR of the USA or JLL of the UMW. But few other unions were as successful, and anti-union employers soon found ways around 7(a). Most popular was the formation of company-dominated "unions," which were in no sense representative collective bargaining agents. When early in 1934, NRA officials approved company-created unions in the auto industry, workers realized they would have to win their own battles.

By almost any reckoning, the NRA was a colossal failure. Dominated from the start by large-business interests, it served them at the expense of the rest of society. Their first concern was to assure their own incomes so they sought to use the codes to guarantee their margins of profit on the basis of restricted production and higher prices. This was scarcity economics and it meant reduced purchasing power. Businessmen could survive in this way under continuing depression conditions, but it would simply perpetuate the hard times, not bring recovery or help anyone else. Given its domination by business interests, the NRA offered little hope of bringing about recovery. As long as businesses were permitted to raise prices to coincide with (or exceed) mandated wage increases, there would be no redistribution of income and no stimulation of purchasing power.

All this is generally accepted. A further question must be addressed. Increasing complaints about the dictatorial actions of the hard-drinking, foul-mouthed Johnson led Roosevelt to ease him out of the NRA in 1934. By this time, his two-day absences for drying out were becoming common. Johnson was already well on the way toward the attitude he would hold in 1938, when he denounced the "one-man Roosevelt Party, conceived with superficial cleverness, but stuck together with spit and tied into a unit with haywire. . . . [T]he Solid South tied in with Northern Pro-Negro policy." When he resigned Johnson praised the "shining name" of Benito Mussolini. Johnson had spoken in 1932 of the need for a temporary dictator and "singleness of control." Others, ranging from Herbert Hoover to Huey Long and Charles Coughlin, charged that the NRA was akin to fascism. It was a plan, Long said, "to regiment business and labor much more than anyone did in Germany and Italy." Such statements were, of course, ridiculously extreme. But the charge remains. The Recovery program centralized power, but left that power largely in private hands. Less than 10 percent of the code authorities included labor representatives, and less than 2 percent had consumer representatives. The NRA contained within it some potential for fascism. Such surely was not the intention of either Roosevelt or his advisers, despite Ronald

Reagan's typically unsubstantiated charge in the 1980 presidential campaign that "the members of the Brain Trust . . . admired the fascist system." Such nonsense aside, there may have been some seeds of fascism in the NRA. The important point is that those seeds never germinated in American soil. In fact, when the business domination of the NRA became apparent, the program's popularity faded.

The original legislation had provided a two-year life span for the NRA. Without the federal agency to back them, the codes would soon wither away. Despite the NRA's obvious failure, Roosevelt had not given up on the idea. Politically he was in no position to do so. It would be admitting failure. So in February 1935 he called for a two-year extension of the NRA. "The fundamental purposes and principles of the Act are sound," the President told Congress. "To abandon them is unthinkable. It would spell the return of industrial and labor chaos." Whether Congress would have agreed on a bill extending the program will never be known. Before the House could vote the Supreme Court made that action unnecessary. On May 27, 1935, in the case of *Schecter Poultry Corp.* v. *United States*, the Court unanimously found the NRA to be, among other things, "an unconstitutional delegation of legislative power." It is difficult to avoid the suspicion that Roosevelt was inwardly relieved when the Court executed the Blue Eagle. Certainly many other New Dealers were. "You know the whole thing is a mess," the President privately told Frances Perkins. "It has been an awful headache. . . . I think perhaps NRA has done all it can do."[6]

The rapid-fire legislation of the First Hundred Days of the New Deal demonstrated Roosevelt's attempt to please everyone: NRA for business and organized labor, AAA for large farm interests, the relief programs for the unemployed, and CCC and TVA for FDR. One politically potent group remained: the middle class. One of the biggest problems confronting this segment of society was the alarming increase in home foreclosures, which had reached a rate of over a thousand a day by Roosevelt's inauguration. The administration moved in June 1933, at the end of the special session of Congress, to protect both hard-pressed homeowners and those who held their mortgages. The Home Owners' Loan Corporation provided refinancing, at low interest rates, of mortgages of middle-income homeowners. The HOLC eventually became involved in 20 percent of all urban dwelling mortgages in the nation. Critics justly charged that the program helped lenders more than homeowners, since it assured repayment of loans, but in many cases did not provide enough help to enable people to keep their homes in the long run. Still, everyone involved was happy: homeowners, banks, real-estate interests, and the President, who in a single stroke assured for himself the support of a large portion of the middle class.

The special session of Congress also aided the middle and upper-middle strata of American society in other ways. The Truth-in-Securities Act of May 1933 required a modicum of honesty from corporations issuing stock. Those floating stock were made responsible for accurately representing information about the company's condition. Investors who could prove deception on the part of a company selling stock were allowed to collect civil damages. Newspapers summed up the thrust of the act: "Let the seller beware." In June, over the bitter opposition of the banking community, Congress passed the Glass-Steagall Act. It required the divorce of commercial from investment banking and, probably more importantly, set up the Federal Deposit Insurance Corporation to guarantee bank deposits. The latter provision soon worked greatly to the advantage of banks, which once again appeared safe repositories for the family nest egg. The FDIC was to be one of the New Deal's most important legacies. Without it a large-scale banking collapse would very likely have occurred in the early 1980s. Of course neither act was of much value to those without funds to deposit or invest.

During the next year-and-a-half, New Dealers turned their attention mainly to administering the programs launched in the Hundred Days. There were, however, a few new departures. The failure of NRA and AAA to produce the intended results, particularly the continuing lag in farm prices, led to renewed protest in the Midwest. The only way to satisfy the spiritual descendants of William Jennings Bryan appeared to be through the old panacea of inflation. Roosevelt had pacified the inflationists by accepting the Thomas Amendment to the AAA bill. This had given him the power to bring about inflation, but he was not obligated to use that power.

In June 1933 an international conference was held in London to deal with Depression-related questions of international trade and finance. Hoover, who believed that the Depression was caused abroad, saw the conference as a great hope for saving the American economy. Roosevelt suffered from no such illusion. He refused to go along with an attempt to stabilize currencies, fearing that this would undermine New Deal attempts to raise domestic prices. The American President virtually broke up the London Economic Conference with a tart message to other world leaders. "The sound internal economic system of a nation is a greater factor in its well being than the price of its currency in changing terms of the currencies of other nations," Roosevelt declared. The United States, in short, would try to solve its own problems, not join in an international scheme to regulate the relative values of currencies. Thus the President retained control over the value of the dollar. It was a power he soon felt constrained to use.

Orthodox economists feared inflation as much as they feared deficit spending. So did New York bankers. But, as some presidents eventually realize, Wall Street is not the nation. Even businessmen in other parts of the country often favored soft money. They were borrowers, whereas the New Yorkers were lenders. It made all the difference.

Roosevelt finally grew tired of listening to his orthodox advisers. Things were getting no better and the old guard economists could offer no suggestions. If there was one thing Roosevelt was steadfastly against, it was inaction. When a new revolt was threatened by the Farm Holiday Association, Roosevelt decided some action was necessary. He later insisted that "if we had continued a week or so longer without my having made this move on gold, we would have had an agricultural revolution in this country." In October 1933 he seized on a plan to buy gold at a high, but changing price, in effect devaluing the dollar by increasing the number of dollars it took to buy an ounce of gold. When James Warburg told Roosevelt that there must be a definite gold price, the President responded: "Poppycock! The bankers want to know everything beforehand and I've told them to go to hell." For the next four months, Henry Morgenthau and Jesse Jones met with Roosevelt each morning in his bedroom to decide on the day's price of gold. The process was less than scientific. One morning Roosevelt decided on a 21-cent increase because, he said with a laugh, "it's a lucky number."

The scheme proved to be no panacea. The price decline halted temporarily, then resumed slowly. In January 1934 the President called a halt, Congress passed the Gold Reserve Act, and Roosevelt established the price of the metal at $35 an ounce, where it remained until 1971.

With no increase in farm prices yet in sight, the pressure from the West for the old Bryan demand for the remonetization of silver became irresistible. In June 1934 the President reluctantly agreed to a Silver Purchase Act, by which the government agreed to buy unlimited quantities of silver at artificially high prices until federal silver holdings equaled one-third the value of the government's gold stock. This legislation made silver mine owners wealthy and provided jobs for a few thousand miners, but was of no discernible benefit to anyone else.

The Hundred Days had ended without the passage of any direct regulation of the stock exchange. When Congress convened in January 1934, such legislation was at the top of the remaining New Deal program. Proposals to curb the Las Vegas syndrome on Wall Street, to end manipulation of the market by insiders, to require stock purchasers to have a reasonable percentage of the money they used to buy securities, and to force brokers and corporations to tell the truth about stocks were greeted with an unprecedented outcry from lower Manhattan. Honesty, Wall Street seemed to be saying, would destroy the stock market. Some, such as Congressman Fred Britten (R, Illinois), charged that "Brain Trusters" were plotting to "Russianize" America.

Yet few Americans were prepared to believe wild accusations coming from the lips of those who had so recently plunged the nation into depression and had even more recently, in the Pecora investigation, been reluctantly admitting their past sins. It was difficult to take seriously arguments made by a group whose leader, New York Stock Exchange President Richard Whitney, could say with a straight face four years after the Crash (and less than five years before he entered Sing Sing after being convicted of larceny), "The Exchange is a perfect institution."

Roosevelt signed the Securities Exchange Act, which had been drafted by James M. Landis, Benjamin V. Cohen, Thomas G. Corcoran, Telford Taylor, and I. N. P. Stokes, into law in June 1934. Business complaints had severely weakened the bill, removing many mandatory provisions and placing more decisions in the hands of the Securities and Exchange Commission, which the act created. This meant that much depended on who was appointed to the commission.

President Roosevelt still hoped to keep the support of business. Therefore his choice as chairman of the SEC was someone businessmen would trust, Joseph P. Kennedy. Less than twelve months before, Kennedy had been party to just the sort of stock manipulation that the SEC was supposed to stop. Most New Dealers were outraged at the choice of Kennedy, but Roosevelt adeptly silenced the in-house criticism by appointing four liberals—Ferdinand Pecora, James Landis, and progressive Republicans Robert Healy and George C. Mathews—to the remaining spots on the SEC.[7]

People who had known Franklin Roosevelt before were amazed at the Hundred Days. "Many of us who have known him long and well," wrote *Nation* editor Ernest Gruening in May 1933, "ask ourselves if this is the same man." "Was I just fooled before the election," wondered Republican editor William Allen White, "or has he developed? . . . I have never had to eat my words before." "He is no more like the man who was here in Wilson's time," wrote someone who had known FDR during the war, "than the capital is like the city it was then." Another who had worked with Roosevelt in the Wilson days insisted, "that fellow in there is not the fellow we used to know. There's been a miracle here." Herbert Feis described the public perception of that miracle: "The outside public seems to believe as if Angel Gabriel had come to earth."

All of this was due in large measure, of course, to Roosevelt's personality and political skill. But it was also to some extent a case of wish fulfillment on the part of the American people. They were desperately hoping for a miracle. Prior to the inauguration, William Randolph Hearst's Cosmopolitan Studios produced a strange and incredibly prescient film called *Gabriel Over the White House*. The movie, directed by Gregory La Cava, later noted for such films as *Stage Door* and *Unfinished Business*, was ready for release by MGM during the interregnum, but Louis Mayer delayed it until March 1, 1933, to avoid problems with Hoover. *Gabriel* portrays an old-style, uncaring president, Judson Hammond (Walter Huston), who worries "when I think of all the promises I had to make to the people to get elected." "Oh, don't worry," an aide reassures him, "by the time they realize you're not keeping them, your term will be over." Hammond gives Hooveresque responses to questions about what he will do to relieve the horrors of the Depression: "As we have gotten out of past depressions—the spirit of Valley Forge, the spirit of Gettysburg, the spirit of the Argonne. America will rise again." Basically he ignores the suffering.

Then Hammond drives his own car in an entirely reckless fashion and has a tire blowout at 100 mph. As a result, he suffers a serious head injury and lies near death. Divine intervention changes him and he emerges from his ordeal as a champion of the poor, inviting the leader of an unemployed army whom he has previously threatened to arrest to come to Washington. The unemployed will be fed at government expense, Hammond says. He proceeds to force Congress to grant him dictatorial powers, saying his dictatorship will be based on Jefferson's definition of democracy: "the greatest good for the greatest number." Hammond speaks directly to the people over the radio, creates an "Army of Construction," appropriates $4 billion, prevents foreclosures, provides direct aid to agriculture, passes a national banking law, repeals the Eighteenth Amendment, and restores law and order. "A plant cannot be made to grow by watering the top and letting the roots go dry," the divinely inspired president says. It was a veritable blueprint for the New Deal. The film was made after Roosevelt's campaign, but well before he took office.

But there was much more in *Gabriel Over the White House*. Hammond forms a national police force to eliminate crime; quick trials and summary executions before firing squads bring a rapid end to crime. International problems are as easily straightened out in this reflection of Hearst's simplistic thinking. Hammond tells the European nations to pay their debts to the United States, or else. He then repudiates the Washington Naval Treaty and says the United States will build a vast new navy. Foreign leaders are invited aboard the presidential yacht to witness a demonstration of American military might, after which they agree to sign a treaty to save the world from war. Pax Americana is established and the Depression ended, so Hammond dies and goes to heaven.

Gabriel Over the White House left no doubt that God was on the side of America—and of William Randolph Hearst. It provided an incredible mixture of the New Deal and fascism. The parallels to what was then beginning in Germany are striking. Although the film was not a big money-maker, it was briefly popular, finishing among the top six movies at the box office during April 1933. The significance of the film lies in what it indicates about the desperate yearning for leadership and the willingness in some quarters to abandon democratic principles in order to get "action, and action now." Clearly Hearst did not speak for the American people, but the ease with which *Gabriel* could blend New Deal–type programs with a "benevolent," militaristic dictatorship indicates how close the United States may have been in 1933 to far more drastic changes than those Roosevelt introduced. Congress demonstrated time and again that spring that it was willing to turn over to the executive powers that went far beyond any a peacetime American president had ever held before. Although Republican opponents condemned Franklin Roosevelt for seizing unconstitutional powers in that crisis, he in fact sought to keep those powers within strict limits. Had a popular new chief executive like FDR wanted to follow the course of the fictional Judson Hammond in 1933, there is little assurance that Congress and the people would not have followed him.[8]

The idea of divine intervention may not have been far from Roosevelt's view of how to explain the early New Deal. He seems to have believed that God had stricken him with polio and spared him for his mission in life. Whatever the merits of such an interpretation may be, the historian is obliged to seek more terrestrial interpretations of events.

One problem with the view that there were two philosophically distinct New Deals, one beginning in 1933 and the other in 1935, is that there was very little philosophy in the New Deal. Franklin Roosevelt, after all, was not an economist or a political philosopher; he was a practicing politician. The First New Deal, accordingly, was not based on philosophy or economic theory, but on political considerations. This is crystal clear in such measures as the Agricultural Adjustment Act and the National Industrial Recovery Act, which were designed to incorporate philosophically and economically conflicting ideas and keep different groups aligned with the New Deal. Economic or philosophic consistency was never the primary objective.

The good politician—and Roosevelt unquestionably was one of the best—always seeks to occupy the center ground. President Roosevelt engaged in a masterful balancing act in 1933 and 1934. Politicians need love, and the best ones are promiscuous to the point of infamy. What FDR sought in his first two years was not majority support, but something approaching consensus. The First New Deal tried to please everyone. Roosevelt's penchant for splitting differences down the middle, blending opposites, and playing one side against the other was evidence of this. It was great politics, at least for a while.

What is good politics, though, is not necessarily good economics. This was one of the basic flaws of the early New Deal. It was not possible to keep competing factions happy and still accomplish much. The early New Deal agencies were often ineffective not only because of contradictory purposes, but also because the wrong people were placed in charge of them. Critics like

Barton J. Bernstein have implied that Roosevelt appointed conservatives to head reform programs in order to hold back change. Such observers contend that Roosevelt wanted only the appearance of substantial reform, not the reality. This interpretation is uncharitable; it is also wrong. Roosevelt was a schemer, all right, but not in this way. His commitment to substantial—although certainly not revolutionary—change was genuine. Rather, the placing of conservatives in charge of reform agencies was part of the President's balancing act, part of his attempt to retain business and conservative support while he undertook change.[9]

This was clever, but proved to be too clever. Keeping conservatives off his back was fine, but to keep political support Roosevelt needed to have his programs work. Placing in charge of the various alphabet henhouses such foxes as Joseph Kennedy at SEC, Hugh Johnson at NRA, and George Peek at AAA was unlikely to make the programs work. Even placing Ickes—who was anything but a fox in a henhouse—over PWA was probably a mistake, since Ickes's concern for spending money carefully prevented it from being spent quickly enough to pull the country out of the Depression. The clearest exception to this generally poor record was Relief Adminstrator Harry Hopkins. The counterproductive appointments, again, were not made because Roosevelt was a poor judge of administrators; they were the almost inevitable result of the President's attempt to please both sides during a major crisis.

The early New Deal made important changes in the American economic setup, but not drastic ones. Roosevelt tried to work within the existing power system, not to transform it. The Emergency Banking Act and the Glass-Steagall Act, despite the bankers' complaints about deposit insurance, greatly strengthened the nation's private banking system. The NRA allowed big businesses to protect their profits through "self-government." The AAA made payments to large landholders and, with Roosevelt's blessing, rejected attempts to alter the rural power structure. The Home Owners' Loan Corporation plainly helped many small homeowners, but this certainly was no attack on the system: it saved mortgage holders as well as homeowners. The federal relief effort, the CWA, PWA, and CCC were all decided departures, but none of them posed a serious threat to existing power relationships. The SEC was not liked by many on Wall Street, but they soon found they could live with it comfortably enough. The TVA was perhaps the biggest "threat" to the established order, in that it had the potential to demonstrate that planning and community cooperation could work and that a government-owned business could compete successfully with private enterprise.

But to fault Roosevelt for missing his chance to bring about drastic changes in the American economic system is to overlook the restraints upon him (even assuming that he wanted such changes, which in most cases he did not). A time of economic collapse, such as 1933, might seem just the time to introduce radical change. It is not. People may be willing to try new ideas; much evidence indicates that a majority was ready for bold new experiments in 1933. But any move toward either socialization or truly effective antitrust action would have been resisted vehemently by business. This would have made the economic collapse even worse in the short run (which might well not be very short). The fact is that, bad as things were in early 1933, they *could* get worse, and drastic change was likely to bring about that undesirable end.

Roosevelt, to be sure, wanted no such fundamental alteration. He sought recovery and more limited reform. Two years after his election he had failed to achieve enough of either, and pressures on him to move further to the left began to mount. Their sources lay in Depression-era life and values.

8· "Fear Itself": Depression Life

To most Americans who escaped the ravages of the Depression, as to almost all Americans today, the unemployed of the 1930s were part of a faceless mass. Many pitied them, some despised them, most tried to ignore them. Few attempted to understand them. Such an understanding must begin with the realization that they were individuals, not statistics. They were a diverse lot, with cleavages along racial, religious, ethnic, sexual, occupational, age, regional, and other lines. Some were proud, others beaten. Some were optimistic, others had lost all hope. Some blamed themselves, others cursed businessmen, politicians, the "system," or "the Interests." They were, to be sure, victims, but they were not *only* victims. In most cases they had no part in the cause of their suffering, but the ways in which they reacted to their plight form a large—although poorly understood—portion of the history of the Depression.

Here I try to follow anthropologist Clifford Geertz's prescription for cultural analysis. "A good interpretation of anything," Geertz has said, "takes us into the heart of that of which it is the interpretation." "Mass unemployment," Cabell Phillips has noted, "is both a statistic and an empty feeling in the stomach. To fully comprehend it, you have to both see the figures and feel the emptiness."[1] The principal goal is to go into the center of the Depression experience and attempt to feel the emptiness; in short, to blend social and intellectual history through an excursion into the minds of working-class Americans.

Undoubtedly the main reason that this topic has been so long neglected is the difficulty of approaching it.[2] Working people are largely absent from the traditional types of historical documentation. Yet many sources do exist. The Depression and its effects upon its victims proved to be an irresistible subject for many sociologists and psychologists in the 1930s. The resulting contemporary investigations are also extremely valuable sources of information.[3] The most important kinds of evidence are those that bring us into contact with individual working-class people of the Depression era. Several varieties of such personal sources are extant. Field investigators sent out by the Federal Emergency Relief Administration and, later, the Works Progress Administration, to report back to Federal Relief Administrator Harry Hopkins on conditions and attitudes among the poor provide us with a wealth of information. The fact that we receive our impressions of working-class thought through the eyes and words of middle-class investigators should make us cautious. Even so, the reports add much to our understanding. Interviewers hired by the WPA Federal Writers' Project collected thousands of personal histories from "ordinary" Americans in the late thirties. These, too, are a significant addition to our knowledge of working-class culture.[4]

The most useful source of direct contact with the people of the thirties is the immense collection of letters that were addressed to public figures, especially to Franklin and Eleanor Roosevelt These communications bring us into direct contact with more than 15 million Depression-era Americans, a majority of them laborers, clerks, and farmers.[5] By weaving together the various types of evidence and using one kind as a check on the indications found in another, we can begin to understand the lives and values of American workers in the Great Depression. What follows is a composite of the Depression experience, using the words of Depression victims from all these sources.

For those workers who had enjoyed at least a taste of prosperity in the 1920s, the initial blow of the Depression was crushing. The twenties had seen the traditional middle-class American values, which taught that success and failure went to those who deserved them and which stressed acquisitive individualism, spread widely among workers. Such workers had been pleased to think that their modest accomplishments in the twenties were the result of their selection—whether by Calvin's God or Darwin's Nature depended upon one's viewpoint—for success. Like the Republican party, which had taken credit for good times and hence found it difficult to escape blame for bad times, Americans who had claimed responsibility for personal gains found it difficult not to feel guilty when confronted with failure.

A widespread attitude of the unemployed early in the Depression was: "There must be something wrong with a fellow who can't get a job." *Sure, I've lost my job, but I'm still a worthy provider. Work will turn up soon.* Every morning up before dawn, washed, shaved, and dressed as neatly as possible. To the factory gates, only to find a hundred others already there, staring blankly at the sign: NO HELP WANTED. The search then became more feverish. One day in 1934 a man in Baltimore walked twenty miles in search of a job. "I just stopped every place," he said, "but mostly they wouldn't even talk to me." *Perhaps an employment agency? A long wait, but it will be worth it to get a job. At last a chance.* The questions: name, age, experience. Yes, well, we'll see what we can do, but there are already more than a hundred men in our files with similar backgrounds, and most of them are younger than you. Employers can be choosy, you know. It's a buyer's market. Why hire a man who is over forty, when there are plenty of unemployed men still in their twenties? Business has to be efficient, after all. "A man over forty might as well go out and shoot himself," said a despairing Chicago resident in 1934.

Gradually those over forty, though fit physically, began to *feel* old and *look* and *act* poor. Keeping up the appearance necessary to secure employment, particularly of the white-collar variety, became increasingly difficult. As an Oklahoma woman put it in a letter to Eleanor Roosevelt in 1934, "The unemployed have been so long with out food-clothes-shoes-medical care-dental care etc-we look pretty bad-so when we ask for a job we don't get it. And we look and feel a little worse each day—when we ask for food they call us bums—it isent our fault . . . no we are not bums." Yet, "with shabby suits, frayed collars, worn shoes and perhaps a couple of front teeth gone," men *looked* like bums. "We do not dare to use even a little soap," wrote a jobless Oregonian, "when it will pay for an extra egg a few more carrots for our children."[6]

As the days without finding a job became weeks, the weeks months, and the months years, it came to be more difficult even to look for work. ". . . You can get pretty discouraged and your soles can get pretty thin after you've been job hunting a couple of months," a Minnesota Depression victim pointed out. First you came to accept the idea of taking a job of lower quality than you thought you deserved. Then you began to wonder just what you did deserve. It came finally, for some, to be a matter of begging: "For God's sake, Mister, when are you going to give us work?" "How," asked the daughter of a long-unemployed man, "can you go up and apply for a job without crying?"

Modern industrial society does not provide a place or position for a person; rather, it requires him to make his own place—and to strive to better it. This is taken to be the measure of one's individual worth. Americans had been brought up on the belief that meaningful work is the basis of life. Without such work, people felt they had no reason for being. "Drives a man crazy," said a seventy-five-year-old former knifemaker, "or drives him to drink, hangin' around." One must, as a St. Louis man said in 1933, "get the job to keep his mind and body whole."

Community attitudes toward the unemployed sometimes added to the feelings of guilt, shame, inferiority, fear, and insecurity. Many of those who remained employed made it plain that they believed that "something is wrong with a man who can't support his family." "Taxpayers" complained of paying for the upkeep of "thieves and lazy, immoral people," "no good for nothing loafers," "human parasites," and "pampered poverty rats."

Although some of the unemployed successfully resisted the psychological effects of such verbal attacks, others were likely to hear internal as well as external voices telling them that they were to blame for their plight. "I'm just no good, I guess," a Houston woman told a caseworker in 1934. "I've given up ever amounting to anything. It's no use." "I'd kinda like to think I could get a job and hold it," an Oklahoma WPA worker said at the end of the Depression. [7]

As scant resources ran out, [8] self-blame often grew into the shame of having to seek assistance. In some areas, people "would almost starve rather than ask for help." Indeed, some of their fellow citizens expected no less from them. "I have had too much self respect for my self and Family to beg anything," wrote a North Carolina man in 1933. "I would be only too glad to dig ditches to keep my family from going hungry." But there were no ditches to be dug. For many, there seemed "little to look forward to save charity," with all the stigma that implied. The loss of one's "good standing" was a matter of great concern. The thought of seeking charity was "very distasteful and humiliating."

Desperation began to take over. For many, nighttime was the worst. "What is going to become of us?" wondered an Arizona man. "I've lost twelve and a half pounds this last month, just thinking. You can't sleep, you know. You wake up about 2 A.M., and you lie and think." When you could sleep, bad dreams were likely. Worry and fear became dominant. Sometimes you would look at your children and wonder what would happen to them. Sheer terror would suddenly overcome you. Some say you appear to be shell-shocked; others tell you that you look like a frightened child. And well you should, because at times that's just the way you feel. Often you cry like a youngster; you try to do it privately, but you know the children hear you at night.

Of course you try to forget. For some, alcohol was a means of escape. It was not much help when you were hungry, though. "It's funny," a nineteen-year-old in Providence said. "A lot of times I get offered a drink. It seems like people don't want to drink alone. But no one ever offers me a meal. Most of the time when I take a drink it makes me sick. My stomach's too empty."[9]

An alternative to drinking was withdrawal from social contacts. Convinced that you are a failure, you try to avoid your friends, fearing that they will look upon you with scorn or, what is sometimes worse, pity. Thus you are unlikely to find out that many of your friends have also fallen victim to the Depression. In this small, hothouse world, self-blame, shame, and self-pity bloom magnificently.

As desperation grows worse the choices narrow. "My children have not got no shoes and clothing to go to school with," a West Virginia man complained in 1935, "and we havent got enough bed clothes to keep us warm." You resort to using old coats in lieu of blankets. *What can be done? What of the children? They are cold and hungry, but* "to do anything desperette now they would never live down the disgrace." "What is a man to do?" You face "a complete nervous breakdown as a result of being idle. . . . What is the next move for a desperate man? To commit some crime in this time of need?" When "all else has failed," one must do something. Is it wrong to steal coal to keep your family warm? Survival becomes the goal, the justification. Much like the slaves of the Old South, some Depression victims developed a distinction between *stealing* (from a fellow sufferer) and what the slaves had called *taking* (what you need and can convince yourself is rightfully yours because its possessor has exploited you or others like you). To some, it was acceptable to get "busy" and bring "home some extra money," as the wife of a Michigan WPA man put it. "I'd steal if I had the guts," declared a Rhode Island boy.[10]

If not crime, what? How long can I take it? Is there no hope? Perhaps the only thing left is to "end it all." If no one will help, "than [sic] I will take my life away," said a Detroit woman in 1935. Suicide at times "seemed the only solution." "The Atlantic calls from our shores that there is plenty of room for us," a Massachusetts woman proclaimed. Suicide would be the ultimate admission of defeat, but it might appear "as the best way out," as it did to a New York woman who stated, "I am not a coward but good Lord it is awful to stand helpless when you need things." "Can you be so kind as to advise me as to which would be the most human way to dispose of my self and family, as this is about the only thing that I see left to do," a Pennsylvania man inquired in 1934. "No home, no work, no money. We cannot go along this way. They have shut the water supply from us. No means of sanitation. We can not keep the children clean and tidy as they should be."

Relatively few, of course, actually took the fatal step, but many Depression victims appear to have considered it. An FERA investigator in New York City reported late in 1934 that "almost every one of her clients" had "talked of suicide at one time or another." The programs of the New Deal may have persuaded some that life might still hold some hope. "You have saved my life, " a New Jersey woman wrote, referring to assistance she had received from the Home Owners' Loan Corporation. "I would have killed myself If I would have lost my house." [11]

Sometimes the decision of whether to seek assistance was a question of socially determined sex roles. An Italian man in Massachusetts, for instance, threatened to kill himself, his wife, and children because he was about to lose his house. It was unacceptable for *him* to ask for help. His wife saved the day by appealing to a neighbor for a loan. The bulk of the help-seeking letters of the thirties were written by women to Eleanor Roosevelt. What was inappropriate behavior for most men—"begging"—was proper for women, either because women were believed to be naturally weak or because a mother seeking help was not showing weakness, but playing her accepted role.

Thousands of the down-and-out, almost all of them women, wrote to Mrs. Roosevelt asking for old clothes. Americans facing adversity clung to their traditions and pride as long as possible, but the Depression forced many to set aside the former and swallow the latter, lest they have nothing at all to swallow. Clothing was considered an area of female responsibility. "Please do not think this does not cause a great feeling of shame to me to have to ask for old clothing," an Iowa woman wrote to the First Lady in 1936. "I am so badly in need of a summer coat and under things and dresses. oh don't think that it is not with a effort I ask you to please send me anything you may have on hand in that line which you don't care to wear yourself." "I can sew and would only be too glad to take two old things and put them together and make a new one," wrote a desperate Philadelphia woman. "I don't care what it is, any thing from an old bunch of stockings to an old Sport Suit or an old afternoon dress, in fact. Any-thing a lady 40 years of age can wear."

Although men were more plentiful among writers asking for direct financial assistance than among those seeking clothing, women appear to have outnumbered men in this category as well. Men might be as pleased as women to receive help, but their expected sex role made it more difficult for them to ask. To do so would be further admission of failure as a provider. [12]

That so many wrote to the Roosevelts seeking help was indicative of the views most Depression-era workers had of the First Family. Such people often saw FDR in a fashion much like the European peasant who, as Oscar Handlin put it, thought "of the religious figure of the sanctified King as his distant protector who, if only he were told, would surely intercede for his devoted subjects." Letters to Roosevelt echoed this attitude. "You honor sir and your royalty. Majesty," began a 1935 letter to the President from an incapacitated black man in Georgia. When he heard Roosevelt speak over the radio in 1932, a Kansas man said, it seemed "as though some Moses had come to alleviated us of our sufferings."

The special relationship between the Roosevelts and the downtrodden made it possible to think that asking for help from that source was somehow different from seeking charity. One might even convince oneself that a modicum of independence was being preserved if help came from one's "personal friends" in the White House. Grasping at hope, a woman could ask Mrs. Roosevelt to intercede with the manager of a contest "and ask him kindly to give me a prize."[13]

When the hope for prizes and direct assistance from the "royal family" flickered out, little was left but to apply for the dreaded dole. Any savings you once had were either lost in bank failures or long since used up.[14] You have asked friends and relatives for a little help more times than is likely to keep them friendly. The grocer has allowed your bill to go up, but now he has said that he can do no more. Pay some of it or go hungry. By now you have been hungry—*really* hungry—for several days. A twelve-year-old boy in Chicago summed it up in a letter: "We haven't paid 4 months rent, Everyday the landlord rings the door bell, we don't open the door for him. We are afraid that will be put out, been put out before, and don't want to happen again. We haven't paid the gas bill, and the electric bill, haven't paid grocery bill for 3 months."[15] *Something* must be done. Survival being prerequisite to independence, the latter must be sacrificed, if only temporarily. So at last it is that painful walk to the local school, which houses the relief office.

You walk by a number of times, trying to get up the nerve to go in. What if your children—or their friends—see you? Finally, it can be delayed no longer. *Why is that policeman there?* Surely *you* have recently felt like breaking something; maybe others are also on the verge of destructive acts. Still, seeing that uniform and gun does not make you any more comfortable. You tell the clerk what you are there for. You are mumbling. Speak up! he says, impatiently. (He is on relief, too, and has few qualifications and little training for the delicate position he holds.) You finally make yourself understood. *(What else would you have been there for? Why did he even have to ask?)* Take a seat. Your name will be called.

The "intake" room is crowded. You sit down, focusing your gaze on one of the holes in your shoes. After a while your eyes, thoughtlessly moving about, make contact with those of another applicant. He looks away as quickly as you do. *How can so many people be failures? . . . What's taking them so long? Do they think I have all day? . . . Come to think of it, I guess I do. What a failure I am! . . . The stink in this place is awful!*

Two hours later you realize that your name is being called—for the second time. You rise slowly and go over to the desk. The questions bother you. *Yes,* FOUR *months since we paid the rent. Yes, we have been evicted before. No, we lost the car months ago. The radio? It's paid for, and it isn't worth enough to keep us fed for a week. Can't we keep it? That's all?* You can go home and wait. An investigator will visit you in a few days. More questions, more embarrassment, further degradation. Pauperization, that's what it is. *How did this happen?* You have become "something anonymous who will presently be more or less fed." *What's that? It may be several weeks before we get any help? How do we eat in the meantime? If we had anything at all left, I wouldn't be here now.*[16]

The shame persists, but eventually it may give way to despair and, then, apathy, particularly among those on direct relief. "Why the Hell should I get up in the morning, lady?" asked a youth of twenty. "What am I going to do with all these days? . . . I've been looking for a job for four years. I've had two. Five months in all. After a while you know it ain't getting you anywhere. There's nothing for us!" Many were bewildered. An FERA investigator described Americans in 1934 as being "terrifyingly patient." "They are sick, mentally and physically," a New York Home Relief Bureau supervisor had said of Depression victims a year earlier. "They have given up even trying to look for work. The majority have become so apathetic that they accept without questioning us whatever we give them, no matter how pitifully inadequate it is or how badly administered."

Such dole recipients were variously characterized as listless, "sinking into indifference," lethargic, and "too docile, too much licked to put up any fight." One FERA investigator described providing relief for such people as "a kind of desperate job like getting the wounded off the battlefield so that they can die quietly at the base hospital."[17]

Apathy, too, was a stage, one beyond which many of the unemployed moved after the New Deal had taken root. Sooner or later those sets of eyes in the relief office would meet. One would see "that there were other fellows who didn't look such a bad sort or low mentality in the same fix he was." It made you feel a little better. "Bit by bit," an FERA investigator reported from Bethlehem, Pennsylvania, late in 1934, "these men discovered that it was bolstering their morale to swap experiences and reactions and to realize that their situation was the result of a social condition, not a personal failure." And if the government had accepted responsibility for providing relief, the problem must not be the fault of the individual.

For such people, resentment began to displace self-blame and apathy. If it is not your fault, why should you suffer the indignities of the relief system? Relief "clients" began to object to the young college women who often served as caseworkers. (Not always without reason. One in California visited "her clients in a very elegant riding costume—breeches, top boots, crop, and all!") "We get work from the Relief as the little young folks thinks we need it," complained a Georgia woman. "They have always been used to plenty. Don't know how hard it is for folks like us."

Among the common criticisms of relief was that recipients were treated as children: given food orders instead of cash, instructed by nutrition experts, investigated by "busybodies," and generally "regimented." "Why should it be 'dished' out to us like we were *little children*, and tell us exactly what every cent should be spent for?" asked a Californian. People who had "always managed to raise their children and feed them without advice from the outside" were unenthusiastic about such lectures. They wanted to be on their own, to have cash to buy what and where they chose, to spend it on beer every now and then, if they so desired. Although relief recipients had already become far more dependent than most of them wished to be, they wanted to retain as much independence as possible, even within the relief system.

What gave relief "clients" the chance to reassert their independence was the opportunity for work relief, first with the CWA and later with the WPA. Self-respect could finally begin to return. When a New York relief investigator told a man who had been receiving grocery orders that there was a CWA job for him, she related, "He grabbed me, swung me right up off the floor, and hugged me." When he went to work, the man left an hour earlier than necessary.

People on WPA jobs spoke with heartfelt conviction about their preference for this type of assistance. "My pride took an awful beating when I had to apply for relief," a fifty-one-year-old Minneapolis man recalled in 1940, "but I feel different about this [WPA]. Here I am working for what I'm getting." "It means," a woman said of the WPA, "that I can look people in the eye because I'm not on a dole . . . it isn't like relief. Being on relief just breaks you all up." Another man spoke of the WPA enabling him "to sleep nights instead of lying awake thinking of desperate things I might do."[18]

By 1935 the attitude of many Depression victims toward relief had changed. Complaints increased. Shame over being on public assistance was replaced in some by anger at the smallness of payments and at relief administrators. A Muncie, Indiana, housewife expressed the latter view when she wrote, "Those in charge of relief have never lain awake at night worrying about unpaid rent, or how to make a few groceries do for the seemingly endless seven days. . . ." "It is always," she continued, "the people with full stomachs who tell us poor people to keep happy."[19]

In the mid-thirties many of the unemployed concluded that relief simply amounted to Depression victims getting what was rightfully theirs. Social workers were reporting as early as 1934 that some people seemed to think "that the Government actually owes it [relief] to them." Lorena Hickok called such recipients "gimmies." Some, an Iowa relief administrator wrote, had "adopted a more demanding attitude" and were "willing for the government to see them through." People on public assistance in Salt Lake City developed a slang of their own. Significantly, they referred to the FERA as "Santa Claus." In many places, groups of angry unemployed people gathered at relief offices and harassed the administrators with their demands for better treatment. [20] Within the context of a basically dependent situation, relief recipients were finding means by which to express their independence.

Whatever the changes in attitudes toward relief and dependence as the Depression continued, the psychological problems for the unemployed remained devastating. For many Americans who avoided the ravages of the Depression, it became an article of faith that relief recipients irresponsibly had children for whom they could not provide. Some conservatives charged that relief women had babies in order to qualify for higher payments. Even FERA investigators were not above accepting such notions. "On the relief rolls," wrote Martha Gellhorn in 1934, "it is an accepted fact that the more incapable and unequipped (physically, mentally, materially) the parents, the more offspring they produce." "Apparently," she concluded in another report, "the instinct of self-preservation is not very well developed in the working class American." [21]

For the victims, however, the problem was far more complex. Some social workers excused poverty-ridden, hopeless young women who had illegitimate children, because "their lives are so empty that they fall a prey to anything which offers momentary escape from the horror of their lives." Although this view was not without some validity, the problem was more complicated. For many "forgotten women" of the thirties, the questions of intercourse, birth control, and having children were among the most gnawing of the Depression years. The wife of a Massachusetts WPA worker (and mother of his eleven children) voiced one aspect of the difficulty: "Ya know down at the Catholic Charities they tell ya your not supposed ta have children if you're on the W.P.A. An' in the church they tell ya you're not supposed ta do anything about it. An' they say you're supposed ta live with your man. Now what's a woman gonna do?"

Even for women without religious qualms about birth control sexual questions caused anguish. A woman in the San Joaquin Valley haltingly told Lorena Hickok of something "that had nearly driven her crazy" and that "she knew was one of the worst problems of women whose husbands are out of work." Almost no one in such circumstances *wanted* to have babies, but "here you are, surrounded by young ones you can't support and never know-ing when there's going to be another. You don't have any money to buy anything at the drugstore. All you have is a grocery order. I've known women to try to sell some of their groceries to get a little money to buy the things needed."

This still did not describe the depth of the problem, however. "I suppose," the woman continued, "you can say the easiest way would be not to do it. But it wouldn't be. You don't know what it's like when your husband's out of work. He's gloomy and unhappy all the time. Life is terrible. You must try all the time to keep him from going crazy. And many times—that's the only way." [22]

Pleasure in the Depression was, to be sure, often limited to such inexpen-sive pastimes. In many places, meat and fruit were rarities. One woman bought a dozen oranges with part of her husband's first CWA check. "I hadn't tasted any for so long," she explained, "that I had forgotten what they were like!" People were gloomy. "I know a party that has got a radio + spends some of his money for beer," a Vermont woman wrote to President Roosevelt. Her family was not so fortunate: "We don't have no pleasure of any kind."

The absence of pleasure sometimes produced family problems. "What about the children who's parents can't give their children the little things in life such as a cone of cream or a 1 *cts* piece of candy or a soft drink once a week," asked a Kentuckian. "Who will get the blame for this neglect The father of course. . . . Do you think it is right that we poor never have the pleasure of a show or a trip back home. Just stay at home and watch others have all the fun good eats fine automobiles town houses, country homes. . . ." Other family problems grew out of the quest for pleasure on empty pocketbooks. "Half the men you have Put to work taken their maney When they get Paid an spends it for whiskey," a Nashville woman com-plained to FDR. "If my husban new that I wrote this he would kill me," she added in a postscript.

The lack of money, work, and self-esteem caused even greater family trou-bles. Unemployment upset the traditional roles of father, mother, and chil-dren. Since the father's position was based upon his occupation and his role as provider, the loss of his job was likely to mean a decline in his status within the family. The man who was without a position was, well, without a posi-tion. It was he who was supposed to provide independence for the family. Having little to do, unemployed men hung around home much of the time. In doing so, they infringed upon the sphere of the wife. If the husband blamed himself for his loss of income, the wife might try to encourage him. At first most did. But as hardships grew, and as the man sitting by the kitchen stove began to irritate his wife, the latter was increasingly likely to see, and point out, faults in her mate. And as his resentment and guilt expanded, he was apt to find more in his wife's actions that displeased him. Quarrels became more numerous.

Being "on relief" stigmatized an entire family, but most especially the father. Male dominance was endangered in the Depression. It asserted itself in odd ways. In some cases, most family resources were devoted to obtaining clothes for the man. "The women," it was concluded, "can stay inside and keep warm, and the children can stay home from school." There were cases, however, where a father was obliged to share his son's clothes. "They're all we've got now," said a North Dakota farmer. "We take turns wearing 'em." The symbolism for the breadwinner must have been apparent.

The traditional role of the mother is far less dependent than that of the father on the family's status in the outside world. The Depression was, accordingly, less harmful to mothers' positions inside their families. John Steinbeck said it well in *The Grapes of Wrath:* " 'Woman can change better'n a man,' Ma said soothingly. 'Woman got all her life in her arms. Man got it all in his head.' " Some women simply took over for their unemployed husbands. In one case, a man first learned of his wife's decision to rent another house "when he came home to find the furniture had been moved." But mothers' roles were also upset by the economic breakdown. Distribution of relief commodities, Chicago social workers pointed out, "deprived the housewife of the privilege of shopping and in a sense destroyed their responsibility as housewives." Nor was it easy for "a mother to hear her hungry babe whimpering in the night and growing children tossing in their sleep because of knawing plain HUNGER," as an Oregon woman put it. "I have laid many a night & cried my self to sleep when I think of what I have to work with," wrote a Pennsylvania mother.

People did their best to maintain traditional roles. If a woman must work for her family to survive, so be it. The reemergence of a family economy of pooled resources was one means of maintaining family independence. "But soon's the men get goin' the wife's through," a Portuguese fisherman in Massachusetts said. "She stays home then. Yes ma'am, we like our wives to be home." Of course spouses who continued to cooperate during the Depression helped each other make it through with a minimum of upheaval. "We got enough ta get along on, and we got each other. That should be enough ta make any body happy," declared a shoe machinery worker. For all the problems, in fact, available evidence indicates that the families of many unemployed men continued to operate under the direction of the traditional head, with little apparent change in internal status. The principal effect of the Depression on internal family relationships, in fact, was to exaggerate the qualities and tendencies already present. The additional strain was often too much for weak families to withstand, but strong relationships usually weathered the hard times successfully.[23]

* * *

Discrimination against women in employment became worse with the Depression. It was easy to assert that women were taking jobs that otherwise would go to male heads of households. Norman Cousins stated this argument in its most simplistic form in 1939: "There are approximately 10,000,000 people out of work in the United States today; there are also 10,000,000 or more women, married and single, who are jobholders. Simply fire the women, who shouldn't be working anyway, and hire the men. Presto! No unemployment. No relief rolls. No depression." Those who made such statements usually had little interest in facts, but most women who worked outside the home during the Depression clearly did so out of necessity. They supported themselves and their families just as did male "breadwinners." Such was the case not only with single women, but also with most working married women, whose husbands were either unemployed or paid too little to provide for their families. Nonetheless, campaigns against hiring married women were common in the 1930s. Fully 77 percent of the school districts in the United States would not hire married women to teach; 50 percent of them had a policy of firing women who married.

Despite the prejudice against women—especially married women—working, their numbers in the work force actually increased, both absolutely and as a percentage of all workers, during the Depression. In 1930, women had represented 24.3 percent of all workers; in 1940, 25.1 percent of the work force was female. Similarly, the proportion of women workers who were married increased in the face of Depression-era discrimination, from 28.8 percent at the beginning of the decade to 35 percent at its end. This seemingly remarkable development resulted from several causes.

Most women who sought employment, before as well as during the Depression, did so because the economic realities of American life obliged them to work. Most families in this country have aspired to an "American standard of living," which has always been ill defined, but is something clearly above mere subsistence. Early in the present century it was not possible for working-class families to reach that level on the wages of one adult male. The income of the father was often supplemented by the wages of children. As child labor declined, wives filled the resulting gap in family income. The living standards of most families improved in the 1920s. When the Depression hit, even those families that did not *need* the wife's extra income in an absolute sense, needed it if they were to stay close to the standard that they had enjoyed during prosperity. As husbands lost their jobs, had their wages cut, or became increasingly fearful that they *might* become unemployed, wives who had not previously worked outside the home sought jobs. Here was a distinct—and often overlooked—irony of the Depression: as jobs became much more difficult to find, far *more* people began looking for work. One estimate held that 2.5 million more people were in the work force in 1937 than there would have been had there been no depression. Most of these new workers were women, so one reason that more women found jobs in the thirties was simply that more sought them.

This might seem to support the claim that women were displacing men from jobs, but another reason for the increase in female workers refutes that argument. Women lost proportionately fewer jobs than men precisely because their types of employment were *not* considered interchangeable. There existed many positions that were identified as "women's work": domestic service, primary education, many clerical and social service jobs. Such situations remained available to women regardless of how many men were out of work. The Depression itself placed women in a relatively better position for obtaining work—poorly paid, of course—than men. "[I]deas that once had consigned women to inferior places in the labor force," historian Alice Kessler-Harris has pointed out, "now preserved for them jobs that menfolk could not get." The economic collapse hit hardest just those sectors of the economy (especially heavy industry) that had barred women workers. The fields in which women were most likely to be employed suffered a lesser decline and, in the case of clerical work (in the new government agencies), social services, and education, actually grew under the impact of the New Deal. A 1940 study found that in the five most depressed industries women represented only 2 percent of the employees. In the employment categories with the smallest drop in employment, on the other hand, women held 30 percent of the jobs. In a strange sense, women might be said to have benefited from past employment discrimination against them.

Before we become too envious of women workers during the Depression, though, it is well to remember what sort of jobs were reserved for them and what they were paid. At the end of the decade fully one-fifth of all women who worked for wages were employed as domestic servants. Live-in maids in the mid-thirties earned less than $8 per week in New York City, the highest-paying locality in the country. Other women workers were better paid, but not by much. One-fourth of the NRA codes permitted lower rates of pay for women than men. The federal government not only allowed discrimination, it practiced it. Men on WPA projects were paid $5 per day; women received only $3.

Women workers during the Depression also had to face increased psychological pressures. Antagonism from male workers and from wives who remained at home was intensified by the generally mistaken belief that women were taking jobs from men. And at a time when their traditional nurturing role seemed especially needed in the home, women who were obliged to work for wages carried a particularly heavy burden of guilt. One study placed the blame for "truancy, incorrigibility, robbery, teenage tantrums, and difficulty in managing children" on the "mother's absence at her job."

Given all the obstacles working wives faced during the Depression, it is not surprising that many people came to associate employment of women outside the home with harsh, undesirable economic conditions. In the thirties an ideal came to be formed among many Americans—women as well as men— of what American family life ought to be like. It was summed up in the answer the vice president of a United Auto Workers local made to a 1939 complaint a union member's wife had made about married women working. "Some day, Dear Sister, I hope we will reach that economic ideal where the married woman will find her place in the home caring for children, which is God's greatest gift to women and her natural birthright," Mike Mannini wrote. Here was an example of a very important part of the origins of what Betty Friedan later called "the feminine mystique." The return of the wife and mother to her "natural" sphere came during the Great Depression to be a goal, the achievement of which would be a sign of the return of "good times."[24]

In those families where there was turmoil during the Depression, the children often suffered. Fathers (and mothers) might take out their frustrations on the children. As the effects of unemployment, shame, and worry became noticeable in parents, children grew more anxious. "The children all seem to be so excitable and high-strung these days," said a New York settlement house kindergarten teacher. "I can't help thinking it's due to the distress at home."

Why do we live like this, a child would wonder. *Things used to be better. We're not even clean anymore. Mama says the relief doesn't give enough for soap. And the bedbugs. In our old house we never had anything like that!* What's wrong with Daddy? Times are hard, they say, but "all the other little girls are getting Easter dresses." "Our friends have skates and we are not able to buy them." *Surely it's not Daddy's fault; he's the greatest. Why, he's been on relief longer than the other kids' fathers—that's* something.

How can you go to school when the other kids know your family has been evicted before and people are saying your father's not paying the rent now? *Why should I be the one who has* "to put a piece of cardboard in the sole of my shoe to go to school"? All the questions in a young mind. "My father he staying home. All the time he's crying because he can't find work. I told him why are you crying daddy, and daddy said why shouldn't I cry when there is nothing in the house. I feel sorry for him. That night I couldn't sleep."

The special times that usually bring joy to children and parents were often the hardest to bear during the Depression. Christmas could be particularly painful. "My little children talking about Santa Claus," a Texas father wrote to the President in 1934, "and I hate to see Xmas come this time because I know it will be one of the dullest Xmas they ever witnessed." A Virginia mother described a similar problem. "My little boy was speaking of Santa

Claus 'He says why is it most children gets pretty toys and so many seems like they are rich and we so poor' This made tears come in my eyes," she said. "Then I told him if we are ever lucky enough to get work we will try to get him something pretty. I have to tell him of some happy day which may come."

While many adults compared Franklin Roosevelt to Lincoln, Moses, or Jesus, for some children the President was Santa Claus. Two Rhode Island boys, for instance, wrote their annual Christmas letter in 1935, but mailed it to Washington rather than the North Pole. They wanted bicycles or microscope-chemistry sets. Other children who sought gifts from the jolly man in the White House were more practical. "We have no one to give us a Christmas presents," wrote a ten-year-old Ohio girl, "and if you want to buy a Christmas present please buy us a stove to do our cooking and to make good bread." Such were the holiday thoughts of some children in 1935.

Although the children of the thirties lived through the same economic hardship as their parents did, it meant different things to the new generation. For one thing, children were largely free from the self-blame and shame that were so common among their elders. Obviously economic problems were not the fault of a child. He could rest assured that *he* had not failed. Adults might have botched things up; perhaps Dad was a failure, but few children felt any personal guilt. The Depression's most significant psychological problem was generally absent in the young.

The hardships many families faced in the thirties led children to assume greater responsibilities at an earlier age than has been customary in the years since World War II. It has been said with accuracy that there were no working-class "teenagers" in the 1930s. The generation had no time for an irresponsible, prolonged adolescence. Challenges had to be met. Often children (especially boys) were called upon to supplement meager family incomes by working after school (or in place of school). When mothers found it necessary—and possible—to get jobs, older children (especially girls) were given the responsibility of looking after their younger brothers and sisters.

Although the loss of any appreciable portion of one's childhood is tragic, there were some compensations for the youth of the thirties. The work thrust upon children in the Depression was likely to instill in them what industrial society commonly considers to be virtues: dependability, self-reliance, order, awareness of the needs of others, and practice in managing money. To the extent that the Depression furthered the development of such qualities in the young, it had a strikingly different effect on the children than on their elders. Ironically, the same family hardship that might weaken the self-reliance of a father could strengthen that quality in his child.[25]

If being a child in the thirties was difficult, but at least on occasion rewarding, being a young adult presented problems with few compensations. Americans have always been future-oriented. If things were not quite perfect at the moment, just wait for tomorrow or next year. This attitude has been especially associated with the young.

In this as in so much else, however, the 1930s were different. Not that optimism did not survive, at least below the surface. Throughout the Depression, the slightest good news was sufficient to activate the latent hopefulness in some Americans. The creation of the CWA and the implementation of the corn loans brightened the outlook in Iowa to the point that an Irish man shouted, "In another 20 days we'll be out of the depression!" In the late spring of 1934, Lorena Hickok temporarily convinced herself that "people are in a pretty contented, optimistic frame of mind. They just aren't thinking about the Depression any more," she said, displaying at least as much optimism as she thought she detected in others. Speaking of the reaction of drought-stricken Colorado ranchers to two cloudbursts, she said, "Funny how people will cheer up if given half a chance!" "If only they will be patient, circumstances will work themselves out, and every-thing will be O.K.," a Wisconsin woman wrote in 1935. Even after a full decade of depression, WPA workers could be found in 1940 expressing faith in the future. "My idea," said an Oklahoma laborer, "is that all this is just a temporary thing, but it'll give us a chance to get another start if jobs will just pick up."

Despite the persistence of such attitudes in some quarters, though, the future looked bleak to many in the thirties. When asked "what his hope for the future was," an ex-truck driver gave a typical answer in 1934: "I just don't know." In the same year, Oklahoma relief recipients were said to "no longer have the 'chin up' attitude." Rather, they "lived in constant fear of what the next day or next week would bring." Young people simply had "nothing to look forward to." Many of the young—at just the stage in life in which the future often appears limitless—were nearly without hope during the Depression years. Older people, FERA investigator Martha Gellhorn pointed out, could "remember an easier life, a less stringent world." They refused "to believe that the end had inevitably come." "But," Gellhorn declared, "these young people have grown up against a shut door."

What hope could the future hold for the young adult of the thirties? Marriage and raising a family appeared out of the question. The CCC was all right for a while, but it was hardly a career. Work relief meant survival, but it offered no chance for advancement and no training for a "real" job. How could you get interested in it? Horatio Alger stories were fine in the old days, but what now? The traditional formula was work, save, succeed; but now you could not even reach step one. It appeared that "we shall never have good times again," we were "permanently licked." It was hard to disagree with the sobering conclusion that "it would be a cinch to run a war these days, with a good many of the world's young men having nothing better to do anyhow than get shot, and at least fed for a bit beforehand, and busy. . . ."

For most, of course, unemployment had to end sometime. The offer of a "real job" often brought tears of joy. "This will be our last week on relief," wept the wife of a skilled worker in Joplin, Missouri, after her husband obtained employment. "Next week we shall be able to take care of ourselves again." Unfortunately, such joy was often short-lived. Long unemployment had taken its physical and psychological toll. People became "nervous, muscularly soft and unconfident of their ability to do the work they formerly did." On a new job, they were so fearful of "making mistakes that they make mistakes and are promptly fired," reported a Chicago settlement official in 1934.[26]

The Great Depression was, of course, an economic disaster for most Americans, but black people suffered a disproportionate share of the burden. The old and true saying that blacks are the last hired and the first fired cut both ways during the Depression. Unemployment in the "prosperity decade" had been much higher among blacks than whites. "The Negro was born in depression," Clifford Burke told Studs Terkel. "It only became official when it hit the white man."

As layoffs began in late 1929 and accelerated in the following years, blacks were often the first to get pink slips. By 1932 black unemployment reached approximately 50 percent nationwide. As with women, some undesirable jobs had long been reserved for blacks. But such jobs became less undesirable when no other work was to be found. Although women's work generally remained just that in the Depression, the same was not the case with some traditionally "Negro occupations." Whites demanded that blacks be discharged as domestic servants, garbage collectors, elevator operators, waiters, bellhops, and street cleaners. A group of whites in Atlanta adopted the slogan "No Jobs for Niggers Until Every White Man Has a Job." A poorly educated Georgia woman spoke for many whites when she wrote to the President in 1935: "negroes being worked ever where instead of white men it dont look like that is rite." A year earlier a white clerk in Marianna, Florida, said in the wake of a lynch mob attack on a store that employed blacks, "A nigger hasn't got no right to have a job when there are white men who can do the work and are out of work." The number of lynchings in the United States rose from eight in 1932 to twenty-eight, fifteen, and twenty in the three succeeding years. A Depression-era study showed a positive correlation between the number of lynchings in the Deep South and economic distress. "Dust had been blown from the shotgun, the whip, and the noose," a *New Republic* article reported in 1931, "and Ku Klux practices were being resumed in the certainty that dead men not only tell no tales but create vacancies."

Those blacks who were able to keep their jobs suffered great hardship as well. A 1935 investigation in Harlem indicated that skilled workers there had experienced a drop of nearly 50 percent in their wages since the onset of the Depression. The lack of employment opportunities in northern cities cut down the extraordinary rate of black migration from the rural South, but more than 400,000 blacks did make the journey in the Depression decade. If jobs were not available in the North, at least there was not as much discrimination in the administration of relief as in the South. The continuing heavy migration of blacks into cities where they could vote, in states with large representation in the electoral college, was a political fact of growing importance.

The political influence of blacks had been minuscule since the end of Reconstruction. They voted in overwhelming majorities for the Republican party, which had come to take the "Negro vote" for granted. The Grand Old Party offered blacks little more by 1930 than the grand old platitudes of Abraham Lincoln, Thaddeus Stevens, and Charles Sumner. The Democrats, however, offered still less. The Democrats had *never* seated a single black delegate at any national convention prior to the New Deal. A few blacks were selected as alternates in 1924, but at the 1928 Democratic National Convention in Houston, the black alternates were seated in an area separated by chicken wire from the white delegates and alternates. Here was a perfect symbol of the racial attitudes of the party.

If there was little cause for blacks to hope for much from the Democratic party, there was not much more reason for optimism about the party's candidate in 1932. Like most northern Democrats, Franklin D. Roosevelt had never said anything about race that might upset southern party leaders. He went along without complaint when President Wilson ordered the institution of a complete Jim Crow system in the Navy. In 1929, FDR issued a public denial that he had eaten lunch with blacks. Both Roosevelt's administration in Albany and his 1932 campaign staff were devoid of blacks. Despite their suffering from the Depression, blacks voted for Hoover by greater majorities against Roosevelt in 1932 than they had against Smith four years before.

Yet a decade later Swedish sociologist Gunnar Myrdal wrote in his classic study of American race relations, *An American Dilemma*, that Roosevelt's presidency had "changed the whole configuration of the Negro problem." Few today would disagree with this assessment. The civil rights revolution that reached fruition in the 1960s had its origins in the Depression years. A number of factors converged to bring about this remarkable result.

In the early New Deal no direct steps were taken toward easing the plight of black Americans. To advocates of legislation to improve race relations, Roosevelt argued, with considerable justification, that pushing such bills would destroy the support of southerners in Congress needed to pass recovery legislation vital to all Americans, black as well as white. "First things come first, and I can't alienate certain votes I need for measures that are more important at the moment by pushing any measures that would entail a fight," Roosevelt said in 1933. "I've got to get legislation passed by Congress to save America," FDR explained to Walter White, the national secretary of the National Association for the Advancement of Colored People. "The Southerners by reason of the seniority rule in Congress are chairmen or occupy strategic places on most of the Senate and House committees. If I come out for the anti-lynching bill now, they will block every bill I ask Congress to pass to keep America from collapsing. I just can't take that risk."

Thus the legislation of the First Hundred Days concentrated on the immediate economic crisis, leaving the specific concerns of blacks unaddressed. The National Recovery Administration's effects on blacks were symptomatic of the impact of the early New Deal on that segment of the population. More than a hundred NRA codes established regional wage differentials under which southern workers (which in many instances meant blacks, because of the job classifications) were paid less than people doing the same work elsewhere. The Blue Eagle did not even cover the occupations in which most blacks were employed: farm labor and domestic service. Eighteen NRA codes included what one NAACP official called the "grandfather clause of the NRA." It established wage scales for types of labor based upon what wages had been at a certain date in the past. Obviously this perpetuated pay discrimination based on racial distinctions in job classifications. And in those instances where NRA codes *did* enforce equal pay for workers of either race, the result was often that blacks lost their "advantage" of working for less and were replaced by whites. Black newspapers had their own versions of what NRA stood for, including "Negro Run Around" and "Negroes Rarely Allowed."

For blacks, the Agricultural Adjustment Administration served mainly to reduce their incomes (which they could stand much less than could their large landholding white neighbors), and force black landowners into tenancy, tenants into sharecropping, and many blacks off the land entirely. These effects were extremely significant. Some 40 percent of all black workers in the United States during the Depression years were farm laborers or tenants. A 1934 investigation estimated the average annual income of black cotton famers of all types at under $200. The AAA was not the *cause* of such deplorable conditions, but it continued them without improvement and in some cases made the problems worse.

Most early New Deal programs included the ideal of decentralized administration or "grass-roots democracy." (No one in the thirties, as far as I am aware, used the term "New Federalism.") Much could be said for the concept in the abstract. In practice, however, it meant that local elites controlled the federal programs in their areas. "[T]he releaf officials here," a black resident of Reidsville, Georgia, wrote to President Roosevelt in 1935, ". . . give us black folks, each one, nothing but a few cans of pickle meet and to the white folks they give blankets, bolts of cloth and things like that." A Georgia official confirmed a discriminatory policy: "There will be no Negroes pushing wheelbarrows and boys driving trucks getting forty cents an hour when the good white men and white women, working on the fields alongside these roads can hardly earn forty cents a day." Relief payments to blacks in Atlanta averaged $19.29 per month, while white relief clients in the same city received $32.66, nearly 70 percent more. A black person in Hattiesburg, Mississippi, summed up the effect of local control in an eloquent, if nearly illiterate, letter to FDR: "i wish you could See the poor hungry an naket half clad's at the relief office an is turned away With tears in their eyes Mississippi is made her own laws and dont treat her destituted as her Pres. had laid plans for us to live." [27]

The need for change should have been obvious. In the 1920s, American popular culture was blatantly racist. Movies portrayed blacks as shiftless, stupid, and laughable. Radio joined in in 1928 with *Amos 'n' Andy*, a series in which white actors spoke the parts of black characters who fit all the white stereotypes of blacks. By 1929, *Amos 'n' Andy* was radio's most popular program, heard by about 60 percent of all radio listeners. Other broadcasts in the decade made frequent use of "darky" jokes. Amusement parks advertised games in which whites could "Hit the Coon and Get a Cigar." Optimists seeking signs of improvement were hard pressed for examples. Perhaps it was a significant reform when *The New York Times* began, early in 1930, to spell "Negro" with a capital "N." Early in the New Deal, though, at least one official of the Federal Housing Administration was still in the habit of telling "darky" and "coon" stories in public speeches. (Administration leaders soon stopped the practice, although it did not die forever, as Nixon-Ford Agriculture Secretary Earl Butz demonstrated in the early 1970s.)

The shift in the attitude of the federal government toward race relations was in large part the work of a few dedicated integrationist reformers, white and black. Unquestionably, the person most responsible for beginning the change in the attitude of the federal government toward blacks was Eleanor Roosevelt. Mrs. Roosevelt had shown no particular concern or understanding for the problems of blacks before her husband became president. But her empathy for the downtrodden led her quite naturally to take up the cause of blacks. She was shocked at the uproar that followed her having lunch with a black woman in Florida in 1933.

In 1927, Eleanor Roosevelt met Mary McLeod Bethune, a black woman who had risen from a sharecropper's family of seventeen children to found Bethune-Cookman College in Florida. The friendship between these two women continued over the ensuing years, and as a result Mrs. Roosevelt's understanding of black problems expanded greatly. She recommended Mrs. Bethune as an assistant to Aubrey Williams at the National Youth Administration, and under the leadership of Williams, a dedicated white liberal from

Alabama, and the influence of Bethune, the NYA became a model of government assistance for blacks.

The First Lady also became friendly with Walter White, the first black
national secretary of the NAACP. With the guidance of Bethune and White,
Eleanor Roosevelt became the leading white advocate of racial integration in
the United States. As such, she found herself the target of virulent abuse from
white racists. One of the harshest was the ditty that put the following words in
the President's mouth, speaking to his wife:

> *You kiss the niggers,*
> *I'll kiss the Jews,*
> *We'll stay in the White House*
> *As long as we choose.*

Eleanor Roosevelt's concern for black people was a reflection of her larger
attitude of compassion, which in turn meshed with the values of cooperation
that were becoming popular among the American people during the Depression years. The "day of selfishness," Mrs. Roosevelt declared in a 1934 speech
to a conference on black education, was over; "the day of working together has
come, and we must learn to work together, all of us, regardless of race or
creed or color. . . . We go ahead together or we go down together." Seen in
this light, the emerging values of the American people seemed to point toward
racial cooperation. But it was not so simple. A move toward racial harmony—
admittedly, a very *small* move—was not the only possible effect of the Depression on racial attitudes. A glance at contemporary events in Germany is
sufficient to remind us that hard times can cause an intensification of racial
and religious animosity. The increase in lynching in the American South in
those years indicates that such a potential existed in the United States as well.
Senator Theodore Bilbo of Mississippi was one of the those Americans who
thought the Nazis had the right idea. "Race consciousness is developing in all
parts of the world," Bilbo declared in 1938. "Consider Italy, consider Germany. It is beginning to be recognized by the thoughtful minds of our age that
the conservation of racial values is the only hope for future civilization. . . .
The Germans appreciate the importance of race values."

That the United States in the Depression moved in the direction of the
values of compassion and cooperation pointed to by Eleanor Roosevelt, rather
than toward the "race values" outlined by Senator Bilbo (who sought a $1
billion congressional appropriation in 1939 to deport all blacks to Africa), was
the result of more than Depression-bred concepts of justice, as important as
they certainly were. The push given the President and his policies by Mrs.
Roosevelt, Mrs. Bethune, Walter White, Harold Ickes, Will Alexander, the
southern white Methodist minister who became head of the Farm Security

Administration, Aubrey Williams of the NYA, and Clark Foreman, a young white Georgian who became FDR's special assistant on the economic status of Negroes, was of great importance. So was pressure from the Communist party and the CIO, both of which were in the forefront of the quest in the thirties for a larger degree of racial equality. In addition, significant pressure came from blacks themselves, both politically and in terms of organization, demonstrations, and even rioting.

The chronological proximity of President Roosevelt's shift to more forceful opposition to racial discrimination with the only major race riot of the decade, that in Harlem in 1935, may have been coincidence. Be that as it may, the growing importance of black voters in national politics surely was directly related to FDR's move to include blacks in his new Democratic coalition. Black voters began their historic desertion of the Republican party in 1934, *before* the Roosevelt administration had done much specifically for them. In the midterm elections of 1934, a majority of black voters cast their ballots for Democrats for the first time. That year Arthur Mitchell became the first black Democrat ever to win a seat in Congress, when he upset incumbent black Republican Oscar De Priest in a Chicago district. Mitchell won using the slogan "Forward with Roosevelt." The fact that Roosevelt at least attempted to prohibit discrimination in some federal programs and that his administration provided significant amounts of relief for blacks were enough to end three-quarters of a century of Republican allegiance. "Let Jesus lead you and Roosevelt feed you," a black preacher advised his congregation in 1936.

In that year, the dramatic shift in black political support was unmistakable. "Abraham Lincoln," the Baltimore *Afro-American* reminded its readers, "Is Not A Candidate in the Present Campaign." Franklin Roosevelt was, and he won an incredible 76 percent of the black vote, roughly reversing the outcome of four years earlier. The change in black voting was more decisive than that of any other group in 1936. As with working-class whites, many blacks who had never voted before were sufficiently impressed with the New Deal to cast their first ballots for Roosevelt. Even in the rural South, many blacks were by this time getting to participate in elections of a sort for the first time, as they voted in AAA referendums on such issues as crop limitations. A new political awareness and hope began to dawn among southern blacks. "They's talked more politics since Mistuh Roosevelt been in than ever befo'," one southern black said of other blacks in his area. "I been here twenty years, but since WPA, the Negro sho' has started talkin' politics."

Unsurprisingly, some Democrats did not welcome the new black members of their party. When a black minister rose to give the invocation at the 1936 Democratic National Convention in Philadelphia, Senator Ellison D. "Cotton Ed" Smith of South Carolina was horrified. "By God, he's as black as melted midnight!" Smith gasped. "Get outa my way. This mongrel meeting ain't no place for a white man!" Smith stormed out of the convention. It was the first time there had been reason for any southern delegate to walk out of a Democratic convention since 1860, but the South Carolinian's action was a foretaste of the future, not a dim reflection of the past. Some southern delegates bolted the Democratic conventions again in 1948 and 1964, as the party gave them considerably more provocation than a black minister's prayer. Senator Smith insisted that he had no objection to "any Negro praying for me, but I don't want any blue-gummed, slew-footed Senegambian praying for me *politically.*" As he later embellished the story for the white folks down home, Smith said that as he left the convention, "it seemed to me that old John Calhoun leaned down from his mansion in the sky and whispered in my ear, 'You did right, Ed.'"

The attitude of such southern reactionaries as "Cotton Ed" Smith to the Democratic alliance with blacks indicates the last critical factor in the Depression-era association between liberalism and the quest for racial justice. Early in the Roosevelt administration, such vehement racists as Theodore Bilbo and John Rankin of Mississippi and Martin Dies of Texas supported the New Deal. But as southern fears grew that Roosevelt was moving toward the twin horrors of socialism and racial equality, racism and economic conservatism became intertwined. Southern conservatives combined red-baiting and race-baiting in their struggle against Roosevelt and his liberal economic policies. Charging that the President sought a second Reconstruction, southern racists created a climate in which racism was plainly identified with conservatism. For economic liberals, this provided one more incentive to come out strongly for greater equality between the races. Racism, particularly as it came increasingly to be associated with fascism and Hitler in the late thirties, was a powerful weapon to use against conservatives. In the 1930s, for the first time since the 1870s, reforms for blacks took their clear place on the liberal agenda. The groundwork was laid, but the "second Reconstruction" so dreaded by such conservative southern senators as Virginia's Carter Glass and North Carolina's Josiah Bailey would not come until a quarter century later.

Although obviously severely limited, the improvements for blacks during the Depression were discernible. In May 1935, as the "Second New Deal" was getting under way, President Roosevelt issued Executive Order 7046, banning discrimination on projects of the new Works Progress Administration. Discrimination continued, but the WPA proved to be a godsend for many blacks. In the later thirties, between 15 and 20 percent of the people working for the agency were black, although blacks constituted less than 10 percent of the national population. This, of course, was a reflection of how much worse off blacks were than whites, but the WPA did enable many blacks to survive. More than that, even minimum WPA wages of $12 a week were *twice* what many blacks had been earning previously.

Harold Ickes's Public Works Administration provided to black tenants a more than fair share of the public housing it built. The PWA went so far as to construct several integrated housing projects. PWA construction payrolls also treated blacks fairly. Some 31 percent of PWA wages in 1936 went to black workers. Ickes first made use of a quota system requiring the hiring of blacks in proportion to their numbers in the local work force. This precedent was followed again (at least in theory) by the wartime Fair Employment Practices Commission and in the civil rights legislation and court decisions of the 1960s and 1970s.

Other foundations were also laid in the New Deal for later victories in the civil rights movement. Roosevelt's Attorney General Frank Murphy created the Civil Rights Section in the Justice Department in 1939. Two years earlier, FDR appointed NAACP attorney William Hastie as the first black federal judge in American history. Robert Weaver, who had just completed a Ph.D. in economics at Harvard, was appointed in 1933 with Clark Foreman to advise the President on black economic problems. Almost a quarter century later, Lyndon Johnson named Weaver as the first black Cabinet member. Roosevelt himself was advised by a group of black leaders who came to be known in the press as his "Black Cabinet." It was, in fact, something considerably less than the name implied, but such an advisory group went far beyond anything any previous president had done in the area. By 1941 the number of blacks in regular (as opposed to WPA) government jobs exceeded their percentage in the population as a whole. But what may have been FDR's most significant legacy to the civil rights movement involved several white appointees. Seven of Roosevelt's eight choices for the United States Supreme Court were advocates of civil rights for blacks. (James F. Byrnes of South Carolina was the exception.) The Roosevelt Court set the stage for the Warren Court of the fifties and sixties.

The New Deal did more for blacks than provide hope for the future. There were measurable improvements at the time. Most telling was the increase in life expectancy at birth. During the 1930s this statistic rose from 63 to 67 years for white women, 60 to 62 for white men, 49 to 55 for black women, and 47 to 52 for black men. While blacks still trailed far behind their white counterparts in this key indicator of health and well-being, they narrowed the gap in the Depression years. The New Deal also helped bring about a drop in black illiteracy, from 16.4 percent at the beginning of the decade to 11.5 percent at the end.

Two well-known incidents late in the Depression symbolized both the gains blacks had made and how far they had yet to go. When, in March 1939, the Daughters of the American Revolution refused to allow black contralto Marian Anderson to give a concert in the organization's Constitution Hall in Washington, administration officials arranged for Miss Anderson to give a free concert at the Lincoln Memorial. An integrated crowd of more than 75,000 attended the event, and more than two-thirds of those asked in a nationwide Gallup poll how they felt about Eleanor Roosevelt's resignation from the DAR in protest over the organization's racist policy approved the First Lady's stand. Little more than a decade before, at the dedication of the Lincoln Memorial, blacks were segregated in a roped-off section across a road from white spectators. A notable change in white attitudes had taken place in the interim.

Less than two years after the Anderson performance, as American industry geared up for war production, A. Philip Randolph, the socialist president of the Brotherhood of Sleeping Car Porters, launched the March on Washington Movement (MOWM). The plan was to stage a massive black march on the capital to press for desegregation of the armed forces and equal opportunity in defense industries. The MOWM was, as historian Richard Dalfiume has said, "something different in black protest." The New Deal had begun a change in the American racial climate, but it had done so in such a way that blacks had been left dependent on whites in the government. Some blacks, like Randolph, were ready by 1941 to insist on doing things for themselves, on making their own gains. The New Deal approach, Ralph Bunche argued, was "in its very nature" a "defeatist attitude, since it accepts the existing patterns while asking favors and exceptions within them." The MOWM amounted to a public notice that some blacks wanted to stop asking for favors and start confronting injustice on their own. The threat of the march was sufficient to lead FDR to issue his famous Executive Order 8802, creating a Fair Employment Practices Commission to investigate charges of discrimination in defense-related industries. In exchange for this, Randolph agreed to call off the march. As it happened, the FEPC in World War II was not very effective and Randolph's militant approach declined. But another precedent had been set, and two decades later Randolph's March on Washington at last took place. Randolph was there to hear Martin Luther King, Jr., deliver his stirring "I Have a Dream" speech.

The rebirth of that dream of true racial equality, which had been crushed with the end of Reconstruction in the 1870s, was the real achievement of the New Deal years in race relations. The dream, of course, remained only that. Black expectations were raised and white liberals were enlisted in the cause. Little of substance had been accomplished by 1941 in bringing about equal rights for blacks, but the seeds of the Black Revolution of the fifties and sixties had been sown.[28]

9·Moral Economics: American Values and Culture in the Great Depression

V alues constitute a turf on which many historians feel uncomfortable. Values, though, as English social historian Edward Thompson has pointed out, "are not 'imponderables' which the historians can safely dismiss with the reflection that since they are not amenable to measurement, anyone's opinion is as good as anyone else's." Rather, values are the critical base on which any society rests. Such values build up over a long period of time, but they are far from being unchangeable. As circumstances change, so do a society's values. New values, however, do not arise out of thin air; they are grounded in the past experiences and beliefs of a people. Any society is likely to have several groups of values from which to choose in reaction to given historical circumstances. These sets of beliefs need not be consistent; their usefulness for dealing with different situations is partially dependent on their being at least somewhat contradictory. Finally, it should be noted that the fundamental beliefs of one segment of a society may differ substantially from those of another portion of the same nation. The values of farmers, for instance, might differ from those of city dwellers, those of one ethnic group from another, or those of industrial workers from those of their employers.

In traditional societies there has usually been a basic belief that economic arrangements should be based upon some concept of morality. One of the distinguishing marks of modern capitalism, on the other hand, has been the divorce of economics from ethics. Professor Thompson has noted that the adoption of the political economy that came to be associated with the name of Adam Smith, in the late eighteenth and early nineteenth centuries, "entailed a demoralizing of the theory of trade and consumption." Smith, who called himself a moral philosopher, advocated a laissez-faire approach because he believed it would produce the greatest benefits for all and so *was* moral. "No society," Adam Smith declared, "can surely be flourishing and happy, of which by far the greater part of the numbers are poor and miserable." Smith condemned "the mean rapacity, the monopolizing spirit of the merchants and manufacturers," who he said ought not be "the rulers of mankind." All of this, however, was quickly forgotten by apologists for the rapacious merchants and manufacturers. Such successors as David Ricardo and Jeremy Bentham quickly abandoned Smith's standard of morality. "Society to Adam Smith," Robert Heilbroner has noted, "was a great family; to Ricardo it was a bitter contest for supremacy." The marketplace came to be seen by most classical economists as a natural realm in which morality had no place. It was not *im*moral, but *a*moral. The results of the free play of the market might sometimes be harsh, but nothing could be done about it. The unrestricted marketplace was not *an* economic system; it was *the* economic system. One might as well try to regulate the weather as attempt to regulate the economy. Such meddling—even though well intentioned—could only make things worse.

It is a bit of marvelous historical coincidence that Smith's *Wealth of Nations* was published in the same year, 1776, that the United States declared its independence. This country has, for a variety of reasons, always been the preeminent home of laissez faire. As a "virgin land," America had from the first been seen as a place of opportunity to start over, without the evils of "decadent" European society. The settlement of the English colonies in North America in the seventeenth and eighteenth centuries coincided with the height of Western civilization's fascination with natural law and natural right philosophies. What better place to restore human society to harmony with the natural order than in the pristine New World?

Adam Smith's "invisible hand," as the economic counterpart of the natural order, was especially appealing to Americans, who already valued their "natural" existence. This view was so generally accepted in the new United States because property ownership was believed to be relatively widespread. If the hope existed (as it did in the minds of such American thinkers as Thomas Jefferson) that most men could become small property holders, then it would be possible to have an economic order that was basically fair but without significant government interference. Nineteenth-century American liberalism rested on this assumption. All the independent American needed or wanted was "a free field and no favor." "Equal rights for all; special privileges for none" was the Jacksonian refrain.

But if these beliefs were based upon the assumption of a wide distribution of productive property (and they *were* so based), how could they apply in an industrial society in which the ownership of productive property was becoming ever more concentrated? To late-nineteenth-century industrialists and their intellectual defenders, there seemed no problem. The system was the system. Individualism was the American way. Social Darwinism supplemented the doctrines of laissez faire (and completed the subversion of the connection Adam Smith had tried to make between laissez faire and morality). "On every ground and at every point," social Darwinist William Graham Sumner declared, "the domain of social science must be defended against the alleged authority of ethical dicta." This was fine for an emerging industrial and financial elite who wanted people to believe that their dominance was "natural," but what of the growing multitudes of propertyless workers? Did they continue to adhere to the standards of Smithean political economy while they suffered from its effects?

Until recently, it was believed that workers in this country accepted the dominant American values associated with individualism. Workers, many labor historians told us, were "wage and job conscious," they sought individual success, did not know the meaning of "enough," and like other Americans, worshiped at the altars of Adam Smith, Horatio Alger, and Andrew Carnegie, if not that of Herbert Spencer. The placing of such emphasis on individualism, I believe, is not so much incorrect as it is misleading.

Most Americans, workers included, have tended toward individualism. To say this, however, is to say very little, because individualism has meant different things to Americans of different classes and in different historical eras. The acquisitive, social Darwinian form of individualism so often associated with the businessmen of late-nineteenth- and early-twentieth-century America was not the individualism that held a place of primacy in the value system of American workers, at least not before the 1920s.

American workers in the period between the Civil War and World War I, labor historian David Montgomery has argued, developed and maintained "popular values antagonistic to acquisitive individualism." Labor reformers in the nineteenth century sought "to impose moral order on the market economy," Montgomery contends. They had a "revulsion toward the consecration of 'selfishness and individualism.'" Other recent labor historians have reached similar conclusions.

Yet to speak, as Montgomery and others do, of a "mutualist ethic" among American workers does not seem quite to hit the mark either. Surely most American workers have rejected the degree of collectivism implicit in that term. The difficulty lies in the juxtaposition of individualism and "mutuality." These are not either/or categories of complete egoism on the one hand and selflessness on the other. Rather, there is a continuum between these extremes. Too often, we tend to think that people must be *either* competitive *or* cooperative. As historian Lawrence Goodwyn has shown, the Populists of the late nineteenth century understood that humankind is *both* competitive *and* cooperative. Both tendencies can coexist within a single individual. Which takes precedence depends in large measure on external conditions.

The key to unlocking the puzzle of individualism versus mutuality is the concept of *independence*. A notion of common interests developed alongside the desire for independence among nineteenth-century American workers. The quest for independence was not rooted in simple acquisitiveness. American working-class values were based upon another sort of individualism: the belief that *each* individual, not just oneself, has rights to be respected; the belief that the measure of a policy or action is its effect on individual human beings, not its result on the balance sheet. Within this framework, workers could, like other Americans, seek success. They could even admire those who achieved it, but *only* if that success was achieved "fairly."

The individualism of American workers was not the amoral individualism of Bentham or Sumner. It was, instead, an individualism distinguished from selfishness. The line may seem a fine one, but the distinction is crucial. American workers sought independence and so were "self-reliant." But they believed as well in justice, equity, cooperation, and what Edward Thompson has called "human reciprocity."

The terminology I am using here is unlikely to be familiar to most readers, but I believe that these distinctions in value systems are essential to comprehending the Great Depression. I shall therefore try to make clearer what I am getting at. We all have our own personal interests and are concerned with our own well-being and our own ambitions. This is not the point. One can be an individual without being an individualist. Philosopher Sidney Hook made the distinction well in 1936 when he noted that Marxism "is hostile to individualism as a social theory, not to individuality as a social value." We can all subscribe to individuality as a social value; it is the social theory of individualism that American workers failed to accept fully. That sort of individualism is based on egoism, that is, the "regard to one's own interest as the supreme guiding principle of action; systematic selfishness." Just as individualism as a philosophy must be distinguished from individuality as a social value, so egoism as a philosophy should not be confused with an egotistical person. One can be personally self-centered to a high degree and still reject the philosophy of egoism. It is a question of whether one advances himself while considering the needs of others or ignoring them. "A good man's egotism," as Sir Charles Sherrington has put it, ". . . is altruism."

Similarly, the terms "amoral marketplace economics" and "moral economics" should be understood to apply to fundamental beliefs about the basis upon which economies ought to be organized. The terms have no necessary connections with personal codes of behavior. Those who believe in letting the unfettered market economy take its course may be very moral on a personal level; they may attend church regularly, be faithful to their spouses, and kind to dogs and small children. But when it comes to the overall operations of the economy, they insist that morality has no place, that nothing should be done to interfere with the "natural" and "impartial" workings of the marketplace. It is an idea as old as the American republic. In his *Federalist* Number 10, James Madison contended that "the rights of property originate" from "the diversity in the faculties of men," and "different and unequal faculties of acquiring property" lead to people possessing it in "differing degrees. . . . The protection of these faculties," Madison insisted, "is the first object of government." In the midst of the Panic of 1893, Charles Kendall Adams, president of the University of Wisconsin, told his students: "In a vast number, if not a majority of cases, suffering has come from improvidence, from extravagance, or from dissipation." Such a belief has been self-serving for most of those who have subscribed to it. They are the "winners," and if they believe that the economic game is being played by the proper rules—the *only* rules—they can be self-righteous about their own success and indifferent to the plight of the "losers." As F. Scott Fitzgerald pointed out, one of the worst characteristics of some among the upper classes is that they are "careless." They feel justified in holding the losers in contempt, in blaming them for their own problems, in telling them that they could find work if they really wanted to. Losers in a perfect, self-regulating system are, by definition, unworthy; they are not "truly needy."

One further caveat: I am not saying that *all* believers in laissez faire insist that morality has no place in economics. Some of them, including Adam Smith, would argue that this *is* moral economics. But most laissez-faire advocates since the early nineteenth century have contended that economics is a science—a "dismal" one, perhaps, but a science nonetheless—not a branch of moral philosophy. "Ordinary" folks have never been quite convinced of this.

Americans are basically pragmatic; as long as the marketplace seems to work, they go along with it. But it works to different degrees for different groups. It has been easy for those who have "won" in the marketplace to defend it as a perfect, self-regulating mechanism in which morality has no role. Those who have not succeeded, though, have clung to the notion that the ultimate justification for an economic policy must be rooted in its moral consequences. The "individualism" of workers has always had ethical and cooperative components, while the individualism of conservative business-men has tended to be amoral, acquisitive, and egoistical. This is not to say that poor working people are inherently "better" than the rich. The poor, like the rich, favor what is best for them. Cooperation can be mutually beneficial. A degree of cooperation and a government moved by compassion are in the interests of workers, much as acquisitive individualism and an unrestricted marketplace feed the self-interest of the successful. That each approach serves the interests of the group more likely to advocate it, however, does not mean that they are ethically equivalent positions. The self-interest of workers hap-pens to coincide with values of justice and compassion.

The interplay between the egoistical, amoral individualism of the owning class and the ethical individualism of most workers is essential to understand-ing many facets of American history. Workers in some periods could seek to gain independence by becoming individual proprietors, hence the emphasis of the Jacksonians on the interests of farmers and small businessmen. At other times, cooperatives appeared to be the best hope. The seeming paradox of the existence of so many cooperative movements—New Harmony, Oneida, the Fourierist and Shaker communities of the early nineteenth century, and the cooperative efforts of the Knights of Labor and the Farmers' Alliances of the late nineteenth century, to name a few—in individualistic America is resolved when we realize that ethical individualists could easily see coopera-tives as the best means of fairly advancing the interests of individual workers, of achieving independence.

American workers have always lived in a society in which they were con-fronted with a set of antagonistic values—those of the marketplace economy. These values were persistently pushed upon workers, since their acceptance of classical political economy and their belief in Alger-style success would keep the owning class safely in power (and since many in the owning class sincerely *believed* in these values).

Very broadly speaking, there have been two opposing sets of values in America. Both are individualistic; but one emphasizes cooperation, the other competition. The categories are far from absolute, but workers have tended to move toward cooperative individualism and businessmen toward acquisitive individualism. Aspects of American history can be illuminated by the realiza-tion that our vast middle class has been pulled toward one or the other of these poles, depending on the particular historical circumstances. During periods

of liberalism—such as the Progressive Era, the New Deal, and the 1960s—
the cooperative values have been in the ascendancy; during times of conservatism—the late nineteenth century is a good example—the acquisitive ethic
has dominated. Similarly, during times of relative prosperity, many in the
middle class have tried to emulate those above them on the social scale and so
adopted their values. The 1920s, 1950s, and 1970s are the leading examples of
such periods in the twentieth century. During hard times, on the other hand,
many in the middle class have identified with the working class. The significance of these general tendencies for the Depression decade is, of course, that
it was a time *both* of liberalism and of economic collapse.

But in the preceding decade, when prosperity combined with a swing of the
pendulum to the right, considerable headway was made—through advertising, installment purchase plans, a rising living standard, and a new emphasis
on consumerism—toward weaning workers from their traditional values and
remolding them into acquisitive, amoral individualists. "Observers were
struck," Irving Bernstein has written of the twenties, "with the materialism
that permeated all levels of American society, including labor; workers shared
with their bosses a devout reverence for the almighty dollar."[1]

The relative success of the "hard sell" of marketplace economics and mate-
rialistic individualism in the 1920s was based upon prosperity. The owning-
class values that had made gains among workers in that decade had their
material props slashed from beneath them in 1929 and subsequently. By the
early 1930s, it was plain to most pragmatic Americans that the marketplace
economy was not living up to its promises.

Often intellectuals find themselves at cross purposes with the popular
mood. So it certainly was for the American intelligentsia in the 1920s. They
condemned the materialism, egoism, and philistinism of a nation of "Bab-
bitts." Many American thinkers and writers in the twenties went so far as to
remove themselves from the society in which they felt so alienated.

The immense social and economic forces of the Great Depression, however, pushed intellectuals and common folk in similar directions. They rarely
met, but they traveled essentially parallel courses in the thirties. Intellectuals
and Depression victims alike criticized the effects of capitalism, although the
latter did not often use such explicit terms. The Depression rapidly undermined many old values and, for a time at least, the American Dream itself.
The economic collapse called, at a minimum, for a readjustment in values.
Some intellectuals in search of new values turned to an idealization of peasant
societies or regional agrarianism in the United States. More turned to the
legacy of Karl Marx. What they all had in common was a search for a life of
community and sharing, as opposed to the acquisitive individualism of modern industrial capitalism.

In the Cold War–McCarthy period, the decade of the thirties was known as the Red Decade. The image originated, in fact, at the time. In 1934 publisher William Randolph Hearst launched what he hoped would be a new Red Scare. He sent spies onto university campuses to ferret out "red" professors and believed he found them at New York University. Hearst also worried about reds in Washington, charging that the Roosevelt administration was "more communistic than the communists." The year 1934 also saw the appearance of a strange book called *The Red Network* by Elizabeth Dilling. It made its contribution to the cause by listing some 1300 red conspirators, ranging from the predictable Eleanor Roosevelt to the startling Mohandas Gandhi and Chiang Kai-shek. Taken together, the charges of Hearst, Dilling, and other "100 percent Americans" in the mid-thirties made the anti-Communist crusade laughable.

But it was not yet over. In 1938 the House of Representatives created a Special Committee on Un-American Activities. The intent of most of those voting to establish the committee appears to have been to investigate the activities of American fascists and Nazi agents in the United States. Committee chairman Martin Dies of Texas, however, was not worried about fascists. He was interested only in the actions of Communists and New Dealers, categories that he saw as largely indistinguishable. Such fascist groups as the Silver Shirts, the Ku Klux Klan, and the Knights of the White Camelia were soon applauding the work of a committee originally intended to investigate them.

In 1941 the title of a book written by Eugene Lyons, *The Red Decade*, kept alive a distorted notion of America in the Depression. In the Cold War climate of the late 1940s and 1950s, the belief that Communists were prominent in the New Deal, as well as on college campuses and in CIO unions, spread widely. As McCarthyism grew in the early fifties, views of the role of Marxism in Depression America became even more distorted. Liberals and defenders of the New Deal felt constrained not only to show that the Roosevelt administration was not riddled with Communists, but also that the New Deal was not influenced by Marxism and that *they*, the New Deal liberals, were fully cognizant of the Communist threat. Thus the three volumes of Arthur Schlesinger's otherwise admirable *The Age of Roosevelt* written in the 1950s suffer from a Cold War mentality that seeks to escape the condemnation of the remnants of McCarthyism. Schlesinger allows that there was an "undue complacency about Communism" in the United States in the late thirties. In a chapter entitled "Growth of a Conspiracy," he says that "the Communist conspiracy" was "a great potential danger to American democracy."

Such assessments greatly overstate the "threat" of Soviet espionage in the thirties. Surely such activities did exist, but there was nothing approaching a dangerous conspiracy. More serious than the overestimation of the conspiracy, though, is the denigration of the importance of Marxist ideas in the decade. In reference to the thirties' radical intellectuals, Schlesinger says: "All shared a profound conviction that, though Karl Marx might have been a formidable social thinker, Marxism in general . . . [was] irrelevant to the United States." This assertion is mistaken. With the exception of some CIO unions, the influence of the Communist party itself was never very great in Depression America, but Marxist *ideas* were very important; indeed, they played a significant role in advancing the cooperative values of the period.

Many American intellectuals were attracted to "Marxism" in the thirties, but there was little agreement over precisely what that meant. Even before the purges of the later thirties and the Nazi-Soviet Pact of 1939, few Americans approved of Stalinism. Some joined the Communist party or at least endorsed its candidates. In September 1932, fifty-two writers, critics, and professors, including Sherwood Anderson, Erskine Caldwell, Malcolm Cowley, John Dos Passos, Theodore Dreiser, Waldo Frank, Granville Hicks, Sidney Hook, Langston Hughes, Lincoln Steffens, and Edmund Wilson, signed an open letter indicating their support for Communist presidential candidate William Z. Foster. The Communists, critic Edmund Wilson said admiringly, "are people who are willing to die for a religion." But few prominent American intellectuals could long tolerate the requirements of the party. Like most of their countrymen, they found the Communists too dogmatic, too authoritarian, and, perhaps, too foreign. Many American intellectuals did like Marxism, though, for its emphasis on class conflict, its explanation of the crises of capitalism, its call for action and personal commitment, and its (at least in their view) moral condemnation of acquisitive individualism. To a considerable extent, Marxism in Depression America was in the eye of the beholder. Each intellectual refashioned the ideas of Marx as he wanted them and then liked what he created.

The Great Depression seemed to many intellectuals who had long been estranged from American bourgeois society a wonderful opportunity to develop new values. Before the Crash, writers were already deeply disturbed by the paradox of technological improvements making conditions worse for large segments of the population. "The better we are able to produce," Stuart Chase wrote in *The New Republic* early in 1929, "the worse off we will be. This is the economy of a mad-house." The Depression confirmed what many intellectuals had been saying for years: an economy built upon acquisitiveness and competition was destructive economically, socially, and psychologically. Samuel Schmalhausen, the associate editor of the Marxist journal *Modern Quarterly*, wrote in 1932 that the American economic system had made a "fetish of individualism," leading to the "dominance of the ego in the affairs of men." The result was a "sick" society. In the early thirties, many among the intelligentsia agreed with him. Capitalism, Sidney Hook maintained, had made man "the basis of society, not social man, but egoistic man." The old economic system, Hook insisted, degraded people and ideas alike "by setting a cash value on them."

The Depression led many intellectuals into believing that some sort of social and ideological apocalypse was at hand. In this sense, it was a thrilling time to be alive. The old world was collapsing and the chance was there to take a hand in molding a new one. The American Dream had turned into a nightmare. Progress, always a central icon in the American secular faith, no longer seemed viable. As they rejected the greed and materialism they associated with American capitalism, scores of leading thinkers turned to Marx for a possible new value system. Marxism was "in the air" in intellectual circles in the thirties, and its spirit was in harmony with the values developing among much of the general public. Intellectuals of all persuasions had to acknowledge the importance and apparent relevance of Marxist thought to the Depression. Marxist vocabulary was in common usage among the thinkers and writers of the decade. Marxists, after all, had predicted the economic collapse and had an explanation for it. Moreover, the Depression left many people feeling that they were being buffeted by powerful forces beyond their control. This lent credibility to the Marxist concept of determinism. Marxism seemed to many in the American intelligentsia of the thirties to support their own moral condemnations of the marketplace economy and to uphold the values of community, justice, and cooperation that so many writers of the period favored.

The goal was, as progressive historian Charles Beard put it in 1935, the "subordination of personal ambition and greed to common plans and purposes." For some (fortunately, not many) as the American Dream faded, it was simply a matter of replacing it with the Russian Dream. The Soviet experiment came to be seen in some quarters as another Puritan "City Upon a Hill." But Joseph Stalin was ill-cast as John Winthrop. Most Americans attracted to Marx soon concluded that they must follow the advice of Edmund Wilson and "take Communism away from the Communists." Marx must be "Americanized."

Through articles in such popular liberal journals as *The New Republic* and *The Nation*, in a host of little magazines—including *Partisan Review, Common Sense, Science and Society, Modern Quarterly, Symposium,* and *Miscellany*—and in their books, such intellectuals as Sidney Hook, Edmund Wilson, John Dewey, Philip Rahv, Lewis Mumford, Robert Lynd, Max Eastman, and Reinhold Niebuhr attempted in the thirties to blend parts of Marxism with the best of the American liberal tradition. They were appalled at the values of the marketplace economy that took away "all sense of social responsibility" and led the individual, in Mumford's words, to "compensate by egocentric getting and spending for the absence of collective institutions and a collective aim." But collectivism to these men did not mean the dissolution of the individual into the mass. On the contrary, Dewey, Hook, Lynd, and others saw socialism as a way to provide the economic security necessary for people to be truly free to express their individuality. Sidney Hook, historian Richard Pells points out, saw Marxism "as a natural extension of ideals that had their roots firmly in the liberal tradition." The intellectuals called for what Niebuhr referred to as "equal justice" and a redistribution of wealth and income to the "disinherited." But they wanted to maintain a large degree of freedom as well.

In all these respects, the leftist intellectuals were basically in tune with the values of the public and the aspirations of the New Deal. Franklin Roosevelt often employed the same class-oriented rhetoric and symbols that the leftists used. The intellectuals were calling for a liberal socialism while FDR was offering a social liberalism. There *were* important differences, but ordinary folks could be forgiven for having difficulty telling them apart and taking what they could get. Both sets of beliefs, after all, were grounded in the moral economic value system that became dominant in Depression America. [2]

Ethical themes were abundant in the letters of Depression victims. "I am in great distress and want," a California man wrote to the President in 1934. "I realize that in the United States, there is enough for all, but on account of selfishness and greed, some are getting, while others are not." "How people can sit down at a banquet and enjoy themselves when millions are going to bed hungry is more than I can understand," said one of Mrs. Roosevelt's correspondents. "Some Gets any thing they want and Some None," a Kansas man complained in a 1934 letter to one of his senators. "[A]ll i want is a square deal," he continued, "i dont want it all Give Every Body a Chance to live Some Lay money up and some going Hungry." "This nation could be made an ideal place to live," a Minneapolis man wrote to Eleanor Roosevelt, "if every one would work together for the common good of every one instead of for selfish purposes." "How about the person who has" been generally unemployed for years "and the one who has had steady, regular employment all the time at a good salary, changing places for a while?" an unemployed Arkansan suggested to Harry Hopkins in 1935. "It seems fair that all get <u>some</u> of the pie."

Specific complaints people made in their letters to the Roosevelts and to government officials often indicated the same resurgence of values based on equity and fairness. This was clearly the case with the common protests concerning the injustice of giving clerical and administrative jobs in relief agencies to those who could "afford to buy fur coats, spend their money on fancy clothes and worthless items of luxury." These positions should instead be "filled by men and women who need the money for their families and their homes." A Nebraska WPA worker wrote Hopkins in 1936 that "it is the rich and not the poor that get the jobs. We are just as capable of doing the work as they are and maybe do the work and not be uptown all hours of the day."

In addition to complaining about who got the good jobs in relief agencies, many workers objected to "higher-ups" being paid too much. "Can't some of these high salaries be cut just a wee bit so the Money allocated for salaries will be more evenly divided," an Ohio "House Wife" asked the President in 1935. "F.D.R. you arprobated [appropriated] it for us Workers. And we want it and are protesting to you," wrote a group of Birmingham WPA workers. "No one is getting the Money but the bosses formons and head mens We workers are not getting it every turn we hafter loose and the big mens gaines." "The big mens are taking it all for them selves," they continued. "You have arprobated it for us where do it go[?]"

Several of the Depression survivors Studs Terkel interviewed in the 1960s recalled a spirit of cooperation among the poor. "A lot of times one family would have some food," Mary Owsley said. "They would divide. And everyone would share." Her daughter, Peggy Terry, expressed the same idea: "But there was a feeling of together." "Black and white, it didn't make any difference who you were," Louis Banks said of hoboes in the Depression, "'cause everybody was poor. All friendly. . . ." And Kitty McCulloch remembered giving away her husband's best suit "to a man who had such shabby clothes." Her husband, she explained, "had three other suits and he didn't have any. So I gave it to him."

That such sentiments were widespread was confirmed by early scientific opinion polls. Nearly 60 percent of the poor questioned in a 1935 *Fortune* survey said that the government should not "allow a man who has investments worth over a million dollars to keep them." (It is not surprising that almost 70 percent of the "prosperous" believed that such wealthy individuals should be left alone.) In the fall of 1937 more than 42 percent of the poor in another *Fortune* poll said that "the federal government should follow a policy of taking money from those who have much and giving money to those who have little." When those who favored such a program "if it doesn't go too far" are included, more than 64 percent of the poor endorsed redistribution.[3]

The Depression-bred values evident in letters and opinion polls were strikingly reflected in the popular culture of the 1930s. This is a realm that has attracted serious historical study only in quite recent years. Further, it is an area in which it may seem difficult to find much convincing evidence about a society's values. Assuming that it is possible to isolate such underlying themes in a movie, book, or song, what does it tell us? Perhaps it provides information about the beliefs of the director, author, or lyricist; but many of us are understandably hesitant to draw conclusions from mass culture about the culture of the masses. Pete Seeger made the point well when he told me, paraphrasing his father, "Music can be made *for* people, *for* the working class, by Tin Pan Alley; and movies can be made *for* the working class by Hollywood. But when it comes to songs made *by* the working class, then you have to look a little harder in this mass production age." Such questions are easier to deal with for an earlier time. Folk culture clearly came from the folk and can more readily be accepted as conveying the values of the segment of the society from which it arises.

Popular culture must be used cautiously in any attempt to get at popular values. But if the same sorts of beliefs and attitudes that are found in the statements, actions, and votes of people in a given historical context emerge repeatedly in the popular entertainment of the day, additional confirmation of those values has been found. Such was decidedly the case in Depression America.

Although music, radio, books, magazines, comics, sports, and other forms of mass entertainment were all significant in the thirties, nothing else was as central to American popular culture in that decade as motion pictures. There are good reasons for concentrating attention on Hollywood. Movies were *the* preeminent form of popular culture in the 1930s. Almost everyone who could afford to (and millions who could not) went to the cinema frequently throughout the decade. During the depths of the Depression in the early thirties, an average of 60 million to 75 million movie tickets were purchased each week. Although part of this remarkable figure represented repeat customers, the number itself corresponds to more than 60 percent of the entire American population. (This compares to a number of weekly movie admissions by the late 1970s equaling less than 10 percent of the population.) Hollywood made more than 5000 feature films during the 1930s. Up to a point, film producers had to reflect changes in popular attitudes. They were guided by the profit motive and so had an incentive to give moviegoers what they wanted to see. Many contemporaries were convinced that film was the most powerful medium of the time. Immediately after the stock market crash, for instance, New York Mayor Jimmy Walker asked movie operators to "show pictures which will reinstate courage and hope in the hearts of the people." If any form of popular culture can shed light on a people's values, surely the Depression-era cinema is the most likely candidate. My perceptions are based on a study of nearly 150 films of the period, including many of the most popular and significant ones.

The most common impression about movies in the Great Depression is that they served as escapism. Depression victims—and those who feared they might soon be such—could pay their dime or quarter and forget the troubles of the real world for a few hours. Of course this is true. It is undeniable that movies provided a temporary escape for millions during the Depression. But they did far more than that. It was, as Arthur Schlesinger, Jr., has rightly said, a time "When the Movies Really Counted," when they were "near the operative center of the nation's consciousness."

In his history of the films of Depression America, *We're in the Money,*

Andrew Bergman insists that the movies of the period served to reinforce the success ethic and values of what I have here termed acquisitive individualism. "Dehumanizing competition," Bergman contends, was glorified in most thirties films. The only exception he finds is King Vidor's *Our Daily Bread* (1934). That film glorifies life on a collective farm and favorably portrays the whole idea of cooperative living. Bergman is right in singling out *Our Daily Bread* for its powerful plea for cooperation and even collectivism, but I think he is quite wrong in suggesting that most films made during the Depression carried a message extolling the virtues of competitive individualism. On the contrary, movie audiences were able to take away from many thirties productions reinforcement of the moral economic values that they were developing on their own.

The first—and most enduring—of the popular genres of the Depression years, the gangster film, makes the point clearly. These movies have generally been taken to have represented one of several viewpoints. Bergman argues that they provided a vehicle for the traditional American story of individual success. Robert Warshow, on the other hand, in his highly perceptive 1948 essay "The Gangster as Tragic Hero," maintains that the ultimate message of the gangster film is that in modern, individualistic, success-oriented society "there is really only one possibility—failure." The gangster, many critics have pointed out, is a figure with whom audiences identified, particularly in the early Depression years. "[T]he gangster speaks for us," Warshow says, "expressing that part of the American psyche which rejects the qualities and demands of modern life, which rejects 'Americanism' itself."

The criminal must either represent the American success ethic or its rejection. We cannot have it both ways. Or can we? "We gain the double satisfaction," Warshow points out, "of participating vicariously in the gangster's sadism and then seeing it turned against the gangster himself." The gangster "is what we want to be and what we are afraid we may become." This insight provides the key to understanding how the public perceived the gangster movie in the early Depression. Americans have always had a love/hate attitude toward individual success. On the one hand, we have a burning desire to succeed; on the other, we despise the successful man who steps on others to get ahead. This amounts to a different way of stating the conflict between the competing American value systems: acquisitive individualism *versus* cooperative or ethical individualism. In a period like the 1920s, the worship of success takes precedence; but in the Depression many Americans concluded, as Warshow put it, "the successful man is an outlaw."

The prototype of the early thirties gangster genre—and its most important example—was *Little Caesar* (1930). Contrary to the popular assumption that the gangster is a film character with which the audience identifies, the central character of this film, Caesar "Rico" Bandello (Edward G. Robinson), is anything but sympathetic. His goals are to make money and, even more, to "be somebody," to be in a position to tell others what to do. Rico destroys anything and anyone who stands in the way of his advancement. He is the epitome of the self-centered, acquisitive man, one who will use any means of "competition" to eliminate (often literally) his rivals. In short, Little Caesar stood in the eyes of early Depression audiences (the movie was released in January 1931) as the symbol of the amoral, greedy businessman. For those who may have missed the connection, Rico makes it explicit as he arrives in the upper reaches of crime: "Yeah, I ain't doin' so bad in this business, so far," he tells his associate. The equation of crime and business was one that Depression viewers appreciated (so much so that in 1933 critic Dwight MacDonald called *Little Caesar* "the most successful talkie that has yet been made in this country").

The message Depression-era audiences were likely to carry away from *Little Caesar* was quite the opposite of reinforcement of the individual success ethic. The film could instead be seen as an implicit condemnation of the amoral marketplace values that dominated the preceding decade. In his drive for the top, Rico has no truck with compassion or human values. "Love, soft stuff!" he says disgustedly to his friend Joe Masara. Rico realizes that the man on the make cannot be soft; he must be able to "dish it out" and "take it." Rico's collapse (like that of American business) is even more rapid than his rise, and begins because of his insistence that Joe must come back to work with him. Although Rico says "this is what I get for liking a guy too much," his real motive was to control Joe and protect himself. Selfishness, not friendship (despite the homosexual undertones in the movie), leads to Rico's demise. As he dies in a shootout—beneath a billboard announcing Joe's success as a performer—Caesar utters his famous last words: "Mother of Mercy, is this the end of Rico?" The obligatory end for the gangster has arrived. The prophecy at the film's outset, where Matthew is quoted ("For those who live by the sword shall also die by the sword"), seems fulfilled. What is often overlooked, however, is that Little Caesar never quite reached the top. One step above him was the head of the city's criminals, appropriately called Big Boy. ("I never saw anybody the Big Boy couldn't get to," says Little Arnie Lorch. "He can fix anything. That's why he's the Big Boy.") The audience— or at least that part of it that noticed—was left with the message that the biggest gangster of them all continues to thrive. The implications for the "big boys" of the economic system in the thirties was apparent.

The same sort of implicit attack on the amoral methods of acquisitive individualism was evident in other films of the early Depression. Chester Morris, the central character in *Corsair* (1931), wants to show his girlfriend that he is "as good a businessman" as her father, who is a stockbroker. To do so, he becomes a pirate! Chester sums up the view of business ethics that was rapidly gaining acceptance in these years: "It doesn't matter how you make your money, it's how much you have when you quit."

But all gangsters in the movies were not alike. If Robinson's Rico was not the sort with whom the viewer was likely to identify, the same could hardly be said of James Cagney as Tommy Powers in *Public Enemy* (1931). Here is the other side of the ambivalence toward the anarchic criminal figure. Viewers could identify with Powers not only because Cagney portrayed a more likable fellow than did Robinson, but because the Cagney character was not entirely self-centered. Powers and another character, Paddy Ryan, are obviously "good" mobsters. "Nobody can do much without somebody else," Ryan says. There is some indication in the movie that Tommy became a criminal because of societal injustice, although this is not explored. In any event, Tom Powers believes in "justice" of a sort—in honor among thieves. He does not go around killing people for fun. (Rico usually had some small reason for his murders, but he obviously enjoyed them.) In the end, Tom is sorry for his life of crime. The sharp contrast with Rico is evident in Powers's dying words: "I ain't so tough." Just so. That is why we like him so much better than Rico. Unlike Little Caesar, Tom Powers is not the completely ruthless reflection of the acquisitive businessman stereotype. The moviegoer was able to take vicarious enjoyment when someone like Powers, with his ultimate sense of justice, "stuck it to" a society that had seemingly become so unjust.

Gangsterism in the early thirties was not, of course, a phenomenon confined to the silver screen. Popular attitudes toward real criminals paralleled the feelings evoked by movie mobsters. Even if they would not admit it, many people identified up to a point with the real gangsters they read about in the newspapers. It was not, however, brutality and selfishness that the public was approving. The popular mood found it agreeable to romanticize the criminals, to see them as social bandits who robbed bankers and gave to the poor. Seeing Depression criminals as Robin Hoods was best exemplified in Woody Guthrie's 1939 song "The Ballad of Pretty Boy Floyd." Guthrie's mythicized Floyd had been unjustly accused of crime and had gone on to become a folk hero:

> There's many a starving farmer the same
>   old story told
> How the outlaw paid their mortgage and
>   saved their little home.

Guthrie's closing verses made the point that many others left unarticulated in their romanticizing of criminals:

> Yes, as through this world I ramble,

> *I see lots of funny men,*
> *Some will rob you with a 6-gun, and*
>   *some will rob you with a pen.*
> *But as through your life you'll travel,*
>   *wherever you may roam,*
> *You won't never see an outlaw drive*
>   *a family from their home.*

In point of fact, few Robin Hoods were roaming the American countryside in the Depression. Floyd, "Baby Face" Nelson, John Dillinger, Bonnie Parker and Clyde Barrow, and the rest were cold-blooded murderers, largely devoid of the human sympathies some observers like to find in them. It must be realized, though, that people who identified with them were making them over in the social bandit image. Their minds created what they wanted to see and then admired it. The songs about the bandits survived, as Eric Hobsbawm has noted that they traditionally did with social bandits in peasant societies. Those songs allowed people to maintain the myths and "the vision of the just society."

Movies could also deal with issues similar to the Guthrie version of how Pretty Boy Floyd became an outlaw because he was wrongly accused. *I Am a Fugitive From a Chain Gang* (1932) is one of the most powerful films of the period. The hero of this Mervyn Le Roy movie, James Allen (Paul Muni), returns from the World War determined to find a better life than his old job as a shipping clerk in a shoe factory. He does not want a job like his life in the Army, being under orders, working in routines. Rather, Jim wants "a man's job"—an expression frequently used to convey the idea of self-respect and independence: "I've learned that life is more important than a stupid, insignificant job." Jim takes to the road seeking an engineering position, but is able to find only occasional employment. Finally he becomes desperate and tries to hock his war medal, but finds a case in the pawnshop is already filled with them.

Jim meets Pete, another "bum," who tells him he knows where they can get some free hamburgers. Jim's real troubles begin when Pete unexpectedly pulls a gun on the diner's proprietor and forces Jim to join in a robbery. Showing no concern for the circumstances, a judge sentences Jim to ten years at hard labor. The action takes place in an unspecified southern state (although scarcely anyone has an accent), and Jim finds himself on a chain gang. On the surface, *I Am a Fugitive* is an effective attack on the horrors of chain gangs. On a slightly deeper level, it carried a more important meaning to Depression audiences. The prison becomes an exaggerated vision of society. Innocent people are treated brutally. The regimented life from which Jim wanted to escape in the Army and factory is even worse in prison. "You even have to get their permission before you can sweat," another inmate tells Jim. While those in power are cruel and unreasoning, the victims show concern for each other and cooperate as much as they can. An older man, Bomber, advises Jim on how to escape and gives him $7, which it took him years to accumulate. Sebastian, a black prisoner, helps Jim bend his shackles. Muni himself presents a more sympathetic character than he had a few months earlier in his more noted role as the Capone-like leading man in *Scarface* (1932).

After his escape Jim (now calling himself Allen James) becomes a 1920s success story, rising Alger-style in a Chicago engineering firm. His only mistake is to fall into the clutches of a "loose woman" who finds out about his past and threatens to expose him unless he marries her, which he does. Finally, after he asks for a divorce, she turns him in. Because Allen has become such a pillar of the community, all of Chicago comes to his defense and the governor refuses to allow extradition. Then an official of the southern state arrives and promises Jim a full pardon if he will voluntarily return and serve ninety days of easy time.

The state goes back on its promise and Jim is outraged: "The state's promise didn't mean anything! It was all lies! . . . Their crimes are worse than mine, worse than anybody's here. They're the ones who belong in chains, not me!" Jim finally escapes again. Now he symbolizes all Depression victims, desperately searching for any kind of work, a social outcast. He constantly feels hunted, and when he returns to Chicago to see the woman with whom he had fallen in love earlier, Jim hears a noise and, believing the authorities are after him, takes his leave. As his face fades, the woman asks, "How do you live?" From the dark comes a hoarse whisper: "I steal!" And the movie *ends*. No other thirties movie has an ending so cold and depressing. *I Am a Fugitive* was the perfect expression of the national mood in 1932: despair, suffering, hopelessness. Few movies have ever represented a year so well. Le Roy's film *was* 1932: hopelessness. America had hit bottom.[4]

The change that the New Deal brought in the nation's mood, its restoration of hope, was clearly paralleled in Hollywood's productions. If the Hoover years had been reflected in the horror and gangster films, in 1932's *I Am a Fugitive* and Tod Browning's *Freaks*, the spirit of the early New Deal was evident in the new popular movies of 1933. It was *the* year of the musical.

In *Gold Diggers of 1933*, the Depression hits show business. As a rehearsal is going on, with the cast singing "We're in the Money," a sheriff comes in to close down the show. The film's story is of the planning and production of a new show, a musical about the Depression. It seems that hard times might be overcome by singing about them. Brad (Dick Powell), the man who supplies the money for the show, turns out to be a member of a wealthy banking family that disapproves of popular music and show people. The film does not indict the rich as a class; rather, it says that their values are wrong. The upper social classes are portrayed as prejudiced, foolish, and believing that money can solve all problems: "Everyone has a price." The story is extremely contrived. Brad's nasty rich brother softens and three aristocrats wind up marrying show girls and, we assume, living happily ever after. The movie concludes with a remarkable attempt by extravagant choreographer Busby Berkeley to make a social statement. As marching World War I soldiers are converted into jobless men "marching" on a soupline, Joan Blondell sings:

> *Remember my forgotten man,*
> *You put a rifle in his hand,*
> *You sent him far away,*
> *You shouted, "Hip Hooray!"*
> *But look at him today.*

If the connection with the New Deal and its restoration of hope were not entirely explicit in *Gold Diggers*, it hit people over the head in another 1933 musical. In *Footlight Parade*, Jimmy Cagney plays a Broadway producer who, as he puts it in song, hears the breadline calling. The salvation from that breadline is made clear in the movie's closing number. Cagney and Ruby Keeler hold up cards showing first the NRA's Blue Eagle, then the warm "nothing to fear" smile of FDR. The other enormously successful Warner Brothers musical of 1933, *42nd Street* (which was chronologically the first of the three), is less precise in its reference to Roosevelt, but shows the almost magical hopes of 1933: Chorus girl Ruby Keeler miraculously learns the leading role in the fictional show *Pretty Lady* in only five hours after the star breaks her leg. Ruby is, of course, a huge success and shuffles off to Buffalo as a new star. The mood here is a far cry from *I Am a Fugitive*, a year before. This sort of optimistic nonsense could not have been sold to audiences in 1932. After the New Deal restored hope, *42nd Street* became the third largest money-maker of 1933.

It is undeniable that the backstage musicals of the New Deal's first year served principally as a means of escape from the worries of hard times. Cultural historian Richard Pells has noted that Busby Berkeley's colossal dance numbers seem like "monuments to collectivism—with their hundreds of anonymous boys and girls, their utilization of massive choruses and gigantic orchestras, rather than soloists and small combos, their faultlessly mechanical precision. . . ." Yet it seems unlikely that many moviegoers carried this message away from his productions, even subconsciously. Instead, the musicals lifted spirits and held out hope for better times. In this regard, they represented Roosevelt's first year almost as effectively as *Fugitive* did Hoover's last year.

Another film reflection of the new optimism of the Hundred Days was far more ironic. Walt Disney was an arch-conservative. His enormously popular 1933 cartoon *Three Little Pigs* was probably intended to be a call for a return to the virtues of Horatio Alger and Calvin Coolidge. But when it was released two months after Roosevelt's inauguration, *Three Little Pigs* seemed to fit in perfectly with the rising optimism of the New Deal. Particularly appropriate to the new President's theme of overcoming fear of the Depression was the cartoon's song, "Who's Afraid of the Big Bad Wolf?" People who suddenly believed that they could defeat the wolf made the song a big hit.[5]

The thoughtless optimism of the musicals and Disney's pigs made the movies of 1933 distinctive. The feelings of optimism trailed off in succeeding years, but faith in Roosevelt remained high. Films in the mid- and later thirties moved more deeply into social problems and the values of Depression America. Several modern critics have argued that Hollywood became in those years the guardian of traditional American values. Most such assessments are made in a tone of disdain. This is based on a misconception of "traditional American culture." There was not, as I have said earlier, *a* traditional American culture, but a variety of values that often contradicted one another. The values that dominated movies in the New Deal years were *not* those of acquisitive individualism.

Hollywood's view of government changed drastically after the New Deal commenced. Whereas government had appeared in early gangster films as inept and, on the state level in *I Am a Fugitive*, as oppressive and evil, the post-1933 film vision of the federal government became extremely favorable. The Feds were now righteous and benevolent. Lawmen had never been the heroes in the movies of the Hoover years. But by the mid-thirties, the very stars who had been criminals a few years before jumped over to the "right side of the law." Edward G. Robinson was transformed from the grasping Little Caesar into a double-agent cop who destroys the gang he joins in *Bullets or Ballots* (1936). In *G-Men* (1935), erstwhile public enemy James Cagney becomes an FBI hero. And Humphrey Bogart, while still frequently playing the bad guy in later thirties movies, popped up in *Crime School* (1938) as a reforming deputy commissioner of corrections.

But if the early Depression view of government had undergone a metamorphosis, the same could not be said of the film portrayals of businessmen, greed, and the rich. If anything, the Hollywood vision of these people and attitudes became more unfavorable. The association of such portrayals with the New Deal was clear. Sometimes it was explicit. In *The President Vanishes* (1934), a president who begins his radio speeches with the familiar, "My

Friends . . . ," declares that "our struggle is against the forces of selfishness and greed." The 1935 MGM production of *A Tale of Two Cities* is true to Dickens in showing Sidney Carton's ultimate selfless sacrifice; it is also chock-full of statements showing the inhumanity and selfishness of the rich and of businessmen, for example: "I am a businessman, think of me as a machine"; "There is no room for sentiment in business"; "There is a sickness today that is called humanitarianism"; "Hunger is an indulgence with these peasants, as the gout is with us"; "What I get from these peasants is barely enough to pay my perfume bill."

The ultimate in the depiction of the values of the Depression is approached in Howard Hawks's morality play *Barbary Coast* (1935). It is not a great film, but it is a crystal-clear rendering of the values of the thirties. Edward G. Robinson as Louis Chamalis is evil incarnate, a mid-nineteenth-century San Francisco version of Rico. As his men are about to wreck the presses of a newspaperman who wants to expose him, Chamalis says: "This is business." When asked why he killed a man, Louis matter-of-factly replies, "for business reasons." On the opposite side is Joel McCrea as James Carmichael, a lover of poetry and people, representing good. Robinson and McCrea contend over the heart of Mary Rutledge (Miriam Hopkins), who represents society, as women so often do. She arrives in San Francisco motivated by greed and is taken in by Chamalis to run a rigged roulette wheel in his gambling house. He calls her "Swan," and as such she is greedy. But, predictably, Hopkins has become good Mary again by the last reel. In a completely selfless act, she offers to stay with Louis if he will let Carmichael, whom she now loves, go. Even Robinson has been at least partially won over to the good values, how-ever, and as he is taken into custody by vigilantes, he tells her to go ahead with McCrea.

Dead End (1937) was one of the more extraordinary productions of the decade. It starkly portrays the life of the urban slum dweller and the contrasts between rich and poor. Two kids who grew up together on the Lower East Side have taken different paths. "Babyface" Martin (Humphrey Bogart) grew up to big-time crime. He has killed eight men. Dave Connell (Joel McCrea) went to college for six years and became an architect, but is unable to find a job. When Babyface returns to the neighborhood and learns of Dave's situa-tion, he says he's glad he "ain't a sap" like him. Babyface is the embodiment of the primitive egoistical business ethic that dominated the 1920s. He tries to teach the local kids how to fight dirty against rival gangs. When the kids say that would not be fair, Babyface is incredulous: "Fair! What's fair? When you fight, you fight to win; and it don't matter how." Clearly, *Dead End*, like so many other thirties movies, was reinforcing viewers' opposition to self-centeredness.

But there is more to *Dead End* than most films with a similar message.

Unlike such earlier productions as *Public Enemy,* for instance, it squarely places on society the responsibility for people "going wrong." Dave complains that people like Babyface, who were once good kids, are labeled "enemies of society." "Well, what do they have to be friendly about?" he asks. After Dave winds up in a fight with Babyface and shoots him, a policeman informs Dave that he will get a large reward. "You mean they'll pay me for it?" he says in a tone of disgust, indicating that society was responsible for making Martin a criminal and now is willing to pay to eliminate him. As an architect, Dave Connell has an answer: build a new society, eliminate the slums and the social conditions that breed crime and make good kids go bad. McCrea was a drastically different leading man from Robinson's Rico. The New Deal–style social consciousness of *Dead End* was evident in many thirties movies: *The Great O'Malley* (1937), *Angels With Dirty Faces* (1938), and the aforementioned *Crime School* (1938), to name a few.[6]

Two Depression-decade directors stand out as the leading examples of those who glorified the traditional, moral American values and condemned the amoral spirit of the marketplace. Since their films have attracted so much attention and are often used by those who charge that American movies in the New Deal years were performing the conservative function of reestablishing the myths of American individualism, it is instructive to analyze the works of Frank Capra and John Ford.

Early in the thirties, Frank Capra achieved great success with comedies in the "screwball" genre. The most notable of these was *It Happened One Night* (1934), which remains the only film ever to win all the major Academy Awards. Andrew Bergman notes in his history of thirties films that the "whackiness" in such films "cemented social classes." Screwball comedy, he says, "was implosive; it worked to pull things together." Up to a point, he is right. In *It Happened One Night,* a down-and-out newspaper reporter (Clark Gable) meets a runaway heiress (Claudette Colbert). Initially separated by their vastly different class backgrounds, the two go through a series of whacky episodes together and fall in love. In the end, her father advises her to forget her planned marriage to another rich man and go off with Gable. Surely there was nothing "class conscious" about such films. To dwell on this obvious fact, however, is to miss the point. Few would make the preposterous argument that rich people are inherently evil. What is far more important than social background is the set of values a person embraces. Most screwball comedies ridiculed not the rich *per se,* but their *values.* And they were often quite effective. The "implosion" that typically took place at the end of such movies consisted of the rich man abandoning his wicked, selfish ways and adopting the values of the "ordinary" people.

Yet there is a critical difference between Capra's films in the first half of the decade—the true screwball comedies—and his later movies. *It Happened One Night*, like *Lady for a Day* (1933), depicts kindhearted people of wealth and power making possible fantastic endings. Capra soon altered his course, claiming that a man who visited him criticized him for not making movies that would serve "God's and humanity's purposes." For the rest of the Depression, Frank Capra tried to meet this challenge. The point of such productions as *Mr. Deeds Goes to Town* (1936) and *Mr. Smith Goes to Washington* (1939) was plain. The rich are powerful, as they were in the earlier movies, but they are no longer screwy, kind, and wonderful. On the contrary, they are the forces of evil, standing in the way of the people and their will. Some among the wealthy might be salvaged, but most were likely to remain opposed to the common people and common decency. There were still cases of the rich being good in the end, but now they began as ruthless, grasping plutocrats who had to be reformed—as in the case of Mr. Kirby (Edward Arnold) in *You Can't Take It With You* (1938). And it happens only because he abandons his old, self-centered values and adopts those of cooperation.

Capra equated traditional, rural American culture with goodness. The moral, naive common man—Gary Cooper as Mr. Deeds or James Stewart as Mr. Smith—is the hero, and the cynical, greedy urban businessman is the villain. But it was not quite as simple as it seemed. Capra did not contend that the "masses" or the "ordinary" people were automatically right. On the contrary, especially in *Mr. Smith*, it is clear that the common people can be misled by the forces of evil. While Capra generally indicated that good would prevail, there was nothing certain about it. In fact, the famous climax of *Mr. Smith* is ambiguous, but perhaps a bit more believable than the conversion of the plutocrat in *You Can't Take It With You*. The convert to what is right in *Mr. Smith* is the corrupt Senator Paine (Claude Rains), not the truly sinister businessman, Jim Taylor (again Edward Arnold). Perhaps Taylor would have converted, too, after the film ended, but that seems unlikely. Rather, the messages *Mr. Smith* left with viewers were that good *could* triumph, but there was no certainty of it; that evil businessmen were still at large, and that if people wanted to achieve a more democratic society, they would have to continue to struggle toward that end.

This was powerful stuff. Few people are unmoved by Senator Smith's corny call for "plain, ordinary, everyday kindness, a little looking out for the other fella, loving thy neighbor." Sentimental, to be sure, but *not* conservative. Anyone who has seen the affirmative reaction of an audience of college students in the 1980s to the climax of *Mr. Smith* cannot doubt the effect on Depression-era moviegoers. The response of modern students is an indication of the existence of a reservoir of humanitarianism below the surface of our culture, even in the cynical age of "looking out for number one." That underground spring was bubbling at the surface during the Depression. Capra's films were a reflection of it, not its cause.

Frank Capra was one of the few leading directors of the later Depression who dealt with contemporary subjects. He reached into the revered past for the names—and characters—of his heroes (Longfellow Deeds, Jefferson Smith); the action, though, was in the present. John Ford, on the other hand, frequently set his stories in the American past.

Ford's liking for the American past and its mythical values is evident in *Stagecoach* (1939), a western that clearly reflected the values of the Depression. The characters aboard the stagecoach appear to be evil—an alcoholic physician, a gambler, a prostitute, an outlaw—but they all prove to be just, humane, compassionate people. The one character who is not a basically fair and benevolent person is, significantly, a selfish banker. Ellsworth Henry Gatewood, the banker, sounds like a spokesman for the Liberty League or the Republican party of the thirties. "And remember this: What's good for the banks is good for the country!" Gatewood exclaims as he steals $50,000 from his own bank. "America for Americans! . . . Reduce taxes! The national debt is shocking!" the crooked banker declares in additional obvious references to the 1930s rather than the late nineteenth century in which the film is set. "What this country needs is a businessman for president!" Gatewood concludes. All of this is in sharp contrast to the values of the prostitute, Dallas (Claire Trevor); the outlaw, Ringo Kid (John Wayne); and Hickok, the whiskey salesman, who speaks of the need to practice "Christian charity, one for the other." In the end, Ringo and Dallas are "saved from the blessings of civilization."

In 1940, Ford addressed contemporary social problems directly by bringing John Steinbeck's *The Grapes of Wrath* to the screen. Although of course not as comprehensive or powerful as the novel, the movie does a remarkable job in presenting the moral economic values of the era. The values of compassion and sharing are evident repeatedly, as in the incident at the truckstop where the proprietor, waitress, and truck drivers all sacrifice to help the hungry Joad family—without letting the Joads know they are helping them. Tom Joad's statement before he takes leave of his mother sounds almost like a verse from the Earl Robinson–Alfred Hayes ballad "Joe Hill." "Well, maybe like Casy says, a fella ain't got a soul of his own, but on'y a piece of a big one—an' then it don' matter. Then I'll be all aroun' in the dark. I'll be everywhere—wherever you look," Tom tells Ma. "Wherever they's a fight so hungry people can eat, I'll be there. Wherever they's a cop beatin' up a guy, I'll be there. . . ." The evils of egoism and the benefits of cooperation are repeatedly emphasized.

The final "social" film of the Depression was Ford's *How Green Was My Valley*, which won the Academy Award as best picture in 1941. The adaptation of Richard Llewellyn's novel is a beautiful and stirring document of working-class culture. The differences between the values of the Welsh coal miners and their employers are made plain. Mr. Morgan remarks that the mine owners will not take advantage of a surplus of workers to cut wages "because the owners are not savages. They are men, too, like us." One of his sons responds: "Men, yes, but not like us. . . . They have power and we have none." The answer, he says, is "a union of all men." At another point in the film, Ianto denounces clergymen: "You make yourselves out to be shepherds of the flock and yet you allow your sheep to live in filth and poverty. And if they at times raise their voices against it, you calm them by telling them their suffering is the will of God. . . . Are we sheep to be herded and sheared by a handful of owners?"

Different messages might be carried away from such films, but they plainly were rejecting the ethic of acquisitive individualism. In both *The Grapes of Wrath* and *How Green Was My Valley*, Ford was quite openly pleading for a society based more on cooperation. Yet some recent social critics have contended that Ford, as one of them (Richard Pells) puts it, "turned out to be the most conservative" director in the Depression era. Similar complaints have been raised about Frank Capra, of whom Pells says, "His was a faith more suited to the individualism of the nineteenth century than to the collectivist dreams of the 1930's." Such assessments are, I think, based upon two fundamental errors: the assumption that new is automatically better than old, and a misunderstanding of at least one meaning of "conservatism."

The former fallacy is an ironic one for a critic of American society to fall into. Scarcely anything, after all, is more American than the equations new = good and old = bad. The popularity of *The Grapes of Wrath* in both its forms, Professor Pells says with more than a little sadness, showed that among the American people there was "some deep yearning for the world as it had been rather than as it might become." This misses the most crucial point. The yearning for the world as it had been—or as people liked to believe it had been—*was* the expression of hope for what it might become. Radical, revolutionary, and reform movements have often been based upon a myth of a "golden age" in the past. When in *How Green Was My Valley* Huw says: "It makes me think of so much that was good, and is gone," the viewer is likely to feel sadness, but the film also builds up anger that the good life of yesterday has been destroyed. The result can be an increased desire to change things. In such ways, the myths of the past become the agenda for the future. This is to say that it was precisely because the myths about American culture *were* myths that they served a progressive rather than a reactionary function. People looked backward to see in front of them.

The longing for an imagined golden age, for a feeling of security, for an identity, was evident in the thirties quest for a sense of place. As Professor Michael Steiner has pointed out, four of the five top-selling novels of the Depression decade—*Gone With the Wind* (1936), *God's Little Acre* (1933), *The Good Earth* (1931), and *The Grapes of Wrath* (1939)—dealt with the search for security in history or on the land. (The fifth book, Dale Carnegie's 1937 volume *How to Win Friends and Influence People*, certainly goes against the grain of the analysis offered here, and this may be a useful place to remind the reader that no claim is being made that *everyone* abandoned the mores of acquisitive individualism during the Depression. "Success" and "self-help" books were plentiful during the Depression, and 750,000 copies of Carnegie's volume were sold in its first year.) The past, like the ownership of a piece of land, offered a refuge for people distressed with the present and fearful of the future. A "sense of continuity with generations gone before," John Dos Passos wrote in 1941, "can stretch like a lifeline across the scary present."

At first blush, films that provided such a sense of continuity certainly appear to have been performing a conservative function. But they were not. Robert Sklar hinted at the reason when he wrote that the young film producers of the thirties were "more deeply entwined with the values not of the American marketplace, but of traditional American culture." The values that filmmakers emphasized were those of an older America, of returning to the cooperative portion of the paradoxical mixture of values in the American culture. Surely there was little in the films of the Depression (except, of course, in *Our Daily Bread*) that pushed collectivism. But there are, fortunately, more than the two options of "rugged individualism" or collectivism. What was evident in the films of Capra and Ford, as well as in many other Depression-era movies, was a call for a kind of cooperative individualism that recognized individuals could achieve a degree of independence and self-respect only by cooperating. "The 1930's," as historian Warren Susman has rightly said, "was *the* decade of participation and belonging." There was a realization that "sticking together" was the way for ordinary people to keep from being oppressed. This was certainly very different from the Herbert Spencer–Ayn Rand sort of individualism, but it was the only way for most people to achieve meaningful independence. Through cooperation, working people did not become totally "free." Rather, they became interdependent. Such a state restored one's dignity and differed fundamentally from dependence upon people who were in a position to dominate. The last word on the Depression's emphasis on cooperative individualism may have been a remark made by Danny Jordan (George Brent) at the end of *Racket Busters*, a less than outstanding 1938 film: "You know, Nora, I've learned one thing from Pops in all this business: People like us, in order to make it, we gotta stick together."[7]

Evidence of many different types points to the conclusion that Americans during the Depression were returning to a set of values at variance with those of amoral individualism and the marketplace. But this shift was not evenly distributed across the American population. The working class appears to have been most imbued with cooperative values, but they also were clearly spreading along with the economic distress among the middle class. Most of the well-to-do, however, appear to have continued their adherence to the amoral marketplace.

On one ethical issue after another, national polls in the thirties indicated that workers favored compassionate government policies. To cite but two examples: In 1935, 89 percent of the poor in a *Fortune* poll said they believed "the government should see to it that every man who wants to work has a job." A plurality of the prosperous in the same survey rejected the idea. In 1936, 74 percent of the people polled in another national survey for *Fortune* favored free, government-supported medical and dental care for those unable to pay.

Such national findings were dramatically confirmed in local in-depth studies of attitudes. For example, a 1936 survey of the attitudes of 600 Chicago residents found a marked "tendency for the middle income group to agree with the lower group on questions pertaining to the present distribution of wealth and influence," a *Public Opinion* article reported. Two of the questions represent the trend. To the inquiry, "Are the things that wealthy businessmen want the government to do usually best for the country as a whole?" 80 percent of the wealthy responded yes; only 20 percent of the lower income group and 23 percent of the middle-income group answered that way. When the 1936 Chicago sample was asked, "Do businessmen and people of wealth have too much influence in running the affairs of the nation?" 80 percent of the lower- and 69 percent of the middle-income people said yes; only 7 percent of the wealthy agreed.

The Chicago study, along with a similar one in Akron in 1938–39 that I discuss in Chapter 13, and evidence from national polls and letters, shows that during the 1930s the values of moral economics were moving up the status ladder (or, perhaps more accurately, many members of the middle class were slipping down that ladder and coming to see their interests as being similar to those of laborers). As one of Mr. Roosevelt's correspondents put it in a 1936 letter, "If you will insist on a tax program that will <u>actually</u> redistribute the enormous and ill-gotten fortunes of this country, the plain people and the middle classes will <u>certainly</u> be with you." The values of moral economics seem to have emerged among a majority of Americans only when distress touched a sufficiently large number of people that it could no longer be ignored. In the apt metaphor used by columnist Ellen Goodman, suffering had reached a "critical mass."[8]

None of this is meant to suggest in any simplistic way that workers were "good guys" with only altruistic impulses and owners were greedy, evil people. Undoubtedly, many workers accepted the amoral values of classical political economy; certainly many of them had in the 1920s. It is equally certain that some in the owning class favored an economy in which morality played a larger role. The points are that the interests of the two classes were divergent and the Depression made the interests of working-class Americans more apparent to them and led many in the middle class to identify with those below them. We are speaking, in any case, of tendencies, not absolute groupings, and the tendency of the lower and middle classes toward a value system different from acquisitive individualism is clear.

Most working- and middle-class Americans in the Depression were not socialists in any strict ideological sense, but certainly they were leaning to the left. All this talk about morality, fairness, equality, humanitarianism, compassion, and moral economics is, admittedly, rather amorphous; but that is how it is with popular values. They do not constitute a coherent ideology. Ideology among those who are not professional intellectuals is like vermouth in a good martini. A hint of it is essential, but too much will spoil the result.

Americans in the 1930s may not have known much about ideology, but they knew what they liked—and what they did *not* like. Their rejection of greed, egoism, and the unfettered marketplace led them toward values through which they could "remoralize" the American economy and society.

10 · Thunder on the Left: Rising Unrest, 1934–35

T he combined effects of the Depression itself and the New Deal programs on American values were profound. The "moral
economic" values that we saw in the last chapter represented far more than an undercurrent
in the mid-thirties. Particularly in 1934 and
1935, they became visible in many ways at the
surface of events. Although Franklin Roosevelt
had ridden the upsurge of egalitarian-human-
itarian values with great skill and had, in fact,
helped shape those popular currents, the flood

tide of demands for economic morality now threatened to submerge the President. Demands that the New Deal move further and more rapidly to the left arose from many quarters in 1934 and 1935. Among the most prominent sources of rumblings of discontent were the factory workers themselves.

The decline of unionization in the face of strenuous employer opposition during the prosperity decade had only been accelerated by the Depression. By early 1933, union membership had dipped to 2 million, down from a high of 5 million thirteen years earlier. Throughout the decline, the American Federation of Labor had refused to take account of the changing technology that made laborers into something closely resembling the interchangeable parts of the assembly lines on which they worked. The majority of workers in mass production industries were no longer skilled, but the AFL continued to cater more to the declining number of craftsmen than to growing legions of mass production workers.

As it always does, widespread unemployment caused a further drop in union membership. A 1933 letter written by Oluf, a friend of Russell Baker's mother, explained why workers could not think about unions, high wages, or better working conditions in hard times: ". . . the War is over with, the good times is over with, them days we did seat a Price on ourself, but to day we just take what we can get and must be satisfact . . . ." But section 7(a) of the National Industrial Recovery Act, with its putative guarantee for collective bargaining rights, provided new hope for effective organization. With the few exceptions noted earlier, however, that hope was dashed by early 1934. It was clear by then that few employers would allow unionization without a struggle. Yet 7(a) along with the New Deal in general had kindled a new spirit among many American workers. The smoldering coals burst into flame in 1934. Nearly 1.5 million workers took part in some 1800 strikes in that year. In some places the growing class conflict reached the point of open warfare. In several struggles unemployed workers joined picket lines. Previously, employers had been able to count on the needs of the jobless to induce them to become strikebreakers. It now seemed that a new class feeling was emerging.

Minnesota was one of the most progressive states in the union during the 1930s. It was under the administration of the avowedly radical Governor Floyd Olson and the nation's most successful third party, the Minnesota Farmer-Labor party (about which more shortly). Yet Minneapolis remained in 1934 an open-shop city. The Citizen's Alliance, an employers' association, reigned supreme. The city's balance of power shifted in the summer of 1934. Led by a group of Trotskyite organizers, a Minneapolis local of the International Brotherhood of Teamsters won a bloody class battle. The victory was attained despite the employers' persistent red-baiting, the strong opposition of the Teamsters' national officials, and the brutal violence of the local police.

The Minneapolis strikers prevailed because the city's working class displayed a remarkable degree of solidarity. But it was not a cheap victory. In one battle alone, two workers were killed and sixty-seven were wounded. Many of the casualties were shot in the back. The bosses were playing for keeps, but so were the workers. They killed two members of a "Citizen's Army" that the employers organized. Two years earlier at Dearborn and Washington, working people had allowed the representatives of the owning class to assault them. Now the workers were ready to fight back. An important change in attitudes had taken place.

Bloodshed helped solidify the ranks of Minneapolis workers. When one of the slain laborers was buried, some 100,000 people, including almost all of the city's organized workers and many middle-class residents, marched in the funeral procession. "Minneapolis truck drivers," it was reported, "would just as soon crack a cop as drink a beer." At one point in the struggle the police abandoned the downtown area and strikers took over the direction of traffic. Wealthy residents began to flee or dig in for the revolution they believed to be starting. In the end, the workers pressured Governor Olson to help win the strike. After an attempt to play both sides, Olson agreed to allow only genuinely essential goods to be transported. This action finally forced the employers to surrender. When news of the settlement reached the workers, they filled the city's streets in a twelve-hour victory celebration.

The victory was well worth celebrating. The workers of Minneapolis had shown what a combination of class solidarity and class politics could achieve. The Minneapolis Central Labor Union had voted its support for a general strike. Almost all unions and a vast majority of the city's workers had been united. Furthermore, some 5000 relief workers, as well as several thousand unemployed members of the Council of Workers, had joined the picket lines. Facing such a united working class, and lacking the accustomed backing of state military forces, the Minneapolis employers had little chance of winning.

The general strike that was partially carried out in Minneapolis occurred full-fledged in San Francisco in 1934. It began among one of the most exploited groups of workers in the city—the longshoremen. Here again, conservative national leaders were repudiated by a union's militant members. The West Coast members of the International Longshoremen's Association (ILA) were so wary of their leaders that they held a rank-and-file convention early in 1934. No paid officer of the union was permitted to be a delegate. The workers fixed their goals and passed a resolution requiring a full membership vote on all future agreements. To further show their distrust of the union officials, the members suspended the president of the San Francisco local of the ILA for being "too conservative." Thus reorganized, the longshoremen early in May struck all ports on the West Coast, effectively closing most of the 2000 miles of shoreline. Only in Los Angeles did strikebreakers make a significant dent in the shutdown.

The employers had no intention of giving in. Large numbers of strike-breakers were imported. The scabs were safe enough on the protected docks. But striking longshoremen "patrolled like vultures" along the waterfront. When they caught a strikebreaker they kicked out his teeth and then laid his leg across a curb and jumped on it.

The San Francisco longshoremen unanimously rejected an agreement the employers had persuaded the all-too-cooperative Joseph P. Ryan, president of the ILA, to sign. The city's owning class then resorted to an old-fashioned Red Scare. Ignoring the unanimity of the laborers, businessmen blamed the trouble on Communist agitators. In the climate of 1934 such charges moved California laborers no more than those of Minnesota. Instead, the maritime workers, almost all of whom had joined the walkout, chose as chairman of their Joint Marine Strike Committee a previously unknown longshoreman named Harry Bridges. Bridges then, as later, faced constant charges of being a Communist. There is little evidence that he ever belonged to the party, but certainly he never hesitated to associate with Communists. Association was sin enough for the employers, but the workers of 1934 in San Francisco could not have cared less. Bridges spoke their language.

The owners resolved to break the strike by force. A major battle was fought on July 5. Like a football game between Stanford and California, it attracted a large crowd of spectators. Refreshments were sold. Belying the carnival atmosphere, however, the entire San Francisco police force was on hand at the waterfront. The curious dispersed quickly when the shooting started. Workers swarmed into the area by the thousands. People fell in the streets, horses ran over them, blood spattered on buildings and pavement, skulls were cracked by nightsticks. Two workers were shot to death. And yet the laborers fought on as if their future depended on the outcome. To a large extent, it did, since the defeat of the strike would have left the longshoremen vulnerable to continued severe exploitation.

Although the workers greatly outnumbered the police, their rocks and bolts could not match bullets and tear gas. The strikers finally had to retreat. "We cannot stand up against police machine guns and National Guard bayonets," Bridges admitted. Still, the laborers refused to give up. The strike committee called for a general strike. The city's labor council, dominated by conservative leaders, approached the idea gingerly. But working-class sentiment for a general strike was overwhelming, as was soon demonstrated at the funeral for the two dead laborers. The procession showed, one reporter observed, how false was the authorities' claim that "everybody was against the longshoremen's strike except a group of radicals." "After the parade had started," he declared, "no one with eyes could doubt that the masses of people were for the strike and defended it." By the time the general strike began on July 16, almost every union in San Francisco had voted to join the walkout. Many had done so unanimously. Bay Area workers had come to see themselves as a class apart from their employers, with interests held in common.

Many San Francisco businessmen welcomed the general strike as an opportunity for totally smashing the city's labor movement. "This strike is the best thing that ever happened to San Francisco," exclaimed one such stalwart. "It's costing us money, certainly. . . . But it's a good investment." Some were fearful, however. One man on the scene offered Roosevelt aide Marvin McIntyre his "guess" that "the leading citizens of San Francisco probably have their wives out of town, and some of them are penned up in the Club which is up on the Hill." He thought, in short, "that the thing [was] . . . pretty much out of hand."

The strike was remarkably effective. A journalist described the city on the first morning of the shutdown: "No street cars were operating, no buses, no taxis, no delivering wagons except milk and bread trucks which were operated with the permission of the general strike committee. No filling stations were open, no theatres, no shops." Many small storekeepers showed that elements of the middle class identified with the workers' goals. Signs appeared in the windows reading: "Closed Till the Boys Win." The only places where food could be obtained were nineteen restaurants that the strikers ordered to remain open for their own feeding. San Francisco was paralyzed.

Class feeling ran high on both sides, but there was no more widespread violence. The general strike had been staged in part to protest the official violence of the preceding weeks. With mass nonviolence working so well, labor had no cause to resort to force. Nor, on the other side, could the police and National Guard be certain of a victory over such mass protest. Only federal intervention could have changed the picture, but Roosevelt did nothing, and the owners held back their forces.

As it happened, the leadership of the general strike had passed from Bridges and the militant Joint Marine Strike Committee to the conservative Central Labor Council. Old-line San Francisco labor leaders had not been so foolish as to resist their members. They had gone along, reluctantly, with the general strike and their positions gave them the leadership. On July 19 the Central Labor Council voted by a narrow margin to accept a government arbitration plan. The general strike ended. Now it was the militant longshoremen who had to go along. Their courage, though, was rewarded three months later when the National Longshoremen's Board reached a settlement very favorable to the union. The ILA gained almost complete control over the hiring halls on the waterfront, which had been the key issue.

The outbreaks in Minneapolis and San Francisco were only the most dramatic episodes in a widespread class confrontation. The message was clear. Roosevelt had given workers hope; they did not intend to let the President, businessmen, or even their own union leaders stand in the way of fulfilling that hope.[1]

* * *

Similar messages were reaching Washington along different frequencies. The 1934 elections have generally been seen as a great mandate for the New Deal. Democrats won 26 of 35 Senate races that year, raising their lead over Republicans in the upper chamber to 69–25 (there were also one Farmer-Laborite and one Progressive). Roosevelt's party increased its strength in the House of Representatives from 313 to 322, while Republican membership dropped from 117 to 103. Progressives won 7 seats and Farmer-Laborites 3. This was the only time in modern American history that the party holding the White House improved its standing in Congress in an off-year election. Republicans were reduced to 26 percent of the Senate seats and less than 24 percent of the House membership. Several prominent New Deal opponents were crushed, sometimes by previously obscure Democrats, such as Harry S Truman in Missouri. "A record number of votes for an off-year election . . . ," *The New York Times* declared, had "literally destroyed the right wing of the Republican Party."

In most respects the *Times* was correct in calling the 1934 results "the most overwhelming victory in the history of American politics." But that victory was not wholly an endorsement of Roosevelt's policies up until that time. Certainly the vast majority of voters demonstrated their preference for the New Deal over conservative Republicanism. When that was the choice, as was the case in most of the 1934 contests, the New Deal usually emerged victorious. But a closer look at some results from that year indicates that the electorate may have been giving its blessings more to economic morality than to the New Deal *per se*. In several states voters were given an opportunity to "send a message to Washington." In those states and localities where the electorate was presented with a realistic alternative to the left of Roosevelt, the response pointed to a growing desire to see the New Deal move further toward a more equitable distribution of wealth and income.

The congressional elections in 1934 saw victories by some thirty-five men who were clearly to the left of the President. Among them were Maury Maverick of Texas, Vito Marcantonio of New York, Ernest Lundeen of Minnesota, and Tom Amlie of Wisconsin. In New York City, Fiorello La Guardia, a nominal Republican with socialist leanings, had already been elected mayor in 1933. And across the nation in the state of Washington, a group favoring a production-for-use economy, the Commonwealth Builders, elected both of the state's United States senators, one each in 1932 and 1934, three congressmen, and nearly half of the state legislators. In Utah the Reform Taxpayers' League, a group advocating redistribution of wealth, dominated the legislature. Other states also showed signs of a trend to the left, but in three—Wisconsin, Minnesota, and California—the desire for policies more advanced than those the New Deal had thus far offered was unmistakable.

Wisconsin had for thirty years been the most socially progressive state in the

nation. The major symbol of Wisconsin progressivism had been the elder
Senator Robert M. La Follette. Except for his third-party presidential campaign in 1924, La Follette and his supporters had remained within the Republican party. After the senior La Follette's death in 1925 his two sons, Robert,
Jr., and Philip, asserted hereditary claim to the leadership of Wisconsin progressivism. Young Bob had taken his father's seat in the Senate. Phil had been
elected governor in 1930, but was defeated in the 1932 Republican primary.
His defeat was the result of a massive switch of Wisconsin's discontented into
the Democratic and Socialist parties. The Grand Old Party was by this time
plainly associated with the name of Herbert Hoover rather than with Bob La
Follette and Teddy Roosevelt. Between 1930 and 1932 the number of Democratic votes in the state leaped from 17,040 to 131,930 and the Socialist ballots
from 11,569 to 31,836. Rank-and-file progressives had abandoned the Republican party. But two more years passed before the La Follettes followed the
lead of their constituency. Then, in the spring of 1934, they formed the
Wisconsin Progressive party.

On many points, the Progressive party supported the New Deal. Yet it was
plainly on the left fringes of the Roosevelt coalition. Bob La Follette outlined
his economic and social views in 1932. "I am not interested in trying to maintain the status quo in our economic life," the young senator declared. "Devices which seek to preserve the unequal distribution of wealth now produced
will halt the progress of mankind and, in the end, will retard or prevent recovery." "We have created a great industrial mechanism," La Follette continued. "It must be run so that its benefits will be more generously and widely
distributed." More like his father than the calm Bob, Phil La Follette was an
active champion of the people. In his first term as governor, between 1931 and
1933, Philip La Follette proposed several schemes, such as unemployment
compensation and farm loans, that foreshadowed the New Deal. The 1934
Progressive platform denounced the existing economic system, with its "cruelty and stupidity."

The new party evoked immediate enthusiasm among the people of Wisconsin. Within less than one month 120,000 citizens had signed petitions to
place it on the state ballot. This was some twelve times the number of voters
needed for the purpose. Many old party politicians had thought the collection
of so many signatures in such a short period of time would be impossible. The
massive support for the Progressives soon convinced President Roosevelt to
put one foot on the bandwagon. FDR endorsed Bob La Follette for reelection
to the Senate, but opposed Phil's bid to regain the governorship.

Bob La Follette's reelection to the Senate was no contest. He carried 66 of
Wisconsin's 71 counties, winning over 50 percent of the vote in 43 of them,
against three opponents. Phil, however, was thought to have little chance of
winning. Many voters were said to believe he was a bit "too full of ideas."

More importantly, Roosevelt was backing Phil's Democratic opponent. This seemed an insurmountable obstacle, but when the ballots were counted Philip La Follette had won back the governor's chair.

The governor's radical rhetoric increased rapidly following his 1934 victory. "We are not liberals!" Phil exclaimed. "Liberalism is nothing but a sort of milk-and-water tolerance. . . . I believe in a fundamental and basic change." "I am a radical," Governor La Follette insisted. "There is no alternative to conscious distribution of income," he declared in 1935. At his inaugural he had said, "It is essential that we recognize the fact that this American principle of popular government, and the constitutions conceived to secure it, were not designed to sustain any particular economic system."

It is true, as Arthur Schlesinger, Jr., has noted, that Phil La Follette's "mood was more radical than his program." But that mood meshed with the attitudes of Wisconsin's working people (and the values of many Americans elsewhere). The governor's radical rhetoric helped persuade the Wisconsin Socialist party to merge into the Progressive party in 1935. La Follette's move toward the left combined with Socialist support resulted in a dramatic increase in urban votes for the governor in 1936. His statewide margin of victory grew in that year, but the sharpest increases were in the urban counties with high concentrations of laborers. When Wisconsin workers were given the option of voting for a "major" party (the presence of the La Follettes made any party major in Wisconsin) to the left of the New Deal, they supported it rather than Roosevelt's Democrats. These discontented Americans did not abandon the President, but their enthusiasm for the "radical" La Follettes leaves little question about which direction they wanted FDR to take. [2]

The Minnesota Farmer-Labor party rose in the early 1920s out of a popular tradition of radical politics in the state. It added urban laborers to the farmers on whom such earlier groups as the Populists and the Non-Partisan League had depended. In so doing, the new party managed to elect two men to the United States Senate during the twenties. Floyd Olson, a Minnesotan who had grown up in poverty, gone to the University of Minnesota Law School, and become county attorney of Hennepin County (Minneapolis) in 1920, was the party's unsuccessful gubernatorial candidate in 1924. By 1930 the Depression ripened conditions for an Olson victory. He was elected governor by an outright majority in a three-way race. After he took office the nation's first Farmer-Labor governor did little to push advanced social or economic programs. Although Olson believed that a growing desire for change existed, he thought it wise to avoid a sharp turn to the left until the people demanded it. But at some point during Olson's wait for the people to catch up to him, they passed him. In order to avoid being turned out of office by discontented voters, the governor had to regroup in 1932.

In the Farmer-Labor platform for that year, Governor Olson sought to rejoin his constituents by moving to the left. The platform declared that capitalism was "on trial for its life," but did not yet convict the system. The specific planks were considerably more progressive than those in the Democratic national platform on which Franklin Roosevelt ran in the same year. Olson's 1932 rhetoric was also to the left of Roosevelt's. In one 1932 speech the governor said capitalism was "steeped in the most dismal stupidity." When conservatives in the state senate held up Olson's relief bills, the governor issued a direct threat. "I shall declare martial law," he warned. "A lot of people who are now fighting the measures because they happen to possess considerable wealth will be brought in by the provost guard. They will be obliged to give up more than they are giving up now," Olson declared. "As long as I sit in the governor's chair, there is not going to be any misery in the state if I can humanly prevent it." "I hope," Olson told a wildly cheering crowd, "the present system of government goes right down to Hell."

The governor's prestige increased as he became more open in his criticism of the economic system. One conservative newspaper unhappily concluded in April 1933, "Floyd B. Olson is the idol of the hour. He can do no wrong." The Minnesota governor mixed endorsements for some of Roosevelt's policies ("A lot of things that used to be called socialism") with criticism of the New Deal for not going far enough. If anyone still doubted Olson's radicalism by early 1934, the governor removed those doubts in his most famous speech. At the Farmer-Labor party's convention in March, Olson gave the keynote address. "Now I am frank to say," he declared, "that I am not a liberal. I enjoy working on a common basis with liberals for their platforms, etc., but I am not a liberal. I am what I want to be—I am a radical. I am a radical in the sense that I want a definite change in the system. I am not satisfied with tinkering, I am not satisfied with patching, I am not satisfied with hanging a laurel wreath upon burglars and thieves and pirates and calling them code authorities or something else." "When the final clash comes between Americanism and fascism," Governor Olson told the enthusiastic delegates, "we will find a so-called 'red' as the defender of democracy."

The mood of the 1934 Farmer-Labor convention meshed with Olson's speech. The delegates adopted a platform that bordered on socialism. Although Olson later backed away slightly from the tone of the platform, there is no doubt that the people of Minnesota went to the polls in November 1934 believing that their choice was among Republicans, Democrats, and radicals. Olson won, and did especially well in working-class areas.

Following his reelection, Olson continued his constructive criticism of FDR's programs, but he suggested that what was needed was "not just a new deal, but also a new deck." Olson toyed for a time with the possibility of a third-party presidential campaign in 1936. The Minnesotan, however, was

not on friendly terms with some of the other likely participants in the formation of a new party. When asked in 1935 about a national third party the
following year, Olson said: "I think I'm a little too radical. Maybe I'll run for
the Senate next year." "How about 1940?" the interviewer asked. Olson
grinned and replied, "Maybe by then I won't be radical enough." The Minnesota governor did consider a Farmer-Labor presidential campaign in 1936
premature. He criticized some "ritualists and leftists" who, he said, wanted to
elect a leftist president "before they even have one Labor alderman in New
York!"

Whatever Olson's plans, he soon met an enemy more formidable than any
politician. Cancer first slowed Olson's pace in 1935, then killed him at the age
of forty-four in August 1936. Although Olson's death was a great disappointment to the downtrodden in Minnesota, the Farmer-Labor party did not ex-
pire with him. On the contrary, 1936 saw the party achieve its greatest
electoral successes. Minnesota Democrats withdrew from the gubernatorial
contest in return for Farmer-Labor support of Roosevelt. Elmer Benson, the
Farmer-Labor candidate for governor, crushed his Republican opponent by
nearly 250,000 votes, more than a 2–1 margin of victory. Nor can this landslide easily be attributed to the Farmer-Labor alliance with Roosevelt. In
twenty-seven counties, including Hennepin (Minneapolis), Benson ran
ahead of the President.

The 1936 Farmer-Labor sweep of Minnesota saw Ernest Lundeen join
Henrik Shipstead in the Senate, party members win five of nine House seats
(and lose another by less than 400 votes), and Farmer-Laborites win all but
one statewide office. Taken together, these results indicate that while most
Minnesotans supported President Roosevelt in the mid-thirties, many of them
wanted more drastic change than the New Deal was producing.[3]

The same message emanated from California in 1934. There another political path open to those who wanted meaningful change was tried. Instead of
forming a third party, discontented Californians took over the Democratic
party.

Novelist Upton Sinclair, a Socialist most of his adult life, was persuaded by
a group of Democrats to change his registration to their party and try to win its
gubernatorial nomination in 1934. Sinclair had run for the office twice before, both times as a Socialist. The highest vote he had obtained under that
party's banner was 60,000. He was now convinced to try another route. "Fifty
percent of the people," Sinclair reasoned, "are going to vote a certain ticket
because their grandfathers voted that ticket. In order to get anywhere, it is
necessary to have a party which has grandfathers." So in September 1933,
Upton Sinclair registered as a Democrat and published a little book with a
long title, *I, Governor of California, And How I Ended Poverty: A True Story*

of the Future. The novelist described how he would be nominated and elected, and how as governor he would create a production-for-use economy in the midst of capitalist California. Sinclair predicted that he would totally eliminate poverty in the state in less than four years.

Utopian? Of course. But perhaps overly optimistic would be a more fitting way to describe Upton Sinclair's End Poverty in California (EPIC) plan. The profit system was unlikely to wither away rapidly, especially if its only opposition was in California. And poverty surely would not be conquered so quickly. But this does not mean that Sinclair was a crank, or guilty of fanaticism, as his political opponents and some later historians have charged. The ridicule to which the EPIC plan has often been subjected is without justification. Sinclair's hopes may have been overly sanguine, but his methods were solid, sensible, and practicable. The poor people of California, at any rate, were impressed with the ideas of this scholar-in-politics. Sinclair's ideas may, in fact, have been the closest political approximation to the dominant values of Depression America.

The central feature of the EPIC plan was the concept of production-for-use. The profit system, Sinclair argued, had produced itself into depression. Under it, increased productivity was a curse rather than a blessing. The workers were not paid enough to buy what they produced. This condition led to unemployment, idle factories, idle farms, warehouses full of products that millions of people desperately needed, and ultimately to the unsettling spectacle of food being destroyed while people went hungry. Sinclair pointed to the absurdity of this and suggested a simple remedy. The state would take over the idle land and factories, and permit the unemployed laborers to use the land and machines to produce for their own needs. This, Sinclair contended, was a direct attack on the profit system.

The Socialist-turned-Democrat proposed the establishment of land colonies to produce food for the unemployed and state factories to meet other needs. The products could then be exchanged in a self-contained system that he hoped would eventually undermine the capitalist world around it. All of Sinclair's proposals were frightening to California conservatives, but the production-for-use economy was clearly the most dire threat. It amounted to the old concept of a "moral economy of provision" as opposed to the political economy of the free market.

The EPIC program spread through California like an old-fashioned Awakening. *I, Governor* sold 225,000 copies in one year, making it at the time the all-time best-seller in California. Three subsequent campaign books brought the fourteen-month total of EPIC volumes to 435,000. EPIC clubs were formed throughout the state. There were almost 2000 of the organizations in existence by election day. The people who marked their ballots for Sinclair knew they were voting against the current economic system. Sinclair ran an open campaign, letting the voters know his opinions on all relevant subjects. He carefully spelled out what he would do if elected. The primary was not a referendum on the New Deal. All of the leading Democrats including Sinclair spoke highly of Roosevelt's efforts. What the primary was is more accurately described as a referendum on whether the New Deal should move further to the left. This, in essence, was the question before voters in the 1934 races in several states.

Two preprimary incidents showed the lengths to which Sinclair's Democratic opponents would go to deny him the nomination. Justus Wardell, one of the other candidates, told a campaign audience that Sinclair had "defied the power of Almighty God." Wardell asserted that Sinclair "had stood in the pulpit of a church and taken out [his] watch and said, 'If there is a God, let him prove it by striking me dead within the next three minutes.'" The person quoted was, in fact, Sinclair Lewis, but such details mattered little to EPIC's foes. Then, two days before the August primary, circulars began appearing all over southern California and in the Bay Area. Distributed mostly in front of churches, the leaflets presented a picture of Sinclair, side by side with a hammer-and-sickle flag. They urged "the Exploited Masses" to vote for Sinclair and said they were sponsored by the "Young People's Communist League." No such organization existed. It was soon discovered that the circulars had been ordered by the headquarters of Sinclair's principal Democratic primary opponent, George Creel. No doubt the fabricated Communist endorsement hurt Sinclair at the polls. The same circular continued to appear throughout the general election campaign, even though EPIC people frequently pointed out its fraudulent nature.

Some of the power of EPIC's appeal was shown by the 350,000 California voters who came into the Democratic party between the beginning of the year and July 1934. Many of these switches were due to Roosevelt's popularity, but most of them appear to have been people wanting to vote for Sinclair in the primary. When the votes were counted Sinclair polled a higher total than any other Democrat in the state's history. He won an absolute majority of the Democratic vote, even though eight other names appeared on the party ballot.

Upton Sinclair emerged from his stunning primary victory as the clear favorite to become California's next governor. The idea of production-for-use had won the minds of the state's laborers, the unemployed, and a large part of the middle class. In September most Californians believed Sinclair's election was "in the bag." "Even our enemies," Sinclair recalled, "conceded it; newspaper correspondents expressed their surprise at how leading businessmen gave up, saying there was no way to 'stop Sinclair.'" The Democratic nominee's friends even began calling him "Governor." But Sinclair realized that the lies were only about to begin in earnest.

The general election campaign against Upton Sinclair in 1934 set a standard for distortion and lies that was not equaled until the 1972 presidential election. Indeed, the whole concept of using advertising techniques, false documents, huge sums of money, inaccurate or wholly fabricated quotations, guilt by association, and other "dirty tricks" was perfected in the 1934 California campaign. Sinclair's novels were dissected, quotations taken out of context, and words snatched from the mouths of the author's fictional characters. Such "evidence" convinced many Californians that Sinclair was an atheist, though he was actually a Christian socialist; that he was a free lover, though he was in fact a devoted husband; and that he was a Communist, though the only thing Sinclair and the Communists had in common was a mutual animosity. California business interests were deeply frightened by Sinclair. They spared no expense in trying to discredit him. Hollywood contributed to the anti-Sinclair campaign in three important ways. Major studios threatened to leave the state if Sinclair won. Movie executives applied pressure on stars to make statements against Sinclair. And the film industry issued several fake newsreels using unknown actors to portray Okies and people with putative Russian accents endorsing Sinclair. Actresses posing as widows appeared on other false newsreels, crying about what would happen to their savings if the Democratic nominee was elected.

Sinclair was defeated, but it is clear that it was not the EPIC plan against which Californians voted. Rather, they voted against atheism, free love, and Stalinism. Moreover, some 879,000 Californians voted for production-for-use despite all the lies about Sinclair. Actually the situation in September, when it appeared that Sinclair would sweep the state, was a more accurate reflection of how Californians felt about EPIC than were the November returns, coming after the all-out slander campaign. Some thirty EPIC candidates were elected to the California legislature while their leader was losing the gubernatorial race. Sinclair's uncharacteristically self-effacing remark after the election—"If we had had a better candidate, we might have won"— was accurate in one sense. A less vulnerable candidate might have kept attention focused on the economic issue.

The Sinclair defeat confirmed the leftward drift of American attitudes in another way. In order to win, the Republican, Acting Governor Frank Merriam, a lifelong arch-conservative, felt constrained to speak favorably of the New Deal, call for a thirty-hour workweek, and endorse the Townsend Revolving Pension Plan. Conservatives had to pose as progressives to have any hope of winning in the mid-thirties. The American political structure as a whole had tilted perceptibly leftward.

In most of the 1934 elections in which plausible candidates to the left of Roosevelt appeared, they won. This was a firm indication of the direction in which many Americans, particularly those on whom Roosevelt's political future depended, wanted to move. The votes for these candidates were not anti-Roosevelt votes—at least not yet. But the possibility that such voters would turn against the President if he did not produce more constructive change was a real one.[4]

While Roosevelt brooded over the meaning of the worker and political uprisings of 1934, even more serious rumblings on the left were threatening him. The strikes, though widespread, were generally local in their individual manifestations. The important political challenges were confined to fewer than ten states. But three movements of national significance were growing stronger every day.

Senator Huey P. Long, Father Charles E. Coughlin, and Dr. Francis Townsend developed immense followings in the mid-thirties. To some observers, their movements represented a frightening potential for fascism in Depression America. Others have insisted that the populist messages of Long and Coughlin, at least, are more properly seen as part of the growing strength at the opposite end of the political spectrum—part, that is, of the thunder on the left.

The notion that these three leaders were gathering the storm troopers for a future fascist America began with contemporary liberals. Raymond Gram Swing, in several articles in *The Nation* and in his 1935 book, *Forerunners of American Fascism*, charged that Long and Coughlin were following in the footsteps of Hitler and Mussolini. Swing admitted that Townsend was not a fascist, but asserted that his movement was helping pave the way for a future demagogue to establish a right-wing dictatorship. This interpretation of the three movements has persisted in the work of liberal historians. Arthur Schlesinger, Jr., writing under the heading "The Dream of Fascism," asserts that the "followers of the demagogues mostly came from the old lower-middle classes, now in an unprecedented stage of frustration and fear, menaced by humiliation, dispossession, and poverty." "They came, in the main," Schlesinger contends, "from the ranks of the self-employed, who as farmers or shopkeepers or artisans, felt threatened by organized economic power, whether from above, as in banks and large corporations, or from below, as in trade unions. To a considerable degree, they came from the evangelical denominations . . . in sum, they seemed to represent Old America in resentful revolt against both contemporary politics and contemporary economics." Alan Brinkley's recent study of Long and Coughlin downplays the threat of fascism but agrees with Schlesinger that the movements were composed principally of "men and women clinging precariously to hard-won middle-class lifestyles; people with valued but imperiled stakes in their local communities."

Such interpretations miss one of the main points about the Depression's effect on American values. As we have seen, the economic collapse slowly led many middle-class Americans to identify their interests with those of people below them on the economic scale. The Depression brought forth among middle-class Americans egalitarian and humanitarian values that they came to share with working-class people. In short, the distinction between the middle class and the working class in the United States—never very precise anyway—became extremely blurred in the Great Depression. Perhaps more important was that the common values this larger group of down-and-out Americans came to share during the Depression were more nearly those previously held by the workers than those of the middle class.

As a young priest, Charles Coughlin was made pastor of a small parish in Royal Oak, Michigan, a suburb of Detroit. He was charged with building a shrine to the Church's newest saint, Therese, the "Little Flower of Jesus." The first obstacle confronting Coughlin was the activity of the Ku Klux Klan in the Royal Oak area. A burning cross greeted the new pastor. To combat the bigotry of the Klan, Father Coughlin sought permission to read his sermons on the radio. The religious program proved a quick success in heavily Catholic Detroit. For three years the "Radio Priest" entertained local audiences but remained unknown outside the Detroit metropolitan area.

Then, in the fall of 1929, Coughlin decided to begin speaking on economic and social questions that had moved him since his college days. The priest obtained time on radio stations in Chicago and Cincinnati, greatly enlarging his audience. In 1930, Coughlin signed a contract with CBS and his sermons were delivered over a sixteen-station network. Father Coughlin's first attacks, in early 1930, were against Communists. This was a safe subject, and the priest's audiences continued to grow. Coughlin next became daring enough to switch from assaults on Bolsheviks to attacks on bankers. He then turned his developing fury on another easy mark, Herbert Hoover. In early 1932 the priest charged that the President was "the bankers' friend, the Holy Ghost of the rich, the protective angel of Wall Street." One such radio address against Hoover was said to have elicited 1.2 million letters to Coughlin from his listeners.

The Radio Priest (a title that most Americans of the thirties would instantly associate with Coughlin) was now a force to be reckoned with in American politics. Coughlin developed his own network of 26 stations from Maine to Colorado. (He had been eased out by CBS and refused time by NBC.) Father Coughlin was just about the biggest thing ever to hit radio. His audience was estimated at 30 to 40 million. He attracted a larger audience than such radio favorites as Rudy Vallee, Gracie Allen, and Amos 'n' Andy. Indeed, he had the largest regular radio audience in the world. No clergyman in history had ever before preached to such a following. The priest employed 106 clerks and 4 personal secretaries to handle his mail, which averaged 80,000 letters per week. A poll taken by a St. Paul, Minnesota, radio station asked if people wanted to hear the priest's program. The response was overwhelming: 137,000 said yes and 400 said no.

If the millions of people listening to Coughlin's broadcasts were protofascists, America was in serious danger of losing democracy in the 1930s. But the thrust of the Radio Priest's sermons in 1934 and 1935 was quite distinct from fascism. Coughlin expressed the basis of his position in these years when he said: "I glory in the fact that I am a simple Catholic priest endeavoring to inject Christianity into the fabric of an economic system woven upon the loom of the greedy." This remained his fundamental public position until at least 1936. He frequently changed his specific panacea, but all were based on the idea of redistributing wealth through monetary manipulation.

To Father Coughlin, international bankers ranked in the devil class right next to Communists. He even lumped the two together, saying capitalism and Marxism were "Siamese twins." The potential for fascism in such statements is undeniable. In this sense, Coughlin was a forerunner of such later right-wing extremist groups as the John Birch Society and those who fear today that a Communist-banker-Jewish-internationalist conspiracy headed by the capitalist Baptist Rockefeller family is trying to seize control of the world. In addition, the priest sometimes made blatantly undemocratic statements. Speaking of his new organization, Coughlin told reporters in May 1935: "I am the Union for Social Justice. There are no representatives here." A year later he affirmed: "If necessary, I shall 'dictate' to preserve democracy." Yet a potential for fascism does not mean that this was the basis of Coughlin's appeal in the mid-thirties.

Coughlin's arguments were simplistic but effective. He based his appeal on traditional American values, promised change, and personalized evil by offering his followers a group of villains they could hold responsible for their problems. When he lashed at the banking community Coughlin was striking a chord to which millions of Americans could respond in the thirties. But the economic problem went far beyond greedy financiers, and Father Coughlin demonstrated that he realized this. In December 1932 he declared that increased productivity without a proper distribution of the profits was the root cause of the Depression. Frequently the priest asserted that concentration of wealth was the nation's most serious problem. Coughlin read his audience statistics claiming that the profits of the wealthy had "increased 66 percent between 1926 and 1932, while wages and salaries dropped 60 percent in the same period. . . . What phrase shall we employ," asked Coughlin, "to term this injustice other than *exploitation of the laboring class*?"

In his early radio career Coughlin held that private property must be defended, but that its owners must accept their social responsibility. By 1934 he seemed to have changed his mind. "Capitalism," the priest declared, "is doomed and not worth trying to save." As an alternative Coughlin organized the National Union for Social Justice. Although the union never became a real political organization (in part because Coughlin loved power too much to delegate any of it), it was a powerful force in the mid-thirties. Being a member of the NUSJ meant little more than being a listener to Coughlin's broadcasts. But the millions of Americans who embraced the organization's principles were thereby endorsing the idea of "social justice," not that of fascism.

When the New Deal was six months old, Coughlin said that FDR ranked in the "American Hall of Fame" with Washington and Lincoln. The priest went so far as to term the New Deal "Christ's Deal" and to state that the alternatives were "Roosevelt or ruin." As time passed, however, Father Coughlin, like many of the nation's workers, lost patience with Roosevelt and his New Deal. During late 1934 and most of 1935, Coughlin's statements on the New Deal bounced faster than a Ping-Pong ball. After charging that the administration was "wedded basically to the philosophy of the money changers," the priest could still tell reporters: "I sincerely hope to be able to support Mr. Roosevelt again." The seemingly final break came in November 1935, when Coughlin stated that the New Deal and the principles of social justice were "unalterably opposed." The Communist-infiltrated New Deal, he said, was "a government of the bankers, by the bankers, and for the bankers." Many of the priest's followers deserted him after his vicious attacks on FDR, but Coughlin responded by increasing the offensive.

By 1936, Coughlin had passed the peak of his popularity, although he was not prepared to admit it. He began to edge more toward fascism, and those who remained his staunch supporters much more nearly fit the lower-middle-class, protofascist description that Schlesinger and Brinkley have applied to his earlier followers. At the convention of the NUSJ held in Cleveland in August 1936, fanatical, emotional followers of the priest "indulged in cries, shrieks, moans, rolling of the eyes, and brandishing of the arms." Some delegates spoke as if Coughlin were Christ come back to earth. Huge pictures of the cleric hung from the rafters. The ultimate came when a resolution was introduced "that we give thanks to the mother of the Reverend Charles E. Coughlin for bearing him."

Such a cult of personality was incompatible with democracy, and Coughlin's popularity began to fall off. In 1938 the priest declared his support for the "corporate state" concept advocated by Benito Mussolini. His anti-Semitism now became open. By 1940, Coughlin was praising Adolf Hitler. All this has led many critics to use hindsight to argue that Coughlin's appeal was a fascist one from the start and that his followers were from the background one would expect to spawn fascists: threatened elements of the lower middle class. Yet studies of the Radio Priest's supporters have indicated that much of his backing came from a lower level and that his appeal was originally one essentially from the left, concentrating on "social justice." [5]

The same cannot be said so easily of the movement that grew up around Dr. Francis E. Townsend, a retired medical doctor who was sure that he had found a cure-all formula for America's economic ills. Townsend had long been something of a utopian (Edward Bellamy's *Looking Backward* was his favorite book), and he now believed he had uncovered the ticket to the promised land. In September 1933, Townsend wrote a letter to the editor of a Long Beach newspaper. In it he explained his "Cure for Depressions." The response to Townsend's letter was enormous. Within a few weeks an entire page of the newspaper was taken up each day with letters discussing Townsend's idea. The good doctor was overwhelmed. He had planned no concrete action following his original letter, but Townsend quickly rose to the task. By January 1934, he had persuaded his former employer, Robert E. Clements, a real-estate dealer, to help him promote the plan. The two men, along with Dr. Townsend's brother, formed a corporation, Old Age Revolving Pensions, Ltd. (OARP).

The Townsend Plan, which the new corporation set out to promote, was disarmingly simple. It proposed to pay every American citizen over the age of sixty $200 each month, provided that he or she had never been convicted of a crime, agreed to give up all other income, and pledged to spend the $200 within thirty days. Townsend contended that his plan would end the Depression and benefit young as well as old. The aged would no longer compete with younger people for jobs, the economy would be stimulated by all the purchases the elderly would make, and everyone would live happily ever after.

There was only one catch. Someone would have to pay for making every senior citizen a king or queen. Townsend's proposal was for a 2 percent "transaction tax," a glorified sales tax that, the doctor said, would be fair because "it taxes everybody alike." That was just the trouble. The tax would be extremely regressive. An enormous sum would be transferred to the one-eleventh of the population that was over sixty. The money would not come, though, principally from those who were already rich, but from the impoverished American consumers. In short, Townsend would help one poor group (the aged) at the expense of another (working-class consumers). The rich would be unharmed, the economy unhelped.

The Townsend Plan was essentially conservative. Unlike Huey Long, or even Father Coughlin, Townsend never seriously proposed to soak the rich. He indicated no desire to challenge the basic tenets of capitalism. "We believe that the profit system is the very mainspring of civilized progress," OARP leaders said. (They were not lying. Robert Clements demonstrated his own dedication to profit by making a small fortune out of the activities of the Townsend Plan, which he fondly called "the racket.")

Townsend offered the American middle class—particularly its older members—a panacea, and he presented it in terms that they could understand. It was very attractive. A married couple, both over sixty years of age, would be given $4800 a year. What this meant can be fully appreciated only when it is realized that 87 percent of all American families had annual incomes below $2500 in 1935. That fact in itself indicates the plan was unworkable.

The Townsend Plan had the distinction of being opposed by the Liberty League, the Socialist party, the Communist party, the National Association of Manufacturers, and the American Federation of Labor. Professional economists were as nearly unanimous as they have ever been in their opposition to the plan. Its annual cost would have been 50 percent more than the combined budgets of all American governments—federal, state, and local—had been in 1932. The sum Townsend proposed to pay to the aged was one-half of the national income for 1934. A sales tax that would have provided sufficient revenue for Townsend's scheme would have amounted to an 80 or 90 percent increase in the final price of consumer goods. The greatest fallacy of the Townsend Plan was the belief that the economy could be balanced through a redistribution of income among the poor. If the plan had been financed through a tax on wealth, instead of one on consumption, a scaled-down version might have been feasible. But recovery could never be brought about, as the New Deal's own social security program would show, by taking from one disadvantaged group to give to another.

All of this mattered little to the plan's followers. The sandcastles that Dr. Townsend built were very pretty and his movement flourished. Public sentiment was ripe for a plan to aid the aged. When asked in December 1935 whether they favored government old-age pensions for needy persons, a whopping 89 percent of a cross section of Americans answered affirmatively. The response to the Townsend Plan was phenomenal. In 1936, Townsend Club leaders claimed a nationwide membership of 3.5 million. In only three months Townsendites collected over 20 million signatures on their petitions. This represented one-fifth of the adults in the United States. No other cause in American history has ever obtained so many signatures on its petitions. Two 1936 public opinion surveys showed even greater support for the doctor's scheme. Approximately one-half of the Americans surveyed early in 1936 favored the plan.

The multitudes who followed Dr. Townsend were not, for the most part, the same people who participated in the other movements discussed in this chapter. The Townsendites were, first of all, old. The overwhelming majority of those who were active in the movement stood to benefit directly if the plan was enacted. Most young people were uninterested in the Townsend scheme. Even more significant than the age of the participants were their predominantly middle-class origins. They came from the ranks of the self-employed—small businessmen and farmers—with some skilled workers, but very few unskilled workers and very few wealthy individuals.

The Townsendites were, in a word, respectable. Most were reported to want a more reputable candidate than Huey Long. Townsend meetings always contained heavy doses of patriotism and religion. Townsend conventions were attended by elderly, Bible-toting prohibitionists. The first resolution passed at the first Townsend convention in 1935 was a rule against smoking in the auditorium. Townsend speakers showed their bourgeois values when they said the plan would "make jobs for young people and take them out of their cigarette-smoking, whiskey-drinking, road-side-petting hell of idleness." If anyone had conducted a survey to see just how many of the young wanted to be rescued from this inferno, its results were not announced.

The Townsend Plan was the least radical of the major panaceas offered the American people in the thirties. It is, therefore, unsurprising that its appeal was to a higher point on the socioeconomic scale than were those of Long and Coughlin. The Townsend Plan marked the stage of discontent that many middle-class people had reached by the mid-thirties. Their unrest was "based on the essential fact that there [was] . . . in this country enough to provide a comfortable living for everyone." As unhappy as many Americans below them on the social scale, the middle-class Townsendites were not yet prepared to go as far.[6]

The popularity of Huey Long's calls for radical redistribution of wealth and income was the most striking example of the widespread thunder on the left of the mid-1930s. Senator Long was a man who evoked extreme emotions of love or hate. The controversy has continued in historical scholarship. Only in the last two decades have more objective studies of Long appeared. Even today, however, neutrality on the subject of Huey Long remains elusive.[7]

Huey Pierce Long, Jr., was reared in a large farm family in the hill country of north-central Louisiana. Huey's father was something of a radical. "There wants to be a revolution, I tell you," the old man said in 1935. "I seen this domination of capital, seen it for seventy years. What do these rich folks care for the poor man? They care nothing—not for his pain, his sickness, nor his death," the senior Long continued. "Maybe you're surprised to hear me talk like that. Well, it was just such talk that my boy was raised under." Such sentiments were not unusual in the Louisiana hill country. The region had been a center of Populist strength in the 1890s. Fifteen years later, the hill country was strong for the Socialist party. In 1912, Long's home parish (county), Winn, cast 35.5 percent of its presidential votes for Eugene Debs.

Young Huey Long adopted the radicalism of his neighbors. In 1918, at the age of twenty-four, Long wrote a letter to the New Orleans Item in which he asserted that "about sixty-five or seventy percent of the entire wealth of the United States is owned by two percent of the people." With "wealth concentrating, classes become defined," he said, "there is not the opportunity for

Christian uplift and education and cannot be until there is more economic reform." Already, Huey Long favored a redistribution of wealth.

The program Long offered the electorate when he ran unsuccessfully for the governorship in 1924 and successfully four years later was aimed at the poor, discontented farmers of upland Louisiana and the smaller number of industrial workers in the state. Long appealed, in fact, to the same groups that had supported populism and socialism. A sociologist who studied Louisiana voting patterns has found a strong correlation between the votes for the Populists, the Socialists, and Huey Long. There is no question that Long's Louisiana supporters came predominantly from the ranks of the poor, both farmers and industrial workers. Long's election was largely the result "of a rising tide of opposition to intolerable economic and social conditions." Huey Long was in two critical ways unlike most southern politicians who appealed to the poor in election campaigns. First, he did not sell out to "the interests" when he took office. Long did more for the underprivileged people of Louisiana than had any other governor in the state's history. He vastly improved education, taxation, roads, medical care, and public services. The second way in which Long differed from other southern "populists" was the nearly complete absence of racism in his public statements.

Absolute power in Louisiana was not Huey Long's goal. It was merely a means to his real end: the presidency of the United States. Long entered the national political arena by winning a seat in the United States Senate in 1931. After solidifying his control of Louisiana, Huey went to Washington in 1932. He campaigned effectively for Franklin Roosevelt in the fall, but broke with the new President soon after the latter took office. Early in FDR's presidency Huey Long told some of his Senate colleagues: "Men, it will not be long until there will be a mob assembling here to hang Senators from the rafters of the Senate. I have to determine whether I will stay and be hung with you, or go out and lead the mob." In another speech Long told the Senate that he would steal if he saw his family starving. "Unless we provide for redistribution of wealth in this country," he declared, "the country is doomed."

By early 1934 the Louisiana senator saw the New Deal as a complete failure. "Not a single thin dime of concentrated, bloated, pompous wealth, massed in the hands of a few people, has been raked down to relieve the masses," Huey complained. In order to pressure Roosevelt to move to the left (and, much more than coincidentally, in order to advance his own presidential ambitions), Long organized the Share Our Wealth Society in February 1934. The organization's appeal was the same one Long had been using all along. He had written to supporters in 1933, pointing out, "I announced when I came here that I had taken my place in the Senate for one main purpose, which was to break up the swollen fortunes of America and to spread the wealth among all our people. . . ." Long was fighting, he said, "only along the line that in the land of too much to eat and wear, everyone should be happy." "The only thing in the way," the senator insisted, "is a few who have more than they need, just to have their vanity and greed satisfied." Later in 1933, Long started a national newspaper, *The American Progress*. In a letter announcing the new journal, the Kingfish (a name Long took from a scheming character on the *Amos 'n' Andy* radio show) continued his arguments on redistributing wealth. "We must fight," Long told his followers, "to avoid the country being opened up on a basis of mere economic slavery for the masses, with the ruling classes greater in power and standing than ever." Like Father Coughlin, Senator Long employed the device of personifying evil. Long described the rich as "pigs swilling in the trough of luxury." Such terms made it easier for Long's followers to visualize the enemy.

The basic thrust of the Share Our Wealth program was the promise to limit the size of fortunes to the degree necessary to provide a $5,000 estate for each "deserving family" in America. Long was not in favor, he said, of "leveling." "We do not propose," he wrote in his *Share Our Wealth* pamphlet, "to guarantee the same income to everybody, but by limiting big fortunes and the hours of toil, we do propose a comfortable living for all." Just what the limit on wealth would have to be remained undecided. In a February 1934 radio speech, Long suggested that $50 million might prove a workable limit; but he added, "It may be necessary, in working out the plans that no man's fortune would be more than $10,000,000 or $15,000,000." A paragon of reason, Huey did not seek to take away anything the rich needed. He would, in fact, leave them "all the luxuries they can possibly use." He proposed merely to confiscate through income and inheritance taxes and an annual capital levy, that for which the rich had no legitimate use. Long told his followers that "the same mill that grinds out fortunes above a certain size at the top, grinds out paupers at the bottom."

Long's figures on the size of fortunes that could be left untouched were grossly unrealistic. The surplus wealth of the nation's rich—while immense by individual standards—was in the aggregate not nearly as great as Long (and most Americans) thought. A study in 1935 estimated that if all wealth in excess of $1 million were taken and given to those with assets of $5000 or less, there would be enough to grant each poor family only $400. Another study suggested that the sort of really drastic "leveling" Long had disavowed would be necessary to give every family a $5000 estate. To accomplish this, it would be necessary to allow no family to have more than $7500, a far cry from the senator's suggestion of $50 million.

Yet none of this mattered much. Most people were not interested in the details (particularly if they brought up unpleasant realities). The plan was simplistic, to be sure, but it did begin to address the largest economic problem in America. The general idea that Long enunciated was in tune with the values of millions of dispossessed Americans. A contemporary writer said that the SOW program "coincides pretty accurately with the aspirations and interests of the common man and, if accepted as sincere and feasible, is calculated to muster an enormous volume of popular support for the Kingfish." That great support was evident almost everywhere. "Every person in the United States who can read, and many who can't," one of Long's most vocal opponents admitted in early 1935, "know at least vaguely who Huey Long is and what he is driving at."

It is doubtful that everyone knew about SOW, but the statistics of the movement were extremely impressive. In February 1935, only one year after its founding, SOW officials announced that there were 27,000 clubs in operation. Long's files contained nearly 8 million names. Mail poured into Long's Senate office in unprecedented quantities. An average of 60,000 letters a week arrived in April 1935. And during one of the Kingfish's verbal assaults on Roosevelt, Long received over 30,000 letters each day for twenty-four consecutive days.

Of such facts are the sleepless nights of presidents made. In the summer of 1935, the Democratic National Committee conducted a secret poll on Long as a possible third-party presidential candidate. The Democrats were shocked to learn that between 3 million and 4 million Americans might vote for Long and wealth-sharing. Even more disturbing to New Dealers were the indications that Long had strong support in the midwestern Farm Belt and in the industrial regions along the Great Lakes (12.5 percent) and even the Pacific coast (12.1 percent). The 1935 poll showed that Long could command a minimum 100,000 votes in New York. It was reported separately that he might have obtained 250,000 votes in Ohio. Such a Long candidacy could throw the election to the Republicans. This was a fate Franklin Roosevelt did not want to see befall his countrymen. The President was already engaged in a secret war against Long. The White House offered encouragement to the senator's opponents in Louisiana, denied patronage to Long's supporters, secured the help of other southern senators in attacking Long, and even had the Justice Department and the FBI investigate the possibility of sending troops into Louisiana to "restore republican government."

Particularly notable in the results of the 1935 secret survey were the indications about Long's followers. Among those on relief, 16.7 percent voted for Long, compared to only 7.8 percent among those not on relief. Again it is clear that the Long appeal, like that of Coughlin, was mainly to the lower reaches of the socioeconomic scale.

Long maintained that a fairer distribution of wealth would strengthen capitalism. When a liberal writer said that it appeared as if Huey wanted to save the rich people he always criticized, Long replied: "That would be one of the unfortunate effects of my program. I'd cut their nails and file their teeth and let them live." The basis of Long's wealth-sharing belief—that "there is enough, yea, there is more than the entire human race can consume, if all are reasonable"—was a production-for-use economy. National opinion surveys confirmed that a majority of poor Americans had come to favor ideas similar to Long's. The 1935 and 1937 *Fortune* polls mentioned in the preceding chapter, which showed the poor opposed by a 2–1 margin to allowing people with investments worth over $1 million to keep them, and a sizable majority of the poor favoring "a policy of taking money from those who have much and giving money to those who have little," left no doubt that there was a large potential constituency for Long.

One of Long's followers in Arizona used phrases similar to those employed by countless others when he called Louisiana "a real democracy." Long, he said, had "lifted Louisiana from the mud of indecent, shameful exploitation by the rich, to a high level of civilization." Yet if there was one thing that Louisiana certainly was not while Huey Long was in charge, it was a democracy. He was, quite simply, a dictator—a popular one who remained dependent upon public approval, but a dictator nonetheless. Long made a mockery of legislative processes, openly telling state lawmakers which bills passed and which were rejected. Although he did much good for the downtrodden people of Louisiana, his methods cannot be excused. Once we begin to allow worthy ends to justify repulsive means, democracy is on its way out. It is safe to speculate that a Huey Long presidency would have been a disaster for the United States.

By 1935, Long was making it plain that he was likely to support an independent presidential candidate the following year. His apparent plan was to siphon enough votes from Roosevelt to elect a Republican in 1936. Long believed that things would get so bad under a Republican administration that the people would turn to him in 1940. The Kingfish would be only forty-six when the new decade began, so there seemed to be plenty of time.

There was not. Before Long's last book, *My First Days in the White House*, could reach his public, an assassin's attack ended any possibility that fiction might become fact. As Long stood talking to aides in a corridor of the Louisiana Capitol in Baton Rouge on the night of September 8, 1935, Carl Weiss, a young physician who saw Huey as a tyrant and whose father-in-law had been wronged by the Long political machine, walked up to the senator and shot him with a pistol. Long's bodyguards responded by emptying their guns into Dr. Weiss. His body was riddled with more than thirty bullets. The senator had been struck by only one shot, under his ribs. He was taken to a nearby hospital and remained conscious until he was operated on two hours later. Although the operation took place with various politicians and Long hangers-on crowding the room, it seemed to be successful. The surgeon, however, had failed to check for damage to Long's kidney, and it later became apparent that internal hemorrhaging was continuing. Too weak to withstand another operation, Huey Long grew steadily weaker; within two days he was dead.[8]

If there was all this discontent on the left in the mid-1930s, it is reasonable to ask why the nation did not move further in that direction. There are several answers, the most fundamental of which was offered by Norman Thomas: "It was, in a word, Roosevelt." There were also, however, other factors in the failure of the left to accomplish more during the Great Depression.

The number of people attracted to one or more of the "radical" schemes or leaders was immense. Surely there was some overlap in the followings of Long, Coughlin, Townsend, Sinclair, Olson, the La Follettes, and other left-leaning leaders and organizations. Yet the principal leaders appealed to different groups and won their greatest number of adherents in different sectors of the population: Long in the South and rural areas, Coughlin in the Midwest and Northeast and among Catholics, Townsend on the Pacific coast and among the elderly. To a considerable extent the membership in these movements was additive. If they were, as some critics called them, the "lunatic fringe," then that fringe was approaching majority status in 1935.

Accordingly, it was the possibility that the demagogues and leftists would unite that struck fear into the hearts of Roosevelt administration political strategists. That danger was never very great. Although they were all—with the partial exception of Townsend—pointing toward essentially the same set of values, the leaders could never have effectively joined forces. A comment labor historian Edward Thompson made about English radicals a century earlier applies to their American counterparts during the Great Depression: "The greatest cause of Radical disagreement was sheer vanity." Such men as Huey Long and Charles Coughlin were addicted to public adulation. Leaders who so loved the limelight were completely incapable of subordinating their personal ambitions and vanity to a greater cause.

Here the largest problem facing the American left in the Great Depression becomes apparent. The values upon which a movement for more fundamental change could have been built were increasingly popular, but no organizational structure existed to translate the changed attitudes into political power. Hence the politics of economic morality became personalized and fell by default to flamboyant leaders who were skilled radio speakers. Long and Coughlin could influence huge numbers of listeners, but they asked little of them other than to listen, write letters, and send money. This was no way to build an effective organization. It involved large numbers of people, but it left discontent passive rather than making it active. For this reason, the Share Our Wealth clubs and the National Union for Social Justice remained little more than "glorified mailing lists." They were unable to generate effective political organizations.

The state political movements to the left of the New Deal demonstrated the possibilities when genuine, effective political organization was combined with a commitment to the values of moral economics. Although the personalities of Floyd Olson, Upton Sinclair, and the La Follettes were important factors in their movements, the ideals were larger than the men. The same could not be said of the Long and Coughlin movements.

If conflict among the prima donnas made unity of the dissenting national movements impossible, this did not mean that the followers were in fundamental disagreement. In some respects, it might seem that the groups were incompatible. As Alan Brinkley has noted, Huey Long spoke in the populist-fundamentalist language that denounced self-indulgent sinners, while Charles Coughlin exploited the urban Catholic view of greedy but puritanical money manipulators. Despite this remarkable divergence, most followers of the demagogues believed that their messages were similar. And in a more basic sense they were. In their symbols, images, and values, the men associated with the "thunder on the left" were making similar noises. The sounds were pleasing to the ears of multitudes of Depression-era Americans.

Yet even in those states where effective political organizations were formed, an insurmountable obstacle beyond personal vanity prevented the launching of a powerful national political organization on the left. The bulk of those who were attracted to the groups and leaders on the left also liked Franklin Roosevelt, at least most of the time. All of the leaders discussed in this chapter faced this problem. Several of them—the La Follettes, Sinclair, Coughlin—tried at times to associate themselves with the President while staking out ground to his left. Huey Long more openly broke with the President and then saw his popularity fluctuate inversely with that of FDR. When Roosevelt was most popular in 1933 and early 1934, Long's prestige suffered a decline. When doubts about Roosevelt's commitment to moral economic values rose in late 1934 and early 1935, Long's strength returned. This relationship was perfectly summed up by a Montana man who wrote to the President early in 1935: "Huey Long is the man we thought you were when we voted for you." [9]

When such danger of massive defections from the New Deal arose, Roosevelt had the inestimable advantage of controlling the largest organization of all—the federal government. He was in a position to win back wavering supporters by taking new actions demonstrating his adherence to the popular values. This he did with the "Second New Deal" of 1935.

11 · "I'm That Kind of Liberal Because I'm That Kind of Conservative": The Second New Deal

E arly in 1935, *Time* magazine said that all indications were that President Roosevelt would move toward reconciliation with business and that reform was virtually at an end. As it turned out, this was precisely the opposite of what happened during the next two years. The fundamental reason for Roosevelt's shift to the left in 1935 is clear. His constituents had already turned in that direction and it was politically necessary for the President to move to catch up with his followers. Roosevelt was many things—patrician, optimist, stamp collector, sailor, among others—but above all he was a politician. He rarely, if ever, made a decision without first thrusting a damp finger into the political wind. In 1934 and 1935 that wind was building up into a gale that no political leader could long ignore. It forced Roosevelt to tack desperately to the leeward in order to keep afloat.

The luxury of consensus government was one of the many privileges that President Roosevelt enjoyed, but he finally had to give it up. As late as the election of 1934, FDR was still aiming for the middle, speaking of "10 to 15 per cent of people" on each extreme who opposed the New Deal. Just before the election, the President addressed the American Bankers Association convention. It was an attempt to placate business opposition. Roosevelt told the bankers that he sought an alliance of major interests in the country, including bankers and government. He pledged to reduce large expenditures as soon as business revived. At the last minute, FDR altered his text, saying, "That is what we call and accept as a profit system." He emphasized "and accept as," his addition to the speech. The bankers were especially pleased with this, and they gave the President a tremendous ovation lasting for several minutes. The treaty between Roosevelt and the bankers proved to be of short duration, though.

There were, to be sure, pressures from both sides in 1934, but the direction in which Roosevelt must turn was clearly to the left. One reason was that businessmen deserted him before he gave up on them. In the dark days of 1933 few captains of industry dared to oppose the dynamic new President. Their own prestige was shattered; his was rising rapidly. At the very least they remained neutral in thought and deed. Many went beyond and cheerfully joined in the alliance FDR offered them. The Economy Act, the Emergency Banking Act, and the NRA were generally pleasing to business interests.

Other parts of the legislative barrage in the Hundred Days were greeted with less enthusiasm, but little open opposition to Roosevelt surfaced until early 1934. Then, however, the combination of the proposed stock exchange legislation and temporary transfer by the President of air mail concessions from private carriers to the Army Air Corps led to the first loud cries of "communism." Since the President himself was too popular to attack directly at this point, early salvos were aimed at his advisers. Some businessmen saw in every professor advising Roosevelt a Communist or, at best, an impractical visionary. The "Brain Trusters"—by now a generic term for all New Dealers, or at least those whom one did not like—were lashed at unmercifully. Opponents portrayed them as power-hungry bureaucrats, carrying the country down a high-speed route to totalitarianism. In the summer of 1934 conservative opponents of the New Deal decided the time had come to end some of the suffering—their own. As John J. Raskob put it, big business must "organize to protect society from the suffering it is bound to endure if . . . no one should be allowed to get rich." With such an understanding of what it meant to suffer, a number of wealthy men launched the Liberty League.

The nucleus of the Liberty League was formed by the same group—Raskob, the Du Ponts, and other backers of Al Smith—who had long sought to turn the Democratic party toward conservatism and switch the tax burden from the rich to the poor and middle class. Jouett Shouse, a corporation lawyer and former congressman closely associated with Raskob, was named chairman. These men had plotted in 1932 to block Roosevelt's nomination. They were, in short, not people who had ever been friendly to FDR or to progressive causes. Their organization quickly became the center of attacks on the New Deal from the right. The league professed to be especially concerned with alleged violations of constitutional rights. It labeled the AAA a "trend toward Fascist control of agriculture," the National Labor Relations Act "unconstitutional," and relief and old-age pensions "the end of democracy." It soon became apparent that the only liberty sought by league members was that of the rich. As Senator William Borah pointed out, they must have been so impressed by the Constitution because "they had just discovered it."

It would be a mistake, however, to assume that big business was solidly opposed to the New Deal. Many sophisticated business leaders, particularly some key figures in New York and leaders of some relatively new businesses, such as Thomas Watson of IBM and Jack Warner and others in Hollywood studios, saw the New Deal as Roosevelt did: as capitalism's savior, not its executioner. FDR had a Business Advisory Council that included in 1935 such luminaries as Winthrop Aldrich of the Chase National Bank, Walter Gifford of AT&T, Gerard Swope of General Electric, and W. Averell Harriman of the Union Pacific Railroad. Boston retail tycoon Edward A. Filene put the pro–New Deal business view most succinctly. "Why shouldn't the American people take half my money from me?" he asked. "I took all of it from them."

Such radical spirits as Lincoln Steffens expressed amusement at the spectacle of businessmen attacking Roosevelt while he was trying desperately to save their system. The President himself saw less humor in the situation. For a time, at least, he was bitter at being called a traitor to his class, a class that he was saving from its own shortsightedness. But he was not yet ready to abandon the hope for consensus. "One of my principal tasks," he believed as late as November 1934, "is to prevent bankers and businessmen from committing suicide!"[1]

Some other Americans did not think the survival of such magnates was worth the trouble. The late second and early third years of a president's first term often constitute an administration's most critical period. The "honeymoon" has worn off and more lasting impressions of a leader are formed.

Such impressions go a long way toward determining whether a president will be reelected. This important period in Franklin Roosevelt's presidency may be dated from late 1934 through the summer of 1935. It was a time in which the President's popularity began to decline, opposition on his left grew, and he finally won back the support of most Americans through a series of actions that are often called the Second New Deal, or the Second Hundred Days.

The motives for Roosevelt's actions of 1935 were many. Business hostility and Supreme Court decisions against such early New Deal legislation as the NRA played their roles. More basic, though, was that the initial Roosevelt programs had been in effect for two years, yet the Depression continued. The National Recovery Administration had provided far more administration than recovery. It seemed to the experiment-minded Roosevelt that the time had come to try something new. The President was not alone in this conclusion. New Deal reformers rapidly perceived the significance of the outcome of the 1934 elections. Shortly after the election Harry Hopkins declared to his staff, "Boys—this is our hour. We've got to get everything we want—a works program, social security, wages and hours, everything—now or never." The reverse side of the opportunity for new policy was the political danger of *not* moving faster and further.

The popularity of Long, Coughlin, and Townsend provided a warning siren for Roosevelt. By early 1935 the signal was shrill and growing in intensity. It was becoming clear that Roosevelt's popularity among working-class Americans was declining. Historian Charles Beard detected a "staggering rapidity" in the "disintegration of President Roosevelt's prestige" in February and March. In April an FERA field investigator reported a dramatic reversal of the positive views toward Roosevelt that she had seen in Camden, New Jersey, in 1934. Martha Gellhorn was shocked: "It surprises me to find how radically attitudes can change within four or five months." In what she considered a typical eastern industrial city, Gellhorn discovered that the workers and unemployed were "no longer sustained by confidence in the President." She found people complaining about low wages. "They say to you, quietly, like people who have been betrayed but are too tired to be angry, 'How does he [FDR] expect us to live on that; does he know what food costs, what rents are, how can we keep clothes on the children . . . ?" Gellhorn asserted that the President was "hardly mentioned now, only in answer to questions." Union and unemployed council leaders said that "if he were up for election tomorrow he would lose."

The Camden poor who had lost faith in Roosevelt were not yet radical, but they were fed up with what they saw as the New Deal's unkept promises. Such was the clear trend in the first half of 1935. In March a Chicago man who had been interviewing the poor for several weeks wrote, "I found that there were quite a few that had turned Democratic in the last election and were beginning to get . . . disgusted with the administration." He told Roosevelt, "There are a great many against you." A Pennsylvania worker agreed. "The forgotten man," he wrote to Eleanor Roosevelt, "is still forgotten. . . . The new deal and N.R.A. has only helped big business." In May a Brooklyn machinist related to Harry Hopkins his disgust with the assistance Roosevelt's program was seemingly providing for big business: "With you demanding the best for those used to the best (just for that reason!) Where's New Deal in that? Where is democracy?"

A Columbus, Ohio, worker summed up the growing feeling of betrayal in 1935 when he wrote to Roosevelt: "We the people voted for you, we had a world of faith in you, we loved you, we stood by you, it was a common thing to hear a man or woman say they would gladly die for you, but it is a different story now. Yes you have faded out on the masses of hungry, idle people. . . . the very rich is the only one who has benefitted from your new deal," he continued. "Why didn't you turn a deaf ear to the United States Chamber of Commers, and turn to the left, and saved millions of starving people, who believed in you. . . . but it is so diferent to day the people are dissappointed, it is common now to hear the people, every where you go say President Roosevelt, has proven to be no deferent from any other President, there all for big business after they get in office." This bitterly disappointed man went on to voice a matter that was of grave personal concern to Roosevelt: his political future. "Today the way people are thinking and talking, if you were to get the nomination in 1936," he declared, "you will be beation by a great land slide." The correspondent was himself considering voting for Huey Long. The impression was widespread that many other voters were leaning the same way. The *Times* of London warned that the people of the United States would soon turn to Long and Coughlin if Roosevelt could not soon bring about improvement.[2]

With a reelection campaign fast approaching, Roosevelt realized that he must decide how best to regain the support of those whose votes he needed to win. This could be done in two ways: by taking action to ease the Depression and by making it clear the administration favored "the forgotten man" and opposed big business. Both tasks were difficult, but in different ways. Few were sure how to accomplish the first, but doing so would make most people happy. Openly opposing business was done easily enough, but it would make powerful enemies.

The quickest way to ease the Depression was by giving adequate **relief**. Roosevelt was greatly troubled, though, by the debilitating effects of the dole. He therefore decided, late in 1934, to seek a massive new appropriation for work relief. The commitment to work relief and the magnitude of the appropriation ($4.88 billion) distinguished the Emergency Relief Appropriation Act of 1935 from earlier New Deal relief efforts. At the time it represented the largest single appropriation in history. Congress passed the act in April. As a result, the President created the WPA, which soon became one of the New Deal's most important agencies. (I deal with the WPA in the next chapter.)

Roosevelt remained hesitant to make a clean break with big-business leadership. This had not been done in 1933, despite its probable popularity, because Roosevelt had no desire to destroy big business. He hoped rather to create a society in which business leaders would cooperate with government. The vision had taken shape in the NRA, but it had not worked. Big business was, if anything, even more unpopular in 1935 than it had been when Roosevelt took office. Opposing "Wall Street"—at least rhetorically and symbolically—was becoming a political imperative.

Testing the waters slowly, FDR decided to launch an attack on perhaps the least popular of all business groups, the utility companies. The worst abuse in the power industry was the pyramiding of holding companies on top of the operating utility firms. These holding companies, which produced nothing and whose sole assets were stocks in lower companies, rarely existed for any function other than to issue stock and inflate profits. By 1932 thirteen such companies controlled 75 percent of the nation's private power interests. The results were huge profits for speculators and grossly overpriced electricity for consumers.

In his 1935 State of the Union speech, President Roosevelt left out a significant word. His text called for the "abolition of the evil *features* of holding companies." By dropping "features" the President—apparently inadvertently—made a much more drastic (and popular) statement. Legislation called the Wheeler-Rayburn bill was drafted to compel the dissolution of all utility holding companies that could not prove they served a valid economic purpose. The bill's key provision, soon known as "the death sentence," drew a distinct line between FDR and big business. Businessmen reacted strongly in defense of their brothers in the utilities.

The utility companies launched a massive lobbying campaign in which the lobbyists were said to outnumber the membership of Congress. Faced with a "death sentence," the utilities went further. They sent a quarter of a million fraudulent telegrams and 5 million letters to congressmen; a whispering campaign was started, suggesting that Roosevelt was on the verge of mental collapse. The pressure worked. The Wheeler-Rayburn bill passed in the Senate, but the House rejected the death sentence. Congress in the thirties was unwilling to outlaw lynching, but when it came to capital punishment for utilities pyramids, the representatives were more compassionate. Finally in late August 1935, a compromise was reached in which the pyramids were, in most cases, to be cut down to smaller units and kept to only one level above the operating company. This was well short of abolishing holding companies, but it was a serious blow against them.

Possibly more important to Roosevelt than the final law was that he had been able to make a tough public stand against a major business abuse. In addition to the direct political benefits this brought the President, it produced an increased business hostility to him. This was all to the good as far as FDR's political future was concerned.

The breach between Roosevelt and big business was achieved by a series of reciprocal actions. After the administration began its attack on utility holding companies, business grew less tolerant of the New Deal. The annual meeting of the United States Chamber of Commerce in late April 1935 showed the extent of anger in some business quarters. Delegates accused the President of trying to "Sovietize America" and voted to oppose a long list of progressive proposals.

Although the administration retained significant friends among big businessmen, the general impression was one of an open break. This made it easier for Roosevelt to do what the political and economic situation dictated—to split the country along its major class cleavage.[3] (This is not to say that Roosevelt was acting in a cynical fashion or that he was not sincere in advocating social programs. Rather, it is to place the greatest emphasis on the political situation dictated by the class-oriented values of the mid-thirties.)

As 1935 progressed, Roosevelt continued to take steps toward the end of identifying himself with the poor and against the uncaring rich. Since his days as governor of New York, Roosevelt had favored government social insurance. But he had failed to move forward on the matter and Congress had taken the initiative in early 1934 with two different versions, one based on payroll taxes, the other on federal grants to the states. The President stalled congressional action by appointing a committee under Labor Secretary Frances Perkins to determine the best form for social insurance. Roosevelt himself favored an all-inclusive "cradle-to-grave" system. He wanted it to be based on contributions, not on general tax revenues. Congress, as usual, followed the path of least resistance, which meant the President lost on the first point and won on the second. Both results were unfortunate for the American people.

Congressional hearings on the bill in the early months of 1935 provided yet another opportunity for businessmen to castigate the New Deal. The cry of "socialism" reverberated throughout the hearing rooms, and business leaders predicted the end of initiative, thrift, and the American way of life. It was mildly entertaining theater, but actually the bill was sufficiently conservative so that all but a few Republicans finally voted for it. Roosevelt signed the act in August 1935.

The Social Security Act was a significant achievement in that it at last acknowledged a modicum of societal responsibility for the care of the aged, unemployed, handicapped, and impoverished. It was also important as a symbolic gesture to demonstrate that Roosevelt's heart was in the right place, no small accomplishment with a presidential election little more than a year away. Although the Townsend organization continued to thrive for more than a decade, Social Security deflated the movement as a threat to Roosevelt.

Despite these gains, four major defects made the Social Security Act a flawed piece of legislation. First, contrary to FDR's wishes, the act did not include everyone. The fears of many southern whites were captured by the *Jackson Daily News*, which declared: "The average Mississippian can't imagine himself chipping in to pay pensions for ablebodied Negroes to sit around in idleness on front galleries supporting their kinfolks on pensions, while cotton and corn crops are crying for workers to get them out of the grass." In order to get southern support for the bill, congressional leaders excluded from the provisions of the law many of the people most in need of protection— farm and domestic workers.

Second, the insurance system was based on payroll taxes, as Roosevelt had insisted. The regressive nature of such taxation is obvious: the lower-income workers paid a far larger percentage of their wages in social security taxes than did those whose incomes were above the maximum taxable level. There was another side to the argument over contributory insurance versus funding from general revenue, though. The latter course would be far more equitable and progressive, but taking the former route ensured that the system would not be cut back by subsequent administrations. Once people had contributed their own money, they saw the Social Security System as a "sacred trust," far different from "charity" programs. The importance of this distinction is apparent nearly a half century later.

Third, the payroll tax was used to build up a fund from which social security payments would eventually be made. This meant simply that purchasing power was being taken out of the economy—and away from those most likely to spend it—when precisely the opposite was desperately needed to stimulate recovery. No payments were scheduled to be made until 1941.

Finally, by creating a hodgepodge state-based network of unemployment compensation, the act helped precipitate the enactment of another regressive type of levy, the sales tax, which spread quickly, particularly in the nation's poorest region, the South.

A system that excluded the neediest, took money from workers, and reduced aggregate demand in the midst of a depression was something less than a model for progressive legislation. Yet the Social Security Act helped, in combination with other parts of the Second New Deal, to win back for Roosevelt the allegiance of the forgotten man.[4]

* * *

Only the need to regain the support of workers led Roosevelt reluctantly and belatedly to endorse perhaps the most important law passed in the 1930s, the Wagner Act. Roosevelt had never been overly sympathetic toward organized labor. As a paternalist, the President wanted to do things *for* workers, not create a situation in which they could help themselves. He had signaled this attitude by naming Frances Perkins, a social worker rather than a unionist, as secretary of labor. Miss Perkins, like most other early New Dealers, was a paternalist (or in her case, perhaps, a maternalist). She acted as if she believed that workers had few good ideas and that expert reformers must think for them.

Accordingly, the emphasis of the early New Deal was upon government programs, some of which would provide benefits for workers. Section 7(a) of the National Industrial Recovery Act was the only nod toward organized labor in Roosevelt's initial program. As it became clear that the promise of 7(a) would go largely unfulfilled, labor's strongest friend in Congress, New York Senator Robert Wagner, sought new legislation to protect unions and those who wished to join them. Wagner was the embodiment of the new urban liberalism that had begun to emerge in the Progressive era and was reaching a level of great influence in the New Deal. Differing in important ways from the rural reformers of an earlier age, urban liberals of the Wagner type were among the foremost advocates of legislation protecting workers, assuring their right to organize, and providing for minimum standards of social welfare.

President Roosevelt, still hoping to hold the middle ground between workers and employers, blocked the Wagner bill in 1934. It was reintroduced in 1935, and still the President wanted no part of it. Now, however, Senator Wagner began skillfully to maneuver the bill through the Senate. Businessmen, already up in arms over the proposals on utilities and social insurance, cried that the passage of the labor law would mean the end of the world, or at least of America as they had known and loved it.

As usual, business fears were overwrought. The law would give the National Labor Relations Board the power to prohibit unfair practices by employers who sought to block unionization, to order and conduct elections to determine if workers wanted to bargain collectively and, if so, whom they wanted to represent them. This in no sense forced unions on unwilling workers; it merely made the government, long a powerful ally of business in labor disputes, an active neutral. This ultimately helped American workers greatly, but it did little harm to employers, most of whom quickly learned to accommodate themselves to the new situation.

Without presidential backing, the Wagner bill was approved in the Senate by the overwhelming margin of 63–12. Seeing that the legislation would pass anyway, President Roosevelt decided to gain whatever credit he could for a popular law that he had never supported. He suddenly announced that the Wagner bill was on his "must" list of legislation. The House passed the bill on a voice vote and Roosevelt signed the National Labor Relations Act on July 5.

By this time, Roosevelt had received another stimulus to move to the left. On May 27, 1935, the Supreme Court announced its unanimous decision that declared the NRA unconstitutional. The case, *United States* v. *Schecter Poultry Corp.*, involved the charge that the company had violated an NRA code by selling diseased poultry, among other irregularities. Inevitably the case came to be popularly known as the "sick chicken case."

The *Schecter* decision has been called "the Black Monday of the New Deal," and has been credited with turning Roosevelt to the left and starting the Second New Deal. All of this is misleading, to say the least. Although Roosevelt later said the decision returned the Constitution to "horse-and-buggy days," his outrage at the verdict centered not so much on the invalidation of the NRA as on the Court's threat to reject other New Deal measures. The *Schecter* case actually helped the President politically by releasing him from a policy that was not working and giving him the opportunity to blame the failure to achieve recovery on "nine old men." Nor was the *Schecter* decision significant in starting the Second New Deal. Roosevelt had decided upon a new work relief program the previous fall, he had called for the enactment of a social insurance system in January, and in March he had demanded the execution of utility holding companies. On May 15 the Senate had passed the Wagner bill and Roosevelt had indicated that he would support such a bill on May 24. More than a week before the Supreme Court ruling newsmen observed a new presidential mood. Roosevelt was clearly moving to the left and trying dramatic new initiatives before the *Schecter* decision, which played at most a minor part in motivating the new policies.[5]

The summer of 1935 also produced other important legislation, such as the Banking Act of 1935, which centralized control of the money market in the Federal Reserve Board, thereby making a coherent government economic policy less difficult, and saw the development of the Rural Electrification Administration, which ultimately would revolutionize farm life by bringing electricity within reach of almost all American farms. But what was probably the most important event of the Second New Deal resulted in a very unimportant piece of legislation.

At the beginning of 1935, Roosevelt had said there was no need for changes in taxation at that time. In February the President rejected a dramatic tax reform package that the Treasury Department had prepared. But the thunder on the left continued to rise, especially around the junior senator from Louisiana, and in the spring FDR spoke privately to Raymond Moley of the need to do something "to steal Long's thunder." In view of Long's demand to "soak the rich," a new tax policy seemed the best way to achieve that end. To undermine Long and save capitalism, Roosevelt told a representative of William Randolph Hearst in May, it might "be necessary to throw to the wolves the forty-six men who are reported to have incomes in excess of one million dollars a year." The President now decided to send a radical-sounding tax message to Congress. The purpose was plainly political; Roosevelt failed even to indicate whether he wanted action in that session of Congress and seems to have been far more interested in the political impact of the message than in actual tax reform. He was prepared, a month after the message, to agree to a congressional adjournment without action on taxes. It might have been better to wait; then he could take a strong stand against the rich in 1936, just before the election.

The tax message went to Congress on June 19, 1935, which is the most convenient time at which to mark the turning point of the New Deal (although Roosevelt's *decision* to move to the left had occurred at least six weeks earlier). On the same day, the House approved the Wagner bill and the Senate passed the Social Security measure. Both of these important events were overshadowed, though, by the presidential message. Roosevelt told Congress that large accumulations of wealth meant "the perpetuation of great and undesirable concentration of control in a relatively few individuals over the employment and welfare of many, many others." Decrying the "unjust concentration of wealth and economic power," the President called for federal inheritance and gift taxes, higher personal income taxes in the upper brackets, and a graduated corporate income tax.

If, as seems apparent, the intention of the wealth tax message was to win back wavering supporters, it succeeded admirably. Public reaction to the proposals was overwhelmingly favorable. More than 80 percent of the people who wrote to Roosevelt about the tax message praised the idea. Their letters make it clear that the view that the tax proposal marked a turn to the left is not simply the product of later historical analysis. Many people commented immediately on FDR's shift. "In this community," a Californian wrote to the President the day after the tax message, "the rank and file stand more resolutely than ever with you since you have begun to turn to the left again." Several letter writers indicated that they had long awaited such a proposal from Roosevelt. It was, one said, "like light in darkness." "Millions of your supporters have been anxiously awaiting such a message," another assured the President. And a Philadelphian informed FDR: "I am now on your bandwagon again, after having slipped off."

Perhaps the best summary of what had been happening to Roosevelt's support in early 1935 and the effect the tax message had in reversing that decline came from an eighty-one-year-old former Republican in Kansas. "Your recent message to Congress furnishes the convincing assurance that the New Deal program means to go to the roots of the evils that plague the nation; that it understands the causes therefor, and proposes to eradicate them," he wrote. "Many early followers" of the New Deal, this Kansan went on, had become "less optimistic. To very many the program was beginning to appear 'half-baked' and doomed to failure." The tax message restored this elderly man's faith in the President and the New Deal. A New Jersey man indicated the political significance of FDR's stance on taxes. "Your message," he wrote to Roosevelt, "has reunited the working class Democrat, overnight for the time being."

With rhetoric producing such results, FDR remained reluctant to push for genuine tax reform. Without strong backing from the White House, the bill was mutilated in Congress. Far from soaking the rich, the "Wealth Tax Act" of 1935 scarcely dampened them. A graduated corporate income tax survived in token form only, and a small estate tax was enacted. The entire final bill increased taxes by only $250 million. The millionaires remained safe from the wolves. The tax act did almost nothing to redistribute wealth, but Roosevelt's original proposals had effectively redistributed political allegiances. Business was more bitter than ever. Roosevelt had burned his bridges to Wall Street, and now had to continue to seek to unify working-class Americans behind him.

This he was at last prepared to do. Late in the year he told Moley that he would continue his "fighting" rhetoric. The President said he hoped that this would keep his "left-wing supporters satisfied." The battle lines for 1936 were now clearly drawn. Roosevelt was casting his lot with the forgotten man (who seems most often to be remembered during and just prior to election years). It would be "us" against "them" in 1936, and FDR clearly wanted to be one of "us."[6]

The primary reason for the Second New Deal was simply the growth of discontent among the workers. The threat from the left had grown since 1932. New Deal programs had brought together the down-and-out and given them ample opportunity to discuss their common plight. The hope the NRA had given workers and then taken away from them had stimulated a new militant drive for organization. And the immense strength of those presenting alternatives to the New Deal, such as Olson, Sinclair, Coughlin, Townsend, and Long, provided foci for the workers' discontent.

Moreover, in 1932, Roosevelt, as the challenger, had been able to benefit from the discontent in the electorate. In 1936 he stood to lose because of that discontent, unless he could perform some fast footwork and catch up with the voters. The result was this flurry of legislation and rhetoric.

Much of the historical scholarship on the Roosevelt era has dealt with the question of whether there were two ideologically distinct "new deals," one from 1933 to early 1935, and the other beginning in 1935. Even among those who have accepted the notion of an identifiable change in direction in 1935, there has been disagreement over the nature of the shift.

Participant Raymond Moley and historian Basil Rauch have contended—from very different perspectives—that Roosevelt turned to the left in 1935. Moley used this interpretation as part of his explanation of his defection from the administration. Arthur Schlesinger, Jr., gave the two new deals view its fullest and best-known statement and altered its meaning when he argued in 1960 that the Second New Deal was more of a turn to the right—a return to the Louis Brandeis–Felix Frankfurter hope "to revitalize the tired old society by establishing a framework within which enterprise could be set free." Schlesinger quotes Frankfurter disciple Thomas Corcoran, pointing out that the Second New Deal was "ideologically far more 'capitalistic' than the First New Deal."

Other historians have avoided the issue of the direction of the New Deal's shift by denying that there was any. Like the contention that there *were* two new deals, the other side of the argument has two rather different versions. One holds that the entire New Deal was pragmatic and contradictory and, hence, there was no basic philosophy to change. The other position, advanced most forcefully by Elliot Rosen, contends that the philosophy of the entire New Deal was carefully spelled out by the Brains Trust in 1932 and, accordingly, there was no shift in 1935.

Those who maintain that there was no significant philosophical shift in 1935 are on firm ground. As I have noted before, Franklin Roosevelt was neither a philosopher nor an economist; he was a politician. Neither his programs of 1933 nor those of 1935 were based on a coherent ideological position. Consistency troubled Roosevelt little. Votes were far more important. The political, rather than philosophic, nature of the Second New Deal is evident. He had tried for the first two years of his presidency to keep everyone happy. By 1935 that was no longer possible. The groups with whom he chose to split—and those he decided not to alienate—leave no doubt that his motivation was political.

Roosevelt finally broke with business in 1935, thus calming the thunder on the left and winning support for 1936. On the other hand, he never split from the southern elite. He refused to make substantive moves toward improving race relations, and he never endorsed the objectives of such organizations as the Southern Tenant Farmers' Union. That group's periodical, *Sharecropper's Voice*, complained in 1936 that under Roosevelt "too often the progressive word has been the clothing for a conservative act. Too often he has talked like a cropper and acted like a planter." The difference was simple. Breaking with the planters would have been as much "the right thing to do" as turning against big business, but while the latter was politically beneficial, the former move would have been politically disastrous, both to New Deal programs and possibly to FDR himself. Far more workers than big businessmen voted, but very few blacks voted in the South, and poor whites in the region could be counted upon to vote Democratic even if the President did not do more for them. A vote-adding machine seemed to be planted in Roosevelt's head. It was always calculating when a decision had to be made.

Roosevelt's shift to the left with the Second New Deal was not an ideological move, but a political one. There was no drastic philosophic reorientation in 1935, but there was a very clear shift in politics, tone, and class identification. The motivation appears to have been a combination of decency and fear. When Roosevelt could no longer get away with playing the middle, he finally had to choose sides. It was easy enough to pick. What was right in this case coincided with what was expedient. Roosevelt simply went in the same direction that a majority of the people at the time was going—toward the left, toward humanitarian, cooperative values.

12· New Hickory: The WPA, the Election of 1936, and the Court Fight

THIS IS THE CAR

HOOVER Promised ME
ROOSEVELT Gave ME
FOR GODS SAKE
DON'T LET LANDON
TAKE IT AWAY

I n October 1935, New Dealers Rex Tugwell and Aubrey Williams made speeches calling on Democrats "to surge forward with the workers and farmers of this nation," and to enlist in the struggle between the "have-nots" and the "haves." Such terms became commonplace in the year before Roosevelt's reelection. Although the President had made no firm shift in ideology and even said in the fall of 1935 that the New Deal had reached a "breathing spell," the political advantage of maintaining a left-leaning posture was too great to pass up.

Whenever Roosevelt thought of trying to re-form an alliance with business, political considerations pushed him further into an anti–big business stance. The election year saw little in the way of new legislation. Members of Congress, like the President, had their eyes on November and their main concern was to end the session early enough to leave them plenty of time to gear up their campaigns. The President did advance his anti-business campaign by calling for a new tax on undistributed corporate profits. Congress passed a watered-down version of the bill before adjourning its lackluster session.[1]

The most important aspect of the New Deal from a political perspective in 1936 was the Works Progress Administration. Created by executive order after the huge Emergency Relief Appropriation of 1935, the WPA was placed under the direction of Harry Hopkins. The President divided the nearly $5 billion made available by Congress in 1935 among several different agencies. Part went to the new National Youth Administration, which gave part-time employment to more than 2 million high school and college students, thus helping them stay in school. The NYA also assisted the 2.6 million young people who were not in school. Harold Ickes's PWA and the CCC received generous slices of the appropriation, too, but the largest share—$1.39 billion—went to the new WPA.

Although there were a sufficient number of make-work projects under the WPA to lend some credence to conservative complaints about one crew digging holes and another filling them up, the shovel-leaning and leaf-raking were only one side of a many-faceted organization. The WPA could not equal the PWA's accomplishments in public building, but it did construct or improve more than 20,000 playgrounds, schools, hospitals, and airfields.

There were, however, serious problems connected with the WPA. Although work relief was far more expensive than direct payments to the unemployed, almost everyone preferred government jobs to a dole. The brief CWA experience had been gratifying. "A workless man," Harry Hopkins observed, "has little status at home and less with his friends." "Give a man a dole," the WPA administrator said on another occasion, "and you save his body and destroy his spirit. Give him a job and you save both body and spirit." Many WPA workers agreed. "Please continue this W.P.A. program," a group of workers in Battle Creek, Michigan, wrote to the President in 1936. "It makes us feel like an American citizen to earn our own living. Being on the dole or relief roll makes us lazy and the funds are not enough to live decent on." A county relief administrator in West Virginia noted as early as 1934 that work relief people "consider themselves as government workers—badly paid, or rather, inadequately employed. The general attitude seems to be," she went on, "that by going on relief one is working for the government. . . . People frequently call me up and say: 'I've been working for you for so long. Can't you do this or that for me[?]'"

Some WPA projects met the goal of sustaining workers' morale; many, unfortunately, did not. Pay was miserable. The nationwide average was $55 a month, much better than FERA relief payments, but an annual income of $660 amounted to barely more than half of a minimum subsistence budget of $1200. Nor was much security provided even for this tiny income. Working hours were often short, thus preventing laborers from obtaining their full potential pay. And there were no guarantees that jobs would continue or that checks would arrive on time. Such problems were frequently subjects of complaint by workers. "[W]hy can't every one be paid regularly as agreed or is it inafficiancy[?]" a Texas WPA worker asked Hopkins in a 1935 letter. "Here in Ft Worth the mens' pay is from 4 to 6 days behind; + some of them have to go home because they are too week to work." A group of Wisconsin workers who said they were "not red, but red-white-and-blue" criticized the President for saying American workers should be paid decent wages and then not doing it.

There were two fundamental reasons for the low wages. The first was obvious: there was not enough money to go around. The second concern was in some respects more significant. Committed as they were (hysterical charges by the Liberty League to the contrary notwithstanding) to maintaining the free enterprise system, Roosevelt and Hopkins wanted to be sure that work relief was not attractive in comparison with private employment. Hence they had to be sure that WPA earnings were kept at a sufficiently low level that the government would not be competing for workers with private enterprise. This was, of course, a rather silly concern while the unemployment rate was in the double digits, but the New Dealers remained convinced that strong incentives must be provided for those on work relief to return to the private sector as soon as *any* opportunity arose.

Yet this policy was in direct conflict with the stated objectives of using work relief to build morale and distinguishing WPA work from charity. Harry Hopkins correctly pointed out that "those who are forced to accept charity, no matter how unwillingly, are first pitied, then disdained" by others. People on direct relief were unable to avoid the stigma attached to charity and the resulting assumption that they were responsible for their own plight. People on the dole had to go through a humiliating "means test." The original hope— fulfilled briefly under the CWA—was that a work relief program could dispense with this demeaning procedure. The goal was summed up by New York social worker William Matthews when he said, "The sooner work relief can be given as nearly as possible the same status as that of work under regular conditions . . . the sooner it will command the respect . . . of the worker. . . ."

The trouble, simply, was that New Dealers wanted on the one hand to make work relief like a "real" job, but on the other to make it *un*like such employment. They sought to make WPA jobs attractive, so as to boost worker morale, at the same time they strove to make them *un*attractive, so as to encourage people to return to private employment. The result, inevitably, was a highly contradictory program. This was embodied in a policy that attempted to provide hourly wages similar to those paid by private businesses for the same sort of work, but limited the total monthly income of a WPA worker to far less than he might hope to make in the private sector. Hence those with the highest-paying jobs were allowed to work the fewest hours per month.

This was no way to provide a sense of security or build morale. WPA planners also failed to understand that manual labor was not a seamless web. Little attempt was made on most projects to match the strength, experience, and ability of a blue-collar worker with the job assigned to him. This was an indication of unconscious discrimination against lower-class people. When it came to the middle-class unemployed—or even to artists and writers—Hopkins and his associates tried to create jobs appropriate to their careers. (Hopkins was partial to artists. His family summered in Woodstock, New York, the noted artists' colony.) Manual laborers, though, were thought of simply as manual laborers.

There were other problems. President Roosevelt had promised when the organization was launched that the work would be "useful . . . in the sense that it affords permanent improvements in living conditions or that it creates future new wealth for the nation." Yet critics soon complained that much of what the WPA did was not "useful." In some cases they were right, but one of the principal reasons was that Roosevelt had pledged that the WPA would not compete with private enterprise. One wonders what such critics would have said if the organization *had* started to do useful things and thus had begun to compete with private business.

Behind the other conservative misgivings lay the fear that bureaucrats like Hopkins—intellectuals who had never "met a payroll" or "faced an electorate"—were using the relief agencies to secure positions of power for themselves. There was also some concern that Hopkins and his assistants wanted to keep large numbers of people on relief so that they would be politically subservient to the WPA. Particularly disturbing to Vice President Garner was the practice of referring to WPA workers as "clients."

Other WPA rules were as constraining as the prohibition on competition with private industry. Concentrating on helping the unemployed get through a "temporary" crisis, New Dealers used all available funds for payrolls and provided scarcely any training to help workers obtain permanent employment. Similarly, the requirement that 90 percent of those hired must come from the relief rolls—well intentioned though it clearly was—served both to discriminate against those who had held out longest against going on the dole and to prevent the employment of skilled workers needed to undertake many "useful" projects. Finally, a WPA rule allowing only one member of a family to be employed discriminated against women (who never represented even one-fifth of WPA workers) and large families. Some of the latter actually found themselves with lower incomes under the WPA than they had received on the dole.

The greatest failing of the WPA, however, was that it never provided work for most of the unemployed (the figure hovered around 30 percent of the jobless on WPA rolls between 1935 and 1940). This left upward of 5 million jobless Americans on the tender mercies and empty treasuries of state and local governments. When he chose the work relief option, President Roosevelt had decided to end federal relief, which he characterized in words worthy of Herbert Hoover (but none the less accurate for that) as "a narcotic, a subtle destroyer of the human spirit." That the states were not up to the task they had amply demonstrated in the early thirties, but Roosevelt dumped back in the laps of the governors and legislatures the "unemployables." The results were similar to those that might be expected if Ronald Reagan had obtained enactment of his New Federalism plan in the 1980s. They are best symbolized by New Jersey's decision to issue licenses to beg to those who could not be helped by exhausted state funds. Also like the New Federalism plan, Roosevelt's 1935 decision that Washington "must and shall quit this business of relief" meant that the states with the greatest needs would have the smallest resources with which to meet them. By the end of the decade, ten poor southern states were paying less than $10 per month per family, considerably less than half the national average.

Despite all of the drawbacks, the WPA was far better than what had gone before it (which is almost to say that it was far better than nothing). For those who got jobs on its projects, the pitiful wages were usually, if not always, better than relief. For all the obstacles to the goal of morale-building, an unemployed person was more likely to maintain a bit of self-respect working on a WPA project than he was receiving direct relief. And the agency did add substantially to the common wealth—material and artistic—of the American people. The WPA was much less than it could have been and it was less innovative than might have been expected in the Depression era. It was, for that matter, a good deal less daring than its precursor, the CWA, had been. Yet it was innovative and daring in some ways, most notably in its attempt to provide public patronage for the arts.[2]

A combination of factors—economic need, resurgent democratic values, Rooseveltian paternalism, and the quest for a distinctly American culture— came together in the mid 1930s to create the most notable experiment of the work relief program, Federal One. This was the use of a small but highly significant portion of WPA funds for an experiment in providing federal support for the arts in America. Although he had no special appreciation for "high culture" himself, as a gentleman Franklin Roosevelt believed fine music, art, and theater were essential to the good life. As part of his general attempt to democratize American life, Roosevelt wanted to make such culture available to the masses.

The 1935 relief appropriation included money designated for use in helping unemployed professionals. The WPA proceeded to set up four programs under Federal One: the Federal Art Project, the Federal Music Project, the Federal Theatre Project, and the Federal Writers' Project. (A fifth, the Historical Records Survey, was made a separate unit in 1936.) Harry Hopkins was among those who thought it was foolish and wasteful to put a concert violinist or a Shakespearean actor to work laying bricks. But Hopkins and a number of those who became involved with the WPA arts projects saw them as far more than a way to provide "suitable" relief work for artistic or educated Depression victims. They saw Federal One as a grand opportunity to fuse "high culture" with American democracy. The relationship between culture and democracy had long been a troubling question in the minds of some Americans. As democrats, some in the American arts community were concerned with bringing the arts to the people at large. At the same time, however, they feared that emphasis on numbers would inevitably lessen quality. Moreover, the dependence of artistic people on wealthy patrons often distanced the arts from "ordinary" folks.

A possible solution to some of these difficulties seemed to be federal patronage of the arts. In any case, private financial support practically dried up during the early Depression. As with so many other areas of American life, the Depression left many artistic people with nowhere else to turn for help but Washington. Dependence on federal financial assistance was not an unmixed blessing, however. Two principal, if vastly different, problems arose. The first was winning public support for the idea. Many people had a hard time accepting singing and acting as work. (We seem to have no trouble accepting the right of performers to make huge sums of money while working privately, but we balk at paying them much smaller amounts from our taxes.) Public support for federal arts projects was never strong. In the end, this proved fatal.

The other problem was the possibility that as Washington began paying the pianist it would want to call the tune. Even if there were no conscious interference—and who could be sure there would not be?—the possibility that bureaucracy would stifle creativity was omnipresent. Yet this possibility never seriously materialized. Instead, the WPA arts projects gave several million Americans their first opportunity to experience "high culture" and many people were enabled to participate in WPA-sponsored community symphonies, amateur theaters, and the like.

The least controversial of the Federal One projects was the Historical Records Survey, which inventoried local government records across the country. It performed a useful service and did so efficiently and without stepping on many conservative toes. The same could nearly be said about the Federal Writers' Project. Writers had originally been left out of the plans for arts projects, but after some of them complained the FWP was created. Although the Historical Records Survey succeeded in using previously untrained personnel, good writing was not so easily obtained. Many self-described "writers" who joined the project might not have been so classified by literary critics. In fact, many people—teachers, librarians, and others from white-collar occupations—who were not writers but did need relief were assigned to the Writers' Project. Trying to make a virtue of necessity—as well as to emphasize the democratic nature of the project—FWP Director Henry Alsberg said, "We must get over the idea that every writer must be an artist of the first class, and that an artist of the second or third class has no function."

Be that as it may, the FWP suffered no shortage of first-class writers. Among those who were employed by the Writers' Project were Richard Wright, Saul Bellow, Ralph Ellison, John Cheever, Jack Conroy, Conrad Aiken, Arna Bontemps, and Margaret Walker. Several of these great talents would likely have gone undeveloped had it not been for the FWP. The project did not allow much creative writing on WPA time, but working hours usually amounted to only thirty per week. "The simple act of providing writers and would-be writers with jobs that gave them a livelihood without unduly taxing their energies," FWP executive Jerre Mangione later contended, "turned out to be the most effective measure that could have been taken to nurture the future of American letters." Richard Wright was perhaps the best example of what the project could do for a young writer. He used his spare time to write *Native Son*, which won him acclaim while he was still an FWP employee. Ralph Ellison summed up the effect of working on the project: "Actually to be *paid* for writing . . . why that was a wonderful thing!"

What they were paid to write was a variety of what has been called "American stuff." Included was a series of inspired state guides. This was part of the mid-thirties revival of interest in all things American. It extended in the work of the FWP to the collection of folklore, studies of ethnic groups, "life histories" of individuals from many backgrounds, and the reminiscences of some 2000 former slaves. The last item, in particular, was a priceless historical treasure that would have been lost if not for the work of the Writers' Project. These efforts, under the guidance of Benjamin Botkin, emphasized the belief that "history must study the inarticulate many as well as the articulate few."

Federal Music Project Director Nikolai Sokoloff was also concerned about the inarticulate many, but he sought to raise them to an appreciation of fine music. An elitist where culture was concerned, Sokoloff of necessity had to reach for a mass audience if he was to find employment for some 15,000 out-of-work musicians. And the wide variation in their talent and skills obliged him to be more eclectic than he desired. Since instrumental music was unlikely to be perceived as carrying leftist messages, the FMP remained less controversial than some of the other WPA arts projects. The Music Project organized orchestras across the nation in cities that had not known them before, but it was prevented by political opposition from taking classical music to many areas its leaders had originally intended to reach. Concerts and music lessons were provided free or for nominal charges.

The accomplishments of the Federal Music Project were significant, but came to far less than some hoped for. Charles Seeger of the Music Project, along with Alan Lomax of the FWP, undertook a remarkable effort to collect and preserve America's folk music. Their accomplishment was magnificent, but Seeger's grand hope to integrate "popular, folk, and academic music into a distinctively American idiom" was never approached. Nor did the advances made by the FMP generally survive. Orchestras formed after World War II appear to have had their roots in WPA symphonies in fewer than ten cities.

More controversial than the historical, writing, or music projects was Holger Cahill's Federal Art Project. Project Director Cahill and his associates were firm believers in the ideal of cultural democracy; they expressed their goal as "art for the millions." Cahill insisted that the audience for plastic arts under the FAP be broadened greatly from those who had frequented galleries and museums in the past. Franklin Roosevelt agreed with the objectives, if not always with the content of the art that was aimed at the millions. The President guessed—optimistically—that only 10 percent of the American people had ever had an opportunity to view a "fine picture." For a brief time the FAP changed that. By 1938 works done by Art Project painters and sculptors were on view in many parts of the country. An FAP exhibit at the New York World's Fair in 1940 was seen by more than 2 million people. The most lasting—and perhaps the most impressive—of the Art Project's achievements were the murals its artists painted in public buildings across the nation. The decisive influence came from Mexican painters of propaganda murals, particularly Diego Rivera and Clemente Orozco, who spent the early years of the Depression being paid large fees by the likes of the Ford and Rockefeller families to paint anti-capitalist murals in such incongruous places as the San Francisco Stock Exchange Club, the Ford-supported Detroit Institute of Arts, the RCA Building in Rockefeller Center, and the Dartmouth College Library. Like the products of other WPA arts projects, the FAP murals represented part of the renewed interest in American life. Victor Arnautoff's "City Life" in San Francisco's Coit Tower is one of the best examples. The subjects of many, however, were too labor-oriented to suit conservatives in Congress. Charges of "Communism" grew louder as the Depression decade neared its end.

The quality of the work done by FAP employees varied widely, of course. So did the opinions of critics on its overall merit. As with the Writers' Project, the Art Project provided a livelihood for some artists who would go on to great careers, among them Jackson Pollock, Willem De Kooning, Anton Refregier, and Yasuo Kuniyoshi. Critical controversy, like that over social content, centered on the murals. Post office murals (most of which were done outside the FAP jurisdiction) tended to celebrate the "masses" and the oppressed laboring class. While Ford Madox Ford, the English art critic, said the quality of FAP work was "astonishingly high," American photographer Alfred Stieglitz said he had nothing against putting unemployed artists on the federal payroll, but they should not be allowed to get near paint. Stieglitz characterized some of the project's work as "the rape of the walls." President Roosevelt, as was his wont, took a middle ground on the murals: "Some of it good," he said, "some of it not so good, but all of it native, human, eager and alive—all of it painted by their own kind in their own country, and painted about things that they know and look at often and have touched and loved." Roosevelt's knack for understanding the public mood was once again evident in this assessment.

If the social content of a mural could raise the eyebrows of members of the House Committee on Un-American Activities, a theatrical production could appear to be outright subversion. The Federal Theatre Project, directed by the former head of the Vassar College Experimental Theatre, Hallie Flanagan, was the most important, the most controversial, and hence, the shortest-lived of the Federal One projects. Flanagan had been a classmate of Harry Hopkins at Grinnell College. One actress who worked with her described her as having "the spirit, the soul, and the dedication, and the drive" of Eleanor Roosevelt. The FTP director was dedicated to building a truly national theater, one that would provide food for thought as well as for actors' stomachs. One of her ideals was to use drama to create public awareness of social problems. Hopkins promised a theater that was "free, adult, uncensored." That was a tall order, but in its brief history the FTP often approached the ideal.

The FTP played a role similar to those of the other arts projects in stimulating and encouraging talents that would remain important for decades after the program's demise. A very abbreviated list of its directors, playwrights, actors, producers, composers, and technicians gives an idea of the FTP's contribution: Orson Welles, Arthur Miller, Dale Wasserman, John Huston, Joseph Cotten, Jack Carter, E. G. Marshall, Will Geer, Arlene Francis, Canada Lee, Howard Da Silva, Burt Lancaster (who began as an aerialist in an FTP circus), John Houseman, Lehman Engel, George Izenour.

Even more important than the individual careers that were spurred on by the FTP was the stimulus the project provided for the American stage through its openness to new ideas. Far more than other government agencies of the Depression era, the Theatre Project treated black Americans as highly capable, basically equal human beings. The FTP established sixteen "Negro Units" around the country. Casts almost always remained segregated (the notable exception being a Newark production of *The Trial of Dr. Beck*), but the roles were not. That is to say that black actors were no longer confined to "Negro" roles. The great departure was initiated by John Houseman, who codirected the Harlem FTP unit with black actress Rose McClendon. When the Federal Theatre began, the Harlem riots of 1935 were only a few months in the past and the usual offensive roles for black performers were wholly unacceptable. Houseman decided to put on a black production of a Shakespearean classic. If the idea was to be accepted it would have to be a first-rate production, and Houseman needed the best possible director. His friend Orson Welles, not yet twenty years old, quickly agreed to take the job. Welles's wife, Virginia, had the inspiration to make the first production *Macbeth*, set in Haiti with Voodoo priestesses as the witches. A troupe of African drummers (including a genuine witch doctor) was hired. At their request WPA requisition forms were filled out for five live black goats, which they proceeded to sacrifice in the theater's basement, so that the skins could be stretched for drums. With such authenticity, the *Voodoo Macbeth* was a smashing success.

Despite a few cases of attempted censorship, the Federal Theatre was remarkably uninhibited in its offerings. Most notable among its innovations were the "living newspapers." These were plays in the new form of documentaries that took a stand on issues of the day, provided information about them, and advocated a course of action. The New York group first put on *Triple-A Plowed Under*, a play that called for farmers and consumers to work together against greedy middlemen. Despite its agrarian subject matter, *Triple-A Plowed Under* was a stunning success, both critically and at the box office. So were such other living newspapers as *Power*, which demanded public ownership of utilities; *Injunction Granted*, a play that dramatized the anti-union actions of the courts; and *Created Equal*, which dealt with conflicts between property owners and citizens throughout American history. Right-wing critics charged that such productions were propaganda for the New Deal—or for something worse. Garrett Garet wrote in *The Saturday Evening Post* in June 1936 that *Triple-A Plowed Under* employed such "logotypes of Communist propaganda" as "hunger" and "starvation." Two months later another piece in the same periodical claimed that the Federal Theatre's "hair [was] full of Communists" and Flanagan was trying to "Russianize" the American stage.

Although the conservative critics finally had their way, the accomplishments of the Federal Theatre Project in its brief history are most impressive. In addition to its remarkable efforts in the legitimate theater, the FTP put on radio drama, children's plays, puppet shows, and circuses. In less than four years, approximately 30 million people attended productions of the FTP. Here, albeit all too briefly, was art for the millions.

The Federal Theatre's success was achieved in the face of constant obstacles and opposition. Some of the problems, though serious, were survivable. Many of the project's best people, for instance, were lured away by private companies. But the freedom and lack of commercial emphasis kept enough talent with the FTP so that this problem could be overcome. Political opposition, though, could not, in the end, be defeated. In 1938 and 1939, in a foretaste of the techniques that were used by Richard Nixon, Joseph McCarthy, and others in the late forties and early fifties, the House Un-American Activities Committee (HUAC) "investigated" the FTP as part of a larger exploration of "un-American propaganda activities" in the nation. It was a classic witch hunt in which the conclusions were reached before any testimony was taken. One Republican on the committee, J. Parnell Thomas of New Jersey, told a news conference before the hearings began that "startling evidence" indicated that the FTP was "serving as a branch of the Communistic organization." What he meant by that was apparent when Thomas added that the Federal Theatre was "one more link in the vast and unparalleled New Deal propaganda machine."

After months of hearings in which people were coaxed to provide hearsay evidence, Hallie Flanagan was finally allowed to testify. She misjudged her interrogators. When she quoted Christopher Marlowe, one of the congressmen interrupted her to ask who Marlowe was and whether he was a Communist. Others laughed, but Flanagan realized that this was tragedy, not comedy. The HUAC report ignored her refutation of the earlier testimony and when the House debated the new WPA budget in 1939, the FTP was cut. The Senate tried to save the project, but it did not survive the conference committee and President Roosevelt had little choice but to sign the relief appropriation bill without the Federal Theatre.

The other arts projects and the WPA itself (rechristened with a more conservative name, Works Projects Administration) limped along until 1943. Their service to the nation was invaluable, but it has been widely recognized only since the 1960s. The arts projects collected a huge amount of raw material that has proved to be of enormous value to subsequent artists and historians. They helped in incalculable ways to lift the spirits of a depressed nation and add to its culture. The WPA as a whole, like its arts projects, was certainly not without serious flaws, but the frequent complaint that it was nothing more than an attempt to provide "bread and circuses" is unjustified. The WPA proved, in fact, to be one of the leading examples of government recognition of the values of Depression America. Its emphasis was on *public* works and arts for the people as a whole. The attitudes behind the expenditures on public buildings and "art for the millions" reflected the decline of self-centeredness evident among Americans of the thirties in so many other ways. These buildings, plays, concerts, and murals were to be *accessible,* to be shared and enjoyed by others. [3]

The President began the election year of 1936 by making it clear that, as far as rhetoric was concerned, the breathing spell for business was over. Roosevelt's annual message to Congress, delivered on the evening of the Court's rejection of the AAA, called upon Congress to "wage unceasing warfare" against "our resplendent economic autocracy" which sought "power for themselves, enslavement for the public." This was only the beginning. Five days later FDR delivered a rousing speech over a radio hookup to some 3000 Jackson Day dinners around the nation. Roosevelt compared himself with the seventh President, saying the American people loved Jackson "for the enemies he had made." "History repeats," Roosevelt declared, picturing himself as a kind of New Hickory. He called upon Americans to keep up the fight against "the forces of privilege and greed."

Talk is cheap, of course, and Roosevelt offered no specific new programs to combat those selfish interests. He was careful to point out repeatedly that the enemy was not businessmen in general, but that small number of financial and industrial leaders whose self-serving dedication to "free enterprise" was unbending. In his budget message the President said the federal budget would soon be balanced. As winter drew to a close, he ordered spending cuts and a reduction in WPA employment. Still, the symbolic importance of FDR's verbal attacks on the "greedy" should not be underestimated. Public response to the Jackson Day speech was overwhelmingly favorable. More than 95 percent of those who wrote to the President about the speech praised his class-tinged phrases. "I am in complete sympathy with your fight on greed and the favored classes," a Philadelphia man wrote to Roosevelt. "At last we have a Man in the White House and not a puppet of organized Wealth," an Oregon woman wrote.

And if Roosevelt's rhetoric was not enough by itself to win the support of the forgotten man, wealthy conservatives were always glad to help. In this regard no group was more obliging than the American Liberty League. Two weeks after Roosevelt's Jackson Day speech, Al Smith, who had completed his graduation from brown derby to white tie and tails, viciously attacked the New Deal before a crowd of twelve Du Ponts and 2000 of their fellow travelers in Washington's Mayflower Hotel. *The New York Times* called this Liberty League confab "the greatest collection of millionaires ever gathered under one roof." The millionaires—and those who aspired to be—who overflowed the hotel's main ballroom that evening were hungry for raw, *red* meat. Smith served up generous portions: "It is all right with me if they want to disguise themselves as Karl Marx or Lenin or any of the rest of that bunch," the Happy

Warrior said of Roosevelt and his followers, "but I won't stand for their allowing them to march under the banner of Jackson and Cleveland." As the crowd roared, Smith could not content himself with that bombast. His peroration brought the faithful in frenzy to their feet: "There can be only one capital, Washington or Moscow. There can be only one atmosphere of government, the clean, pure fresh air of free America, or the foul breath of Communistic Russia." This was sheer poppycock, and few people outside the select Mayflower audience would swallow it. The impact was hardly what the Liberty League had had in mind. Smith and company simply made it easier for Roosevelt to paint the 1936 election as a contest, not between Washington and Moscow, but between Roosevelt and the Du Ponts, between compassion and selfish indifference. If the Democratic National Committee had to choose the most effective way to spend its limited funds, it should have considered contributions to the league.

Rich businessmen would not have achieved their positions had it not been for their ingenuity. They demonstrated this quality in 1936 by finding ever new ways to aid Roosevelt inadvertently. There had been significant gains in recovery the year before the election. But when conservatives warned of an economic boom and said inflation was now the great danger, they merely convinced more people of their own callousness, and thus made Roosevelt all the more attractive. Such businessmen gave Roosevelt just the dramatic foil he needed for his role as champion of the people. That it worked was demonstrated in the comments many "ordinary" Americans made in letters to the Roosevelts. An Indiana admirer, for example, wrote to Mrs. Roosevelt in 1935 that she liked the President because "his most bitter opponents are the (Rich) the Chambers of Commerce Principaly the manufacturers." In May of that year, Tugwell expressed the view that a sweeping attack the United States Chamber of Commerce had made on the New Deal was "perhaps one of the best things which has happened politically." Given the climate of opinion, it seems unlikely that the Liberty League's warning early in the election year that Roosevelt sought "redistribution of income on a grand scale" did the President any political harm.

Yet early in the year polls showed the President's popularity was low. Republicans convinced themselves, as politicians usually do at the dawn of an election year, that their prospects were good. One problem remained, however: finding a candidate. This was not as easy as it may sound. Herbert Hoover was eager for a chance to vindicate himself, but few Republican leaders—as much as some of them might like the former President's philosophy—were up to the level of self-deception necessary to think the voters could be convinced to accept the man many of them blamed for the Depression. And few other potential candidates were available. There were only seven Republican governors in the entire nation, and only one of these had been reelected in 1934. This qualification made Alfred M. Landon of Kansas the "most available" man. Landon was, in fact, the only GOP governor of a state west of the Mississippi, an area Roosevelt had swept in 1932. Therefore Republican leaders, who wanted to shed the party's disastrous image as the tool of eastern financiers, had another reason to look to Landon.

Whatever image the Republican leaders might create, their true colors were shown by their reference to Landon as "the Kansas Coolidge." The name said little about the governor, but spoke volumes about what many Republicans saw as the ideal chief executive.

Alf Landon was no Coolidge. Actually he had a progressive record and had supported much of the New Deal. Such sins were overlooked by the GOP powers not only because Landon was about all that was available, but because the Kansan had a reputation as a fiscal conservative. He had run Kansas on a balanced budget (albeit with three-fourths of the public funds expended in the state in 1935 coming from Washington, which led a Roosevelt adviser to point out that although the President "has not yet balanced his budget . . . he certainly has balanced Governor Landon's").

The Republican party was prepared to seek victory by nominating someone who did not see Roosevelt as an agent of Lucifer, but delegates to the party's 1936 convention demonstrated what a reluctant compromise this was by cheering wildly during a speech by Hoover. The former President castigated Roosevelt for preaching "the gospel of class hatred." The Democrat's reelection, Hoover warned, would lead to "the succeeding states of violence and outrage by which European despotisms have crushed all liberalism and all freedom." Despite several minutes of boisterous screams of "We want Hoover," the convention eventually returned to the real world and nominated Landon without opposition.[4]

Roosevelt had more to worry about than Republicans, however. One factor that had scared him into his new, class-oriented course the year before was the rise of the demagogues. The Second New Deal and Huey Long's death had eased the threat, but successful politicians never feel secure. Father Coughlin continued early in the election year to vacillate between attacks on Roosevelt and praise for him; Dr. Townsend was irate over what he called the "wholly unfair, inadequate and unjust" Social Security program; and the Reverend Gerald L. K. Smith was claiming the mantle of Long and the leadership of the Share Our Wealth movement. Smith, who had latched onto the Long entourage in 1934, after a career as a preacher in Indiana and Louisiana, had proved to be an effective organizer for the SOW Society. As such, he was an asset to Long. Still, he made the Kingfish nervous. This is understandable. Smith liked to wear Huey's used clothing and, one Long aide claimed, at least once slept on the floor near the senator's bed "just so he could be close to

Huey." The Reverend Mr. Smith was not likely to fill the shoes of Huey Long figuratively, even if he did so literally. The possibility that he would unite with Coughlin and Townsend continued to worry Democrats, though. Early in 1936 such an alliance still appeared capable of taking many votes away from the Democrats, so much so that some wealthy Republicans secretly financed an effort to create a Coughlin-Smith-Townsend party for the 1936 campaign.

The alliance did ultimately come into being, but the Democrats' fears proved to be greatly inflated. In June 1936, apparently at the urging of Coughlin, Representative William Lemke of North Dakota announced his candidacy for the presidency. The vehicle for Lemke's campaign was called the Union party. It began with the backing of Townsend and Smith, but was essentially a combination of Coughlin's organization with militant agrarians of the northern Plains. Lemke, a sincere populist, soon found himself in uncomfortable company. Coughlin's fascism began to show; Smith never made much of an attempt to hide his. By mid-October the self-anointed heir to the Kingfish was proclaiming a nationalist movement to "seize the government of the United States." "The democratic method is a lot of baloney," Smith declared, "it doesn't mean a thing."

With backers like these, "Liberty Bill" Lemke (unkind critics liked to say that the nickname derived from the fact that the congressman's head was in a condition similar to that of the famous Philadelphia Bell) may appear fortunate to have won 2 percent of the national vote. Like other third-party candidates, though, Lemke almost certainly had more support than was indicated by the votes counted for him. People are generally reluctant to "throw away their votes." In August 1936, Lorena Hickok reported that many Iowans with whom she talked had told her: "I'd vote for Lemke, only I don't think he can win. And I'd rather have Roosevelt than Landon." When the size of the Long, Coughlin, and Townsend movements in 1935 is considered, it becomes clear that Lemke's low vote total was not the result of a rejection of wealth-sharing or "social justice" by the voters, but principally of a growing awareness of the fascism of Smith and Coughlin. Most of the discontented Americans who had been attracted to the demagogues in 1935 apparently voted for Roosevelt a year later.[5]

This, of course, was exactly what the President wanted discontented voters to do. To assure this, he needed continued economic improvement and a strong identification as the defender of the down-and-out. To accomplish the first, he instructed government officials to do whatever was necessary to keep crop prices up and to be sure that there were no large reductions in WPA employment before the election. The second ingredient in FDR's recipe for victory was obtained easily enough. The President made a series of "non-political" visits to victims of floods and drought, emphasizing the humanitarian concern of his administration. And, above all, Roosevelt continued to lash at big business and portray himself as the friend of the working class.

In the latter effort, FDR had much help. Landon was the first Republican presidential candidate to face two problems that would plague his successors for more than a generation: the specter (all too alive in the 1936 campaign) of Herbert Hoover and the question of whether, as Barry Goldwater put it twenty-eight years later, to offer voters a choice or an echo. Landon preferred to endorse the goals of the New Deal, but to criticize the inefficiency and poor administration of government programs. After following this course for a time, Landon realized that it looked like "me-tooism." He then joined with other Republicans in direct assaults on the New Deal. It did not work. Alf Landon was no great speaker. (The most memorable line in his campaign was "Wherever I have gone in this country, I have found Americans.") He denounced the Social Security program, but accepted its basic premise, thus alienating its supporters without gaining the confidence of its opponents. The Republican nominee went on to warn that the New Deal would lead to the guillotine. Landon aides insisted that Roosevelt was backed by Moscow. GOP national chairman John D. M. Hamilton solemnly warned voters that ballots cast for the President would further the "International Communist Conspiracy." Republican campaigners informed workers that Social Security would soon be robbing money from their pay envelopes and that the system would bring regimentation to America. Such misrepresentations, half-truths, and bald-faced lies backfired. Figuratively, at least, many Americans believed that some of their rich neighbors deserved nothing so much as the guillotine; few Americans believed that Moscow was behind the President, but such stories enhanced Roosevelt's image as an opponent of business. And when employers placed copies of the GOP attack on social security in pay envelopes, workers saw more clearly than ever the links between big business and the Republicans.

Given the sharp class division, businessmen could be counted upon for fewer financial contributions than usual to the Democratic cause. (Bankers, who had provided one-quarter of Roosevelt's 1932 campaign funds, supplied only 3 percent in 1936.) Part of the slack was taken up by Roosevelt's most important new ally, organized labor. Following the passage of the Wagner Act, many union leaders clearly saw the stake they had in keeping Roosevelt in office. Labor gave over $770,000 to the Democratic campaign in 1936, with nearly two-thirds of the total coming from John L. Lewis's United Mine Workers. Lewis and other unionists also formed Labor's Non-Partisan League to hold rallies, distribute literature, and get out the vote for FDR. The President, never before noted as a great friend of organized labor, proudly displayed a union card given to him in New York at the beginning of October.

The Roosevelt campaign in 1936 mobilized blacks, Jews, Catholics,

women, intellectuals, and independent and Republican progressives, to join
with labor and the traditional Democratic strength in city machines and the
South. It was a new sort of campaign, and the coalition formed in it made the
New Deal party dominant in American politics for more than forty years. The
1982 congressional elections indicated that the Roosevelt coalition has life in
it still.

The Republicans also introduced a new and lasting feature of presidential
campaigns in 1936. For the first time the methods used to sell soap and soft
drinks were tried on a large scale in marketing a presidential candidate. The
effort to sell Alf Landon to the American people was extensive and expensive.
The Republicans outspent the Democrats, $14 million to $9 million. Despite
its failure, the massive advertising campaign had won a place for itself in
American elections. The days of the H. R. Haldemans and David Gergens
were still beyond the horizon, but American politics was on a path that led in
that direction.

For his part, Roosevelt played up the class differences in the election and
stepped up his "us-against-them" rhetoric. In his acceptance speech, the President drew the battle lines sharply. Denouncing the "economic royalists" and
"privileged princes" who sought to impose a "new industrial dictatorship,"
FDR said that Americans must take away the power of the "overprivileged."
He warned that these people were an "enemy within our gates" and pledged to
continue to struggle against them. "Private enterprise," Roosevelt declared,
had become "too private. It became privileged enterprise, not free enterprise."
The President admitted that mistakes had been made, but said his administration was warm-hearted and "lives in a spirit of charity." "Charity literally
translated from the original," he said, "means love, the love that understands,
that does not merely share the wealth of the giver, but in true sympathy and
wisdom helps men to help themselves." Once again FDR and his speech-
writers had struck the chord of the values so many Depression-era Americans
had adopted. "This generation of Americans," Roosevelt declared, "has a
rendezvous with destiny." The crowd of 100,000 roared its approval.

And so it went through the campaign. The President continued to emphasize class in his speeches, and the enthusiastic crowds greeting him almost
everywhere he went reached unprecedented size. In 1932 people had voted
against Hoover; now they clearly were voting for Roosevelt. People were heard
shouting, "He gave me a job," or "He saved my home." The only places
where FDR was booed on the campaign trail were in the Wall Street area and
at his alma mater. This hurt his cause not at all. At Harrisburg, Pennsylvania,
as at so many other campaign stops, Roosevelt linked himself to the Depression-era values: "Ours has been a program of one for all and all for one." In
the traditional end of the campaign speech in New York's Madison Square
Garden, the President summed up the theme of the campaign: The election

was a contest between "the millions who never had a chance" and "organized money." The "forces of selfishness and of lust for power," Roosevelt said, had "never before in all our history . . . been so united against one candidate as they stand today. They are unanimous in their *hate* for *me—and I welcome their hatred.*"

Roosevelt had turned the presidential election into a contest between the haves and the have-nots. In Depression America the latter were obviously far more numerous. Nonetheless, the highly respected *Literary Digest* straw poll, which had been correct in each of the four previous presidential elections it had forecast, predicted that Landon would win by an electoral college margin of 370–161. The actual balloting, however, gave Roosevelt the largest electoral vote victory ever recorded in a contested election, 523–8. The popular vote went to FDR by the huge margin of 27,751,841 to 16,679,491. The President had won 60.8 percent of the ballots cast. Landon carried only Maine and Vermont, leading to Democratic national chairman James Farley's famous play on the old campaign saying, "As Maine goes, so goes the nation." "As Maine goes," Farley quipped after the election, "so goes Vermont." From the other side of the political fence, newspaperwoman Dorothy Thompson remarked: "If Landon had given one more speech, Roosevelt would have carried Canada, too."

The explanation of how the previously reliable *Literary Digest* poll could be so utterly wrong tells much about the mood of the electorate in 1936. In many areas of the nation the people polled were chosen from lists of automobile owners and from telephone books. This skewed the poll toward upper-income groups. Even in areas where a truly random selection of voters was conducted, the well-to-do were more likely to return their ballots. This, of course, had always been the case with *Literary Digest* polls, but in the past it had not mattered. That it did matter in 1936 is a strong indication that socioeconomic class made a difference that year as at no time since at least the Jacksonian era. In short, Roosevelt's appeal to class had worked. His huge margin of victory came largely from people—presumably poor—who had not believed it mattered to vote in 1932, but now wanted to express their support for the New Deal. Approximately 6 million more people cast ballots in 1936 than had done so four years before; fully 5 million of these voted for FDR.

The 1936 Roosevelt vote increased in each successively lower-income group, varying from only 42 percent of the upper-income voters to 80 percent of the votes of union members, 81 percent of unskilled workers, and 84 percent of the people on relief. As the poor clustered around Roosevelt, the wealthy moved their wagons into an ever tighter circle around the Republican party. The Du Pont family donated more than half a million dollars to the GOP that year. It did not help. Their home city of Wilmington, Delaware, long a Republican bastion, voted Democratic. In Muncie, Indiana, where the Lynds noted in 1936 "perhaps the strongest effort in the city's history by the local big businessmen (industrialists and bankers) to stampede local opinion in behalf of a single presidential candidate," the results were similar. Muncie went for the Democratic presidential candidate for the first time since the Civil War, giving FDR nearly 60 percent of its votes. "We workers licked the big bosses here," one laborer told the Lynds, ". . . by our majority vote for Roosevelt."

The 1936 election showed that class had become, at least temporarily, the dominant element in American politics. On one class issue after another in the mid-thirties, the difference of opinion between Democrats and Republicans was striking. Asked in January 1936 if they favored an amendment to the Constitution allowing the federal government to regulate agriculture and industry, 69 percent of those classifying themselves as Democrats said yes; 88 percent of the Republicans said no. Similar differences were recorded on many other issues. The reason most often cited by voters for supporting Roosevelt was: "He helped the working classes."

After the 1936 election it was clear that a fundamental shift in the American political alignment had occurred. The depression of the 1890s had made the Republicans the majority party in the United States. Now another depression, along with Roosevelt's attempts to deal with it, had made the Democrats the majority party. Outside the South the nation had split politically along class lines. In the South most voters of all classes remained Democrats, but elsewhere the rich tended toward the GOP and the poor and lower-middle income groups flocked into the party of the New Deal. Obviously such shifts were far from absolute. Many poorer Americans retained their Republican loyalties, and certainly a number of those who were well-to-do remained Democrats. But the shift was one of the most marked in American political history. It seems appropriate to give workers the last words on the 1936 election. "Mr. Roosevelt," one forgotten man said, "is the only man we ever had in the White House who would understand that my boss is a son-of-a-bitch." An electrician in the nation's capital vastly overstated the case, but pointed up the distinction in values that many Americans saw between the two sides in 1936, when he said of the election: "On the one side is pure and unadulterated greed and cruelty. On the other the crying need of a lost humanity."[6]

"Wait until next year, Henry," President Roosevelt had said to Treasury Secretary Morgenthau in May 1936, "I am going to be really radical . . . I am going to recommend a lot of radical legislation." Now the way appeared to be clear. The Democratic majorities in Congress had swelled to 333–88 in the House and 75–16 in the Senate (and most of the 13 representatives and 4 senators from minor parties were to the President's left). Roosevelt seemed to be in a position to move further to the left.

In his second inaugural address, Roosevelt indicated that new proposals would be forthcoming, that he would do something about the "one-third of a nation ill-housed, ill-clad, ill-nourished." That he could get away with a statement like this, not in criticism of an incumbent, but after having been president for four years himself, is one of the most impressive measures of Roosevelt's powerful appeal.

As it happened, though, the radical action the President took in 1937 was not in the direction of new social programs. He had been painfully reminded in the preceding two years that there was a third branch of the government. His mandate from the people and the bulging Democratic majorities in Congress could be neutralized by five old men on the Supreme Court. Before he could try any new programs, Roosevelt believed he must protect what remained of the old by ending Court opposition.

The idea was not new. When the possibility had arisen in February 1935 that the Court might strip Congress of the power to regulate the currency by negating the devaluation of the dollar, Roosevelt had prepared a message to nullify the decision. Attorney General Homer Cummings had suggested that if the decision went against the government Congress should immediately be asked to increase the number of justices and produce a favorable majority. But the Court upheld the government's action and both Roosevelt's speech and Cummings's idea went unused.

Later in 1935 and in 1936, however, it became clear that if the Supreme Court were not brought under control it would dismantle the New Deal. The background of the Court struggle of 1937 must be understood before Roosevelt's proposal can be explained. Through FDR's first term the Supreme Court continued to bear the imprint of Warren G. Harding, who had appointed the Chief Justice, Charles Evans Hughes, and three other justices during his two-and-one-half years as president. As in the case of Richard Nixon a half century later, Harding's Court appointments allowed his influence to live on long after his personal disgrace. After Roosevelt took office the judiciary was the only branch of government in Republican hands. In 1933, Republican federal judges outnumbered Democrats by more than 2.5 to 1. During his first term Roosevelt had no opportunity to alter this at the highest level. This was the first time in American history that a president had served four or more years without an opportunity to appoint a single Supreme Court justice. (Since Roosevelt finally did get to make appointments the distinction of being the only president to serve a full term and never appoint a Supreme Court justice goes to Jimmy Carter.) In their four-year administrations, Taft had appointed five justices and Hoover three. All this would have counted for little if the Court had not embarked upon an unprecedented spree of reversals of congressional actions. Between 1920 and 1933 the Court had invalidated portions of acts of Congress twenty-two times. When it is remembered that in the republic's first seventy-six years the Court had taken such action only twice, the extent of judicial activism after 1920 becomes plain. As Senator Norris said, the Supreme Court had turned into "a continuous constitutional convention." The Chief Justice also put it well. "The Constitution," Charles Evans Hughes said, "is what the judges say it is."

Confronted with the opposition of the Court in 1935, FDR had considered submitting a constitutional amendment either to give new powers to Congress or to limit the power of the Court. The alternative, which Roosevelt found "distasteful" at the end of 1935, was to follow Cummings's suggestion of ten months before and "pack" the Court with liberal judges. Ultimately, however, Roosevelt came to realize that the problem lay not in the Constitution, but in the Court's interpretations. Accordingly, he gave up on the idea of seeking an amendment and during the election year he said little about what could be done about the Court.

Roosevelt's overwhelming victory in 1936 was a misfortune for the nation and for him. Understandably, it convinced the President that his popularity was immense and that he could do no wrong. He believed the public would always be on his side. Coming now rather easily to identify his wishes with those of the American electorate, Roosevelt saw the Court as blocking the will of the people and decided to act.

Without consulting congressional leaders (who, after all, did not speak for *all* the people the way the President did), Roosevelt submitted a Court "re-form" proposal on February 5, 1937. The idea was essentially Roosevelt's own; the details were worked out by Attorney General Cummings. The objective was transparent enough: FDR wanted to create a Court majority that would approve New Deal legislation, but he did not admit this. His proposal was, as a newspaper favorable to the New Deal said, "too damned clever." He moved at the issue obliquely, seeking the power to appoint a new justice for every one with ten years' service on the Court who did not retire within six months after his seventieth birthday. The reason, the President disingenuously declared, was that the Court was overburdened and the aging judges could not keep up with the workload.

What Roosevelt requested was in no sense unconstitutional. It is clearly within the power of Congress to alter the size of the Supreme Court; it had, in fact, been done several times in the nineteenth century. The proposal met with a howl of outrage all the same. Appearing to be an open grab for power that would upset the balance of the American system of government, Roosevelt's "Court-packing" plan gave closet conservatives, heretofore afraid to attack the New Deal, a grand opportunity to assail the President.

Conservative opposition was expected, of course, and in itself would have concerned Roosevelt little. But many moderates and liberals—Senator Norris, William Allen White, and Oswald Garrison Villard, to name a few—

soon joined the chorus of criticism. The reasons were several. One was the way FDR introduced the proposal. It seemed almost as if, with his new mandate from the voters, the President was ready to treat Congress the way Huey Long had treated the Louisiana legislature. A second reason for opposition was Roosevelt's "clever" approach of indirect assault on the Court. The Court, as Hughes soon showed, was not falling behind in its work and, in any case, adding judges was more likely to slow than to speed deliberations. In raising the age question Roosevelt made another blunder. Louis Brandeis, one of the New Deal's most consistent supporters and a highly respected liberal, was over eighty and the oldest justice. Nor were senators, many past or fast approaching seventy themselves, likely to agree that public officials ought to retire at that age.

Finally, and most importantly, liberals shared with conservatives a genuine fear that Court-packing would upset the American constitutional government. In one sense making the Court responsive to Congress and the President was a move toward greater democracy, but it was an unchecked democracy that could lead to a pseudodemocratic absolutism. Talk about the possibility that dictatorship might lie down the road for the United States was no longer confined to hysterical right-wingers. Many remembered uncomfortably what Roosevelt had said in the closing speech of his campaign a few months before: "I should like to have it said of my second Administration that in it these forces [of selfishness and of lust for power] met their master." In the eyes of most Americans, the world of 1937, replete as it was with Hitlers, Stalins, and Mussolinis, had quite enough "masters." Even those who had no fears that Roosevelt might move toward absolute power shuddered at the thought of creating such a precedent for later abuse by a reactionary president. George Norris wondered how he would have reacted if "Harding had offered this bill." Such people doubted that the immediate benefits of curbing the Court were worth the dangers the plan would create for the future. For a task that required the sculptor's chisel, it seemed Roosevelt wanted to wield a sledgehammer. As much as he admired TR, the younger Roosevelt still sometimes confused soft-speaking problems with those calling for the big stick.

A crusade against the Court plan developed rapidly. Conservative Republicans wisely contained their urge to take the lead in denouncing the proposal. That job was left to Democrats whose motives were above suspicion, particularly to such impeccable progressives as Montana Senator Burton K. Wheeler. Brandeis and Hughes lent their prestige to the opposition. The Chief Justice responded to Roosevelt's charges of inefficiency in a public letter. Hughes left no doubt that there was no need to enlarge the Court.

Despite all the clamor President Roosevelt—still savoring his mandate—remained calm and confident. "All I have to do," he assured Jim Farley, "is to devise a better speech, and the opposition will be beating a path to the

White House door." Before such pleasant events could occur, however, a series of actions by the Court intervened to seal the fate of the packing scheme. Justice Owen J. Roberts, who had joined with the conservatives in striking down several New Deal laws, had a change of heart. At the end of March the Supreme Court announced a 5–4 decision upholding a Washington State minimum wage law similar to a New York law the Court had disallowed a year before. Since the decision had been completed before Roosevelt made his proposal, Roberts's "switch in time that saved nine" was not a response to the President's threat. Rather, it seems to have been an acknowledgment of the election results. In mid-April the Court upheld the Wagner Act, again by a 5–4 margin. Then in May conservative Justice Willis Van Devanter announced his intention to retire, finally giving Roosevelt an opportunity to appoint a member of the Court. A few days later the Court approved the Social Security Act. If only Roosevelt had waited a few months . . .

But now the President's prestige was committed, and he refused to give up. A bitter Senate debate ensued, with Roosevelt's support crumbling. Finally, after majority leader Joe Robinson died in July, the President had to abandon the fight and accept (in an attempt at face-saving) an innocuous substitute bill to speed up the judicial process.

This, it may safely be said, was not Franklin Roosevelt's finest hour. The casualties were many. A congressional session that had promised to be one of glorious new programs enacted by a liberal President with an overwhelmingly supportive Congress was wasted. The Court scheme united the Republican party, no small feat, and one party members were unlikely to have accomplished without Roosevelt's generous assistance. But that was the least of it. The Court battle saw the rebirth of a conservative coalition of Republicans and southern Democrats. This coalition blocked most liberal legislation from 1937 onward. In the midst of the fray, it seemed that Roosevelt had achieved his objective of ending Court opposition to the New Deal. Within two and a half years the Court enjoyed a Roosevelt majority with the appointments of Hugo Black, Stanley Reed, Felix Frankfurter, William O. Douglas, and Frank Murphy. Black, Frankfurter, and Douglas would ultimately prove to be among the ablest justices in the Court's history. If victory it was, however, it was a very costly one. Roosevelt had gained a Court, but had expended much of his political capital.

Perhaps the most critical casualty of the Court battle was Franklin Roosevelt's aura of invincibility. The Court-packing defeat was to FDR what the Battle of Adrianople had been to the Roman legions, what the Russian campaign had been to Napoleon, and what the Vietnam War would be to the United States. It showed that Roosevelt could be beaten. After leaving the New Deal once—and living to tell about it—it was much easier for a senator to oppose Roosevelt again. The New Deal, what was left of it, would never be the same.[7]

13· The CIO and the Later New Deal

A	lthough the Court battle was the catalyst responsible for the rapid precipitation of a conservative coalition, other events in 1937 also served to reinvigorate the right. The most significant of these developments, and perhaps the most important change of the decade, was the emergence of industrial unionism.

The craft unionists who dominated the AFL had been slow in making any attempt to organize the growing millions of mass production

287

workers in such basic industries as steel, automobiles, and rubber. Yet the widespread unrest in 1934 demonstrated the eagerness of many unskilled workers to organize and improve their conditions. American workers in 1934 and 1935 were taking matters into their own hands and creating a movement from the bottom up. Eventually, though, any movement needs leadership.

There was no particularly good reason for predicting that John L. Lewis would provide that leadership. As president of the United Mine Workers since 1919, Lewis had demonstrated his ability to lead and to fight, but he had also shown little tolerance for rank-and-file discontents and had taken a conservative stance on most economic issues. He was a noted anti-Communist during the twenties. A staunch Republican, Lewis had supported Hoover in 1932. One fact emerged from Lewis's confusing past: he was emphatically his own man. That was fortunate, for he admired no one as much as himself.

Lewis ruled the UMW as an absolute monarch. Once he had chosen a course of action, he would let nothing deter him. This did not mean, however, that he would never change course. When he chose a new objective, he pursued it as single-mindedly as he had the rapidly discarded former goal.

As the Depression dragged on, Lewis, like other labor bosses, found himself far to the right of his membership. Workers were demanding organization and new economic policies; Lewis remained a Republican—but not for long. President Roosevelt was not the only one who heard the angry voices of workers in the streets; Lewis's ears were not as prominent as his eyebrows, but they were even more useful, since they were often close to the ground. Characteristically, the UMW boss made a dramatic reversal and tried to catch up with his followers. Adept opportunism was one of the by-products of Lewis's supreme egotism. Rising working-class discontent demanded a "radical" labor leader; Lewis stepped forward. His dogmatic nature quickly infused sincerity into his newfound class feelings. "I don't give a hang what happened yesterday," he once declared. "I live for today and tomorrow." Lewis forgot the past completely and made himself champion of the American working class between 1935 and 1940.

The unskilled workers were ready for effective organization. Beyond the opportunity provided by the Wagner Act's provisions for representation elections and against anti-union practices, the reluctance of the man in the White House to use federal troops against workers further aided unionization of the mass production industries. The only sensible way to organize them was on an industrial basis. However, such leaders of the AFL as William Green, John Frey, and Matthew Woll remained, at best, too timid to fight strongly for the organization of the unskilled. At worst, the AFL officials were elitists who did not want to contaminate their "aristocracy of labor" with the dregs of the mass production industries. This latter position was strongly argued by AFL Vice President John Frey: "To mingle highly skilled and lower skilled into one organization is as impractical as endeavoring to mix oil and water, for the oil will presently seek the higher level." By the mid-thirties, the water had risen so high that it was threatening to drown Frey and his AFL colleagues.

The struggle for industrial unionism was not new. Its origins in the United States date back at least to the Knights of Labor in the early 1880s and continue through Eugene Debs's American Railway Union, the Socialist Trade and Labor Alliance, the Industrial Workers of the World, and the Communist labor organizations of the twenties and early thirties. Within the AFL itself, the conflict between craft and industrial organizers had existed from the beginning in the 1880s.

The workers were ready in the mid-1930s for industrial unionism. They were "pounding on the doors" of the CIO before the organization was even begun. The frightened bosses could speak all they wanted about "agitators," "Communists," and "radical leaders" stirring up the workers. The simple fact was that it was the workers themselves who drove union leaders to action.

Action of a sort came in October 1935. John L. Lewis was determined to force the issue of industrial unionism at the annual AFL convention in Atlantic City. Lewis proposed that the AFL commit itself to the "industrial organization of mass production workers." The federation's majority of conservative craft union bosses voted Lewis's idea down, but he got 38 percent of the votes, a surprisingly good showing under the circumstances. And Lewis knew how to turn defeat into victory. At the last session of the convention, a delegate from the Rubber Workers was speaking in favor of industrial jurisdiction for his union. "Big Bill" Hutcheson, president of the Carpenters' Union, interrupted to say that the issue of industrial unionism had already been settled. Lewis called Hutcheson's action "small potatoes." Moments later, as Lewis walked past the Carpenters' table, Hutcheson called him a bastard. Lewis replied with a quick right jab that knocked Hutcheson down and left him bleeding. The punch in the jaw made national headlines. It brought the issue of industrial unionism to the public's attention. As CIO publicist Len De Caux later observed, the people "did follow sporting events." A member of Hutcheson's own union expressed the effect of the event on many workers. "Congratulations," he wired Lewis, "sock him again."

The next day Lewis met with a group of unionists interested in industrial organization. A few weeks later, still within the federation, a Committee for Industrial Organization was launched. The CIO was not a homogeneous group. Old-line union leaders were somewhat uneasy about the young and rebellious who flocked into the CIO. But such rebellious workers soon pushed the organization on to its early, stunning victories. "Much of Lewis' sense of urgency in 1935," labor historian David Brody has noted, "sprang from his awareness of the pressure mounting in the industrial ranks."

The CIO remained within the AFL for a year. During that time Lewis tried to prevent a split of the labor movement. He did this not because he was prepared to submit to the old guard leadership, but because he expected to lead a huge expansion in union membership among the unorganized. This would, he believed, put him at the head of the movement and it was obviously better to lead a united labor organization than to direct half a movement after a split. But old guard intransigence prevented Lewis from succeeding within the AFL, and the CIO unions were suspended by the parent organization in September 1936. The grounds for the suspension of the unions were that the CIO constituted a "dual organization" threatening the unity of the federation and that the CIO unions were "fomenting insurrection" within the AFL, violating their "contracts" with the federation, and engaging in "rebellion" by acting in ways contrary to the decision of the Atlantic City convention. The CIO, now rechristened the Congress of Industrial Organizations, became a separate coalition of industrial unions.

The first great CIO strike—against the giant rubber manufacturers in Akron, Ohio, in 1936—showed how rebellious rank-and-file laborers were at this time. It is significant that this initial CIO strike was launched by "native" Americans of Appalachian background, not by immigrants. This was no conspiracy fomented by "foreign radicals." At the end of 1935, Goodyear announced plans to go back from a six- to an eight-hour day, with the same daily pay. The workers rebelled. The sit-down—refusing to work but staying in the factory to prevent scabs from taking over—was used spontaneously by workers in three different Akron companies (Firestone, Goodyear, and Goodrich) in January and February 1936. The sit-downs were successful against two companies, but not at Goodyear. Goodyear celebrated its resistance by laying off seventy workers in mid-February. The workers there sat down again, ready this time for a fight to the finish. One of them put the feelings of his fellows concisely: "I favor shutting her down!" And shut her down they did, although the leaders of the United Rubber Workers had opposed the sit-down in favor of a conventional picket line. The workers, nevertheless, were united. Fourteen thousand went on strike; only 300 remained at work.

Although the strike was a sign of how much the men in the factories had the jump on their "leaders," the CIO stepped in quickly and gave the workers much help. Other unions also sent organizers and money to aid the Rubber Workers. The CIO gave the word "union" a new meaning. As one CIO leader has recalled, in the AFL days union "had only meant pot bellied grafters with diamond stickpins—little cliques of gravy train snobs with a corner on cushy jobs—high initiation fees, long apprenticeships, rituals, all sorts of tricks to avoid sharing the goodies." This image was broken—for a time— when the CIO came on the scene. For the most part, CIO unions did not discriminate against blacks, women, or ethnic minorities. The new organization bridged the gap between native and immigrant workers. The common experience of depression came to outweigh ethnic hostilities. (Not for everyone, of course. Opponents of the new organization later used a tune from Walt Disney's *Snow White* [1938] to sing:

> *Hiho, hiho, hiho!*
> *Don't join the CIO*
> *And pay your dues to a*
> *   bunch of Jews*
> *Hiho! Hiho!*)

The Goodyear strike lasted a little over a month, until late March 1936. When the company gave in on a number of demands, the CIO leaders urged the Akron workers to accept. The local Rubber Workers were reluctant, but they followed the advice of the national leaders. Continuing local discontent was clear from a number of unauthorized sit-downs after the men had returned to their jobs. Such "wildcat" upheavals were not to bring final victory over Goodyear until 1941.

The CIO had easily passed its first test in Akron. Too much of the credit (or blame, in the eyes of some) for the labor upheaval has been placed with John L. Lewis and his associates. The key figures in the CIO at this time, in addition to Lewis, who had been named the organization's chairman, were Charles P. Howard of the Typographical Union (the first CIO secretary), Philip Murray of the Miners, Sidney Hillman of the Clothing Workers, David Dubinsky of the Ladies' Garment Workers, and Max Zaritsky of the Hatters. Their leadership greatly helped the organization of the basic industries. Another vital factor was the friendly attitude of the federal government. But the real thrust came from the bottom, where discontent of volcanic proportions existed.[1]

Just how volcanic such forces were soon became evident in the auto industry. Automobile production brought the assembly line to its epitome. The line set the laborers' pace, making them mere factors in the productive process, with no individuality and little humanity. Charlie Chaplin's *Modern Times* (1936) perfectly represented what had happened to workers in modern industry. Chaplin as a factory laborer has become part of the mechanical process. He continues to turn nonexistent bolts after the assembly line has shut down. A Chevrolet worker in Flint, Michigan, made the same point: "Where you used to be a man, . . . now you are less than their cheapest tool." The speed of the lines was periodically increased. "We didn't even have time to go to the toilet," one laborer complained. "You have to run to the toilet and run back." The wife of an auto worker told how the speedup affected home lives: "Yes, they're not men any more, if you know what I mean." The only difference one worker could see between his General Motors plant and a prison was that the workers were allowed to go home at night.

Complete alienation was common among such workers, and with it sometimes came radicalism. By 1936 the automobile laborers could take their frustration no longer. They demanded action, regardless of their leaders' advice. In April of that year, the United Auto Workers' convention elected several leftists to the union's General Executive Board. The convention also refused to bar Communists from union office, called for the establishment of a farmer-labor party, and came close to refusing to endorse President Roosevelt for a second term. The November election of the very liberal Frank Murphy as governor of Michigan gave the auto workers in that state the encouragement they needed to strike.

Up to that point the auto union had responded little to the new opportunities for organization that had opened up. As in the rubber industry, the real drive came from the workers themselves. Worker pressure forced the CIO to turn away from the steel to the auto industry in its national organizing campaign. As early as November 1936, a spontaneous strike against General Motors broke out in Atlanta. It spread in the ensuing weeks to Kansas City, then Cleveland, and finally GM's main plants at Flint.

The CIO and the national leaders of the UAW yielded reluctantly to rank-and-file pressure, but they were obliged to do so for the sake of their own prestige. As it was, a sit-down strike began in Flint on December 30, 1936, in advance of the date set by the national leaders. The rubber workers' sit-down tactic of the preceding spring had become increasingly popular. It had much to recommend it. It was safer and more comfortable than outside picketing, it kept plants shut down, and it made it difficult for employers to break a strike without doing the same to their own equipment. Beyond that, as Sidney Fine, the leading historian of the sit-down, has pointed out: "The sit-down strike satisfied the urge for recognition of the depersonalized and alienated automobile worker. Looking at the idle machine beside which he sat, he could believe, for the first time perhaps, that he was its master rather than its slave."

Fine's observation helps explain why sit-downs were more popular with laborers than with their leaders. The latter also were often inhibited by their respect for private property and fear of adverse official and public reactions. The man on the job had less concern for such ideological, legal, or tactical niceties. Indeed, a 1938–39 study of the views of residents of Akron toward corporate property found that rank-and-file workers had little respect for it. In the Akron survey some 1700 persons were interviewed. Each was told eight stories involving the "rights" of corporate property (and conversely the rights of workers). After each story the respondent was asked his opinion of the incident related. In each case a score of zero indicated complete opposition to corporate property and a score of four complete approval. Thus a combined score of less than eight (an average of less than one on each story) signified very little sympathy with the concept of corporate property. Sixty-eight percent of the CIO Rubber Workers fell into this category while only one percent were found in the classification of strong support of corporate property rights. The business leaders of Akron held drastically different views on the subject. Not a single businessman fell into the classification of strong opposition to corporate property; 94 percent received ratings in the range of extremely high support for the rights of property.

The supervisor of the Akron investigation concluded that workers had been moved toward disapproval of corporate property by events of the Depression. The laboring class appeared in the study to be humanitarian and nonviolent, but it would "approve violence if there were wrongdoers that it thinks could be met in no other way." The attitudes of Akron working people toward "the rights of the wealthy, the 'big interests,' the banks," were sharply distinguished from those toward small property holders. "Classes," the Akron researcher concluded, were "becoming prime factors, at least in certain areas of opinion."

Businessmen were horrified by labor's new militancy, particularly by the sit-down tactic. They saw it as an assault on private property, and perhaps the most frightening development yet in the thirties. As they did often in the decade, conservatives were overreacting, but there was a genuine basis for their fear. The sit-down strike lent itself to the development of a new sense of cooperation among the workers. A left-wing psychologist, whose observations may have been partly wishful thinking, noted an interesting phenomenon among the Flint strikers: increasingly they were saying "we" instead of "I." When the strikers sang such favorite songs as "Solidarity Forever," many of them meant what they said.

The sit-down was no picnic. The strikers were separated from their families for long periods of time. They lived in constant fear of attacks by police or vigilantes. Yet the sense of kinship, the feeling of struggling for a great cause, and the adventure of it all made the experience a happy one for many strikers. One wrote, "I am having a great time, something new, something different, lots of grub and music."

Few of the sit-downers had any revolutionary intentions. But their actions had revolutionary implications. The workers' growing sense of community brought those implications home to many. Strikers began to act as if the plants belonged to them. One striker expressed a feeling that must have been disturbing the sleep of many capitalists across the country. "We learned we can take the plant," he said. "We already knew how to run them. If General Motors isn't careful we'll put two and two together." Socialists and Communists were plentiful in the ranks of the strikers, should any of the brothers need help in arithmetic. But most of the Marxists, like the other workers, were, for the moment, more interested in creating a strong union than in pushing their ideologies.

The occupation of two GM plants in Flint continued without physical challenge for almost two weeks. Then, on January 11, 1937, a clash between police and strikers took place outside one of the factories. As in other such battles, the workers fought with rocks, bottles, and door hinges, while the police began with tear gas and soon resorted to pistols and riot guns. Despite the technological advantages enjoyed by the forces of law and order, the workers won this "Battle of Running Bulls." Casualties included fourteen workers, two spectators, and nine policemen. No one was killed.

Governor Murphy sent the National Guard into Flint after the Battle of Running Bulls. But Murphy's motives were like those of Minnesota's Olson. He wanted to protect the strikers, not evict them. Some of the Guardsmen showed their feelings as the strike ended when one truckload of the militia began singing "Solidarity Forever." Agreement with management on union recognition and wages still proved to be difficult, and the strike dragged on through the rest of January. Continued stalemate might have resulted in the defeat of the UAW. So the unionists made a daring forcible seizure of another key Chevrolet plant in Flint on February 1. Ten days later, after Governor Murphy refrained from enforcing an injunction GM obtained to evict the strikers, a negotiated settlement was reached. John L. Lewis himself conducted the negotiations for the union.

The UAW did not win everything it wanted in the agreement, but it was clearly a victory for the workers. The strikers' determination and unity had brought General Motors to its knees. GM was able to produce only 151 automobiles in the entire country during the period February 1–10. After the settlement was made the strikers gathered with families and friends for a well-deserved victory celebration. One CIO organizer in the strike said of the celebrants, "These people sang and joked and laughed and cried, deliriously joyful. . . . Victory . . . meant a freedom they had never known before."

The results of the GM strike were monumental. It was the acid test of the CIO. A steel organizer said during the auto strike that the steel workers "hesitate to stick out their necks. 'Wait till you win the auto strike. Then we'll join.'" And join they did, in steel and autos and other industries. The membership of the UAW itself skyrocketed in the eight months after the GM strike from 88,000 to 400,000. In March 1937 there were 170 sit-down strikes involving 167,210 workers across the nation.

The most remarkable event to take place in the wake of the GM strike was the surrender—without a strike—of U.S. Steel to the CIO. The great bastion of the open shop signed an agreement with the Steel Workers' Organizing

Committee (SWOC) on March 2, 1937. There were many reasons for the about-face in U.S. Steel's labor policy, but certainly one of the most important was the UAW victory over GM.

It appeared in March 1937 that the CIO's back-to-back agreements with the giants of the nation's two greatest industries would open the way for a clean union sweep of the basic industries. The CIO, having been ejected from the AFL, was on its own. The future seemed bright. Such leading corporations as General Electric, Firestone, and RCA were soon brought under CIO contracts. But more trouble lay ahead. A number of companies, led by Ford, Goodyear, and Republic Steel, steadfastly refused to recognize unions. Nor was bloodshed over. When the smaller steel companies failed to follow U.S. Steel's lead, the SWOC struck "Little Steel" in the spring of 1937. Sixteen strikers met violent deaths during that bitter struggle.

The worst incident in the Little Steel strike took place on Memorial Day at Republic's South Chicago mill. SWOC was attempting to conduct a legal picket line in front of the Republic mill. The police, who were being fed at company expense, prevented peaceful picketing at the mill gates. On Memorial Day the union held a meeting protesting the police restrictions. When the meeting broke up someone suggested that they proceed to the main gate at Republic and set up a mass picket line. As the crowd marched toward the mill to put this motion into effect, a small army of police met them. The two groups walked to within a few feet of each other and talked over the situation. After a few minutes of discussion, a demonstrator back in the crowd threw a tree branch toward the police. Before the missile reached them the police fired three shots in the air. The marchers immediately responded by hurling rocks and sticks at the officers. The latter then fired about 200 rounds of ammunition into the workers at very close range. Those demonstrators who remained mobile after this barrage fled across a field. The police pursued, continuing to shoot, and beat those who fell. When the massacre ended, ten workers lay dead from gunshot wounds. None of the ten was shot in the front. Thirty other demonstrators were wounded by gunshots; twenty-eight more were hospitalized for other injuries. Only three policemen required hospital treatment.

The Memorial Day massacre and other killings of steelworkers showed that the labor euphoria of early 1937 had not been entirely justified. The 1937–38 recession further dampened the organization drive. Not until the imminence of war in 1941 forced it upon them did Ford—with its talented corps of goons—Goodyear, and several of the steel companies agree to recognize unions.

There were other problems. Middle-class Americans, generally sympathetic to unionization in the mid-thirties, were upset by the sit-down tactic, which they saw as an attack on private property. Despite his overall pro-labor stance, in the midst of the Little Steel strike Roosevelt himself proclaimed "a plague on both your houses" (the CIO and the companies). "It ill behooves one who has supped at labor's table," Lewis responded, "to curse with equal fervor and fine impartiality both labor and its adversaries when they become locked in deadly embrace." Then in 1939 the Supreme Court outlawed the sit-down strike, taking from the CIO its most effective weapon.

Still, the success of the CIO was remarkable. Here John L. Lewis emerges once more as the critical figure. For millions of unorganized, unskilled workers he was Moses. The labor upheaval of the thirties would not have followed the course it did without Lewis. It was a genuine uprising among the workers themselves, but without Lewis's leadership it might have failed completely. Or it might have gone much further. For Lewis's role was that of a manager of discontent. As sociologist C. Wright Mills once said, "Even as the labor leader rebels, he holds back rebellion. He organizes discontent and then he sits on it, exploiting it in order to maintain a continuous organization. . . . He makes regular what might otherwise be disruptive." [2]

Such a mission was filled not only by Lewis personally, but also by the CIO as an organization. Many workers had lost their faith in the system. This was not often expressed in words, but the actions of the workers who took to the streets spoke loudly. Rank-and-file workers had gradually moved considerably to the left of their leaders. Some of those leaders—Lewis, Hillman, and Dubinsky among them—followed their members in the mid-thirties and launched the CIO. The leaders of the new organization began talking about industrial democracy, exactly what the American workers wanted to hear. Those CIO unionists who looked forward to the day when workers would transform society received respectful hearings from the rank and file; some looked on those leftists as prophets.

The CIO channeled into constructive action the discontent that was so widespread among working Americans in the thirties. The achievement of the organization should not be underestimated; the benefits mass production laborers have enjoyed in recent decades because of the CIO upheaval are numerous. The accomplishments of the CIO probably proved of more lasting benefit to the American worker than did any single New Deal program. The industrial unions provided mass production workers with a power that could represent them against the previously unchecked might of giant corporations. Employees could no longer be fired without cause; their benefits gradually increased to the point where they provided some security for their families; and the wages of production workers rose to a level where many of them could claim middle-class status in the post–World War II decades.

For all the horror the CIO induced among business leaders, in the end they, too, benefited from it. The organization directed the workers' essentially egalitarian discontent into streams that became in time acceptable, if unpalatable, to American capitalism. The economic royalists found that they could survive as economic parliamentarians. When the decade's class struggle subsided, new (and some old) union leaders rose on the backs of their members and made the CIO an industrial version of the AFL. The union administrators were generally happy to work with reformed captains of industry. Capitalism's problems led to worker unrest, worker unrest produced the CIO, the CIO helped resuscitate capitalism, and a revived capitalism devitalized the CIO. Working-class discontent ebbs and flows with prosperity and depression. With the return of prosperity, unions gradually resumed their parochial concerns. Ultimately, the CIO wed the AFL and begat George Meany.

As conservatives brooded over Court-packing and sit-down strikes, a more persistent issue continued to trouble them. By 1937 it seemed to many Americans—by no means all of them conservatives—that recovery had been achieved. True, unemployment was still distressingly high (in the double digits), but maybe we (or, rather, the unemployed) would just have to learn to live with that. Harry Hopkins estimated that year that 4 to 5 million Americans would remain jobless *after* recovery had been achieved. Production was now above 1929 levels, stock prices and profits were up, and many agreed with South Carolina Senator James Byrnes when he said in May, "the emergency has passed." If this was so, then surely there was no excuse for continuing the alarming deficits in the federal budget. And what of the relief programs that were creating a class of lazy, dependent Americans? The time had come at least to cut back on relief.

With recovery seemingly so far along (in his recent campaign Roosevelt himself had stressed economic gains heavily), congressional conservatives attempted in the spring of 1937 to pare down Roosevelt's request for an additional $1.5 billion for the WPA. Although the House attached a restrictive amendment to the bill, the final version gave the President everything he sought. The conservatives had shown more strength than before, but not enough.

In one sense it did not matter. Roosevelt had already cut WPA rolls following his reelection. Nonsensical talk of runaway inflation increased in 1937. (The following year Joseph P. Kennedy told Henry Stimson that he "lay awake nights" because he feared that "Roosevelt's inflation" would undermine his fortune and leave his children with nothing. The patriarch of the Kennedy clan was one of the few in the Depression who could find nothing to fear but fear itself.) The President's fiscal conservatism took firm hold of him. By August the number of people on WPA projects had been cut in half, leaving about 1.5 million people so employed. PWA operations virtually ceased. At about the same time, the Federal Reserve System tightened credit.

All this occurred while unemployment still hovered around the 9 million mark, representing about 14 percent of the civilian work force.

If these policies were not sufficient to bring disaster, 1937 also saw the start of the mischievous effects of the social security tax. Some $2 billion was taken out of the pockets of consumers during the year in order to begin the pension fund. None of it was yet to be returned to the economy. The result of all these misguided economic policies was the "recession" of 1937–38. "Recession," in this case at least, was a euphemism for "new depression." It was a term that would last through the Eisenhower years, despite an attempt by Leon Keyserling, a member of President Truman's Council of Economic Advisers, to substitute "downward correction." In the sixties, presidents seeking to avoid the stigma of presiding over recessions spoke of "economic downturns." The contribution of Gerald Ford's economic adviser, Alan Greenspan, was: "This is not a recession, it is a sideways waffle." By the Carter administration, the public would be treated to "pauses in recovery." The ultimate seemed to have been reached when President Carter's chief inflation fighter, Alfred Kahn, was reprimanded for using the dreaded Hoover word "depression." Kahn pledged to substitute "banana" thereafter. Ronald Reagan went Kahn one better in mid-1983 when he termed 9.5 percent unemployment "recovery." A depression by any other name smells as foul.

In August 1937 the stock market collapsed again, with the Dow Jones average dropping from 190 to 115 over the next two months. Production, sales, and employment also plummeted. By March 1938 the unemployment lists had added 4 million new (and rejoining) members, raising the unemployment level again toward 20 percent. The President did not know what to do. Charges and countercharges were flung back and forth. Conservatives and businessmen insisted Roosevelt's "radical" policies had undermined business confidence. The President and some of his advisers blamed the new collapse, which by some measures was even sharper than that of 1929, on a "strike of capital." Opportunities for investment abounded, this explanation contended, but businessmen were refusing to invest because they wanted to undermine Roosevelt's support.

In truth, although both the lack of business confidence and business desires to discredit the New Deal may have played parts in the new recession, most of the blame belonged on the White House doorstep. Roosevelt's sharp cutback in spending clearly precipitated the collapse. Probably realizing this, even if he did not admit it to himself, the President was badly shaken. He suddenly found himself in a situation similar to that which had faced Hoover at the beginning of the decade. FDR had understandably—if foolishly—taken full credit for the recovery of 1935–37. In 1935 he had proclaimed, "Yes, we are on our way back—not just by pure chance. . . . We are coming back more soundly than ever before because we are planning it that way." Like the Republicans before him, Roosevelt, having claimed credit for the good, now had to accept responsibility for the bad. He even began to sound like his predecessor. FDR insisted privately in October 1937 that he knew conditions were good. "Fundamentally sound," he might have said. "Everything will work out all right if we just sit tight and keep quiet," FDR told his Cabinet. Hoover probably gained no satisfaction from this, but he would have been justified if he had.

As economic conditions worsened, the President continued to vacillate. Businessmen and fiscal conservatives urged further retrenchment; New Dealers demanded a return to heavy spending. Always favoring a balanced budget, FDR tried for a time to restore business confidence by promising new budget slashing. At the same time, however, he tried to return to his class-based rhetoric of 1936. In January 1938 he promised to continue the fight "to curb the power and privileges of small minorities." These evil people, Roosevelt hastened to add, were "a mere handful of the total of businessmen and bankers and industrialists." Still unclear on whether to spend or cut back, Roosevelt decided to follow another course. Egged on by such Brandeisian advisers as Assistant Attorney General Robert Jackson, Leon Henderson, who served as Harry Hopkins's economic assistant, and the expert legal draftsmen Benjamin V. Cohen and Thomas Corcoran, the President attacked that small minority who had, he thought, subverted the economy. Trust-busting was likely to be popular and it might obviate the need for choosing between the spenders and the conservatives.

But conditions would not allow Roosevelt an easy way out. At the end of March 1938, the stock market took a new and precipitous drop. Unemployment continued to soar. The President could wait no longer. Hopkins persuaded him that spending was the only solution, and in mid-April Roosevelt asked Congress for a new $3 billion spending program to expand WPA, restart PWA, and assist other agencies. Faced with economic chaos in an election year, Congress quickly voted for a $3.75 billion appropriation. Within a few months economic indicators were again on the rise, seemingly confirming the analysis of the deficit-spending advocates. These people were already being referred to as Keynesians, but John Maynard Keynes actually had little to do with New Deal policy. The leading advocates of deficit spending close to Roosevelt were Marriner Eccles of the Federal Reserve and Harry Hopkins. Neither was directly influenced by Keynes. Eccles later said he had never heard of Keynes when he first began advancing "Keynesian" views and that he had never read more than small portions of Keynes's work at any time in the thirties.

Roosevelt had already verbally committed himself to an assault on monopoly. In late April he sent Congress a series of recommendations to curb monopolies. Congress responded by approving a full-scale investigation of the concentration of power in the American economy. The public seemed pleased. Letters reaching the White House after the President's message indicated that many Americans who had again become disillusioned with the New Deal were cheered by the attack on monopoly. "The hope that had almost ceased to glow," wrote a Tennessee man, "now burns anew."

There was little reason for such hope. Roosevelt remained unsure of his economic policy. Calling for a "study" of a problem is a way to avoid action on it. As Raymond Moley pointed out, the President's request for an investigation was "the final expression of Roosevelt's personal indecision about what policy his administration ought to follow in its relations with business." It put off (permanently, as it turned out) "the adoption of a guiding economic philosophy."

The Temporary National Economic Committee, created in response to Roosevelt's message, investigated the economy for the next three years, but offered no concrete recommendations. Under its chairman, Senator Joseph O'Mahoney of Wyoming, it served precisely the purpose Moley indicated. The next few years did witness a greatly expanded antitrust campaign, but this was due more to the zeal of Thurman Arnold, the new assistant attorney general for the Antitrust Division of the Justice Department, than to any commitment by Roosevelt. Arnold's barrage of antimonopoly action produced few results (other than getting Arnold kicked upstairs), however, since corporations were soon able to have suits dismissed on the grounds that they interfered with military production.[3]

It might have been expected that the new collapse in the economy in 1937–38 would lead to greater discontent and demand for change. On the surface, at least, such was not the case. One reason is readily apparent. Much Depression-bred discontent was now channeled into the development of CIO unions in the mass production industries. The success of the UAW and SWOC with General Motors and U.S. Steel had been aided by the relative prosperity of early 1937. With the new collapse, manufacturers faced with growing inventories were no longer frightened by strike threats. The "recession" put the CIO on the defensive after mid-1937.

The second reason that the renewed economic disaster failed to move the country further to the left is that Roosevelt had successfully identified himself with the left. To the extent that his decisions were responsible for the new collapse, Roosevelt was actually playing a conservative role in early 1937. Yet he continued to talk as the champion of the common man. When the bottom fell out of the economy, it was quite natural for many people to blame Roosevelt and the New Deal, the more so when for several months the President seemed to have no solution to offer.

The recession gave conservatives in the Senate and the House new hope, but they never became a stable voting bloc. They disagreed on many issues and were often kept apart by partisanship. They generally wanted to restore America to what they imagined it had been like before 1933. The conservatives were also united in opposing deficit spending, except where it helped special interests in their states or districts. Thus they were unable (and in many cases unwilling) to stop Roosevelt's spending proposal of April 1938. Similarly, expenditures for farm subsidies, no matter how large, were rarely given a second look by the conservatives, most of whom represented rural areas.

There were, however, farm programs and, then, there were farm programs. Most rural representatives in Congress were far more concerned with the interests of large landowners than with those of small farmers, tenants, sharecroppers, or farm workers. The latter groups generally had to look to the executive branch for whatever assistance they might hope to get from the government. In the early stages of the Second New Deal, just after agreeing to the firing of most of the pro-tenant members of the AAA staff, Roosevelt had used part of the money from the Emergency Relief Appropriation to create the Resettlement Administration. Placed under the leadership of ardent New Deal planner Rexford Tugwell, the RA unenthusiastically continued the subsistence homestead colonies that had begun at Eleanor Roosevelt's urging but had been left an unwanted stepchild in Harold Ickes's Interior Department. The new agency also oversaw the construction of "greenbelt" towns near three major cities, Washington, Milwaukee, and Cincinnati. Communal farms were established in such localities as New Madrid, Missouri; Casa Grande, Arizona; and Lake Dick, Arkansas. The major goal of the Resettlement program, as its name indicated, was to relocate poor farmers to better land and provide expert advice and equipment. It was a noble idea, but a lack of funds prevented the RA from giving a new start to even one percent of the 500,000 families it intended to help.

In 1937, Congress passed the Bankhead-Jones Farm Tenancy Act, which replaced the RA with a new organization, the Farm Security Administration. The FSA proved to be another noble experiment. It provided loans for tenants to become family farmers, helped poor farmers improve their land, and sought to better the conditions facing migrant farm workers. By 1941 the agency had spent $1 billion in such efforts. The FSA, like the RA before it, made sincere efforts to prevent racial discrimination in its operations. All of this ensured that the agency would face increasing criticism from planters and their representatives in Congress. Like its predecessor, the FSA never had nearly enough money to have an appreciable effect on the massive problems of the rural poor.

When Tugwell was placed in charge of the RA, he realized that many of its programs were tempting targets for conservative critics. To try to blunt some of the inevitable complaints, he established an Information Division to put out positive propaganda about the Resettlement Administration's programs. One result was the bringing together of a remarkable group of photographers in the organization's historical section. Tugwell placed his former Columbia University teaching assistant, Roy Stryker, in charge of the program. The consequence was a national treasure of documentary photographs of rural life, Depression conditions, and ultimately, of America itself. The historical section was carried over into the FSA, and the wonderful collection of photographs is generally referred to under the Farm Security Administration label.

The FSA photographs, several of which are reproduced in this volume, represented an achievement that in some ways paralleled the accomplishments of the WPA arts projects. There were, however, significant differences. The photographers were certainly artists, but they were dealing more directly with unfiltered reality than were the Federal Art Project mural painters or the directors in the Federal Theatre Project. A more important difference was that the FSA photographers were not on relief. They were hired solely for their professional talents, not because they were without a job. The monument left by Dorothea Lange, Ben Shahn, Walker Evans, Marion Post Wolcott, Carl Mydans, Russell Lee, John Vachon, Arthur Rothstein, and the other FSA photographers represents today one of the most important collections of documents on Depression America. Even if the RA/FSA had done nothing else, this effort would easily secure its place as an important contribution of the New Deal.

The same members of Congress who pinched pennies for RA and FSA and who usually complained about New Deal extravagance were less stingy when it came to large farm owners. After the Supreme Court struck down the original AAA processing tax in 1936, a new bill was hastily drawn up to pay farmers for conserving soil. They would do this by planting such soil enrichers as soybeans and clover instead of the overproduced staples. This end run around the Supreme Court worked constitutionally, but failed agriculturally. With crop surpluses multiplying and a friendlier majority on the high bench, Roosevelt called late in 1937 for a new AAA law. The main problem here came not from legislators intent on cutting back on the administration proposal, but from farm bloc representatives seeking to enlarge the program. In February 1938, Congress passed the bill, which allowed the secretary of agriculture to establish acreage allotments for growers of staple crops. It established the basis of American agriculture policy for decades to come. Even so, the surpluses continued to mount. Export subsidies were authorized in mid-1938, but the overflow rose until World War II temporarily solved the problem.

Aside from the farm bill, FDR's only major successes in the Seventy-fifth Congress of 1937–38 were a housing bill and wages and hours legislation. Both of these trophies emerged from Congress already well tarnished. Despite an acute need, low-cost housing had never been a top priority in Roosevelt's plans. The agrarian myth held too high a place in the President's heart for him to get enthusiastic about rebuilding urban slums. The PWA had originally been given responsibility for dealing with this problem, but it accomplished little. The National Housing Act of 1934 set up a separate agency, the Federal Housing Administration, which was quite helpful in insuring loans for middle-class people seeking to buy houses or to make home improvements. The FHA was of no assistance to those in need of low-income housing.

While FDR remained uninterested in the housing problem, Senator Wagner pushed persistently for a federal housing act. As in the case of the labor relations bill, Roosevelt was late in joining the cause of the New York senator. Unlike the labor bill, however, the housing measure needed presidential support, With it, the Wagner-Steagall Housing Act became law in the summer of 1937. It established the United States Housing Authority, which could make loans for the construction of low-cost dwellings. Conservatives had placed crippling amendments on the bill, however, greatly restricting the USHA's effectiveness. The results of the act corresponded more nearly to Roosevelt's than Wagner's commitment to it.

Although there had been overwhelming support in 1935 for the National Labor Relations Act, proposals to place a floor under wages and a ceiling over hours enjoyed a smaller constituency. The President himself had long favored such a fair labor standards bill, but two important groups within the New Deal coalition were unenthusiastic. Southerners feared that their region would lose its primary attraction for industry—its pitifully low wage scale. And although it might seem surprising at first glance, organized labor was lukewarm toward the proposal. Some union leaders feared that minimum wages would in effect become maximum wages. They also wanted to gain increases through union bargaining rather than government decree.

During the early months of 1938, conservatives on the House Rules Committee prevented the bill from reaching the floor. Not all southerners opposed the legislation, however, and this provided a means of getting it through. Claude Pepper of Florida, one of the strongest supporters of the New Deal in the Senate, was in the midst of a tough primary race in the spring of 1938. The White House encouraged Pepper to speak out clearly for the wages and hours bill. This he did, and when he won a smashing victory in May, other members of Congress began to see the wisdom of supporting Fair Labor Standards legislation. Before conservatives let the bill pass, though, they weakened it. Domestic workers and farm laborers were excluded from its provisions, as they had been from the Social Security Act. Many other categories of workers were similarly exempted. Tongue in cheek, one representative suggested an amendment to the bill. "Within 90 days after appointment of the Administrator," it would read, "she shall report to Congress whether anyone is subject to this bill."

The bill outlawed, at long last, the use of child labor in interstate commerce. It set standards of 25 cents per hour and 44 hours per week, which must be improved within two years to 40 cents and 40 hours. Even such low wage standards were of more than passing interest to 12 million workers covered by the new law who had been making less than 40 cents an hour. The Fair Labor Standards Act was less than the President wanted, but it did establish the principle of government regulation of these matters. The defects and exclusions might be remedied in the future. Roosevelt signed the bill into law on June 25, 1938.

As Congress became less tractable President Roosevelt's patience wore thin. He had been especially hurt by the desertion on the Court plan of many Democrats he had supported. It was a poor issue to make into a test of loyalty, but Roosevelt "stayed mad" at the Court "deserters." The President seemed bent on what one critic called "high school girl revenge." On a deeper level, both Roosevelt and some of his advisers wanted a realignment of the parties, with all liberals becoming Democrats and conservatives of various stripes joining the Republicans. Many conservatives also hoped for such a change in party composition. The 1938 primaries became the testing ground for this attempt to sort out the confusing American party setup.

Of the thirty-four Senate elections in 1938, Republicans were incumbents in only three, and all of them were considered "safe" for the GOP. (How could they be otherwise if they had remained in Republican hands six years before, in 1932?) Therefore any improvement for Roosevelt in the upper house would have to come from the replacement of conservative Democrats by liberals. Some of Roosevelt's assistants intervened in early primaries, and late in June the President himself used a fireside chat to launch what came to be known as his "purge" of conservative Democrats. The attempt to rid the party of legislators unfriendly to the New Deal is generally considered to have been a disaster for Roosevelt. Of the four pro–New Dealers who were seriously challenged by more conservative opponents, though, three won. Southern liberals Lister Hill of Alabama, Claude Pepper of Florida, and Hattie Carraway of Arkansas demonstrated that the New Deal was not entirely unpopular in the South. In Idaho a New Dealer lost, but the victor tried to link himself to FDR, endorsed the Townsend Plan, and was an isolationist, which was a popular position to take in the state. In addition to all this, large numbers of Republicans crossed over in the primary to vote against the New Deal candidate.

New Deal Senators Alben Barkley of Kentucky and Elmer Thomas of Oklahoma were also victorious. Clearly, it was not in the defeat of New Deal supporters that Roosevelt's plans for the 1938 primaries failed. The administration targeted five conservative Democrats for defeat: Guy Gillette of Iowa, Frederick Van Nuys of Indiana, Walter George of Georgia, "Cotton Ed" Smith of South Carolina, and Millard Tydings of Maryland. All five were renominated.

The story, however, is not as simple as it appears. Roosevelt did not personally intervene against Gillette or Van Nuys. The former made a point of not attacking the President, insisting only that he would not be a rubber stamp. Van Nuys was renominated by state party leaders who were loyal to Roosevelt but could find no suitable alternative candidate. It was, therefore, on the contests in Georgia, South Carolina, and Maryland that the "purge" focused. Roosevelt spoke publicly against the three conservative incumbents. But the President had not added to his persuasive abilities in the South earlier in the year when in a Georgia speech he had compared southern feudalism to fascism. Liberals in the three states failed to come to the aid of Roosevelt's candidates. Most significant was the stress that George and Smith placed on their commitment to most of the New Deal. They appealed to voters on the traditional issues of racism and state independence. Off-year elections are usually decided on local issues and personalities. The conservative victories were therefore something far short of repudiations of the New Deal. Although Tydings does not fit so neatly into this analysis, he too emphasized state independence and not being a "rubber stamp."

"Outside interference" is almost always resented in state elections. Roosevelt was, however, successful in one important House primary. Representative John J. O'Connor of New York, chairman of the Rules Committee, which had blocked Roosevelt's desires on several occasions, was defeated. The President found solace in this victory, saying "Harvard lost the schedule but won the Yale game." A comforting thought, no doubt, but wishful thinking all the same. The attempted purge could only help convince other Democrats that they could oppose the President and survive. Despite all the ambiguities, the failed purge was a serious political setback for Roosevelt and hopes for any further reform.

The general election in 1938 brought even worse news to the White House. The Republicans, so recently the subject of numerous obituaries, gained 13 governorships, 8 seats in the Senate, and 81 in the House. The overriding reason was the new economic collapse. American voters tend to blame the party in power when things go wrong. Yet surface appearances are again deceptive. Democrats continued to do well among the lower income groups, and they won 75 percent of the Senate races and 61 percent of the House contests. Moveover, many Republicans who won had to move toward the left in order to do so. A minimum of 40 of the 169 successful Republican House candidates in 1938 owed their victories at least in part to their (often hypocritical) endorsements of the Townsend Plan. And Roosevelt could justly claim to be the first two-term President since the one-party days of James Monroe who had kept a majority in Congress throughout his administration.[4]

14 · "Dr. New Deal" Runs Out of Medicine: The Last Years of the Depression, 1939–41

As he signed the Wages and Hours Act into law in June 1938, President Roosevelt sighed: "That's that." Indeed it was. The New Deal's last major step had been taken. The domestic program for dealing with the Depression had ended. Remarkably, it had done so without curing the Depression.

In 1939, a full decade after the Crash, 9.4 million Americans remained unemployed. This figure constituted 17.2 percent of the work force. Few would have predicted it in the heady days of 1933, or even in 1935 or 1936 (and many people fail to realize it today), but the Great Depression outlived the New Deal. This is certainly not to say that the *effects* of the New Deal were over in 1939. Roosevelt's reforms profoundly altered the United States and their consequences continue to be felt most perceptibly a half century later. But, by 1939 the New Deal as a continuing source of innovation was through.

The New Deal did not, of course, wither away in 1939. Large parts of it remained vital and some programs were expanded. A look at the varying treatment Congress accorded to different parts of Roosevelt's policy in the late thirties provides an indication of some of the fundamental problems in the New Deal approach.

President Roosevelt had proposed in June 1937 the creation of six new regional development authorities, which were quickly dubbed "little TVA's." This was perceived as a challenge to free enterprise and the reborn conservative coalition nipped it in the bud, although several more limited federal hydroelectric projects were allowed to be completed. The defeat was unfortunate for the nation, as much good might have been accomplished through these agencies, but it was entirely in keeping with the general rule of congressional disposition of New Deal proposals in the late thirties.

The "recession" of 1937–38 threw a scare into the Congress as well as the White House, and the President's special message in April 1938 calling for a dramatic return to deficit spending and a rapid easing of credit was welcomed on Capitol Hill. By 1939 most economic indexes had returned to their relatively high early-1937 levels. Deficit spending had proved its efficacy once more, but this did not make it any more palatable to congressional conservatives—or to Franklin Roosevelt.

Once the emergency was passed (which, it should be remembered, left nearly one-sixth of the work force unemployed), Congress began again to tighten the reins on spending. This did not amount to the imposing of unwelcome restrictions on the President. Instead, Roosevelt joined in the new budget-cutting of late 1939 and early 1940. He rejected the advice of economist Lauchlin Currie, an administrative assistant to the President, that more spending on housing, health, and welfare was necessary to avert a new collapse. The only proposal along these lines that Roosevelt made in early 1940 was for a small hospital construction program for depressed areas. Even this modest suggestion was quickly lost in the shuffle.

What President Roosevelt was shuffling in 1939 and 1940 was no longer the New Deal deck, but that of military preparedness. If a balanced budget remained a higher priority than sufficient social spending, defense against the fascist menace was most important of all. The irony, of course, was that FDR and Congress finally began to restore prosperity by spending on military needs at levels they had rejected for social needs. As early as the beginning of 1939, the President signaled that his quest for significant reforms was over. "We have now passed the period of internal conflict in the launching of our program of social reform," he said in his annual message. "Our full energies may now be released to invigorate the processes of recovery in order to preserve our reforms, and to give every man and woman who wants to work a real job at a living wage."

What remained to be done, Roosevelt seemed to be saying, was to improve those programs already in place, not to devise new ones. The meaning of this approach, given the sentiment in the Seventy-sixth Congress of 1939–40, was that programs with powerful constituencies or a broad range of beneficiaries would be enhanced, while those that helped only the poor would be cut. Social welfare experts had long maintained that a "program for the poor is a poor program." This became clear in 1939, when the Senate (in a 47–46 vote) slashed $150 million from the President's proposed relief appropriation. As soon as it seemed "safe" to cut back on relief, Congress did so. The Relief Act of 1939 also ordered that all workers who had been employed on WPA projects for eighteen consecutive months must be terminated. The old notion that anyone who really tried could find a private job seemed again to be in the ascendancy. The result was the dismissal of more than 775,000 WPA workers in July and August 1939. A survey three months later found that fewer than 100,000 of them had succeeded in finding private employment. The capital sentence Congress passed on the Federal Theatre Project in the 1939 relief bill showed that unpopular programs were likely to go the way of those that helped only the poor. The Senate further showed its growing opposition to relief by launching an investigation of alleged political corruption in the WPA. The result was the passage of the Hatch Act of 1939, which forbade all political activity by federal employees.

The contrast with the fate of programs affecting more powerful interests is striking. Large farmers continued to receive more help from the government than any other group. Just after Congress slashed relief spending in the summer of 1939, Roosevelt wrote to Joseph Kennedy: "The silly Congress gave me three hundred million more than I wanted for farm subsidies." By 1940—before the impact of the war—farm income stood at $4.2 billion, up from a low of $1.9 billion in 1932, and federal subsidies further supported the income of those farmers who owned enough land to benefit significantly.

The Social Security System provided much-needed assistance for many destitute Americans, but its main purpose was to provide "social insurance" for the vast middle class. Here was a program—as many politicians have been reminded in recent years—with a powerful constituency. While relief for those on the bottom was being cut late in the Depression, programs for the middle class under Social Security were expanded. Payments under the Old Age benefit provisions were moved up to begin in 1939. In that year also, some categories of widows were placed under an Old Age and Survivors Insurance Plan. Many such widows were certainly very poor; some were not so poor. The former probably benefited from the latter being in the program. Other poor people also made gains because of the expansion of certain Social Security programs. The amount of federal matching funds available for state Aid to Dependent Children (ADC) programs, for example, was significantly increased in 1939. The fact remains, though, that by the end of the decade programs for the poor had come to seem once again more expendable than many other types of activity in which the federal government was engaged, and many efforts to aid the destitute were left up to the states. Where that could lead was evident in the grand totals of 104 families in Mississippi and 85 in Texas on the ADC rolls in 1940, five years after the program was enacted.[1]

The New Deal had no climax; like the old soldier (or sailor) Franklin Roosevelt had always wanted to be, it simply faded away. This remarkable happening demands explanation. FDR had received the greatest mandate yet enjoyed by an American president in 1936; his personal charm and effectiveness were, if anything, more polished than before. Yet he was unable to accomplish much in his second term.

The most obvious explanation was growing congressional opposition. This is somewhat surprising, in view of the huge Democratic majorities elected with Roosevelt in 1936. Such large majorities can, however, breed factionalism. Congressmen naturally resented the idea that they were rubber stamps; they were jealous of the growth of presidential power. In the 1933–35 period, the crisis was so great that few legislators dared to oppose the President's program. By 1937, though, the economy seemed better and opposition safer. Then when conditions again grew worse, conservatives believed they had all the more reason for opposing the New Deal.

A second-term president normally begins to lose leverage with Congress, since members of his party do not expect him to be again heading a ticket on which they will run. This process was rapidly accelerated in Roosevelt's case because of his ill-advised introduction of the Court "reform." To many on Capitol Hill, already upset at the flow of power down Pennsylvania Avenue, Roosevelt's attempt to pack the Court raised the possibility of dictatorship in democratic garb. This, more than anything else, explains the remarkable rise in hostility toward presidential proposals from early 1937 onward. Had it not been for the Court plan, it is unlikely that Roosevelt's subsequent call for executive reorganization would have met so much opposition.

Fears of southern and rural Democrats were especially heightened by what they correctly saw as a dramatic transformation of their party in the thirties. Suddenly their party was a largely northern, urban, labor party, interested to a degree in the problems of minorities. Faced with this change, it was only natural that many southern and rural members of the party rebelled.

Perhaps the most important reason for the dichotomy between Roosevelt's landslide and his difficulties in Congress was simply that it was far easier to bring together the disparate elements of the "Roosevelt Coalition" behind a presidential candidate—particularly one as politically skilled as FDR—than to get them to agree on specific proposals in Congress. Labor unions, southerners, blacks, Catholics, relief recipients, farmers, and intellectuals might back the same man for president; they were unlikely to support the same legislative proposals.

A second explanation often cited for the ending of the New Deal is the growing American concern with foreign affairs in the late thirties. Although it is undeniable that the growth of fascism and the power of Germany and Japan, the Ethiopian War, the Spanish Civil War, and the war in China were significant to Roosevelt, there is little evidence that a desire for a more active foreign policy led him to slow down his domestic program voluntarily. While it is true that Roosevelt would need the backing of many of those who opposed his domestic policy if he were to gain approval for an easing of neutrality legislation and the development of a military preparedness program, two facts dispel the notion that he made a trade to obtain that support: First, the New Deal was in obvious decline *before* foreign policy assumed primacy; and second, the more conservative members of Congress were, with a few isolationist exceptions, generally eager to approve a bolder foreign and military policy. Foreign affairs seem to have offered Roosevelt an almost welcome escape from the increasingly unfathomable socioeconomic problems at home, but international problems did not *cause* abandonment of social reform. World War II would provide for the American people a release similar to that which earlier foreign questions had given FDR.

It is sometimes asserted, as a third explanation, that the American people had grown tired of the New Deal by 1937. Such emotional exhaustion does occur in a society, as the 1920s, 1950s and late seventies–early eighties periods of American history attest. Yet both opinion polls on social issues and the letters I have reviewed suggest that a substantial constituency for further change remained in 1937 and 1938.

We are left with a fourth explanation as the most important cause of the decline of the New Deal: Roosevelt had played out his hand by 1936. The attempt—if we may change the metaphor—to bandage the economic system without making fundamental changes had reached its limits. It was not until the end of 1943 that FDR said that "Dr. New Deal" had been replaced by "Dr. Win the War," but six years earlier it was already apparent that the former physician had run out of curative medicine. Large numbers of Americans remained, to be sure, "ill-housed, ill-clad, ill-nourished," as the President noted in 1937. But what did he propose to do about it?

When Roosevelt's legislative proposals from 1937 onward are examined, it becomes clear that one of the principal reasons few new departures were made in his second term is that few were proposed. Roosevelt was not unaware of the continuing need for progress. "If liberal government continues over another ten years," he told a reporter in 1938, "we ought to be contemporary somewhere in the late Nineteen Forties." Yet FDR himself did little more to advance liberal government. Aside from the wages and hours legislation and the two attempts to increase presidential power (the Court plan and executive reorganization), Roosevelt's second-term program concentrated on modifying what already existed: more relief spending, alterations in Social Security, "little TVA's," and a reassembled AAA. The creation of the FSA and USHA were not his ideas. In mid-1939 the President told Treasury Secretary Morgenthau that he was "sick and tired of having a lot of long-haired people around here who want a billion dollars for schools, a billion dollars for public health." [2]

It is beyond question that congressional opposition played a significant role in bringing down the curtain on the New Deal. Foreign problems and emotional drain may have served as supporting actors. But the star of the final act was, fittingly, Franklin D. Roosevelt himself.

Those out of political power almost always seem to find reason to be hopeful. The Republicans' hopes in 1936 had been groundless, but two years later rain at last fell on the political dustbowl through which the Depression-era Grand Old Party had been suffering. In the midterm elections of 1938, the Republicans won 81 new seats in the House of Representatives, nearly doubling their all-time low total of 88 in the previous House. The Republicans also added 8 new senators (giving them 23), and more than tripled their number of governors by making a gain of 13 that raised their total to 18. This hardly meant that the GOP was healthy. The party lost 24 of the 32 Senate races and still held barely 40 percent of the House.

Signs of life in the previously limp elephant, though, were clearly evident after the 1938 revival. There were new faces that might attract a national following. Thomas E. Dewey, who had earned such a reputation as a crusading district attorney in New York that Humphrey Bogart played a character based on him in the 1937 film *Marked Woman*, narrowly lost that state's highest office to the apparently unbeatable Governor Herbert Lehman. At thirty-six, Dewey seemed certain to have a bright future. Even more intriguing for Republicans looking to future national tickets was Harold Stassen, who was elected governor of Minnesota by a plurality of almost 300,000 votes after a serious split in the Farmer-Labor ranks. Stassen, though, could offer no help for 1940. He was thirty-one when he won the Minnesota race and would not be old enough to seek the presidency two years later. A more likely competitor for the 1940 nomination was the new forty-nine-year-old senator from Ohio, Robert A. Taft. The son of the former President immediately assumed a position of leadership in the national Republican party.

Remarkably, the early leader in the polls was Dewey, a man just over the constitutional minimum age requirement and one who had never held an office higher than that of county district attorney. When Dewey formally declared himself to be in the race in December 1939, Harold Ickes noted that the young New Yorker had "thrown his diaper into the ring." The voters in several states in the spring of 1940, however, indicated that they thought Dewey had been weaned; he won most of the primaries he contested. By the beginning of May, polls showed Dewey to be the choice of 60 percent of all Republicans. But Dewey remained short of the 500 delegates necessary for nomination. Senator Taft seemed to be his only serious rival by late spring.

Some corporate leaders were dissatisfied with both Dewey and Taft. They feared that President Roosevelt—whose name many of them declined to utter, replacing it with "That Man"—might run again. If he did, the Republicans must find someone who would be able to beat him. Perhaps they could take a page from the cynical course of their predecessors, the Whigs, a century before. In 1840 the Whig party had defeated the party of Andrew Jackson by finding a candidate they could recreate in the Hero's mold. With the help of a depression, William Henry Harrison had ridden the symbols of the log cabin and hard cider to victory over Jackson's successor, Martin Van Buren. By late 1939 some Republicans were exploring the possibility of using similar tactics to unseat Roosevelt in 1940.

Wendell Willkie hardly seemed a likely—or even a possible—Republican presidential nominee. His father had been a backer of William Jennings Bryan. Wendell Willkie himself had been a delegate to the 1924 Democratic convention and had worked in Newton Baker's behalf in 1932. The current (1938–39) edition of *Who's Who in America* at the time of the 1940 Republican convention *still* listed him as a Democrat. Herbert Hoover had not been sufficiently Republican to suit many party leaders in 1928, but his Republicanism was not nearly as new as that of Willkie in 1940. It was not that the GOP bosses did not welcome converts who had suddenly seen the light (they could hardly do otherwise, considering their decidedly minority status by this time). Rather, the problem of the Old Guard was well stated by former Senate majority leader James Watson, who told Willkie in 1940: "Well, Wendell, you know that back home in Indiana, it's all right if the town whore joins the church, but they don't let her lead the choir the first night."

If his late rebirth as a Republican was not enough to disqualify him for consideration for the nomination, Willkie was also both a Wall Street lawyer and the president of a utility company. Two more unpopular positions in the eyes of most Americans during the Depression would be hard to imagine. In fighting the TVA, Willkie had nurtured an image as the New Deal's most prominent innocent victim. Despite all this, he had a reputation as something of a liberal. That just might make him marketable to the voters. And the very Wall Street and utility connections that might make him suspect to many voters provided resassurance to the men who got behind Willkie's candidacy.

These people who began working behind the scenes for Willkie's nomination included Russell Davenport, the managing editor of *Fortune* magazine; Charlton MacVeagh and Thomas W. Lamont of J. P. Morgan and Company; Lammont Du Pont; Joseph N. Pew of the Sun Oil Company; Ernest T. Weir of Weirton Steel; and Edgar Monsanto Queeny of Monsanto Chemicals. It was an impressive board of directors. Joining them in the camp were Republican national chairman John D. M. Hamilton (who, it will be recalled, had in 1936 equated a vote for Roosevelt with support for the "International Communist Conspiracy"), Congressman Bruce Barton of New York (whose fame stemmed from his advertising career and *The Man Nobody Knows*, and who had in a 1932 letter to President Hoover called FDR just "a name and a crutch"), and the arch-conservative Congressman Joe Martin of Massachusetts, who would be permanent chairman of the 1940 convention.

With such men as these behind him, Wendell Willkie had the inside track to the Republican nomination, even though as late as two months before the convention he did not have a single publicly announced delegate. In addition to his behind-the-scenes support, Willkie benefited from the change in the war in Europe. All of the other major Republican contenders were clearly identified as isolationists. When the Nazis launched their blitzkrieg across the Low Countries and France in May 1940, the stock of isolationists fell rapidly, if not as far as the Dow Jones had dropped eleven years before. Isolationism seemed much less realistic by the time the Republican delegates gathered in Philadelphia late in June. Just three days before the convention opened, France capitulated to German terms and signed an armistice. It was not easy to picture young Tom Dewey leading a nation at war.

By this time, the Willkie operation, while carefully maintaining the outward appearance of amateurism, was working very well. The campaign had gone public in March in an issue of Davenport's *Fortune*. In a long article (largely written by Davenport), Willkie endorsed most goals of the New Deal, but indicated that he could make it work by removing its anti-business bias. He asserted that the New Deal Democrats had developed "a vested interest in depression." This was a politically powerful argument, the more so when Willkie called for going beyond the New Deal to build a "New World." The *Fortune* issue also contained a proposed petition calling, in so many words, for the unleashing of free enterprise. Republicans liked the idea, of course— they always have. It was much the same plea that Ronald Reagan used forty years later. Unfortunately for Willkie, the memory of what unfettered free enterprise had led to in 1929 was much fresher in 1940 than in 1980. (Certainly the fact that the incumbent Democrat was far more popular in 1940 than his counterpart four decades later had something to do with the difference in outcomes, too.) In 1980 a majority of voters accepted the argument and so had to relearn the results of Coolidge economics through harsh experience.

The people behind Willkie were busy in other ways. Some 2000 Willkie clubs, largely (although secretly) organized by local electric power companies, sprouted up around the country. When the convention itself opened, the galleries, streets, and hotel lobbies were swarming with young Willkie supporters, chanting "We Want Willkie," and giving out buttons and pamphlets bearing the same message. A promotion of cigarettes or mouthwash could not have been better handled; the connection of Bruce Barton with the Willkie campaign was not coincidental. Many of the "Willkie Girls" in Philadelphia for the convention were in fact employees of Wall Street firms who had been given a week's vacation plus expenses to go and cheer for Wendell.

Despite another attempt by Herbert Hoover to redeem himself with the voters, the Republican contest proved to be a three-way-race. Dewey led on the first ballot but faded quickly, and the field narrowed to Taft and Willkie. Taft came very close to victory, but Willkie claimed the nomination on the sixth ballot. He was not an opponent the Democrats could take lightly.[3]

If the age and experience of the leading Republican presidential hopefuls in 1940 were a commentary on the sad state of that party at the end of the New Deal, the Democrats seemed to have little more to offer in the way of proven leadership. When the original Roosevelt Cabinet was being assembled in 1932–33, James Farley told reporters: "There won't be any presidential possibilities in the Roosevelt Cabinet." He was right, and so it had remained. FDR was the master of his own show and his personality so dominated the administration that others did not arise as clear presidential possibilities. What was true of the Cabinet was also true of the rest of the Democratic party. Franklin Roosevelt was like a sun illuminating the Democratic heavens, and the other stars were not visible while he was shining. Further, the New Deal's alterations in power relationships lowered the prestige of those who might have been expected in earlier years to emerge as presidential aspirants. The primacy of the executive branch in the New Deal shifted attention from the Democratic leaders in Congress. The ranks of governors, whence many a previous president had come, were overwhelmingly Democratic in the 1930s, but the scope of state activity had become so circumscribed by the expansion of federal authority that few of them were able to gain much national attention.

By 1939 this was clearly a problem. There had long been speculation that Roosevelt might break the tradition begun by George Washington and run for a third term. If he did, though, it would provide the Republicans with a powerful issue. The complaints that FDR aspired to dictatorship would certainly increase; gleeful Republicans would attempt to link Roosevelt's name with those of Hitler, Mussolini, and Stalin. And what if the opposition succeeded? What an ignominious end it would be for Roosevelt's presidency if he sought a third term and was defeated.

The President looked for a suitable successor. His first concern was that the candidate must be a liberal, someone who was committed to continuing New Deal social and economic policies. Roosevelt realized that there was no assurance the Democrats would remain a progressive party. His two terms had moved the party decidedly in that direction, but eight years were not enough to assure a lasting association. The President's first choice to succeed him was Harry Hopkins, who met Roosevelt's requirements but was not popular with Democratic politicians. In an attempt to boost Hopkins's chances, FDR appointed him secretary of Commerce in 1938. The following year, however, Hopkins's health deteriorated markedly and the President was obliged to give up the idea.

Others were quite willing to run but were less to Roosevelt's liking. The President's longtime political adviser and operative, Jim Farley, hoped to succeed his boss. Roosevelt urged him to run for the New York governorship in 1938 in order to build a base, but Farley refused. Roosevelt began to push the idea that Farley's Catholic faith would prevent him from being elected. Intent on ensuring that the New Deal not appear to be repudiated, FDR wanted to take no chances on the religious issue leading to the defeat of the party's nominee.

The only possibility worse for Roosevelt than seeing the voters repudiate the New Deal would be if his own party did so. The nomination of Vice President Garner would amount to just that, and Roosevelt was absolutely opposed to the seventy-one-year-old Texan's candidacy. FDR was pleased when John L. Lewis publicly called the Vice President a "labor-baiting, poker-playing, whiskey-drinking, evil old man." Roosevelt was less enthusiastic about the things the CIO leader said about *him*.

Every time the President went over the list of possible Democratic standard-bearers for 1940, he eliminated all of them. A phenomenon common among people in positions of great authority had been at work on Franklin Roosevelt for several years. In the face of the extraordinary crisis, he had concentrated power in the executive branch. For a time, this worked fairly well. He encouraged his subordinates to be candid; criticism was accepted. But the longer a person is president, particularly if all decision making is focused on him, the more likely he is to believe in his own infallibility. Roosevelt came at times to speak of himself in the third person: "The President thinks . . ." The general problem grew worse in 1936. By that time, Louis Howe was the only man who would persist in telling Roosevelt that he was wrong. Howe's death in April left the yes-men unchallenged. This was followed by the election campaign. The adoration of the crowds on his trips and the unprecedented size of his victory seem to have convinced Roosevelt more than ever that he represented the will of the people.

Presidential hubris became more of a problem during Roosevelt's second term. *He* spoke for the people; the Supreme Court did not. Neither, perhaps, did the Congress. The frequency of FDR's vetoes—505 in his first eight years—is startling when his huge congressional majorities are remembered. It is not difficult to believe that by 1940, Roosevelt had convinced himself that no one else *could* be a good president; in short, that he was indispensable. Such feelings intensified as the world crisis worsened.

Even if one of the Democratic possibilities could handle the growing likelihood of war, Roosevelt had to worry about whether such a candidate could defeat the Republican nominee. The President appears to have sincerely feared for the future of the country if an isolationist Republican were elected in 1940. (On election night when he knew he had won, FDR said to Joseph Lash: "We seem to have averted a *Putsch*, Joe.")

It was a delicate situation. If Roosevelt sought the nomination, he might be defeated on the third-term/potential dictatorship issue. If he were to run, it would have to be on the basis of a draft by the party and the people, a summons to duty that he could not reject. So Roosevelt continued throughout the first half of the election year to say that he was not a candidate and had no desire to do anything after January 1941 but return to Hyde Park. Yet the President declined Farley's suggestion that he do "exactly what General Sherman did many years ago—issue a statement saying [you] would refuse to run if nominated and would not serve if elected." If the people insisted, FDR told Farley, he could not refuse them.

The President's failure to take the Sherman pledge kept most other potential candidates out of the race, and his encouragement to several different men prevented any one of them from emerging from the pack as a leading contender. Others might orchestrate the "draft" at the convention in Chicago—the party was left with no alternative if it wanted to win in November—while Roosevelt sat in Washington insisting that he was not interested. God, the President told his chief aides, would provide a candidate. To almost everyone but FDR, this was all an elaborate fiction. He very much wanted to be called by the party and the people to serve an unprecedented third term. It is doubtful that he admitted to himself that he was manipulating the situation to assure such an outcome.

When the convention opened on July 15, Mayor Edward J. Kelly, the boss of Chicago's Democratic machine, made a highly unusual welcoming speech in which he told the delegates that "the salvation of the nation rests in one man." Later, the convention's permanent chairman, Senator Alben Barkley of Kentucky, read a speech Roosevelt had prepared for him, saying that the President did not wish to remain in office. As Barkley reached the end of his address, the huge amplifiers in the building came on with shouts of "We want Roosevelt," "Illinois wants Roosevelt," "America wants Roosevelt," "Everybody wants Roosevelt," "The *world* wants Roosevelt," and so forth. A reporter traced the voice to the basement and found that the man doing the shouting was the city's superintendent of sewers, Thomas F. Garry, acting on orders from Boss Kelly. The "voice from the sewer" accomplished part of its purpose. A Roosevelt demonstration was launched on the convention floor, but the delegates did not go on to nominate him by acclamation as he may have hoped. The next evening the President easily won renomination, with 946 votes to 72 for runner-up Farley, who showed his party loyalty by moving to make the nomination unanimous.

The real drama of the convention was yet to come. A new vice-presidential candidate had to be chosen, since Garner was not willing to continue in the position and Roosevelt would not have had him even had Garner been willing. The President had encouraged the hopes of several men, but was intent upon having someone he could be sure would carry on liberal programs. He finally decided on Henry Wallace, but let no one except Hopkins know of the decision until after the President's own renomination was secured. When word of the choice reached the convention, both delegates and other potential candidates were irate. Wallace was not popular with the politicians, but opposition was derived even more from the desire of the delegates to rebel against Roosevelt's control. William B. Bankhead of Alabama, the speaker of the House, refused to bow out of the race. Jeers and screams of discontent arose from the floor during the speeches nominating Wallace. The vote itself was close, and Roosevelt prepared a statement of withdrawal in case the convention rejected Wallace. He meant it, at least to the point that he would withdraw in order to force the convention to redraft him—and Wallace as well. Wallace narrowly won, though, and Roosevelt was able to lead an unhappy party toward the November showdown with Willkie.[4]

President Roosevelt's strategy for the 1940 campaign was simple: he would act as president, not as a politician. It is, in fact, one of the most remarkable points about the 1940 election that both candidates attempted, at least initially, to act as nonpartisans, men "above" politics. It proved to be an easier task for the President than his challenger.

The first step in FDR's plan was taken before either party had chosen its nominee. Four days before the Republicans convened in June, the President appointed two prominent members of their party to his Cabinet. Henry Stimson, who had been secretary of War under President Taft and Herbert Hoover's secretary of state, again assumed leadership of the War Department. Frank Knox, Alf Landon's running mate in 1936, accepted the post of secretary of the Navy. It was a master political stroke as well as a solid administrative move. Roosevelt was forming a bipartisan government to deal with the war crisis in Europe. It was a sign of things to come. Throughout the campaign, Roosevelt used his position to the fullest advantage. "Mr. Roosevelt can act," journalist Turner Catledge pointed out, "while Mr. Willkie can only talk, and talk for the most part about the President's acts."

As Willkie talked—to the point of completely losing his voice—the President continued to act. Roosevelt toured military bases and new defense plants, emphasizing both his efforts to bolster the nation's preparedness (making clear that the goal was to keep us *out* of the war) and the creation of new jobs that resulted from military spending. While on such tours Roosevelt made "non-political" speeches and allowed news photographers to take pictures of him beside tanks, ships, and bustling assembly lines.

When the Republican nominee talked during the campaign, it was usually extemporaneously. The only major exception was his initial address at his hometown of Elwood, Indiana, a carefully planned statement of his campaign themes. In this speech Wendell Willkie came out firmly as a liberal. He explicitly accepted most goals of the New Deal. Any assessment of the impact of the Depression and the New Deal on American values must take note of the fact that the Republican party, including some of its more conservative elements, determined that their only hope for victory in 1940 was to endorse Roosevelt's goals and nominate a candidate who would identify himself as a liberal. Willkie condemned the pre-1929 business structure and monopolistic practices. He endorsed regulation of business, government-protected collective bargaining, minimum wages and maximum hours laws, social security, and unemployment insurance. His chief difference with Roosevelt was to charge that the New Deal inhibited enterprise. "I say that we must substitute for the philosophy of distributed scarcity, the philosophy of unlimited productivity."

This was a campaign theme with some potential, but Willkie's attempt to be a Republican as well as a nonpartisan candidate led him to move in an increasingly conservative-isolationist direction as the campaign progressed. His tongue grew more loose as he traveled around the country. After a particularly intemperate Willkie attack on the President's foreign policy, the challenger's press secretary, Lem Jones, produced what was to become the Willkie campaign's most unfortunate legacy. Jones put out a statement saying that Willkie had "mis-spoken himself." The phrase was to be heard again often following the campaign statements of another Republican challenger forty years later.

By mid-October, Willkie seemed to be gaining strength, principally by exploiting fears that Roosevelt might lead the United States into the European war. It was time for the President to enter the struggle personally. Nothing, in any case, could keep the old campaigner in Franklin Roosevelt from taking to the hustings in the final two weeks before the election. It proved to be one of Roosevelt's most effective brief political efforts. The President ignored the third-term issue, hoping the voters would do likewise. (Most of them did.) He reminded the nation—and particularly the more than one-third of it that remained in poverty—of what he had done for it. In a brilliant speech in Philadelphia on October 23, he pointed to apparent Republican hypocrisy: "The tears, the crocodile tears, for the laboring man and woman now being shed in this campaign come from those same Republican leaders who had their chance to prove their love for labor in 1932—and missed it." He went on to tick off the list of items that Willkie claimed to favor but that Republicans had tried to prevent over the past decade.

A few nights later, at Madison Square Garden, Roosevelt introduced the most famous line of the campaign, ridiculing the arch-conservative backers of the putatively liberal Willkie with the rhythmic repetition of the names "Martin, Barton, and Fish" (the last named being New York Congressman Hamilton Fish). Roosevelt and his supporters used this cadence throughout the remainder of the campaign, always to good audience effect. His best speech, though, was saved for last. Closing the campaign in Cleveland, the President recited the accomplishments of the New Deal, his vision for the future, and his allegiance to the working class: "I see an America where factory workers are not discarded after they reach their prime, where there is no endless chain of poverty from generation to generation."

Although both candidates had started out portraying themselves as liberals and each had sought the support of workers, by the end of the campaign the class division was at least as sharp as it had been in 1936. Many workers came to resent Willkie's attack on a President who they believed was their friend and champion. When Willkie toured working-class areas he was greeted with boos and not infrequently found himself the target of projectiles ranging from tomatoes and eggs to light bulbs and rocks.

When the votes were counted it was clear that a solid majority still backed the New Deal President. Willkie had done considerably better than Landon four years before, but he still took less than 45 percent of the popular vote and only 82 electoral votes to Roosevelt's 449. Nor was there any doubt about the continuing political division along class lines. An American Institute of Public Opinion survey conducted after the election found that 80 percent of those on relief had voted for Roosevelt, as had 60 percent of those who said they would be able to survive without relief for one month or less if they lost their jobs. At the other end of the wealth scale, those who said they could survive without relief for from three years to forever split 61–39 percent for Willkie.

Political analyst Samuel Lubell found even more striking evidence of class-based political divisions. In every city in which Lubell interviewed voters, Roosevelt received an overwhelming share of the vote in wards with average rentals below $45 per month. In areas with typical rents above $60 per month, the Democratic vote dropped sharply. A UAW member in Detroit put the reason succinctly: "I'll say it even though it doesn't sound nice. We've grown class conscious."

So had the more well-to-do (although they had always tended to be more class conscious than workers). As Henry Steele Commager once noted of Roosevelt's four victories, "On each occasion, the majority of the wise, the rich and the well-born voted the other way." The continuation of this political split between rich and poor in 1940 helped immeasurably to assure that the New Deal coalition that had coalesced in 1936 would continue to dominate American politics for years to come.[5]

The military buildup of 1940–41 did more to revive American industry and reduce unemployment than had any New Deal program. This is not, though, the reproach of Roosevelt's policies that it may seem. It simply means that the deficit-spending, "demand-side" approach that the New Deal had used timidly was shown to work when employed boldly. Rather than representing a reversal of the New Deal prescription, the military spending of 1940 and subsequent years represented a much larger dose of the same medicine.

The cure did not come quickly. The 1940 average for unemployment was 8.1 million (14.6 percent of the work force), and even in 1941 as the defense industries moved into high gear, the mean unemployment rate was 9.9 percent, representing 5.6 million jobless people who wanted to work. Industrial production, which had surpassed its 1929 level just before the 1937–38 recession, soared 30 percent above its 1929 level in 1941.

All of this might be taken to indicate that Adolf Hitler was more responsible for ending the Great Depression in the United States than Franklin Roosevelt was. In a roundabout way, such an argument is correct. The Nazi threat induced Roosevelt at last to let go enough of his insistence on trying to balance the budget so that the Keynesian prescription was finally allowed to work. The last irony of the Depression era is that Hitler, in a very indirect sense, saved the reputation of the New Deal and the Roosevelt presidency. Without the military boom in response to the German war machine, Roosevelt's presidency would probably have been remembered as compassionate and helpful but ineffective in solving the fundamental problems of the Depression. This in no sense means that the Depression *could* not have been solved without the threat of war, but that it took the danger to convince Roosevelt and the Congress to spend at the level necessary to bring about recovery.

Although 1941 was a year dominated by the concerns of war abroad and the growing likelihood that the United States would be drawn into the conflict, it was also very much a year of the Depression. While people were encouraged by the trend back toward prosperity, they generally remained fearful that it would not continue. In response to a national survey in the summer of 1941 that asked if the respondent was financially "better off or worse off than last year," only 30 percent answered "better," 20 percent said "worse," and fully one-half said "the same." The source of the boom, after all, was clear for all to see, and it appeared unlikely to outlast the military crisis. The nation seemed to be faced by the horrible choice of war or depression.

There was no longer much talk of reform in 1941. More immediate problems had to be faced. This did not mean that there was any significant change in the Depression-era values. Certainly there was an increase in patriotic themes in popular culture in the last years of the Depression. But the American values that were emphasized in such successful films as *Sergeant York* (1941) were, in important respects, similar to those of the earlier social films of the thirties. Gary Cooper as Alvin York has a religious experience that leads him to oppose greed and violence and return love to those who wrong him. York opposes war and seeks conscientious objector status when he is drafted to fight in World War I. After a long talk with an officer who tells him that pacifism is a good thing, but sometimes it is necessary to fight to protect what we believe in, York decides to join the Army and becomes a hero by *saving* lives. *Sergeant York* does not abandon Depression-era values, but marks a transition by showing viewers that under some circumstances war may be compatible with those values—in fact, fighting may be necessary to defend them. Nor was there any decline in the popularity of movies with a direct social message, such as the previously discussed *Grapes of Wrath* (1940) and *How Green Was My Valley* (1941).

It is clear that the Depression-bred moral economic values remained strong in 1940–41. A Gallup poll in May 1941 found that a cross section of Americans believed by more than a 2–1 margin that "there is too much power in the hands of a few rich men and large corporations in the United States." If those values declined in the early 1940s, it was *after* the Depression had ended. And there is no imprecision about when that took place. The Great Depression is one of the most neatly demarcated events in our history. It began in New York City on a series of days in October 1929, and decisively ended on December 7, 1941, near Honolulu.

American participation in World War II began in the frame of reference of the Depression-era values, as our entry into the First World War had taken place in the context of progressivism. If the first war was fought with idealist expectations that led to rapid disillusionment, the second war was fought in a way more in keeping with the "practical idealism" of the Depression. Expectations of bringing about the millennium were lower in the 1940s, but there was a much more certain feeling that we were on the side of right, on the side of the values that had reemerged in the 1930s.

This meant that there was an attempt to keep the spirit of liberalism alive during World War II, as exemplified by Harry Hopkins, Vice President Henry Wallace, and such congressional liberals as Senator Robert Wagner, in the hope that the values of the thirties could be revived after the conflict ended. Some liberals, such as Rex Tugwell, in fact, hoped that the war might help to advance their cause. Perhaps it would lead to a greater sense of cooperation, a further decline in individualism, and greater government direction of the economy. It did. Some redistribution of income was achieved during the war as a result of full employment and high taxes on the upper income brackets. The economy was brought under more government control than at any other time in American history. Maximum prices and rents were administered by government agencies. Unions became more powerful than ever before.

But just as World War I had killed the Progressive Era's spirit of sacrifice, the second war stretched beyond their limits the capacities of most Americans for selflessness. Although the cooperative spirit of the war led some liberals to be more self-assured than they had been before, conservatives were becoming more prominent in Washington. Such men as Henry Stimson, James Byrnes, Edward Stettinius, and Dean Acheson were far less concerned with social issues than had been the New Dealers of the previous decade. Various New Deal agencies—the Civilian Conservation Corps, the Works Projects Administration, and the National Youth Administration—expired during the war. In order to promote efficient production, big-business leaders were given a voice in policymaking that they had not enjoyed since the early thirties. Some liberals remained hopeful, but Archibald MacLeish spoke for many when he wrote in 1944: "It is no longer feared, it is assumed, that the country is headed back to normalcy, that Harding is just around the corner, that the twenties will repeat themselves."[6]

It was not to be that bad. Harry Truman, not Warren Harding, was just around the corner, and a few more reforms were added in the later forties. The Employment Act of 1946 committed the American government to a Keynesian countercyclical policy. But it took the turn of only one more corner to find Richard Nixon and Joe McCarthy. If the fifties were not the twenties reborn, they were certainly a new age of materialism and egoism. As with previous eras of reform, though, the Great Depression left a legacy that could not be wiped out in the subsequent period of reversion to self-centeredness. It remained an inheritance for America that endures into the 1980s.

15·Perspective:
The Great Depression
and Modern America

It is obvious that the Great Depression of the 1930s marked a dramatic change in the course of American history. Questions concerning the nature of that change remain open. The writing of history is a process of simplification; it becomes art when it avoids *over*simplification and makes the complex flow of events comprehensible. Imposing clarity and order where there was in fact confusion is necessary, but it can be misleading. Academic observers of the New Deal, for example, have sought co-

323

herent patterns in the Roosevelt programs. They have come up with such explanations of the New Deal policies as the division of them into the "three R's": Relief, Recovery, and Reform; or into ideologically distinct First and Second New Deals. The First New Deal has been said to have emphasized planning and the Second New Deal has been identified as a turn back toward restoring a competitive economy.

None of this has ever seemed quite satisfactory—and with good reason. We have tried to fit both Roosevelt and the American people into coherent intellectual and ideological categories. Neither the President nor most of the people were intellectuals; nor were they ideological. Franklin D. Roosevelt was, as I have emphasized repeatedly in this volume, a politician. The digestion of that simple fact makes understanding an admittedly complex man and a complex era considerably more manageable. For one thing, it means that an understanding of Depression America is to be found more in the values of the people than in the philosophy of a leader. This is in no sense to deny the importance of Franklin Roosevelt. It is only to point out that the political context in which he operated in the 1930s—that is, the changing mix of American values in the Depression—was of even more significance than was Roosevelt himself. FDR was so dominant and important in the Depression decade precisely because his leadership meshed with the moral economic values of American society in those years.

All that said, though, it is necessary to review the impact of the two Depression-era Presidents before we return to the values of the time and the ways in which they have affected us in the last half century. That presidential leadership was of tremendous significance is shown by even the most casual comparison of the mood of the country under Herbert Hoover with that after Roosevelt took office. It is beyond doubt that without Roosevelt, the history of the 1930s would have been vastly different. It is nearly as certain that the subsequent development of the United States would have been altered in important ways. If one imagines—it requires a great leap of imagination—a Hoover victory in 1932, or that another Democrat, say John Nance Garner, had become president in 1933, it is difficult to picture anything like what happened in the remainder of the thirties. No other American political figure in this century has had an impact as great as that of FDR.

One of the critical differences between Hoover and Roosevelt was hinted at in mid-1982 when, in the face of a new economic decline, Treasury Secretary Donald Regan explained why he always tried to be "bullish on America." "If you do not offer people a ray of hope," said the former chairman of Merrill Lynch, "if you don't offer them the promise that things will get better, then you have got no chance of success." It was not that Herbert Hoover did not *try* to offer hope of better things, it was rather that he was unable to do so in a credible fashion. Roosevelt had the ability to restore hope. This was partly a difference of style and personality, but it also reflected a more fundamental difference between the men. The difference was, most simply, that Hoover was an ideologue (the last such to be elected president until Ronald Reagan, although Hoover's ideology was quite different from Reagan's) and Roosevelt was a pragmatist. Hoover was greatly concerned with intellectual consistency; Roosevelt was eclectic. This did not mean that FDR was a crass, unprincipled politician. He was a "commonsense idealist"—two qualities he often associated. One of the factors that made Roosevelt a great leader was that his beliefs so neatly coincided with popular values in the thirties. For a good politician, principle must usually yield to expediency. But during the Depression, the two frequently coincided. What was good, decent, fair, and just—what was "right"—was also what a majority of people wanted and, hence, what was expedient.

Roosevelt was self-centered, but genuinely concerned with others. To close associates, the President even referred to himself as "Papa." Like any affectionate father, Roosevelt sought to help those entrusted to his care. After saying something that hurt one of his subordinates (which he did rather frequently), he would usually telephone the injured party and have a soothing chat. On one occasion in 1935 at Warm Springs, Roosevelt waved aside a wheelchair and walked down a ramp in front of other patients. It took great strength and will to withstand the pain this must have caused, but Roosevelt apparently believed that it would be encouraging to the other disabled people. His concern for others seems to have been the result of a combination of noblesse oblige and the effects of his own struggle with polio.

Despite his exceptional political ability and his verbal capacity to hurt those around him, Roosevelt was usually a humane man. He was even, in his own way, something of a moralist, who could on one level play dirty politics with the best of them, but on another liked to believe in the basic goodness of people. At times he almost seemed innocent, a naive optimist. He had great faith that he was doing the best he could. He could rationalize his own or subordinates' tactical sleight of hand because he was confident that the end would be the advancement of the American people (and, of course, of himself). FDR's confidence in his own ability and in human capacity in general led him to reject the notion that depressions are inevitable. Economic laws, Roosevelt said in a 1932 speech, are made by human beings, not nature. *Something* could be done; it *must* be done.

The paradoxical combination of self-centeredness and humanitarian concern that Roosevelt exhibited led to an extraordinarily personal government. Establishing, through radio contact and the feedback of letters from the public, a kind of "intimacy" with the public, Roosevelt saw himself as the one true spokesman for the American people. Roosevelt's personal government established a bad precedent, but in 1933 and the years immediately following, it was one of the few things that could have given people the will to carry on.

From the start, FDR began to centralize power. He made all important decisions himself. A White House clerk calculated that Roosevelt made thirty-five or more decisions for every one Coolidge had made. Instead of giving anti-Depression tasks to old, constitutionally oriented departments, FDR created new "emergency" agencies, which were more firmly under his control. Among the problems this practice led to was that creating new agencies became at times an end in itself, a way to avoid solving problems. The new agencies also started an almost uncontrolled growth of bureaucracy, which accelerated during World War II. Under Roosevelt, at least, a personal touch served to somewhat humanize what would otherwise have been (and what would soon become) an unfeeling federal bureaucracy.

The burgeoning executive branch worked better under Roosevelt than it would in later years. This was due in part to the President's accessibility. He was always willing to hear new ideas; he constantly sought sources of information outside the normal channels. Roosevelt's seeming readiness to listen to any idea opened the floodgates for new thoughts and new thinkers. Intellectuals took on an importance in the White House that they had not enjoyed since the days before Jackson, when Jefferson and the Adamses themselves fit into that category. Even Woodrow Wilson, himself a professor, had not given intellectuals the prominence they had in the New Deal.

Indeed, one of Franklin Roosevelt's most remarkable achievements was to bring together political currents that had been antagonistic throughout most of American history. Theodore Roosevelt had begun to blend Hamiltonian means into Jeffersonian ends; Franklin Roosevelt carried this combination much further. More significant, though, was FDR's combination of Jefferson and Jackson, or even John Quincy Adams and Jackson. The antagonism between the Jacksonian "common man" and the intellectual elite that Jackson associated with Adams in the 1828 campaign had become deeply embedded in American politics during the ensuing century. By employing intellectual advisers to try to reach Jacksonian ends, Franklin Roosevelt brought together the plowman and the professor. This was no easy feat. Although many intellectuals had joined the progressive movement earlier in the twentieth century, the elite educational institutions remained staunchly conservative when FDR took office. When he returned as President for visits to Groton, Roosevelt was greeted with a formality that could not conceal the hostility of both students and alumni. The catcalls that met Roosevelt at Harvard during a 1936 campaign visit have already been mentioned. And when Brain Truster Adolf A. Berle was asked to speak at the twenty-fifth reunion of his class at the Harvard Law School in 1941, his classmates shouted him down. Berle was not even able to finish his talk.

Yet such hostile receptions for Roosevelt and his aides at exclusive schools were more a reflection of upper-class hostility to the New Deal than of intellectual disaffection. Like so many other departures of the Roosevelt years, the marriage of intellectuals to liberalism was to continue for decades after the New Deal ended. The association had become so nearly complete by the 1960s that it may be hard for many readers to imagine that it was ever otherwise. But it was, and the alliance of intellectuals and the poor that seems so natural today was another of FDR's contributions. The "establishment" of the 1930s was anything but liberal, but Roosevelt's actions convinced bright young people that government should be active and humane. This was the source of the "liberal establishment" that irked conservatives in later decades.

President Roosevelt's use of intellectual advisers went hand in hand with his centralization of decision making and concentration of power at the federal level and in the executive branch. The growth in presidential power during the New Deal marked the start of the modern presidency. The basis was there in the powers used by Lincoln, the first Roosevelt, and Wilson, but FDR was an activist president to a degree that went far beyond these predecessors. Beginning with Roosevelt, presidents have been expected to take a prominent role in the legislative process, to present a "program" to Congress. The person of the president as leader, the man on horseback, came to be the sine qua non of paternalist liberals. Tugwell clearly stated the importance of the leader to liberals of this stripe: Subordinates had to go along with Roosevelt even if they did not agree with him. "Nothing could be done at all unless we hung together under a leader . . . we had no real right to make judgments."

One result of Roosevelt's utter dominance of American liberalism was that no other leader could emerge from his shadow. "No head rose high enough and big enough," Frances Perkins recalled, ". . . to offer any alternative." The consequences of this went far beyond the third-term question in 1940. After Roosevelt's death in 1945 liberals drifted for years, awaiting a new leader of his style and stature. They thought that they could accomplish little without such a dashing champion. Although many liberals believed they had found a new leader, worthy of the FDR tradition, in Adlai Stevenson, it was not until 1960 that a "new FDR" emerged from the unlikely source of Joseph Kennedy's family.[1]

Economic problems were, of course, paramount in the 1930s. Although Franklin Roosevelt's lack of classical economic knowledge opened him to new ideas, he never came to understand the new economics that was emerging all around him in the decade. Since at least 1928 the assumptions of laissez-faire economics had been under attack. In that year William Trufant Foster and Waddill Catchings published their popular economic volume, *The Road to Plenty*. In it they indicated that when business declined, government intervention in the economy was necessary in order to place in the hands of consumers a sufficient amount of money to buy what was being produced. In the boom of 1928 few took heed. After the Crash, though, Foster's theories seemed to deserve a hearing. His advice to government was simple and would have been effective: increase government spending and tax away some of the surplus income of the rich. Foster's most telling argument was that everyone knew "what would happen if war were declared today." Billions would be spent and the Depression would be over. Why wait for a military war, Foster asked, when we could achieve the same end by fighting famine. Neither Hoover nor Roosevelt ever quite believed that the nation could spend itself into prosperity, and in the end it took the war to which Foster had alluded to prove his point.

Foster's ideas were adopted by Utah banker Marriner Eccles. After Roosevelt appointed Eccles as a governor of the Federal Reserve System in 1934, spending had an effective advocate close to the President. Eccles's importance grew in 1935, but Roosevelt remained firm in his belief that a balanced budget must be achieved as soon as possible.

Meanwhile, there was a simultaneous battle within the administration between those, like Tugwell, who advocated planning, and disciples of Louis Brandeis, who sought a restoration of competition. The latter's views gained somewhat after the NRA failed. The main backers of this approach (aside from the aged Justice Brandeis himself) were Felix Frankfurter of the Harvard Law School and the "little hot dogs" he sent to Washington. Among these former Frankfurter students, the most important were Thomas G. Corcoran and Benjamin V. Cohen. Their thrusts against concentration were reflected in the Wheeler-Rayburn bill and the tax policies of the administration from 1935 onward, Roosevelt's verbal assault on monopoly in 1938, and Thurman Arnold's antitrust suits in the closing years of the Depression.

This switch from the Berle-Tugwell position to the Brandeis-Frankfurter view is often cited as the ideological shift of the First to the Second New Deal. For the intellectuals involved, no doubt there was an ideological change. But Roosevelt and such nonideological aides as Hopkins and Ickes had no trouble getting along with both groups. This was because these men represented the essence of the New Deal: a humane, cooperative impulse that was not ideological. This was the general mood of the public as well. Roosevelt, the compassionate politician, naturally favored this concept of a better deal, too. He was willing to join with the "hot dogs" after the Blue Eagles failed, particularly since the Brandeisians' anti–big business attitudes seemed to fit the public mood and, hence, would be politically useful.

Thus, working- and many middle-class Americans, Hopkins, Ickes, and to a large extent Roosevelt himself found a common cause. The planners and competitors also favored greater equality, but each in their own separate ways.

The Brandeisians seem to have been closer to the popular feeling of the mid-thirties, which naturally enough sought its equality, if possible, with a large dose of individual freedom.

As spending increased in 1935, some observers believed they discerned the hand of John Maynard Keynes at work. Keynes's theories on using fiscal and monetary policies to cool overheated economies and to warm cooling ones were similar to the ideas of Foster and Catchings. But Roosevelt never accepted the idea, no matter who offered it. There is little doubt that a full-scale Keynesian program *could* have ended the Depression. The fact remains, though, that it was only at the height of the war, in 1943, that average unemployment for the year finally dipped below its 1929 level. The moral of the story seemed clear enough: If warfare means prosperity, Foster, Eccles, and Keynes were right. We could spend our way out of depression. The lesson was learned well. Military spending helped keep us out of depression from the early forties to the beginning of the eighties. (There were, of course, many other reasons for the relative prosperity of the post–World War II period, including cheap energy, a backlog of savings, growing consumer demand, new industries, and low inflation.) Unfortunately, this was less than half of the Keynesian prescription. It could—and did—become politically popular to spend, but what was to be done when the economy overheated? Keynes called for a reversal of the fiscal and monetary policies he prescribed for bad times. But what politician would vote for collecting more in taxes than the government was spending?

Roosevelt and other traditionalists had been right in their feeling that large deficits could not continue forever. Although the fear of inflation had been ludicrous in 1937, sooner or later it would become a problem if deficits were not compensated for. When a man from Texas who pictured himself as a new Roosevelt took over in the 1960s and tried to outdo his idol in lavish domestic programs, fight a war at the same time, and not raise taxes to pay for it, inflation finally *did* become a major problem.

Yet despite Lyndon Johnson's overheating of the economy, inflation had risen to an annual rate of only 4.7 percent when he left office in 1969. The really serious, runaway inflation of the 1970s began only with the combination of the Arab oil embargo of 1973–74 (and the consequent leap in energy prices) with Richard Nixon's huge grain sales to the Soviet Union, which contributed substantially to a 20 percent jump in food prices in 1973. These pressures added spectacularly to the inflationary flames Johnson's deficits had kindled. The Organization of Petroleum Exporting Countries threw more of their oil on the fire in 1979, when energy prices shot upward by another 37 percent. In so doing, OPEC joined with the efforts of one of its members, Iran, to complete the discrediting of Jimmy Carter and pave the way for the election of a man committed to dismantling the New Deal and returning, as much as possible, to the days of Calvin Coolidge.

It is an extraordinary irony that the first firm ideological opponent of the New Deal and Keynesianism to occupy the White House since Franklin Roosevelt was the one who finally created a deficit so large that it exacerbated an already bad economy and brought on a serious collapse. There can be no question that Ronald Reagan's economic policies of drastic tax cuts combined with increased spending (although shifted from social programs to the military) and tight money were a major cause of the "recession" of the early 1980s, easily the worst such economic disaster since the Great Depression. Plainly it was more than coincidence that the increase in unemployment began in precisely the same month (July 1981) that Reagan's economic program was enacted. Ronald Reagan performed the striking feat of demonstrating anew that "supply-side" (i.e., Coolidge-Mellon) economics does not work and at the same time showing that excessive use of one side of the Keynesian formula (deficit spending) can lead to disaster.

In fact, Keynesianism had offered a temporary way out of the Depression, but by itself it could provide no permanent solution. The fundamental problem in the economy remained maldistribution of income. That maldistribution continues to be severe, but as the following table indicates, there have been some significant changes in income distribution in the United States since 1929. There have been important reductions in the shares going to the top 5 percent and the top 20 percent. Most of these declines in the relative positions of the richest Americans took place during the Great Depression and World War II, with less dramatic drops being registered in the 1960s. Interestingly, though, the redistribution from the top fifth went mostly to the second and third fifths: to the middle class. The shares going to the lower two income fifths increased somewhat during World War II, but have not improved since. Although the poorest Americans have not benefited greatly, it is reasonable to conclude that the redistribution from the richest to the middle-income brackets helped sustain purchasing power in the postwar years of relative prosperity. Ronald Reagan's 1981 imitation of Andrew Mellon's tax cuts favoring the rich reversed this beneficial trend, and did so quite intentionally.

The apparent vindication of Keynesianism in World War II led to its rapid conquest of the field. Unmodified laissez faire nearly expired in the Roosevelt years. Some Republicans continued thereafter to hold aloft the tattered banner of the unfettered marketplace, but Eisenhower made no attempt to dismantle the New Deal, Goldwater was crushed when he suggested he might try, and Nixon shocked many when he announced in 1971 that he was a Keynesian. Even Ronald Reagan ran into firm opposition when he attempted to tamper with the more basic parts of the New Deal legacy, such as Social Security. And Reagan himself—although he would never admit it—used

PERCENTAGE SHARE OF MONEY INCOME
RECEIVED BY EACH INCOME FIFTH OF AMERICAN
FAMILIES AND UNATTACHED INDIVIDUALS

Year	Lowest Fifth	Fourth Fifth	Middle Fifth	Second Fifth	Highest Fifth	Top 5 Percent
1981	4.6	10.6	16.7	24.3	43.7	16.5
1978	4.9	10.8	16.7	24.0	43.5	16.8
1970	4.9	10.9	16.4	23.8	44.1	16.1
1960	4.6	10.9	16.4	22.7	45.4	19.6
1950	4.8	10.9	16.1	22.1	46.1	21.4
1946	5.0	11.1	16.0	21.8	46.1	21.3
1941	4.1	9.5	15.3	22.3	48.8	24.0
1935–36	4.1	9.2	14.1	20.9	51.7	26.5
1929	(12.5)		13.8	19.3	54.4	30.0

Compiled from: U.S. Department of Commerce, Bureau of the Census, *Historical Statistics of the United States, Colonial Times to 1970* (Washington: Government Printing Office, 1975), Series G-319-336, p. 301, and *Current Population Reports*, P-60, No. 85 (Table 14), No. 120 (Table 5), and No. 134 (Table 4).

Keynesianism when he induced a recession to curb inflation. Oddly, although Roosevelt never became a Keynesian, his administration created a new orthodoxy, of which conscious government use of fiscal and monetary policy was a primary part.

Yet the real "solution" to the Depression that emerged from the New Deal and the military spending of World War II was, basically, to return to an old and comfortable American assumption: more or less constant expansion. The economic boom of World War II allowed Americans to opt once more for the easy solution of an ever expanding pie. With the return of prosperity and the coinciding swing of the pendulum away from social concerns and toward a more self-centered outlook and a complacent sense that the economic problem had been licked, the values of the Depression era declined.

Two principal factors are often cited as having kept up growth and prevented a new depression in the postwar years. One is that enough Keynesianism had been learned that government usually moved in the correct direction during critical periods to reverse recessions. The other is that many programs established by the New Deal—unemployment compensation, Social Security, welfare payments, deposit insurance, and so forth—worked automatically to counter economic downturns. Both of these facts were of great importance in keeping the economy in relative health from the early 1940s to the late 1970s, but both were seriously undermined by the policies of the Reagan administration.

Two other phenomena were of at least equal significance in creating and maintaining the greatest economic boom in the history of the world. Both served to persuade what might otherwise have been a reluctant public and Congress to spend at high enough levels to keep up sufficient demand. One was the Cold War, which from the early 1950s kept military spending at high rates even while the nation was at peace. At times when neither congressional nor public opinion was given to supporting heavy spending for social programs, the need to defend ourselves from the Communist threat in fact helped protect us from the possibly more immediate danger of economic collapse. In the years between the Korean War and the early 1970s, a majority of Americans usually seemed ready to believe that the country could never have too much defense. The resulting government spending played no small part in keeping the economy on a general rise during those years.

Even more significant in the great postwar economic boom, though, may have been another coinciding boom: that of babies. The phenomenal explosion in births in the years 1946–64 fueled the demand needed to keep the American economy growing. "A civilian market growing by the size of Iowa every year," *Fortune* magazine noted in 1951, "ought to be able to absorb whatever production the military will eventually turn loose." Seven years later, *Life* headlined its cover story: "Kids, Built-In Recession Cure—How 4,000,000 A Year Make Millions In Business." The Cold War and the Baby Boom combined to keep the economy strong enough that its occasional slips remained within the bounds of what mild Keynesianism could correct. Both phenomena, however, added to the reliance on an ever expanding economy. Should that growth ever slow appreciably, a new crisis would be inevitable. We are now facing that crisis.[2]

The economic impact of Franklin Roosevelt's actions as president have been immense and lasting. The same can readily be said of his political achievements. Politics was the area in which FDR considered himself an expert. The changes he helped effect in this realm were monumental.

Winning the election in 1932 was no particular accomplishment, of course. The Depression had assured a Democratic victory. After coming into office, though, Franklin Roosevelt began a dramatic alteration of American politics. He focused public attention on genuine problems for the first time in more than a decade. More even than in the Populist and Progressive eras, American politics became issue-oriented in the 1930s. The Depression itself was largely responsible, to be sure, but it should be remembered that the Republicans and many important Democrats sought to ignore economics and concentrate the 1932 campaign on such diversions as prohibition. Roosevelt's personal role cannot be discounted.

Although immigrants had long played a part in urban machine politics, and ethnic groups had had some impact in the Progressive era, national politics before 1933 remained—despite the Al Smith nomination in 1928—largely the province of property-owning, Anglo-Saxon Protestant males. The New Deal began the slow process of bringing other Americans into the democratic process. Roosevelt's goal was to create a lasting coalition of interest groups that would assure his party majority status for decades to come. With the help of the Depression he succeeded. The economic collapse of the 1930s did for the Democratic party what the depression of the 1890s had done for the Republicans.

Creating such a lasting majority was an exceedingly difficult task. The bedrock of the Democratic party had long been the Solid South. For a Democrat to reject the South was unthinkable; for the South to reject the Democratic party was worse. The "Southern Way of Life," with its complete white domination, was tied to the one-party system.

At first, Roosevelt and southern Democrats got along famously. He was, after all, a part-time Georgian. Southern delegates had put FDR over the top to win his 1932 nomination. They were generally pleased with the AAA, and relief programs seemed no great threat in the beginning. Soon, however, doubts arose. The attempts by Ickes, Hopkins, and other New Deal relief administrators to see that blacks were not discriminated against in the dispensing of government funds rubbed many white supremacists the wrong way. Relief rates, as low as they were, often exceeded the criminally low pay scales southern whites offered black employees. As Eleanor Roosevelt's beliefs in a greater degree of racial equality came to be better known, she became for many southern whites the world's single most hated person, known simply as "That Woman" to thousands who considered the utterance of her name improper for ladies and gentlemen.

In the general euphoria of 1936, southern Democrats allowed the abrogation of the party's requirement that a presidential nominee receive the support of two-thirds of the delegates. The rule had for a century given southerners a veto over Democratic nominees. When Roosevelt introduced his Court plan the following year, many southerners believed that the President secretly wanted to appoint justices who would upset the racial order of their region.

Although the section's long-standing paranoia made the situation look more threatening than it was, southerners were correct in seeing a fundamental change in their position in the Democratic party. With the huge Democratic majorities elected in 1936, the southerners found themselves a distinct minority within their own party. Still, the need to maintain a one-party system seemed absolute. The changes in the Democratic party in the thirties were enough to scare southerners, but not yet sufficient to cause them to abandon the party of their grandfathers. The move of blacks, labor unions, Catholics, and Jews into the Democratic party did, however, provide some strange company for southern conservatives. The possibility of a formal alliance between southerners and Republicans lay open. What Barry Goldwater, Richard Nixon, and John Mitchell, the architects of the "southern strategy," would try to accomplish in the 1960s was clearly foreshadowed by the events of the thirties.

The greatest trouble of all in trying to appeal to opposing groups came with the President's early attempt to keep both big business and the working class on his side. It did not succeed, and early in 1935, facing mounting pressure from the left, Roosevelt seems to have made a decision similar to that made by Nixon in the early 1970s on the advice of aide Patrick Buchanan: "Cut . . . the country in half; . . . we would have far the larger half." Roosevelt's division had the redeeming feature that at least the enemy he singled out—the reactionary rich—had clearly done harm or been indifferent to the plight of a majority of Americans. America's upper crust responded to Roosevelt's rhetorical attacks with bitterness unmatched in the annals of twentieth-century presidents. Two famous cartoons illustrated the feelings of the wealthy toward one they viewed as an apostate. One by Dorothy McKay in *Esquire* for November 1938 showed an upper-class youngster writing "ROOSEVELT" on the sidewalk. His tattletale sister was informing on him. "Mother," she exclaimed, "Wilfred wrote a bad word!" In a similar vein, Peter Arno drew in *The New Yorker* two groups of well-to-do people at a club. "Come along," the first urged the second. "We're going to the Trans-Lux to hiss Roosevelt." On a copy of this cartoon, FDR wrote "Grand."

With his class-oriented actions and talk of 1935 and 1936, Roosevelt had crossed a political Rubicon. The rise of the CIO and the wave of sit-down strikes in 1937 took place while the President's fortunes were tied up with the working class, whether he continued to like it or not.

He had, though, little reason not to like it. The coalition formed of labor unionists, relief recipients, blacks, southerners, ethnic and religious minorities, intellectuals, and sometimes farmers has dominated American politics since the thirties. Even as the South split along class lines in the 1970s, with many of the better-off whites in the region becoming Republicans, a majority could still be formed in 1976 of the remaining parts of the "Roosevelt Coalition." And the outcome of the 1980 election, while unquestionably marking at least a temporary shift to the right, was far more a repudiation of Jimmy Carter than it was the death knell of the New Deal and the majority that the Depression and Roosevelt had put together. By the 1982 off-year elections, the half-century-old New Deal coalition was able once more to demonstrate enough strength that *The New York Times* could proclaim editorially: "'Liberal' Is No Longer a Dirty Word."[3]

That political concerns motivated so many of Franklin Roosevelt's actions is disturbing to some observers. Critics can condemn FDR for opportunism. Obviously, that is just what it was, but perhaps that is not as bad as most of us think. Opportunism may play a crucial role in democracy. The President must lead, but if he wants to be reelected he must conform finally to the popular will rather than to a preconceived plan of his own. It is possible that Roosevelt's relative success and his great popularity were functions of his being more of a politician (in the best sense of the word) and less of an ideologue than many of his critics liked or recognized.

Discussions of the New Deal's place in history in recent years have concentrated on its conservative aspects—that is, its success in keeping the system running. Aside from inducing apoplexy in surviving right-wing Roosevelt-haters, the most serious problem with this view is its present-mindedness. The troubles that paternalist liberalism produced in the 1960s and 1970s should not be used to condemn the reforms made in the 1930s.

There can be no doubt that the New Deal performed a marvelous job of conservation: it saved American capitalism at the time of that economic system's worst crisis to date. To accept this, however, is not to say as some leftist historians have in the last two decades that things would have been better had the reforms of the Roosevelt administration never occurred. It may very well be regrettable that the New Deal did not do more, particularly that it did nothing effective to strike at the maldistribution of wealth and income that continues to plague the American economy. But some reform is better than none. Making things worse is not a way to make them better; the reelection of Hoover in 1932 would have been a disaster; allowing the poor to starve is not a way to make their lives better.

Of course the New Deal defused discontent; doubtless this was one motive for relief expenditures. This is, however, much easier to condemn from the friendly confines of Stanford or Columbia several decades after the fact than it was from a WPA project in the midst of the Depression. It also seems unfair—and more than a little inconsistent—to criticize the New Deal both for not helping workers and for aiding them sufficiently to undermine their discontent.

This said, however, a basic question about the New Deal must be asked: Whom did it help? Of the early measures, the NRA aided big business, the AAA helped large landowners and hurt tenant farmers, the Emergency Banking Act and the FDIC helped bankers and depositors, the HOLA aided lenders and homeowners, the SEC helped stock investors, and the so-called economy bill helped no one, except perhaps some befuddled classical economists. The only things in the First New Deal that directly benefited the really poor were the TVA, the Farm Credit Administration (which saved many small farmers), and the relief programs.

Considering these facts, many observers have wondered why Franklin Roosevelt was loved most by those he helped least. It is a legitimate and important question. One answer is simply that the provision of relief was in itself so much more than the federal government had done before for the down-and-out that they naturally appreciated it. In addition, there was the Second New Deal. The benefits of the Wagner Act, Social Security, and the later Fair Labor Standards Act were not shared by Americans at the very bottom of the economic ladder, but these acts did reach further down than most of the First New Deal legislation. Next to Roosevelt's fatherly image, the WPA was the most important factor in tying the poor to the New Deal. For all its problems, the WPA seemed to most who worked for it to mean one thing: the government had finally remembered the "forgotten man."

The New Deal created the welfare state. Never again would it be seriously argued that society had no responsibility for the unemployed, the aged, and the infirm. The government might not do *much* for them, but it would not let them again completely fend for themselves. Even Ronald Reagan, a half century later, found it necessary to pay lip service to the idea of a federal "safety net" for the "truly needy." The federal government's relationship to the American people was drastically altered. "Washington"—previously the name of the first president, numerous other people, a state, and various landmarks and towns, including one on the Potomac River—suddenly came in the 1930s to have a new meaning for most Americans. It was the source of income for many, the collector of social security taxes for more, and the stimulator of the economy for almost all. "The government" now always meant the national government. The United States became, through the New Deal, an "it" instead of a "they." No longer "these United States," the nation more than ever before became *the* United States.

The New Deal did even more than this. By making the Depression livable, it preserved a free, democratic society in an age when the survival of such societies was by no means assured. This laudable end was achieved at considerable expense, though. The trend toward centralized power was one that held the potential for subverting democracy, as events of the sixties and seventies showed.

Moreover, the methods employed by the New Deal were generally not designed to maximize participation. Based as they were on the concept of paternalism, most New Deal programs edged America closer to dependence on competition between big government, big business, big labor, and other such institutions. Those who belonged to none of these organizations were left out of the theory of pluralism that grew out of the Roosevelt years; and most of those in the groups, such as union members, also had little say in the affairs of their institutions. Pluralism was but one legacy of the New Deal. I have discussed many others. Such bequests are not difficult to find, since most of them still survive. Indeed, the New Deal defined the limits of political debate for at least a half century.

For all it did, for all it changed, the New Deal never succeeded in its primary goal: ending the Depression. Roosevelt himself had stated the objective best during the 1932 campaign. In his April "Forgotten Man" radio address, the candidate declared: "A real economic cure must go to the killing of the bacteria in the system rather than to the treatment of external symptoms."[4] This Dr. New Deal never accomplished; he was quite effective in easing symptoms, but the bacteria remained untouched. Necessary as analgesics were in the thirties, they may, as painkillers often do, have done a long-term disservice to the patient. Deadening the pain lessened the urgency of finding the cause and cure of the affliction. This is not to belittle the accomplishments of the New Deal; it is simply to indicate that more might have been done.

But *could* more have been done? The changes brought by the Depression and the New Deal were immense. Franklin Roosevelt's role in those changes was certainly large. Yet in Roosevelt's first term, Congress was often to his left, not merely agreeing to presidential proposals but pushing more substantial changes on its own. The National Labor Relations Act, the Wagner-Steagall Housing Act, and the creation of the FDIC were all congressional initiatives. The NRA had been a response to the certainty of more drastic action in Congress.

Whether or not more could have been achieved in the political atmosphere of the Depression years, it is beyond question that the economic collapse and Franklin Roosevelt's response to it decidedly altered the course of the nation. The simplest and most meaningful statement that can be made about the New Deal is that it brought into our government the sense of compassion that arose among so many Americans during the Depression and left that sense of caring as a legacy to subsequent generations of Americans.

Perhaps the chief impact of the Great Depression was that it obliged the American people to face up to the necessity of cooperative action because it took away, at least temporarily, the easy assumptions of expansion and mobility that had decisively influenced so much of past American thinking. Those assumptions had generally made most Americans feel that it was unnecessary to inquire much about the degree of justice in their economic system. For a time during the Depression, the nation confronted that basic question and began to answer it by moving toward the "moral economic" values I described earlier.

Americans have always been basically pragmatic. They were willing to accept an unfettered marketplace economy so long as it seemed to be working— so long, that is, as it appeared to be living up to Adam Smith's original moral belief that it eventuated in the common good. For many industrial workers, it was apparent as early as the immediate post–Civil War era that laissez faire and the marketplace did not produce *their* common good. By the 1880s and 1890s, many farmers in the South and Great Plains had reached a similar conclusion. Both of these groups moved in the late nineteenth century toward values based on a greater degree of cooperation. For the vast "middle class" of the United States, however, it took the Great Depression to convince them— at least for a while—that the marketplace was not benign in its workings.

During the Depression America moved toward community-oriented values simply because so many were in need. With up to one-fourth of the work force unemployed, an even larger percentage of the population (when dependents are figured in) without a regular source of income, and more still in constant fear that they might be next to lose their jobs, most people came to realize that they faced a common predicament. People became much less willing to "go it alone" with no thought of the consequences for others. They became less selfish and more compassionate.

When I speak of the compassion of the thirties as contrasted to the egoism of the twenties, I certainly do not mean to imply anything approaching the sort of absolute dichotomy posed by such extremists as Ayn Rand. It is not an either/or situation. If the prosperity decade had some men who approached the megalomania of Rand's *Fountainhead* characters, Gail Wynand and Howard Roark, the utterly selfless people of the Depression decade—epitomized by Melanie Hamilton in *Gone With the Wind*—were entirely fictional. The quest for justice in the Great Depression implied no desire to destroy the individual or to impose totalitarian collectivism. It merely meant that people sought a greater degree of sharing, a more ethical, cooperative individualism; not at all an obliteration of the self, but a recognition of the rights, needs, and humanity of others. President Roosevelt stated it well in 1936: "I believe in individualism . . . —up to the point where the individualist starts to operate at the expense of society."

John Steinbeck put the emerging quality beautifully: "The baby has a cold. Here, take this blanket. It's wool. It was my mother's blanket—take it for the baby. This is the thing to bomb. This is the beginning—from 'I' to 'we.'" Steinbeck went to the heart of the economic influence on the change in values from prosperity to depression: "For the quality of owning freezes you forever into 'I,' and cuts you off forever from the 'we.'"

The initial impact of the Depression was, of course, devastating for most people. They quickly rejected the acquisitive individualism associated with the business ethic of the twenties, but they were slower to see just what they might replace it with. Self-blame was a natural outgrowth of the self-congratulation of the preceding era of prosperity. The turning point came in 1933. Franklin Roosevelt and the New Deal provided hope to go with the hard times. Hope is a necessary ingredient in any significant movement for change. The shift in attitudes beginning with the Hundred Days was reflected in movies, union militancy, "thunder on the left," declining self-blame, new attitudes toward relief, and many other ways. This change has sometimes been misinterpreted as a return to the values of competitive, acquisitive individualism. In fact, those values were more firmly rejected after the New Deal provided hope of a more just society than they had been before Roosevelt's inauguration. What happened was a return to the partly mythical older values of justice, cooperation, and moral economics. Since these older values were reshaped in the context of the 1930s, they amounted to a new cooperative approach, although one with clear roots in the pre-marketplace economy.

The circumstances out of which the reforms of the Great Depression arose differed in several important respects from those of earlier American reform eras. Most obviously, such earlier successful reform movements as Progressivism occurred in times of relative prosperity, while the New Deal took place under just the opposite conditions. Progressivism was much more a series of reforms initiated from above *for* those in the lower ranks of society. The Depression-era reforms were pushed from below, by those who needed them. If Progressivism was, as historian Charles Forcey has said, a "strange mixture of guilt and moral fervor," the New Deal was characterized only by moral fervor, and that of a different sort. Inspired as they were by those who were the victims of the economic collapse, the reforms of the Depression years were in no sense a product of guilt. Those who pushed for the changes were not the guilty parties in the Depression, and after 1933 most of them understood this. As victims, those demanding change during the Depression were not thinking in terms of giving, but of sharing.

Another distinction between the mood of the Progressive era and the values of the Great Depression deserves mention and leads us into a new perspective on the values of the Depression era. The reformers of the earlier period had, as Otis Graham has put it, "a strong appetite for adventure." Certainly Theodore Roosevelt's "urge for great 'male' exploits" is beyond question. The emphasis that Americans placed on supposedly "male" qualities had always been high. One of the highest "male virtues" was competition, trying to win, seeking "success." Indeed, much of Western society since the beginnings of industrialization in the eighteenth century had become separated into "male" and "female" spheres. The former was closely associated with the emerging marketplace political economy. The division of labor that Adam Smith postulated was carried further and led to a division of human qualities into those appropriate for men and those proper for women. The male sphere, which has dominated Western and especially American society for the past two centuries, placed a high value on aggressiveness, toughness, competition, and pursuit of self-interest. The female sphere, on the other hand, emphasized cooperation, sharing, compassion, service to others, self-denial—in short, the traditional Judeo-Christian ethic. Such qualities were necessary for human survival, but would get in the way of the pursuit of success in the marketplace. Hence, they were confined to the sphere of women, which was coextensive with the home and the church. In the most simplified terms, the male sphere in the industrialized world was the amoral marketplace, the female world the place where morality was still to reign—but where it was to remain confined, a haven for men from the brutal struggle outside.

Students of public opinion in the early 1980s have noted a "gender gap" on a series of topics ranging from nuclear disarmament through Ronald Reagan to social welfare programs. The element that seems to tie together the concerns of women on these varied issues, pollsters tell us, is a desire for "fairness" and "morality." These findings are suggestive about the rise of "moral economic" values during the Great Depression.

In certain respects, the Depression can be seen as having effected a "feminization" of American society. The self-centered, aggressive, competitive "male" ethic of the 1920s was discredited. Men who lost their jobs became dependent in ways that women had been thought to be. Women in films in the early Depression, for example, were portrayed as totally dependent. In *Faithless* (1932), Tallulah Bankhead attempts to find work but meets nothing but "No Help Wanted—This Means You" signs. She marries, but neither she nor her husband is able to find work. Bankhead is obliged to sell herself in order to survive. The message is the same in such other early Depression films as *Susan Lenox, Her Fall and Rise* (1931) and *Blonde Venus* (1932): women —Greta Garbo and Marlene Dietrich, respectively—are totally dependent and must prostitute themselves to get ahead. A similar fate seemed to have befallen many men by 1932. Like women, they rejected the success-oriented life, became passive, and in an economic sense, expressed a willingness to prostitute themselves in order to survive.

As in so many other ways, 1933 was the turning point. With the New Deal the nation moved from passive acceptance of the Depression's effects to active attempts to overcome them. It may not be coincidental that 1933 was also the year in which Hollywood's only "different" woman of the decade—Mae West—burst forth. In *She Done Him Wrong* (1933), West is *not* a dependent woman. She is in complete control. Yet it is not a simple role reversal, for Mae West does not use "male" qualities to get ahead. She is a representative of the poor; bighearted and generous, she helps people. [5]

If men in the Depression found themselves much more often in the traditional position of women—on the bottom, in a state of dependence—they also moved toward the "feminine" values I have here called "moral economics." When, with the New Deal, they got beyond passivity and became active in their quest to improve their situation, Depression victims tended to do so through "female" values. They sought to escape dependence not through "male," self-centered, "rugged" individualism, but through cooperation and compassion.

The division between female and male values is, of course, essentially another way to look at the effects of the Depression on American values that I have been concerned with throughout this book. It does, though, cast a slightly different light on the subject, and it may help us to see what has become of those values in the more than four decades since the Great Depression ended.

First, it must again be made clear that I am not speaking about absolute distinctions or suggesting that women are inherently "better" than men, any more than I am saying that the poor are automatically better than the rich. Obviously some women adopt so-called masculine values and some men adhere to "feminine" values, just as many of the poor at times adopt the acquisitive, competitive ethic and many of the rich are compassionate. I am speaking about tendencies. The situation in which the poor find themselves has led many of them to see the benefits of basing the economy on moral considerations. Similarly, for a variety of societal reasons, women have been encouraged to be compassionate. (I have neither the inclination nor the expertise to enter the thicket of whether there may be a biological as well as a social basis for the difference, on the average, between the values of men and women.) Depression conditions strengthened the attraction of the values of the poor for the sinking middle class and the values associated with women for men.

If reformers in the Progressive era remained essentially "masculine" in their outlook, but those demanding change from below during the Depression were adopting more "feminine" values, it would seem that another fundamental difference between these reform eras has been identified. This distinction can also be made between the motivation for reform in the Depression and that in the subsequent liberal period of the 1960s. The leaders of the later period had as great an "urge for 'male' exploits" as did such Progressives as Theodore Roosevelt. John F. Kennedy's reputation for such things is too large to require repetition here. Lyndon Johnson's internal conflict between female compassion and male toughness and his continuing fear of appearing to be a "sissy," which have been detailed by Doris Kearns, ultimately led to tragic consequences as he sought to demonstrate his "manhood" in far-away places. Spurred on by concern over the mistreatment of black Americans and the effects of the "vigorous" foreign policies of JFK and LBJ, a growing number of Americans—particularly younger ones—turned in the 1960s toward values of compassion, equity, and justice. But the "Movement" of the sixties was fundamentally different from that of the thirties. In the 1960s prosperity reigned and most of those who demanded change had themselves grown up surrounded by material abundance. The liberalism of the sixties was based upon the assumption of an expanding economic pie. President Kennedy even revived an old term for this cherished American belief when he spoke of a New Frontier. A majority in the sixties was willing to help others because they thought that this could be done without harming themselves.

When the American economic pie stopped growing in the 1970s, much of the population was ready once again to turn inward. As at the end of the Progressive era, the people grew tired of sacrifice for others and returned to concern with the self. The "me" generation came into dominance.

In the seventies and eighties, the American people have again been confronting the prospect of limits. The 1973–74 Arab oil embargo, inflation, a decline in productivity, and a general change from an industrial to high technology economy have combined to create an unfamiliar situation for Americans. The future no longer seems certain to be better than the past. The initial reaction of most appeared to be almost the opposite of that which occurred when a similar conclusion was reached in the Depression.

Postwar American society has been so permeated by the values of acquisitive individualism (despite the survival of some residue of the social concern of the Depression) that few of us have escaped it. The mass media bombard us with a self-centered ethic of consumption, and advertisers are far more skillful than they were in earlier decades in convincing us that we *need* what, without their assault on our senses, we would not even know we *wanted*. Given this framework, it should not have been especially surprising when many Americans greeted the new economic problems associated with limits by "looking out for number one." If we had to accept that things *in general* would not get better, we could still assume the good—and improving—life for ourselves.

If, as I have contended, the Great Depression led many middle-class Americans to see their interests as coinciding with those of the poor, the same has plainly not been the case in recent years. Middle-class Americans in the thirties identified with the Joads; in the seventies they aspired not only to keep up with the Joneses, but to try to catch up with the Rockefellers. Americans of moderate means have been encouraged to live beyond those means, to try to emulate those above them on the income scale. Products are purchased not merely for their use or enjoyment, but to demonstrate one's position in society. "The pressure on all these people to dispose of their cash as they do," *The New Republic* observes, "does not come from a sudden prosperity. . . . The pressure comes, rather, from a social ethos for which the highest value is style." That ethos is diametrically opposed to the one that dominated in the Great Depression. The official crowning of the social ethos of style was the election of Ronald Reagan in 1980. The Reagan administration has lifted much of the remaining stigma from the practice of acquisitive individualism. More even than a return to the doctrine of social Darwinism, this seems to represent the development of what might be called "social Calvinism." The successful see themselves as the economically Elect and the unemployed as the socially damned. The former need not concern themselves about the latter. By concentrating on increasing their own success, they further prove that they are among the Chosen. As John D. Rockefeller once put it: "The good Lord gave me my money."

The indicators of the turning inward to private concerns in the latest conservative swing were ubiquitous by the late 1970s. While the New Deal had persistently reflected Depression-era America's desire for *public* projects, by the 1970s there was a noticeable decline in interest in the commonweal. Public transportation systems were allowed to decay while citizens spent ever greater sums on private cars and the fuel to operate them. Budgets for public education were cut while the wealthy—and those who aspired to be—demanded tax credits for their children to attend private schools. Voters from California to Massachusetts passed referendums limiting the amount of taxes that could be collected to support public projects. Public libraries were often among the first targets of state and local budget cutters.

Politics in recent years has been increasingly dominated by single-interest groups. "Today everyone is imitating the National Rifle Association," Charles Peters wrote in *The Washington Monthly* in 1983. "That's the way to have a successful lobby. It's also the way to ruin America." The major concerns of the National Rifle Association are, in fact, among the best examples of the contrast between the community-oriented values of the thirties and the "every man for himself" attitude of the seventies and eighties. Instead of accepting that the provision of security is a responsibility to be undertaken by society, many Americans—including President Reagan—maintain that individuals armed with everything up to and including armor-piercing bullets should provide protection for their families. That way lies the road to anarchy, not community.

The private concerns of Americans in the 1970s and early 1980s were evident also in the growth of career orientation among college students. They sought ways to "plug into" the system, not to challenge it. Many of the terms that became clichés in these years made the same point: "assertiveness training," "getting in touch with myself," "open marriage," "my space." So did the fads, cults, and "therapies" of the period: health foods, est, "consciousness raising," Esalen, and so forth. Former Yippie Jerry Rubin, whom the media once made a symbol of in the 1960s, became a much better representative of the seventies when he said he had learned "to love myself enough so that I do not need another to make me happy." Predictably, the results of such an attitude (although, of course, most people would not put it so bluntly) included an increase in the divorce rate and a decline in the birthrate. Marriage requires a willingness to sacrifice, share, and consider the needs of another.

And children, after all, can disrupt one's "lifestyle." They demand that a parent give of his time and himself. It was a sacrifice many seemed unwilling to make.

The mood of egoism has become worse in modern American business than it was in the 1920s. American corporate executives today seek to construct personal images as "winners." They show little loyalty, even to their companies. Competition has gone beyond that between companies and come to be between individual executives. Success is defined in the management textbook *Routes to the Executive Suite* as "not simply getting ahead," but "getting ahead of others." The "winning image" is usually achieved by concentration on short-term profitability. Corporate executives have worked at what Harvard economist Robert Reich calls "paper entrepreneurialism"—the manipulation of stock and finances—rather than at increasing productivity. Such attitudes have played a large role in the weakening of the American economy.[6]

If the values of Americans in recent years seem closer to those of the 1920s than those of the Depression, there are other disturbing parallels between the economic situation leading into the Depression and that we face in the 1980s. Any study of the Great Depression ought to address the question that seems to be on so many minds today: Can it happen again? Indeed, is it *already* happening again?

That the values of acquisitive individualism that helped create the climate for the Depression appear again to have been dominant in recent years is not a good sign. Nor is it comforting to know that we have a president who admires Calvin Coolidge, believes in the economic policies that were in effect in the 1920s, and wants to weaken the social programs that have helped prevent large economic collapses throughout the postwar years.

Clearly the economic slump of the early 1980s is the worst since the Great Depression. The previous post-Depression peaks of unemployment were 7.9 percent in the recession of 1948–49, 7.5 percent in the 1957–58 recession, and 9.0 percent in the 1973–75 recession. All those records were left far behind in the early 1980s. In December 1982 the jobless rate hit 10.8 percent. Approximately 12 million Americans seeking jobs were unable to find them, the largest absolute number of unemployed Americans since 1933. Moreover, several million more had either given up and stopped looking (and so were classified as "discouraged," rather than unemployed) or were working part-time when they wanted full-time jobs. Some 6 million of those without work had exhausted their unemployment benefits. Certain industries, such as automobile, housing, and steel, are, as this is written, at Depression levels, as are the states of Michigan and West Virginia and localities in many industrial states. Bankruptcies in 1982 reached the highest level since the bottom of the Great Depression in 1932. More than 200 American financial institutions—banks and savings and loan associations—closed their doors in 1982.

There were also disturbing impressionistic signs reminiscent of the Great Depression. By late 1982 an estimated 50,000 migrants a month were taking to American highways searching for work in other regions. Some of these were going *to* the very areas—Oklahoma and Texas—from which "Okies" fled in the thirties, but for many California remained the land of promise. Some of the migrants of the eighties were being called not "Okies," but "black tag people," because of the color of their Michigan license plates. Many Americans—perhaps 2 million—in 1982–83 were again homeless, living in vans, cars, or under bridges. In several cities, tent colonies of jobless families—now dubbed "Reagan ranches" rather than "Hoovervilles"—were established. The head of the Northern Ohio Salvation Army told a congressional hearing at the end of 1982 that people in Cleveland were sleeping in the organization's deposit boxes. "What do you say to a husband and wife and three children sleeping in an old car on the road desperately looking for work, the temperature in the teens . . . ?" he asked. Half of the men in New York City's shelters for the homeless in 1982 were reported to be high school graduates and 20 percent of them were college graduates. The number of "customers" at soup kitchens multiplied dramatically in 1982. In Cleveland alone, the number of soup kitchens leaped from three in early 1981 to more than thirty only two years later. The lines at many such establishments stretched for blocks like an eerie vision of the breadlines of the thirties. Many of those standing in the soup kitchen lines were previously "respectable" folks who said they had never taken "handouts" before and had to swallow their pride because they were hungry and had no means to buy food. "I just don't like people knowing how bad off we are," explained a man at an Elyria, Ohio, soup kitchen. The Christmas wishes of Depression-era children were echoed in a December 1982 report from Sears, Roebuck that one of the most common requests their store Santas were receiving from children was to "help their parents find a job or pay bills."

The sense of *déjà vu* made itself felt in other ways. Median farm income dropped from $18,483 in 1979 to only $15,755 in 1980. By December 1982 the parity ratio was down to 54, the lowest since records began to be kept in 1910. This means that farmers today have only 54 percent of the relative buying power their forebears had in 1910–14. When the Farmers Home Administration attempted to auction off the dairy equipment of a bankrupt western Illinois farmer in November 1982, some one hundred other farmers came to the sale and shouted down the auctioneer, thus preventing the sale. Similar confrontations took place in farming communities throughout the Midwest. Earlier in 1982 farmers in Oto, Iowa, slashed the tires of a truck Internal Revenue agents were using to seize machinery from a debt-plagued farmer. American Agriculture Movement (AAM) groups in some areas were talking about other forms of direct action, such as burning grainfields. Early in January 1983 police had to use tear gas to disperse a crowd of AAM members in

Springfield, Colorado, who attempted to prevent the forced sale of a farm. At about the same time, a district director of the United Steelworkers of America in the Pittsburgh region declared: "If we don't start doing something for these people [the unemployed], there's going to be a revolution." And the sheriff of Allegheny County, Pennsylvania, proclaimed a moratorium on foreclosures of owner-occupied homes because he "sympathized with the plight of the unemployed."

Nor was the worldwide outlook much brighter. In 1982 unemployment reached post-Depression record levels in most industrial countries. "I just came back from a tour of many of our depressed areas," Canada's minister of employment said in mid-1982, "and I can tell you that watching mature men with good skills go on soup lines is not something I found very rewarding." Even West Germany and Japan were not immune. Perhaps most ominous of all the troubling indicators is the extremely fragile condition of the international banking structure. Between 1972 and 1982 international indebtedness increased tenfold, rising to some $2 *trillion*. Brazil and Mexico owe more than $80 billion each. Nine leading American banks have lent approximately one-half of their total capital to Mexico. International bankers have made extremely unwise loans, much as did their predecessors in the 1920s. The results are already apparent in the virtual bankruptcy of such countries as Poland and Mexico. Brazil, Argentina, Yugoslavia, Chile, and others may not be far behind. A collapse of the international financial system is a distinct possibility.

We are also seeing a disturbing turn toward the sort of self-destructive economic nationalism and protectionism that exacerbated the Great Depression. Attempts by the trade ministers of the member nations of the General Agreement on Tariffs and Trade (GATT) in late 1982 to head off a trade war met with little success. Political pressures for protectionism in nations with high unemployment only appeared likely to increase.

Economist Lester Thurow put it simply—and frighteningly—in October 1982: "Today, once again, we are faced by the impossible—not one of those brief, isolated American recessions, but a long-term, world-wide malaise." Even those who were supposed to be optimistic found it difficult to see a bright future. Martin S. Feldstein, chairman of President Reagan's Council of Economic Advisers, said late in 1982 that it might take six years to bring unemployment back down to the 6 to 7 percent range. "Things are going to get better if we stick with this program," Treasury Secretary Donald Regan said in mid-1982. "In the late 1980's or early 1990's, there will be a brighter tomorrow." Some Americans could be forgiven for thinking that this was not a particularly hopeful forecast. Ronald Reagan himself was not very reassuring in November 1982 when he remarked that the economy was "in a hell of a mess."

Worse is the fact that as 1983 went on it began to look more and more like "recovery" would occur, but would have little effect on the level of unemployment. (Nor should anyone miss the fact that such recovery as there was was the result of increased *demand*, not a "supply side" panacea. Consumer spending leaped by 18 percent between March and May 1983.) In May President Reagan told an audience of Cuban-Americans in Miami that no special programs were needed for Hispanics or other depressed groups because "a rising tide lifts all boats." Six days earlier, though, the chief executives of most of America's leading corporations said at a meeting of the Business Council at Hot Springs, Virginia, that they would "rehire few of the workers they laid off in the recession, no matter how strongly the economy recovers." The rising tide of the 1980s, it appeared, would lift yachts, but not dinghies.

Nothing was more debilitating for the unemployed of the eighties than to hear talk about recovery while they faced the prospect of continued, perhaps more or less permanent, joblessness. The stock market soared upward in 1982 and 1983, reaching many record highs as unemployment rates hovered near the post-Depression peak. During the year 1982, the Dow Jones industrial average gained 171 points while the ranks of the jobless swelled by 2.5 million people and the poverty rate rose to 15 percent, the highest level since Lyndon Johnson's War on Poverty took effect in 1965. And—adding the proverbial insult to the injuries already inflicted upon the unemployed—the Reagan administration seemed to care little about their plight. A president whose response to unemployment was to say that he saw twenty-five pages of "Help Wanted" ads in the Sunday paper was not showing the compassion so often demonstrated by Franklin Roosevelt in the 1930s. President Reagan sounded more like a member of the Liberty League than the one-time supporter of FDR that he is. Echoing the words of John Raskob a half century earlier, Reagan told a June 1983 news conference, "[W]hat I want above all is that this country remains a country where someone can always get rich. That's the thing that we have and that must be preserved." (Compare Raskob's 1934 statement, pp. 251–52, above.)

For all the similarities between the situation in the early eighties and that of the Great Depression, though, there are also significant differences. In some respects unemployment may not be quite as devastating today as it was in the thirties. Unemployment compensation and other social programs help. So does the fact that in 1982 almost 60 percent of the unemployed were in families with more than one wage earner.

One cause of the collapse in the 1920s was the rapid growth in productivity with wages not keeping pace. That clearly has not been a problem in the 1970s and '80s. There exists today a tremendous excess capacity in many basic American industries, far more than was the case in 1929. In late 1982 factories were running at 67.8 percent of capacity and the American steel industry was operating at less than 35 percent of capacity. These facts undermined attempts to bring about recovery by stimulating investment. There is no reason to invest in new plant when so much already in existence is unused. Another critical difference between the Depression and the economic problems of the 1980s is that the Coolidge-Mellon tax cuts took place in a time of low federal spending; the Reagan tax cuts were implemented at a time of large deficits and growing spending. This has meant that the high unemployment of the eighties has occurred in the midst of unprecedented federal deficits. Hence the Keynesian solution is much more difficult to implement. Nor is consumer spending likely to do the trick. With fear of unemployment high, those with jobs tend to reduce their spending and increase their saving. Here again is the classic fallacy of composition—behavior that is prudent for the individual is destructive in the aggregate.[7]

Part of the trouble is that while most conservatives in the postwar years have ignored the problem of maldistribution and depended upon a growing economy, many liberals came by the 1960s to concentrate *only* on the division of the pie, not on its size. Questions of distribution are fundamental, but so are those of productivity. We need a more equitable distribution of wealth, not of poverty. If we are to succeed economically and morally, we must concern ourselves *both* with the size of the pie *and* with how it is sliced.

There are no easy solutions to our current economic problems, but the Great Depression does have lessons to teach us that can be useful in facing the crisis of the eighties. One, clearly, is that "supply-side" or Coolidge-Mellon economics is precisely the wrong medicine. More important, though, is the relevance of the Depression-era values for Americans today. The self-centeredness of the 1970s was one of the sources of our present economic problems, just as the similar attitudes of the twenties had helped to bring on the Great Depression. New York Mayor Edward Koch complained late in 1982 of a nationwide "outbreak of selfishness. . . . President Reagan," Koch said, "has initiated a regressive philosophy of government in which the concept of federal burden-sharing is being eliminated. And people are being told to watch out for themselves."

There are some encouraging signs that the economic crisis of the eighties may have started to rekindle the cooperative spirit of the thirties. In his January 1983 inaugural address as governor of New York, for example, Mario Cuomo spoke in words reminiscent of the man who preceded him to Albany fifty-four years earlier. "It has become popular in some quarters to argue that the principal function of government is to make instruments of war and to clear obstacles from the way of the strong," Governor Cuomo noted. "It is said that the rest will happen automatically. The cream will rise to the top. . . ." The New York governor rejected this view. "We can, and we will, refuse to settle for just survival and certainly not for just survival of the fittest," he declared. Calling the state a "family," Cuomo said both blessings and pains must be shared "equitably, honestly and fairly" by all. He decried "the massive inequity of the new redistribution of national wealth" resulting from President Reagan's policies. (Economist Robert Lekachman has pointed out that Reagan's redistribution is similar to Roosevelt's "with the trifling difference that FDR sought to alleviate poverty and Ronald Reagan enthusiastically enriches further the already obscenely rich.")

Mario Cuomo may not be another Franklin Roosevelt, but he was not alone in voicing such themes during the economic crisis of the eighties. As columnist Ellen Goodman has pointed out, "There is nothing like hunger to sharpen the senses, and the consciences." Poverty in America in 1983 was again approaching the "critical mass" at which the values of compassion and community might ignite. Yet there was also the disturbing possibility that once the unemployment rate stopped rising, so would the fear among the 90 percent of the work force that remained employed. If a majority became convinced that unemployment was no threat to them, could we be confident that many members of the "me generation" might not choose to close their eyes to the problems of their impoverished neighbors? Regardless of what the economic future holds in store, we would be better off if we could regain the values of Depression-era Americans.

No better evidence that some significant residue of those humane values of the 1930s persists in modern America could be offered than the fact that as the election year of 1984 approached, Ronald Reagan began to voice concern about the poor. Ignoring the obvious truth that his own economic policies and cuts in social programs were the root causes of a renewal of malnutrition in the United States, Reagan said in the summer of 1983 that he was "perplexed" and "deeply concerned" to find that hunger plagues millions of Americans. Few take such statements from Reagan seriously, but they demonstrate that, even after the "Reagan Revolution," it is politically necessary to at least pretend to subscribe to the enduring values of compassion that reached their peak in the Great Depression.

As he did so often, Franklin D. Roosevelt spoke in words that perfectly reflected the spirit of the time when he accepted the 1936 Democratic presidential nomination. These words, I believe, speak directly to Americans in the 1980s: "Governments can err; Presidents do make mistakes, . . . but better the occasional faults of a Government that lives in a spirit of charity than the consistent omissions of a Government frozen in the ice of its own indifference."[8] Surely we could all benefit from a greater practice of the values summarized by those words. The Great Depression has no more important lesson to teach modern America.

NOTES

FOREWORD

1. Josephine Herbst, "Moralist Progress," *Kenyon Review*, 28 (Autumn 1965), 776.

CHAPTER 1
HISTORICAL CURRENTS AND THE GREAT DEPRESSION

1. Arthur M. Schlesinger, *Paths to the Present* (New York: Macmillan, 1949), 77–92; Herbert Hoover, *The New Day: Campaign Speeches of Herbert Hoover, 1928* (Palo Alto, Calif.: Stanford University Press, 1928), 213; Robert S. McElvaine, "Liberalism Is Not Dead," *The New York Times*, Sept. 20, 1980; Robert S. McElvaine, "Where Have All the Liberals Gone?" *Texas Quarterly*, 19 (Autumn 1976), 202–13; Charles Forcey, *The Crossroads of Liberalism: Croly, Weyl, Lippmann, and the Progressive Era, 1900–1925* (New York: Oxford University Press, 1961), xi–xiv; Otis L. Graham, Jr., *An Encore for Reform: The Old Progressives and the New Deal* (New York: Oxford University Press, 1967), 181–82.

2. Charles Hoffman, "The Depression of the Nineties," *Journal of Economic History*, 16 (June 1956), 151; Herbert Gutman, *Work, Culture and Society in Industrializing America* (New York: Knopf, 1976), 61; Gerald N. Grob, *Workers and Utopia: A Study of Ideological Conflict in the American Labor Movement, 1865–1900* (Evanston, Ill.: Northwestern University Press, 1961), 176–79, 184; David Montgomery, *Workers' Control in America: Studies in the History of Work, Technology, and Labor Struggles* (Cambridge and New York: Cambridge University Press, 1979); Alan Dawley, *Class and Community: The Industrial Revolution in Lynn* (Cambridge, Mass.:

Harvard University Press, 1976), 89; Richard Hofstadter, *The American Political Tradition: And the Men Who Made It* (New York: Knopf, 1948; 2d ed., Vintage, 1973), 239; Lawrence Goodwyn, *Democratic Promise: The Populist Moment in America* (New York: Oxford University Press, 1976); Richard Hofstadter, "Manifest Destiny and the Philippines," in Daniel Aaron, ed., *America in Crisis* (New York: Knopf, 1952), 173–74; Allan Nevins, *Grover Cleveland: A Study in Courage* (New York: Dodd, Mead, 1932), 332; Elliot A. Rosen, *Hoover, Roosevelt and the Brains Trust: From Depression to New Deal* (New York: Columbia University Press, 1977), 309; David Brody, *Steelworkers in America: The Nonunion Era* (Cambridge, Mass.: Harvard University Press, 1960; reprint ed., New York: Harper & Row, 1969), 4; Carl N. Degler, "American Political Parties and the Rise of the City: An Interpretation," *Journal of American History*, 51 (June 1964), 42, 49; Samuel P. Hays, *The Response to Industrialism, 1885–1914* (Chicago: University of Chicago Press, 1957), 46; Walter Lippmann, *Drift and Mastery* (New York: Mitchell Kennerly, 1914; reprint ed., Englewood Cliffs, N.J.: Prentice-Hall, 1961), 135.

3. Robert H. Wiebe, *The Search for Order, 1877–1920* (New York: Hill & Wang, 1967), xiii; Richard Hofstadter, *The Age of Reform: From Bryan to F.D.R.* (New York: Knopf, 1955), ch. IV, 64; Gutman, *Work, Culture and Society*; Dawley, *Class and Community*; David Montgomery, *Beyond Equality: Labor and the Radical Republicans, 1862–1872* (New York: Knopf, 1967); Ferdinand Tönnies, *Community and Society*, ed. and trans. by Charles P. Loomis (New York: Harper & Row, 1957; orig. German ed.: 1887); Graham, *Encore for Reform*, 74, 22, 82–83, 70, 65, 84, 107, 144–45; Forcey, *Crossroads of Liberalism*, xvii; Irwin Yellowitz, *Labor and the Progressive Movement in New York State, 1897–1916* (Ithaca, N.Y.: Cornell University Press, 1965); William E. Leuchtenburg, *Franklin D. Roosevelt and the New Deal, 1932–1940* (New York: Harper & Row, 1963), 339.

That other groups besides the middle-class elements emphasized by Hofstadter and George Mowry (*The California Progressives* [Berkeley: University of California Press, 1951]) were prominent in the highly complex Progressive era has been demonstrated by J. Joseph Huthmacher, "Urban Liberalism and the Age of Reform," *Mississippi Valley Historical Review*, 49 (Sept. 1962), 231–41; Melvyn Dubofsky, *When Workers Organize: New York City in the Progressive Era* (Amherst: University of Massachusetts Press, 1968); Michael Paul Rogin and John L. Shover, *Political Change in California: Critical Elections and Social Movements, 1890–1966* (Westport, Conn.: Greenwood, 1970); Samuel P. Hays, "The Politics of Reform in Municipal Government in the Progressive Era," *Pacific Northwest Quarterly*, 55 (Oct. 1964), 159–69; Gabriel Kolko, *The Triumph of Conservatism: A Reinterpretation of American History, 1900–1916* (Glencoe, Ill.: Free Press, 1963); James Weinstein, *The Corporate Ideal and the Liberal State, 1900–1918* (Boston: Beacon, 1968); and Robert H. Wiebe, *Businessmen and Reform: A Study of the Progressive Movement* (Cambridge, Mass.: Harvard University Press, 1962).

4. Hofstadter, *Age of Reform*, 275–82; Rosen, *Hoover, Roosevelt, and the Brains Trust*, 93; Edwin G. Nourse, *American Agriculture and the European Market* (New York: McGraw-Hill, 1924), 236; Henry F. May, *The End of American Innocence* (New York: Knopf, 1959); Graham, *Encore for Reform*, 46–47; Allen F. Davis, "Welfare, Reform, and World War I," *American Quarterly*, 19 (Fall 1967), 516, 533; William E. Leuchtenburg, *The Perils of Prosperity, 1914–1932* (Chicago: University of Chicago Press, 1958), 41–42; David M. Kennedy, *Over Here: The First World War and American Society* (New York: Oxford University Press, 1980), 93–143; David Burner, *Herbert Hoover: A Public Life* (New York: Knopf, 1979), 96–113; Albert U. Romasco, *The Poverty of Abundance: Hoover, the Nation, the Depression* (New York: Oxford University Press, 1965), 43.

5. Geoffrey Perrett, *America in the Twenties: A History* (New York: Simon & Schuster, 1982), 72–78; Frederick Lewis Allen, *Only Yesterday: An Informal History of the 1920's* (New York: Harper & Brothers, 1931), 16; David Burner, "1919: Prelude to Normalcy," in John Braeman,

Robert H. Bremner, and David Brody, eds., *Change and Continuity in Twentieth Century America: The 1920's* (Columbus: Ohio State University Press, 1968), 3–31; Leuchtenburg, *Perils of Prosperity*, 124; William Preston, *Aliens and Dissenters: Federal Suppression of Radicals, 1903–1933* (Cambridge, Mass.: Harvard University Press, 1963); Robert K. Murray, *Red Scare: A Study in National Hysteria* (Minneapolis: University of Minnesota Press, 1955); David Brody, *Labor in Crisis: The Steel Strike of 1919* (Philadelphia: Lippincott, 1965); Gene Smith, *When the Cheering Stopped: The Last Years of Woodrow Wilson* (New York: Morrow, 1964).

6. George Soule, *Prosperity Decade: From War to Depression, 1917–1929* (New York: Holt, Rinehart and Winston, 1947); Samuel Hopkins Adams, *Incredible Era: The Life and Times of Warren Gamaliel Harding* (Boston: Houghton Mifflin, 1939); Andrew Sinclair, *Prohibition: The Era of Excess* (Boston: Atlantic–Little, Brown, 1962); Laurence Greene, *The Era of Wonderful Nonsense* (Indianapolis: Bobbs-Merrill, 1939); James W. Prothro, *Dollar Decade: Business Ideas in the 1920's* (Baton Rouge: Louisiana State University Press, 1954); Henry Steele Commager and Richard B. Morris, Editors' Introduction to John D. Hicks, *Republican Ascendancy, 1921–1933* (New York: Harper & Row, 1960), viii–x; Paula S. Fass, *The Damned and the Beautiful: American Youth in the 1920's* (New York: Oxford University Press, 1977), 3, 5; Henry F. May, "Shifting Perspectives on the 1920's," *Mississippi Valley Historical Review*, 43 (Dec. 1956), 412; J. Joseph Huthmacher and Warren I. Susman, eds., *Herbert Hoover and the Crisis of American Capitalism* (Cambridge, Mass.: Schenkman, 1973), xii; Donald R. McCoy, *Calvin Coolidge: The Quiet President* (New York: Macmillan, 1967), 414, 413, 417; Malcolm Cowley, *Exile's Return: A Narrative of Ideas* (New York: Viking, 1951), 309; Robert S. McElvaine, "The Coolidge Model: What Better Choice?" *The Boston Globe*, June 27, 1981.

7. Leuchtenburg, *Perils of Prosperity*, 97, 96; McCoy, *Coolidge*, 299, 160–61, 99, 290, 272, 421, 418, 413–14, 421–22; William Allen White, *A Puritan in Babylon: The Story of Calvin Coolidge* (New York: Macmillan, 1938), 150–67; x; George E. Mowry, *The Era of Theodore Roosevelt and the Birth of Modern America, 1900–1912* (New York: Harper & Row, 1958), 110, 232; Burner, *Hoover*, 219n; McElvaine, "Where Have All the Liberals Gone?" 206; H. L. Mencken, "Calvin Coolidge," *American Mercury* (April 1933); Peter R. Levin, *Seven By Chance: The Accidental Presidents* (New York: Farrar, Straus, 1948), 262, as quoted in McCoy, *Coolidge*, 419.

8. Burner, "1919: Prelude to Normalcy," 12; Graham, *Encore for Reform*, 39, 156; Huthmacher and Susman, *Herbert Hoover and the Crisis of American Capitalism*, vii–ix; Herbert Hoover, *Memoirs: The Cabinet and the Presidency, 1920–1933* (New York: Macmillan, 1952), 167–73; Rosen, *Hoover, Roosevelt and the Brains Trust*, 48, 164; Romasco, *Poverty of Abundance*, 44, 141; Milton Derber, *The American Ideal of Industrial Democracy, 1865–1965* (Urbana: University of Illinois Press, 1970), 285, 205–06, 281, 208, 203, 260, 273; Morrell Heald, "Business Thought in the Twenties: Social Responsibility," *American Quarterly*, 13 (Summer 1961), 126–39; David Brody, "The Rise and Decline of Welfare Capitalism," in Braeman, Bremner, and Brody, *Change and Continuity in Twentieth Century America: 1920's*, 150, 155, 176; David Montgomery, *Workers' Control in America*, 32–33, 113–14, 44, 160; W. Jett Lauck, *Political and Industrial Democracy, 1776–1926* (New York: Funk & Wagnalls, 1926), 279 ff., as quoted in Derber, *American Ideal of Industrial Democracy*, 225, 267–68; Harry Braverman, *Labor and Monopoly Capital: The Degradation of Work in the Twentieth Century* (New York: Monthly Review Press, 1974), 87n; Daniel Nelson, *Managers and Workers: Origins of the New Factory System in the United States, 1880–1920* (Madison: University of Wisconsin Press, 1975), 65–66; Brody, *Steelworkers in America*, 268, 275; Perrett, *America in the Twenties*, 49–50; Irving Bernstein, *The Lean Years: A History of the American Worker, 1920–1933* (Boston: Houghton Mifflin, 1960), 147–52, 157–65; David Montgomery, "To Study the People: The American Working Class," *Labor History*, 21 (Fall 1980), 510; Lincoln Steffens, as quoted in

Huthmacher and Susman, eds., *Herbert Hoover and the Crisis of American Capitalism*, ix–x; Elmer Davis, "Confidence in Whom?" *Forum*, 89 (Jan. 1933), 31; Burner, *Hoover*, 247.

9. Genesis 41:25–36; Allen, *Only Yesterday*, 3, 53; Bruce Barton, *The Man Nobody Knows: A Discovery of the Real Jesus* (New York: Grosset & Dunlap, 1925), x–xi, 143; Leuchtenburg, *Perils of Prosperity*, 188–89, 200, 187; Otis Pease, *The Responsibilities of American Advertising: Private Control and Public Influence, 1920–1940* (New Haven: Yale University Press, 1958; reprint ed., New York: Arno, 1976); David M. Potter, "Advertising: The Institution of Abundance," *Yale Review*, 43 (Autumn 1953), 49–70; Stuart Ewen, *Captains of Consciousness: Advertising and the Social Roots of the Consumer Culture* (New York: McGraw-Hill, 1976), 170, 173–74; *The Saturday Evening Post*, Dec. 14, 1929, as quoted in *ibid.*, 161; John Stuart Mill, as quoted in Daniel T. Rodgers, *The Work Ethic in Industrial America, 1850–1920* (Chicago: University of Chicago Press, 1978), 120; Zelda Fitzgerald, as quoted in Leuchtenburg, *Perils of Prosperity*, 242; Simon N. Patten, *The New Basis of Civilization* (New York: Macmillan, 1907), ch. VII, as quoted in Rodgers, *Work Ethic*, 121; Derber, *American Ideal of Industrial Democracy*, 200; Allan Nevins, *Ford: The Times, The Man, The Company* (New York: Charles Scribner's Sons, 1954), 512–41; Carol Gelderman, *Henry Ford: The Wayward Capitalist* (New York: Dial, 1981), 395, 290.

10. Romasco, *Poverty of Abundance*, 202, 99; Forcey, *Crossroads of Liberalism*, ix; Fass, *The Damned and the Beautiful*, 231–34, 25, 21, 77, 262–68, 375, 22, 50, 23, 370; Leuchtenburg, *Perils of Prosperity*, 187, 180, 229; Leo Marx, *The Machine in the Garden: Technology and the Pastoral Ideal in America* (New York: Oxford University Press, 1964); Ewen, *Captains of Consciousness*, ch. VI; "Mr. Grundy," "Polite Society," *Atlantic Monthly*, 125 (May 1920), 608, as quoted in Fass, *The Damned and the Beautiful*, 35; Barbara Welter, "The Cult of True Womanhood: 1820–1860," *American Quarterly*, 18 (Summer 1966), 151–74; John R. McMahon, "Unspeakable Jazz Must Go," *Ladies' Home Journal*, 38 (Dec. 1921), 116, as quoted in Fass, *The Damned and the Beautiful*, 22; Allen, *Only Yesterday*, 76, 96, 95, 98–99, 88, 77, 94; Robert S. Lynd and Helen Merrell Lynd, *Middletown: A Study in Modern American Culture* (New York: Harcourt, Brace, 1929), 114; Graham, *Encore for Reform*, 72, 122; John R. McMahon, "Back to Pre-War Morals," *Ladies' Home Journal*, 38 (Nov. 1921); Hofstadter, *Age of Reform*, ch. I; Lawrence W. Levine, *Defender of the Faith: William Jennings Bryan—The Last Decade, 1915–1925* (New York: Oxford University Press, 1965) 324–57; Ray Ginger, *Six Days or Forever? Tennessee v. John Thomas Scopes* (Boston: Beacon, 1958); Gelderman, *Henry Ford*, 290–91, 397.

11. Soule, *Prosperity Decade*, 124; Rosen, *Hoover, Roosevelt and the Brains Trust*, 338; Gilbert C. Fite, "The Farmers' Dilemma, 1919–1929," in Braeman, Bremner, and Brody, eds., *Change and Continuity in Twentieth Century America: 1920's*, 67; Arthur S. Link, "What Happened to the Progressive Movement in the 1920's?" *American Historical Review*, 64 (July 1959), 845–46; Bernstein, *Lean Years*, 47, 59, 476, 239, 10, 65, 190–243; Lynd and Lynd, *Middletown*, 56–57, 59; U.S. Department of Commerce, Bureau of the Census, *Historical Statistics of the United States, Colonial Times to 1970* (Washington: Government Printing Office, 1975), Series D-85-86, p. 135; Derber, *American Ideal of Industrial Democracy*, 200–01, 285, 282, 272; Leuchtenburg, *Perils of Prosperity*, 193–94; E. P. Thompson, *The Making of the English Working Class* (New York: Pantheon, 1963), 708; Brody, *Steelworkers in America*, 198, 264, 250–51; Leo Wolman, *Ebb and Flow in Trade Unionism* (New York: National Bureau of Economic Research, 1936), 16; Montgomery, *Workers' Control in America*, 100, 160–61; Braverman, *Labor and Monopoly Capital*, 10; Mark Perlman, "Labor in Eclipse," in Braeman, Bremner, and Brody, eds., *Change and Continuity in Twentieth Century America: 1920's*, 103–45; Robert H. Zieger, *Republicans and Labor, 1919–1929* (Lexington: University of Kentucky Press, 1969); Nelson, *Managers and Workers*, 120; Selig Perlman, *A Theory of the Labor Move-*

ment (New York: Macmillan, 1928), 275; Stanley B. Mathewson, *Restriction of Output Among Unorganized Workers* (New York: Viking, 1931), 30–52.

12. Arthur M. Schlesinger, Jr., *The Crisis of the Old Order, 1919–1933* (Boston: Houghton Mifflin, 1957), 177, 62–63; McCoy, *Coolidge*, 314–21, 417, 415; Leuchtenburg, *The Perils of Prosperity*, 96–97, 132–33, 234; Jordan A. Schwartz, *The Interregnum of Despair: Hoover, Congress, and the Depression* (Urbana: University of Illinois Press, 1970), 236–37, 228, 106–07; Hicks, *Republican Ascendancy*, 97, 53–54, 106; Lynd and Lynd, *Middletown*, 88; Rosen, *Hoover, Roosevelt and the Brains Trust*, 26–28, 2.

CHAPTER 2
WHO WAS ROARING IN THE TWENTIES?

1. John Kenneth Galbraith, *The Great Crash: 1929* (Boston: Houghton Mifflin, 1954; 3d ed., 1972), 2, 176, 8, 178; Peter Temin, *Did Monetary Forces Cause the Great Depression?* (New York: Norton, 1976), xii, 14–16, 169–70, 31–33; W. W. Kiplinger, as quoted in David Burner, *Herbert Hoover: A Public Life* (New York: Knopf, 1979), 248; Jude Wanniski, *The Way the World Works: How Economies Fail—and Succeed* (New York: Basic Books, 1978); *The Wall Street Journal*, Aug. 28, 1979, April 7, 1982; Milton Friedman and Anna Jacobson Schwartz, *A Monetary History of the United States, 1867–1960* (Princeton: Princeton University Press, 1963); Milton Friedman and Anna Jacobson Schwartz, *The Great Contraction, 1929–1933* (Princeton: Princeton University Press, 1965); Milton Friedman and Anna Jacobson Schwartz, "Money and Business Cycles," *Review of Economics and Statistics*, 45 (Feb. 1963), 52; Charles P. Kindleberger, *The World in Depression, 1929–1939* (1973; reprint ed., Berkeley and Los Angeles: University of California Press, 1975), 20, 291, 22; Herbert Hoover, *Memoirs: The Great Depression, 1929–1941* (New York: Macmillan, 1952), 2, 4, 61–96; Joseph A. Schumpeter, *Business Cycles: A Theoretical, Historical and Statistical Analysis of the Capitalist Process* (New York: McGraw-Hill, 1939), v. II, 794, 908–11; *The Wall Street Journal*, Oct. 12, 1979; John Maynard Keynes, *The General Theory of Employment, Interest, and Money* (New York: Harcourt, Brace, 1936), 323; Alvin H. Hansen, *Fiscal Policy and Business Cycles* (New York: Norton, 1941); Thomas Wilson, *Fluctuations in Income and Employment* (London: Pitman, 1942), 156.

2. Albert U. Romasco, *The Poverty of Abundance: Hoover, the Nation, the Depression* (New York: Oxford University Press, 1965), 40, 81–82, 85, 4; Galbraith, *Great Crash*, 153–54; Elliot A. Rosen, *Hoover, Roosevelt and the Brains Trust: From Depression to New Deal* (New York: Columbia University Press, 1977), 308–09; Andrew Mellon, as quoted in Hoover, *Memoirs: The Great Depression*, 30; Gilbert Seldes, as quoted in William E. Leuchtenburg, *The Perils of Prosperity, 1914–1932* (Chicago: University of Chicago Press, 1958), 250; Stuart Chase, "The Case for Inflation," *Harper's*, 165 (July 1932), 206; E. J. Hobsbawm, *Industry and Empire: An Economic History of Britain Since 1750* (New York: Pantheon, 1968), 179; Jude Wanniski, "The Crash and Classical Economics," *The Wall Street Journal*, Oct. 26, 1979; Wanniski, *The Way the World Works*, 123, 302, 18–39, 124–25, 84–86, 132–37, 146; Daniel T. Rodgers, *The Work Ethic in Industrial America, 1850–1920* (Chicago: University of Chicago Press, 1978), 120; Jean-Jacques Rousseau, *The Social Contract*, as quoted in Bertrand Russell, *A History of Western Philosophy* (New York: Simon & Schuster, 1945), 696; *The Wall Street Journal*, Oct. 28, 1977; Burner, *Hoover*, 248n.

3. Kindleberger, *World in Depression*, 293–95, 35, 39–42, 38, 54–56, 77–78, 74–75, 292–93, 306–07, 47–53, 296–97, 26–27; Edward Hallett Carr, *The Twenty Years' Crisis, 1919–1939: An Introduction to the Study of International Relations* (New York: Macmillan, 1939, 2d ed., 1946), 234; William Appleman Williams, *The Tragedy of American Diplomacy* (Cleveland: World, 1959; rev. ed., New York: Dell, 1962), 104–59; John Maynard Keynes, *The Economic*

Consequences of the Peace (New York: Harcourt, Brace, 1920); Étienne Mantoux, *The Carthaginian Peace; or the Economic Consequences of Mr. Keynes* (New York: Charles Scribner's Sons, 1952), 45, 168–69; Donald R. McCoy, *Calvin Coolidge: The Quiet President* (New York: Macmillan, 1967), 190, 416; Herbert Feis, *The Diplomacy of the Dollar, 1919–1939* (New York: Norton, 1950), 42; J. W. Beyen, *Money in Maelstrom* (New York: Macmillan, 1949), 45; Galbraith, *Great Crash*, 192, 14, 187; Richard Hofstadter, *The American Political Tradition: And the Men Who Made It* (New York: Knopf, 1948; 2d ed., Vintage, 1973), 379, 396–97; Rosen, *Hoover, Roosevelt and the Brains Trust*, 348.

4. Burner, *Hoover*, 107; Frank Freidel, *Franklin D. Roosevelt: Launching the New Deal* (Boston: Little, Brown, 1973), 86n; Romasco, *Poverty of Abundance*, 98, 114, 99–100, 103; Kindleberger, *World in Depression*, 106, 83–85, 97, 107, 93–94; John D. Hicks, *Republican Ascendancy, 1921–1933* (New York: Harper & Row, 1960), 195–201; Theodore Saloutos and John D. Hicks, *Agricultural Discontent in the Middle West, 1900–1939* (Madison: University of Wisconsin Press, 1951), 399–402; Willard W. Cochrane, *The City Man's Guide to the Farm Problem* (Minneapolis: University of Minnesota Press, 1966).

5. Adolf A. Berle, Jr., and Gardiner C. Means, *The Modern Corporation and Private Property* (New York: Macmillan, 1932, 1948), v, vii, 32, 345, 350–51; Gardiner C. Means, "The Growth in the Relative Importance of the Large Corporation in American Life," *American Economic Review*, 21 (March 1931), 10; Berle memorandum, "The Nature of the Difficulty," in Beatrice B. Berle and Travis B. Jacobs, eds., *Navigating the Rapids, 1918–1971* (New York: Harcourt, Brace, 1973), 32–50; President's Research Committee on Social Trends, *Recent Social Trends in the United States* (New York: McGraw-Hill, 1933), v. I, 241.

6. Maurice Leven, Harold G. Moulton, and Clark Warburton, *America's Capacity to Consume* (Washington: Brookings Institution, 1934), 54–56, 93–94, 103–04, 123; Galbraith, *Great Crash*, 180, 182, 191; Robert J. Lampman, *The Share of Top Wealth-Holders in National Wealth, 1922–1956* (New York: National Bureau of Economic Research, 1962); James D. Smith and Steven D. Franklin, "The Concentration of Personal Wealth, 1922–1969," *American Economic Review*, 64 (May 1974), 162–67; Jonathan H. Turner and Charles E. Starne, *Inequality: Privilege and Poverty in America* (Santa Monica, Calif.: Goodyear, 1976), 36–38; Gilbert C. Fite and Jim E. Reese, *An Economic History of the United States* (Boston: Houghton Mifflin, 1959; 3d ed., 1973), 506; Simon Kuznets, *National Income: A Summary of Findings* (New York: Bureau of Economic Research, 1946), 97–106; Arthur M. Schlesinger, Jr., *The Crisis of the Old Order, 1919–1933* (Boston: Houghton Mifflin, 1957), 67–68; Leuchtenburg, *Perils of Prosperity*, 193, 200, 174; Temin, *Did Monetary Forces Cause the Great Depression?*, 4, Table 1; Kindleberger, *World in Depression*, 61.

7. Galbraith, *Great Crash*, 81, 112, 11, 57–58, xiv, 8–9, 12, 18, 83, 14–17, 22, 71, 61, 73, 5; John J. Raskob, "Everybody Ought to Be Rich," *Ladies' Home Journal*, 46 (Aug. 1929), 9; Frederick Lewis Allen, *Only Yesterday: An Informal History of the 1920's* (New York: Harper & Brothers, 1931; New York: Perennial Library, 1964), 225–35; Friedman and Schwartz, *Monetary History of the United States*, 298–99; Kindleberger, *World in Depression*, 59–60, 69–70, 108, 75–76, 113; Berle and Means, *Modern Corporation and Private Property*, 60; Robert Sobel, *Panic on Wall Street: A History of America's Financial Disasters* (New York: Macmillan, 1968), 355, 360–61, 356–59; Robert Sobel, *The Great Bull Market: Wall Street in the 1920s* (New York: Norton, 1968), 123; Romasco, *Poverty of Abundance*, 32; Hoover, *Memoirs: The Great Depression*, 14, 16; McCoy, *Coolidge*, 290; *The Wall Street Journal*, Sept. 19, 1929; Charles Merz, as quoted in Leuchtenburg, *Perils of Prosperity*, 244.

8. Kindleberger, *World in Depression*, 108, 124–25; Galbraith, *Great Crash*, 75, 99, 111, 89, 97, 101, 103–08, 114–17, 123, 127–31, 140, 3; Burner, *Hoover*, 247; Garet Garrett, "Wall

Street and Washington," *The Saturday Evening Post*, 202 (Dec. 28, 1929), 6–7; Wanniski, *The Way the World Works*, 133, 137.

9. Milton Friedman, as quoted in "How the Slump Looks to Three Experts," *Newsweek*, 75 (May 25, 1970), 78–79; Galbraith, *Great Crash*, 191, 94–95; Kindleberger, *World in Depression*, 125–27; Michael Harrington, *Socialism* (New York: Saturday Review Press, 1972), 257; Temin, *Did Monetary Forces Cause the Great Depression?*, 172, 178; J. M. Kenworthy, "The Way Back to Prosperity," *Current History*, 36 (April 1932), 129.

CHAPTER 3
IN THE RIGHT PLACE AT THE WRONG TIME?

1. Russell Baker, *Growing Up* (New York: Congdon & Weed, 1982), 91; Albert U. Romasco, *The Poverty of Abundance: Hoover, the Nation, the Depression* (New York: Oxford University Press, 1965), 212; *New York Review of Books*, 14 (June 18, 1970), l; David Burner, *Herbert Hoover: A Public Life* (New York: Knopf, 1979), 332, 339n, 250, 58, 58n, 256; *The New York Times*, Oct. 21, 1964; *The Wall Street Journal*, Feb. 22, 1982; *The New York Times*, Oct. 1, 1982; Jude Wanniski, *The Way the World Works: How Economies Fail—And Succeed* (New York: Basic Books, 1978), 141, 145; *The Wall Street Journal*, Oct. 26, 1979.

2. Richard Hofstadter, *The American Political Tradition: And the Men Who Made It* (New York: Knopf, 1948; 2d ed., Vintage, 1973), 384; Kent Schofield, "The Public Image of Herbert Hoover in the 1928 Campaign," *Mid-America*, 51 (Oct. 1969); Herbert Hoover, *The New Day: Campaign Speeches of Herbert Hoover, 1928* (Palo Alto: Stanford University Press, 1928); Romasco, *Poverty of Abundance*, 202; Joan Hoff Wilson, *Herbert Hoover: Forgotten Progressive* (Boston: Little, Brown, 1975), 270; Anne O'Hare McCormick, as quoted in Romasco, *Poverty of Abundance*, 203; Burner, *Hoover*, 211; Carl N. Degler, "The Ordeal of Herbert Hoover," *Yale Review*, 52 (Summer 1963), 581.

3. Burner, *Hoover*, x, 8, 9, 60, 6, 12, 13, 16, 19–20, 54, 44, 73–80, 93–95, 115, 102, 82, 93, 151, 138, 152, 157; Wilson, *Hoover: Forgotten Progressive*, 14–15, 7–9, 281, 10–11; Degler, "Ordeal of Herbert Hoover," 579–80, 564; William Appleman Williams, *The Tragedy of American Diplomacy* (Cleveland: World, 1959; rev. ed., New York: Dell, 1962), 136–37; Hofstadter, *American Political Tradition*, 374, 371, 377; John Maynard Keynes, *The Economic Consequences of the Peace* (New York: Harcourt, Brace, 1920), 247; Michael Kammen, *People of Paradox: An Inquiry Concerning the Origins of American Civilization* (New York: Knopf, 1972; reprint ed., Oxford University Press, 1980), 174–75, 195; *The New York Times*, April 2, 1920.

4. Elliot A. Rosen, *Hoover, Roosevelt and the Brains Trust: From Depression to New Deal* (New York: Columbia University Press, 1977), 35–36; Robert H. Wiebe, *The Search for Order, 1877–1920* (New York: Hill & Wang, 1967), 170; *The New Republic*, 44 (Sept. 19, 1925); Burner, *Hoover*, 192, 63, 143–45, 173–78, 164–65, 234, 192–93, 146, 111–13; Hofstadter, *American Political Tradition*, 406, 388; Wilson, *Hoover: Forgotten Progressive*, 5; Herbert Hoover, *Principles of Mining* (New York: Hill, 1909); Robert H. Zieger, *Republicans and Labor, 1919–1929*, (Lexington: University of Kentucky Press, 1969); Zieger, "Labor, Progressivism, and Herbert Hoover in the 1920's," *Wisconsin Magazine of History*, 47 (Spring 1975), 196–208; Romasco, *Poverty of Abundance*, 33–34; J. Joseph Huthmacher and Warren I. Susman, eds., *Herbert Hoover and the Crisis of American Capitalism* (Cambridge, Mass.: Schenkman, 1973), ix; Herbert Hoover, *American Individualism* (Garden City, N.Y.: Doubleday, Page, 1922); Degler, "Ordeal of Herbert Hover," 565; Arthur M. Schlesinger, Jr., *The Crisis of the Old Order* (Boston: Houghton Mifflin, 1957), 83–85.

That Hoover was a genuine progressive is far from universally accepted. Elliot Rosen flatly states that "Herbert Hoover was no progressive." Rosen insists, in fact, that Hoover was "anxious to proceed along the lines of Social Darwinism, modified by what appeared to be a civilized set of ground rules for a competitive era" (*Hoover, Roosevelt and the Brains Trust*, 40, 43). I disagree. "Progressive" is a term of such breadth that it is impossible to exclude Hoover; and if "Social Darwinism" is to be stretched sufficiently to include him, it will become as meaningless as "progressive."

5. Murray N. Rothbard essay in Huthmacher and Susman, eds., *Herbert Hoover and the Crisis of American Capitalism*, 35–58; Ellis W. Hawley essay in *ibid.*, 3–35; Hawley, "Herbert Hoover, the Commerce Secretariat, and the Vision of an 'Associative State,' 1921–1928," *Journal of American History*, 61 (June 1974), 116–40; Wilson, *Hoover: Forgotten Progressive*, 6, 278, 15, 280, 159; Romasco, *Poverty of Abundance*, 7, 16–20, 201–03, 188, 209; Hofstadter, *American Political Tradition*, 384, 399, 372, 385, 400; Burner, *Hoover*, 20, 159, 139–41, 66, 329–30, 273–74, 185, 276–77; Hoover, *The New Day*, 164–65; William Appleman Williams, "What This Country Needs . . . ," *New York Review of Books*, 15 (Nov. 5, 1970), 7–11; William Appleman Williams, *The Contours of American History* (Chicago: Quadrangle, 1966), 425–50; Robert F. Himmelberg essay in Huthmacher and Susman, eds., *Herbert Hoover and the Crisis of American Capitalism*, 59–85; Karl Mannheim, *Ideology and Utopia* (1936, New York: Harcourt, Brace, 1951), as cited in Hofstadter, *American Political Tradition*, 407–08n; Degler, "Ordeal of Herbert Hoover," 569–72; William Starr Myers, ed., *The State Papers and Other Writings of Herbert Hoover* (Garden City, N.Y.: Doubleday, Doran, 1934), v. I, 499.

6. Jordan A. Schwartz, *The Interregnum of Despair: Hoover, Congress, and the Depression* (Urbana: University of Illinois Press, 1970), 156, 142–45, 40; Degler, "Ordeal of Herbert Hoover," 571, 578; Myers, ed., *State Papers of Hoover*, v. II, 57–72; Romasco, *Poverty of Abundance*, 172, 199–200; Rosen, *Hoover, Roosevelt and the Brains Trust*, 169; Hofstadter, *American Political Tradition*, 394; Hoover letter to Walter Trohan, April 13, 1962, as quoted in Wilson, *Hoover: Forgotten Progressive*, 268; *ibid.*, 269–72; Burner, *Hoover*, 99, 98, 59–60, 97, 92, 150, 255; Bernard Baruch, as quoted in *ibid.*, 151; Silas Bent, "Mr. Hoover's Sins of Commissions," *Scribner's*, 90 (July 1931), 9.

7. William Allen White, as quoted in Degler, "Ordeal of Herbert Hoover," 580; Burner, *Hoover*, 78, 257, 253; Romasco, *Poverty of Abundance*, 146, 36, 229, 221–22, 37–38; Schwartz, *Interregnum of Despair*, 105, 47–49, 12–13; Harris G. Warren, *Herbert Hoover and the Great Depression* (New York: Oxford University Press, 1959; reprint ed., Westport, Conn.: Greenwood, 1980), 53–55; Arthur Krock, "President Hoover's Two Years," *Current History*, 34 (July 1931), 488–94; Degler, "Ordeal of Herbert Hoover," 578; Hofstadter, *American Political Tradition*, 373; Schlesinger, *Crisis of the Old Order*, 242; Herbert Hoover, *Memoirs: The Great Depression, 1929–1941* (New York: Macmillan, 1952), 195; Gerald D. Nash essay in Huthmacher and Susman, eds., *Herbert Hoover and the Crisis of American Capitalism*, 110.

8. Donald R. McCoy, *Calvin Coolidge: The Quiet President* (New York: Macmillan, 1967), 382–92; Burner, *Hoover*, 190, 193–94, 204–05, 201, 199, 207; Richard Hofstadter, "Could a Protestant Have Beaten Hoover in 1928?" *Reporter*, 22 (March 17, 1960), 31; Schlesinger, *Crisis of the Old Order*, 126–29; William E. Leuchtenburg, *The Perils of Prosperity, 1914–1932* (Chicago: University of Chicago Press, 1958), 234, 238, 240, 233; Paul A. Carter, "The Campaign of 1928 Re-Examined: A Study in Political Folklore," *Wisconsin Magazine of History*, 46 (Summer 1963), 264; John William Ward, *Andrew Jackson: Symbol for an Age* (New York: Oxford University Press, 1955), 46–78; Samuel Lubell, *The Future of American Politics* (2d rev. ed., Garden City, N.Y.: Doubleday, 1956), 29–43; Carl N. Degler, "American Political Parties and the Rise of the City: An Interpretation," *Journal of American History*, 51 (June 1964), 41–59; John D. Hicks, *Republican Ascendancy, 1921–1933* (New York: Harper & Row, 1960), 213; Rosen,

Hoover, Roosevelt and the Brains Trust, 35–36; Hofstadter, *American Political Tradition*, 379–80; Schwartz, *Interregnum of Despair*, 5; Silas Bent, "Will the Democrats Follow the Whigs?" *Scribner's*, 86 (Nov. 1929), 473–79; John Kenneth Galbraith, *The Great Crash: 1929* (Boston: Houghton Mifflin, 1954; 3d ed., 1972), 20; "Acceptance Speech by Secretary of Commerce Herbert C. Hoover, San Francisco, August 11, 1928," in Arthur M. Schlesinger, Jr., and Fred L. Israel, eds., *History of American Presidential Elections, 1789–1968* (New York: Chelsea House, 1971), v. III, 2683, 2689.

On Al Smith and the 1928 campaign, see also Oscar Handlin, *Al Smith and His America* (Boston: Little, Brown, 1958); Roy V. Peel and Thomas C. Donnelly, *The 1928 Campaign: An Analysis* (New York: R. R. Smith, 1931); and Lawrence H. Fuchs, "Election of 1928," in Schlesinger and Israel, eds., *History of American Presidential Elections*, v. III, 2585–609.

9. Burner, *Hoover*, 212–13, 252–53; Romasco, *Poverty of Abundance*, 24–25, 27–29, 48–49, 26, 36, 227–28; Hofstadter, *American Political Tradition*, 391–92; Walter Lippmann, as quoted in Romasco, *Poverty of Abundance*, 35; George Soule, *Prosperity Decade: From War to Depression, 1917–1929* (Holt, Rinehart and Winston, 1947), 312; Schwartz, *Interregnum of Despair*, 52, 13, 50, 164–65; *The New York Times*, Oct. 26, 1929, May 23, 1932, May 28, 1932; Degler, "Ordeal of Herbert Hoover," 568; Myers, ed., *State Papers of Hoover*, v. I, 578, 585.

10. Burner, *Hoover*, 199, 208, 314–15, 309–12; Herbert Hoover, *Memoirs: The Cabinet and the Presidency, 1920–1933* (New York: Macmillan, 1952), 56; McCoy, *Coolidge*, 391; Hoover to Mrs. Sinclair Lewis, Oct. 22, 1937, as quoted in Burner, *Hoover*, 330; Hofstadter, *American Political Tradition*, 339; Degler, "Ordeal of Herbert Hoover," 581; Schwartz, *Interregnum of Despair*, 40; *Public Papers of the Presidents of the United States: Herbert Hoover, 1932–33* (Washington: Government Printing Office, 1976), 751; Schlesinger, *Crisis of the Old Order*, 437.

11. Steve Neal, article in *Chicago Tribune Magazine*, Jan. 10, 1982, summarized in Thomas E. Cronin, "News Notes," *Presidential Studies Quarterly*, 12 (Spring 1982), 293; Hoover autobiographical fragment, as quoted in Wilson, *Hoover: Forgotten Progressive*, 282; William Allen White, "Herbert Hoover: Last of the Old Presidents or First of the New?" *The Saturday Evening Post*, 205 (March 4, 1933), 6–7; Walter Lippmann, "The Permanent New Deal," *Yale Review*, 24 (June 1935); Degler, "Ordeal of Herbert Hoover," 563, 573–74; Wilson, *Hoover: Forgotten Progressive*, 274; "Hoover Plays His Part," *The New Republic*, 61 (Dec. 11, 1929), 56; Romasco, *Poverty of Abundance*, 231–34, 199–200, 211; Hofstadter, *American Political Tradition*, 407, 377; Burner, *Hoover*, 264, 276, 177–88, 208, 236–44, 256–57, 417: n.7; Rosen, *Hoover, Roosevelt and the Brains Trust*, 40, 168, vii; Thomas E. Dewey, oral history, Herbert Hoover Presidential Library, West Branch, Iowa, as quoted in Burner, *Hoover*, 329; Paul Y. Anderson, "Congress Takes a Holiday," *The Nation*, 129 (July 3, 1929), 13–14; Schwartz, *Interregnum of Despair*, 47–49, 74; Huthmacher and Susman, eds., *Herbert Hoover and the Crisis of American Capitalism*, xi.

CHAPTER 4
NATURE TAKES ITS COURSE

1. David Burner, *Herbert Hoover: A Public Life* (New York: Knopf, 1979), 248, 250; Russell Baker, *Growing Up* (New York: Congdon & Weed, 1982), 67; Maurice Niveau, *Histoire des faits économiques contemporains* (2d ed., Paris: Presses Universitaires de France, 1969), 231, as quoted in Charles P. Kindleberger, *The World in Depression, 1929–1939* (1973; reprint ed.: Berkeley and Los Angeles: University of California Press, 1975), 135; Harris G. Warren, *Herbert Hoover and the Great Depression* (New York: Oxford University Press, 1959; reprint ed., Westport, Conn.: Greenwood, 1980), 115–17; Carol Gelderman, *Henry Ford: The Wayward Capitalist* (New York: Dial, 1981), 292; Peter Temin, *Did Monetary Forces Cause the Great Depression?*

(New York: Norton, 1976), 4, Table 1; Albert U. Romasco, *The Poverty of Abundance: Hoover, the Nation, the Depression* (New York: Oxford University Press, 1965), 133, 57, 34, 59–60, 64, 74, 8; Jordan A. Schwartz, *The Interregnum of Despair: Hoover, Congress, and the Depression* (Urbana: University of Illinois Press, 1970), 3–4; Daniel Willard, as quoted in Romasco, *Poverty of Abundance*, 140; U.S. Department of Commerce, Bureau of the Census, *Historical Statistics of the United States, Colonial Times to 1970* (Washington: Government Printing Office, 1975), Series E-135, pp. 210–11, Series D-85-86, p. 135; *Public Papers of the Presidents of the United States: Herbert Hoover, 1930* (Washington: Government Printing Office, 1976), 171–79.

2. Herbert Hoover, *Memoirs: The Great Depression, 1929–1941* (New York: Macmillan, 1952), 30–31, 97; Andrew Mellon, Sept. 9, 1928, as quoted in John Kenneth Galbraith, *The Great Crash: 1929* (Boston: Houghton Mifflin, 1954; 3d ed., 1972), 20; Richard Hofstadter, *The American Political Tradition: And the Men Who Made It* (New York: Knopf, 1948; 2d ed., Vintage, 1973), 393; Berton Hersh, *The Mellon Family: A Fortune in History* (New York: Morrow, 1978); Herbert Hoover, *Memoirs: The Cabinet and the Presidency, 1920–1933* (New York: Macmillan, 1952), 58–60; Galbraith, *Great Crash*, 31; Burner, *Hoover*, 208, 263, 257; Schwartz, *Interregnum of Despair*, 89, 16–17, 35, 30–31, 150; Kindleberger, *World in Depression*, 37; Richard Whitney, as quoted in Arthur M. Schlesinger, Jr., *The Crisis of the Old Order* (Boston: Houghton Mifflin, 1957), 178, 242; Julius H. Barnes, "Business Looks at Unemployment," *Atlantic*, 148 (Aug. 1931), 242; Walter H. Hart, Annapolis, Md., to Hoover, Sept. 19, 1931, President's Organization for Unemployment Relief (POUR) General Correspondence, Tray XVI-1, National Archives, Washington, D.C. (reproduced in Robert S. McElvaine, ed., *Down and Out in the Great Depression: Letters from the "Forgotten Man"* [Chapel Hill: University of North Carolina Press, 1983], 38–39); Caroline Bird, *The Invisible Scar* (New York: McKay, 1966), 30: H. H. Franklin, Syracuse, N.Y., to Col. Arthur Woods, Chairman, President's Emergency Committee for Employment (PECE), Jan. 9, 1931, PECE Central Files, Tray I-1, National Archives; John W. Black, Minneapolis, Minn., to Walter Newton (Secretary to President Hoover), Nov. 9, 1931, POUR General Correspondence, Tray XVI-1 (reproduced in McElvaine, *Down and Out*, 39–41); Mrs. H. D. Crowell, East Orange, N. J., to Woods, Nov. 1930, PECE Central Files, Tray I-1; Dewey W. Grantham, Jr., "Recent American History and the Great Depression," *Texas Quarterly*, 6 (Winter 1963), 12–28; Henry Ford, as quoted in Gelderman, *Ford*, 293; *The New York Times*, Nov. 24, 1931; Romasco, *Poverty of Abundance*, 178–81, 117–18, 50–51, 240: n.23, 89–90, 77–79, 194–95, 145–48, 57, 162–66; Irving Bernstein, *The Lean Years: A History of the American Worker, 1920–1933* (Boston: Houghton Mifflin, 1960), 332; copy of POUR advertisement enclosed with letter from H. L. Crutchfield, Rome, Ga., to Walter Gifford, March 16, 1932, POUR General Correspondence, Tray XVI-1.

3. Romasco, *Poverty of Abundance*, 149, 166–71; Arthur T. Burns, as quoted in *ibid.*, 159; Patrick J. Hurley, as quoted in *ibid.*, 131; Schlesinger, *Crisis of the Old Order*, 242; Bernstein, *The Lean Years*, 331; Kentucky miner to Arthur Garfield Hays, *The Nation*, 134 (June 8, 1932), 651; William E. Leuchtenburg, *Franklin D. Roosevelt and the New Deal, 1932–1940* (New York: Harper & Row, 1963), 3; Nathan Miller, *FDR: An Intimate History* (Garden City, N.Y.: Doubleday, 1983), 2; *Advance*, 18 (March 1932), 13; Bird, *Invisible Scar*, 24; K. F. Liljergren, "American Guarantee of Equity," *American Federationist*, 39 (June 1932), 638; the Rev. George L. Willets, Columbus, Ohio, as quoted in *United Mine Workers' Journal*, 43 (June 1, 1932), 9; Fred Kramer, Centralia, Ill., to Woods, Jan. 28, 1931, PECE Central Files, Tray I-1; Edward T. Johnson, New Haven, Conn., to Hoover, Aug. 1, 1931, POUR General Correspondence, Tray XVI-1; Elmer C. Warriner, Avalon, Pa., to Hoover, Oct. 1930, PECE Central Files, Tray XIII-15; Calvin C. Wood, Denver, Col., to Woods, Jan. 15, 1931, PECE Central Files, Tray XIII-15; David J. Fleming, Bronx, N.Y., to Sen. Robert F. Wagner, Feb. 14, 1931, Robert F.

Wagner Papers, Drawer Q-4, Georgetown University Library; B. E. Minter, New York, N.Y., "An American Jeffersonian Democrat," to Wagner, Dec. 3, 1930, Wagner Papers, Drawer Q-4.

4. Sherwood Anderson, *Puzzled America* (New York: Charles Scribner's Sons, 1935), ix; Marquis Childs, "Main Street Ten Years After," *The New Republic*, 73 (Jan. 18, 1933), 263–65; Remley J. Glass, "Gentlemen, the Corn Belt!" *Harper's*, 167 (July 1933), 199–209; Louis Adamic, *My America, 1928–1938* (New York: Harper & Brothers, 1938), 298; "Talk of the Town," *The New Yorker*, 8 (June 25, 1932), 5; Mrs. M. E. Brink, Oil City, Pa., to Woods, Dec. 15, 1930, PECE Central Files, Tray I-1 (reproduced in McElvaine, *Down and Out*, 47–48).

5. Kindleberger, *World in Depression*, 77–78, 133, 146–70; E. E. Schattschneider, *Politics, Pressures and Tariffs: A Study of Free Private Enterprise in Pressure Politics as Shown by the 1929–30 Revision of the Tariff* (New York: Prentice-Hall, 1935), 293; Hoover, *Memoirs: Cabinet and Presidency*, 291–99; John D. Hicks, *Republican Ascendancy, 1921–1933* (New York: Harper & Row, 1960), 220–23; Warren, *Hoover and the Great Depression*, 84–87, 92–94; Broadus Mitchell, *Depression Decade: From New Era through New Deal* (New York: Holt, Rinehart and Winston, 1947), 61–62, 72–76; Galbraith, *Great Crash*, 110; Frank W. Taussig, *The Tariff History of the United States* (New York: Putnam, 1892, 1931), 500–21; Schlesinger, *Crisis of the Old Order*, 164; *The New York Times*, June 16, 1930; Hoover, *Memoirs: Great Depression*, 61–80; Elliot A. Rosen, *Hoover, Roosevelt and the Brains Trust: From Depression to New Deal* (New York: Columbia University Press, 1977), 67–90.

6. Schwartz, *Interregnum of Despair*, 18–21, 232, 53–59, 151, 73, 99–101, 106–41, 145, 164–73; Schlesinger, *Crisis of the Old Order*, 224; Burner, *Hoover*, 308, 280–82, 253; Joan Hoff Wilson, *Herbert Hoover: Forgotten Progressive* (Boston: Little, Brown, 1975), 273; Arthur W. MacMahon, "Second Session of the Seventy-first Congress," *American Political Science Review*, 24 (Nov. 1930), 936-37; George H. Nash, "Herbert Hoover's Balanced Budget," *The Wall Street Journal*, June 12, 1980; Roy Chapin, Feb. 17, 1932, as quoted in Schwartz, *Interregnum of Despair*, 116–17; *The New York Times*, March 13, 1932; Jude Wanniski, *The Way the World Works: How Economies Fail–and Succeed* (New York: Basic Books, 1978), 141; E. Cary Brown, "Fiscal Policy in the 'Thirties': A Reappraisal," *American Economic Review*, 46 (Dec. 1956), 868–69; Arthur M. Schlesinger, Jr., "The Revolution that Never Was," *The Wall Street Journal*, Oct. 24, 1979; Romasco, *Poverty of Abundance*, 222–26.

7. James Stuart Olson, *Herbert Hoover and the Reconstruction Finance Corporation, 1931–1933* (Ames: Iowa State University Press, 1977), 29, 33, 116–17, 58–61; Gerald Nash, "Herbert Hoover and the Origins of the Reconstruction Finance Corporation," *Mississippi Valley Historical Review*, 46 (Dec. 1959), 455–68; Burner, *Hoover*, 275; Romasco, *Poverty of Abundance*, 189–90, 93; Rosen, *Hoover, Roosevelt and the Brains Trust*, 276–79, 297; Schlesinger, *Crisis of the Old Order*, 237–38.

8. Robert S. Lynd and Helen Merrell Lynd, *Middletown in Transition: A Study in Cultural Conflicts* (New York: Harcourt, Brace & World, 1937), 20; David A. Shannon, ed., *The Great Depression* (Englewood Cliffs, N.J.: Prentice-Hall, 1960), 111, 122; *Justice*, 12 (Nov. 1931), 9; Schlesinger, *Crisis of the Old Order*, 172, 176, 460, 265, 255–65; *American Federationist*, 38 (Aug. 1931), 923–24; *Justice*, 14 (June 1932), 10; Schlesinger, "The Revolution that Never Was"; *American Federationist*, 39 (Sept. 1932), 981; Bernstein, *The Lean Years*, 416, 421–22, 432–34, 440–54; Mary Heaton Vorse, "Rebellion in the Corn Belt: American Farmers Beat their Plowshares into Swords," *Harper's*, 166 (Dec. 1932), 3; George R. Leighton, "And If the Revolution Comes . . . ?" *Harper's*, 164 (March 1932), 467; Burner, *Hoover*, 263–64, 309–12; Oakley Johnson, "After the Dearborn Massacre," *The New Republic*, 70 (March 30, 1932), 172–74; Gelderman, *Henry Ford*, 304–05; *Advance*, 18 (March 1932), 13; Roger Daniels, *The Bonus March: An Episode of the Great Depression* (Westport, Conn.: Greenwood, 1971); Donald Lisio,

The President and Protest: Hoover, Conspiracy, and the Bonus Riot (Columbia: University of Missouri Press, 1974), 56; "A Real American," to Woods, Nov. 8, 1930, PECE Central Files, Tray XIII-15.

CHAPTER 5
THE LORD OF THE MANOR

1. Charles A. Beard and Mary R. Beard, *The Rise of American Civilization* (New York: Macmillan, 1927), v. II, 99–121; Richard Hofstadter, *The American Political Tradition: And the Men Who Made It* (New York: Knopf, 1948; 2d ed., Vintage, 1973), 421; Paul K. Conkin, *The New Deal* (New York: Crowell, 1967, 1975), 1–19; Nathan Miller, *FDR: An Intimate History* (Garden City, N.Y.: Doubleday, 1983), 153n.

2. Frank Freidel, *Franklin D. Roosevelt: The Apprenticeship* (Boston: Little, Brown, 1952), 4–14, 19, 37–43, 29, 48, 52–57, 25n, 61n, 62–63, 72–73, 75–77, 85; Joseph Alsop, *FDR, 1882–1945: A Centenary Remembrance* (New York: Viking, 1982), 29–30; Edward Pessen, "Social Structure and Politics in American History," *American Historical Review*, 87 (Dec. 1982), 1296; James MacGregor Burns, *Roosevelt: The Lion and the Fox* (New York: Harcourt, Brace & World, 1956), 3–21; Rita Halle Kleeman, *Gracious Lady: The Life of Sara Delano Roosevelt* (New York: Appleton-Century, 1935), 222; Barbara Welter, "The Cult of True Womanhood: 1820–1860," *American Quarterly*, 18 (Summer 1966), 151–74; Arthur M. Schlesinger, Jr., *The Crisis of the Old Order, 1919–1933* (Boston: Houghton Mifflin, 1957), 317–29; Hofstadter, *American Political Tradition*, 415.

3. Freidel, *Roosevelt: The Apprenticeship*, 86–116, 155–56, 163–65, 179–91, 24; Miller, *FDR*, 61–69; Josephus Daniels, *The Wilson Era: Years of Peace, 1910–1917* (Chapel Hill: University of North Carolina Press, 1944), 124, 130; Burns, *The Lion and the Fox*, 71–80; Frank Freidel, *Franklin D. Roosevelt: The Ordeal* (Boston: Little, Brown, 1954), 51–91; Kenneth S. Davis, *FDR: The Beckoning of Destiny, 1882–1928* (New York: Putnam, 1972), 607–30.

4. Freidel, *Roosevelt: The Ordeal*, 92, 99–103; Freidel, *Roosevelt: The Apprenticeship*, 81; Joseph P. Lash, *Eleanor and Franklin* (New York: Norton, 1971), 273; Alfred B. Rollins, Jr., *Roosevelt and Howe* (New York: Knopf, 1962), 181–86; Robert Jackson Diary, March 3, 1932, as quoted in Elliot A. Rosen, *Hoover, Roosevelt and the Brains Trust: From Depression to New Deal* (New York: Columbia University Press, 1977), 217–18; Frances Perkins, *The Roosevelt I Knew* (New York: Viking, 1946), 29; Eleanor Roosevelt, *This I Remember* (New York: Harper & Brothers, 1949), 69, 25; James Roosevelt, with Sidney Shalett, *Affectionately, F.D.R.: A Son's Story of a Lonely Man* (New York: Hacourt, Brace & World, 1959), 158; Eleanor Roosevelt, *This Is My Story* (New York: Harper & Brothers, 1937), 162; Davis, *FDR: Beckoning of Destiny*, 676–81.

5. Lash, *Eleanor and Franklin*, 24, 29–33, 44, 59, 63, 74, 121–41, 152–53, 197, 175, 179, 212, 219, 146, 154–69, 194, 220–27; Freidel, *Roosevelt: The Apprenticeship*, 66–71, 77, 79; Archibald MacLeish, *The Eleanor Roosevelt Story* (Boston: Houghton Mifflin, 1965), Introduction; Miller, *FDR*, 152–54; Elliott Roosevelt and James Brough, *An Untold Story: The Roosevelts of Hyde Park* (New York: Putnam, 1973), 77–94, 316–17; Burns, *The Lion and the Fox*, 67–68; James Roosevelt, *My Parents: A Different View* (Chicago: Playboy Press, 1976), 99–104; Elliott Roosevelt and James Brough, *Mother R: Eleanor Roosevelt's Untold Story* (New York: Putnam, 1977), 19–38; Robert S. McElvaine, ed., *Down and Out in the Great Depression: Letters from The "Forgotten Man"* (Chapel Hill: University of North Carolina Press, 1983); Joseph P. Lash, *Love, Eleanor: Eleanor Roosevelt and Her Friends* (New York: Doubleday, 1982); Doris Faber, *The Life of Lorena Hickok, E. R.'s Friend* (New York: Morrow, 1980).

6. Lash, *Eleanor and Franklin*, 276; Burns, *The Lion and the Fox*, 91–104, 123; Freidel,

Roosevelt: The Ordeal, 176–78, 199, 200, 250–56, 268; Freidel, *Roosevelt: The Apprenticeship*, 89–90; Rollins, *Roosevelt and Howe*, 233–44; Frank Freidel, *Franklin D. Roosevelt: The Triumph* (Boston: Little, Brown, 1956), 43–46, 53–54, 101–12, 162–63, 218–27, 167–70; Jordan A. Schwartz, *Interregnum of Despair: Hoover, Congress, and the Depression* (Urbana: University of Illinois Press, 1970), 71; Rosen, *Hoover, Roosevelt and the Brains Trust*, 12.

7. Florence King, *Southern Ladies and Gentlemen* (New York: Stein & Day, 1975), 12; Anonymous, Cambridge (no state given), to FDR, June 22, 1936, FERA Central Files, Box 86, National Archives, Washington, D.C. (reproduced in McElvaine, *Down and Out*, 224); Anonymous, Glendale, Calif., to FDR, Jan. 4, 1936, FERA Central Files, Box 87; A. Graham, Jr., Seattle, Wash., to FERA, Dec. 12, 1934; FERA Central Files, Box 4 (reproduced in McElvaine, *Down and Out*, 59–60); Ilene Hinchaw. Lawndale, Calif., to FDR, Feb. 1, 1934, CWA Administrative Correspondence, Box 54, National Archives (reproduced in McElvaine, *Down and Out*, 57–58); "A Friend," Chicago, Ill., to Ben Whitehurst, Sept. 20, 1935, FERA Central Files, Box 88.

8. Martha Gellhorn, "Report to Mr. Hopkins," Harry Hopkins Papers, Box 60, Franklin D. Roosevelt Library, Hyde Park, N.Y.; David McCullough, "The Legacy: The President They Couldn't Forget," *Parade*, Jan. 31, 1982; William E. Leuchtenburg, "Ronald Reagan's Liberal Past," *The New Republic*, 188 (May 23, 1983), 21; Henry Steele Commager, "Roosevelt: Will His Legacy Survive Reagan?" *Los Angeles Times*, Jan. 24, 1982; NBC Nightly News, Jan. 23, 1982; Associated Press dispatch, Jan. 24, 1982; Fillmore H. Sanford, "Public Orientation to Roosevelt," *Public Opinion Quarterly*, 15 (Summer 1951), 189–216; Will Rogers, as quoted in George Wolfskill, *Happy Days Are Here Again! A Short Interpretive History of the New Deal* (Hinsdale, Ill.: Dryden, 1974), 17.

9. Gellhorn, "Report to Mr. Hopkins," Hopkins Papers, Box 60; Marat Moore, "Coalmining Woman," *Southern Exposure*, 9 (Winter 1981), 46; Lucy K. Schuette, Cedarburg, Wisc., to ER, March 5, 1934, Eleanor Roosevelt Papers, Box 2691, FDR Library (reproduced in McElvaine, *Down and Out*, 218–19); Tex Moore, Wichita Falls, Texas, to FDR, Jan. 4, 1935, FERA Central Files, Box 4; Anonymous, Eureka Springs, Ark., to ER, April 1936, FERA Central Files, Box 86; Laura O'Donnell, Denver, Co., to ER, June 14, 1936, ER Papers, Box 2725; Burns, *The Lion and the Fox*, 133; *The New York Times*, March 9, 1936; Arthur M. Schlesinger, Jr., *The Politics of Upheaval* (Boston, Houghton Mifflin, 1960), 273–74; "A Friend of you both," Kokomo, Ind., to ER, Oct. 28, 1935, FERA Central Files, Box 88.

10. Samuel I. Rosenman, ed., *The Public Papers and Addresses of Franklin D. Roosevelt* (New York: Russell & Russell, 1938–50), v. I, 646; John Dewey, "The Future of Liberalism," *School and Society*, 41 (Jan. 19, 1935), 75; Otis L. Graham, *An Encore for Reform: The Old Progressives and the New Deal* (New York: Oxford University Press, 1967), 112n; Schwartz, *Interregnum of Despair*, 189; George Creel, *Rebel at Large: Recollections of Fifty Crowded Years* (New York: Putnam, 1947), 270; Walter Johnson, ed., *Selected Letters of William Allen White, 1899–1943* (New York: Holt, 1947), 345; Freidel, *Roosevelt: The Apprenticeship*, 31; Rosen, *Hoover, Roosevelt and the Brains Trust*, 105.

11. Rosenman, ed., *Public Papers and Addresses*, v. II, 15–16; Charles P. Kindleberger, *The World in Depression, 1929–1939* (1973; Berkeley and Los Angeles: University of California Press, 1975), 303; Steve Neal, in *Chicago Tribune Magazine*, Jan. 10, 1982, reported in Thomas E. Cronin, "News Notes," *Presidential Studies Quarterly*, 12 (Spring 1982), 291–93; John Gunther, *Roosevelt in Retrospect: A Profile in History* (New York: Harper & Brothers, 1950), 5, 50; Walter Lippmann, in New York *Herald Tribune*, Jan. 8, 1932; Schlesinger, *Crisis of the Old Order*, 452; Hofstadter, *American Political Tradition*, 412; R.J.C. Butow, "The FDR Tapes," *American Heritage*, 33 (Feb.–March 1982), 8–24.

CHAPTER 6
"AND WHAT WAS DEAD WAS HOPE"

The chapter title is taken from Oscar Wilde's *The Ballad of Reading Gaol* (New York: Dutton, 1928), 72.

1. Elliot A. Rosen, *Hoover, Roosevelt and the Brains Trust: From Depression to New Deal* (New York: Columbia University Press, 1977), 288; Jordan A. Schwartz, *The Interregnum of Despair: Hoover, Congress, and the Depression* (Urbana: University of Illinois Press, 1970), 159, 236, 193–94; Albert U. Romasco, *The Poverty of Abundance: Hoover, the Nation, the Depression* (New York: Oxford University Press, 1965), 128; Irving Bernstein, *The Lean Years: A History of the American Worker, 1920–1933* (Boston: Houghton Mifflin, 1960), 467; *The New York Times*, Nov. 20, 1931; William Allen White, *A Puritan in Babylon: The Story of Calvin Coolidge* (New York: Macmillan, 1938), 439; David Burner, *Herbert Hoover: A Public Life* (New York: Knopf, 1979), 307–08.

2. Fred L. Israel, *Nevada's Key Pittman* (Lincoln: University of Nebraska Press, 1963), 96; Frank Freidel, *Franklin D. Roosevelt: The Triumph* (Boston: Little, Brown, 1956), 311; Freidel, *Franklin D. Roosevelt: Launching the New Deal* (Boston: Little, Brown, 1973), 154n; Robert S. Allen, "Texas Jack," *The New Republic*, 70 (March 16, 1932), 119–21; Schwartz, *Interregnum of Despair*, 185–87; Rosen, *Hoover, Roosevelt and the Brains Trust*, 18–24, 114, 4n, 123–30, 130–40, 144, 153–75, 197–201, 205, 210–11; Samuel I. Rosenman, ed., *The Public Papers and Addresses of Franklin D. Roosevelt* (New York: Russell & Russell, 1938–50), v. I, 625, 632, 646, 642; *The New York Times*, April 14, 1932; Arthur M. Schlesinger, Jr., *The Crisis of the Old Order, 1919–1933* (Boston: Houghton Mifflin, 1957), 292–93; Raymond Moley, *The First New Deal* (New York: Harcourt, Brace & World, 1966); Raymond Moley, *After Seven Years* (New York: Harper & Brothers, 1939; reprint ed., Lincoln: University of Nebraska Press, 1971), 15; Rexford Tugwell, *The Brains Trust* (New York: Viking, 1968); Moley memorandum, May 19, 1932, Raymond Moley Papers, Hoover Institution on War, Revolution, and Peace, Stanford University, Palo Alto, Calif., as quoted in Rosen, *Hoover, Roosevelt and the Brains Trust*, 141.

3. Freidel, *The Triumph*, 291–311; Rosen, *Hoover, Roosevelt and the Brains Trust*, 31–39, 228–34, 250–65, 270–72, 306; Schwartz, *Interregnum of Despair*, 60–62; William Gibbs McAdoo, *Crowded Years* (Boston: Houghton Mifflin, 1931), 44, 291; Martha H. Swain, *Pat Harrison: The New Deal Years* (Jackson: University Press of Mississippi, 1978), 27–28; T. Harry Williams, *Huey Long* (New York: Knopf, 1969), 572–73, 581; Edward J. Flynn, *You're the Boss* (New York: Viking, 1947), 100–01; Schlesinger, *Crisis of the Old Order*, 306–07; Rosenman, *Public Papers and Addresses*, v. I, 647–59.

4. Burner, *Hoover*, 316–17, 312; Schwartz, *Interregnum of Despair*, 196–98, 201, 204; Huey Long, as quoted in Schlesinger, *Crisis of the Old Order*, 430; *Public Papers of the Presidents of the United States: Herbert Hoover, 1932–33* (Washington: Government Printing Office, 1977), 656–80, 750–51; Rosenman, *Public Papers and Addresses*, v. I, 669–84, 693–711, 742–56, 795–812, 734–35, 742; Moley, *After Seven Years*, 48; Rosen, *Hoover, Roosevelt and the Brains Trust*, 267, 345, 138.

5. Herbert Hoover, *Memoirs: The Great Depression, 1929–1941* (New York: Macmillan, 1952), 176–216; *New York Evening Post*, Feb. 6, 1933, clipping in Huey Long Scrapbooks, v. 19, Louisiana State University Library, Baton Rouge; William E. Leuchtenburg, *Franklin D. Roosevelt and the New Deal, 1932–1940* (New York: Harper & Row, 1963), 23–24; *Time*, Feb. 1, 1982, 30; Schwartz, *Interregnum of Despair*, 205, 229, 206, 97–98, 222; Burner, *Hoover*, 319, 269–73, 321–24; Rosen, *Hoover, Roosevelt and the Brains Trust*, 3; John Kenneth Galbraith, *The Great Crash: 1929* (Boston: Houghton Mifflin, 1954, 1972), 118, 156–59, 184–85;

Harris G. Warren, *Herbert Hoover and the Great Depression* (New York: Oxford University Press, 1959; reprint ed., Westport, Conn.: Greenwood, 1980), 113; Schlesinger, *Crisis of the Old Order*, 457, 478–79; Susan Estabrook Kennedy, *The Banking Crisis of 1933* (Lexington: University Press of Kentucky, 1973), 20–21, 30–39; Milton Friedman and Anna Jacobson Schwartz, *The Great Contraction, 1929–1933* (Princeton: Princeton University Press, 1965), 3–21; Romasco, *Poverty of Abundance*, 68–70, 85–86, 80–81.

CHAPTER 7
"ACTION, AND ACTION NOW"

1. *The New York Times*, March 3, 1933, March 4, 1933; Samuel I. Rosenman, ed., *The Public Papers and Addresses of Franklin D. Roosevelt* (New York: Russell & Russell, 1938–50), v., II, 11–16, 61–66; Edmund Wilson, *The Shores of Light* (New York: Farrar, Straus & Young, 1952), 498–99; Dixon Wechter, *The Age of the Great Depression, 1929–1941* (New York: Macmillan, 1948), 229; J. Fred MacDonald, *Don't Touch That Dial! Radio Programming in American Life, 1920–1960* (Chicago: Nelson-Hall, 1979), 41; Frank Freidel, *Franklin D. Roosevelt: Launching the New Deal* (Boston: Little, Brown, 1973), 214–15, 234, 194–95, 219, 184, 226, 225, 234, 443, 236; Arthur M. Schlesinger, Jr., *The Coming of the New Deal* (Boston: Houghton Mifflin, 1959), 13; Raymond Moley, *After Seven Years: A Political Analysis of the New Deal* (New York: Harper & Brothers, 1939; reprint ed., Lincoln: University of Nebraska Press, 1971), 155; Susan Estabrook Kennedy, *The Banking Crisis of 1933* (Lexington: University Press of Kentucky, 1973), 152–202; William Starr Myers and Walter H. Newton, *The Hoover Administration: A Documented Narrative* (New York: Charles Scribner's Sons, 1936), 356; Herbert Hoover, *Memoirs: The Great Depression, 1929–1941* (New York: Macmillan, 1952), 215; Bernard Sternsher, *Rexford Tugwell and the New Deal* (New Brunswick, N.J.: Rutgers University Press, 1964), 75; Theodore G. Joslin, *Hoover Off the Record* (Garden City, N.Y.: Doubleday, Doran, 1934), 364–65; *The Wall Street Journal*, March 4, 1933.

2. Freidel, *Roosevelt: Launching the New Deal*, 237–54, 140–42, 147–50, 159, 249, 303, 312–13; Rosenman, *Public Papers and Addresses*, v. II, 49, 16; William E. Leuchtenburg, *Franklin D. Roosevelt and the New Deal, 1932–1940* (New York: Harper & Row, 1963), 47, 64; Moley, *After Seven Years*, 153; *The New York Times*, May 19, 1933; Schlesinger, *Coming of the New Deal*, 8–13, 15, 17–20; *The New York Times*, Sept. 11, 1932; Ray Tucker, "The National Air," *Collier's*, 93 (Jan. 27, 1934), 22; *The New Republic*, 90 (April 7, 1937), 251–52; Otis L. Graham, Jr., *An Encore for Reform: The Old Progressives and the New Deal* (New York: Oxford University Press, 1967), 171–72, 24, 27, 178; *Time*, 119 (Feb. 1, 1982); Charles Forcey, *The Crossroads of Liberalism: Croly, Weyl, Lippmann, and the Progressive Era, 1900–1925* (New York: Oxford University Press, 1961); George N. Peek and Samuel Crowther, *Why Quit Our Own?* (New York: Van Nostrand, 1936), 20; Elliot A. Rosen, *Hoover, Roosevelt and the Brains Trust: From Depression to New Deal* (New York: Columbia University Press, 1977), 156, 304; James T. Patterson, *Congressional Conservatism and the New Deal* (Lexington: University Press of Kentucky, 1967), 4–6; E. Pendleton Herring, "First Session of the 73rd Congress," *American Political Science Review*, 27 (Feb. 1934), 65–83.

3. Van L. Perkins, *Crisis in Agriculture: The Agricultural Adjustment Administration and the New Deal, 1933* (Berkeley and Los Angeles: University of California Press, 1969), 73; Freidel, *Roosevelt: Launching the New Deal*, 85–86, 89–90, 308–39; Christiana McFadyen Campbell, *The Farm Bureau and the New Deal* (Urbana: University of Illinois Press, 1962), 51; *The Complete Presidential Press Conferences of Franklin D. Roosevelt* (New York: Da Capo, 1972), v. I, 44 (March 15, 1933); *The New York Times*, March 19, 1933; Jordan Schwartz, *1933: Roosevelt's Decision: The United States Leaves the Gold Standard* (New York: Chelsea House, 1969); Schles-

inger, *Coming of the New Deal*, 40, 199–203, 74–84; Moley, *After Seven Years*, 160; Leuchtenburg, *Roosevelt and the New Deal*, 72–78, 136–40, 170–71; Carey McWilliams, *Factories in the Field* (Boston: Little, Brown, 1939); Donald Worster, *Dust Bowl: The Southern Plains in the 1930s* (New York: Oxford University Press, 1979); John Steinbeck, *The Grapes of Wrath* (New York: Viking, 1939; Penguin, 1976), 40, 50; Paul E. Mertz, *New Deal Policy and Southern Rural Poverty* (Baton Rouge: Louisiana State University Press, 1978), 5–13; Lois Bray, Leachville, Ark., to Norman Thomas, April 6, 1934, Norman Thomas Papers, Box 10, New York Public Library (reproduced in Robert S. McElvaine, ed., *Down and Out in the Great Depression: Letters from the "Forgotten Man"* [Chapel Hill: University of North Carolina Press, 1983], 74–75): Donald H. Grubbs, *Cry From the Cotton: The Southern Tenant Farmers' Union and the New Deal* (Chapel Hill: University of North Carolina Press, 1971); Gilbert Fite, *George N. Peek and the Fight for Farm Parity* (Norman: University of Oklahoma Press, 1954), 251–52.

4. James T. Pattterson, *America's Struggle Against Poverty, 1900–1980* (Cambridge, Mass.: Harvard University Press, 1981), 56–60; Schlesinger, *Coming of the New Deal*, 264–78, 282–88, Robert Sherwood, *Roosevelt and Hopkins: An Intimate History* (New York: Harper & Brothers, 1948); Leuchtenburg, *Roosevelt and the New Deal*, 120–25; Raymond Moley, *The First New Deal* (New York: Harcourt, Brace & World, 1966), 271; Eric F. Goldman, *Rendezvous with Destiny* (New York: Knopf, 1952; rev. ed., Vintage, 1955), 257; Harold Ickes, *Autobiography of a Curmudgeon* (New York: Reynal and Hitchcock, 1943); Freidel, *Roosevelt: Launching the New Deal*, 154–55; Harry Hopkins, *Spending to Save* (New York: Norton, 1936); "W.P.A. Workers of Battle Creek," Michigan, to FDR, April 5, 1936, FERA Central Files, Box 86; Lorena Hickok to Harry Hopkins, from Des Moines, Iowa, Nov. 25, 1933, Hickok to Hopkins, from Birmingham, Ala., April 2, 1934, and Hickok to Hopkins, from Raleigh, N.C., Feb. 14, 1934, all in Lorena Hickok Papers, Box 11, FDR Library; Gov. Floyd Olson (Farmer-Labor, Minnesota) to Hopkins, June 22, 1934, Harry Hopkins Papers, Box 61, FDR Library; Rosenman, *Public Papers and Addresses*, v. V, 19–21.

5. Leuchtenburg, *Roosevelt and the New Deal*, 174; Rosenman, *Public Papers and Addresses*, v. IV, 65; Schlesinger, *Coming of the New Deal*, 336–40, 319–34; Paul K. Conkin, *The New Deal* (2d ed., New York: Crowell, 1967, 1975), 45; Moley, *The First New Deal*, 5, 323–34; John A. Salmond, *The Civilian Conservation Corps, 1933–1942* (Durham, N.C.: Duke University Press, 1967); Freidel, *Launching the New Deal*, 256–66, 162–66, 350–54; Frances Perkins, *The Roosevelt I Knew* (New York: Viking, 1946), 177–81; C. H. Prichett, *The Tennessee Valley Authority* (Chapel Hill: University of North Carolina Press, 1943); David E. Lilienthal, *TVA: Democracy on the March* (New York: Harper & Brothers, 1944); Gordon R. Clapp, *The TVA: An Approach to the Development of a Region* (Chicago: University of Chicago Press, 1955); John H. Kyle, *The Building of TVA* (Baton Rouge: Louisiana State University Press, 1958); Marguerite Owen, *The Tennessee Valley Authority* (New York: Praeger, 1973); North Callahan, *TVA: Bridge Over Troubled Waters* (New York: Barnes, 1980).

6. Rosenman, *Public Papers and Addresses*, v. II, 246, 164; Freidel, *Roosevelt: Launching the New Deal*, 408–35; *Time*, 21 (April 17, 1933); Ellis W. Hawley, *The New Deal and the Problem of Monopoly* (Princeton: Princeton University Press, 1966), 21–25, 472–75, 33, 53–55, 57–58, 104, 67, 132, 61, 123–24, 127–31; Perkins, *The Roosevelt I Knew*, 192–96, 252–53; Schlesinger, *Coming of the New Deal*, 95, 108–10, 125–26, 152–53; Moley, *First New Deal*, 284, 290; Hugh S. Johnson, *The Blue Eagle from Egg to Earth* (Garden City, N.Y.: Doubleday, Doran, 1935), 196–204; Dorothy Thompson, in the New York *Herald Tribune*, Jan. 24, 1938, as quoted in Hawley, *New Deal and the Problem of Monopoly*, 472; Gabriel Kolko, *The Triumph of Conservatism: A Reinterpretation of American History, 1900–1916* (Glencoe, Ill.: Free Press, 1963); Robert H. Wiebe, *Businessmen and Reform: A Study of the Progressive Movement* (Cambridge, Mass.: Harvard University Press, 1962), 80–85, 186–90; James Weinstein, *The*

Corporate Ideal in the Liberal State, 1900–1918 (Boston: Beacon, 1968); Richard H. Pells, *Radical Visions and American Dreams: Culture and Social Thought in the Depression Years* (New York: Harper & Row, 1973), 81; Leuchtenburg, *Roosevelt and the New Deal*, 65–66; "The NRA Prosperity March," as quoted in Hawley, *New Deal and the Problem of Monopoly*, 54; Harvard Sitkoff, *A New Deal for Blacks: The Emergence of Civil Rights as a National Issue: The Depression Decade* (New York: Oxford University Press, 1978), 109; Goldman, *Rendezvous with Destiny*, 160–61; James F. Ragland, "Franklin D. Roosevelt and Public Opinion, 1933–1940" (PH.D. dissertation, Stanford University, 1954), 249; Alan Brinkley, *Voices of Protest: Huey Long, Father Coughlin, and the Great Depression* (New York: Knopf, 1982), 155; William E. Leuchtenburg, "Ronald Reagan's Liberal Past," *The New Republic*, 188 (May 23, 1983), 21; Richard Hofstadter, *The American Political Tradition: And the Men Who Made It* (New York: Knopf, 1948; 2d ed., Vintage, 1973), 435.

7. Schlesinger, *Coming of the New Deal*, 297–98, 440–45, 232–52, 456–70; Leuchtenburg, *Roosevelt and the New Deal*, 53, 60; C. Lowell Harriss, *History and Policies of the Home Owners' Loan Corporation* (New York: National Bureau of Economic Research, 1951), 35–39; Moley, *After Seven Years*, 175–84; *Business Week*, (Dec. 9, 1933), 16; John Kenneth Galbraith, *The Great Crash: 1929* (Boston: Houghton Mifflin, 1954; 3d ed., 1972), 164–72; Frank Freidel, *Franklin D. Roosevelt: The Apprenticeship* (Boston: Little, Brown, 1952), 37; Freidel, *Roosevelt: Launching the New Deal*, 442–43, 340–50, 483.

8. Oswald Garrison Villard, "Mr. Roosevelt's Two Months," *New Statesman and Nation*, May 13, 1933, as quoted in Schlesinger, *Coming of the New Deal*, 21; *The New York Times*, March 26, 1933; William Allen White to Harold Ickes, May 23, 1933, as quoted in Leuchtenburg, *Roosevelt and the New Deal*, 62; Schlesinger, *Coming of the New Deal*, 21; Herbert Feis to Henry Stimson, March 15, 1933, as quoted in Freidel, *Roosevelt: Launching the New Deal*, 312; *Gabriel Over the White House* (1933, Gregory La Cava, MGM); Andrew Bergman, *We're in the Money: Depression America and Its Films* (New York: New York University Press, 1971; reprint ed., Harper & Row, 1972), 15, 116–20.

9. Otis L. Graham, "Historians and the New Deals, 1944–1960," *The Social Studies*, 54 (April 1963), 133–40; Arthur M. Schlesinger, Jr., *The Politics of Upheaval* (Boston: Houghton Mifflin, 1960), 385–408; Basil Rauch, *The History of the New Deal, 1933–1938* (New York; Creative Age Press, 1944); Jerrold S. Auerbach, "New Deal, Old Deal, or Raw Deal: Some Thoughts on New Left Historiography," *Journal of Southern History*, 35 (Feb. 1969), 18–30; Hawley, *New Deal and the Problem of Monopoly*, 107; Barton J. Bernstein, "The New Deal: The Conservative Achievements of Liberal Reform," in Barton J. Bernstein, ed., *Towards a New Past: Dissenting Essays in American History* (New York: Vintage, 1968), 263–88; Frances Fox Piven and Richard A. Cloward, *Regulating the Poor: The Functions of Public Welfare* (New York: Vintage, 1971); Howard Zinn, ed., *New Deal Thought* (Indianapolis: Bobbs-Merrill, 1966), xxv.

CHAPTER 8
"FEAR ITSELF"

1. Clifford Geertz, *The Interpretation of Cultures* (New York: Basic Books, 1973), 18; Cabell Phillips, *From the Crash to the Blitz, 1929–1939* (New York: Macmillan, 1969), xii.

2. Among the books that have begun to provide us with the raw material for the basis of an understanding of working-class culture in the Great Depression are Studs Terkel, *Hard Times: An Oral History of the Great Depression* (New York: Pantheon, 1970); Alice and Staughton Lynd, *Rank and File: Personal Histories by Working-Class Organizers* (Boston: Beacon, 1973); Tom E. Terrill and Jerrold Hirsch, eds., *Such As Us: Southern Voices of the Thirties* (Chapel Hill: Univer-

sity of North Carolina Press, 1978); Ann Banks, ed., *First-Person America* (New York: Knopf, 1980); and Richard Lowitt and Maurine Beasley, *One Third of a Nation: Lorena Hickok's Reports on the Great Depression* (Champaign: University of Illinois Press, 1981).

3. Philip Eisenberg and Paul F. Lazarfeld, "The Psychological Effects of Unemployment," *Psychological Bulletin*, 35 (June 1938); Alfred Winslow Jones, *Life, Liberty and Property* (Philadelphia: Lippincott, 1941); Robert S. Lynd and Helen Merrell Lynd, *Middletown in Transition: A Study in Cultural Conflicts* (New York: Harcourt, Brace, 1937); Arthur W. Kornhauser, "Attitudes of Economic Groups," *Public Opinion Quarterly*, 2 (April 1938), 260–68; Ruth Shonle Cavan and Katherine Howland Ranck, *The Family and the Depression: A Study of One Hundred Chicago Families* (Chicago: University of Chicago Press, 1938); Mirra Komarovsky, *The Unemployed Man and His Family* (New York: Dryden, 1940); E. Wight Bakke, *Citizens without Work* (New Haven: Yale University Press, 1940); Bakke, *The Unemployed Worker* (New Haven: Yale University Press, 1940); Jessie A. Bloodworth and Elizabeth J. Greenwood, *The Personal Side* (1939; reprint ed., New York: Arno, 1971); Howard B. Woolston, "Psychology of Unemployment," *Sociology and Social Research*, 19 (March–April 1935), 335–40; Flora Slocum and Charlotte Ring, "Industry's Discarded Workers (A Study of 100 St. Louis Relief Families)," *Sociology and Social Research*, 19 (July–Aug. 1935); Edward A. Rundquist and Raymond F. Sletto, *Personality in the Depression: A Study in the Management of Attitudes* (Minneapolis: University of Minnesota Press, 1936); Gabriel Almond and Harold D. Lasswell, "Aggressive Behavior by Clients toward Public Relief Administrators: A Configurative Analysis," *American Political Science Review*, 28 (Aug. 1934), 643–55.

4. Oral history interviews conducted thirty-five to forty-five years after the events being described, such as Terkel's *Hard Times* and the Lynds' *Rank and File*—useful as they unquestionably are—are less reliable than testimony given at the time, either through letters or interviews. It seems inevitable that the years between the Depression and the Terkel and Lynd interviews, particularly the long period of relative affluence from World War II through the 1960s, will have colored people's recollections of the thirties. See Fred Davis, *Passage through Crisis* (Indianapolis: Bobbs-Merrill, 1961).

5. A sampling of these letters is available in Robert S. McElvaine, ed., *Down and Out in the Great Depression: Letters from the "Forgotten Man"* (Chapel Hill: University of North Carolina Press, 1983).

Herman Kahn, former director of the Franklin D. Roosevelt Library, estimated that there were some 15 million letters from the public in Hyde Park. Many more are housed in the National Archives and elsewhere. During the early years of the Depression, Roosevelt annually received letters equaling a rate of 160 per 10,000 literate adults in the American population. This was nearly four times greater than the next-highest level in American history, that of 47 per 10,000 literate adults writing to Woodrow Wilson during World War I.

In most periods of American history, well-educated, upper-class people have been disproportionately represented among those who have written letters to political figures. This was not the case during the New Deal years. An analysis of the mail addressed to FDR and received in a week in March 1934, found 46 percent coming from laborers, 14 percent from clerks, and 15 percent from farmers. A combined total of only 20 percent were from businessmen and professionals. Poorly educated, working-class people need a stronger motive to write than do their more learned and affluent countrymen. The Depression provided them with such a motive and the Roosevelts gave them reason to hope that their thoughts and pleas might be heard and answered.

Leila A. Sussmann, *Dear FDR: A Study in Political Letter-Writing* (Totowa, N.J.: Bedminster, 1963), 72, 60, 11, 87, 135–41; Ira Smith, *Dear Mr. President* (New York: Messner, 1949), 150; FERA, "Analysis of General Run of All Mail Addressed to President Roosevelt, March 23–27, 1934," cited in Sussmann, *Dear FDR*, 140–41.

6. Lorena Hickok, Report to Harry Hopkins on Maine, Sept. 21–29, 1933, Lorena Hickok Papers, Box 11, Franklin D. Roosevelt Library; John A. Garraty, "Unemployment During the Great Depression," *Labor History*, 12 (Spring 1976), 147; Hickok report dated "June 1(?), 1934(?)," but actually written in late 1934, Hickok Papers, Box 11; Thomas Steep, Report to Hopkins from Chicago, Nov. 10, 1934, Harry Hopkins Papers, Box 66, FDR Library; Mrs. Sanderson, Oklahoma City, Okla., to ER, June 10, 1934, Eleanor Roosevelt Papers, Box 2691, FDR Library (reproduced in McElvaine, *Down and Out*, 189–92); "One of the Unwashed," Oregon, to ER, Feb. 28, 1935, FERA Central Files, Box 91, National Archives (reproduced in McElvaine, *Down and Out*, 211).

7. "Henry E.," age 43, former salesman and clerical worker, Minnesota, interviewed by Miss McEachern, Minnesota WPA, Feb. 1940, "Interviews of Project Workers in Twelve States," WPA Division of Information Files, Box 482, National Archives; Steep to Hopkins, from Chicago, Nov. 10, 1934; Hickok, Report to Hopkins on Ohio, Oct. 10, 1935, Hickok Papers, Box 11; Louisa Wilson, Report to Hopkins on Detroit, Nov. 17, 1934, Hopkins Papers, Box 67; Solomon Diamond, "A Study of the Influence of Political Radicalism on Personality Development," *Archives of Psychology*, no. 203 (June 1936), 10–12; Caroline Bird, *The Invisible Scar* (New York: McKay, 1966), 197; Daniel T. Rodgers, *The Work Ethic in Industrial America, 1850–1920* (Chicago: University of Chicago Press, 1978); interview with Albert Beaujon, age 75, former knifemaker, Thomaston, Conn., ca. 1938, WPA Federal Writers' Project, Living Lore Collection, Archive of Folk Song, Library of Congress; Ralph R. Connor, St. Louis, Mo., to Hopkins, Dec. 2, 1933, Civil Works Administration Central Files, Box 54, National Archives; Glen H. Elder, Jr., *Children of the Great Depression* (Chicago: University of Chicago Press, 1974), 51; "A Taxpayer," New York, N.Y., to FERA, Jan. 3, 1936, FERA Files, Box 87; Anonymous, Evansville, Ind., to FDR, Sept. 7, 1935, FERA Files, Box 88; Minnie A. Hardin, Columbus, Ind., to ER, Dec. 14, 1937, ER Papers, Box 2735 (reproduced in McElvaine, *Down and Out*, 145–47); Terkel, *Hard Times*, 5; Hickok, Report to Hopkins on Houston, Tex., April 13, 1934, Hickok Papers, Box 11; 38-year-old laborer, interviewed by Carl W. Held, Information Service Department, Oklahoma WPA, Feb. 1940, WPA Division of Information Files, Box 482.

8. Which was often far more rapidly than could have been anticipated, because life savings were wiped out in bank failures. This sometimes made Depression victims more bitter than did other hardships. David M. Maynard, Report to Hopkins on Dayton, Ohio, Dec. 6, 1934, Hopkins Papers, Box 66. "I had enough money in the bank to take care of myself," complained the Oklahoma City woman quoted earlier, "but the bankers got it—hundreds were the same— we have lost our homes—but it wasent our fault," Mrs. Sanderson, Oklahoma City, to ER, June 10, 1934.

9. Hickok, Report to Hopkins on Maine, Sept. 21–29, 1933; James T. Bagley, Charlotte, N.C., to Hopkins, Nov. 28, 1933, CWA Files, Box 54; J. C. Swindler, Riverside, Calif., to General Hugh Johnson, Nov. 23, 1933, CWA Files, Box 55; Mrs. Grenobia Vincent, Weldon, N.C., to ER, Jan. 21, 1935, ER Papers, Box 2220 (reproduced in McElvaine, *Down and Out*, 109–10); Ben L. Beaver, Egan, Texas, to Hopkins, Dec. 5, 1933, CWA Files Box 54; Hickok, Report to Hopkins, Phoenix, Ariz., May 4, 1934, Hickok Papers, Box 11. The man quoted had been a small businessman before the Depression, but by this time had long been one of the unemployed. Bruce McClure, Report to Hopkins on Lawrence County, Pa., Fall 1934, Hopkins Papers, Box 66; A. Graham, Jr., Seattle, Wash., to FERA, Dec. 12, 1934, FERA Files, Box 4 (reproduced in McElvaine, *Down and Out*, 59–60); Hickok, Report to Hopkins from Rock Springs, Wyo., Sept. 3, 1934, Hickok Papers, Box 11; Wayne Parrish, Report to Hopkins on New Jersey, Dec. 1, 1934, Hopkins Papers, Box 66; Hickok, Report to Hopkins from Lincoln, Neb., Nov. 18, 1933, and Hickok, Report to Hopkins on West Virginia, Aug. 16–26, 1933, both in Hickok Papers, Box 11; Martha Gellhorn, Report on Rhode Island, Dec. 1934, Hopkins Papers, Box 66.

10. Elder, *Children of the Great Depression*, 54, 60; Bird, *Invisible Scar*, 39; George W. Kearns, Martinsburg, W.Va., to Sen. M. M. Neely (D—W.Va.), Jan. 23, 1935, FERA Files, Box 5 (reproduced in McElvaine, *Down and Out*, 130–31); Mrs. Post, Cambridge (no state given), to FDR, May 16, 1934, FERA Files, Box 4 (reproduced in McElvaine, *Down and Out*, 158); Ralph R. Connor, St. Louis, Mo., to Hopkins, Dec. 2, 1933, CWA Files, Box 54; Ed Paulsen, in Terkel, *Hard Times*, 34; "W.P.A. Workers wife," Kalamazoo, Mich., to Hopkins, Nov. 21, 1935, FERA Files, Box 88; Gellhorn, Report on Rhode Island, Dec. 1934. On "taking" by slaves, see Lawrence W. Levine, *Black Culture and Black Consciousness* (New York: Oxford University Press, 1977), 131.

11. "An Obscure Couple," Kingston, N.Y., to Hopkins, May 1935, FERA Files, Box 90; Mary L., Detroit, Mich., to FDR, Oct. 2, 1935, FERA Files, Box 88; "Florence B.," age 28, former packager of candies and cookies, displaced by automation, interviewed by Miss McEachern, Minnesota WPA, Feb. 1940, WPA Division of Information Files, Box 482; Mrs. F. E. Gray, Beverly, Mass., to ER, Dec. 4, 1934, ER Papers, Box 612 (reproduced in McElvaine, *Down and Out*, 103–04); "123986," New York, N.Y., to FDR, March 1936, FERA New Subject File, 002; Joseph S. Hall, Latrobe, Pa., to Bruce McClure, Secretary, CWA, April 4, 1934, CWA Files, Box 54 (reproduced in McElvaine, *Down and Out*, 159); Parrish, Report to Hopkins on New York City, Nov. 17, 1934, Hopkins Papers, Box 66. The suicide rate increased in the Depression years. It was noticeably higher in all the years of the thirties than it had been in the twenties or has been at any time since 1941. By 1932, the rate had increased to 17.4 per 100,000, up from 14 per 100,000 in 1929. U.S. Chamber of Commerce, Bureau of the Census, *Historical Statistics of the United States, Colonial Times to 1970* (Washington: Government Printing Office, 1975), Series B-166, v. I, 58. Gellhorn, Report to Hopkins on Camden, N.J., April 25, 1935, Hopkins Papers, Box 66; Mrs. J. Graziano, Montvale, N.J., to ER, Aug. 28, 1934, ER Papers, Box 612 (reproduced in McElvaine, *Down and Out*, 58).

12. Vito Cacciola, cobbler, Beverly, Mass., interviewed by Merton R. Lovett, Jan. 12, 1939, WPA FWP Living Lore Collection. For the help-seeking letters to Mrs. Roosevelt, see File 150.1, Eleanor Roosevelt Papers. Mrs. Alfred Westphal, Aurelia, Iowa, to ER, n.d. (ca. June 1936), ER Papers, Box 2220; "E.T.," Philadelphia, Pa., to ER, Feb. 19, 1935, FERA Files, Box 91 (reproduced in McElvaine, *Down and Out*, 164). Other good examples of such letters include Mrs. Albina Martell, Waterbury, Vt., to ER, Jan. 19, 1934, ER Papers, Box 2197 (reproduced in McElvaine, *Down and Out*, 75); Mrs. Jno. Trimble, Goff, Kans., to ER, May 10, 1935 (reproduced in McElvaine, *Down and Out*, 75); and Mrs. J. N. Tony, Athens, Ga., to ER, Nov. 25, 1935, both in ER Papers, Box 2220. On the connection between asking for help and seeing oneself as a failure, see for example, Mrs. C. D. Cockerham, Winnsboro, La., to ER, Oct. 29, 1935, ER Papers, Box 645 (reproduced in McElvaine, *Down and Out*, 69–70).

13. Oscar Handlin, *The Uprooted* (Boston: Atlantic–Little, Brown, 1951, 1973), 181; "Colored," Marietta, Ga., to FDR, Oct. 27, 1935, FERA New Subject File, 002 (reproduced in McElvaine, *Down and Out*, 90–91); P. F. Alston, Arkansas City, Kans., to ER, Nov. 25, 1934, ER Papers, Box 600; Mrs. Charles Clontz, Summerville, Pa., to ER, April 1935, ER Papers, Box 645 (reproduced in McElvaine, *Down and Out*, 70–71).

14. "Contrary to an erroneous popular impression, workers on urban relief rolls in 1934 were not industrial misfits who had never worked nor persons with an irregular work history. . . . Over half of the men had worked 10 years or more at their usual occupation." WPA, *Urban Workers on Relief*, Research Monograph IV, Part I (Washington: Government Printing Office, 1936), 32.

15. Anonymous, Chicago, Ill., to Mr. and Mrs. Roosevelt, Feb. 1936, FERA Files, Box 87 (reproduced in McElvaine, *Down and Out*, 117).

16. The foregoing scene of applying for relief is based on a general background of information

in letters and other sources and specifically on Hickok, Report to Hopkins on New York City, Oct. 2–12, 1933, and Hickok, Report to Hopkins on Houston, Tex., April 4–12, 1934, both in Hickok Papers, Box 11, and Gellhorn, Report to Hopkins on Massachusetts, Nov. 1934, Hopkins Papers, Box 66.

17. Gellhorn, Report on Rhode Island, Dec. 1934; Hickok Report, "June 1(?), 1934(?)"; Hickok, Report to Hopkins on New York City, Oct. 2–12, 1933; Gellhorn, Report to Hopkins on Massachusetts, Nov. 1934; William Haber, State Emergency Relief Commissioner of Michigan, to Hopkins, Dec. 4, 1934, Hopkins Papers, Box 61; Hickok, Report to Hopkins on Philadelphia (from Allentown, Pa.), July 14, 1935, Hopkins Papers, Box 68; Gellhorn, Report to Hopkins on North Carolina, Nov. 19, 1934, Hopkins Papers, Box 66. On apathy among Depression victims, see also Arthur M. Schlesinger, Jr., *The Crisis of the Old Order* (Boston: Houghton Mifflin, 1957), 252; Marquis Childs, "Main Street Ten Years After," *The New Republic*, 73 (Jan. 18, 1933), 263–65; and Jones, *Life, Liberty and Property*, 71.

18. Hazel Reavis, Report to Hopkins on Bethlehem, Pa., Dec. 7, 1934, Hopkins Papers, Box 66; Hickok, Report to Hopkins from Salt Lake City, Utah, Sept. 1, 1934, Hickok Papers, Box 11; Anonymous, Atlanta, Ga., to FDR, Aug. 14, 1935, FERA Files, Box 89; Hickok Reports to Hopkins: Pennsylvania, Aug. 6, 1933, Cheyenne, Wyo., Sept. 9, 1934, and Salt Lake City, Sept. 1, 1934, Hickok Papers, Box 11; "An S.E.R.A. Worker," Los Angeles, Calif., May 13, 1935, FERA Files, Box 90; Hickok Reports to Hopkins: Upstate New York, Sept. 12–19, 1933, Des Moines, Iowa, Nov. 25, 1933, and Cleveland, Ohio, Sept. 22, 1935, Hickok Papers, Box 11; Hickok , Memo to Hopkins, "On 'the State of the Nation' in the Great City of New York," Dec. 29, 1933, Hickok Papers, Box 11; "Paul D.," age 51, former streetcar conductor, and "Florence B.," interviewed by Miss McEachern, Minnesota WPA; 58-year-old former building contractor, Detroit, interviewed by Frederic S. Schouman, Michigan WPA, all Feb. 1940, WPA Division of Information Files, Box 482. Many other interviews in this collection support the same point.

19. George Orwell noted a similar change in the attitude of the unemployed in Great Britain by 1937. *The Road to Wigan Pier* (New York: Harcourt, Brace, 1958), 80. Lynd and Lynd, *Middletown in Transition*, 111–12.

20. Hickok, as quoted in Arthur M. Schlesinger, Jr., *The Coming of the New Deal* (Boston: Houghton Mifflin, 1958), 275; E. H. Mulock, Administrator, Iowa E.R.A., "Statement of Relief Conditions and Employment Prospects in Iowa as of November 15, 1934," (letter to Hopkins, Nov. 27, 1934), Hopkins Papers, Box 61; Hickok, Report to Hopkins from Salt Lake City, Sept. 1, 1934; Frances Fox Piven and Richard A. Cloward, *Regulating the Poor: The Functions of Public Welfare* (New York: Pantheon, 1971), 61–62. Many studies of the attitudes of Depression victims indicate the existence of this demanding, relief-as-a-right group, as one of several categories of recipients. See Melvin J. Vincent, "Relief and Resultant Attitudes," *Sociology and Social Research*, 20 (Sept.–Oct. 1935), 27–33; Eisenberg and Lazarfeld, "The Psychological Effects of Unemployment," 372; Cavan and Ranck, *The Family and the Depression*, 195; Woolston, "Psychology of Unemployment," 335–40; and Slocum and Ring, "Industry's Discarded Workers (A Study of 100 St. Louis Relief Families)," 524–25.

21. Bird, *Invisible Scar*, 32; Gellhorn, Report to Hopkins on South Carolina, Nov. 5, 1934, and Gellhorn, Report to Hopkins on New Hampshire, Dec. 2, 1934, both in Hopkins Papers, Box 66. Gellhorn, it may be relevant to note, seems to have had a remarkable ability to find syphilis and morons among the poor. In her limited surveys she discovered more of each than seems remotely credible. Her solution to both "problems": a massive sterilization program for "cretins." Gellhorn reports to Hopkins, *passim.*, Hopkins Papers, Box 66.

22. Henry W. Francis, Report to Hopkins from Williamson, W.Va., Dec. 7, 1934, Hopkins

Papers, Box 66; Mrs. Howe, age 39, wife of WPA worker, Lynn, Mass., interviewed by Jane E. Leary, July 27, 1939, WPA FWP Living Lore Collection; Hickok, Report to Hopkins from Salt Lake City, Sept. 1, 1934.

23. Hickok, Report to Hopkins from Sioux City, Iowa, Dec. 4, 1933, Hickok Papers, Box 11; Mrs. A. J. Ferguson, Fair Haven, Vt., to FDR, June 1934, FERA Files, Box 4 (reproduced in McElvaine, *Down and Out*, 165–66); "A Democrat Voter," Louisville, Ky., to FDR, May 8, 1936, FERA New Subject File, 002 (reproduced in McElvaine, *Down and Out*, 175–76); "Just a Friend," Nashville, Tenn., to FDR, Nov. 27, 1935, FERA New Subject File, 002 (reproduced in McElvaine, *Down and Out*, 127); Steep, Report to Hopkins from Chicago, Nov. 4, 1934, Hopkins Papers, Box 66; Elder, *Children of the Great Depression*, 91–92; Parrish, Report to Hopkins on New York City, Nov. 24, 1934, Hopkins Papers, Box 66; Hickok, Report to Hopkins from Dickinson, N. Dak. and Minot, N. Dak., Nov. 1, 1933, both in Hickok Papers, Box 11; John Steinbeck, *The Grapes of Wrath* (New York: Viking, 1939; Penguin, 1976), 467; Elder, *Children of the Great Depression*, 83, 88, 101, 106; Steep, Report to Hopkins from Chicago, Nov. 17, 1934; "One of the Unwashed," Oregon, to ER, Feb. 28, 1935, FERA Files, Box 91; Mrs. Charles Clontz, Summerville, Pa., to ER, April 1935, ER Papers, Box 645 (reproduced in McElvaine, *Down and Out*, 70–71); Joseph Captiva, fisherman, Provincetown, Mass., interviewed by Alice Kelly, Feb. 1939, and Patrick J. Ryan, shoe machinery worker, Lynn, Mass., interviewed by Jane K. Leary, July 20, 1939, both in WPA FWP Living Lore Collection: Komarovsky, *The Unemployed Man and His Family*; Louis Adamic, *My America, 1928–1938* (New York: Harper & Brothers, 1938), 283–93; Cavan and Ranck, *The Family and the Depression*, 7–8.

24. Norman Cousins, "Will Women Lose Their Jobs?" *Current History and Forum*, 41 (Sept. 1939), 14; Alice Kessler-Harris, *Out to Work: A History of Wage-Earning Women in the United States* (New York: Oxford University Press, 1982), 257–59, 254, 260–61, 251, 270–71, 262–63; Susan Ware, *Holding Their Own: American Women in the 1930s* (Boston: Twayne, 1982), 21–50; Ware, *Beyond Suffrage: Women in the New Deal* (Cambridge, Mass.: Harvard University Press, 1981); Ruth Milkman, "Women's Work and Economic Crisis: Some Lessons of the Great Depression," *Review of Radical Political Economics*, 8 (Spring 1978); Jeane Westin, *Making Do: How Women Survived the '30s* (Chicago: Follett, 1976); Winifred D. Wandersee, *Women's Work and Family Values, 1920–1940* (Cambridge, Mass.: Harvard University Press, 1981), 84, 101–02, 1–3, 88, 97; John B. Parrish, "Changes in the Nation's Labor Supply," *American Economic Review*, 29 (June 1939), 332; Parrish, "Women in the Nation's Labor Market," *Quarterly Journal of Economics*, 54 (May 1940), 528; *Local No. 2 Edition*, UAW-CIO, Nov. 15, 1939, as quoted in Kessler-Harris, *Out to Work*, 269; Betty Friedan, *The Feminine Mystique* (New York: Norton, 1963).

25. Elder, *Children of the Great Depression*, 52, 71, 29; Beran Wolfe, "Psycho-analyzing the Depression," *The Forum*, 87 (April 1932), 212; Hickok, Report to Hopkins on New York City, Oct. 2–12, 1933; Hickok, Report to Hopkins on Pennsylvania, Aug. 7–12, 1933; Hickok Papers, Box 11; Clarabell Van Busick, age 11, Rushyhania, Ohio, to ER, March 29, 1935, ER Papers, Box 2220 (reproduced in McElvaine, *Down and Out*, 118–19); Lucille Ledbetter, age 12, Blacksburg, S.C., to ER, Jan. 19, 1934, ER Papers, Box 2197 (reproduced in McElvaine, *Down and Out*, 116); Hickok, Report to Hopkins from Salt Lake City, Sept. 1, 1934; Larry Van Dusen, in Terkel, *Hard Times*, 106–07; Anonymous, age 12, Chicago, Ill., to Mr. and Mrs. Roosevelt, Feb. 1936, FERA Files, Box 87 (reproduced in McElvaine, *Down and Out*, 117); Ned Stribling, Sulphur Springs, Tex., to FDR, Dec. 11, 1934, FERA Files, Box 5 (reproduced in McElvaine, *Down and Out*, 72); Anonymous, Beaverdam, Va., to FDR, Oct. 23, 1935, FERA Files, Box 88 (reproduced in McElvaine, *Down and Out*, 170–71); John Garlacy and John Lemch, Woonsocket, R.I., to FDR, Dec. 23, 1935, FDR Papers, Alphabetical File, 1933–36, Box 2,

FDR Library; Anonymous, Warren, Ohio, to FDR, Dec. 22, 1935, FERA Files, Box 88 (reproduced in McElvaine, *Down and Out*, 116).

26. Hickok, Report to Hopkins from Fergus Falls, Minn., Dec. 5, 1933; Hickok, Report to Hopkins, "Enroute, Memphis to Denver," June 17, 1934, all in Hickok Papers, Box 11; Mrs. Luella Comstock, Merrill, Wisc., to ER, Sept. 10, 1935, ER Papers, Box 645; 30-year-old laborer on Oklahoma WPA project, interviewed by Carl W. Held, Information Service Department, Oklahoma WPA, WPA Division of Information Files, Box 482; Steep, Report to Hopkins from Chicago, Nov. 10, 1934, Hopkins Papers, Box 66; Carl Giles, Administrator, ERA, Oklahoma, to Hopkins, Nov. 15, 1934, Hopkins Papers, Box 61; "Working Girls League," Winona, Minn., to Hopkins, June 23, 1936, FERA Files, Box 86; Gellhorn, Report on Rhode Island, Dec. 1934; Parrish, Report to Hopkins on New York City and New Jersey, n.d. (ca. Dec. 1934), Hopkins Papers, Box 66; Hickok, Report to Hopkins from Syracuse, N.Y., Aug. 5, 1935, Hopkins Papers, Box 68; Lynd and Lynd, *Middletown in Transition*, 476, 455; George R. Cody, State Emergency Relief Administrator, Rhode Island, to Hopkins, Dec. 4, 1934, Hopkins Papers, Box 61; Gellhorn, Report on Rhode Island, Dec. 1934; Hickok, Report to Hopkins, "June 1(?), 1934(?)"; Lea D. Taylor, as reported in Steep, Report to Hopkins on Chicago, Nov. 17, 1934. Belief in the Alger myth was relatively weak among the poor in the 1930s. See Hadley Cantril and Mildred Strunk, eds., *Public Opinion, 1935–1946* (Princeton, N.J.: Princeton University Press, 1951), 829.

27. Clifford Burke, in Terkel, *Hard Times*, 82; Harvard Sitkoff, *A New Deal for Blacks; The Emergence of Civil Rights As a National Issue: The Depression Decade* (New York: Oxford University Press, 1978), 41, 35–38, 93, 40–41, 44–46, 54–55, 53–54, 50–51, 48–49; Anonymous, Canton, Ga., to FDR, July 22, 1935, FERA New Subject File, 002, National Archives (reproduced in McElvaine, *Down and Out*, 94); Raymond Wolters, *Negroes and the Great Depression: The Problem of Economic Recovery* (Westport, Conn.: Greenwood, 1970), 116–17, 126–27, 130–31, 39; Arthur F. Raper, *The Tragedy of Lynching* (Chapel Hill: University of North Carolina Press, 1933), 30–31; Hilton Butler, "Lynch Law in Action," *The New Republic*, 67 (July 22, 1931), 257; Frank Freidel, *Franklin D. Roosevelt: The Triumph* (Boston: Little, Brown, 1956), 276; Gunnar Myrdal, *An American Dilemma: The Negro Problem and Modern Democracy* (New York: Harper & Brothers, 1944), 74; Frank Freidel, *FDR and the South* (Baton Rouge: Louisiana State University Press, 1955), 36; Walter White, *A Man Called White* (New York: Viking, 1948), 169–70; Arthur F. Raper, *Preface to Peasantry* (Chapel Hill: University of North Carolina Press, 1936), 56; Anonymous, Reidsville, Ga., to FDR, Oct. 19, 1935, and Anonymous, Hattiesburg, Miss., to FDR, FERA New Subject File, 002 (reproduced in McElvaine, *Down and Out*, 83, 88).

28. John B. Kirby, *Black Americans in the Roosevelt Era: Liberalism and Race* (Knoxville: University of Tennessee Press, 1980), 230, 76–96, 8–11, 49–53, 234; Sitkoff, *New Deal for Blacks*, 29, 59–61, 80–81, 72–73, 106, 77–78, 179–83, 88–96, 109, 116, 112–14, 332–33, 69–72, 104–05, 66–69, 331, 65–66, 216–43, 331–32, 76, 89, 326–27, 33, 334, 82–83; Erik Barnouw, *A Tower of Babel: A History of Broadcasting in the United States to 1933* (New York: Oxford University Press, 1966), 225–30; J. Fred MacDonald, *Don't Touch That Dial! Radio Programming in American Life, 1920–1960* (Chicago: Nelson-Hall, 1979), 27; *The New York Times*, editorial, March 7, 1930; Joseph P. Lash, *Eleanor and Franklin* (New York: Norton, 1971), 512–35; Tamara K. Hareven, *Eleanor Roosevelt: An American Conscience* (Chicago: Quadrangle, 1968), 112–29; Eleanor Roosevelt, "Address," The National Conference on Fundamental Problems in the Education of Negroes, Washington, D.C., May 9–12, 1934, as quoted in Kirby, *Black Americans in the Roosevelt Era*, 78; Theodore G. Bilbo, as quoted in Sitkoff, *New Deal for Blacks*, 117; Morton Sosna, *In Search of the Silent South: Southern Liberals and the Race Issue* (New York: Columbia University Press, 1977), 60–87; Ralph J. Bunche, *The*

Political Status of the Negro in the Age of FDR, Dewey W. Grantham, ed., (Chicago: University of Chicago Press, 1973), xxii; Richard M. Dalfiume, "The 'Forgotten Years' of the Negro Revolution," *Journal of American History*, 55 (June 1968), 99; Ralph Bunche, "Programs, Ideologies, Tactics," 559–560, as quoted in Kirby, *Black Americans in the Roosevelt Era*, 234n; Richard M. Dalfiume, *Fighting on Two Fronts: Desegregation of the Armed Forces, 1939–1953* (Columbia: University of Missouri Press, 1969), 121.

CHAPTER 9
MORAL ECONOMICS

1. E. P. Thompson, *The Making of the English Working Class* (New York: Vintage, 1963), 444; Michael Kammen, *People of Paradox: An Inquiry Concerning the Origins of American Civilization* (New York: Knopf, 1972; Oxford University Press, 1980); E. P. Thompson, "The Moral Economy of the Crowd in the Eighteenth Century," *Past and Present*, no. 50 (Feb. 1971), 89–90, 136; John L. Hess, "The Compleat Adam Smith," *The Nation*, 232 (May 16, 1981), 596–97; Robert L. Heilbroner, *The Worldly Philosophers* (New York: Simon & Schuster, 1953, 1961), 45, 52–54, 62; Henry Nash Smith, *Virgin Land* (Cambridge, Mass.: Harvard University Press, 1950, 1970); Leo Marx, *The Machine in the Garden: Technology and the Pastoral Ideal in America* (New York: Oxford University Press, 1964); David W. Noble, *The Progressive Mind, 1890–1917* (revised ed., Minneapolis: Burgess, 1981), 2, 12; Richard Hofstadter, *Social Darwinism in American Thought* (Philadelphia: University of Pennsylvania Press, 1944; revised ed., Boston: Beacon, 1955); Selig Perlman, *A Theory of the Labor Movement* (New York: Macmillan, 1928), 169; Gerald Grob, *Workers and Utopia: A Study of Ideological Conflict in the American Labor Movement, 1865–1900* (Evanston, Ill.: Northwestern University Press, 1961), 161–62; Milton Derber, *The American Ideal of Industrial Democracy, 1865–1965* (Urbana: University of Illinois Press, 1970), 34; David Montgomery, *Workers' Control in America: Studies in the History of Work, Technology, and Labor Struggles* (Cambridge and New York: Cambridge University Press, 1979), 153; David Montgomery, *Beyond Equality: Labor and the Radical Republicans, 1862–1872* (New York: Knopf, 1967), 445, 447; Leon Fink, "Workingmen's Democracy: The Knights of Labor in Local Politics, 1886–1896" (PH.D. dissertation, University of Rochester, 1977); Alan Dawley, *Class and Community: The Industrial Revolution in Lynn* (Cambridge, Mass.: Harvard University Press, 1976); Herbert G. Gutman, *Work, Culture and Society in Industrializing America* (New York: Knopf, 1976); Lawrence Goodwyn, *Democratic Promise: The Populist Moment in America* (New York: Oxford University Press, 1976), xiii; Goodwyn, *The Populist Moment in America: A Short History of the Agrarian Revolt in America* (New York: Oxford University Press, 1978), xxiii; Thomas Dublin, *Women at Work: The Transformation of Work and Community in Lowell, Massachusetts, 1820–1860* (New York: Columbia University Press, 1979), 48, 56–57; Sidney Hook, *From Hegel to Marx* (New York: Reynal and Hitchcock, 1936), 303; Richard H. Pells, *Radical Visions and American Dreams: Culture and Social Thought in the Depression Years* (New York: Harper & Row, 1973), 139; *Oxford English Dictionary* (London: Oxford University Press, 1933), v. III, E-59–60; Charles Sherrington, *Man on His Nature* (Cambridge: Cambridge University Press, 1953), 278; James Madison, *Federalist* No. 10 (1788); Charles Kendall Adams, as quoted in Irwin Wyllie, *The Self-Made Man in America* (New Brunswick, N.J.: Rutgers University Press, 1954), 158; Irving Bernstein, *The Lean Years: A History of the American Worker, 1920–1933* (Boston: Houghton Mifflin, 1960), 316–17; Daniel Rodgers, *The Work Ethic in Industrial America, 1850–1920* (Chicago: University of Chicago Press, 1978), 125.

2. Arthur M. Schlesinger, Jr., *The Politics of Upheaval* (Boston: Houghton Mifflin, 1960), 84–87, 94–95, 207, 162, 165; Walter Goodman, *The Committee: The Extraordinary Career of the*

House Committee on Un-American Activities (New York: Farrar, Straus & Giroux, 1968); Pells, *Radical Visions and American Dreams*, 77, 46, 73, 28, 76, 111, 98, 117, 101, 55, 138–40, 125, 116, 66, 25, 126–27, 108, 120–25, 132–33, 139, 80; Edmund Wilson, "Foster and Fish," *The New Republic*, 65 (Dec. 14, 1930), 162; Stuart Chase, "Skilled Work and No Work," *The New Republic*, 58 (March 20, 1929), 123; Samuel Schmalhausen, "Psychoanalysis and Communism, " *Modern Quarterly*, 6 (Summer 1932), 63–69, and "Psychological Portrait of Modern Civilization," *Modern Quarterly*, 6 (Autumn 1932), 85–95, as quoted in Pells, *Radical Visions and American Dreams*, 100; Hook, *From Hegel to Marx*, 161; Sidney Hook, *Towards the Understanding of Karl Marx* (New York: Day, 1933), 99–101; Charles Beard, "The Educator in the Quest for National Security," *Social Frontier*, 1 (April 1935), 14, as quoted in Pells, *Radical Visions and American Dreams*, 115; Edmund Wilson, "An Appeal to Progressives," *The New Republic*, 65 (Jan. 14, 1931), 238; Lewis Mumford, *Technics and Civilization* (New York: Harcourt, Brace, 1934), 392, as quoted in Pells, *Radical Visions and American Dreams*, 108; Reinhold Niebuhr, *Moral Man and Immoral Society* (New York: Charles Scribner's Sons, 1932), 231–38.

3. George Henry Melcher, Topanga, Calif., to FDR, Feb. 19, 1934, CWA Central Files, Box 55, National Archives; "A lover of the poor," Hudson, N.Y., to ER, March 1935, FERA Central Files, Box 91; Pat Geer, Lakin, Kans., to Sen. George McGill (D—Kans.), March 30, 1934, CWA Files, Box 54; H. S. Avery, Minneapolis, Minn., to ER, Jan. 4, 1934, ER Papers, Box 2676, FDR Library; "One of the unemployed," Arkansas, to Harry Hopkins, July 4, 1935, FERA Files, Box 89; "UNEMPLOYED WELL-WISHERS," Tacoma, Wash., to FDR, Sept. 29, 1935, FERA Files, Box 88; "A W.P.A. Worker," Lincoln, Neb., to Hopkins, July 21, 1936, FERA Files, Box 86; "A House Wife," Columbus, Ohio, to FDR, Feb. 8, 1935, FERA Files, Box 91; "We the Workers of thes Projects," Birmingham, Ala., to FDR, March 2, 1936, FERA Files, Box 87; Mary Owsley, Peggy Terry, Louis Banks, Kitty McCulloch, in Studs Terkel, *Hard Times: An Oral History of the Great Depression* (New York: Pantheon, 1970), 46, 47, 41, 39; *Fortune* surveys, July 1935 and Oct. 1937, in Hadley Cantril and Mildred Strunk, eds., *Public Opinion, 1935–1946* (Princeton: Princeton University Press, 1951), 1040, 1041.

4. Pete Seeger, interview with the author, July 1, 1981, Holmdel, N.J.; Andrew Bergman, *We're in the Money: Depression America and its Films* (New York: New York University Press, 1971; reprint ed., Harper & Row, 1972), xi, xvi, 167–69, 6–10, 15, 93–96; Gerald Mast, *A Short History of the Movies* (Chicago: University of Chicago Press, 1971; 3d ed., 1981), 218–19; Siegfried Kracauer, *From Caligari to Hitler* (Princeton: Princeton University Press, 1966), 5; John Kenneth Galbraith, *The Great Crash: 1929* (Boston: Houghton Mifflin, 1954; 3d ed., 1972), 120; Charles R. Hearn, *The American Dream in the Great Depression* (Westport, Conn.: Greenwood, 1977), 78; Frederick Lewis Allen, *Since Yesterday* (New York: Harper & Brothers, 1940), 223–24; Arthur M. Schlesinger, Jr., "When the Movies Really Counted," *Show*, 3 (April 1963), 77; *Our Daily Bread* (1934, King Vidor, United Artists); Robert Warshow, "The Gangster as Tragic Hero," in Warshow, *The Immediate Experience* (New York: Doubleday, 1962), 127–33; *Little Caesar* (1930, Mervyn Le Roy, Warner Brothers); Robert Sklar, *Movie-Made America: A Social History of American Movies* (New York: Random House, 1975), 179–81; Pells, *Radical Visions and American Dreams*, 270–71, 273–74; Dwight MacDonald, "Notes on Hollywood Directors, Part II," *Symposium* (July 1933), 293–94; *Corsair* (1931, Roland West, United Artists); *Public Enemy* (1931, William Wellman, Warner Brothers); L. Glen Seretan, "Social Banditry in Depression America" (paper delivered at 1980 annual meeting of the Organization of American Historians, San Francisco); Eric Hobsbawm, *Bandits* (New York: Delacorte, 1969), 13–14, 19–23, 34–36, 109–15; Joe Klein, *Woody Guthrie: A Life* (New York: Knopf, 1980), 123–24; Alan Lomax, Woody Guthrie, and Pete Seeger, eds., *Hard-Hitting Songs for Hard-Hit People* (New York: Oak Pubns., 1967), 114–15; E. J. Hobsbawm, *Primitive Rebels* (New York:

Norton, 1959), 28; *I Am a Fugitive From a Chain Gang* (1932, Mervyn Le Roy, Warner Brothers); *Scarface* (1932, Howard Hawks, United Artists); John Baxter, *Hollywood in the Thirties* (New York: Barnes, 1968), 59; Lewis Jacobs, *The Rise of American Film* (New York: Harcourt, Brace, 1939; Teachers College Press, 1968), 486.

5. *Freaks* (1932, Tod Browning, MGM); *Gold Diggers of 1933* (1933, Mervyn Le Roy, Warner Brothers); *Footlight Parade* (1933, Lloyd Bacon, Warner Brothers); Bergman, *We're in the Money*, 62–65, 32–38; *42nd Street* (1933, Lloyd Bacon, Warner Brothers); Pells, *Radical Visions and American Dreams*, 282; *Three Little Pigs* (1933, Walt Disney); Sklar, *Movie-Made America*, 204, 182–84.

6. Sklar, *Movie-Made America*, 175, 192; Pells, *Radical Visions and American Dreams*, 278–79; Bergman, *We're in the Money*, 83–88, 119, 149–60; *Bullets or Ballots* (1936, William Keighly, Warner Brothers); *G-Men* (1935, William Keighly, Warner Brothers); *Crime School* (1938, Louis Seiler, Warner Brothers); *The President Vanishes* (1934, William Wellman, Paramount); *A Tale of Two Cities* (1935, Jack Conway, MGM); *Barbary Coast* (1935, Howard Hawks, United Artists); Baxter, *Hollywood in the Thirties*, 95; *Dead End* (1937, William Wyler, United Artists); *The Great O'Malley* (1937, William Dieterle, Warner Brothers); *Angels with Dirty Faces* (1938, Michael Curtiz, Warner Brothers).

7. *It Happened One Night* (1934, Frank Capra, Columbia); Bergman, *We're in the Money*, 133–34, 138–39, 145; Sklar, *Movie-Made America*, 207, 211, 191–92; *Lady for a Day* (1933, Frank Capra, Columbia); *Mr. Deeds Goes to Town* (1936, Frank Capra, Columbia); *Mr. Smith Goes to Washington* (1939, Frank Capra, Columbia); *You Can't Take It With You* (1938, Frank Capra, Columbia); Pells, *Radical Visions and American Dreams*, 278–81, 215; *Stagecoach* (1939, John Ford, 20th Century-Fox); Mast, *Short History of the Movies*, 243–44; *The Grapes of Wrath* (1940, John Ford, 20th Century-Fox); John Steinbeck, *The Grapes of Wrath* (New York: Viking, 1939; Penguin, 1976), 463; *How Green Was My Valley* (1941, John Ford, 20th Century-Fox); Michael C. Steiner, "Regionalism and the Larger Society: The Need for a Sense of Place During the Great Depression" (paper delivered at the 1981 meeting of the American Studies Association, Memphis), 7, 18, 9; James D. Hart, *The Popular Book* (New York: Oxford University Press, 1970), 255-56; Warren I. Susman, "The Thirties," in Stanley Coben and Lorman Ratner, eds., *The Development of an American Culture* (2d ed., New York: St. Martin's, 1983), 236, 245; John Dos Passos, *The Ground We Stand On* (New York: Harcourt, Brace, 1941), 3; *Racket Busters* (1938, Lloyd Bacon, Warner Brothers).

8. *Fortune* surveys, July 1935 and Oct. 1936, in Cantril and Strunk, *Public Opinion, 1935–1946*, 893, 439; Arthur W. Kornhauser, "Attitudes of Economic Groups," *Public Opinion Quarterly*, 2 (April 1938), 261–65; W. Smith, Sharon, Conn., to FDR, July 5, 1935, PPF 200-B, Box 45; Ellen Goodman, "The Contrast Is Too Great," *The Boston Globe*, Jan. 11, 1983.

CHAPTER 10
THUNDER ON THE LEFT

1. Irving Bernstein, *Turbulent Years: A History of the American Worker, 1933–1941* (Boston: Houghton Mifflin, 1971), 218–52, 261–98, 252–59; Russell Baker, *Growing Up* (New York: Congdon & Weed, 1982), 86; Anne Ross, "Labor Unity in Minneapolis," *The New Republic*, 79 (July 25, 1934), 284–86; "Revolt in the Northwest," *Fortune*, 13 (April 1936); Arthur M. Schlesinger, Jr., *The Coming of the New Deal* (Boston: Houghton Mifflin, 1958), 387–89; Herbert Solow, "War in Minneapolis," *The Nation*, 139 (Aug. 8, 1934), 160–61; Anne Ross, "Minnesota Sets Some Precedents," *The New Republic*, 80 (Sept. 12, 1934), 121–23; Samuel Yellen, *American Labor Struggles* (New York: Harcourt, Brace, 1936), 330–35; Robert Cantwell, "San

Francisco: Act One," *The New Republic*, 79 (July 25, 1934), 280; Charles A. Madison, *American Labor Leaders* (2d ed., New York: Ungar, 1962), 404–33; Donald MacKenzie Brown, "Dividends and Stevedores," *Scribner's*, 97 (Jan. 1935), 52–56; Memoranda on conversations between James A. Moffett and Marvin McIntyre, July 14, July 16, July 17, 1934, Frances Perkins to FDR, July 17, 1934, and Radio Washington to Naval Aide to the President, all in FDR Official File 407-B, Box 25, FDR Library; Robert Cantwell, "War on the West Coast: The Gentlemen of San Francisco," *The New Republic*, 79 (Aug. 1, 1934), 308–10.

2. *The New York Times*, Nov. 6, 1934; Alan Brinkley, *Voices of Protest: Huey Long, Father Coughlin, and the Great Depression* (New York: Knopf, 1982), 204; Louis Adamic, "La Follette Progressives Face the Future," *The Nation*, 140 (Feb. 20, 1935), 213–14; The Unofficial Observer (J. Franklin Carter), *American Messiahs* (New York: Simon & Schuster, 1935), 111–14; Donald R. McCoy, "The Formation of the Wisconsin Progressive Party in 1934," *Historian*, 14 (Autumn 1951), 72–87; McCoy, *Angry Voices: Left-of-Center Politics in the New Deal Era* (Lawrence: University of Kansas Press, 1958), 46–49; Arthur M. Schlesinger, Jr., *The Politics of Upheaval* (Boston: Houghton Mifflin, 1960), 106–08; Edward N. Doan, *The La Follettes and the Wisconsin Idea* (New York: Rinehart, 1947), 181, 171, 186, 188–89; Wisconsin Secretary of State, *Blue Book of the State of Wisconsin, 1935* (Madison: Wisconsin Department of State, 1935), 618; Louis Adamic, "A Talk with Phil La Follette," *The Nation*, 140 (Feb. 27, 1935), 244; Michael Paul Rogin, *The Intellectuals and McCarthy: The Radical Specter* (Cambridge, Mass.: MIT Press, 1967), 75–76, 78, 82.

3. George H. Mayer, *The Political Career of Floyd B. Olson* (Minneapolis: University of Minnesota Press, 1951), 17–25, 239, 4–16, 20–36, 43–56, 76–77, 92–96, 108–09, 132–33, 142, 149, 280–301; Schlesinger, *Politics of Upheaval*, 99, 101; Herbert Lefkowitz, "Olson: Radical and Proud of It," *Review of Reviews*, 91 (May 1935), 40; John Janney, "Minnesota's Enigma," *American Magazine*, 120 (Sept. 1935), 107–09, Charles Rumford Walker, *American City: A Rank-and-File History* (New York: Farrar and Rinehart, 1937; reprint ed., Arno, 1971), 66–67; McCoy, *Angry Voices*, 55, 79; *The New York Times*, Dec. 10, 1934; Carter, *American Messiahs*, 97–99; Charles R. Walker, "Governor Olson's Last Interview," *The Nation*, 144 (March 20, 1937), 319; State of Minnesota, "Abstract of Votes Polled for State Officers by Counties," 1934, 1936, provided by the office of the Secretary of State, St. Paul.

4. Upton Sinclair, *I, Governor of California, And How I Ended Poverty: A True Story of the Future* (Los Angeles: Sinclair, 1933), 6, 59, 13–17; Sinclair, *I, Candidate for Governor: And How I Got Licked* (Pasadena: Sinclair, 1934), 6–7, 22, 29–30, 34, 66, 44, 52–57, 45–47, 64, 156, 97–98; Clarence McIntosh, "Upton Sinclair and the EPIC Movement, 1933–1936" (PH.D. dissertation, Stanford University, 1955), 53–54, 144–45, 131–34, 152–58, 94–95, 89–90, 233, 263, 322–23, 159, 225; E. P. Thompson, "The Moral Economy of the English Crowd in the Eighteenth Century," *Past and Present*, no. 50 (Feb. 1971), 76–136; Norman Thomas to Upton Sinclair, May 1, 1934, and Jerry Voorhis, San Dimas, California, to Thomas, April 2, 1934, both in Norman Thomas Papers, Box 10, New York Public Library; Bernard K. Johnpoll, *Pacifist's Progress: Norman Thomas and the Decline of American Socialism* (Chicago: Quadrangle, 1970), 135–37; Daniel Bell, *Marxian Socialism in the United States* (Princeton: Princeton University Press, 1967), 161–62; Upton Sinclair, "End Poverty in Civilization," *The Nation*, 139 (Sept. 26, 1934), 351; Arnold Peter Biella, "Upton Sinclair: Crusader" (PH.D. dissertation, Stanford University, 1954), 246–48; California Secretary of State, *Statement of Vote at Primary Election Held on August 28, 1934* (Sacramento: State of California, 1934), 4–7; Louis Ashlock, San Francisco, to Lorena Hickok, Nov. 24, 1934, Harry Hopkins Papers, Box 67, FDR Library; Charles E. Larsen, "The EPIC Campaign of 1934," *Pacific Historical Review*, 27 (May 1958), 127–47; *The New York Times*, Nov. 8, 1934; Upton Sinclair, "The Future of EPIC," *The Nation*, 139 (Nov. 28, 1934), 616–17; Upton Sinclair, *The Lie Factory Starts* (Pasadena: Sinclair, 1934); Schlesinger, *Politics of Upheaval*, 120.

5. Raymond Gram Swing, *Forerunners of American Fascism* (New York: Messner, 1935), 40, 45, and *passim*.; Schlesinger, *Politics of Upheaval*, 69, 20; Brinkley, *Voices of Protest*, 196–203, 208, 135, 137, 178–79, 191, 113, 143–44, 187, 124–26, 259; David H. Bennett, *Demagogues in the Depression: American Radicals and the Union Party, 1932–1936* (New Brunswick, N.J.: Rutgers University Press, 1969), 32–34, 54–55, 43, 41, 38, 78–79; Charles J. Tull, *Father Coughlin and the New Deal* (Syracuse: Syracuse University Press, 1965), 4, 6–8, 20, 41, 43, 96, 19, 52, 39, 96, 102–03, 243–44; Charles E. Coughlin, *Eight Lectures on Labor, Capital and Justice* (Royal Oak, Mich.: Radio League of the Little Flower, 1934), 10–11, 56–57, 34; Sinclair, *I, Candidate for Governor*, 91; Sheldon Marcus, *Father Coughlin: The Tumultuous Life of the Priest of the Little Flower* (Boston: Little, Brown, 1973); Charles E. Coughlin, *A Series of Lectures on Social Justice* (Royal Oak, Mich.: Radio League of the Little Flower, 1935), 144; Jonathan Mitchell, "Father Coughlin's Children," *The New Republic*, 88, (Aug. 26, 1936), 72–74; Gary Marx, "The Social Basis of the Support of a Depression Era Extremist: Father Coughlin" (Berkeley: University of California Survey Research Center, Monograph 7, 1962), 2, 10–32, 40, 80, 101–02, 109, 126; Robert S. McElvaine, "Thunder Without Lightning: Working-Class Discontent in the United States, 1929–1937" (PH.D. dissertation, State University of New York at Binghamton, 1974), 227–31, 305–06, n. 51.

6. Bennett, *Demagogues in the Depression*, 153, 159, 173–74, 168, 8–9, 175, 167; Abraham Holtzman, *The Townsend Movement: A Political Study* (New York: Bookman, 1963), 35–36, 44–45, 28, 39, 84, 48; Old Age Revolving Pensions, Ltd., *The Townsend Plan: National Recovery Program* (Washington: OARP, Ltd., 2d ed., 1936), 4–5, 7, 70, 77, 35; Carter, *American Messiahs*, 86–87, 81, 88, 85; Swing, *Forerunners of American Fascism*, 127–29; Schlesinger, *Politics of Upheaval*, 38; American Institute of Public Opinion surveys, Dec. 14, 1935, March 7, March 14, 1936, in Hadley Cantril and Mildred Strunk, eds., *Public Opinion, 1935–1946* (Princeton: Princeton University Press, 1951), 541–42; "A Dem. A Voter. A Citizen by Birth. A White man & not Blessed with any Criminal record either," Pueblo, Colo., to Harry Hopkins, Feb. 6, 1935, FERA Central Files, Box 91, National Archives; Nancy Gresham, Eugene, Ore., to ER, Nov. 8, 1934, Eleanor Roosevelt Papers, Box 612, FDR Library.

7. Examples of anti-Long books are T. O. Harris, *The Kingfish: Huey P. Long, Dictator* (New York: Pelican, 1938) and Harnett T. Kane, *Louisiana Hayride: The American Rehearsal for Dictatorship, 1928–1940* (New York: Morrow, 1941). All previous works on Long were superseded by T. Harry Williams, *Huey Long* (New York: Knopf, 1969), which is far more balanced than the older studies. Williams's monumental biography must, however, be classified as judiciously pro-Long. Alan Brinkley's *Voices of Protest: Huey Long, Father Coughlin, and the Great Depression* (New York: Knopf, 1982) achieves greater objectivity and neutrality than any other study of Long.

8. Schlesinger, *Politics of Upheaval*, 43, 58–60, 66; Perry H. Howard, *Political Tendencies in Louisiana, 1812–1952* (Baton Rouge: Louisiana State University Press, 1957), 112–14, 126–29; Williams, *Huey Long*, 44, 602–69, 742, 692, 700–01, 697–98, 6, 693–94, 864–76; Carter, *American Messiahs*, 20, 21, 22–23; Brinkley, *Voices of Protest*, 33–34, 44, 149, 180, 73–74, 208, 284–86, 79, 69, 174–75; Hugh Davis Graham, ed., *Huey Long* (Englewood Cliffs, N.J.: Prentice-Hall, 1970), 56; Huey P. Long, *Every Man a King* (New Orleans: National Book Co., 1933), 290–91; Huey Long form letters, dated June 22, 1933, July 1, 1933, and undated, Huey Long Papers, Duke University Library, Durham, N.C.; *American Progress*, March 29, 1934; Huey P. Long, *Share Our Wealth* (Washington, D.C., no publisher, n.d.), 3–5, 1, 14, 8, 31; Raymond Gram Swing, "The Menace of Huey Long: III. His Bid for National Power," *The Nation*, 140 (Jan. 23, 1935), 98–100; Buel W. Patch, "National Wealth and National Income," *Editorial Research Reports*, 1 (April 20, 1935), 287–304; Robert R. Doane, *The Measurement of American Wealth* (New York: Harper & Brothers, 1933), 25; Hodding Carter, "How Come Huey Long? I. Bogeyman," *The New Republic*, 82 (Feb. 13, 1935), 14; James A. Farley, *Jim Farley's*

Story: The Roosevelt Years (New York: McGraw-Hill, 1948), 51; Rodney Dutcher, "Washington Daily Revue," Nov. 8, 1935, clipping in Long Papers, Duke; Fortune surveys, July 1935 and October 1937, in Cantril and Strunk, eds., Public Opinion, 1040–41; E. D. Sibley, letter to the editor, Arizona Daily Star (Tucson), Jan. 25, 1933, clipping in Huey Long Scrapbooks, v. 19, Louisiana State University Library, Baton Rouge; Huey Long, My First Days in the White House (Harrisburg, Pa.: Telegraph Press, 1935).

9. The Reminiscences of Norman Thomas, part 1, p. 65, Columbia Oral History Project, as quoted in David A. Shannon, The Socialist Party of America: A History (New York: Macmillan, 1955), 248; E. P. Thompson, The Making of the English Working Class (New York: Vintage, 1963), 624, 626–27; Brinkley, Voices of Protest, 206, 209, 106, 211, 193, 179, 150, 213, 144–45, 67–68, 74; Marshall McLuhan, Understanding Media: The Dimensions of Man (New York: McGraw-Hill, 1964), 7–32, 297–307; W. E. Warren, Montana, to FDR, Feb. 14, 1935, Official File 1403, FDR Library, as quoted in Brinkley, Voices of Protest, 198.

CHAPTER 11
"I'M THAT KIND OF LIBERAL BECAUSE I'M THAT KIND OF CONSERVATIVE"

1. Time, 25 (Feb. 18, 1935), 14–15; The New York Times, Oct. 25, 1934; Arthur M. Schlesinger, Jr., The Coming of the New Deal (Boston: Houghton Mifflin, 1958), 446–55, 485–89; William E. Leuchtenburg, Franklin D. Roosevelt and the New Deal (New York: Harper & Row, 1963), 91–92; Frederick Lewis Allen, Since Yesterday: The 1930s in America (New York: Harper & Row, 1939; Perennial Library, 1972), 192; George Wolfskill, Revolt of the Conservatives: The American Liberty League, 1933–40 (Cambridge, Mass.: Harvard University Press, 1962); Elliot A. Rosen, Hoover, Roosevelt and the Brains Trust: From Depression to New Deal (New York: Columbia University Press, 1977), 266–67; Otis L. Graham, Encore for Reform: The Old Progressives and the New Deal (New York: Oxford University Press, 1967), 147.

2. Leuchtenburg, Roosevelt and New Deal, 117; Charles A. Beard, "The President Loses Prestige," Current History, 42 (April 1935), 64–71; Martha Gellhorn, Report to Harry Hopkins from Camden, N.J., April 25, 1935, Hopkins Papers, Box 60, FDR Library; Anonymous, Chicago, Ill., to FDR, March 13, 1935, FERA Central Files, Box 91, National Archives; Joseph W. Churbock, Loyalhanna, Pa., to ER, March 4, 1935, Eleanor Roosevelt Papers, Box 2697, FDR Library; Anonymous, Brooklyn, N.Y., to Hopkins, May 23, 1935, FERA, Box 91; "From a Democrat," Columbus, Ohio, to FDR, May 1935, FERA, Box 90; Alan Brinkley, Voices of Protest: Huey Long, Father Coughlin, and the Great Depression (New York: Knopf, 1982), 214.

3. Arthur M. Schlesinger, Jr., The Politics of Upheaval (Boston: Houghton Mifflin, 1960), 305–24, 272; Paul K. Conkin, The New Deal (New York: Crowell, 1967; 2d ed., 1975), 64; Samuel I. Rosenman, ed., The Public Papers and Addresses of Franklin Roosevelt (New York: Russell & Russell, 1938–50), v. IV, 23, 98–103; Leuchtenburg, Roosevelt and the New Deal, 156–57.

4. Edwin E. Witte, The Development of the Social Security Act (Madison: University of Wisconsin Press, 1962); Schlesinger, Coming of the New Deal, 301–15; Roy Lubove, The Struggle for Social Security, 1900–1935 (Cambridge, Mass.: Harvard University Press, 1968); George Martin, Madam Secretary: Frances Perkins (Boston: Houghton Mifflin, 1976), 341–356; Conkin, The New Deal, 58–60; Leuchtenburg, Roosevelt and the New Deal, 131–33, 154, 165; Jackson (Miss.) Daily News, June 20, 1935; James T. Patterson, America's Struggle Against Poverty, 1900–1980 (Cambridge, Mass.: Harvard University Press, 1981), 60, 67–77.

5. Frances Perkins, The Roosevelt I Knew (New York: Viking, 1946), 303–10; J. Joseph Huthmacher, Senator Robert F. Wagner and the Rise of Urban Liberalism (New York: Athe-

neum, 1968, 1971); Irving Bernstein, *Turbulent Years: A History of the American Worker, 1933–1941* (Boston: Houghton Mifflin, 1971), 322–51; Bernstein, *The New Deal Collective Bargaining Policy* (Berkeley: University of California Press, 1950), 84–128; Schlesinger, *Coming of the New Deal*, 403–06; Leuchtenburg, *Roosevelt and the New Deal*, 158–61.

6. Schlesinger, *Politics of Upheaval*, 325–34; Raymond Moley, *After Seven Years: A Political Analysis of the New Deal* (New York: Harper & Brothers, 1939; reprint ed., Lincoln: University of Nebraska Press, 1971), 305–14; New York *Herald Tribune*, June 23, 1935; Rosenman, *Public Papers and Addresses*, v. IV, 270–77; Robert S. McElvaine, "The Effects of Economic Depression on Working-Class Attitudes: The 1930's," in *Papers of the American Historical Association, 1977* (Ann Arbor: University Microfilms, 1978); Joseph T. McKenna, Philadelphia, Pa., to FDR, n.d. (ca. June 1935), J. M. Salzer, Willows, Calif., to FDR, June 20, 1935, the Rev. Walter Moore, East Chicago, Ind., to FDR, n.d. (ca. June 1935), A. U. Shirk, Little Neck Hills, Long Island, N.Y., to FDR, June 21, 1935, H. M. Beeler, Philadelphia, Pa., to FDR, June 27, 1935, Enoch P. Philips, Eureka, Kans., to FDR, June 22, 1935, all in FDR Papers, President's Personal File, #200-B; "Reactions to Radio Addresses," Message to Congress, June 19, 1935, Box 45, FDR Library.

7. Moley, *After Seven Years*, 300–14; Basil Rauch, *The History of the New Deal, 1933–1938* (New York: Creative Age Press, 1944); Schlesinger, *Politics of Upheaval*, 392–408; Otis L. Graham, Jr., "Historians and the New Deals: 1944–1960," *The Social Studies*, 54 (April 1963), 133–40; Leuchtenburg, *Roosevelt and the New Deal*, 162–66; William H. Wilson, "The Two New Deals: A Valid Concept?" *Historian*, 28 (Feb. 1966), 268–88; Rosen, *Hoover, Roosevelt and the Brains Trust*, 114–20; *Sharecropper's Voice*, July 1936, as quoted in Schlesinger, *Coming of the New Deal*, 379; Graham, *Encore for Reform*, 92.

CHAPTER 12
NEW HICKORY

1. Arthur M. Schlesinger, Jr., *The Politics of Upheaval* (Boston: Houghton Mifflin, 1960), 502–04, 488; Raymond Moley, *After Seven Years: A Political Analysis of the New Deal* (New York: Harper & Brothers, 1939; reprint ed., Lincoln: University of Nebraska Press, 1971), 317–18, 330–31; William E. Leuchtenburg, *Franklin D. Roosevelt and the New Deal, 1932–1940* (New York: Harper & Row, 1963), 170–71.

2. Harry L. Hopkins, *Spending to Save: The Complete Story of Relief* (New York: Norton, 1936), 114, 109; "W.P.A. workers of Battle Creek," to FDR, April 5, 1936, FERA Central Files, Box 86, National Archives (reproduced in Robert S. McElvaine, ed., *Down and Out in the Great Depression: Letters from the "Forgotten Man"* [Chapel Hill: University of North Carolina Press, 1983], 127); Henry W. Francis, Report to Harry Hopkins, from Clarksburg, W.Va., Dec. 1, 1934, Hopkins Papers, Box 66, "One of the many workers + a leagionaire," Ft. Worth, Tex., to Hopkins, Nov. 21, 1935, FERA Central Files, Box 88; "American Workers," Wisconsin, to Hopkins, FERA Central Files, Box 89; Anonymous, Suffolk, Va., to Hopkins, FERA Central Files, Box 88 (reproduced in McElvaine, *Down and Out*, 135); James T. Patterson, *America's Struggle Against Poverty, 1900–1980* (Cambridge, Mass.: Harvard University Press, 1981), 63, 59, 62; Harry L. Hopkins, "They'd Rather Work," *Collier's*, 96 (Nov. 16, 1935), 7; William W. Bremer, "Along the 'American Way': The New Deal's Work Relief Programs for the Unemployed," *Journal of American History*, 62 (Dec. 1975), 636, 645, 638–39, 641; Samuel I. Rosenman, ed., *The Public Papers and Addresses of Franklin D. Roosevelt* (New York: Russell & Russell, 1938–50), v. V, 19; Caroline Bird, *The Invisible Scar* (New York: McKay, 1966), 197–99; Frances Fox Piven and Richard A. Cloward, *Regulating the Poor: The Functions of Public*

Welfare (New York: Pantheon, 1971; Vintage, 1972), 109; Josephine C. Brown, *Public Relief, 1929–1939* (New York: Holt, 1940), 386–89.

3. Jane DeHart Mathews, "Arts and the People: The New Deal Quest for a Cultural Democracy," *Journal of American History,* 62 (Sept. 1975), 319, 335, 320, 329, 327, 334n, 324, 332, 316, 320, 328, 325, 337, 333, 339, 331; Alfred Kazin, *On Native Grounds: An Interpretation of Modern American Prose Literature* (New York: Reynal and Hitchcock, 1941), 363–518; Ann Banks, ed., *First-Person America* (New York: Knopf, 1980), xviii–xix, xx; Jerre Mangione, *The Dream and the Deal: The Federal Writers' Project, 1935–1943* (Boston: Little, Brown, 1972), 255–56, 244, 46–49; Malcolm Cowley, "Federal Writers' Project," *The New Republic,* 167 (Oct. 21, 1972), 23–26; Charles I. Glicksberg, "The Federal Writers' Project," *South Atlantic Quarterly,* 37 (April 1938), 158–69; Marguerite D. Bloxom, ed., *Pickaxe and Pencil: References for the Study of the WPA* (Washington, D.C.: Library of Congress, 1982), 37, 29, 45; Janelle Jedd Warren-Findley, "Of Tears and Need: The Federal Music Project, 1935–1943" (PH.D. dissertation, George Washington University, 1973), 319–20; Joe Klein, *Woody Guthrie: A Life* (New York: Knopf, 1980), 145–50; Alan Lomax, Woody Guthrie, and Pete Seeger, eds., *Hard-Hitting Songs for Hard-Hit People* (New York: Oak Pubns., 1967), 11; Cornelius Baird Canon, "The Federal Music Project of the Works Progress Administration: Music in a Democracy" (PH.D. dissertation, University of Minnesota, 1963), 165–66; Francis V. O'Connor, comp., *Art for the Millions: Essays from the 1930s by Artists and Administrators of the WPA Federal Art Project* (Greenwich, Conn.: N.Y. Graphic Society, 1973); Richard D. McKinzie, *The New Deal for Artists* (Princeton: Princeton University Press, 1973); Helen A. Harrison, "American Art and the New Deal," *Journal of American Studies,* 6 (Dec. 1972), 289–96; J. C. Furnas, *Stormy Weather: Crosslights on the Nineteen Thirties; An Informal Social History of the United States, 1929–1941* (New York: Putnam, 1977), 73–80; "A Sampler of New Deal Murals," *American Heritage,* 21 (Oct. 1970), 45–57; Karal Ann Manning, *Wall-to-Wall America: A Cultural History of Post Office Murals in the Great Depression* (Minneapolis: University of Minnesota Press, 1982); Leuchtenburg, *Roosevelt and the New Deal,* 128, 127; Jane DeHart Mathews, *The Federal Theatre, 1935–1939: Plays, Relief, and Politics* (Princeton: Princeton University Press, 1967), 3–43; John O'Connor and Lorraine Brown, *Free, Adult, Uncensored: The Living History of the Federal Theatre Project* (Washington, D.C.: New Republic Books, 1978), 2, 8–9, 18–19, 26–29, 10–15, 31–35; Hallie Flanagan, *Arena* (New York: Duell, Sloan and Pearce, 1940), 51–80, 342, 356–73; John Houseman, *Run-Through* (New York: Simon & Schuster, 1972), 176, 183–85, 189–205, 175n, 245–81; John Houseman, lecture at Millsaps College, Jackson, Miss., Sept. 23, 1982; Garrett Garet, "Federal Theater for the Masses," *The Saturday Evening Post,* 208 (June 20, 1936), 8–9, 84–86, 88; Harrison G. Fiske, "The Federal Theater Doomboggle," *The Saturday Evening Post,* 209 (Aug. 1, 1936), 23, 68–72; Robert S. McElvaine, "America Suffers a Change in Values," *Los Angeles Times,* Oct. 28, 1981.

4. Rosenman, *Public Papers and Addresses,* v. V, 8–18, 38–44; A. W. Gudal, Philadelphia, Pa., to FDR, Jan. 8, 1936, and Mrs. A. H. Fasel, Estacada, Ore., to FDR, Jan. 18, 1936, both in President's Personal File, #200-B, FDR Library; *The New York Times,* Jan. 26, 1936; Richard Hofstadter, *The American Political Tradition: And the Men Who Made It* (New York: Knopf, 1948; 2d ed., Vintage, 1973), 288; "A Friend of you both," Kokomo, Ind., to ER, Oct. 28, 1935, FERA Central Files, Box 88, National Archives; Schlesinger, *Politics of Upheaval,* 273–74; *The New York Times,* March 9, 1936.

5. Warren Moscow, *Roosevelt and Willkie* (Englewood Cliffs, N.J.: Prentice-Hall, 1968), 22–23; T. Harry Williams, *Huey Long* (New York: Knopf, 1969), 734–35; Alan Brinkley, *Voices of Protest: Huey Long, Father Coughlin, and the Great Depression* (New York: Knopf, 1982), 172; David H. Bennett, *Demagogues in the Depression: American Radicals and the Union Party,*

1932–1936 (New Brunswick, N.J.: Rutgers University Press, 1969); Bennett, "The Year of the Old Folk's Revolt," American Heritage, 16 (Dec. 1964), 48–51, 99–107; Lorena Hickok, report to Harry Hopkins from St. Louis, Aug. 21, 1936, Hopkins Papers, Box 68, FDR Library.

6. Schlesinger, Politics of Upheaval, 524–47, 559–61, 571–644; Leuchtenburg, Roosevelt and the New Deal, 178–96; Samuel Lubell, The Future of American Politics (2d ed., Garden City, N.Y.: Doubleday, 1956), 51, 45, 46; Rosenman, Public Papers and Addresses, v. V, 230–36, 553, 566–73; Moscow, Roosevelt and Willkie, 38; Robert S. Lynd and Helen Merrell Lynd, Middletown in Transition: A Study in Cultural Conflicts (New York: Harcourt, Brace & World, 1937), 360, 359, 44; American Institute of Public Opinion Surveys, Jan. 18, 1936, and Dec. 7, 1936, both in Hadley Cantril and Mildred Strunk, eds., Public Opinion, 1935–46 (Princeton: Princeton University Press, 1951), 344, 599; F. V. Eastman, Washington, D. C., to "Secretary to Mrs. F. D. Roosevelt," Nov. 2, 1936, ER Papers, Box 2719.

7. Rosenman, Public Papers and Addresses, v. VI, 4; Joseph Alsop and Turner Catledge, The 168 Days (Garden City, N.Y.: Doubleday, Doran, 1938); Leuchtenburg, Roosevelt and the New Deal, 232–39; James T. Patterson, Congressional Conservatism and the New Deal (Lexington: University of Kentucky Press, 1967), 77–127; Otis L. Graham, Encore for Reform: The Old Progressives and the New Deal (New York: Oxford University Press, 1967), 43.

CHAPTER 13
THE CIO AND THE LATER NEW DEAL

1. Melvyn Dubofsky and Warren Van Tyne, John L. Lewis: A Biography (New York: Quadrangle/New York Times, 1977), xiv–xvi, 217–21, and passim.; Charles A. Madison, American Labor Leaders (2d ed., New York: Ungar, 1962), 177, 182, 185; Irving Bernstein, The Lean Years: A History of the American Worker, 1920–1933 (Boston: Houghton Mifflin, 1960), 123; Saul Alinsky, John L. Lewis: An Unauthorized Biography (New York: Putnam, 1949), 14; Len De Caux, Labor Radical: From the Wobblies to CIO (Boston: Beacon, 1970), 120, 226–27, 216, 214–15, 229–30; Cecil Carnes, John L. Lewis: Leader of Labor (New York: Speller, 1936), 126; David Brody, "The Emergence of Mass Production Unionism," in John Braeman, Robert H. Bremner, and Everett Walters, eds., Change and Continuity in Twentieth Century America (Columbus: Ohio State University Press, 1964), 243–62; James O. Morris, Conflict Within the AFL: A Study of Craft Versus Industrial Unionism 1901–1935 (Ithaca, N.Y.: Cornell University Press, 1958), 4, 150–52, 210–11; Irving Bernstein, Turbulent Years: A History of the American Worker, 1933–1941 (Boston: Houghton Mifflin, 1971), 386–404, 590–94, 595–602; Mary Heaton Vorse, Labor's New Millions (New York: Modern Age, 1938), 5–8, 17–18, 28–29; Samuel Lubell, The Future of American Politics (2d ed., Garden City, N.Y.: Doubleday/Anchor, 1956), 48–50; Art Preis, Labor's Giant Step: Twenty Years of the CIO (New York: Pioneer, 1964), 45–46; Walter Galenson, The CIO Challenge to the AFL: A History of the American Labor Movement, 1935–1941 (Cambridge, Mass.: Harvard University Press, 1960); Edward Levinson, Labor on the March (New York: Harper & Brothers, 1938); J. C. Furnas, Stormy Weather: Crosslights on the Nineteen Thirties: An Informal Social History of the United States, 1929–1941 (New York: Putnam, 1977), 99.

2. Modern Times (1936, Charles Chaplin); Richard H. Pells, Radical Visions and American Dreams (New York: Harper & Row, 1973), 284; Sidney Fine, Sit-Down: The General Motors Strike of 1936–1937 (Ann Arbor: University of Michigan Press, 1969), 59, 56–57, 62–63, 90–91, 96, 99, 133–41, 146–48, 121–22, 157–58, 171, 174, 220–23, 1–13, 239, 318, 266–71, 274, 279, 280, 297–303, 310–12, 327–31; Edward Levinson, "Labor on the March," Harper's, 174 (May 1937), 642–50; Bernstein, Turbulent Years, 522–23, 529–30, 432–73, 485–90; De Caux, Labor Radical, 227–28, 254–55, 242–45; Alfred Winslow Jones, Life, Liberty and Prop-

erty (Philadelphia: Lippincott, 1941), 332, 342, 378–79; Solomon Diamond, "The Psychology of the Sit-Down," *New Masses*, 23 (May 4, 1937), 16; C. Wright Mills, *The New Men of Power: America's Labor Leaders* (New York: Harcourt, Brace, 1948; reprint ed., Kelley, 1971), 8–9.

3. William E. Leuchtenburg, *Franklin D. Roosevelt and the New Deal, 1932–1940* (New York: Harper & Row, 1963), 263, 257–60; Henry Stimson Diary, Yale University Library, July 27, 1938, quoted in Otis L. Graham, *An Encore for Reform: The Old Progressives and the New Deal* (New York: Oxford University Press, 1967), 19; Samuel I. Rosenman, ed., *The Public Papers and Addresses of Franklin D. Roosevelt* (New York: Russell & Russell, 1938–50), v. VII, 305–32; Lawrence Edwards, Cumberland Gap, Tenn., to FDR, April 30, 1938, FDR Papers, President's Personal File, #200-B, FDR Library; Raymond Moley, *After Seven Years: A Political Analysis of the New Deal* (New York: Harper & Brothers, 1939; reprint ed., Lincoln: University of Nebraska Press, 1971), 376; Ellis W. Hawley, *The New Deal and the Problem of Monopoly* (Princeton: Princeton University Press, 1966), 149; Thurman Arnold, *The Bottlenecks of Business* (New York: Reynal and Hitchcock, 1940).

4. James T. Patterson, *Congressional Conservatism and the New Deal* (Lexington: University of Kentucky Press, 1967), 188–249; Leuchtenburg, *Roosevelt and the New Deal*, 140–41, 257, 135–37; Arthur M. Schlesinger, Jr., *The Coming of the New Deal* (Boston: Houghton Mifflin, 1959), 369–81; Sidney Baldwin, *Poverty and Politics: The Rise and Decline of the Farm Security Administration* (Chapel Hill: University of North Carolina Press, 1968), 204–07; Paul Conkin, *Tomorrow a New World: The New Deal Community Program* (Ithaca, N.Y.: Cornell University Press, 1959), 305–25; F. Jack Hurley, *Portrait of a Decade: Roy Stryker and the Development of Documentary Photography in the Thirties* (Baton Rouge: Louisiana State University Press, 1972), 32–34, viii–ix, 50–94, and *passim.*; Hank O'Neal, *A Vision Shared: A Classic Portrait of America and Its People, 1935–1945* (New York: St. Martin's, 1976); Walker Evans, *Photographs for the Farm Security Administration, 1935–1938* (New York: Da Capo, 1973); James Agee and Walker Evans, *Let Us Now Praise Famous Men* (1941; New York: Ballantine, 1969).

CHAPTER 14
"DR. NEW DEAL" RUNS OUT OF MEDICINE

1. James MacGregor Burns, *Roosevelt: The Lion and the Fox* (New York: Harcourt, Brace & World, 1956), 343, 416; U.S. Department of Commerce, Bureau of the Census, *Historical Statistics of the United States to 1970* (Washington: Government Printing Office, 1975), Ser. D-85, 86, K-284, pp. 135, 484; James T. Patterson, *Congressional Conservatism and the New Deal* (Lexington: University of Kentucky Press, 1967), 288–324; Samuel I. Rosenman, ed., *The Public Papers and Addresses of Franklin D. Roosevelt* (New York: Russell & Russell, 1938–50), v. VIII, 1–12; James T. Patterson, *America's Struggle Against Poverty, 1900–1980* (Cambridge, Mass.: Harvard University Press, 1981), 60–61; Francis Fox Piven and Richard A. Cloward, *Regulating the Poor: The Functions of Public Welfare* (New York: Random House, 1971; Vintage, 1972), 80, 113, 116–17; William E. Leuchtenburg, *Franklin D. Roosevelt and the New Deal, 1932–1940* (New York: Harper & Row, 1963), 270; Floyd Riddick, "First Session of the Seventy-sixth Congress," *American Political Science Review*, 33 (Dec. 1939), 1022–43; FDR, to Joseph P. Kennedy, Aug. 5, 1939, in Elliott Roosevelt, ed., *F.D.R.: His Personal Letters, 1928–1945* (New York: Duell, Sloan and Pearce, 1950), v. II, 911.

2. Patterson, *Congressional Conservatism*, 325–37; Leuchtenburg, *Roosevelt and the New Deal*, 197–251; Robert S. McElvaine, ed., *Down and Out in the Great Depression: Letters from the "Forgotten Man"* (Chapel Hill: University of North Carolina Press, 1983); Anne O'Hare McCormick, "As He Sees Himself," *The New York Times Magazine* (Oct. 16, 1938), 2; John M.

Blum, *From the Morgenthau Diaries: Years of Urgency* (Boston: Houghton Mifflin, 1965), 41–42.

3. Hugh T. Lovin, "The Fall of Farmer-Labor Parties, 1936–1938," *Pacific Northwest Quarterly*, 62 (Jan. 1971), 25; Warren Moscow, *Roosevelt and Willkie* (Englewood Cliffs, N.J.: Prentice-Hall, 1968), 27, 33, 101, 70, 52–53, 63, 56–61, 55, 68, 95, 96, 106; Robert E. Burke, "Election of 1940," in Arthur M. Schlesinger, Jr., and Fred L. Israel, eds., *History of American Presidential Elections, 1798–1968* (New York: Chelsea House, 1971), v. IV, 2923–25, 2928; Burns, *The Lion and the Fox*, 432; Harold Ickes, *The Secret Diary of Harold Ickes* (New York: Simon & Schuster, 1954), v. III, 92; David Burner, *Herbert Hoover: A Public Life* (New York: Knopf, 1979), 408n; Leuchtenburg, *Roosevelt and the New Deal*, 313; Wolcott Gibbs and John Bainbridge, "St. George and the Dragnet," *The New Yorker*, 16 (May 25, 1940), 24; "Editorial: Business-and-Government," *Fortune*, 21 (April 1940), 46–47; Wendell L. Willkie, "We, the People," *Fortune*, 21 (April 1940), 64–65, 162–73.

4. Moscow, *Roosevelt and Willkie*, 71–79, 2, 43, 110–11, 117–18. 127; Robert E. Sherwood, *Roosevelt and Hopkins: An Intimate History* (New York: Harper & Brothers, 1948); Burns, *The Lion and the Fox*, 414, 425–28; Burke, "Election of 1940," 2934–35; Joseph P. Lash, *Eleanor Roosevelt: A Friend's Memoir* (Garden City, N.Y.: Doubleday, 1964), 194.

5. Burke, "Election of 1940," 2938, 2944; Turner Catledge, as quoted in Moscow, *Roosevelt and Willkie*, 151; Moscow, *Roosevelt and Willkie*, 138, 143, 145, 160, 147; Burns, *The Lion and the Fox*, 441, 447; *The New York Times*, Sept. 7, 1940, Sept. 17, 1940, Aug. 26, 1940, Sept. 20, 1940, Oct. 26, 1940; Rosenman, *Public Papers and Addresses*, v. IX, 485–95, 499–510, 544–53; American Institute of Public Opinion (AIPO) survey, Dec. 25, 1940, in Hadley Cantril and Mildred Strunk, eds., *Public Opinion, 1935–1946* (Princeton: Princeton University Press, 1951), 896; Samuel Lubell, *The Future of American Politics* (2d ed., Garden City, N.Y.: Doubleday/ Anchor, 191, 1956), 54–55, 60; Henry Steele Commager, *The American Mind* (New Haven: Yale University Press, 1950), 354.

6. *Historical Statistics to 1970*, Ser. D-85, 86, p. 135, Ser. F-126, p. 232; AIPO surveys, July 1941 and May 1941, in George H. Gallup, ed., *The Gallup Poll: Public Opinion, 1935–1971* (New York: Random House, 1972), v. I, 286–87, 277; *Sergeant York* (1941, Howard Hawks, Warner Brothers); Richard Polenberg, *War and Society: The United States, 1941–1945* (Philadelphia: Lippincott, 1972), 73–75; Archibald MacLeish, "Defeatist Liberals," *The New Republic*, 110 (March 6, 1944), 302.

CHAPTER 15
PERSPECTIVE

1. *Time*, 120 (July 26, 1982), 36; Elliot A. Rosen, *Hoover, Roosevelt and the Brains Trust: From Depression to New Deal* (New York: Columbia University Press, 1977), 377, 305, 198–99; FDR, to George H. Dern, Feb. 2, 1933, as quoted in Frank Freidel, *Franklin D. Roosevelt: Launching the New Deal* (Boston: Little, Brown, 1973), 137; Samuel I. Rosenman, ed., *The Public Papers and Addresses of Franklin D. Roosevelt* (New York: Russell & Russell, 1938–50), v. I., 657; Frank Freidel, *Franklin D. Roosevelt: The Apprenticeship* (Boston: Little, Brown, 1952), 37n; Otis L. Graham, *Encore for Reform: The Old Progressives and the New Deal* (New York: Oxford University Presss, 1967), 185–86; Frances Perkins, *The Roosevelt I Knew* (New York: Viking, 1946), 125–34; Robert S. McElvaine, "Where Have All the Liberals Gone?" *Texas Quarterly*, 19 (Autumn 1976), 202–13.

2. William Trufant Foster and Waddill Catchings, *The Road to Plenty* (Boston: Houghton Mifflin, 1928); Arthur M. Schlesinger, Jr., *The Crisis of the Old Order* (Boston: Houghton

Mifflin, 1957), 134–36, 186–89; Ellis W. Hawley, *The New Deal and the Problem of Monopoly* (Princeton: Princeton University Press, 1966), 283–92, 420–55; Arthur M. Schlesinger, Jr., *The Coming of the New Deal* (Boston: Houghton Mifflin, 1958), 440–42; Schlesinger, *The Politics of Upheaval* (Boston: Houghton Mifflin, 1960), 220–24, 385–423; John Maynard Keynes, *The General Theory of Employment, Interest and Money* (New York: Harcourt, Brace, 1936); Barbara R. Bergman, "Who's to Blame for the Economy?" *The New York Times*, Oct. 17, 1982; Lester C. Thurow, *The Zero-Sum Society: Distribution and the Possibilities for Economic Change* (New York: Basic Books, 1980; Penguin, 1981), 17; "More Booms Ahead," *Fortune*, 43 (April 1951), 81; "Rocketing Births: Business Bonanza," *Life*, 44 (June 16, 1958), cover, 2, 83–89; Landon Y. Jones, *Great Expectations: America and the Baby Boom Generation* (New York: Coward, Mc-Cann & Geoghegan, 1980; Ballantine, 1981), 41.

3. Schlesinger, *Politics of Upheaval*, 424–43; Frank Freidel, *F.D.R. and the South* (Baton Rouge: Louisiana State University Press, 1965); Florence King, *Southern Ladies and Gentlemen* (New York: Stein & Day, 1975), 12; Jonathan Schell, *The Time of Illusion* (New York: Knopf, 1975), 185; *Esquire*, 10 (Nov. 1938); Stephen Early, "Below the Belt," *The Saturday Evening Post*, 211 (June 10, 1939); Schlesinger, *Coming of the New Deal*, 569; "The Center, Re-discovered: 'Liberal' Is No Longer a Dirty Word" (editorial), *The New York Times*, Nov. 4, 1982.

4. Barton J. Bernstein, "The New Deal: The Conservative Achievements of Liberal Reform," in Barton J. Bernstein, ed., *Towards a New Past: Dissenting Essays in American History* (New York: Pantheon, 1968), 263–88; Frances Fox Piven and Richard A. Cloward, *Regulating the Poor: The Functions of Public Welfare* (New York: Pantheon, 1971); Piven and Cloward, *Poor People's Movements: How They Succeed and Why They Fail* (New York: Pantheon, 1977), 41–175; Studs Terkel, *Hard Times: An Oral History of the Great Depression* (New York: Pantheon, 1970), 34; John Kenneth Galbraith, *American Capitalism: The Concept of Countervailing Power* (Boston: Houghton Mifflin, 1952); Rosenman, *Public Papers and Addresses*, v. I, 625.

5. David W. Noble, *The Progressive Mind, 1890–1917* (rev. ed., Minneapolis: Burgess, 1981), x; Ayn Rand, *The Fountainhead* (Indianapolis: Bobbs-Merrill, 1943), 547, 565; Rosenman, *Public Papers and Addresses*, v. V, 480–89; John Steinbeck, *The Grapes of Wrath* (New York: Viking, 1939; Penguin, 1976), 165–66; Lawrence Goodwyn, *The Populist Moment* (New York: Oxford University Press, 1976), 61; Charles Forcey, *The Crossroads of Liberalism: Croly, Weyl, Lippmann, and the Progressive Era, 1900–1925* (New York: Oxford University Press, 1961), xvii; Graham, *Encore for Reform*, 47n; Frances H. Coker, "Women and Men: An Unfinished Job" (paper presented at Millsaps College Friday Forum, March 19, 1982); Jessie Bernard, *The Female World* (New York: Free Press, 1981), 84–91; Carol Gilligan, *In a Different Voice: Psychological Theory and Women's Development* (Cambridge, Mass: Harvard University Press, 1982); Ellen Goodman, "A Political Gender Gap," *The Boston Globe*, Oct. 19, 1982; *Faithless* (1932, Harry Beaumont, MGM); Andrew Bergman, *We're in the Money: Depression America and Its Films* (New York: New York University Press, 1971; reprinted ed., Harper & Row, 1972), 50–54; Paul Rotha and Richard Griffith, *The Film Till Now* (London: J. Cape, 1930), 438–39; *Susan Lenox, Her Fall and Rise* (1931, Robert Z. Leonard, MGM); *Blonde Venus* (1932, Josef von Sternberg, Paramount); *She Done Him Wrong* (1933, Lowell Sherman, Paramount).

6. Doris Kearns, *Lyndon Johnson and the American Dream* (New York: Harper & Row, 1976), 33, 40; Robert J. Ringer, *Looking Out for Number 1* (New York: Funk & Wagnalls, 1977); Goodwyn, *Populist Moment*, xiv; Robert S. McElvaine, "America Suffers a Change in Values," *Los Angeles Times*, Oct. 28, 1981; "And a Happy New Year," *The New Republic*, 188 (Year-end, 1982), 5–6; John D. Rockefeller, as quoted in George Will, "In Defense of the Welfare State," *The New Republic*, 188 (May 9, 1983), 21; Charles Peters, "A Neoliberal's Manifesto," *The*

Washington Monthly, 15 (May 1983), 13; "Gaga Over Guns," *The New Republic*, 188 (May 30, 1983), 9; Christopher Lasch, *The Culture of Narcissism: American Life in an Age of Diminishing Expectations* (New York: Norton, 1978), 30, 14, 44–47; Jerry Rubin, *Growing (Up) at Thirty-Seven* (New York: M. Evans, 1976), 56; Eugene Emerson Jennings, *Routes to the Executive Suite* (New York: McGraw-Hill, 1971), 3, as quoted in Lasch, *Culture of Narcissism*, 44; Robert B. Reich, *The Next American Frontier* (New York: Times Books, 1983), 140–72.

7. *The New York Times*, Nov. 6, 1982, Dec. 16, 1982, Dec. 31, 1982, Jan. 4, 1983, Nov. 30, 1982, Nov. 21, 1982, May 16, 1983, Apr. 2, 1983, June 29, 1983, July 10, 1983; *The Wall Street Journal*, Nov. 24, 1982; *Clarion-Ledger* (Jackson, Miss.), Nov. 25, 1982, Dec. 16, 1982, Oct. 10, 1982; Daniel Yergin, "Unemployment: The Outlook Is Grim," *The New York Times*, July 13, 1982; James Reston, "A Talk With Schmidt," *The New York Times*, Nov. 17, 1982; TRB, "Yuletide Gloom," *The New Republic*, 188 (Year-end, 1982), 4; *The Washington Post*, Nov. 29, 1982; Lester C. Thurow, "The Great Stagnation," *The New York Times Magazine*, Oct. 17, 1982; *Time*, 120 (July 26, 1982), 36; Damon Darlin, "America's New Poor Swallow Their Pride, Go to Soup Kitchens," *The Wall Street Journal*, Jan. 11, 1983; TRB, "Eroding Banks," *The New Republic*, 188, (Feb. 21, 1983), 4; Lester Thurow, "Economics First," *The New York Times*, Nov. 15, 1982; "Reagan's Pressure Points," *The New Republic*, 189 (Aug. 29, 1983), 5; CBS Radio News, May 20, 1983; Haynes Johnson, "Elegant Breakfast, Lines of Jobless Mark Disparity in Progress, *The Washington Post*, Aug. 7, 1983; Ellen Goodman, "The Contrast Is Too Great," *The Boston Globe*, Jan. 11, 1983.

8. *The New York Times*, Dec. 18, 1982, Jan. 2, 1983; Sydney H. Schanberg, "Not Just the Fittest," *The New York Times*, Jan. 4, 1983; James Reston, "A Different Voice," *The New York Times*, Jan. 5, 1983; Goodman, "The Contrast Is Too Great"; Robert Lekachman, *Greed Is Not Enough: Reaganomics* (New York: Pantheon, 1982), 3; TRB, "Frustration," *The New Republic*, 188 (May 30, 1983), 6; Anthony Lewis, "Reagan Sheds Reagan," *The New York Times*, Aug. 7, 1983; Rosenman, *Public Papers and Addresses*, v. V, 235.

INDEX